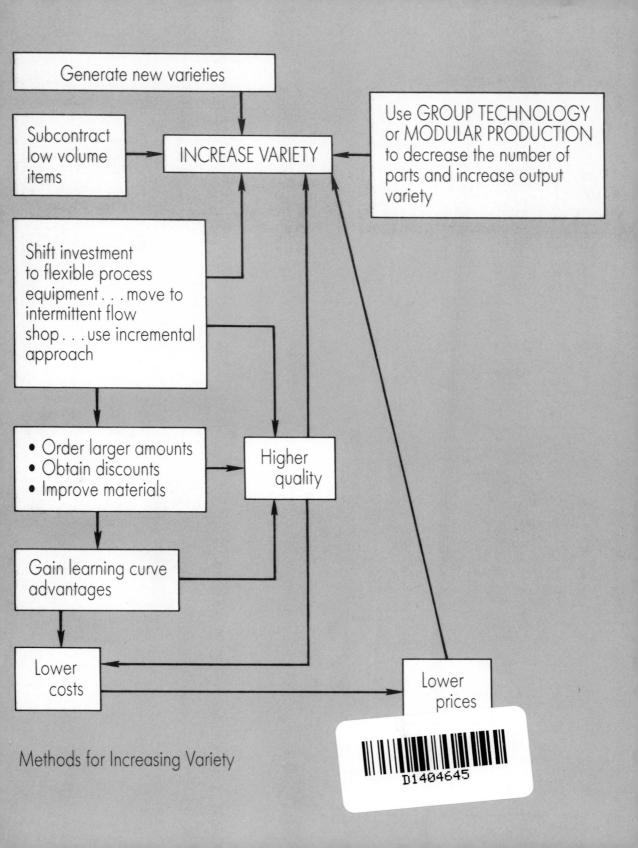

Methods for Increasing Variety

MANAGING
PRODUCTION
AND
OPERATIONS

MANAGING PRODUCTION AND OPERATIONS

Martin K. Starr
Columbia University

PRENTICE HALL, Englewood Cliffs, New Jersey 07632

Library of Congress Cataloging-in-Publication Data

Starr, Martin Kenneth,
  Managing production and operations/Martin K. Starr.
  p. cm.
  Includes bibliographies and index.
  ISBN 0-13-551284-0
  1. Production management. I. Title.
TS155.S75872 1988
658.5—dc 19   88-9736

Editorial/production supervision and
Interior design: Robert C. Walters
Cover design: Karen Stephens
Manufacturing buyer: Margaret Rizzi

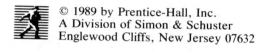 © 1989 by Prentice-Hall, Inc.
A Division of Simon & Schuster
Englewood Cliffs, New Jersey 07632

Printed in the United States of America
10 9 8 7 6 5 4 3 2 1

ISBN 0-13-551284-0

Prentice-Hall International (UK) Limited, *London*
Prentice-Hall of Australia Pty. Limited, *Sydney*
Prentice-Hall Canada Inc., *Toronto*
Prentice-Hall Hispanoamericana, S.A., *Mexico City*
Prentice-Hall of India, Private Limited, *New Delhi*
Prentice-Hall of Japan, Inc, *Tokyo*
Prentice-Hall of Southeast Asia Pte. Ltd., *Singapore*
Editora Prentice-Hall do Brasil, Ltda, *Rio de Janeiro*

This Book is dedicated to the people who are devoted to changing the education of MBA's . . . so that they can provide role models that are globally competitive.

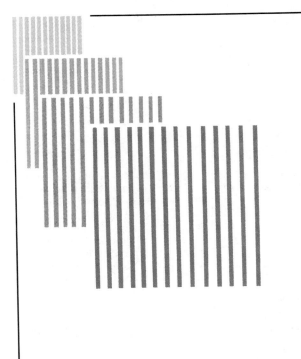

Contents

Chapter 5
Capacity Planning and Forecasting Demand   173

SUMMARY

Section 5.1   The Breakeven Concept and Capacity Planning   174

Input/Output Models of Revenues and Costs · Output and Revenue · Interfunctional Models · The Process and Fixed Costs · Inputs and Variable Costs · Functional Areas and Revenues and Costs · The Breakeven Chart · Analysis of the Linear Breakeven Model · *Case:* Personalized Hand-Held Calculators · Breakeven Related to Work Configurations · Linear Breakeven Equations · Analysis of Nonlinear Breakeven Model · PROBLEM SET

Section 5.2   The Breakeven Decision Model   197

Decision Theory · Analysis and Synthesis · Strategies · States of Nature · Setting Up the Decision Matrix · Adding Forecasts to the Decision Matrix · Decision-Making under Risk (DMUR) · Decision Matrix and the Breakeven Chart · *Case:* Alpha Airlines · Flow Shop Air Travel: An Example · PROBLEM SET

Section 5.3   Capacity Planning: Combining Economies of Scale and Price/Demand Elasticities   218

Price Elasticity and Substitutability · The Economics of Scale Model · The Learning Curve · Merging the Models · *Case:* Ace Rahm Company · Variant A: Linear/Total Cost (TC) and Revenue (R) · Variant B: Linear TC and Non-Linear R · Variant C: Nonlinear TC and R · Variant D: Price Elasticity/Capacity Analysis · REFERENCES

PART III—SETTING STRATEGIC P/OM MISSIONS

Chapter 6
Quality Management   229

SUMMARY
When Is Quality Free and When Is It Costly?   231

Section 6.1   The Dimensions of Quality   233

Two Different Quality Viewpoints · Functional Qualities · Nonfunctional Qualities · Quality Function Deployment and Companywide Quality Control · The Tradeoffs of Cost and Quality · PROBLEM SET

Section 6.2   Inspection and Acceptance Sampling   244

Costs of Defective Inputs · One Hundred Percent Inspection · Acceptance Sampling Terminology · *Case:* Proportional Sampling at Farmers' Bank · Negotiation between Supplier and Buyer: Alpha and Beta Risks · The Cost of Inspection · Design of Operating Characteristic (OC) Curves ·

PART IV—DESIGN OF P/OM OPERATING SYSTEMS

Chapter 10
Production Planning for the Flow Shop   492

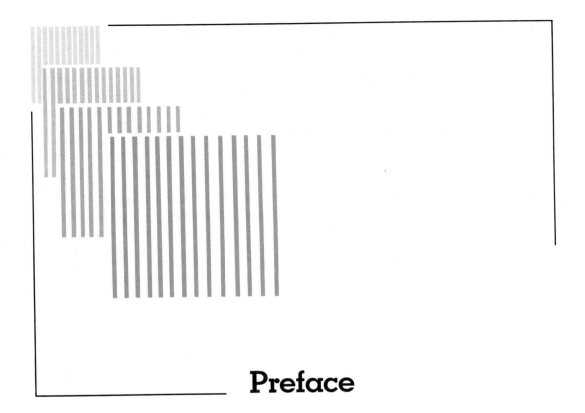

Preface

Managing production and operations has become one of the most important functions for globally competitive companies. The emphasis is on **managing.** The leverage arises from the product and/or service interaction with the increasingly high technology of the process.

"Production" refers to manufacturing. "Operations" refers to services. The field of production and operations management is well-known as P/OM.

Our P/OM text reflects a bond of similar interests on the part of manufacturing and service industries. There is a convergence of concepts and techniques between them that needs to be explored. There is increasing dependence between them that needs to be explained.

Books about P/OM usually are entitled Production and Operations Management. The title of this text puts managing first. This is meant to indicate the active role of managing the system through changing times of global competition rather than allowing P/OM the passive role of doing what has been done in the past. The manager as a compass, and not as a weathervane . . . is the simple model that catches the idea of this book.

Managers of manufacturing and service industries have a lot in common. Both want their customers to be satisfied and loyal. They know that customer loyalty has to be earned, and that loyalty is based on providing superior products (goods or services) at the best possible price. Superior products result from careful planning, leaving nothing to chance, from the highest competitive standards, from team play by all employees and from attention to detail. All these ideas apply to management excellence for providing competitive goods and services. The text describes how these ideas are applied by leading competitive companies such as Disney, Ford, McDonald's, Toyota, and Xerox, and a great number of medium-sized firms in the U.S., such as Apple Computer, Armstrong World Industries, McCormick & Co., Nike, and Tandem Corporation.

Manufacturing is changing. Wasteful production can no longer be tolerated. New computer-driven equipment requires information coordination at a level never previously encountered. Manufacturing decisions have become the major basis for **competitive leverage in the marketplace.** Customers generally make intelligent choices. They perceive product qualities correctly and they know what the competition offers. The company that delivers the product with high quality at a reasonable cost, quickly eliminates competitors that are unable to match such performance. Because the technology situation is in great flux, the ability of management to adapt to change is the key to its success.

Many manufacturing companies in the U.S. (such as AT&T, Cincinnati Milacron, John Deere, Eastman Kodak, Ford Motor, General Motors, Hewlett-Packard, IBM, and Xerox) have embarked upon major changes in their production systems so that they can deliver the most competitive product. They have restructured closing inefficient plants, or downsizing them. Using new technologies of adaptive automation, they have refitted and refixtured the saveable old plants and facilities. They have started up new ventures with computerized equipment, and management has accepted different ideas about how to cooperate with their workers in pursuit of mutually consistent objectives.

Service procedures have changed a great deal in the past. They can be expected to change even faster in the future. The reason is that competition in the service sector was just starting to get tough as the 1990's started. This is in comparison with manufacturers who had been experiencing severe competitive challenges to be the best producers (or not survive) since the 1970's. Because of competitive pressures in the financial services sector, commercial and investment banks increasingly turned to computers and new methods to speed-up their operations.

The trend of service industries in the U.S. losing global market share continues in 1989, thereby contributing to the trade deficit. As a result service industries are moving more of their operations offshore to Ireland (Travelers Insurance Co.), Barbados (AMR Caribbean—AMR Corp. owns American Airlines), and Southeast Asia (Mead Data Corp—Ohio-based Mead Corporation). The offshore moves are reminiscent of similar steps taken by manufacturers in the early 1980's, to decrease costs, to improve productivity, and to increase quality.

Computers and people are tied together in **information processing networks.** These can range from local telephone networks to global communications via satellite. Competition to provide financial services has grown and continues to grow on a global scale with competing firms in Europe, the Pacific Basin and North America. Telecommunications plays a large role in the production systems of those in the financial services business. These telecommunication-driven production systems must be fast, correct, and friendly to customers and workers alike. The ability of management to absorb such new technologies and to change the way that the business is run is the key to its success.

Similar types of analysis extend to other kinds of services including transportation, health care, education, advertising, market research, insurance, and utilities. Often, the interface (**contact**) between a company's customers and that company's service products is the employee with a smile on his or her face, and adequate training to fulfill the service mission.

The level of personal contact is usually much higher in services than in manufacturing. Also inventories of goods in manufacturing are tangible, and therefore, easier to measure than inventories of services which are sometimes as intangible as creative ideas or legal advice.

Given the differences between goods and services, the similarities are also striking. Many service organizations have tangible inventories. Manufacturers would have contact with their customers (much as service organizations do) if they ran the retail stores that sell their products. For example, the AT&T telephone stores, and computer stores have a lot in common with fast food outlets.

Manufacturers have a lot to learn about dealing with customers. Service organizations have a lot to learn about the production aspects of their businesses.

The study of production and operations must address both the manufacture of goods and the provision of services. Over time, manufacturing has become increasingly dependent upon services to keep its equipment running with appropriate software, and to keep its computer-controlled machines maintained and functioning. Service is also essential for the customer using the company's products. In a similar way, service operations are becoming more like the new kind of factories that require synchonizing people, materials and information products to keep them competitive in terms of quality, cost, delivery, variety, and innovations. With the remarkable **convergence between services and manufacturing** that is occurring, it is competitively damaging to deal with one and not the other.

This text is written to inform students about how to manage production and operations responsibilities in the environment described above. The competition exists on a global scale since countries seek to offset the costs of their imports with revenues derived from exports. On balance, international agreements support global trade and even though sentiment for protectionism arises from time to time, and in various places, it is self-limiting.

There are three distinct phases of P/OM systems that apply to all processes which provide goods and services, namely:

1. PLANNING the P/OM process,
2. STARTING UP the P/OM process, and
3. CONTROLLING, or running that process.

These production system phases are related to the marketing product life cycle stages, mainly:

1. GROWTH of demand volume,
2. MATURITY, which has stable volume, and
3. WITHDRAWAL of the product from the market.

Education for P/OM must relate all production process phases and marketing product stages in a rapidly changing environment. Winners are Fast Response Organizations that consistently stay ahead of the competition. This is the P/OM agenda for achieving world class status.

There are different types of processes. Some processes put materials and information together and others take them apart. Many do both. There are large, small and in-between volumes of output. In the background, product and process technology change at different rates. Competitive strategies are aggressive, volatile and difficult to anticipate. Education for managing P/OM systems must capture this whole dynamic picture.

To be ready for what will happen next is not enough. To be ahead of what will happen next (i.e, the ability to manage Fast Response Organizations) is the prime objective of education. To teach how P/OM contributes to **proactive strategies** rather than to reactive strategies requires the ability to deal with the total dynamic system.

To accomplish this objective, the text is developed in 4 parts.

Part I: Basic Models and History of P/OM
Part II: Managing Production and Operations
          Systems Through their Life Cycle Stages
Part III: Setting Strategic P/OM Missions
Part IV: Design of P/OM Operating Systems

Part I sets the frame for understanding the development of the theory of production and operations. The theory is highly-developed and well-understood by the best of the global competitors. It is not possible to be competitive without understanding the existing theory.

Part II examines P/OM strategies for Life Cycle Management. In this context, managing change is crucial, as is portfolio management to balance cash flow. Project management is the technique needed to start-up a new process or change an existing process. Conventional project management tends to overlook quality which damages competitiveness.

Part II then moves on to consider the work configurations and capacity planning required to support the strategic missions of the organization. Life cycle planning, to be as effective as possible, involves forecasting for short and long-term planning, productline portfolio planning and project management to bring competitive ideas into being. Being effective means doing the right things first. Then, having chosen to do the right things, doing those things in the right way.

Part III expands on the means for setting P/OM's strategic missions. These means include the management of quality, materials, human resources and facilities. Chapters 6 through 9 deal with controlling resources to achieve strategic missions. These chapters are dedicated to the maintenance of resources and to the improvement of their condition. Quality attainment is a critical part of mission definition so it is given the lead-off position. All other strategic missions including cost containment and service levels are related to quality. This is the notion of total quality control (TQC) which includes all mission elements.

Human resource management is essential to keep a winning team. This text emphasizes humanistic elements of the theory of production. Facilities management requires more than remedial maintenance, and more than preventative maintenance. It requires up-dating and improvement. The materials resource involves supplier relations. In many ways, it is equivalent to visualizing suppliers as extensions of the firm, on the same team, and subject to the same expectations that exist within the company.

Part IV concludes with the design of the major operating systems including flow shops, job shops and the new technologies of flexible process systems. These chapters relate to running the process system in the right way.

The production planning (design) chapters describe what must be considered by P/OM managers when the process is in place and every effort is made to use it efficiently. For example, scheduling production so that flows are smooth and continuous as with Just-in-Time (JIT) and with Material Requirements Planning (MRP). At the same time, work in process (WIP) is to be minimized. Bottlenecks are recognized and waiting lines removed, as in OPT.

There are 12 chapters. Within each of these chapters there are major sections that can be grouped in various ways and treated as lesson modules or teaching units. From this structure, one can obtain the necessary number of modules for various course lengths and different course orientations and levels.

Some teachers like to concentrate on a broad spectrum of the fundamentals, whereas others prefer to advance certain topics in depth. The organization of the book allows a great deal of choice for the instructors.

The book supplies current facts that build upon each other. P/OM is a field that demands knowledge of techniques which can only be applied by a manager who understands the conceptual foundations and interactions of product quality, quantity, variety and cost.

At the same time, P/OM is a functional field that interacts with all other functional fields of business. This means that some aspects of finance, marketing, accounting, etc., must be understood by P/OM students. If we did not use the systems approach to achieve integration, this would be too complex to attempt.

Because of its systems integration, this book can deal with the complex issues that challenge production and operations managers. It can make the benefits of P/OM knowledge available to students at the beginning of their academic training in business. In this way, students can integrate the subject of P/OM with their other courses in accounting, finance, marketing, etc.

The motivation for students is evident. Production and operations decisions can provide major competitive advantage. Companies compete with respect to their products (goods or services). Competition starts with the process that makes or delivers what is sold to the customer. Production quality affects marketing and sales success. If accounting measures the wrong aspects of a system's productivity, then production costs can rise while quality diminishes. So, it is important to understand how we make what we sell. In the educational process, we should learn about P/OM as soon as possible, rather than later on. Otherwise, there is a real danger of producing, marketing and financing the sizzle, not the steak.

To maximize student interest in P/OM early on, it is essential that the text:

1. Require no complex math or statistics to explain production techniques. Yet, it must provide relevant techniques in an interesting way by using math concepts, computer applications and graphs.
2. Explain what software exists for applying the production techniques. A special appendix discusses software that is referred to throughout the text.
3. Be readable, understandable and involving.
4. Motivate students to want to read it.

We do not need complex math to teach real-world applications of P/OM. Much of the underlying math is already in place in the form of computer programs which permit close approaches to optimal scheduling, inventory planning, project planning, line balancing, forecasting, quality control, etc.

Readability is enhanced when a text refers to actual experiences with known companies and institutions. This book combines what is known about production theory with the success and failures of actual practices by business and industry.

As for motivation, students will be motivated to study if it is clear to them that there will be opportunity to apply what they are reading. Textbooks will turn students off if they cannot figure out how to use the materials they are learning about in order to take charge of a real situation. By taking charge we mean, planning for, starting-up, controlling and improving a realistic competitive situation.

The improvement must have value. This text repeatedly demonstrates that such opportunities do exist and will continue to exist in the future.

Question: What significant opportunities exist for P/OM in the 1990's?

Answer: The 1990's require new leadership in production and operations management. Such leadership is required to meet the challenges of emerging competitors who use production strategies to gain the upper hand in securing loyal customers and thereby, superior market shares, revenues and profits.

Question: How does this book help students understand how to apply the materials about which they are learning?

Answer: This book uses focused applications and cases for explanations of the concepts and techniques. Focusing cuts out nonessentials and, by using applications, addresses most of the steps that one must understand in order to go from problem to solution. Many textbooks do not surface the real problem nor can they then explain how to solve that problem. They give the details of how to bail the boat rather than plug the hole.

Writing about applications of P/OM calls forth a different sequence of reasoning than writing about techniques without applications. A conceptual framework is needed to begin the discussion. This must be followed by a logic that is organized, simple, and problem-related. Further, some redundancy is helpful to reinforce essential concepts which underlie the application.

In short, students are motivated to read the book because they can apply what they read to improve the competitive advantage of their organizations. They achieve the competitive advantage through greater productivity, better quality, lower costs, less variability, more flexibility, and overall better strategic planning.

There are numerous short cases. They provide quantitative situations with worked-out solutions. Problems are given at the end of the topical sections within each chapter. There are more than 250 problems, and 20 percent of these problems have their answers furnished in the text. This is meant to provide the student with feedback for learning, positive reinforcement of specific concepts, and to encourage students to practice applying what they have learned. An Instructor's Manual provides solutions and discussion for the remaining problems, as well as sample exams of both the quantitative and essay-type.

A major theme of the book is how to choose and use the best possible process configurations. These include FLOW SHOPS (intermittent or continuous), JOB SHOPS, FLEXIBLE MANUFACTURING & PROCESSING SYSTEMS, PROJECTS, and combinations.

This covers the new as well as the more traditional ways that work can be done. The book emphasizes that most of the time there are broad options as to how to make goods or provide services, but habit dictates choice when options are not recognized. It is necessary to be open to the options to be able to choose the best one. Choosing proactively instead of reactively can provide winning competitive advantages.

Many individuals deserve my thanks and appreciation for their help. These include the manuscript reviewers whose insightful comments often led to improvements. Loren M. Starr provided important spreadsheet analyses for capacity planning in Chapter 5. Doctoral candidate Sandy Cohn provided useful comments on quality control in Chapter 6. Never to be forgotten are the many MBA students who used these materials in manuscript form and helped shape the book through their interactions. Finally, there are numerous companies in the U.S. and abroad whose executives made a significant contribution to the ideas presented in this book.

Martin K. Starr

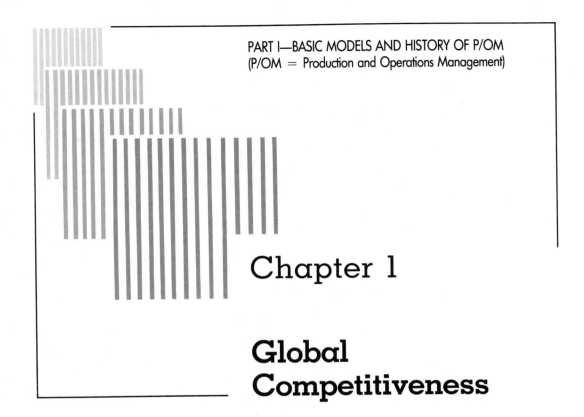

Chapter 1

Global Competitiveness

CHAPTER
SUMMARY

This chapter describes the basic model of production and operations systems. The history of P/OM is examined, so that the development of the theory of production and operations can be understood. Using the history of production systems we can better recognize why productivity is so crucial an issue.

Section 1.1 The Productivity Problem

Industrial Systems

The twentieth century is outstanding among all centuries for the massive and pervasive changes in the way of life of a rapidly expanding population. The basis for production of food and clothing and shelter, of sports equipment and entertainment devices, of home furnishings and kitchen equipment, moved from small craft workshops to mechanized industrial systems. Then, in another leap forward that has just begun, it moved from mechanical feats to electronic, computer-controlled systems capable of displaying increasing amounts of **artificial intelligence.**

There are still parts of the world where production processes remain in the hands of artisans, but that too is rapidly disappearing. At the same time, technology continues to develop in the industrialized portions of the world, and now is spreading from goods to services. Transport and telecommunications are excellent examples of technologized service functions. So is the fast food industry. Hospital activities, library functions, and even the dissemination of education are undergoing related changes. Computer technology is transforming regional P/OM systems into global P/OM systems. Consequently, it behooves us to know how to manage global P/OM systems, and to understand that P/OM systems are *all changing, constantly,* in both developed and developing countries. Managing such economically important and dynamic systems properly is a real challenge.

Input–[Transformation]–Output Model

To begin with, we must understand the elements of P/OM systems. Because questions often capture issues better than statements, we begin with three basic ones: What are P/OM systems? What concepts are fundamental to their success? What criteria are useful for evaluating P/OM systems?

Question 1: What are P/OM systems?

Answer 1: P/OM systems are systems for doing work. There are many kinds of work; the dictionary lists such forms of work as fermenting, moving, molding, sewing and embroidering, kneading, calculating, and cultivating. You can sense nineteenth- and early twentieth-century commerce influencing the definition of the word. Perhaps a newer dictionary would add driving, flying, and computer programming to the list.

Work involves configurations of people, materials, energy, and machines that are used to achieve **transformations.** The key to productive P/OM systems are intelligent, well-designed transformations. Here are some examples:

- When materials are transformed (such as wood being cut, metal being worked, or liquid being mixed), work is being accomplished.
- When information is processed (such as letters being typed or statements being filed or check processing), transformations are being accomplished.

When people are treated (served food at Pizza Hut, X-rayed at the clinic, have teeth filled by the dentist, go up by elevator, are entertained at Disney World, or are transported by bus), transformations are being accomplished. Assume that you had fun at Disney World and felt it was worth the price. If Disney is making a good profit while providing a quality product, the transformation is well-designed and the system's productivity is reasonable. Maybe it could be better. The quest to continually improve Disney World is unlikely to stop with the present management. The same can be said for Hewlett Packard, IBM, 3M, McDonald's, Delta Airlines, and so on.

P/OM systems include transportation, distribution, mining, communication, manufacture, assembly, packaging, caring for the sick, running libraries and schools. The key to understanding specific production systems (e.g., how to make molasses or train an MBA) is knowing what transformations must be used to do the job right, and how to design the transformation processes and utilize people, machines, buildings, books and manuals, and so on, efficiently.

Question 2: What concepts are fundamental to the success of P/OM systems?

Answer 2: Most important is the concept of the **input-output system.** This concept or model includes three factors:

1. What is to be worked on (called inputs)
2. How the work is accomplished (called the P/OM transformation process)
3. What is produced (called outputs)

Second, there are the interrelationships between the costs of the inputs and the process and the revenues obtained from the outputs.

There are many forms of inputs and as many kinds of outputs, but until the late 1970s, there were only three basic ways to get work done. These three fundamentally different arrangements of the P/OM process are the project, the flow shop (including continuous-process chemical flow shops), and the job shop. To these we add the newest form of doing work (**flexible and programmable systems**), which is computer-technology-driven. We shall elaborate on each of these work configurations throughout the book, and examine their special characteristics. But it is essential that we have some idea, at the start, of the way in which they differ.

- A **project** is done once (writing a book).
- The **flow shop** has highly repetitive operations; one common term for a dedicated flow shop process is **mass production.**
- The **job shop** produces a variety of outputs in small batches.

Question 3: What criteria are generally useful for evaluating the quality of P/OM systems?

Answer 3: Productivity is a particularly good measure to use if it is put into the strategic terms that facilitate the manager's job. The strategic concept of productivity of a process is measured in terms of profit margin and market share. It takes into account the long- and the short-term results, and includes the competitive effect as well. Specific elements that enter into the assessment are the investment in the process, the costs of the inputs, and the value of the outputs, now and estimated into the future. Other criteria include the extent of customer loyalty, employee motivation and commitment, and community support for the management team, the work system and its outputs.

The kind of productivity referred to above is managerial, strategic, and related to effectiveness. No one knows how to put together in a single measure all the factors that contribute to productivity as a *measure of effectiveness*. It is different from the productivity measure that the U.S. Bureau of Labor employs, which is measurable and regularly measured. Economists and industrial engineers are associated with productivity as a *measure of efficiency*. This productivity measure employs concepts that are tactical and that can be measured directly, although not without difficulty. Both kinds of productivity measures are helpful, and they will be discussed in more detail below. Here it is necessary to point out that for globally successful P/OM systems, it is recommended that both approaches be used. Effectiveness is fuzzy but it must come first, before efficiency, which is measured according to standards.

So the answer to question 3 is that satisfactory criteria for evaluating P/OM systems require two steps. The first step is at the strategic level, with difficult evaluations that are interactively dependent for all the functional areas. There is no simplistic evaluation formula. The second step is at the tactical level, with efficiency measures which can be obtained, but may be of marginal value.

The input-output systems model allows us to examine the status of the inputs in some detail. How much do they cost compared to what competitors are paying? How much waste is there in the input system? Are materials sitting around, blocking passageways and being pilfered? What are their delivered qualities, and how reliable are the delivery dates? These are good questions, some of the many that can be asked about inputs. Let us, however, turn to questions about the way the work is to be done—about the transformation process. Does it have the right mixture of people and technology? Does it change readily as new technology arises to replace the old equipment? For example, will the new computer run the system without rewriting all the existing software? How much is invested in the work configuration (the transformation process)? What output capacity have we purchased? How does that capacity relate to the breakeven point? We are asking questions that use words and ideas we haven't gotten to yet. We have done this to create a feeling for what is involved in evaluating the total process. When we know these concepts, we can apply them.

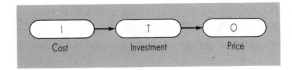

Input—Transformation—Output Model

What about the outputs? Do our customers really prefer them to competitors' products, and if so, why? Are we consistent in the quality of our products? If we are doing a good job, our work configuration is producing products that have sufficient value, to some group, to make it worth our while (profitable enough) to continue to produce that product.

Linkage Model

Another view of the input-output system is that of a model linking suppliers and their inputs to the firm, with its transformation process. At the other end of the model, the transformation process ships output to customers. Linking vendors and customers is the producer—located, as it should be, in the middle of the system. This viewpoint brings home the fact that customers are really dealing with suppliers, and vice versa. At the center of this **linkage model** is the producer, receiving inputs and shipping product. The customers can pay their bills, which allows the company to pay its suppliers and its employees. This version of the input-output model is described by Michael Porter in his book *Competitive Strategy*. We use the interconnectedness of the concept to further reinforce the necessity for the systems view when dealing with P/OM systems.

What Is Productivity?

Although much knowledge exists about production systems and operations management, there has been and continues to be a serious productivity problem in the world. This problem has afflicted many developing countries, where knowledge of good techniques to produce even

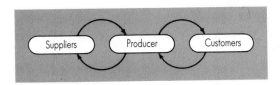

Producer's Linkage Model

food or clothing is missing. One of the great contributions of the United States to world agriculture has been the teaching of methods to increase crop yields and quality. Manufacturing in developing countries has generally been run by multinational corporations, most of which originate from the United States and Western Europe. (At least, this was the pattern throughout the 1960s.) When global competitors began to move out of the Pacific Basin countries, and especially Japan and Korea, another category of countries with productivity problems emerged. These were the highly developed industrialized nations that were accustomed to dominating markets for durables and industrial goods.

Productivity as it is defined by economists is given below; you can see that it is strictly a measure of P/OM efficiency.

Productivity refers to a comparison between the quantity of goods or services produced and the quantity of resources employed in turning out these goods or services.[1]

Thus, productivity is a ratio of output to input:

$$\text{Productivity} = \frac{\text{Output}}{\text{Input}}$$

There are different kinds of productivity efficiency measures. Output can be compared in ratio to the man-hour inputs required to achieve that level of output. This is called **labor productivity.** There is a question of how labor productivity, in the economists' sense, relates to the strategic well-being of the firm. Does it matter if the workers are happy with their jobs?

Surveys are taken from time to time of employees' feelings and attitudes about work. Some of these indicate that an average employee defines work as that which one has to do in order to get paid. In such cases, work is considered as something one would rather not do. Perhaps in the short term, satisfactory labor productivity can obtained despite the fact that the work force is negatively motivated. In the long run, and with respect to the strategic measure of productivity, this is not the case. With proper management, work can be a challenge; something to look forward to doing, and perhaps even pleasant. There are various motivations that can make a person look forward to working. The best global competitors know how to motivate employees (and train them, which is related) to produce quality work. All those who would be successful global competitors had best learn how to make work rewarding to employees. For the most successful, work might even be fun. It should show up in both types of productivity measures.

---

[1]Soloman Fabricant, *A Primer on Productivity* (New York: Random House, 1969), p. 3.

Alternatively, output can be compared to the combination of worker and machine hours required to achieve that level of output. This is called **total productivity.** The latter measure of output per unit of labor and capital reflects the overall efficiency of the production system. Total productivity is computed by using a sum of weighted worker hours and weighted machine hours, where larger weights reflect higher salaries and more expensive equipment. Output is generally measured in terms of its value (corrected for inflation). It is important to know that the type of production system used will affect the amount of output obtained per unit of labor and capital.

Further, it has been widely observed that when productivity increases, the per unit costs of production output go down. When productivity falls, if the payroll stays the same, there is less output to sell or fewer services to distribute, and the cost of each unit of output has increased. Declining productivity can play a major role in creating inflationary pressures. The producer raises prices to cover increased costs. The same goods and services cost more than they did before. Demand falls off as prices mount, which further increases costs (see Fig. 1–1). The process can prove relentless, and the seeds of recession are planted.

Poor productivity cannot be accepted. It is unnecessary. High productivity is available for those who will provide adequate management. The theory of production may not yet be complete, but it is well ahead of practice in many places in the United States. There are more than enough examples of successful companies, and the seeds of failure have become recognizable.

The economic production of goods and services is always based on the belief that demand exists for the output of the production system. Therefore, it is worth studying alternative designs of how the job might be done in order to choose the best one. Figure 1–2 is an illustration of P/OM as the transformation of a set of inputs that are available (at a cost) to a set of outputs that are wanted (at a price). The inputs typically consist of some combination of labor and capital (to invest in the transformation process). There are also expenditures for materials and energy. In the United States, labor costs tend to be a small percentage of total operating costs; materials and overhead are a large percentage. These overhead

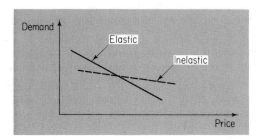

FIGURE 1-1. Demand elasticity with changes in price (quality fixed)

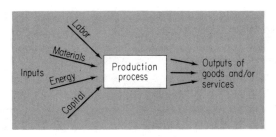

FIGURE 1-2. The production system

costs are partly depreciation (which we will examine later on) and partly administration costs.

There is the other way to measure productivity (namely, in terms of effectiveness and efficiency, in that order). This is the fuzzier, strategic measure which has more appeal to managers than the economist's measure. The production system requires a process for converting an appropriate set of inputs into the desired set of outputs. Here there is opportunity for creative ideas to prevail. Good systems reasoning tells us that the process and its goods and/or service outputs should be designed together to produce the best possible production system. "Best possible" means that demand is fully satisfied, output quality is high, there is a winning competitive position (e.g., market share is maximum), and the cost of output is lowest. Thus profits or benefits are at a maximum. Realistically, "best possible" is some combination of these good effects, because seldom can they all be obtained together. We will develop some ideas concerning how to measure such strategic interplays later on.

As repeatedly stated, the P/OM process can be services or manufacturing. It can be a data processing system or an airline or a mining process. Further, the goods or services do not have to be sold for profit. They can be production outputs of a public sector. That is why we speak about maximum benefits.

Price Elasticities

The economic concept of elasticity relates price with demand. In straightforward terms, **elasticity** is the way in which demand changes as price goes up or down. It is a truly complicated relationship about which there is only limited knowledge. But enough is known to make it imperative to measure elasticity and to relate that measure to production planning. This step is essential to achieving high productivity. And it is necessary that we also understand how **quality** affects that relationship. When we understand this highly interrelated system of quality, costs, and prices, we can explain how different types of production systems have different strategic productivities and different cost structures.

Whether in the public or the private sector, production costs money.

It is always desirable that the production system be able to produce as inexpensively as possible, given the specifications of required quality and output volume to be sustained. There are important relations between prices, costs, output volumes, quality levels, and share of market. The share of market is an indicator of competition that can be affected by various factors, but price is one of the most important of these. In general, we know that as price increases, demand decreases. Figure 1–1 illustrates a situation where demand elasticity to a change in price is great (solid line) and another situation where demand is relatively inelastic to price changes (dashed line). Elasticity measures, in this case, the degree to which demand increases or decreases in response to a change in price. The more elastic demand is to price changes, the more critical it is that production costs be kept low so that a low price can be charged. This is especially true when there is a great deal of competition, since share of market decreases much as demand does when the price we charge is higher than that of our competitors. Figure 1–3 shows what such a curve might look like.

The notions we have been discussing apply to public as well as private systems. For example, when the cost of public transportation rises, the number of users decreases. If bus fares go up, the share of market held by buses decreases compared to all other means of transportation. Public systems often compete with each other as well as with private systems for time, expendable income, etc.

Planning with Price Elasticities

When demand is price-elastic, a low price is required to generate enough demand to consume all production output. Figure 1–4 shows why a high volume of output is needed to keep production costs low and productivity high. It is critical to plan output volume and price with these concepts in mind. Consider the sequence:

1. Select a production process and an output volume.
2. Determine the per unit production costs, which are a function of the process and its output volume.

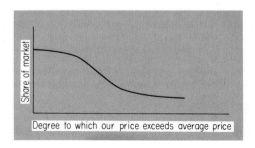

FIGURE 1-3. Share of market elasticity with changes in price

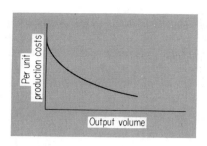

FIGURE 1-4. Per unit production costs decrease with increasing output volume

3. From the production costs, determine a satisfactory selling price (include estimates of marketing and administrative costs plus required profit).

4. Determine the demand that will be generated by the selling price and the customers' perceived quality. Note that the process chosen plays a major role in determining the quality levels that can be achieved.

5. If demand is too low to consume existing process output capacity, then determine at what price (and quality) demand would match capacity. Note that another process might yield superior quality products which could command a higher price.

If demand is greater than production output, selling price can be raised. Demand would decrease, as would share, but profits would increase. Other alternatives exist as well. For example, we could increase production output to match demand. This should also result in higher profits if per unit production costs decrease sufficiently to offset added investments in the production facilities.

Going back and forth between output volume, per unit production costs, selling price, and demand, can a satisfactory match be found? Planning like this is central to the systems approach to operations management. Operations management helps us to get the lowest per unit production costs possible for a given volume of output, as the next section explains.

Cost Leverage

The price that can be charged for goods or services must equal or exceed the costs of producing the goods or providing the services. Therefore, costs form a base upon which all price structures are built. The design of the total production system has many facets which, if recognized, can be used to maintain minimum costs. By missing a few such opportunities, the organization provides cost leverage to its competitors. If some companies have overlooked specific opportunities to design minimum cost systems, then the advantages of cost leverage accrue to those companies sharp enough not to miss these items.

The kinds of opportunities we are discussing include inventory policies, scheduling work, plant layout, purchase quantities, and, in general, all the production operations that are required to produce the goods and/or services that are in demand. **P/OM** is the term we use to describe our knowledge of the best possible way to design a process to maximize the cost leverage of the organization.

Before we study the different kinds of operations in the production of goods and services, we should note that efficient operations are a goal to be achieved after it is entirely clear that the operations being used are the correct ones. It is essential to design an effective system of operations that can be made as efficient as possible. The systems view of the production process is required to shed light on what constitutes the effective interrelations of operations. The question to be asked is this: For a chosen output volume, what kind of production system is to be used? This is a systems question about the configuration of the production facility. The answer regarding the type of P/OM system is not arbitrary; it is based on the character of the output technology and the existing facilities of competitors.

The type of system to be used for a given output volume will greatly influence costs (which in turn affect price). But if large, efficient competitive facilities exist, it may not be possible to attain a sufficient share of market and thereby sufficient volume to allow any form of low-cost configuration to be used. What if the large competitors were not so efficient? Could we use cost leverage to gain a price advantage and thereby a large enough share of the market to support a high volume? Or might we produce a product of superior quality at a high price? Does new technology exist, allowing us to lower costs by a large enough increment to warrant changing the type of P/OM system?

Types of P/OM Systems

The character of production models will differ markedly for the four different kinds of P/OM systems: the flow shop, the job shop, the flexible and programmable shop, and the project shop. Later, we shall discuss the special structure of each type of shop. For the moment, let us go a little further in explaining them. The flow shop exists when the same set of operations is performed in sequence repetitively. The job shop exists where the facilities are capable of producing many different jobs in small batches. The flexible and programmable shop is a cross between the flow shop and the job shop because the technology allows small numbers of many different products to be produced. The project is a major undertaking that is usually done only once and that consists of many steps that must be coordinated.

The flow shop employs special-purpose equipment (designed specifically to mass-produce a particular item or provide a special service). The job shop contains general-purpose equipment (each unit is capable of doing a variety of jobs). The flexible and programmable shop uses computer-driven equipment to provide general-purpose flexibility at the cost of special-purpose equipment, but without being locked in to a limited and dedicated product line. The project shop, like the flow shop, requires a sequence of operations, except that the sequence is not repeated.

Let us look at some examples. The production line for automobiles is a flow shop; so is the check processing operation at a large bank. The machine shop that makes hundreds of different gears in batches of 50 at a time is a job shop; so is the typical office operation for mailing 50 letters to special customers. John Deere's Flexible Manufacturing System can make seven different crankshafts one at a time with no penalty for changing from one model to another; the word processor (which exemplifies a flexible programmable office system) can merge hundreds of names with five types of letters. Building a bridge, or sending astronauts to the moon, or putting on a play are all projects. Many other examples of each kind of P/OM system will be given throughout the text.

Models of Production Systems

Throughout this text, we describe the different kinds of problems that each type of P/OM system encounters and the methods that are useful to resolve them. To do this effectively, we introduce a variety of models of P/OM systems. By models we mean that important elements of a particular kind of situation or problem have been identified and named. Often, the relationships of these problem elements to one another and to the managers' goals and objectives are also identified and clearly stated in specific terms. Each model is comprised of elements and relationships that have been fully articulated. Let us further develop this concept of models in general and then relate it to one of the fundamental models of production systems—namely, the cost structure of input-output systems.

Some Background on Models

A model is a representation of reality. It is constructed in such a way as to explain the behavior of some aspects of that reality. A model is employed because it is always less complex than the actual situation; it is a convenient way of studying the interacting complexities of the real world. That is why planes are flown in wind tunnels or small ships towed through tanks filled with mercury (which fairly well simulates how water would act with the big ship). Flight simulators allow pilots to be trained to handle situations that in reality could be dangerous or even fatal. In all cases, the model must be a good representation of those dimensions that are related to the systems objectives; otherwise, it will not be useful and therefore will not be used.

Without question, the recognition that we can employ models has increased their use, and the use of models has altered the nature of P/OM. Many successful models have been developed in the P/OM field. Undoubtedly, the manufacturing function is represented by the most complete set of problem-solving and decision-making models that exist in any organizational division of industry.

Models can be physical (such as architectural models of buildings, designer's prototypes of autos, maps, charts, and blueprints) or abstract (such as organization charts and systems of mathematical equations). The total unification of the P/OM field would be achieved if we could write out the entire system of equations to describe the effect of all relevant factors on the systems objectives. (These equations would certainly have to contain probability or risk statements.)

All the relevant variables would interact with each other much as they would in the real world. Given such equations, it would be theoretically possible to solve them and to determine the optimal course of action for the organization.

At this time it is impossible to write, let alone solve, such a total system of equations. But at least in theory, a production department equation, a total enterprise equation, a national equation, or a world equation might be written. The theoretical possibilities are not challenged or altered by the scope of the undertaking, even though the practical limitations become formidable at a level far below that of the production department's system.

Because we are unable to produce or solve such equations, it is essential that we structure our thinking to parallel the underlying meaning that is implicit in the total system. Fortunately, we are able to do this to some extent. We are able to put into conceptual form the rules for achieving high performance. That is the extent to which models can help us with strategic issues. For tactical or efficiency issues, the models can help a great deal. The notion that effectiveness goes before efficiency can be emphasized at this time.

**PROBLEM
SET**

1. Total productivity between 1889 and 1970 increased in the United States at an average annual rate of 1.7 percent. During the same period, labor productivity grew at an average annual rate of 2.4 percent. How can this be explained? (Do the same for 1970–1985.)

   Answer: Capital investment per worker hour worked went up. The increased investment includes both tangible capital in the form of machines and less tangible capital investments in education and general improvement of the work force.

2. What two production principles account for the high level of produc-

tivity obtained in the United States before 1950? What third principle began to take effect around 1965? Did it continue throughout the late 1980s without change?

Partial Answer: See pp. 16–22 and p. 27.

3. Company A, which has priced its service at the competitive average, is about to make a small increase in price. Company B has traditionally considered itself as offering a premium service and accordingly has charged premium prices. Company B now intends to make a large increase in its price. Which statement below generally is correct?

    a. Company A will lose little share of market, while Company B will experience a sharp drop in market share.

    b. Company B will lose little share of market, while Company A will experience a sharp drop in market share.

    c. Neither Company A nor Company B will lose more than a little share of market.

    d. Both Company A and Company B will experience a sharp drop in their respective market shares.

4. There is a sequence of relationships between production volume, costs, prices, demand, and so on. Explain this sequence and draw a figure to illustrate the fact that each factor affects every other one.

5. Define P/OM. How does P/OM relate to the systems view of the production process?

6. Explain what a model is and why it is used in P/OM.

7. It has been stated that P/OM models apply to both goods and services. What differences exist between goods and services? Explain the possible significance of such differences to the operations manager.

8. From Fig. 1–5, curve A, what happens to demand for product A when price goes from 50¢ to 60¢?

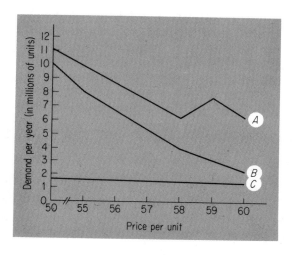

FIGURE 1-5.

Answer: At first demand is highly elastic, decreasing until the price of 58¢ is reached. Then a kink occurs in the demand curve. Between 58¢ and 59¢ demand rises, but begins to fall again above 59¢.

9. Production management is said to be cost conscious. In what way can this attitude lead to poor decisions?

10. Name several input-output systems. Discuss their components and describe the process used to transform inputs.

11. In psychology, stimulus-response experiments are frequently utilized. What kind of a system is this? Why is it used? Does it have any implications with respect to the utilization of people and machines in a production system?

Answer: A stimulus-response system is another commonly encountered form of input-output system. It is used by physiologists and psychologists to provide an effective model for studying human behavior patterns. In production we encounter it as a basis for the design of systems where people and machines must work together. The literature on human factors will provide many examples of the way in which this approach is utilized.

Section 1.2 How P/OM Relates to Global Competitiveness

The management of production methodology holds the key to global competitiveness. By **production methodology** we mean the way that work gets done. Work can be concerned with both the production of goods and the providing of services. In common usage, the word *production* is associated with the manufacture of goods, and the word *operations* is associated with the providing of services. The problems of managing the production of goods and the providing of services have many similarities.

There are also important ways in which these areas differ. At the same time, manufacturing is becoming increasingly dependent on services, and the service sector is utilizing technology and methodology characteristic of manufacturing. The combined field of study is often called P/OM. This acronym stands for production and operations management. It also stands for production and operations managers, singular or plural.

The output of the production system is called its product (or product line). In recent common usage, the output of the service process is also called its product. There are advantages to calling the salable output of production and operations by the single word *product*. Both goods and services are competing in their respective marketplaces. In fact, services are more readily designed, packaged, priced, and delivered when they are seen as products.

Production methodology has been changing rapidly in recent years. These changes reflect new developments in **production theory.** In part, these changes in the way work is done are driven by the enormous increase in computer power that is available at ever lower costs. These changes are also based on new concepts that arise because of technological innovation.

Our understanding of how new technology affects the way work can be done is only part of the story. We also understand how important it is to secure competent workers who are committed to achieving the highest levels of product quality at the most competitive price. In addition to acquiring new views about human resource participation, production and operations managers have gained new understanding about the critical aspects of vendor and customer relationships.

To be competitive, an organization's production and operations systems must be designed, planned, and controlled on the basis of the most current and highly developed formulation of production theory. This knowledge is not casually picked up, nor is it related to having many years of experience. On the contrary, people with years of experience with procedures based upon incorrect production theory often are most difficult to change or retrain.

Training of production and operations managers to meet future challenges is essential if our organizations are to compete successfully on a global scale. The chart below gives some insight as to how production theory and methodology have developed over 500 years. It will be noted that since 1960, the leading forms of production methodology have become a global achievement, supported by national policies, in many instances.

Highlights of P/OM History

1500	Benvenuto Cellini (craftsmanship/apprenticeship)
1780	Eli Whitney (interchangeable parts)
1890	Frederick W. Taylor (scientific management)
1910	Henry Ford (sequenced assembly)
1920	Walter Shewhart (statistical quality control)
1940–1960s	The era of successful job shops (USA and Western Europe)
1950–1980s	Growth of computer technology
1960–1980s	Global changes in the way work is done (flow shop processes are supported by government policies, especially in Pacific Basin nations)
1980–2000	Growth of flexible manufacturing and office systems (global appearance of this newest technology)

It is essential to understand why global competition is so intimately related to production and operations. Early economic theory recognized that international trade would take place between countries each of which specialized in certain products. Country A would sell wheat to country B. In return, B would sell A its milk and butter. The basis of the trade was that A can produce wheat more cheaply than B, while B has an economic advantage in producing milk and butter. It is the production function differentials in each country that allow a win-win situation. Both countries stand to gain by using their domestic production resources to supply international markets.

The real situation is far more complicated. Nevertheless, the fundamentals of global competition are market-driven. Trade takes place because customers are price, quality, and delivery sensitive. A and B trade because each is able to offer a better buy to the other in the items for which they are specialized. This explanation for trade was described long ago by a man known as Ricardo. He called the effect *comparative advantage*.

The explanation emphasized price, although quality, delivery, service, and so on were implicitly assumed to be satisfactory. However, the satisfaction that relates to commodities is no longer sufficient to characterize customer expectations for consumer goods and services. In these cases, satisfaction is directly related to the benefits available from competitors.

Consumers want to buy the best values. These values are benefits divided by prices. Such values are direct outcomes of the production process and the operations systems used. Prices are reflections of production costs. Quality is the child of the production process. Delivery is responsive to production scheduling and inventory policies.

Service is just another important aspect of the complex of elements that are bundled together under the term quality. To emphasize this fact, we often hear about *total quality control*, which literally means to include every aspect of quality as perceived by the customer and as affected by everything that goes on as part of the production process. We will have much opportunity to delve into the P/OM's responsibility for total quality control (TQC).

Total quality control is not a simple concept. It involves doing the job right the first time. It is essential to be able to measure qualities to distinguish between acceptable product and defective product. Scheduling production for delivery assumes that good product goes out the door. Total quality control plays a major role in production scheduling. A particularly demanding form of production scheduling is called Just-in-Time (JIT), and TQC is required to support the no-waste goals of JIT.

So much change has occurred in P/OM within the 1980–1990 decade that it is essential to understand the history of this change. Many systems for production and operations are holdovers from another time. In fact, the majority of managers in the world have been trained in methods for doing work that may no longer make sense.

The ways of doing work that we associate with personal achievement—the way we study and learn, the way we cook and serve a meal, the way we clean the house and make a bed, the way we drive to work—all are increasingly different from the production and operations environment that makes economic sense. As the gulf widens, instinctual approaches to getting the job done are increasingly counterproductive. And the background for understanding all of the changes in production theory reside in the history of P/OM.

History of P/OM

The capability of P/OM processes to deliver goods and services has changed in many ways over time. The history that follows shows how gradually the present state of production theory was developed. Many facilities all over the world can be found to be operating at older stages in the history of development. Other facilities are at the cutting edge. Most are evolving, trying to catch up with competitors that have successfully adopted new technologies and new methodologies. Often, the P/OM-advantaged competitor is an ocean's distance away from its markets. Yet in many cases the best facilities are run by overseas companies operating in the U.S. domestic market. How did all of this come to pass?

Artisans, Apprentices, and Trainees. Let us begin with the Renaissance (ca. 1300–1500), when a rebirth of intellectual and productive vitality occurred in Europe that swept away the dark, closed medieval world and fostered great accomplishments in the arts and sciences. Production centered around crafts and craftsmen (also known as artisans). Trainees were known as apprentices.

The various craft guilds, were primarily organizations designed to protect and foster the interests of the artisans. Perhaps an even more important function of the guilds was to study, collect, and codify the best practices and to enhance skills by training apprentices in the best possible way. The training of apprentices emphasized knowledge of how to work with materials (from Cellini's silver to the shoemaker's leather). Whatever was known by the master artisans was transmitted, with much time and attention, to the apprentices. The methods and procedures for training were matters of the utmost importance.

Today the care and feeding of trainees has dwindled in significance in the United States, and in some parts of Western Europe as well. In Japan, however, apprenticeship remains important for a variety of specialty and artistic products. This may account for the fact that in many Japanese firms, selection and training for manufacturing and services receives much more attention than in the United States. What happens when the two meet in a joint venture? A joint venture of Toyota and General Motors was established in Fremont, California, in 1984. It was called NUMMI (New United Motor Manufacturing, Inc.). Toyota took responsibility for production at this former GM site, which had been closed after a history of labor disputes between management and a strong union. Toyota accepted the union and hired former workers when it reopened the Fremont plant. Toyota used great care in hiring. Training of workers was intense and took many months. In fact, a long period of time elapsed before there was any output. Meanwhile, everyone was participating in the training program. After the plant opened, its performance was rated as being among the best of all automobile plants in the country. *The key point is that we have to find ways to emphasize training for excellence which includes knowing what must be taught and knowing how to teach what must be taught to everyone who should know it.*

Does the apprenticeship model help? It should, because it emphasizes the fact that criteria for excellence must be learned from the master product makers. In them resides existent knowledge about the qualities that count and how to achieve these qualities. How did they become the caretakers of the wisdom? We know that they themselves first had to undergo the necessary training from the masters who preceded them. Their shared knowledge allowed them to recognize, identify, and agree upon levels of skill.

The apprenticeship model assumes that improvement of skills is possible through training. Learning takes place through observation, emulation, and instruction. While skills can be taught, enough time must be allowed to practice and improve. The process is sufficiently complex to justify the master status, so learning how to become a master takes time. One does not become a master of a process in four school terms. The master of business administration is not equivalent to the master of the apprentice.

Our ideas about production and operations are the result of conditioning of generation after generation of owners and managers, over hundreds of years. Conjure up a factory in medieval Italy, where the first aspects of an industrial *evolution* appeared. It probably did not look too different from a shoe repair parlor today. It was not big enough and it did not have enough machinery to resemble a factory.

But while the coming into existence of such establishments could hardly be called a revolution, the signs of industry had begun to appear. The view that industry exists when factories and plants are developed as places where people come together to work is being challenged and changed by relatively people-free work processes, which we will be discussing.

Another classic P/OM viewpoint, inherited from the not-so-distant past, is that controlling the cost of labor plays a critical role in determining the economic success of any business. With the advent of the factory, individual workers no longer owned, nor could they sell, what they produced.

They earned piecework wages for their product output, or else they were employed and received a salary for their time. It behooved management to be as efficient as possible, and in some well-documented instances of sweatshops, around the turn of the century, to be as ruthless as possible, in order to maximize profit. The union-management confrontations that arose created a business and societal environment in which adversarial relationships between workers and managers became the norm.

Since global competitors have found ways to avoid having adversarial relationships between their workers and managers, U.S. production and operations managers must also learn how to substitute cooperation for antagonism. It should also be noted that the substitution of technology for direct labor creates additional factors to be considered.

The Key Factor Underlying Change: Invention. From Italy, the rudiments of industrial activity spread north to Augsburg, Lyons, Bruges, Antwerp, and Amsterdam, and west to England during the sixteenth and seventeenth centuries. By the beginning of the nineteenth century, with the utilization of steam-driven machines, industrialization in England became so rapid and dramatic that it could best be described as an industrial revolution.

Why did this revolution occur in England? A complex of factors can help to explain why, including the presence of coal, a growing population with high unemployment, a limited agricultural output, the existence of investment capital, the growth of trade with colonies, and interest and belief in scientific methods. The interest and belief in scientific methods led to product and process inventions that were tied to the applied research of the times. Invention was the catalyst for technological change. Mechanical inventiveness was the focus of the era. New machines were developed using mechanical principles that could lift more weight, cut metals, create fabrics, and transport cargo and people. Power generation was also at the center of invention for this time, and the power was used to turn motors and run engines.

During the 1970s and 1980s an industrial revolution of another sort took place in the Asian countries of the Pacific Basin. It could be said that the catalyst was again invention, but it was far less technological invention than production and operations theory development. To understand this, we examine the way in which production theory started to develop from the era of the craft guilds to the present systems of high-quality, smooth-flowing production outputs.

Interchangeable Parts: Beginning of Production Theory Technological invention was the keystone; hand labor in every field began to be replaced by machinery. The effects of this industrial revolution gradually spread to the North American continent. Change came slowly because a variety of factors impeded the growth of American industry. These included a fundamental dependence on agriculture, as well as English hostility toward the industrialization of its colony. In 1798, however, American industry received an enormous impetus. Eli Whitney developed and engineered the notion of *interchangeable parts* for the manufacture of rifles. Within a short time, sewing machines, clocks, and other products were utilizing these principles. There was no shortage of American inventiveness, and industry began to prosper.

What does interchangeability mean? It means that the parts or components of one production item can be used in another. For example, headlights, fenders, tires, and windshield wiper blades are not made specially for each car. One 60 watt bulb is like another and does not have to be fitted to each socket.

How does interchangeability come about? The answer is by shaping, cutting, forming, and making all parts within *tolerance limits*. How big does the threaded part of a lightbulb have to be before it gets too large to be able to be inserted and screwed into the lamp socket? Name it, and you have specified the *upper tolerance limit* for that product. How small can the threaded part be so that the bulb does not wobble around in the lamp socket? Smaller than that is unacceptable, so that is the *lower tolerance limit*. Note that the design tolerances of the lamp socket must be specified correctly so that an acceptable (within tolerances) bulb will fit an acceptable (within tolerances) socket.

To achieve interchangeability on an industrywide basis, *standards* must be set for all shared parts of commonly produced products. In other words, standards are necessary for interchangeability to exist among several producers. For example, consumers expect to purchase standard lightbulbs, no matter what the brand name, which will fit all of their standard lamps. Standards, both within a company and intra-industry, must include the specification of tolerance limits.

Product designers set tolerance limits on every dimension that affects perceived product quality. In other words, designers establish the range (e.g., 1.50 inches ± .02) within which the production process must operate for a product to function properly. Tolerance limits are designer's limits; they are the dimensional latitudes that will allow the product to function as is intended.

All product elements which affect consumers' perceptions of quality must be understood by the designers. The list of important qualities may be very long (see Figure 6–2).

At the time of Eli Whitney, as you may guess, the concept of interchangeability was not well understood, nor was it readily achieved. Designers have to specify tolerances that will allow the product to work *and that can be produced by the process*. When we come to the chapter on quality, we will have much more to say about the subject of matching product design tolerances to the capabilities of workers and machines.

Understanding quality goals and their achievement has become fundamental to being a world class producer. Successful global competitors set high quality goals and achieve these goals by the only means possible, excellence in production and operations management.

Only recently, service industries have begun to introduce the notion of tolerance limits for the important perceived qualities of their products. It is not hard to see how well the notion of acceptable tolerances applies to the expected qualities of McDonald's hamburgers or a trip to the Caribbean on American Airlines. It also works when applied to information systems and office operations.

Synchronization and Control of Process Flows: Production Theory Continues to Evolve. In the early 1900s, Henry Ford introduced the moving assembly line. Based on a relatively high level of component interchangeability, Ford succeeded in achieving almost total synchronization of the production process flows. By means of these two principles (interchangeability and synchronization), industrial empires emerged. Continuous flow industries in chemicals and petrochemicals were also developing.

U.S. and Japanese Production Processes. The major portion of production and operations activities in the United States utilized batch processes. Batch work with small lots does not lend itself to the kind of synchronization that applies to the automobile industry or the continuous flows of chemical processes. As the Japanese export industry began to recover from the devastation of World War II, it eschewed batch-type production systems and specialized instead in high-volume, serialized flow shops which simply extended the concept and application of assembly synchronization to manufacturing and assembly systems. The Japanese pioneered in the further development of production theory, and most of their developments have now been absorbed on a international basis.

Changes in production theory continued as technological developments moved rapidly ahead during the 1980s. The new challenges and opportunities that are associated with *flexible or programmable systems* trace their origins to the birth of electronic computing in the late 1940s. By 1988, computors had become highly cost effective for managing much of the information required to plan and run production systems and to operate numerically controlled machines. Computers provided management with a third production principle, that of systems' controllability. Further, the improvement of computers permitted the resolution of many problems by using methods that would otherwise have been unusable because of the computational burden.

The Japanese had gained an advantage by using flow shops while the Western world's production systems remained predominantly job shops. However, with the emergence of new flexible manufacturing technology, the playing field was leveled once again.

What Happened to P/OM from 1890 to 1950? To this point we have presented in capsule form the technological changes that brought the production field into being. (See the References at the end of the chapter for a list of books that deal with the history of technology.) Now let us consider the growth in management's understanding of the proper use of production systems. About a hundred years after Eli Whitney had obtained a United States government contract for "ten thousand stand of arms," Frederick Winslow Taylor (1865–1915) began a concerted attack on existing production management practices.

Taylor and his associates developed principles and practices that ultimately revolutionized the field of production and operations management. His work was essentially analytic and stressed the development of standards and improved efficiency. Taylor's initial studies related to the cutting of metals. Many thousands of experiments were undertaken, and the results were recorded and analyzed. To carry out these experiments, Taylor and his group had to identify the relevant variables in the metal-cutting process. Taylor thus laid the groundwork for an era of operations-oriented analyses. However, it was not until the 1950s that the term *operations management* appeared, and then it was in response to the need to find a name to describe the application of operations research to production problems.

In line with this thinking, operations that included an operator could be studied. The operator was thought of as an extension of the machine. Taylor found that the repetitive task of moving iron castings from one place to another could be achieved at a lower cost by improving the way in which the job was done and by giving the operator an incentive for increasing output.

The time was ripe to be concerned about operations, operators, and their organization. In France, Henri Fayol was attempting to develop theories of management. In the United States, at about the same time, Henry Towne, Harrington Emerson, George Shepard, and others were working with new concepts for managing. The emphasis was on the role and utilization of manpower in the enterprise. Taylor concentrated on the analysis of operations and operators. He labeled his efforts *scientific management*.

Henry L. Gantt (1861–1919) was an associate of Frederick Taylor. Gantt also was concerned with operators and operations in a basically analytic sense, but he added a new dimension. Gantt recognized the fact that a process was a combination of operations. He developed methods for sequencing operations which are still in use (the Gantt load chart and the Gantt layout chart).

A large group of operation specialists developed, and foremost among these was the team of Frank and Lillian Gilbreth. Lillian Gilbreth was a psychologist. Her training mitigated against a purely mechanical view of the operator-machine team. In her work we find the seeds for the growing recognition of the importance of behavioral factors. Working together, the Gilbreths categorized operations in a way that permitted these categories to be independent of the specific job. For example, *search, grasp, release,* and so on, were work components that could be put together in different ways to create different operations. In order to study each job and break it into its proper components, Frank Gilbreth began using motion picture records, and thereby advanced the cause of reliability and validity in the measurement of work. Later use of predetermined or synthetic time standards was based on these earlier efforts.

Eventually, operation specialists were called *methods engineers,* and more affectionately by the popular press, *efficiency experts.* The application of exclusively operation-oriented analysis continued unabated for many years, but gradually the emphasis shifted to the concept of a process that was composed of operations. Then, at both the operations and process levels of analysis, several new dimensions were added. First came the realization that risk and uncertainty exist and that they should play a part in production planning. It behooved engineers and production department managers to accept this change and to apply it to their own situations.[2]

Undoubtedly the greatest impact on P/OM resulted from Walter Shewhart's invention in the 1920s of statistical quality control (SQC). Deming and Juran participated in the development of this theory, and later they played a crucial role in its implementation in Japan after World War II. With SQC, at last the economic implications of Whitney's contribution of the interchangeability of parts was resolvable.

Tolerances and specifications required technological capabilities that could be analyzed in cost and profit terms. More than this, Shewhart's work demanded application of the systems principle. Deming actively developed this systems approach during the period 1950 through 1985.

It was not immediately recognized that the operation in isolation had been transcended. However, with the passing of time it became evident that product design, materials, equipment, labor skills, employee attitudes, work flow, and environmental factors interacted with consumer requirements of quality and price, and with financial considerations pertaining to the allocation of resources. Other statistical developments that affected P/OM included the use of sampling plans for inspecting materials, work sampling, and much later, queueing theory, inventory theory, and other operations research (OR) techniques.

Second, and also in the period of the 1920s and 1930s, psychological factors were understood to be much more complex than had been thought to be the case. F. J. Roethlisberger, reporting on the Hawthorne studies,[3] tells how the productivity of workers increased, whether desirable or undesirable changes were made in their working environment (in this case the illumination of the work area).

The result of the study, it was hypothesized, could be traced to the fact that the morale of workers increases when attention is paid to them.

---

[2]For an interesting discussion of this history, see H. F. Smiddy and L. Naum, "Evaluation of a 'Science of Managing' in America," *Management Science,* I (October 1954), pp. 1–31.

[3]The studies were sponsored by Harvard University and began in 1924 at the Hawthorne Works of the Western Electric Company, in Chicago.

As morale increases, so does productivity. The original corps of scientific management people believed that they could intuit the responses of workers without having to study these behaviors. The field of industrial relations has grown to be an accepted contradiction to this idea.

The strength of the labor movement helped to convince management that it did not live in an egocentric world where the premise that "papa knows best" could be consistently applied. Therefore, not only were employees recognized to be as complex as employers, they were also recognized as being people. Much P/OM history and present-day effort is still involved with these developments. We speak now about man-machine (people-machine) systems wherein the behaviors of workers must be integrated with the attributes of machines in some "best possible" way. The recognition of the individual's psychological and physiological makeup is of paramount importance when mechanization and computer-augmented systems are involved. Furthermore, the consumer is recognized as a complex being to whom a product must be fitted in many different ways. The employee's relationship to equipment and workplace environment is also vital. Therefore, the field of human factors analysis continues to receive much attention.

A third new force resulted from the growth in interest and knowledge of the field of economics. Governmental planning during the Depression years of the 1930s triggered deep involvement with fundamental questions concerning the role of the government in welfare planning, and the responsibilities of the industrial community in this regard.

Economic analysis formed the base for the planning function. An important achievement in economic analysis occurred in the 1930s when Walter Rautenstrauch,[4] an industrial engineer and professor at Columbia University, invented the planning device known as a **breakeven chart.** It was one of the first tools for economic analysis that became available to production and operations managers. It permitted and, in fact, encouraged an integration or synthesis of the planning function.

Modifications of the breakeven chart that introduce risk occurred as a result of interest in **decision theory,** which underlay the development of operations research (OR) and management science (MS). Operations research was an offspring of World War II; prior to 1940, the name OR did not exist. We can better understand the name operations research when we consider Operation Alpine Violets (the code name for the German plan to send reinforcements to Albania), or Operation Dynamo (the code name for the plan of the British Admiralty to evacuate Dunkirk).

The approach began in Britain, where it is still called operational research. Scientists from many fields were recruited by the American and British governments to assist in the resolution of complex problems of logistics and military strategy. Logistic problems for the military are con-

---

[4]W. Rautenstrauch and R. Villers, *The Economics of Industrial Management* (New York: Funk & Wagnalls, 1949).

cerned with transporting, sheltering, and supplying troops. These scientists were successful in spite of the fact that they had little training in military systems. The reason is that they were methodologists willing and able to borrow knowledge and method from any and every field of scientific endeavor. Where no useful analogs existed, new ones were developed.

In the early 1950s, industrial interest in nonmilitary applications of OR led to the formation of The Institute of Management Sciences (TIMS). The field of management science, in turn, supported the development of P/OM, where the accent is not on research, but squarely on the practical application of decision-making techniques to the operational requirements of the production department.

Prospects for P/OM

At first, the production departments that employed the P/OM approaches were those of manufacturers, with standard (old-style textbook) types of problems. But this began to change as methods were modified and expanded. The modifications in methods enabled the P/OM personnel to apply their models in new ways to many different kinds of problems (e.g., nonmanufacturing, service-oriented, and even public sector problems).

P/OM methods are spreading to all kinds of work systems, as there is increased understanding that production activities are required and used by every organization. Bankers are rapidly accepting the concept that banking is a production system, where the inputs and outputs are information. P/OM methodology is totally applicable and is being rapidly absorbed by the banking community as we move to credit cards and eventually to the checkless society.

Without P/OM techniques, the fast food service industry could not exist. Transportation, communication, public health, agriculture, and many other socially productive endeavors have been giving up their traditional ways of doing the job and have hired people with P/OM skills, who can organize the work flows to be as efficient as present knowledge allows.

Production and operations managers have been radically improving productivity worldwide. The capabilities of P/OM have been extended to developing countries whose need for productivity improvement is intense. A basic principle is to adopt the flow shop configuration wherever possible. Developing countries, lacking managerial skills, can gain great advantages by specializing and thereby concentrating the use of their management talent. The flow shop has many completed decisions already built into it by predesign, further relieving the need for management skills.

The cumulative effect of many poorly run jobs is low productivity. If the same level of investment funds were channeled into a few flow shops, productivity would be high, yielding the potential for successful world trade. Another, more recent, basic principle is to adopt the new flexible and programmable technologies slowly but surely, so that learning can take place.

The prospects are good that P/OM methods will correct the poor productivity record of service systems. Increasingly, the flow shop configuration will be adopted. Deviations from systematic patterns can be partly the responsibility of the customer. For example, the standard service is x. If you require special attention, please stay on the line and an operator will get to you shortly. For another example, the standard product has a red decal. If you want a different color, send for our kit of decals.

Where the job shop remains a necessity, it will be made an efficient job shop. Applying to the production of both goods and services, FPS-type computer-controlled equipment often will be able to deliver job shop variety with flow shop economy. The application of new technologies to services provides great opportunities and challenges which are almost untapped at the present time.

The prospects are good that most public systems will be managed by P/OM methods, thereby improving the public sector's productivity and decreasing the waste of resources. Large amounts of the public's funds are expended on public works. Such projects will be better managed because P/OM techniques are being used that focus on the achievement of satisfactory tradeoffs between cost and time. Hospitals, schools, police and fire departments, waste disposal and water management systems, the Post Office all have inventories to manage, quality to control, work to schedule, output to deliver, facilities to lay out, workers to pay, and breakeven points to determine.

The prospects are good that industries worldwide will use the best P/OM methods and that flow shop configurations and FPS will predominate because of their competitive advantage. Thus, the productivity of the private sector will increase, allowing marked reductions in the costs of goods and services to consumers.

Flexible and Programmable Production Technology

Our earlier analysis of the upsurge in mechanical invention about a hundred years ago is of particular interest when we consider the present situation with respect to a current, similar surge in invention. Starting about 1950, computer inventions started a new era for all kinds of production and operations. Microchips became increasingly powerful and inexpensive. Inventions began to appear which attached the computer's abilities to machinery. Cutting, shaping, and forming tools can be driven by computer, as can typewriters and card catalogs in libraries. Virtually no system remains unaffected by computer enhancements.

Both services and manufacturing are affected by the development of mechanical and electric systems controlled by computers. Car ignitions, electric typewriters, and compact disk players are all examples of mechanical systems interacting with semiconductor chip controllers.

The combination of mechanical and electronic systems led to the development of machines called **robots** to assist with work in the 1980s. The concept of robots, of course, arose much earlier. The word is derived from the Slavic word *robotnik,* which means worker. It was used in the early 1900s when Karel Capek wrote a popular play, *R.U.R.,* which stood for Rossum's Universal Robots. This was a science fiction work that extrapolated future events based on present trends in industrial development. In the late 1980s, robots functioned well, both as stand-alone equipment, doing material handling chores, and also as augumenters of conventional equipment.

PROBLEM
SET

1. Imagine that you are Postmaster General and that planning for the future of the Post Office system is your responsibility. On your desk are forecasts of computer and telecommunication capability expectations from 1995 to 2000.

   What might the future be like? Is such speculation useless or purposeful? Has science fiction been successful in predicting the future? What will you do about managing the future of the Post Office?

2. What are the main elements in the development of a theory of production?

3. How does a theory of production differ from a theory of operations?

4. Prepare a survey report on the number and types of robots that are at work in different parts of the world. Are robots used in the same way for all applications?

5. In an accounting and auditing firm, how may P/OM affect organizational profitability? *Note:* Accountants are often called knowledge workers.

REFERENCES

ABERNATHY, WILLIAM J., K. B. CLARK, AND A. M. KANTROW. *Industrial Renaissance.* New York: Basic Books, 1983.

ARNOLD, HORACE LUCIEN, AND FAY LEONE FAUROTE. *Ford Methods and the Ford Shops.* New York: The Engineering Magazine Company, 1915.

BARNARD, CHESTER I. *The Functions of the Executive.* Cambridge, Mass.: Harvard University Press, 1935.

BEARD, MIRIAM. *A History of Business.* Ann Arbor: The University of Michigan Press, Vol. 1, 1962; Vol. 11, 1963.

BURLINGAME, ROGER. *March of the Iron Men.* New York: Grosset & Dunlap, 1938.

COHEN, STEPHAN S., AND JOHN ZYSMAN. *Manufacturing Matters: The Myth of a Post-Industrial Economy.* New York: Basic Books, Inc., 1987.

CROMBIE, A. C. *Scientific Change*. New York: Basic Books, 1963.

DRUCKER, PETER F. *The Practice of Management*. New York: Harper & Row, 1954.

——. *The Age of Discontinuity*. New York: Harper & Row, 1969.

HALBERSTAM, DAVID. *The Reckoning*. New York: William Morrow, 1986.

HERTZ, DAVID B. *New Power for Management*. New York: McGraw-Hill, 1969.

MUMFORD, LEWIS. *Technics and Civilization*. New York: Harcourt, Brace & World, 1934.

——. *The Myth of the Machine*. New York: Harcourt Brace Jovanovich, 1970.

NEWMAN, WILLIAM H. *Administrative Action*. Englewood Cliffs, N.J.: Prentice-Hall, 1950.

——, AND CHARLES E. SUMMER. *The Process of Management*. Englewood Cliffs, N.J.: Prentice-Hall, 1961.

NOBLE, DAVID F. *A Social History of Industrial Automation*. New York: Knopf, 1984.

PARKINSON, C. NORTHCOTE. *Parkinson's Law*. Boston: Houghton Mifflin, 1957.

PETERS, TOM, AND R. H. WATERMAN, JR. *In Search of Excellence*. New York: Basic Books, 1983.

SARTON, GEORGE. *A History of Science*. Cambridge, Mass.: Harvard University Press, 1959.

SCOTT, BRUCE R., AND GEORGE C. LODGE (eds.). *U.S. Competitiveness in the World Economy*. Boston: Harvard Business School Press, 1985.

SINGER, CHARLES, E. J. HOLMYARD, AND A. R. HALL (eds.). *A History of Technology*, 5 Vols. London: Oxford University Press, 1954–58.

SIU, R. G. H. *The Tao of Science*. New York: Wiley, 1957.

STARR, MARTIN K. *Management: A Modern Approach*. New York: Harcourt Brace Jovanovich, 1971, and Life Office Management Association, 1975.

——. "Productivity Is the USA's Problem." *California Management Review,* 16 (Winter 1973), pp. 32–36.

STRASSMAN, W. PAUL. *Risk and Technological Innovation*. Ithaca, N.Y.: Cornell University Press, 1959.

USHER, A. P. *A History of Mechanical Inventions*. Boston: Beacon Press, 1959.

WALKER, CHARLES R. *Modern Technology and Civilization*. New York: McGraw-Hill, 1962.

WANG, AN. *Lessons: An Autobiography*. Reading, Mass. Addison-Wesley, 1986.

WATERMAN, ROBERT H., JR. *The Renewal Factor*. New York: Bantam Press, 1987.

WHYTE, WILLIAM H., JR. *The Organization Man*. New York: Simon and Schuster, 1956.

WILSON, MITCHELL. *American Science and Invention*. New York: Bonanza Books, 1960.

WOLF, A. *A History of Science, Technology, and Philosophy in the 16th and 17th Centuries,* Vols. I and II. New York: Harper & Row, 1951.

——. *A History of Science, Technology, and Philosophy in the 18th Century,* Vols. I and II. New York: Harper & Row, 1961.

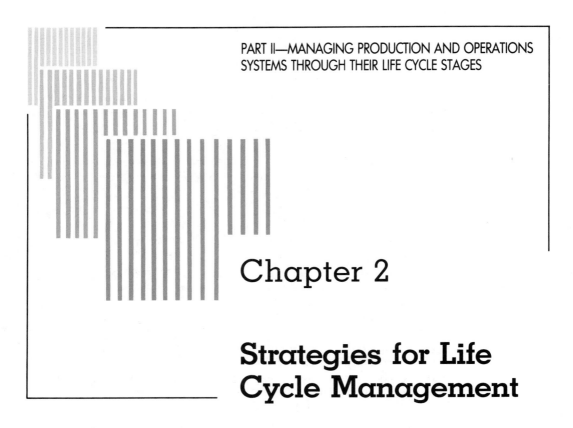

Chapter 2

Strategies for Life Cycle Management

PART
SUMMARY

The intent of Part II is to develop appreciation for the big differences that exist in what constitutes good management of production and operations—in accord with the life cycle stage of the system.

CHAPTER
SUMMARY

Chapter 2 focuses on the life cycle stages of products and processes. The discussion deals with the management of both goods and services (called products) at different points in their evolution. Section 2.1 looks at the R&D inputs to start up, including some background on patents. If successfully launched, the system grows to maturity, where demand is relatively stable. Section 2.2 provides project management methods which are at the heart of beginning something new or changing from one system to another. The section develops charts of steps to be taken in the pre-market startup stages and during the in-market P/OM stages of the product's life. Section 2.3 examines the cash flow implications of the various life cycle stages and considers the portfolio of products characterized by

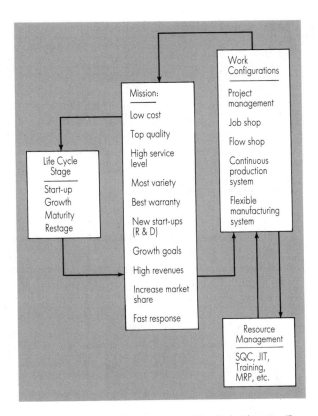

Planning Model. This figure connects Life Cycle Planning (Part II) with Setting Strategic Missions (Part III) with Design of P/OM Operating Systems (Part IV).

differing life cycle stages that would provide adequate (balanced) net cash flow to keep the business running.

Summary of the Life Cycle Stages

P/OM must deal with all of these stages:

Startup and Growth
Maturity
Restaging (plan for modification of the existing product/process strategies)
Withdraw market support (from existing product)
Terminate distribution (of existing product)
Replacement (use same process for new startup)

Section 2.1 Managing Change

The speed with which products go through the life cycle stages has been increasing. In many instances the rate of change is so fast that the situation is best described as volatile. Fast passage through the life cycle stages challenges all functions and levels of management. Short life cycle stages pose particularly difficult problems for P/OM because of the extensive lead times required to convert investments in facilities and equipment into functioning process systems.

Entrepreneurs and Intrapreneurs at Startup

The first life cycle stage is called *startup*. Startup products (both goods and services) must be developed from ideas to realities. Innovative ideas may be a dime a dozen. To shape these ideas into successful market entries at a cost that provides profit incentives requires managerial skills associated with **entrepreneurs** or **intrapreneurs**. A distinction can be drawn between these two kinds of startup change agents as follows: Entrepreneurs start a new business on their own, whereas intrapreneurs are sponsored by a company with lots of available resources. Both need to deal with all aspects of P/OM and marketing. The entrepreneurs also need to work hard at getting financial and human resource support, whereas, generally, the intrapreneurs already have such support.

Feasibility Studies at Startup for Evaluating Designs and Design Changes

Startup is a time when all of the cash flow is out. Often, there are some forms of **R&D** expenses to convert ideas into practical products and to remove technical uncertainties. There usually are **market research** costs to test customer reactions to alternatives and to reduce marketing uncertainties about the price and design of the product. There should be costs associated with determining feasibility and of producing the **feasibility study** that puts all the information together in a coherent statement. The feasibility study does more than state "OK" or "no go": It leads to suggested changes in both product and process designs, as well as marketing plans and P/OM strategies.

Cash Flow and Return on Investments

The generally accepted criteria for what constitutes a successful feasibility study is financial; namely, there should be sufficient long-term positive cash flow, high-level returns on investment (ROI) or returns on assets (ROA), and if there is equity financing, high-level returns on equity

(ROE). Excellent companies are expected to achieve a consistent ROE of 18 percent or better. These performance criteria set standards for achievement which test the mettle of even the most venturesome startup agent. Once the honeymoon period is over, attainment of financial objectives becomes imperative, unless dependence on equity markets is minimized by self-ownership. Even then, if such firms want to borrow money from banks or other financial institutions, some adherence to the ROI rules can be anticipated.

One of the oft-cited problems of living by such rules is that they tend to favor low-risk investments and they lead to short-term management decisions (quarter by quarter). To overcome the problem, it is essential that the startup products be supported by a portfolio of successful mature products (see Section 2.3).

As soon as the feasibility of new products is established, there will be some outflows of funds as the investments determined by the feasibility study are made for process facilities and equipment. These investments are described as being fixed costs because they will be incurred no matter what product volume is achieved. For example, when you buy a building, its cost will be the same whether you use it successfully or not. Depending on the work configuration that is chosen, the fixed costs will be larger or smaller. When there are high fixed costs at startup, there is more initial risk involved than when high levels of liquidity are maintained. Accepting that risk is rational when the potential return is large enough to warrant it. In all cases, good marketing and production planning can reduce the initial risk.

The Dynamics of Startup and Growth

All products that survive must go through the initial life cycle stages of startup and growth. The cycles apply whether the product is market-driven (actually, pulled by the market from the process) or R&D-driven (actually pushed to and through the process to the marketplace by internally generated product and process design innovations). Market-driven means that the product moves into the marketplace in response to a consumer need that is not being fulfilled. The successful product finds its niche and thereby secures market share. This applies to industrial products as well as to retail products for consumers of goods and services. The competition offers products that are nearly substitutable, but the special added features that are expected to cause some consumers to switch to the new alternative are readily identified.

With consumer package goods, the special feature may be a new flavor, a better package, or a different size. For example, to be competitive, P & G, Lever Brothers and Colgate continually introduce new formulations of toothpaste. Some of the formulations may pose difficult production problems, such as getting different colored stripes of toothpaste to

34

Managing
Production and
Operations
Systems
Through Their
Life Cycle
Stages

come out of the tube, or shifting the packaging operations from metal to plastic tubes. Still, these companies are all very familiar with making toothpaste, and a lot of the same equipment and knowledge can be used independent of the formulation.

There are more P/OM uncertainties in consumer package goods start-ups than in starting up the production of commodities such as corn and wheat (farmer planting crops) or iron ore (mining). There are even more P/OM uncertainties when the product has high technology content and has never before been seen by consumers. This kind of situation is epitomized by the Sony case.

Sony's Video Cassette Recorder Startup

R&D design driven systems often deliver a product that is unique. When this happens, it is necessary to create a market from scratch for the new product. The uncertainty is high enough to warrant caution in plant investment. This usually implies higher product costs and less quality than expected from major plant investments. The quandaries are difficult to resolve. For example, when the video-cassette recorder (VCR) was first introduced by the Sony Corporation, no market existed.

Consumers had never before seen such a machine. The startup for VCRs was risky, involving a lot of new technology and weak market research support. Market research produces "iffy" results when the product is entirely new to the consumers. Although riskier than the startup for a different kind of toothpaste formulation, the rewards of successfully creating an entirely new VCR marketplace were greater.

Risks in R&D-driven startups are of at least two types. First, the market may not respond to the new product. Second, competition can enter by copying the same technology. The competitive entry risk can be substantially reduced if that product has the protection of a **patent** (see pp. 47–53 for more details about patents).

Alternatively, the process might be able to be kept secret. Sony's Betamax format was not protected against Matsushita's VHS entry. Sony no longer had a monopoly, and its competitors eventually obtained a major share of the market. Sony alone paid for all the research leading to the VCR introduction. These costs, which the imitators did not incur, gave the imitators additional margin to develop distribution channels for the VHS size tape. If Sony's production process was such that it could have produced a sufficient volume of VCRs to meet the rapidly growing demand, at the lowest competitive price and highest quality, then being first into the market probably would have allowed them to fend off the competition.

Functional Areas Must Coordinate Activities. Planning for life cycle stages requires that every functional area participate (see Figure 2–1). Coordination is required to link production and marketing efforts with those of the research department, engineering, human resource management, accounting, and finance. Many new goods or services derived by R&D require such costly investment (finance decision) for the transformation process (run by P/OM) that it is essential to pretest them carefully (using market research). For example, the freeze-dried coffee-making process entails a hefty investment. Before a commitment is made, market research should unequivocally determine that consumers can perceive the difference between freeze-dried and other forms of coffee, and that a substantial number prefer it.

As another example, before a new subway line is built, much data should be collected and analyzed to estimate the probable number of riders that will choose this method of transport. On the other hand, a new bus route can be instituted directly on an experimental basis. If a mistake has been made the buses can be rerouted, but the subway requires making an inflexible, nonreversible investment commitment.

Similarly, the decision to produce a new blend of instant coffee using an existing production facility has far less risk than the decision to invest in a costly new production process such as freeze-dried coffee requires. P/OM considerations must interact with financial, marketing, R&D, and engineering considerations for success with the *startup* life cycle phase. In the mature stage, there is less emphasis on R&D and engineering.

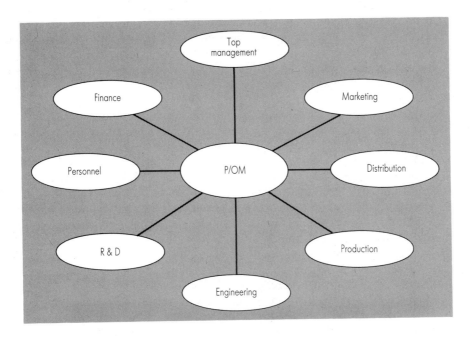

FIGURE 2-1. Interfunctional Cooperation

36

Managing
Production and
Operations
Systems
Through Their
Life Cycle
Stages

A critical aspect of the first life cycle stage is the *growth* that follows startup. The growth stage begins when the product (or products) are ready to be launched. When the products are introduced to the market, they have to be accepted by a sufficient number of users, within a reasonable time period. The definition of a reasonable time period is related to marketing factors such as purchase cycle (how long between purchases), size of market, number of competitors, and so on. How long the window of opportunity stays open affects all P/OM and market planning. All functional area managers had better be marching to the same drummer.

With consumer package goods, this means putting a lot of product (say 100 million units of a new soap or shampoo) into consumers' hands within three months to six months. That is the allowable period for growth. Production must be able to deliver several times that amount of high-quality product. Production must also be able to deal with the initial rollout of product which is sent as samples to potential consumers. The rollout is timed to be almost simultaneous with TV and printed ad campaigns. Coordination between marketing and P/OM is essential.

As we stated previously, a new consumer product or service must build awareness quickly and sufficiently. Companies are prepared to spend a lot on advertising and promotion in order to secure enough new customers to provide the growth momentum required to attain the potential level of market share. Uniqueness is a loyalty-building factor that contributes to successful startup and subsequent growth. Such uniqueness is usually the result of creative but practical research and development (R&D).

Higher quality and lower cost products than previously available command consumer attention. Such advantages are usually the result of superior production and operations procedures. The interactions of product design and process design must be considered, since such interactions are always inherent in the launching of new products and important to the ultimate success of new product introductions.

Inventory and P/OM Scheduling. As customer demand grows, the production process must have the capacity to meet all, or at least part of, that demand. If only part of the demand is met by the company's production process, then the remainder has to be filled from the company's inventory (if there is enough stock on hand) or by purchasing the product from suppliers. Deciding on what production capacity to have over time, is complicated by the lead times required to bring that capacity on line. It is difficult and challenging to make the right decisions during the dynamic growth period (Chapter 5 examines the capacity planning problem).

Purchase Cycle Effect. The rate of change of the life cycles can be different for various products. It helps to ask such questions as: How long will it take to go through the startup period, and when does the growth period end? The length of the purchase cycle (defined again—the repurchase interval) is usually positively correlated with the length of the growth period.

Assume that the purchase cycle for toothpaste is six weeks. The growth period for a new brand of toothpaste might last six months. At least when they first became available, videocassette recorders had a long purchase cycle and an even longer growth period. At this time, the purchase cycle may be five years, and the growth period is still going on, for the product class.

Project Management for Startup

The first life cycle stage, which we have been discussing, is startup and growth. Project management concepts and techniques are used to plan and control startup and growth decisions. Section 2.2, and Chapter 3 in its entirety, are devoted to project management.

Managing for Competitiveness: The Mature Stage

The second life cycle stage is associated with product maturity. Established goods or services require solving a different set of P/OM decision problems than the startup and growth cycle. It is essential to maintain the high level of demand which resulted from growth over time. Vulnerability to new competition, which can afford to offer consumers a change, poses real problems, since the established goods or services are more certain of the success of the status quo than they are of modifications to the proven product or service mix. However, if the established company, with its mature product, strives for continual improvements, price can be lowered and quality raised. Such changes can act as deterrents to the entry of new competitors.

On the other hand, successful mature products are often called **cash cows,** because their major expenses are behind them, and they provide regular and consistent cash flow for the firm to use in pursuing new business (startup and growth).

Vulnerability. An established product or service must maintain its market. It must hold on to its existing customers. Even small downturns can affect its profitability because, having finished growing, it is vulnerable to economic changes and competitive actions.

Uniqueness diminishes in importance for mature products. To rate the title of ''mature,'' the product has to have a history of many purchase cycles, and in that time, the product has become familiar to almost all potential consumers. High quality, good service, and reasonable cost become critical for the maintenance of the mature product's share of market.

Product quality is always important, but it is less important during startup and growth than it is during maturity. We expect that competition will be at its highest level. Not only will it manifest itself in cost com-

38

Managing
Production and
Operations
Systems
Through Their
Life Cycle
Stages

petitiveness, but in having high product quality and many productline varieties as well. The work configurations that bestow advantages under such circumstances are the well-designed flow shop (treated in Chapter 10), or the flexible and programmable system (treated in Chapter 12).

Volatility. Before 1950, most products could expect to spend years in the mature life cycle stage if they made no serious mistakes. The product achieved and maintained an established franchise with loyal customers. Because of inherent market stability, changes to improve the product could be brought about slowly. By 1985, the rate of change had speeded up so that some products never achieved maturity. There was startup, growth, and then restaging or replacement.

When the mature life cycle stage lasted for many years, there was no need to rush into new product introductions, forcing completion of critical P/OM decisions in a short time (see pages 31–32, 41). Those times have changed. As a result, the premarket startup production stages which are the responsibility of the P/OM department are often completed under great time pressure or are called into play hastily and even unexpectedly.

The Restaging Effort

The third life cycle stage is called restaging. It is an effort to halt the decline in sales volume and/or market share that every mature product begins to experience sooner or later. In the 1980s, the mature stage of product life was greatly diminished in length, as compared to the 1970s and earlier. This was especially true of technology-based products. For example, until the rate of microchip inventions begins to level off, the speedup of each new chip product (e.g., 64K, 256K, 1MB, 4MB) through its life cycle stages can be expected to continue.

Restaging is difficult because it requires finding product alternatives (as viewed by consumers) which are made from essentially the same process as was being used before. It is the perception of difference by consumers that counts.

Therefore, restaging is often viewed as a marketing function, which is unfortunate because P/OM holds many important cards for using the process to differentiate the product. Materials can be changed. Special features and services can be added. Innovations derived from a coordinated effort by P/OM and marketing are likely to be far more successful than from either function alone.

Stopping Production and Distribution

The fourth life cycle stage is associated with the decision to stop production and withdraw market support from the product. This raises the question of how to use existing personnel and facilities for alternative products. Management often deals with this situation by shutting down plants and laying off workers. However, if properly prepared with life cycle planning, a replacement startup product usually is in the wings, ready to take its place, using retrained workers with modified equipment and facilities.

The fifth life cycle is the termination of distribution. Rapid reduction of inventories must be planned. Startup and growth of the replacement product is similar in some ways to the first life cycle stage for an entirely new product. However, the differences are that the prior market development is already in place as is the production process.

Work Configuration Considerations

Production decisions concerning what work configuration to use (see pages 26–28) are tightly interrelated with market conditions. For startup, the market size is small, growing quickly, and often volatile. This is entirely different from the larger size and relative stability of the mature product's market.

The most usual scenario is to employ project management to startup a job shop. Then, as demand grows and success seems attainable, the additional investment for a flow shop or flexible manufacturing system can be justified. However, it is not reasonable to assume that this scenario applies all of the time.

It is quite possible that the specifications for a startup production process work configuration should be that of a flow shop or flexible manufacturing system. It is not reasonable to specify the kind of production process without knowing about the marketplace and its elasticities of demand volume with respect to price, quality, advertising, promotion, distribution, and so on.

The startup design of the production process affects the consumers' first perceptions of the new product's quality and price. From the managers' point of view, the efficiency of the production process will determine how much gross profit is available to support lower prices and higher qualities, as well as advertising, promotion, and distribution. Consequently, it is essential to understand production-marketing interactions before we can proceed to examine the various fundamental classifications for the design of P/OM work configurations.

Public Sector and Service Applications

Startup and growth issues apply to goods and services, and to both the public and private sectors. The marketplace concept of supply and demand is valid in all these categories. The production process that will supply the particular marketplace must be based upon the existing demand and the growth of that demand at given price levels.

40

Managing
Production and
Operations
Systems
Through Their
Life Cycle
Stages

For example, how many riders will the subway have if the fare is $2? How many people will rent a VCR movie if the charge is $5? Decisions will have to be made in the light of how much capital investment is required to start up (build a subway or rent a store) and what level of operating costs will be needed to continue to grow (running the subways or the VCR rental store).

At present, almost 100 percent of all public systems are either pure projects or project-managed startups of a job shop. A pure project is used when the service is offered, or required, only once (a national vaccination program or building a new rapid transit system). The job shop is used when the service is regularly available in individual units or in small batches (running the new rapid transit system, providing city bus service, selecting a trial jury, putting out a fire, or obtaining license plates when you buy your car).

The costs of supplying almost all ongoing public services on a job shop basis are high. This applies to the delivery of mail, intercity transport, police and fire protection, and public health. With increasing population size, it has become imperative to design public system flow shops that can achieve high-level productivity (efficiency) with no decrease in the quality of the outputs demanded by society. The computer capability offers the prospect of regularizing public activities so that they come closer to a flow shop than a job shop. New emphasis can be placed on using public sector startups that will lead to more efficient forms of service.

In general, productivity in the public sector is poorer than in the private sector. In general, the productivity of service industries is poorer than that of manufacturing industries. None of them is free of inefficiency. Even at the present time, a majority of manufacturing production processes in the United States and Western Europe are job shops. A variety of sources estimate that about 75 percent of the dollar value of goods manufactured in the United States are attributable to small batches produced by job shops. Later on, we will explain why this means that in the marketplace, costs are higher and service is poorer. Consumer dissatisfaction makes it easy for an aggresive competitor to rapidly gain a growing share of market. Such competition typified the 1980s, with much of that competition coming from the Pacific Basin countries.

Manufacturing in the private sector is generally more productive than operations in the service industries (such as education, transportation, and banking and financial services). Global competition is just beginning in these areas. We can expect to see many innovative startups in the service industries, both from within the United States and from abroad, over the next decade. Whatever the industry, the key points to remember are that the marketplace is where the production and/or operation system is judged.

The product, the process, and the marketplace evolve together through the life cycle stages. While it may not always be the same, there is an appropriate production work configuration for each stage in a product's life cycle. Therefore, before we begin to examine the characteristics of different production system configurations, we shall continue to explore the life cycle properties of the goods and services that are produced.

Life Cycle Sales Volume Curve

A life cycle sales volume curve (shown in Fig. 2–2) illustrates the market situations of growth, maturity, and decay. Mature products will be found on the portion of the curve that is close to the saturation (or maximum potential) level for those particular goods or services. New products must move up the growth portion of the curve fast enough to achieve their share potential (i.e., the saturation level).

Obsolete products are represented by the dashed portion of the curve, which depicts the declining sales (or the decay region) of the life cycle stage curve. We see on the curve the point at which the product or service is restaged. If the effort to market an improved version to reverse an expected (or actual) decline in demand is successful, then the curve starts to move up again.

New Product Failures, Barriers to Entry, and Value Added

During the 1980s, new products and services experienced increasingly higher failure rates. Claims to new product features were not sufficiently appealing to cause consumers to switch from the product to which they were already loyal. Fierce competitive pricing was often used to cripple

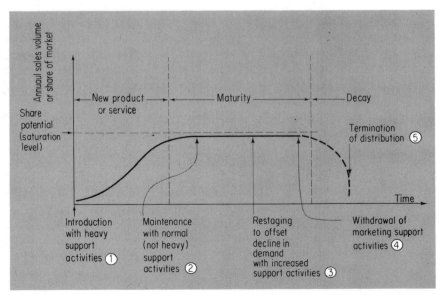

FIGURE 2-2. The marketing evolution of goods and services

42

Managing
Production and
Operations
Systems
Through Their
Life Cycle
Stages

the new entry's effort to secure market share. Superior quality is the hallmark of mature products if they have been managed in such a way as to continuously improve both the product and the process.

Such quality provides barriers to the entry of new products. Specifically, the production process of the mature product can be a flow shop which is economically justified by the required high level of output volume. If the new competitive entry is being produced by a job shop, it may not be able to match the quality or cost of the mature product being produced by a flow shop.

On the other hand, if the new entry has qualities that are superior to the existing market leaders, then the ramparts can be breached. For example, non-U.S. companies had achieved 30 percent of the automobile market by 1987. Detroit's auto makers had never believed that such a market share was possible for nondomestic manufacturers. If they had foreseen the success of imports, they would never have allowed their network of dealers to sell the imports. Once the imported cars had achieved distribution, a large number of customers were able to judge the quality of the imports, which they then wanted to own. Successful products deliver better values to consumers. This means higher levels of desired qualities per dollar spent. As in the case of imported cars, many customers recognize and choose what they consider to be superior dollar value options.

Changes in the economy can produce chaotic conditions which inhibit the growth that is essential for the success of the new product. Trouble with the startup production process can lead to erratic delivery or inconsistent quality, and if such troubles are not remedied fast enough, the required growth can never be achieved. The share of market is permanently damaged (i.e., the share potential that originally existed becomes unachievable). Still, it may be the case that in spite of high failure rates, the optimal strategy for a company is to introduce many new products. Although each new product has a relatively high likelihood of failure, the one product that is a success provides sufficient payback to support the whole program.

This kind of approach requires a life cycle management capability to cope with the great number of new products that are consistently being introduced. This approach also raises many questions about the kind of production system that can support such a high variety of quality products while delivering them at low cost. Figure 2–9 illustrates the cash flow of a portfolio of products, each at different stages in their life cycles.

Some companies follow this pattern; others take quite a different view. They utilize careful analysis and deliberation before the introduction of a single product (or a few products), all of which have been shown through market research tests to have relatively high probabilities of success. Production factors must be considered carefully because of the large amount of value added by the production process. **Value added** is that part of the product's total cost that is not purchased in the form of materials and components from suppliers. Value added is built into the product by direct labor and by the use of machinery to provide desired services or (in manufacturing) transforming materials into what the customer purchases. To get a perspective on value added, consider that for a company whose product is information, a typist at a word processor is adding value.

It is often said that services use more direct labor and less equipment, but this generalization falls apart when you think about airlines providing customers with physical distance transformations, hospitals' use of expensive equipment, and even the procedures of fast food restaurants. The value added by labor and equipment is the basis for profit margins. Each supplier in the purchasing chain receives its profits (from its customers) for the value it has added.

Variety and Focus

Variety is constrained by the desire to maintain a production *focus*. The reason for a production focus is that it offers more learning about certain kinds of processes. Instead of being jack-of-all-trades and master of none, production systems with focus allow people to become perfectionists. Larger volumes of similar operations support improvement programs and training. In many instances, the larger volumes bestow discounts such as carload shipping rates and supplier discounts. **Focus** in production systems provides better profit margins for output of the production process; focus clarifies what the company should make and what it should buy.

The question of which approach, or combination of approaches, is better for the company's short- and long-term strategy is a problem that must involve life cycle management considerations. The problem is a tough one under the best of circumstances. A major stumbling block lies in the inability to develop good forecasts for marketplace demand. Test marketing may be able to supply useful forecasts, but at the real cost of delaying introduction while the test market is set up and run.

Circular Reasoning for Production Volume

The production costs for alternative work configurations can be derived under the assumption that believable predictions of production volume requirements will be available. Circular reasoning is at work, since:

Sales volume is a function of price and quality,
Price is set with cost (and competitive qualities) in mind,
Cost is a function of the work configuration, and
Work configuration is chosen in line with sales volume . . .
Sales volume is a function of price and quality, . . .

44

Managing
Production and
Operations
Systems
Through Their
Life Cycle
Stages

The factors work together. Also, note that profit margin is derived by combining price, cost, and volume:

$$\text{Profit margin} = \text{volume (price} - \text{cost)}$$

These connections and interrelationships will be treated in detail (see pages 222–227). Circular reasoning can be used to converge on a solution, or to show that no solution exists. Thus, life cycle management involves a sequence of analytic steps that examine the interactions among production, marketing, personnel, accounting, and finance. The key is to include all relevant factors and consider them as a *system*.

How R&D Supports Successful Startups

Research and development (R&D) can be critical creative functions responsible for initiating new products and services. To provide such support, you have to do enough R&D, and what is done has to be the right kind. With respect to whether there is enough R&D done, total government and industry spending for R&D in the United States would seem to have increased tremendously over the past few years. Consider the interval from 1975 to 1986. The 1975 expenditures were about $34 billion. Some 45 percent of this sum was for R&D in industry—$15 billion. Of this $15 billion, less than 4 percent was spent on pure research (see below). According to the National Science Foundation, R&D expenditures in 1986 had risen to $118.6 billion.

The percent increase ($118.6 − $34)/$34 = 249% appears to be substantial. An estimate by Battelle (an Ohio-based research organization) for 1987 R&D expenditures was $127.4 billion. This represents an increase of 7.4 percent from the 1986 level of $118.6. Using 3 percent as the 1987 inflationary rate, the real rise in R&D spending is a little above 4 percent, and this is just a bit higher than the national average for the past ten years. Therefore, the real increase in R&D spending from 1975, after correcting for some severe periods of inflation, is much lower than the indicated 249 percent.

About 50 percent of the total R&D expenditure is for government research. Private industry spends about 47 percent of the total, and the remaining 3 percent is spent by universities. Of the government part of the bill, about 80 percent goes for military research. There is debate about how much and how quickly, if ever, military research affects the private sector. A significant portion is ''confidential,'' and a large part is irrelevant to civilian applications. Further, a really small portion of private sector funding is spent on pure research. Also, as will be discussed below, the applied portion of the private sector research may not be producing the kind of technological changes that fuel economic growth. In summary, we cannot point to the seemingly enormous national expenditure on R&D as the key to competitive advantage in a global economy.

Still, the total U.S. R&D budget is larger than that of any other country in the world, even though its per capita spending is not. With such expenditures, one might expect that a booming economy would result. But this has not occurred, and instead global competition has created a U.S. trade deficit running $140 billion per year. Although explanations include the large percentage of R&D expenditures that go to military projects, the more telling issue involves the poor use of R&D funds by industry. It is to be noted that for many years U.S. auto companies led all U.S. companies in R&D expenditures. But although they spent billions of dollars, they could not protect their share of market from global competitors.

What Is the Difference between Pure and Applied Research? Pure research is a generator of ideas. It has no immediate or obvious utility, and is therefore equatable to the pursuit of knowledge for the sake of increased understanding. Pure research findings (for example, knowledge about photon behavior) form a base upon which creative applied research thinking (for example, the concept of lasers) can be launched.

Only large companies can afford to engage in substantial amounts of pure research. The investments are too large, the risks are major, and the payoff is usually many years away. At the same time, when the payoff is realized, it is frequently substantial. Before AT&T's breakup, Bell Labs epitomized the great pure research laboratory supported by industry. No longer a protected monopoly, AT&T cannot afford such pure research. Similarly, other companies that formerly spent substantial sums on pure research have ceased to do this in order to be more competitive in the short run.

Since industry tends to shun pure research expenses, there is constant social pressure on government to support such research activities. Part of this spending is through the universities. Nevertheless, in constant dollars, government support of pure research has been decreasing. Also, on a per capita basis, many countries do more pure industrial research than the United States does.

In practice, applied research has little to do with pure research results. Immediate commercial advantage is what industry wants. Although this orientation provides short-term profits, in the long run it can lead to a noncompetitive national economy. Rather than decrying the lack of pure research, perhaps more stress should be placed on the degree to which applied research deals with fundamental issues. Projects should emphasize real product and process design improvements. Projects which enhance marketing efforts should not be classified as applied research. Many companies that claim to have large applied research budgets are suspect in how they use such funds, based on their performance in introducing changes and improvements.

The D in R&D stands for *development*. It is the conversion of applied research results into feasible and economically viable P/OM systems. It alters the production process in terms of materials, equipment, and peo-

46
Managing
Production and
Operations
Systems
Through Their
Life Cycle
Stages

ple. Development efforts interface research people and engineers with production and operations managers.

The R&D Function Is Critical to Life Cycle Management. What is needed is a portfolio of products at different stages. Ideally, some pure research would be going on with the promise of conversion to applied research within ten to twenty years. Applied research should span a spectrum of potential implementation ranging from one to ten years. Development of applied research ideas would range from immediate to three years. (Section 2.3 examines the portfolio concept.)

R&D Is Applicable to the Service Function. Artificial intelligence and expert systems apply to information services. Medical research is constantly changing hospital procedures. Telecommunication and computer networking research is altering the basic foundations of information transfer and interactions.

All R&D Work Does Not Succeed. Talented people who understand their field have a greater chance of success. But talent is not easy to define. The use of psychological tests has shown no sign of pinpointing the requisite characteristics for ingenuity and creativity. However, as we proceed along the path from pure research to applied research and then to development, the kind of creativity that is required becomes less difficult to discuss. Also, the ability to forecast the time and effort that will be required to complete a project improves.

Budget Appropriation for R&D Is One of the Most Difficult Control Areas in an Organization. Because the outcome of pure research is unknowable beforehand, the question of how much to allocate to which projects is based on conjecture. The intangibility dissipates as projects move toward development stages. But in all R&D, estimates of time and cost are crucial matters. It has been found that schedules of time and cost for applied research and development are subject to a "slippage factor." Figure 2-3 compares predicted and actual results for the length of time required to complete a project, as a function of the manpower allocations that are made.

We see that the number of employees increases at the beginning of the project, then remains constant, and ultimately falls off sharply when the job is near completion. If PERT-type project management controls are lacking (see pp. 97–114),[1] the actual results seldom conform to the schedule. It takes significantly longer to complete the job than had originally been scheduled. Slippage occurs, often as much as 50 percent. Because of increased manpower requirements, costs are also much greater than had been anticipated. Why does slippage occur so generally?

---

[1]PERT-type project controls can help alleviate the slippage problem, but even PERT is ineffective as the project includes more pure research and less development work.

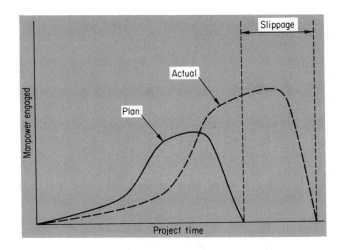

FIGURE 2-3. Typical manpower buildup and phasing out for development project

At the beginning of a project the desire to excel in fulfilling the project's requirements causes people to take many more steps than they would indulge in at a later point when the pressure of a completion date is upon them. As time grows shorter, the project participants dispense with frills and special investigations. They begin to follow the original schedule, but it is too late. Consequently, a crash program is undertaken which costs more and leads to unplanned delays. The uniformity of slippage in many actual projects appears to confirm the fact that fundamental behavioral relations are involved.

Patents as Barriers to Entry

During startup, every effort should be made to get a patent. If it is obtained, then competition is eliminated during the growth stage and for a long period of maturity. The patent grants the advantages of a monopoly to the firm. Patentability is of major concern during the early life cycle stages. It is particularly important for small and medium-size firms that are vulnerable to the competitive onslaughts of resource-rich large firms.

There are tough qualifications for patent protection. The rules for qualification change over time, often as a result of court rulings. Patents, when granted, drastically change the life cycle character of new products or services by altering the competitive environment.

The award of a patent allows early consideration of using a flow shop, if the competition-free situation provides a basis for aggregating enough demand. The patent holder can attract sufficient financing to develop a low-cost, high-quality process, and therefore to insure a profitable operation. However, there are many examples of patents that never achieve

48

Managing
Production and
Operations
Systems
Through Their
Life Cycle
Stages

sufficient demand. If the cases could be described, it would be found that usually lack of management skills is at fault. Management of products through life cycle stages is the most demanding aspect of management in general. It is a lot less difficult if you have a patent, but the patent is no substitute for smart decisions reached by interfunctional communication.

Here are some basic facts concerning patents. The patent law (established in 1836) acts in two ways: (1) as a reward for research efforts, and (2) as a penalty for imitating someone else's patented work even if that fact is unknown to the imitator. The intention of the patent law[2] is to encourage the development of new ideas into practical products that will succeed in the marketplace. The patent law is not arbitrary, but various court decisions over time have indicated that ambiguity exists in the interpretation of what is patentable. Nevertheless, it has always been intended that an individual or a company should be encouraged to develop new products and processes, and that a degree of protection for a reasonable period of time should be given inventors so that their ideas and their work cannot be imitated by competitors.

Without the patent law, there would be little incentive to spend large sums of money for the development of entirely new products and services. Large expenditures of time and money are required to research and develop a new product. If a company, having had no expenditure of research funds, could copy someone else's idea and begin to produce it, then, in effect, the first company would be subsidizing the second company. This would be unlikely to happen to any company more than once. The imitators could put all their funds behind the promotion of their product. The innovator would have spent the bank on research.

The patent law is intended to protect the innovator. More than four million patents have been granted by the U.S. Patent Office, which is under the jurisdiction of the U.S. Department of Commerce. New additions are being made at the rate of approximately 1700 patents granted per week.[3]

Consider two companies that are both working on the same kind of product idea. Company A does not intend to investigate or obtain a patent, whereas company B has taken all necessary steps to obtain patent protection. Company A is unaware of the fact that company B has a patent pending[4] that covers the new product developments of company A. Therefore, company A proceeds to produce this new item. Assume that the product is an instant success. Company A sells one million units in the first year. Meanwhile, company B receives its patent on the product and sues company A for treble damages. The triple damage claim, if upheld

---

[2]This law was passed pursuant to Congress's power under Article 1, Section 8, Clause 8, of the Constitution of the United States.

[3]As of December 1987.

[4]*Patent pending* means that the patent has been applied for and that the formal papers are on file in the Patent Office. The term has no effect in law.

by the courts, can entitle a company which holds a patent that is *infringed upon* by another company to triple reimbursement on all losses sustained by that company as a result of the patent infringement. This severe penalty can drastically alter a company's financial solvency, and in some cases it can produce bankruptcy.

Patents are granted for the invention of new machines, processes, and products for 17 years from the date that the patent is granted.[5] Design patents, concerned with the style, ornamentation, and appearance of manufactured articles, can be granted for 3½, 7, or 14 years, as requested by the applicant. U.S. Patents are granted to "The first to perfect," which is out of line with the rest of the world, which grants patents to "the first file."

Patent Search

The Patent Office maintains records of all patents that have been granted, and publishes the Manual of Classification. It has more than 300 main classes, which are broken down into about 60,000 subclasses. (Copies of the Manual can be purchased from the U.S. Government Printing Office.) Further, on a weekly basis, the Patent Office issues the *Official Gazette (OG)*. The *OG* lists new patents that have been granted. It permits keeping abreast of recent developments in particular fields. The "searching" process can stimulate new ideas. Figure 2-4 illustrates a typical page of patent announcements in the *Official Gazette*.

Although computerized, the Patent Office is not responsible for an improper search. However, the Patent Office really tries to assist the inventor. Searching is not an operation to be undertaken by the untrained person. A patent attorney trained in Patent Office classification and knowledge of court rulings is in a much better position to conduct a thorough search. Large companies usually employ patent attorneys full time to conduct searches. Smaller companies and individuals can obtain the services of patent attorneys who charge fees to conduct a search. Should the search reveal possible infringement of a patent, the attorney is usually in a position to advise the client on the prospects of continuing with the development of the product. This could include licensing arrangements.

The Patent Process

Protection of Originality Claim. The right to hold a patent begins with **proof of originality.** This means that the date of filing for a patent is not significant. It is most important to be able to prove the date when the idea of the invention was first conceived. It is also desirable to be able to prove the dates of written descriptions, blueprints and drawings, work-

---

[5]A patent is not renewable except by a special Act of Congress.

50

Managing
Production and
Operations
Systems
Through Their
Life Cycle
Stages

1312   OFFICIAL GAZETTE   APRIL 21, 1987

4,658,637

**CELL FOR ANALYZING A FLUID WHICH IS
CONDENSABLE, AT LEAST IN PART**

Bernard Ollivaud, Ligne, and Jean-Marie Lebas, Basse Gou-
laine, both of France, assignors to Alsthom, Paris, France
Filed Oct. 23, 1985, Ser. No. 790,592
Claims priority, application France, Oct. 23, 1984, 84 16196
Int. Cl.⁴ G01N 25/00

U.S. Cl. 73—61.3   5 Claims

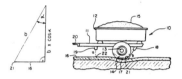

1. In a cell for analyzing a fluid which is condensable, at least
in part, said cell forming a volume in which the fluid is inserted, said volume being delimited firstly by an outer envelope and secondly by an upper piston slidably mounted in a
sealed manner in said outer envelope and means for slidably
shifting said upper piston for adjusting the pressure of the fluid
being analyzed, lower means within said outer envelope for
adjusting the level of the gas/liquid separation surface, said
outer envelope including portholes for displaying and measuring the level of said surface, means provided between the
piston and said lower means for inserting the fluid to be analyzed into said volume and for emptying said volume of said
fluid, the improvement wherein said means for slidably shifting
said upper piston comprises a rod of a first control actuator
linked to said upper piston, and said lower means for adjusting
the level of said gas/liquid separation surface includes a lower
piston slidably mounted within said outer envelope connected
to a rod of a second control actuator.

4,658,638

MACHINE COMPONENT DIAGNOSTIC SYSTEM

Thomas G. Plahmer, Waukesha, Wis., assignor to Rexnord Inc.,
Brookfield, Wis.
Continuation-in-part of Ser. No. 721,097, Apr. 8, 1985, Pat. No.
4,620,185. This application Jul. 7, 1986, Ser. No. 882,324
Int. Cl.⁴ G01N 3/56

U.S. Cl. 73—7   14 Claims

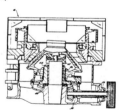

1. In a system for monitoring a machine having an internal
circulating fluid and various replaceable, wearable components, such that the fluid is common to said wearable components, the process of monitoring the condition of circulating
fluid to pinpoint malfunctioning components comprising:

(a) distributing a distinct trace element indicator material in
close proximity to each wearable component;
(b) establishing acceptable cumulative levels of indicators
from all wearable components in said fluid;
(c) sampling said fluid; and
(d) analyzing said sample of said fluid by means capable of
distinguishing between various indicators to detect the
presence and changes in the amount of the particular
indicator or indicators which signify a specific malfunctioning component.

4,658,639

**METHOD AND APPARATUS FOR MEASURING LOAD
BEARING CAPACITY OF TRAFFIC-CARRYING
SURFACES**

Peter W. Arnberg, Odeng 75, 11322 Stockholm, Sweden
Filed Sep. 16, 1985, Ser. No. 776,502
Claims priority, application Sweden, Sep. 17, 1984, 8404663
Int. Cl.⁴ G01N 3/40

U.S. Cl. 73—84   24 Claims

1. A method for measuring the load bearing capacity of a
traffic-carrying surface, comprising the steps of:
(a) continuously transporting a load along said surface;
(b) measuring the elevation of the surface in front of the load
with respect to a first reference elevation to produce a first
measured value;
(c) measuring the elevation of the surface behind the load
with respect to a second reference elevation to produce a
second measured value; and
(d) determining the difference between the first and second
measured values.

4,658,640

**ACCELERATION DETECTING SYSTEMS FOR
INTERNAL COMBUSTION ENGINES**

Yoshinobu Kido, Higashihiroshima, and Toshihiro Yamada,
Hiroshima, both of Japan, assignors to Mazda Motor Corpo-
ration, Hiroshima, Japan
Filed Jan. 31, 1986, Ser. No. 824,762
Claims priority, application Japan, Feb. 3, 1985, 60/19086
Int. Cl.⁴ G01M 15/00

U.S. Cl. 73—118.2   10 Claims

1. An acceleration detecting system for an internal combustion engine comprising;
air flow determining means for determining intake air mass
flow in an inlet channel provided to the engine and producing an output signal corresponding to the determined
intake air mass flow,
first variation detecting means for detecting variations in the
output signal of said air flow determining means at intervals of a first predetermined period,
first comparing means for comparing the variation detected
by said first variation detecting means with a first predetermined value to find a first condition wherein the variation detected by said first variation detecting means is
equal to or larger than the first predetermined value,
second variation detecting means for detecting variations in
the output signal of said air flow determining means at
intervals of a second predetermined period shorter than
said first predetermined period or continuously,

FIGURE 2-4. A typical page from the *Official Gazette* of the United States Patent and
Trademark Office

ing prototypes, and operating tests. Witnesses to these dates are the most effective proof from the point of view of the courts. Thus, even though a patent may not be sought, a company should maintain adequate records of all inventions (properly attested to by witnesses) for its own protection.[6]

Working Model. At the time the patent application is issued, the Patent Office can insist that a prototype or working model be furnished with the patent application.

Patent Application. In addition to the Formal Papers, which is primarily a petition for the patent, a description of the invention is required, called the Specification, and also an explicit definition of the invention called Claims. Drawings will be attached if they provide clarification. Skill is required to write the Specification. The description is supposed to be clear enough so that an individual who is skilled in the particular area covered by the patent could construct the invention and utilize it.

Novelty. The patent courts have over the years interpreted the requirement of novelty in a variety of ways. The definition of novelty has varied from a difference imposed on a basic theme to something that is entirely new. In any case, the claims that are made must distinguish the difference between the invention under consideration from all other efforts in this same area.

Utility. The patent law requires that a patentable invention should have utility. Here again semantic problems lead to interpretations which differ over time. It is difficult to determine what constitutes social utility. The issue that must be decided is how to determine what is useful for the public. The courts have exercised a great deal of influence in determining what utility is in terms of patent litigation.

Time Limitation. It might be expected that the granting of a patent should obligate the inventor to produce the item in question, in sufficient volume and within a reasonable period of time. After all, competitors have been barred from producing the product. Surprisingly, the interpre-

---

[6]As a service to inventors, the Office instituted the Disclosure Document Program under which the Office will accept and preserve documents which may be used as evidence of the dates of conception of inventions for two years. The documents will be destroyed after two years unless they are referred to in related patent applications within the period. Inventors have used various means to attempt to establish such dates, prior to the submission of their patent applications, for use as evidence in any further controversy. This has included the practice of mailing to themselves or to other persons registered envelopes containing disclosure statements.

52

Managing
Production and
Operations
Systems
Through Their
Life Cycle
Stages

tation of the court does not support this point of view.[7] Therefore, if a company obtains a patent on an invention that competes with its present product line, strictly with the intention of keeping it out of production and out of competitors' hands, this does not constitute a violation of the patent laws.

When the conditions required by the patent law are met, a patent is granted. This guarantees protection for 17 years. Frequently, companies attempt to extend the period of protection by a procedure that is known as **fencing in.** In this case, the basic patent idea is divided into as many components as possible. Patents are obtained, one at a time, on each of the component parts. At the end of the first 17-year period, a second basic notion is patented. The procedure is repeated as long as possible.

Another form of action with the same purpose is to patent a basic idea and then at a later time to patent improvements of the basic idea. Thus, when the basic idea becomes public property, the first improvement is protected. A company that attempts to produce the basic product without the improvement is operating at a competitive disadvantage which is likely to deter its entering the market.

Only people can obtain patents, not corporations. This means that when a company develops a new idea in its laboratory, the idea must be credited to an individual or individuals. The individuals apply for the patent. The company achieves protection by requiring that its employees sign an agreement, as a condition of employment, which states that all patents obtained by the employee as a result of his work with the company are to be assigned to the company by the employee (see Fig. 2–4).

Patents: An Overview

To conclude, let us note some additional points about patents. *First,* company size tends to be correlated with the number of patents the company holds. Larger companies hold a disproportionate share of patents. This trend can be explained by the costly research facilities that are

---

[7]Chief Justice Stone, in a Supreme Court case construing the federal patent statutes, indicated that prior Court decisions and the Constitution of the United States support the position that "failure of a patentee to make use of a patented invention does not affect the validity of a patent." (*Special Equipment Co.* vs. *Coe, Commissioner of Patents,* 324 U.S. 370, 65 Sup. Ct. 741 [1945].)

In defining the nature of a patent grant, the Court stated: "The patent grant is not of a right to the patentee to use the invention, for that he already possesses. It is a grant of a right to exclude others from using it." Mr. Justice Douglas, in a dissenting opinion, argued that to permit a patentee to suppress the use of one patent to enlarge its monopoly on another is contrary to the limited monopoly control permitted by legislative grace, a block in the development of technology, and irreconcilable with the purpose of the Constitution of the United States, "to promote the Progress of Science and useful Arts." (Art. 1, Sect, 8, Cl. 8.)

required, at present levels of knowledge, to come up with patentable inventions. This does not mean that all of the patents obtained by the large companies are benefiting the consumer.

Second, the percentage of patents granted each year by the U.S. Patent Office to foreign interests continues to grow. This is indicative of the fact that U.S. research efforts represent a decreasing percentage of world research efforts. According to the *Wall Street Journal* (Jan. 23, 1987), "Japan produces more than twice as many patents per capita as the U.S. does." In 1986, 45 percent of all patents granted by the U.S. Patent Office were to foreign citizens.

Third, the emphasis of many companies has shifted from product development and improvement to cost savings. Also, efforts to comply with governmental regulations concerning pollution control, food and drug testing requirements, unsafe product designs, and so on have changed the focus of research and development, with consequent alterations in the kinds of patent applications that are made.

Fourth, in spite of the growth of international trade, there is no fundamental reciprocity between nations with respect to patent protection. It has been disappointing that a common patent system was not developed with the European Economic Community, and worldwide as well. It remains customary for U.S. companies to apply separately for patent protection in various countries, rather than having a worldwide policy that would require only a single patent search and application to be made.

Fifth, there have been many signs that U.S. organizations are less interested in innovation than their public relations departments allow.[8] Still, life cycle management is much different when a broadly based patent has been obtained than when no patent protection exists at all. With patent protection, there is time to build up the size of the market to a point that flow shop activities can be sustained. Viewed in this light, the holding of a patent not only protects against early growth-stage competitive actions, but also allows the patent-holding organization to achieve a significant competitive advantage in production efficiency when the patent expires. In the same sense, process patents can offer one organization a flow shop capability that other organizations cannot obtain.

Sixth, it should be noted that contrary advice is given by some knowledgeable individuals who contend that patents give away information to potential competitors. They maintain that the knowhow of making and delivering the product should be kept as secret as possible. To these individuals, the competitive edge does not reside in the product design, but in the way that the business is run. Adding support to this position is the fact that global competitors often act as if they were immune to penalties for violating patents held in countries other than their own.

---

[8]See Donald A. Schon, *Technology and Change* (New York: Delacorte Press, 1967).

Section 2.2 Pre-Market and In-Market Production Phases

Every product or service must go through three pre-market production phases. **Pre-market** means everything that must be done before the product is distributed and sold. We will call these phases I-A, I-B, and I-C. These are the preparations required of P/OM during the startup life cycle stage and before the in-market production phases II-A and II-B can begin. All the phases are listed below:

Pre-Market Phases

I–A Product and service development (Fig. 2–5)
I–B Process development (Fig. 2–6)
I–C Implementation of operations (Fig. 2–7)

In-Market Phases

II–A Operating the system
II–B Redesigning the process

A graphic picture is developed of each pre-market production phase to explore its characteristics and to learn the involvement of P/OM. Fig-

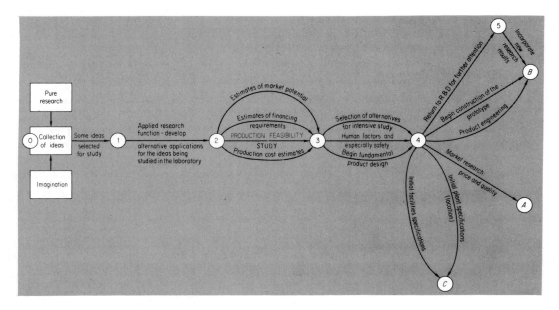

FIGURE 2-5. Model PERT network for the design of a production system: Stage I-A-product and service development

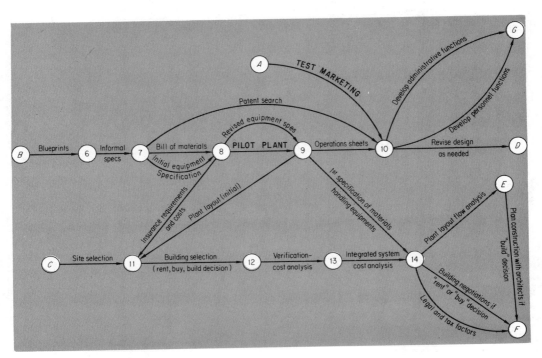

FIGURE 2-6. Model PERT network for the design of a production system: Stage I-B-process development

ures 2–5, 2–6, and 2–7 show sequences of activities that are typical of production systems. With minor revision, they apply to particular goods or service systems.

Feasibility Analysis

Our diagrams are critical path or PERT-type charts that are now always employed by project managers. We shall deal with the definition of terms and the technical aspects of using PERT charts for project management in Chapter 3. However, at this point the diagrams are used to describe a sequence of activities appropriate for determining feasibility at the pre-market production phases.

Figure 2–5 traces many of the steps that are crucial for the successful development of new products and services (Phase I-A). Starting with 1 in Fig. 2–5 and including most of the paths of Fig. 2–6, we find that the considerations usually required for feasibility analysis of a new product or service appear in the diagram.

Feasibility studies are essential to plan production and operations start-ups. They begin early in the planning process (note: 2 to 3) and are

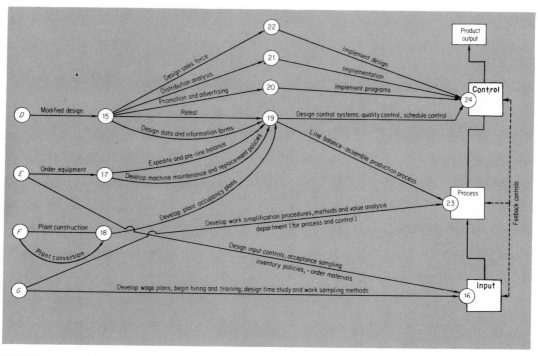

FIGURE 2-7. Model PERT network for the design of a production system: Stage I-C—implementation of operations

continued at increasing levels of depth throughout the pre-market period of activity. These studies are responsible for [go/(no go)] determinations for the entire project as well as for parts of it. They lead to major and minor revisions of plans. The practice of using feasibility studies has been established over many years. Feasibility studies for flow shops (and major projects) are pursued with much greater vigor than those for job shops. This is because the cost of errors in planning the flow shop (and major projects) can be enormous and they are difficult to correct. This is not so for the job shop.

The new product or service originates with a combination of ideas and research (Note: 0 and 1). Often, the stimulus is a competitive development. The intention is to produce a copy of the competitor's product or service. As we have noted previously, if the originator has no patent protection, the imitator can benefit substantially by obtaining a reasonable market share without having to invest heavily in research and development. On the other hand, whoever is first to enter the market has distinct advantages.

These notions help to explain why financial managers may seem to withhold support from major new undertakings, waiting for competitors to underwrite development costs and test market responses. Conversely, they also explain why marketing managers request unreasonable production delivery schedules in order to assure being first in the marketplace. The key to success is communication of objectives and coordination of efforts between P/OM, financial management, and marketing management.

Figure 2–6 provides network representation for Phase I-B, which is process development. Two critical activities should be amplified. The first, test marketing (Note: A → 10), is the main pre-market activity of marketing. Production must supply sample goods and services in ample quantities to be tested. But this results in a quandary: How can you supply production output to be tested when the production facility is not in place? Conversely, how can custom-made output stand in for the real thing so that test market results are credible? This problem is more serious for the flow shop than for the job shop, because the flow shop entails much greater investment. Nevertheless, even in the job shop, significant expenditures may be required for specially trained individuals, costly tools and dies, and materials that cannot be purchased in small quantities.

Often, to resolve the dilemma of whether or not to employ a flow shop, a pilot plant (Note: 8 → 9) is built. The **pilot plant** is a copy on a smaller scale of the eventual production process. More realistic estimates of the costs of production can be obtained by using the pilot plant than from custom-made, job shop output. Consequently, better pricing strategies can be tested. Also, the output samples are more nearly like the actual output of the finalized, full-scale production system.

In Fig. 2–7 we see the third stage of our pre-market production activities, called implementation of operations. These third-phase steps represent the activities required to actualize the decisions made in prior stages. Beginning with events D, E, F, and G, the components of the actual facility are assembled and set up in working order. Thus, the end product of the overall planning sequence is the operating system, 16 → 23 → 24.

Once assembled, the system must be operated as in Phase II-A. All of the activities shown in Figs. 2–6 and 2–7 will be explained in the text. The PERT charts provide organization and a basis for understanding activities, but each activity requires clarification and explanation.

The Design of Products and Services

New product or new service development begins with a collection of ideas. Wearing their innovators' hats, managers choose some of these ideas for further study. Various ways of converting ideas into applications are investigated in the laboratory. Promising alternatives must be checked for such factors as production feasibility in a technological sense, acceptability of the production costs, financing requirements, and possible prices and qualities related to marketability. In addition, human factors concerned with both product and process are considered from various points of view, including attractiveness, ease of use, and safety.

58

Managing
Production and
Operations
Systems
Through Their
Life Cycle
Stages

From the alternatives, one or more possibilities are selected for further study because of encouraging evaluations. Design is begun in earnest, and a basic decision is reached concerning the product or service design. Thus begins the developmental phase. Occasionally, the managers in charge of the project request further help and guidance from R&D. Product development requires product engineering, which includes detailed cost specification, the beginning of intensive market research, and the inception of plant and facilities specification. At this point we reach a boundary between product and process development. It is not that the product development phase is finished. Rather, it is integrated with the further specification of the process. The procedure should become iterative, as shown in Figure 2–8.

Service development frequently requires many of the same steps. Office outputs should be designed and checked to verify that they are serving the intended purpose. In designing the office, the question arises as to whether it will be essentially a job shop or a flow shop office. Mail-order companies have most of the clerical work so thoroughly routinized that these activities practically constitute a flow shop. As another example, the design of a transportation system (be it airline, railroad, trucker, or steamship line) must specify the product (i.e., what kind of cargo), what ratio of cargo to passengers, what kind of delivery service, and what kind of service to passengers. The delivery process must also be carefully designed. All supporting facilities must be developed so that they can provide high-quality services, as promised.

Prototypes, Pilot Plants, and Test Markets

An important and exciting phase of the development process for products occurs when the output design prototype is made. This is a fully developed physical model of the goods or services. It is intended to embody most of the significant characteristics that will be found in the final product. Many kinds of prototypes are used. For example, the prototype of an automobile is frequently made of clay. This model of the chassis reveals the styling and appearance of the automobile so that it can be

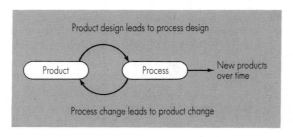

FIGURE 2-8. Product and Process Planning

evaluated on a visual basis. Many important qualities are not captured by the prototype, and the process for producing the product has been by-passed. Consequently, the prototype is best viewed as a step in the information gathering process, and not as a final basis for decision-making.

A separate, hand-tooled model of the engine and other moving parts of the system will also be required. At a still later point, a handcrafted automobile will be developed that represents a total assembly as it will eventually come from the production line. There is a scaling problem with prototypes. It is well known to engineers that a reduction in scale can produce behaviors that do not accurately describe the performance of the final system. When possible, engineers transform the results obtained from experiments with scale models to overcome the inherent distortions.

The same kind of thinking should be applied to all prototypes. Differences in physical size must be properly rationalized as they affect performance. Scaled-down inputs and outputs may not behave in linear proportion to the full-scale system. Materials-aging experiments require a reduction of time, as do most fatigue tests, but the effects of artificially compressing time must be completely understood if the prototype is to be used to predict the performance of the full-scale unit operating in real time. Even for styling and appearance, the scaled-down prototype can mislead design judgment.

In the case of a process (for example, a chemical plant), an advanced prototype will take the form of a pilot plant. This pilot plant is a scaled-down model of the final plans for the processing unit. It is similar to the final unit in all respects, but on a reduced scale. Pilot plants may involve expenditures of millions of dollars. In such cases, they usually represent models of full-scale units that cost hundreds of millions of dollars. If the pilot plant produces negative results, the plans can be reworked or discarded. The purpose of a pilot plant is to spend a relatively small sum of money (say $1 million) in order to avoid far larger penalties (say $20 million) that could occur if such precautions were not taken.

Since prototypes must be evaluated with care, a test market is often set up and supplied with sample production output. It is difficult to design a test marketing situation that incorporates all relevant features existing in the full-scale market. However, by using statistical sampling theory, a reasonable approximation often can be obtained.[9] A group of people is chosen whose behavior is expected to approximate the behavior that would be found on a national scale. The test market may be divided into two parts on a matched sample basis. That is, two areas are chosen, supposedly identical and each representing the full market. Both are given different alternatives (e.g., taste formulations and package designs) to evaluate. In this way, it is possible to obtain information concerning which design alternative is likely to be the most acceptable.

---

[9]See, for example, Frederick F. Stephan and Philip J. McCarthy, *Sampling Opinions—An Analysis of Survey, Procedures* (New York: Wiley, 1958), and William G. Cochran, *Sampling Techniques,* 2nd ed. (New York: Wiley, 1963).

60
Managing
Production and
Operations
Systems
Through Their
Life Cycle
Stages

Prototypes, test markets, and pilot plants represent a boundary where research and development, production, finance, and marketing all come together in a crucial test situation. Production and operations managers must be thoroughly familiar with the use of such methods for testing technological feasibility, market reactions, and estimates of production costs. Only in this way is it possible to reduce uncertainty before major financial commitments are made. The costs of testing alternative actions can be figured in terms of direct expenditures, which should always be matched against the costs of not conducting such tests (i.e., the penalties of making serious mistakes).

Process Design

The efficiency of operations is dependent upon the design of the processes of which they are a part. Therefore, we wish to generalize about the life-cycle properties and broad systems characteristics of process design.

First, the product line or service mix should be created with the process design in mind. Each should be successively altered (iterative thinking is used) until a best combination is achieved. Iterative thinking is repetitive analysis of a sequence of steps aimed at converging on an acceptable solution. In this case, product or service determines process, which then alters the initial output specifications, leading to further changes in process design, and so on.

For example, the cost of producing a flashlight battery by a flow shop method is determined to be too high to support the demand required to absorb the flow shop volume. Consequently, a change in the design of the battery is proposed, but this change requires an alteration in the process, and so on. The use of the systems approach for product/process design can pay off handsomely for the extra work involved.

Second, process design must ultimately deal with every detail of what is to be done, how, when, and where. Such detailed study is essential for products. Nothing will occur until a decision has been made for every activity, step by step, that is physically required to produce output. The same requirement cannot always be levied for service systems, where it is often harder to pin down exactly what service is to be rendered. This aspect of designing service systems is especially true when people play an important part in the service process (for example, bank tellers, store checkout clerks, airline reservation personnel, and fast-food order takers). Therefore, before a new service is launched, stress should be placed on achieving as totally detailed a description of service elements as possible.

Third, much greater effort can be justified in designing flow shop processes than can be warranted for designing even relatively high-volume batch jobs in the generalized job shop. Process design goes on continuously in the job shop as new orders are received. Each new job shop order requires some set of operations that can be sequenced together from the modular productive capabilities of the general-purpose equipment on the job shop floor.

Process design and development occur during the pre-marketing phases of the life cycles of products and services. In conjunction with designing production output, the task is systems-oriented and requires coordination with other functions. Through implementation (Phase I-C), we achieve an operating production process (Phase II-A) that produces the right outputs (i.e., there is demand for them) with high productivity.

Running a system takes one kind of talent. Designing and building the system calls upon another set of talents: those of project management. Both aspects of P/OM are changing. However, the technology of designing and building is changing faster than the technology of running systems. Computer-aided design (called CAD) and computer-aided manufacturing (called CAM) and computer-aided engineering (called CAE) are just a sample of the project management changes that have occurred. There is less and less to be learned from past experience; but there is also a lot of risk in pioneering projects that have skimpy precedents.

Success in the project design phase prohibits fractionation, segmentation, or splintering of the system components. Like an orchestra or ballet, all the players must coordinate their activities. Decisions reached in false isolation are dangerous. To help prevent overlooking potentially critical aspects, a number of questions relevant to the design process are raised below. The list is intended to illustrate the variety of issues that should be considered. Many decisions are not consciously made, and the resulting activities occur by default. Further, the list should reveal the interrelationships that bind decisions together, so that a conclusion on one point removes the possibility of deciding about another. Some questions are broad, others are narrow. The level of detail should move from the broad, strategic considerations to the narrow, tactical issues. Then a decision on detail does not block the possibility of achieving the best solution to a major consideration. *Do the right thing before you do the thing right.* The answer to any question should involve the total system. Through synthesis,[10] a process design of real excellence can emerge.

With Respect to the Output

1. What product has been chosen? Why? (Should there be one or more outputs?)
2. Are the attributes of the product (output) completely specified? To what extent are they unique?
3. If they are unique, why has no other company done this before?
4. Why does the opportunity exist? (For how long has it existed?)

---

[10]See p. 198.

62

Managing
Production and
Operations
Systems
Through Their
Life Cycle
Stages

5. Are the estimates that account for the choice of the specified output accurate and believable? (Is there consensus on this point?)
6. How will the output be distributed and by whom?
7. How will quality be assessed and high quality assured?
8. How does the production schedule relate to anticipated demands?
9. What mechanisms and policies have been set up for production schedule control?
10. Has a policy been developed with respect to patent protection? (What are the pros and cons for getting a patent?)

With Respect to Human Resources

11. What are the human resource requirements?
12. Are there tradeoffs to be considered between employees and machines?
13. Is the relationship between employees and machines likely to change because of technological factors? (Alternatively, when will it change?)
14. What are the expected productivities, and what are the commensurate costs?
15. Have the patterns of work been thoroughly studied?

With Respect to Materials

16. Can the choices of input materials be thoroughly justified?
17. Are these choices likely to change because of technological factors?
18. Have all subcontracting possibilities been considered? (Has global sourcing been included?)
19. Are there alternative sources for the same materials? (Has global sourcing been included? Do volume discounts offset work in process (WIP) costs?)
20. Have adequate inventory management policies been developed?

With Respect to the Process

21. What specific equipment and facilities will be needed? (What is available?)
22. How adequately have sources of equipment supply been investigated?
23. How accurately have equipment costs and productivity been estimated?
24. What equipment capacities and sizes have been estimated for the process?
25. What space requirements have been determined for the total process?

26. Is the plant layout based on short- or long-term assumptions?

27. Should preventive or remedial maintenance be used?

28. How much maintenance will be required? (Has this been considered with respect to equipment selection?)

29. What are the work in process inventory storage requirements? (Do they fluctuate?)

30. Has the designed process flow been totally justified? How flexible and amenable to change are the lines of flow?

31. Is the basis for materials-handling equipment decisions short- or long-term?

32. Have equipment setup times been estimated accurately? Can they be reduced?

With Respect to Location

33. Has consideration been given to both supply of input materials and demand for output products in locating a plant site?

34. Has the cost of studying the plant location or relocation problem been included?

35. Have insurance rates and taxes been determined with respect to plant selection?

36. Have the costs, availability, and apparent skills of labor been compared for the various location possibilities? (Has equipment selection been made with this in mind?)

37. What importance have transportation problems and shipping costs played in reaching a location decision? (Can the basis for this decision change?)

38. What zoning restrictions and town or state ordinances exist that might affect the location decision? (Do water, air, or noise pollution considerations deserve attention?)

39. How available and costly will utility services be, such as sewage, water, oil, gas, heat, and electricity? (Will process demands be stable or grow?)

40. Have incorporation fees and procedures been considered?

41. Has the cost of shutting down and moving been taken into account?

42. What consideration has been given to long-run land values?

43. Have the effects of inflation been taken into account?

44. Have building costs been properly compared with plant purchase and plant rentals?

45. Should climate have any influence on the location decision?

46. Has there been a thorough evaluation of specific site factors, including drainage, exposure, and so forth? (Has the ecological impact been evaluated?)

64

Managing
Production and
Operations
Systems
Through Their
Life Cycle
Stages

47. What lot dimensions will be required? Has room for expansion been provided?

48. What internal space divisions have been determined?

49. Is a railroad siding a necessary feature? How many floors should the building have?

50. What colors will be used for walls, ceilings, floors, and machines? Have illumination needs been properly assessed?

51. What construction materials will be used? Who will control the construction schedule?

52. Has the effect of decisions on competitors been properly surveyed?

53. Have all relevant questions been asked? Have all these questions been answered?

54. Is the chosen course of action the best possible way to proceed?

Implementation is greatly facilitated by the use of project management methods which help to organize and schedule all necessary activities and which provide awareness of what is happening, as well as controls to rectify problems as they develop. A further requisite is agreement concerning strategies and goals among all managers participating in the implementation process.

Implementing (I-C) the Operating System (II-A)

When the production system is ready to go, most of the fixed costs are already committed. Distribution channels have been secured, and marketing has either started to communicate with potential consumers or is about to do so. In some cases, especially in job shop systems, it is possible to let the production system grow in stages: first distribute the product or service in the Northeast; then (if successful after six months) expand to the Midwest, and so on.

With the flow shop, such stepwise planning is often inefficient. Assessment of competitive actions is essential in all cases to provide strategic timing for actions. Cash flow should be mapped out in accordance with the dynamics of life cycle estimates.

We plan a production system down to the finest possible details of operations. Then we implement our plans. These two steps constitute a project. When reading Chapter 3, bear in mind that one of the most important projects is that of designing and implementing the startup of a production system.

Designing (planning) and implementing the production system is one distinct responsibility of production and operations management. Running the system (operating the production process) is a second, distinct type of activity. Operating the production system means controlling the input/process/output (see node 24 in the PERT network of Fig. 2–7). Control is exercised in line with predetermined policies and standards of performance. Productivity must be monitored continuously. Schedules of operations are designed to deliver the desired quantity of product or service output with specific quality levels.

Redesigning the Process (II-B)

The design of products or services can often be changed during their lifetimes by making minor modifications in the processes. This is less true for the flow shop than for the job shop, but it still applies to some extent. The alteration of product or service (called restaging when accompanied by changes in marketing strategies) often is needed because of competitive actions. New tools and fixtures, retraining of personnel, and different inventories and equipment can be required, according to the case. In some instances, the extent of change may be nothing more than printing the word "new" on the package.

If flow shop design is the basic configuration, there is less flexibility to make large changes. It is more important for the flow shop than for the job shop, therefore, that the question of what changes might someday be called for be carefully considered and that the original process design allow for them to be achieved. The job shop, on the other hand, is well suited for product or service redesign, since its facilities are general-purpose (meaning that they were chosen to be as adaptable as possible for varied production outputs).

Flexible and programmable systems offer a different kind of versatility. Within a class of output types, it is very easy to change from one product to another. Between output classes (e.g., products requiring fundamentally different machines) there is no flexibility, despite the FPS name. FPS is an important alternative if the investment in such equipment and the costs of supporting software can be justified. Consequently, we find yet another criterion for deciding between the flow shop, the job shop, and the FPS shop. If no changes of consequence are anticipated for the output, or if changes can be predicted that are feasible to allow for in the flow shop process design, then the flow shop configuration is a very attractive alternative. As the importance of change increases, and as the lack of ability to predict what that change might be increases, the desirable process configuration moves toward ever greater degrees of job shop flexibility. Finally, if the importance of change is great and there is the ability to predict what those changes might be, then FPS is a strong candidate.

How Responsive in Restaging Should the Production System Be to Changes in What the Market Wants?

An auto manufacturer had a successful marketing policy of selling only compact cars. Then the marketplace, which had been demanding mostly small cars, rapidly shifted to larger ones. It would

66
Managing
Production and
Operations
Systems
Through Their
Life Cycle
Stages

be costly to convert its flow shop production line from compact to full-size cars. Even partial redesign of the product line and the production process would take time, and the move would be risky.

It had been expected that the high cost of fuel would be a boon to the compact car market, but then the price of gasoline fell sharply and stayed low. The company's marketing strategy had seemed right on target, but that was doubtful now. When would gasoline prices go up again? Was there a possibility that the shift to large cars might be temporary?

Careful coordination between marketing and production planning is essential. Are there any strategies that have been overlooked, such as luxury fittings for compacts or importing larger cars from abroad? If not, the best conversion plan must be found. It must be acceptable to production (budget) and successful for marketing (sales volume, share, and profit).

As another example, if a particular raw material becomes scarce on the world market, a substitute must be found. The product or service that uses the substitute material must be test marketed. If it is satisfactory, the production system has to be altered accordingly. Production is required to make up enough units of product or to provide enough service capacity for consumption by the test markets. Since it is for a test, this output is necessarily produced by job shop production methods.

Similarly, governmental regulation (such as the removal of saccharin from diet soft drinks, or the ban of detergent phosphates by municipalities, or the control of noise levels for aircraft, or the requirement for seat belts and pollution deterrents for automobiles) can lead to relatively rapid shifts in product and service designs. Often these require substantial and costly changes in the production process. Speed is generally of the utmost importance so that distribution levels can be maintained.

·PROBLEM
SET

1. What activities would you convert (and how) to make Figs. 2–5, 2–6, and 2–7 applicable to service systems instead of manufactured product systems?

2. How does the market research activity $4 \longrightarrow A$ in Fig. 2–5 concern P/OM? In many organizations, whatever market research is done is unknown to the production department. Does this make sense? Explain.

   Answer: Market research provides answers concerning the qualities of goods and services that people prefer, and the prices that they are willing to pay to obtain these qualities. P/OM can determine the per unit cost advantages of different production systems configurations. Thus, it is essential to know the production cost and quality capabilities before reaching any decision. Consequently, it is a weak managerial system that does not include P/OM inputs when designing the market research questionnaire as well as when analyzing the survey results.

3. What is meant by the statement, "The product line or service mix should be created with the process design in mind"? In this context, explain the use of iterative thinking.

4. The use of seat belts in cars decreases the severity of accidents. Another study indicates that the use of seat belts increases the number of accidents—as a result of increased confidence of drivers who take chances they would not otherwise because they are aware of the protection provided by seat belts. At an executive meeting (topic: auto design) you are asked to comment on this finding, providing the viewpoint of P/OM.

5. Smoking filtered, low-tar cigarettes should decrease the risk of cancer. There is evidence of the logic of this statement. However, a recent study has shown that smokers of filtered, low-tar cigarettes (feeling more confident that they are safer with these cigarettes) puff more often and inhale more deeply. As a result, their statistical cancer risk has increased.

   Another study indicates that smokers of low-tar cigarettes smoke more cigarettes in order to obtain the same amount of nicotine that they formerly got from regular cigarettes. Thus, their statistical cancer risk has increased. At an executive meeting (topic: cigarette product line design) you are asked to comment on these findings, providing the viewpoint of P/OM.

6. What is the relation of the implementation of a product or service marketing strategy to P/OM?

   Answer: The production facility may not be able to provide quality and/or quantity in line with the expectations of marketing. For example, there have been real situations where the demand has been far too great. Production could not supply the required output volume. Consequently, distribution dried up and demand dropped off permanently. In other cases, output volume requirements have been met but quality was inconsistent. Sometimes costs are high, forcing up prices. Coordination is essential if marketing plans are to be backed up by P/OM capabilities.

7. What kind of pilot plants might be appropriate for
   a. Public transportation systems
   b. A chain of new hotels
   c. Fast-food franchisers
   d. A cosmetic manufacturer

8. Name some of the pros and cons of using test marketing for each of the systems listed in Problem 7. Explain how test marketing can affect pilot plants, and vice versa.

Section 2.3: Balancing Cash Flow with Portfolio Management

During the early life cycle stages, cash flow is out of pocket to pay for the startup and fuel the growth. The cash to do this should come from products that are in their mature stages. A balanced portfolio of products has enough mature products to supply the needs of the right number of startups and growing products.

Because of the increased rate of change going through the life cycle stages, it has become increasingly important that the cash flow of an organization be managed well. Managed well means that the cash requirements of the company to meet debts (i.e., payroll, purchase obligations, rentals, interest payments, telephone) must be balanced by cash receipts, over time. Bringing a new product or service into being often involves significant outlays of funds against which the return on investment (ROI) will be delayed by months or years. Thus, cash flow management hinges on adequate life cycle planning for the portfolio.

Figure 2–9 captures some of the elements of this critical requirement, couched in terms of the product portfolio. By our convention, the term product applies equally well to goods or services.

Accounting for Present Value

We have talked about balancing cash flows over time so that within any specific period, the cash receipts (plus funds from the bank and by other borrowing) match the debts of the organization (which include payroll, purchases, rents, and interest owed). For balancing cash flows, it is convenient to work in cash terms without discounting the value of money. That is because a dollar that must be spent a year from now is correctly offset by a dollar that will be earned a year from now. However, we should note that a dollar spent or earned today is worth more than a dollar spent or earned a year from now. The difference between the dollar now and the dollar next year is determined by the discounting factor.

The Make or Buy Decision

To explain discounting, let us compare two plans. If the first plan is used, the company will make a particular component of the product. To do so, it will buy equipment and train a workforce. The alternative is to buy the product component from a supplier. Many factors determine the best solution to this problem, including the desire to maintain knowledge and expertise in the company, and control over quality and deliveries and

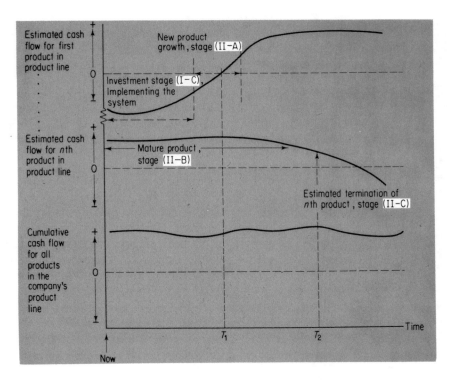

FIGURE 2-9. Life cycle management to balance cash flows of the product line. This figure shows that the first product in the product line is producing a larger outflow of cash than an inflow. At time T_1, it is expected to break-even. Thereafter, it should produce profit. There are n products in the product line. Each has its own cash flow pattern. Thus, the nth product is mature and profitable at a stable level until some time after T_1, when its profit is expected to begin to falter. A small restaging effort will be made with the expectation that it will halt only temporarily the decline in demand. Estimated termination of this nth product is time T_2. At the bottom is the cumulative cash flow curve representing the sum of all positive and negative flows from the n products.

price. But underlying all qualitative considerations is the comparison of discounted cash flow for each alternative.

To *make* the product component requires a large outlay of cash immediately. This is needed to buy equipment and the space to put it in. Also, there will be regular installments of cash outflow paid to workers, for raw materials, power costs, and so on. To *buy* the product from a supplier does not entail the same up-front costs. While the price per piece is higher since it includes profit for the suppliers, payments are made in small amounts with each invoice. These two kinds of costs are not incurred in the same way. Some method is required to compare costs that are immediate or within a short period with those that represent a stream of costs over a longer period of time. Immediate costs result from making; a stream of smaller costs results from buying.

70

Managing
Production and
Operations
Systems
Through Their
Life Cycle
Stages

Similarly, we require a way of comparing the income that will be obtained over a period of time from alternative product designs. Assume that one product has an expected life of five years. The second design promises a smaller income stream, but taken over a ten-year life. Consider the value of improvements, such as a process design or an inventory system change. Each requires a given expenditure now and will produce different streams of savings over various periods of time. We must calculate the present value of the savings and then compare it against the expenditure to see whether either or both of the proposed improvements is worthwhile.

A method of discounting is required to resolve the issues that have been raised. The premise upon which discounting is based is that a sum of money to be received at some future time has less value than the same sum of money owned at the present time. Essentially, this method provides for a comparison between an investment made in the present and a stream of smaller payments made over a period of time.

We can either derive the **present value** (or worth) of the stream of payments and compare it to the investment, or we can determine what stream of payments (perhaps borrowed from the bank) would be equivalent to the investment. In both cases, an interest rate and an interval of time must be specified. The length of time over which the monetary stream is reckoned will affect the conclusions.

To Buy or Rent?

To illustrate, assume it is possible to buy a plant for $1,000,000. An alternative is also offered, to rent at $80,000 per year. The question that we wish to answer is: How do these plans compare? It is our purpose to measure the stream factors (annuities) in the same terms as the investment.

First, we must obtain an estimate for the interest value of money. For example, 6 percent per year would be the amount that could be obtained by investing a given sum of money in savings bank certificates. The estimate of this interest rate will vary depending upon the size of the company, its growth potential, and capital requirements. Some companies can earn much higher returns simply by plowing back all available cash into their production output. We shall employ the 6 percent rate, recognizing that it is not easy but necessary to determine the appropriate rate of interest.

We ask the question: What is the present value of an $80,000 per year rental payment stream as a function of the length of the time period that is employed? The formula for present value that we utilize is:

$$PV = N \sum_{n=1}^{n} \left(\frac{1}{1 + r} \right)^n$$

where

PV = present value

N = \$80,000, the yearly rental value

r = interest rate, 6 percent per year

n = the planning horizon of n years, (n = 0, 1, 2, . . . , n).

Expanding the summation, which must still be multiplied by N, we obtain

$$PV = \sum_{n=1}^{n} \left(\frac{1}{1+r}\right)^n = \text{the sum of terms: } \left(\frac{1}{1+r}\right)^1 + \left(\frac{1}{1+r}\right)^2 + \ldots + \left(\frac{1}{1+r}\right)^n$$

The equation for PV assumes that the first rental payment is made at the end of the period. Consequently, each dollar paid out at the end of the first year costs us less than a full dollar—\$0.94. If we had that dollar at the beginning of the period, we could have invested it at 6 percent per year. At the end of the year we would have \$1.06, but we would be required to pay out only \$1.00. The actual cost would be \$1.00 − 0.06 = \$0.94. Thus, by deferring payment we decrease the cost of such payments to us. If the payments start at the beginning of the period, the first payment would be one dollar (N times), and we would add this to the series of numbers that are summed.

Table 2–1 shows the way in which present value changes as a function of the time period. Tabled values are available for different interest rates and time periods—see, for example, R. S. Burington, *Handbook of Mathematical Tables and Formulas,* 5th ed. (New York: McGraw-Hill, 1973). Such tables make present value analysis very easy.

What kind of a commitment does the company want to make to the future of the new product? In general, to buy a plant for manufacturing, or to buy an office building to contain the service organization is a stronger commitment (and a longer one) than to rent the facility.

We see that in the twenty-fourth year the rental stream of \$80,000 per year is equivalent to the purchase price of \$1,000,000. Thus, it takes about twenty-four years to balance the investment proposal. It is likely that the decision would be to rent, because a planning period of twenty-four years is long, and up to that time it is less expensive to rent the facility. In so many years a lot of things can change. It is risky to buy, unless the real estate independently is a good investment.

The buy or rent example could as easily have been an example of the make or buy problem. Say that to make the component would cost \$1 million at the start, whereas to buy the components from suppliers would cost \$80,000 per year. The decision would be to buy from suppliers. Yet, as was previously noted, various qualitative factors should be considered.

72

Managing
Production and
Operations
Systems
Through Their
Life Cycle
Stages

TABLE 2-1 PRESENT VALUES
(where $r = 0.06$ and $N = 80,000$)

n (years)	Column 1 $\left(\dfrac{1}{1 + 0.06}\right)^n$	The Sum of Column 1 $\sum\limits_{n=1}^{n} \left(\dfrac{1}{1 + 0.06}\right)^n$	$N \times$ the Sum of Column 1 $(80,000) \sum\limits_{n=1}^{n} \left(\dfrac{1}{1 + 0.06}\right)^n$
1	0.943	0.943	75,440
2	0.890	1.833	146,640
3	0.840	2.673	213,840
4	0.792	3.465	277,200
5	0.747	4.212	336,960
6	0.705	4.917	393,360
7	0.665	5.582	446,560
8	0.627	6.209	496,720
9	0.592	6.801	544,080
10	0.558	7.359	588,720
11	0.527	7.886	630,880
12	0.497	8.383	760,640
13	0.469	8.852	708,160
14	0.442	9.294	743,520
15	0.417	9.711	776,880
16	0.394	10.105	808,400
17	0.371	10.476	838,080
18	0.350	10.826	866,080
19	0.331	11.157	892,560
20	0.312	11.469	917,520
21	0.294	11.763	941,040
22	0.278	12.041	963,280
23	0.262	12.303	984,240
24	0.247	12.550	1,004,000
25	0.233	12.783	1,022,640

Will the company be as competitively able if it loses the knowhow of the component's manufacture?

Many informed people question the rote use of discounting analysis to reach decisions such as the make or buy decision just discussed. This is because decisions based purely on discounting methods avoid large expenditures now, and prefer immediate revenues. As a result, strategies that make big expenditures to achieve maximum competitive capability in the future will get turned down if strictly quantitative criteria are used. If discounting is combined with intelligent evaluation of the qualitative factors, the problem of polarizing the firm to risk avoidance behavior is eliminated.

A computing formula for the present value of a stream of payments at the end of the nth year is also available:

$$PV = N \left[\frac{(1 + r)^n - 1}{r(1 + r)^n} \right]$$

It is easy to use with pocket calculators, some of which are designed specifically to yield *PV*. This saves computing and adding each one of the stream of numbers. Carrying our thinking one step further: If an infinite period of time is utilized ($n = 00$), then the series of payments converges, so that the sum can be well approximated by N/r. Thus, for our example, the value of the payment stream over an infinite time period is:

$$PV = \frac{N}{r} = \frac{\$80,000}{0.06} = \$1,333,333$$

If an infinite planning horizon had applied to the prior analysis, meaning that we expect to keep paying $80,000 forever, then it would be better to invest $1 million.

A variety of possibilities exist for choosing the span of the discount period. What factors underlie an appropriate choice? In the case of the buy versus rent decision, one basic question is: How long will the purchased facility be utilized? A second important question is: When does the sum of the rental stream equal the purchase price? A third factor must also be considered: What is the resale value of the purchased facility at the time that it will no longer be used?

When the cost of the purchased facility less the discounted resale (at the *n*th year) is greater than the sum of the rental stream (for *n* years), we prefer to rent. Even when they are equal, we might prefer to rent because uncertainties have not been taken into account, and renting allows us greater flexibility to change what we are doing. On the other hand, if an increase in rent might occur, our preference could switch to buying (or building). When the cost of the equipment to make a component plus the discounted cash outflow to pay labor and materials is less than the discounted cash payments to suppliers (for *n* years), we prefer to make the component. As before, we must be sure to consider intangibles.

An important corollary is that only products or services that are very likely to have a long mature stage in the market can justify large immediate expenditures for special-purpose equipment which has poor (if any) resale value. Further, because flow shop planning generally involves much longer term investment commitments than job shop planning, the effects of using discounting will operate against using flow shop work configurations.

Flexible and programmable systems have large immediate expenses, but because of their flexibility can be altered to meet market changes. Therefore, they enjoy a longer planning horizon. Software costs with FPS represent a continuous stream of cash outflow which is needed to take advantage of the process flexibility.

With reference to the example, without discounting it would take only 12.5 years for the rental payments of $80,000 to equal the purchase price of $1,000,000 ($1,000,000 / 80,000 = 12.5). With discounting, it takes 24 years. Clearly, discounting works to the disadvantage of immediate purchase decisions except where a relatively long period of commitment to

74

Managing
Production and
Operations
Systems
Through Their
Life Cycle
Stages

a facility can be made. And, as we have previously said, long-term commitments characterize the flow shop and not the job shop (or the project). FPS is somewhere in between.

The **portfolio concept** ties together the various products' cash flows so that the firm always has enough money to meet its obligations. That is what is meant by cash flow management. Although life cycle management is concerned with the marketing stages of the company's products and services, we see that these marketing dimensions directly interact with financial planning for process decisions. Cash flow management balances the discounted income streams derived at the various stages of product and service life against the discounted purchase investments and streams of expenses that are incurred to support production, distribution, and sales.

The Payoff Period

Some organizations do not use discounting when determining how long it will take to recover an investment—the **payoff period.** This is the length of time required before an investment pays for itself—that is, before it begins to produce additional capital for the company. If the computation of the payoff period is performed without discounting, we have:

$$\text{Payoff period} = \text{investment} \div \text{income per time period}$$

This straight computation, which ignores the discounting effect, will indicate a shorter period than would be obtained if discounting were used. Thus, for example, if the investment required for a new product or service is \$630,000 and it is expected to produce an income stream of \$580,000 per year, the payoff period (without discounting) would be:

$$630,000/80,000 = 7.9 \text{ years}$$

However, when discounting is taken into consideration, we can see (from Table 2–1) that a period of 11 years would be required for the investment to pay for itself. Generally speaking, it is advisable to utilize discounting for such computations. However, it must be pointed out that the payoff period will be critically affected by the choice of interest rate.

If a 5 percent rate per year is used, then less than 11 years would be required to pay off the investment. If the rate is 3 percent per year, then the result would be less than 10 years. If 10 percent per year is used, then about 16 years is required (see Table 2–3).

A variety of criteria can be employed for investment decisions. The choice depends upon the life cycle character of the production output and the process configuration. Thus, for example, we can describe three criteria for accepting an investment.

$$\frac{\text{Annual income stream}}{\text{Investment}} \geq r \quad (4\text{-}1)$$

$$\frac{\text{Required income stream at present value for } n \text{ years}}{\text{Investment}} \geq 1 \quad (4\text{-}2)$$

$$\frac{\text{Required income stream at present value for lifetime}}{\text{Investment}} \geq f \quad (4\text{-}3)$$

where $f > 1$.

The first formulation is the inverse of the payoff period computation. It expresses the fact that the annual return on our investment must be equal to or greater than the interest rate that could be obtained by using an alternative investment. The planning period, in this case, is just one year. This criterion at best might be acceptable for short-term investments in batch production of the job shop. The second formulation is based upon the selection of a period of time n. We require that the breakeven point occur in the nth year. This criterion is appropriate for both job shops with standard items in inventory (not custom production) and low-investment flow shops. The third formulation represents the number of times that we would like the income stream to pay for a given investment over its lifetime. Here, the planning period is infinite. This criterion is appropriate for high-investment flow shops and flexible and programmable systems where mature products and services have long lifetimes.

Each criterion can result in different decisions. Production and operations management should be aware of the significance of the planning period and the investment criterion used. A consistent policy that is generally understood and agreed to by participants in the company is a necessary requirement for successful operations.

The Difference between Products and Services

The differences between products and services is less than one might suppose. True, in general, products like food and toothpaste can be stored, whereas services like hotel rooms and the work of a carpenter can not be put in the cupboard. Nevertheless, all products have services built into them; this includes durable goods such as typewriters and refrigerators, and consumables such as shoes and cornflakes.

The production of goods does not necessarily require larger investments than the production of services. On the one hand, there is a class of service functions that is labor-intensive. An employment agency or a travel agency can have minimum investments and almost no fixed assets.

76

Managing
Production and
Operations
Systems
Through Their
Life Cycle
Stages

On the other hand, there are many capital-intensive service organizations. Telephone companies, electric power utilities, airlines, hotels, railroads, and hospitals require sizable investments.

Upon careful consideration, it turns out that although there are differences between products and services, the differences are often unimportant for production and operations management planning. The differences within each category leading to alternative production configurations (project, FPS, flow shop, and job shop) will have greater influence on decision-making, planning, and controlling. The difference between providing goods and services will have greater importance for marketing and distribution, and may even have an impact on the organizational characteristics and managerial style. However, for production and operations management, the generality of the P/OM function emerges, and the paramount issue is how to configure the system and how to run it.

PROBLEM
SET

1. Examine the situation of the compact car manufacturer discussed on pp. 65–66. Assume that the price of compacts had risen so that full-size cars were not much more expensive than compacts. Why might this have happened? Consider this problem in terms of labor productivity, total productivity, and price elasticity.

2. What is the pattern of net cash flow of a municipality? Detail some of the major cash inflows and outflows and specify their timing. How does this pattern differ from that of a company selling a product such as toothpaste?

3. Is it likely that the cash flow pattern of a job shop is the same as that of a flow shop? Explain your answer.

4. Give an example of a product or service with which you are familiar that has gone through all five stages of the marketing evolution pictured in Fig. 2–2.

5. When would we be indifferent as to whether we should buy an automobile costing $9000 or lease its use at $540 per month? Assume an interest rate of 1 percent per month. (See Table 2–2).

6. Assume that a cosmetic manufacturer rushes many new product formulations into the marketplace knowing that most will just recover the initial investment within a year. Thereafter they must be withdrawn, or they will begin to accumulate an increasing net loss for the company. The reason for this strategy is that about 1 out of 7 times the new entry become highly profitable over at least a two-year period. In cash flow terms, discuss what might be the best sequencing of new product releases. Make any other recommendations to management that might be appropriate.

7. Why is ROI regarded so highly by managers as an important measure of performance? In the same context, evaluate brand share, sales volume, and net profit.

TABLE 2-2   TABLE OF PRESENT VALUES

$(r = 0.12/\text{yr} = 0.01/\text{mo.})$

n (months)	$\left(\dfrac{.1}{1 + 0.01}\right)^n$	$\displaystyle\sum_{n=1}^{n}\left(\dfrac{1}{1 + 0.01}\right)^n$	n (months)	$\left(\dfrac{1}{1 + 0.01}\right)^n$	$\displaystyle\sum_{n=1}^{n}\left(\dfrac{1}{1 + 0.01}\right)^n$
1	0.9901	0.9901	13	0.8787	12.1337
2	0.9803	1.9704	14	0.8700	13.0037
3	0.9706	2.9410	15	0.8613	13.8651
4	0.9610	3.9020	16	0.8528	14.7179
5	0.9515	4.8534	17	0.8444	15.5623
6	0.9420	5.7955	18	0.8360	16.3983
7	0.9327	6.7282	19	0.8277	17.2261
8	0.9235	7.6517	20	0.8195	18.0456
9	0.9143	8.5660	21	0.8114	18.8570
10	0.9053	9.4713	22	0.8034	19.6604
11	0.5963	10.3676	23	0.7954	20.4559
12	0.8874	11.2551	24	0.7876	21.2434

8. Determine the present value of an income stream that is associated with a new product, where anticipated revenue changes as follows:

Years after Release	Revenue (millions $)
1	0.2
2	0.5
3	1.2
4	1.8
5	2.0
6	1.0
7	0.6
8	0.0

(Use the table on p. 79. This assumes that a discounting factor of 0.06 per year is applicable.)

Answer: This is a straightforward problem using the methods described in the text (see pp. 70–74).

Year	Revenue (million $)	Discount Factor 6%	Present Worth (million $)
1	0.2	0.943	0.1886
2	0.5	0.890	0.4450
3	1.2	0.840	1.0080
4	1.8	0.792	1.4256
5	2.0	0.747	1.4940
6	1.0	0.705	0.7050
7	0.6	0.665	0.3990
8	0.0	0.627	0.0000

Total Present Worth = 5.6652

TABLE 2-3 TABLE OF CUMULATIVE PRESENT VALUES

$$\sum_{n=1}^{z}\left(\frac{1}{1+r}\right)^{n}$$

Interest Rate (r)

Year n	.030	.035	.040	.045	.050	.055	.060	.065	.070	.080	.090	.100	.110	.120
1	0.9709	0.9662	0.9615	0.9569	0.9524	0.9479	0.9434	0.9390	0.9346	0.9259	0.9174	0.9091	0.9009	0.8929
2	1.9135	1.8997	1.8861	1.8727	1.8594	1.8463	1.8334	1.8206	1.8080	1.7833	1.7591	1.7356	1.7125	1.6901
3	2.8286	2.8016	2.7751	2.7490	2.7233	2.6980	2.6730	2.6485	2.6244	2.5771	2.5313	2.4869	2.4438	2.4019
4	3.7171	3.6731	3.6299	3.5876	3.5460	3.5052	3.4652	3.4259	3.3873	3.3122	3.2398	3.1699	3.1025	3.0374
5	4.5797	4.5151	4.4519	4.3900	4.3295	4.2703	4.2124	4.1558	4.1003	3.9928	3.8897	3.7909	3.6960	3.6049
6	5.4172	5.3286	5.2422	5.1579	5.0758	4.9956	4.9174	4.8411	4.7665	4.6230	4.4860	4.3554	4.2307	4.1115
7	6.2303	6.1146	6.0021	5.8928	5.7865	5.6831	5.5825	5.4847	5.3894	5.2065	5.0331	4.8686	4.7124	4.5639
8	7.0197	6.8740	6.7328	6.5960	6.4633	6.3347	6.2099	6.0889	5.9715	5.7468	5.5350	5.3351	5.1463	4.9678
9	7.7861	7.6078	7.4354	7.2689	7.1080	6.9524	6.8019	6.6563	6.5155	6.2471	5.9955	5.7593	5.5373	5.3285
10	8.5303	8.3167	8.1110	7.9129	7.7219	7.5378	7.3603	7.1891	7.0238	6.7103	6.4179	6.1448	5.8895	5.6505
11	9.2527	9.0016	8.7606	8.5291	8.3066	8.0928	7.8871	7.6893	7.4990	7.1393	6.8055	6.4954	6.2068	5.9380
12	9.9541	9.6634	9.3852	9.1188	8.8635	8.6188	8.3841	8.1590	7.9430	7.5364	7.1611	6.8140	6.4927	6.1947
13	10.6350	10.3029	9.9858	9.6831	9.3938	9.1174	8.8530	8.6001	8.3581	7.9041	7.4873	7.1037	6.7502	6.4239
14	11.2962	10.9207	10.5633	10.2231	9.8989	9.5900	9.2953	9.0142	8.7459	8.2446	7.7866	7.3671	6.9823	6.6286
15	11.9380	11.5176	11.1186	10.7398	10.3800	10.0379	9.7126	9.4031	9.1084	8.5599	8.0611	7.6065	7.1913	6.8113
16	12.5612	12.0943	11.6525	11.2343	10.8381	10.4626	10.1063	9.7682	9.4471	8.8519	8.3130	7.8242	7.3796	6.9744
17	13.1662	12.6515	12.1659	11.7075	11.2744	10.8650	10.4777	10.1111	9.7638	9.1222	8.5441	8.0220	7.5493	7.1202
18	13.7536	13.1899	12.6596	12.1603	11.6900	11.2465	10.8281	10.4330	10.0597	9.3724	8.7562	8.2019	7.7021	7.2502
19	14.3239	13.7101	13.1343	12.5937	12.0858	11.6081	11.1587	10.7353	10.3362	9.6042	8.9507	8.3655	7.8398	7.3663
20	14.8776	14.2127	13.5907	13.0084	12.4627	11.9509	11.4705	11.0191	10.5947	9.8188	9.1292	8.5141	7.9639	7.4700
21	15.4152	14.6983	14.0295	13.4052	12.8217	12.2758	11.7647	11.2856	10.8362	10.0175	9.2929	8.6493	8.0757	7.5626
22	15.9371	15.1674	14.4515	13.7849	13.1635	12.5838	12.0422	11.5359	11.0620	10.2014	9.4431	8.7722	8.1763	7.6452
23	16.4438	15.6207	14.8573	14.1483	13.4891	12.8757	12.3041	11.7709	11.2729	10.3718	9.5809	8.8839	8.2671	7.7190
24	16.9357	16.0587	15.2474	14.4960	13.7992	13.1524	12.5511	11.9915	11.4701	10.5295	9.7073	8.9854	8.3488	7.7849
25	17.4134	16.4819	15.6226	14.8288	14.0946	13.4146	12.7841	12.1987	11.6544	10.6756	9.8233	9.0777	8.4224	7.8438
26	17.8771	16.8907	15.9833	15.1472	14.3759	13.6632	13.0039	12.3932	11.8266	10.8108	9.9297	9.1617	8.4887	7.8963
27	18.3273	17.2857	16.3301	15.4519	14.6437	13.8989	13.2113	12.5759	11.9876	10.9360	10.0274	9.2380	8.5485	7.9432
28	18.7643	17.6674	16.6636	15.7435	14.8989	14.1222	13.4070	12.7474	12.1380	11.0519	10.1169	9.3073	8.6023	7.9851
29	19.1887	18.0361	16.9843	16.0226	15.1418	14.3339	13.5916	12.9084	12.2786	11.1593	10.1991	9.3704	8.6508	8.0225
30	19.6007	18.3924	17.2926	16.2896	15.3732	14.5346	13.7657	13.0596	12.4100	11.2587	10.2745	9.4277	8.6945	8.0559

TABLE 2-4 TABLE OF PRESENT VALUES $\left(\dfrac{1}{1+r}\right)^n$

Year n	.030	.035	.040	.045	.050	.055	.060	.065	.070	.080	.090	.100	.110	.120
							Interest Rate (r)							
1	0.9709	0.9662	0.9615	0.9569	0.9524	0.9479	0.9434	0.9390	0.9346	0.9259	0.9174	0.9091	0.9009	0.8929
2	0.9426	0.9335	0.9246	0.9157	0.9070	0.8985	0.8900	0.8817	0.8735	0.8574	0.8417	0.8265	0.8116	0.7972
3	0.9151	0.9019	0.8890	0.8763	0.8638	0.8516	0.8396	0.8279	0.8163	0.7939	0.7722	0.7513	0.7312	0.7118
4	0.8885	0.8714	0.8548	0.8386	0.8227	0.8072	0.7921	0.7773	0.7629	0.7351	0.7084	0.6830	0.6588	0.6355
5	0.8626	0.8420	0.8219	0.8025	0.7835	0.7652	0.7473	0.7299	0.7130	0.6806	0.6500	0.6210	0.5935	0.5675
6	0.8375	0.8135	0.7903	0.7679	0.7462	0.7253	0.7050	0.6854	0.6664	0.6302	0.5963	0.5645	0.5347	0.5067
7	0.8131	0.7860	0.7599	0.7348	0.7107	0.6875	0.6651	0.6435	0.6228	0.5835	0.5471	0.5132	0.4817	0.4524
8	0.7894	0.7594	0.7307	0.7032	0.6769	0.6516	0.6274	0.6043	0.5820	0.5403	0.5019	0.4665	0.4340	0.4039
9	0.7664	0.7337	0.7026	0.6729	0.6446	0.6177	0.5919	0.5674	0.5440	0.5003	0.4605	0.4241	0.3910	0.3606
10	0.7441	0.7089	0.6756	0.6440	0.6139	0.5855	0.5584	0.5328	0.5084	0.4632	0.4224	0.3856	0.3522	0.3220
11	0.7224	0.6850	0.6496	0.6162	0.5847	0.5549	0.5268	0.5002	0.4751	0.4289	0.3876	0.3505	0.3173	0.2875
12	0.7014	0.6618	0.6246	0.5897	0.5569	0.5260	0.4970	0.4697	0.4441	0.3972	0.3556	0.3187	0.2859	0.2567
13	0.6810	0.6394	0.6006	0.5643	0.5304	0.4986	0.4689	0.4411	0.4150	0.3677	0.3262	0.2897	0.2575	0.2292
14	0.6611	0.6178	0.5775	0.5400	0.5051	0.4726	0.4423	0.4141	0.3879	0.3405	0.2993	0.2634	0.2320	0.2046
15	0.6419	0.5969	0.5553	0.5167	0.4810	0.4480	0.4173	0.3889	0.3625	0.3153	0.2746	0.2394	0.2090	0.1827
16	0.6232	0.5767	0.5339	0.4945	0.4581	0.4246	0.3937	0.3651	0.3388	0.2919	0.2519	0.2177	0.1883	0.1631
17	0.6050	0.5572	0.5134	0.4732	0.4363	0.4025	0.3714	0.3429	0.3166	0.2703	0.2311	0.1979	0.1697	0.1457
18	0.5874	0.5384	0.4937	0.4528	0.4156	0.3815	0.3504	0.3219	0.2959	0.2503	0.2120	0.1799	0.1528	0.1301
19	0.5703	0.5202	0.4747	0.4333	0.3958	0.3616	0.3306	0.3023	0.2765	0.2317	0.1945	0.1635	0.1377	0.1161
20	0.5537	0.5026	0.4564	0.4147	0.3769	0.3428	0.3118	0.2838	0.2585	0.2146	0.1785	0.1487	0.1241	0.1037
21	0.5376	0.4856	0.4389	0.3968	0.3590	0.3249	0.2942	0.2665	0.2416	0.1987	0.1637	0.1352	0.1118	0.0926
22	0.5219	0.4692	0.4220	0.3797	0.3419	0.3080	0.2775	0.2502	0.2258	0.1840	0.1502	0.1229	0.1007	0.0827
23	0.5067	0.4533	0.4058	0.3634	0.3256	0.2919	0.2618	0.2350	0.2110	0.1703	0.1378	0.1117	0.0907	0.0738
24	0.4919	0.4380	0.3901	0.3477	0.3101	0.2767	0.2470	0.2206	0.1972	0.1577	0.1264	0.1015	0.0817	0.0659
25	0.4776	0.4232	0.3751	0.3328	0.2953	0.2623	0.2330	0.2072	0.1843	0.1460	0.1160	0.0923	0.0736	0.0588
26	0.4637	0.4089	0.3607	0.3184	0.2813	0.2486	0.2198	0.1945	0.1722	0.1352	0.1064	0.0839	0.0663	0.0525
27	0.4502	0.3950	0.3468	0.3047	0.2679	0.2356	0.2074	0.1827	0.1610	0.1252	0.0976	0.0763	0.0598	0.0469
28	0.4371	0.3817	0.3335	0.2916	0.2551	0.2234	0.1957	0.1715	0.1504	0.1159	0.0896	0.0694	0.0538	0.0419
29	0.4244	0.3688	0.3207	0.2790	0.2430	0.2117	0.1846	0.1610	0.1406	0.1074	0.0822	0.0631	0.0485	0.0374
30	0.4120	0.3563	0.3083	0.2670	0.2314	0.2007	0.1741	0.1512	0.1314	0.0994	0.0754	0.0573	0.0437	0.0334

80

Managing
Production and
Operations
Systems
Through Their
Life Cycle
Stages

9. Develop a table for $n = 1, \ldots 10$ and $\sum_{n=1}^{n} \left(\frac{1}{1 + 0.10} \right)^{n}$ similar in structure to the table for 0.06 shown on p. 78.

Answer: For the student's convenience, we present Tables 2–3 and 2–4. Table 2–3 provides the cumulative present value (for the worth today of one dollar paid regularly at the end of each of n years). It is given in terms of interest rates ranging from .03 to .12, and from 1 to 30 years. Table 2–4 provides the present values from which the cumulative present value table (2–3) is derived. It is the value today of a dollar that will be paid at the end of the nth year, at interest rate r.

REFERENCES

ALDERSON, WROE. *Marketing Behavior and Executive Action.* Homewood, IL: Richard D. Irwin, 1957.

AMSTUTZ, A. E. *Computer Simulation of Competitive Market Response.* Cambridge, Mass.: The M.I.T. Press, 1967.

ASIMOW, MORRIS. *Introduction to Design.* Englewood Cliffs, N.J.: Prentice-Hall, 1962.

BIERMAN, HAROLD, AND SEYMOUR SMIDT. *The Capital Budgeting Decision,* 2nd ed. New York: Macmillan, 1966.

BREALEY, RICHARD, AND STEWART MYERS. *Principles of Corporate Finance.* New York: McGraw-Hill, 1981.

CHASE, R. B., AND N. J. AQUILANO. *Production and Operations Management (A Life Cycle Approach),* 4th ed. Homewood, Ill.: Richard D. Irwin, 1985.

DREYFUSS, HENRY. *Designing for People.* New York: Simon & Schuster, 1955.

FORRESTER, JAY. *Industrial Dynamics.* Cambridge, Mass.: The M.I.T. Press, 1961.

FOSTER, G. *Financial Statement Analysis,* 2nd ed. Englewood Cliffs, N.J.: Prentice-Hall, 1986.

FRIEDLAND, SEYMOUR. *The Economics of Corporate Finance.* Englewood Cliffs, N.J.: Prentice-Hall, 1966.

GERLACH, J. T., AND C. A. WAINWRIGHT. *Successful Management of New Products.* New York: Hastings House, 1968.

GHISELIN, BREWSTER. *The Creative Process.* New York: The New American Library, 1960.

GLEOG, G. L. *The Design of Design.* Cambridge, Eng.: Cambridge University Press, 1969.

GORDON, W. J. J. *Synectics.* New York: Harper & Row, 1961.

GREEN, P. E., AND D. S. TULL. *Research for Marketing Decisions,* 3rd ed. Englewood Cliffs, N.J.: Prentice-Hall, 1974.

HARRIS, R. D., AND M. J. MAGGARD. *Computer Models in Operations Management,* 2nd ed. New York: Harper & Row, 1977.

HERTZ, DAVID B. "Risk Analysis in Capital Investment." *Harvard Business Review* (January–February 1964), pp. 95–106.

JOHNSON, ROBERT W. *Financial Management,* 3rd ed. Boston: Allyn and Bacon, 1966.

KAUFMANN, A., M. FUSTIER, AND A. DREVET. *L'Inventique, Nouvelles Methodes de Creativité.* Paris: Entreprise Moderne D'Edition, 1970.

LONGMAN, K. A. *Advertising.* New York: Harcourt Brace Jovanovich, 1971.

LUCE, R. DUNCAN. *Individual Choice Behavior.* New York: Wiley, 1959.

MACHLUP, FRITZ. *The Production and Distribution of Knowledge in the United States.* Princeton, N.J.: Princeton University Press, 1962.

MAO, JAMES C. T. *Quantitative Analysis of Financial Decisions.* London: Macmillan, 1969.

MAYER, MARTIN. *Madison Avenue U.S.A.* New York: Harper & Row, 1958.

MILLER, DAVID W., AND MARTIN K. STARR. *Executive Decisions and Operations Research,* 2nd ed. Englewood Cliffs, N.J.: Prentice-Hall, 1969.

MONTGOMERY, D. B., AND G. L. URBAN. *Applications of Management Science in Marketing.* Englewood Cliffs, N.J.: Prentice-Hall, 1969.

————, AND ————. *Management Science in Marketing.* Englewood Cliffs, N.J.: Prentice-Hall, 1969.

MORTON, J. A. *Organizing for Innovation.* New York: McGraw-Hill, 1971.

NEWTON, NORMAN T. *An Approach to Design.* Cambridge, Mass.: Addison-Wesley, 1951.

QUIRIN, G. DAVID. *The Capital Expenditure Decision.* Homewood, Ill.: Richard D. Irwin, 1967.

SANDKULL, BENGT. *Innovative Behavior of Organizations: The Case of New Products, SiAR.* Lund, Sweden: Student litteratur, 1970.

SCHON, DONALD A. *Technology and Change.* New York: Delacorte Press, 1967.

SHUBIK, MARTIN. *Strategy and Market Structure: Competition, Oligopoly, and the Theory of Games.* New York: Wiley, 1959.

SMITH, VERNON. *Investment and Production.* Cambridge, Mass.: Harvard University Press, 1966.

STARR, MARTIN K. "Product Planning from the Top Variety and Diversity." *University of Illinois Bulletin,* 65: Proceedings, Systems: Research and Applications for Marketing (July 26, 1968), pp. 71–77.

————. *Product Design and Decision Theory.* Englewood Cliffs, N.J.: Prentice-Hall, 1963.

TERBORGH, GEORGE. *Business Equipment Policy.* Washington, D.C.: Machinery and Allied Products Institute, 1958.

VAN HORNE, JAMES C. *Financial Management and Policy.* Englewood Cliffs, N.J.: Prentice-Hall, 1971.

WALTERS, J. E. *Research Management: Principles and Practice.* Washington, D.C.: Spartan Books, 1965.

WESTON, J. F. *The Scope and Methodology of Finance.* Englewood Cliffs, N.J.: Prentice-Hall, 1966.

WILLIAMS, J. D. *The Compleat Strategyst.* New York: McGraw-Hill, 1954.

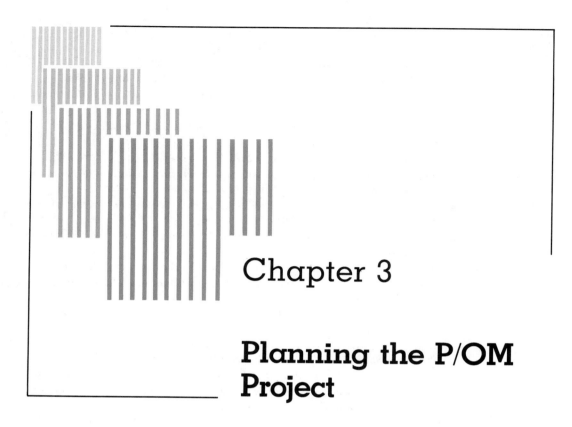

Chapter 3

Planning the P/OM Project

CHAPTER SUMMARY This chapter deals with project management. There are many examples of projects, but they all share certain common properties. The dictionary defines a project as "a planned undertaking." Project managers have much more to say about the nature of projects. Section 3.1 examines the character of projects. Gantt charts, developed by Henry L. Gantt in the 1890s, have been used to manage projects for 100 years and are still in use. Stronger project management methods called PERT and Critical Path Methods were introduced in the 1950s. Section 3.2 explains how both kinds of project management systems work. Project management using PERT allows control over resource allocations that was unavailable with Gantt charts. This is explained in Section 3.3, where the discussion treats tradeoffs between cost and time, as well as moving resources to where they are needed from where they are not.

In Section 3.1 we begin with relevant differentiating characteristics of projects. This is followed by some history of project management. We have introduced the Gantt chart, and have explained how it is used.

Critical paths methods are introduced in Section 3.2, including:

1. The construction of PERT networks.
2. Methods and problems of activity time estimation.
3. How to use the $(T_L - T_E = 0)$ algorithm of 0 slack to determine the critical path.
4. Working with variance measures of activity times to target completion time to fall within a range x percent of the time.
5. How to expedite slippage by means of schedule control, but only when necessary (i.e., it is seldom used for slack time activities).

Resource leveling is introduced in Section 3.3, and the following concepts are explained.

1. Resource leveling by trading off resources to get a more even balance among project activities.
2. Resource leveling by trading off resources to decrease the overall project completion time.
3. Resource leveling and resource peaking through the use of cost/time tradeoff functions to change project completion times and to gain sensible cost control over project activities.

Of course, there is more to project management, but anyone understanding what has been described in Chapter 3 can put into practice a major capability to deal effectively and productively with project systems.

Section 3.1 Management of Projects

Projects are a form of doing work. They are distinctly different from flow shops, which yield high-volume output at a minimum cost. The flow shop is not a feasible design configuration if demand is too low. The project satisfies the demand for *one* thing, but it is usually a big thing, like a building. Many job shops produce a few items in a batch, and never run the same thing again. That situation gets close to being a project. Getting the software in place for a new use of the FPS is a project. Perhaps someday software will be produced by flow shop methods, or even by FPS methods.

Types of Projects and Gantt Charts

Neither flow shop nor job shop nor FPS configurations can take care of what needs to be done when the circumstances for a project exist. What are those circumstances? Output volume is one unique, complex system. Per unit costs of the output can be gigantic, but there is only one unit (or at best a few). There is no variety, since there is only one output.

84

*Managing
Production and
Operations
Systems Through
Their Life Cycle
Stages*

Productivity is measured by how many people take how long to complete the project.

Projects are not rare; every individual deals with projects of different levels of complexity, such as moving into a new home, building a cabinet, writing a book, reading a book, programming software, cooking a meal, constructing a stereo set from a kit, or making a dress from a pattern. Organizations encounter the need for project management whenever they consider introducing a new product or service. Thus, development work requires project management. Whether the ultimate production system is going to be a flow shop or a job shop (or some combination of the two), in all cases project management is needed to formulate, design, and actualize plans.

The two main types of P/OM activities are (a) planning, designing, redesigning, and implementing the system, and (b) operating the system. Type (a) activities must be employed to start up (or change) any kind of production system. But there are many types of institutional projects other than that of setting up a production process. Some organizations do nothing but manage projects; that is the business in which they have specialized. These projects can be as varied as NASA's plans to develop the Space Station, planning to build a monorail between Los Angeles and San Diego, constructing a computer-operated, voice-responsive supertanker in Korea, converting a telecommunication system to satellites and fiber optics, starting up a chain of Mexican fast-food restaurants in the Northeast United States, building the Alaska pipeline, or designing and starting up petroleum refineries all over the world.

The life cycles of products and services start with the introduction of a new design. If there is sufficient demand at the market price, then the product or service, if properly managed, becomes mature. It becomes established in production procedures and well known in the marketplace, with a loyal following. All of this was inherent in the original definition of the project. Each project poses quite special conditions, but the methods for managing any and all projects are remarkably similar.

Most organizations are poorly prepared for projects, because their managers consider their primary function to be something else. A conflict exists. The training and skills (and perhaps the mental set and innate abilities) of flow shop managers differ from those of job shop managers. Both differ from those of project managers. The issue, then, is how to prepare an organization that sees itself as a flow shop or as a job shop for those project management responsibilities that most surely will occur. For example:

1. When we talk about setting up decision rules for inventories, we incorporate the standards and procedures that will be used by management to operate the inventory system. Setting this up is a project.
2. Consider what is involved in carrying out the decision to build a new facility that requires major investment outlays for construction and equipment. Both building and financing are interrelated projects.

3. A major market research study is to be conducted in order to assess the value of listing nutritional information on the labels of food products. This study, starting with data collection and ending with analytic reports, is a project.

Our present purpose is not to talk about specific project situations, but to highlight the extent to which variations exist. Our ultimate purpose is to introduce the methods that are applicable for managing complex projects.

Awareness of the Project Management Role

Models that organize the complex information required to know when to do what in a project have been available for more than thirty years. Then why is it that some projects are completed without the benefit of these models? The answer is that some managers do not know about project models. They have been trained in operating production systems and not in project management. Also, they do not recognize their projects for what they are; they see them as important but temporary distractions from the main line of their activities.

Production personnel tend to view operations as their primary concern. Market researchers view questionnaire formulation, sample selection, and statistical analysis as their primary concern. Public managers are concerned about politics and dissatisfied constituencies. Financial managers concentrate on return on investment, debt ratios, price earnings, inflation, and taxes. In each case the concerns are valid, but they obscure the project management roles played by all these individuals. On the other hand, companies that specialize in managing projects are fully conversant and adept at using the most appropriate forms of project models.

Basic Rules for Project Management

Project management models are neither difficult to understand nor to use. But there are some basic rules to follow:

1. Project objectives must be clearly stated. They should be reduced to the simplest possible terms. There are often many participants in a project, and unless knowledge about objectives is shared by all participants, the project is likely to encounter many reverses. Much time will be spent finding out what everyone is trying to do.

2. Expertise is required to outline the steps of the project designed to deliver the specified results. Accurate time and cost estimates for all project activities are essential. Slippage from schedule can sometimes mean real trouble, whereas at other times it can be tolerated. Project management requires that you know which is which.

86

*Managing
Production and
Operations
Systems Through
Their Life Cycle
Stages*

3. Duplication of activities should, in general, be eliminated. Under some circumstances, however, parallel path activities are warranted.

   a. If a major conflict of ideas exists and there is urgency to achieve the objectives, it is sometimes reasonable to allow two or more groups to work independently on the different approaches. Preplanned evaluation procedures should exist so that as soon as possible, the program can be trimmed back to a single path.

   b. At the inception of a program (during what might be called the exploratory stage), parallel path research is frequently warranted and can be encouraged. All possible approaches should be considered and evaluated before large commitments of funds have been made.

   c. When the risk of failure is high—for example, survival is at stake—or when the payoff incentive is sufficiently great with respect to the costs of achieving it, parallel path activities can be justified for as long a period of time as is deemed necessary to achieve the objectives.

4. Project management should carefully evaluate the sequence of activities that constitutes the program. An effective organization should be set up to monitor and control accomplishments as compared to expectations.

5. One person should be responsible for all major decisions. This project manager must understand the nature of the problem and the technological, marketing, and production constraints. Multiple decisionmakers can produce chaotic conditions.

6. The project moves through many phases. Different functional areas of interest must be integrated and coordinated. For example, a supplier's inventory policy can create delivery delays; insufficient quality controls can result in defective parts, which can stop a cascade of interdependent activities; national distribution of a new product requires extensive backup stock; sales levels are affected by promotional and advertising timing, which must be coordinated with production output.

Project management of large, complex systems requires the support of a well-organized management information system. Existing project management methods are information systems that utilize data bases which are updated on a regular basis.

1. The project methods categorize and summarize a mass of information that relate to precedence of activities, and their time and cost.

2. Project methods organize problem areas, making all relevant variables explicit so that administrators can communicate with each other about the project.

3. The information systems require estimates of cost and time for every project stage.

4. The methods structure projects—so that details will not be forgotten, so that actions will be taken in appropriate sequence, so that intelligent allocations of resources will be made, and so that control over accomplishments will be ensured.

5. Alternative strategies can be tested by various methods to determine how sensitive a particular strategy is to technological uncertainties and to the actions competitors might take.

6. Project methods can assess the effects of possible errors in estimates.

Extent of Repetitive Environment

As you can observe from the brief listing above, project decisions result in actions that are seldom repeated under similar circumstances. Thus, the decision to move a plant to a new geographic area is a major commitment that is best described as a project. As each step is accomplished or a stage is completed, it is unlikely ever to be repeated again in the same form. Developing the first space station is a project, long-term and nonrepetitive. Earning a bachelors degree or an MBA degree are consummate projects. Contrast these with the decision to place an order for materials used by a flow shop to make a high-volume production item— for example, purchasing continuous feed forms for the premium processing operations of an insurance company, or hamburger meat for McDonald's. Such ordering decisions are made repeatedly. There are special inventory models for flow shops, others for job shops and FPS systems, and still others for projects.

We can see why the type of methodology employed for projects as compared to systems with repetitive operations would be different. The flow shop has preprogrammed decision rules, which are repeated over and over again. Job shop methodology lends itself to a repetitive sequence of different decision situations. When repetition exists, there is a reasonably stable system, providing historical evidence that can be used for forecasting the future. Gradual changes in strategies can be introduced, because penalties accumulate over a period of time. No such gradual changes are available for the project.

Degree of Reversibility

By the nature of ''big'' projects, large investments are required. This means that a mistake can be serious. A company can be competitively crippled or rendered bankrupt. There exist ruin thresholds in long-term planning situations where a single decision can push the company across a threshold from which there is no return. Short-cycle decisions, repeated

88

*Managing
Production and
Operations
Systems Through
Their Life Cycle
Stages*

over and over again, can also result in ruin when the decision repeatedly imposes even a small penalty on the company. But generally corrective action can be taken so that a new and better decision is substituted for the old one. If it is noticed that rejects, customer returns, back orders, machine idle time, setup costs, or absenteeism are increasing, steps can be taken to correct these weaknesses long before any gates are passed.

Nonreversibility characterizes project management and the flow shop, distinguishing them from the job shop and from FPS, which have output flexibility, as well as good resale value for facilities. Project decisions about what to do (what activities to use) and when to do it are frequently founded upon nothing more than informed opinion. If differences of opinion exist, the reasons for the differences are vital. The reasons may be expressible only in qualitative terms. But this in no way permits an executive group to dismiss differences of opinion. Reasons for disagreements about complex project decisions are exceedingly difficult to uncover. Almost without exception, systematic analysis is an absolute necessity.

Belief in estimates may be of a low order. Nevertheless, some set of estimates is essential. Every project requires them. Two considerations, especially applicable to long-term planning situations, can be derived when the degree of belief in predictions is low. First, there should be a preference for decisions that promise greater flexibility. That is, other things being equal, decisions that permit corrective actions to be taken at a future date are preferred to decisions that cannot be changed. A strategy that can produce a catastrophic outcome—although with very small likelihood—will be avoided, even though it has a higher potential benefit. This is because the penalty for irreversibility is likely to outweigh simple profit or benefit considerations. Second, there is a preference for decisions that promise a reasonably good expected outcome, across a broad spectrum of "likely" situations that may arise, as compared to decisions that produce exceptionally good expected outcomes with situations that are unlikely to occur.

The Gantt Project Planning Chart

Project planning has always been a critical function for business in particular and society in general. Serious errors can lead to catastrophes. No one will forget the tragedy of the space shuttle *Challenger* in January 1986. It is therefore not surprising that a great deal of both theoretical and practical effort has been expended to define and develop methods that can adequately deal with the problems involved in potential ruin situations.

Around 1900, an objective method for project planning was developed by Henry L. Gantt, a colleague of Frederick W. Taylor, the "father" of P/OM methods and measurement. The problems Gantt and P/OM people of his time faced had considerably less complexity than the problems presently encountered in project management. Gantt's methods were fine for his time. In our world, Gantt's trial and error approach provides a means of organizing our thinking, but it does not satisfy the need for controlling complex situations, where seemingly small errors can produce crises. Furthermore, Gantt's method requires that someone familiar with all aspects of the project use his or her instincts and knowhow to make decisions. The problem with this idea is that projects having even an average level of complexity are too big to handle in this way. Even so, Gantt has not been forgotten, because the methods and charts he developed provide the foundation for the more powerful computer-driven planning programs.

A great number of computerized project planning models have become available in recent years. They are superior to the older methods. Yet many flow shop and job shop managers, when faced with a project, still use the Gantt chart to manage that project, if they use any systematic method at all.

Figure 3–1 shows the structure of a Gantt Project Planning Chart. Figure 3–3 pictures a chart in actual use. The project planner uses the charts in two ways. First, to set down—a priori—the steps of work that must be followed in order to bring to fruition a nonrepeating set of activities that constitutes the project system. Second, to monitor the way in which the steps of the plan are being carried out—that is, to track the

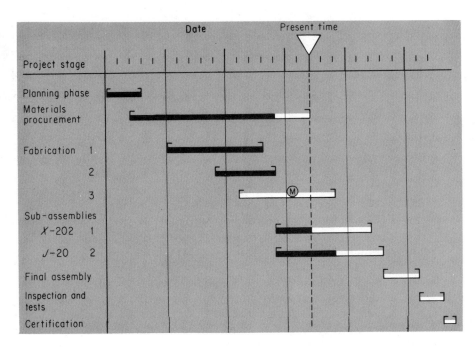

FIGURE 3-1. A Gantt project planning chart.

status of the project over a period of time. These two purposes permeate all project management. They can be translated as:

1. Making the plan
2. Carrying the plan to completion

Gantt Chart Symbols

There are some conventional symbols used in the construction of Gantt charts. Within any organization, these are usually modified in accordance with the particular circumstances of that organization. This flexibility makes sense as long as all users within the organization are aware of the modifications. See Fig. 3–2 for the basic elements of the traditional Gantt chart.

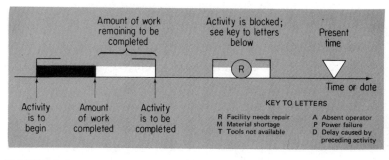

FIGURE 3-2.

In all projects technological sequences constrain the arrangement of activities with which a project shall be accomplished. Usually, there are many constraints on the project sequences that can be used. The project planners determine which activity sequences will be used, so they must know the technological restrictions. From the set of all possible arrangements, they would like to find the best one.

Figure 3–3 illustrates a specific project, bringing to market a new car. The project manager begins by listing the required stages or jobs that are the component building blocks of the project. These must be sequenced in some sensible order if the project is to be completed. The first of these stages can allow for further development of the project design. In such a case, the Gantt chart is later redrawn if an improved sequence can be found. It is worth noting that four years elapse from the beginning to the end of the project. If this span of time can be reduced, it provides the reducer with a competitive edge.

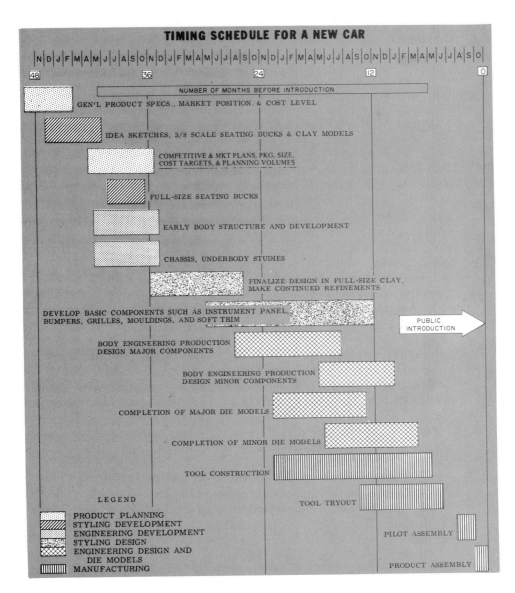

FIGURE 3-3. Project planning chart for new car introduction [Courtesy Chrysler Corporation]

Certain steps can be accomplished faster or slower, depending upon the number of people employed, the kinds of facilities used, and so on. The way in which resources are allocated to the various steps of a project will determine how long it takes to accomplish each phase and how much it will cost. Taken together, both of these points spell out the fact that for any given project there is at least one best sequence to be followed and one best allocation of resources to the various activities with respect

92

*Managing
Production and
Operations
Systems Through
Their Life Cycle
Stages*

to a specific set of cost and time objectives. The Gantt method requires that the intuition and good judgment of the project manager be responsible for approximating such an optimal project plan.

The Evolution of Project Planning Methods

At the time of the building of the pyramids in ancient Egypt some foresight had to be exercised. The planning methods that were used have never been recorded. (Is it likely to be the same project methods that were used to build the Colossus at Rhodes?) These projects were so big there is no doubt that some planning method was employed. To begin with, the project of building a pyramid was conceived. Then, in logical order, the builders had to specify where to build, what materials to use, what labor would be required at each stage (that is, labor to select the site, to clear it, to bring in the necessary materials, and then to construct the pyramid).

If the plan was to be carried through efficiently, each of the stages would have to dovetail properly. If not, at various stages materials might be lacking, or an adequate supply of manpower would be missing. From the point of view of the Egyptians, the logistics of the problem were enormous. Materials had to be carried from great distances, and at these faraway locations individual quarrying operations had to be set up. Work gangs were required at the quarries to transport giant blocks and at the building site to construct the pyramid. It is evident that many of these operations coexisted in time, so a general administration was required to see that the total operation was properly integrated.

The steps to build a pyramid represent a good example of the kind of elements involved in present-day projects. But the design, construction, and launching of an Apollo moon shot or the development of a large manufacturing system require coordination and dovetailing to a much greater degree. In the first place, many more factors are involved, and second, time losses are now of extreme importance.

It is true that if the construction teams on the site of the pyramids were not supplied with sufficient building materials, a penalty was suffered. Enormous quantities of food had to be transported to these locations in order to keep the slaves alive. This effort taxed the resources of the kingdom. However, there was no competition to be first into the market with a completed pyramid. There were no legal contracts with penalties to be paid if the pyramid was not completed at a stated time. There may have been best seasons for doing the work, but such constraints were less severe than the planetary window for getting a Jupiter probe into orbit.

Gantt project planning methods might have been able to help the pyramid builders, but they cannot succeed in our present complex, project-planning efforts. Because of competitive factors, we recognize that the ability to reach the marketplace as quickly as possible with a new product or service can be a major influence on its success or failure. Excessive planning periods pose the threat of producing an obsolete product if development takes too long. For example, in the aircraft industry and in the computer field, delay in carrying out a major plan can produce long-lasting harmful results. So there is good reason to learn about PERT and critical path methods.

The Contact Lens Case— Lensmasters

Design of the sequence of activities often must conform to more than technological feasibility. Here is an example. Lensmasters is well established in the contact lens field but has played follow-the-leader when it comes to the newest soft contact lens, which has been obtaining a significant share of the contact lens market. After much procrastination, a licensing agreement was worked out so that Lensmasters can produce and distribute soft lenses by paying a reasonable royalty.

To get into production and distribution, a Gantt planning chart was drawn up. There is a problem, however. The way that the Gantt chart was constructed, it turns out that most of the activities required to bring soft lens production on-line occur at about the same time.

The manager noted that although all these activities could be done almost simultaneously, there is not sufficient personnel to commit to the project at one time. The manager returned the Gantt chart to its originators and requested that they find a new sequence of activities so that the drain on company resources would be level instead of peaked.

This case requires knowledge of resource leveling which is discussed on p. 117.

Resource leveling is a desirable way of restructuring activities when there are resources allocated to activities which do not have to be completed right away. The resources can be shifted to activities that must be finished right away if those additional resources can help to reduce the time to completion. In other cases, it might pay for a company to mount a major effort, doing as many things as possible simultaneously, to get into the marketplace before the competition.

Use of Gantt Charts

The chart is equivalent to the plan. In the planning phase, adjustments are made to the basic set of steps, the order in which they are to be used, the allocation of resources to each step, and the estimated times for completing each job. As a general rule, materials, plant, facilities, labor, power, and so forth are required. A statement of actual or desirable resource availability allows for intelligent planning of the sequence. Once these steps have been completed, the planning process moves on to the detailed level of assigning specific resources and facilities in order to produce the chosen result. Elapsed time to complete all the steps is usually considered to be of major consequence.

That is where the second purpose of the Gantt chart appears. Along the top of the chart is a time scale. This time scale can be general, in the sense that it represents a sequence of days, or weeks, or months. On the other hand, calendar dates can be associated with the time scale so that it represents particular points in time.

The former approach is useful when estimates of total time involved are required and when the starting point in real time is unknown. For example, assume that capital has to be raised to finance the project, but no one can estimate when the necessary monetary assets will be acquired. Plans will be launched at the completion of this stage, but because the completion date of that stage cannot be set, only an abstract time plan can be constructed.

Usually, cost and time estimates are supplied for completing all steps in the project. Such estimates are based upon specific commitments to a particular pattern for the allocation of resources. When a starting date is specified, calendar time can be utilized for the time scale. When real time is used, then it is very convenient to use the project plan as a check or control over what is actually happening so that revisions in the basic plans can be developed as required. There are penalties for delays occurring as a result of poor integration of the planning elements. We cannot afford to have a press shop staffed and waiting with all the necessary tools and dies at their disposal while the research laboratory is still determining the proper materials to be used. Opportunity costs such as these can occur in many different ways in the project planning cycle. The project manager can do a lot to reduce such opportunity costs.

The left-hand column of the Gantt chart lists all the activities that must be done. This is the operational sequence of activities required for the design of our system. It is the project's plan. If we make a mistake here we may destroy the project's viability. It could put us out of business. It is also essential to bear in mind that a competitor may have a project plan similar to ours—or destructive to ours. If this plan is without error, or if it meets the objectives on time and ours does not, or if the competitor is able to complete various steps in less time than it takes us, or if the competitor is a better project planner than we are and finds ways to accomplish various activities in parallel while we serialize them, it is likely that we will lose the game.

Figure 3–1 indicates that a number of the steps can be operating simultaneously even though they begin at different times. To recognize this fact, observe the number of project activities that are intersected simultaneously by any given time line. Sometimes a fraction of a job must be completed before the next step can begin. Often, stages can begin simultaneously. When the constraints are technological, it is not strange if, in a particular case, two-thirds of one prior stage and one-eighth of another prior stage must be completed before a third stage can be started.

Accomplishments: Planned vs. Actual

How does the plan measure up to the actuality? The darkened portion of each activity box represents the percentage of completion of each phase at a particular point in time designated by the time arrow. With succeeding days, the dark portion is lengthened until at completion the box is entirely filled. Thus, we have a running record of accomplishments.

The true course of projects never runs perfectly smoothly. Unexpected situations arise, and difficulties may delay certain phases. Typically, while some things lag, others spurt, and so some phases are ahead of schedule while others are behind. Specifying the activities of a project and the estimated times is a prior operation, but it is also an ongoing operation.

Constant refinement with new data is essential. Regular review is needed in order to adjust and update the record of accomplishment. In rare instances, an entirely new project sequence must be developed because of difficulties that arise.

It will be noted that in Fig. 3–1 the arrow appears on the second day of the fourth week. Usually that arrow is moved along on a daily basis, in effect saying, "This is today." We look down at each of the activities and see that the dark bars indicate how much of the job has been completed. The materials procurement stage lags; the second subassembly, J-20, is ahead of schedule. One has not even begun (Fabrication 3), although according to plan it should have almost been done.

We have now reviewed the elements of project planning in terms of the Gantt chart. It is an effective way of keeping track of what has happened in terms of what we thought should have happened. It is also a suitable control and accounting device. But what is lacking is that there is no suitable way of using the Gantt chart to determine how resources might have been allocated in a superior fashion. For example, consider two parallel activities, called x and y. If employees had been shifted from x to y, it might have been possible to accomplish y in a shorter period of time. Correspondingly, x would have taken longer. Is this better?

Another possibility would be to permit certain delays to occur in order to reduce costs. With the Gantt chart we have not succeeded in associating costs with the various activities or with the overall project. Problems amenable to Gantt chart methods cannot possess the complexities familiar in present-day project management situations. Let us therefore consider next a project planning approach used since the late 1950s. It is called the critical path method.

PROBLEM
SET

1. A crash vaccine production activity has been instituted. Roughly 200 million doses are to be readied for the inoculation program, which starts in 8 months. One normally associates the flow shop with such high production volumes (and rates). Nevertheless, the characteristics

96

*Managing
Production and
Operations
Systems Through
Their Life Cycle
Stages*

of a project are very much in evidence. What is the best classification in this case? Explain.

2. List three projects and explain why they qualify as such. Describe the character of these projects, being careful to differentiate them from flow shops and job shops.

3. It has been stated in the text that there are two main types of P/OM activities: (a) planning, designing, redesigning, and implementing the system; and (b) operating the system. Describe the different kinds of managerial activities that would be best associated with each. Do you think that all of the (a) activities belong together, or would you create a third category?

4. A mass producer of paper products plans to construct another plant. A consulting firm with a strong project orientation has been retained to oversee the activities of the site selection and plant design committee. The committee is composed of executives with flow shop experience. How should the members of the committee be made aware of the special characteristics of project management?

5. In certain projects, it is considered advisable to duplicate specified activities. Thus, two groups would be charged with completing the same activity. Would you allow the groups to be in communication with each other? Explain your answer, making certain to identify the objectives of such parallel path activity.

6. Why should one person be responsible for all major project decisions? How does the flow shop differ from the project in this regard?

   Answer: Coordination is an absolute requirement for successful project management. In the flow shop, much of the coordination has been predesigned and is incorporated in the system.

7. "Sunk costs" are those which cannot be recovered by a decision to stop (or alter) a project. Discuss the degree of reversibility and ruin thresholds of projects in terms of "sunk costs."

8. Using Fig. 3–3, analyze the Gantt chart, "Timing Schedule for a New Car." Why are major die models completed before minor die models? Should competitive marketing plans be finished two years before public introduction? Tool tryout is started before tool construction is finished; does this make sense? Raise additional questions of this type and try to answer them.

9. With reference to the Gantt chart in Fig. 3–3, how can we be sure that no step has been omitted by mistake? What way is there to tell that the sequence of activities in Fig. 3–3 is as good as can be had?

   Answer (to both parts of the question): Consult as many knowledgeable people (including consultants) as can be identified. Check Gantt and PERT charts of prior introductions. The Gantt chart in Fig. 3–3 is more of a public relations piece than a viable project management approach. A detailed PERT-type system of activities would be used in actual practice.

Section 3.2: Critical Path Methods

Network analysis methods such as PERT and critical path are significantly stronger for project planning than Gantt charts. The weaknesses of Gantt charts provided the focus for important developments in the planning of complex projects. A method was required that would permit optimal or near-optimal sequencing of activities and utilization of resources. An appropriate methodology was found in the area of network analysis. Starting about 1957, two similar approaches to large-scale project planning were begun at separate locations and for different reasons. These were:

PERT—Program Evaluation Research Task
CPM—Critical Path Method

PERT was developed by the U.S. Navy Special Projects Office in conjunction with Booz, Allen and Hamilton. It was one of the first of the network methods, and was used for the Polaris project. CPM was developed by E.I. duPont de Nemours and Company and Remington Rand at about the same time (circa 1957) and was used to plan the construction of a plant. Many other names and acronyms appeared later on (e.g., RAMPS, PEP, IMPACT). They were all abbreviations for project planning methods. The differences between the approaches arose primarily as a consequence of the original job for which the method was developed. All share the notion of a critical path, and it is for this reason that we have chosen to call this section "Critical Path Methods" (CPMs). PERT is the most familiar of all to project managers, and we shall therefore discuss the PERT variant of critical path methods.

How to Construct PERT Networks

Three steps are required to utilize network models.

1. All the elements, variously called jobs, steps, tasks, or activities, that are required to bring the project to fruition must be detailed.
2. A precise sequencing order (drawn as a precedence diagram) needs to be determined. Precedence is based on technological feasibility, administrative capabilities, equipment and workforce availabilities, and managerial objectives. The rationale for sequential constraints should be made explicit.
3. The time (and cost) to perform each task or activity must be estimated. The method of estimation for time and cost must be detailed, and related to specifications of the project's quality.

When all this information has been assembled, a PERT network (as shown by Fig. 3–4) can be constructed.

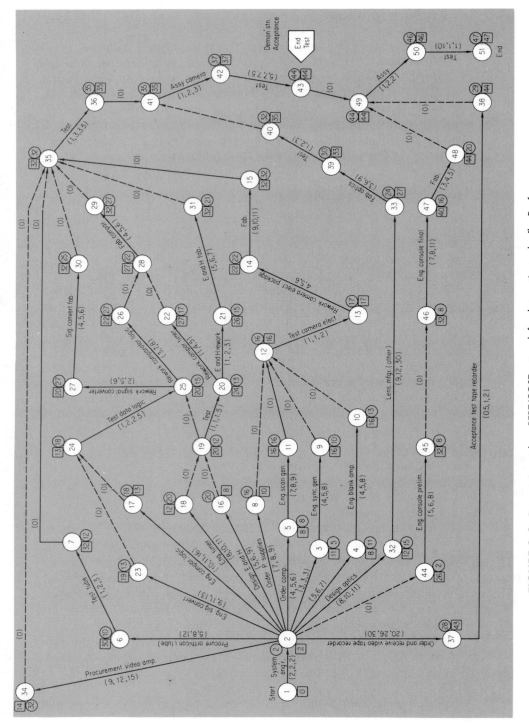

FIGURE 3-4. Datomatic reader—PERT/COST network for datomatic reader [by Professor William J. Abernathy, Harvard University, Graduate School of Business Administration. Reproduced by permission.]

Detail is essential for the successful use of CPMs. Activities are broken down into their components. All relevant activities must be included. Various estimates are required for each activity, with the result that for normally complex projects, a gigantic amount of information is generated. Fortunately, computer programs have been developed that readily handle the information required for most network systems.

Many applications of critical path methods can be found for production management projects. A service organization may want to develop a new service center. In the construction industry, CPM is well known (for example, see Fig. 3–5).

Government agencies have found critical path methods so useful that they frequently require this approach from companies working on government contracts. This is particularly true when an integrated effort on the part of several companies is needed (see Fig. 3–4).

We use the network approach as a means of unifying the totality of activities, problems, decisions, and operations that constitute the project management field. This gives us a planning tool that is operational from the very inception of enterprise activity.

CPMs may be expected to deliver **turnkey systems** on time: at the appointed time, to make the system work, turn the key and it should start to run. It does not always work that way. Bugs crop up and startup is delayed. Global competitors have developed **continuous project support systems.** This means that the project is never completed, since product and process improvement is an ongoing effort. Further, all functional areas participate simultaneously in fast-response organizations (FRO's).

This requires multifunctional, parallel-path CPMs, which has been characterized as new-product rugby. In this context, the conventional project management approach is likened to a relay race, where each function completes its activities before handing the baton over to the next functional area. Figure 3–6 illustrates the continuous, multifunctional project that delivers the operating process system.

Network Representation: Activities Labeled on Nodes

Project planning begins with a list of all activities. Then, it is necessary to describe precedence relations—which activities must precede or follow other activities. A network of arrows and nodes can be drawn to represent a specific sequence of project activities. One form of network can be constructed by considering each activity to be a node (each of the small circles in Fig. 3–7 is a node). The arrows (also called arcs) describe the order or precedence of the activities. We call this an **activity-oriented network.** Figure 3–7 is equivalent to a list of project activities, each of which has been numbered and arranged according to node precedence.

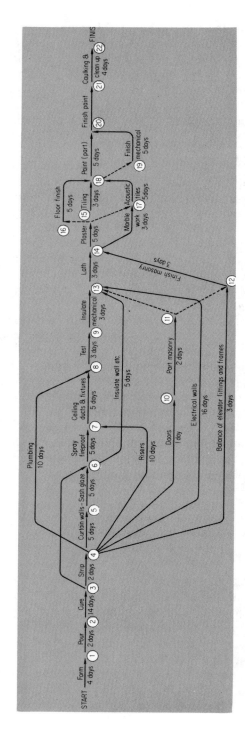

FIGURE 3-5. CPM diagram for a construction of a typical floor in a multistory building [Reprinted from *Engineering News-Record*; copyright, McGraw-Hill, Inc., January 26, 1961, all rights reserved.]

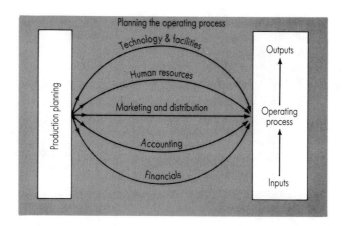

FIGURE 3-6. Continuous multifunctional PERT.

Thus:

Activity	Which Activities Must Immediately Precede
X	none
A	X
B	A
C	A
D	B, C

Network Representation: Activities Labeled on Arcs

An alternative technique exists for drawing networks. In this case, the activities are represented by the arcs (for example, refer to Figs 3–8a and 3–8b). The nodes are events that mark either the beginning of one or more activities or the completion of one or more activities, or both. We call these **event-oriented networks.**

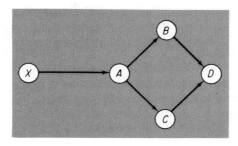

FIGURE 3-7. The activities X, A, B, C, and D have been arranged according to a specific set of precedence relations.

102

*Managing
Production and
Operations
Systems Through
Their Life Cycle
Stages*

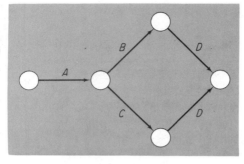

FIGURE 3-8a. An infeasible, event-oriented network.

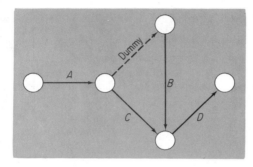

FIGURE 3-8b. The infeasible event-oriented network in Fig. 3-8a can be made feasible using a dummy activity.

It is easier to draw up an activity-oriented network, where the activities are represented by nodes. However, for the computational requirements of PERT, it is necessary to employ an event-oriented network having nodes that can be identified with specific starting and finishing times. The reason for this will become evident when we discuss critical path computations (pp. 107–111). For the moment, let us note that every event node in the PERT network will be identified with a two-part scorecard of event calendar dates or clock times.

There is a problem in drawing some event-oriented networks. For example, if two activities, say B and C in Fig. 3–8a, are preceded by the same activity A, and are followed by another common activity D, then the event-oriented network would require that two arcs be labeled activity D. This cannot be permitted for computational reasons. The PERT network algorithm cannot deal with two separate arcs both being called by the same name. Therefore, we must redraw this network and insert what is called a **dummy activity,** represented by a dashed line in Fig. 3–8b. Now there is only one activity D, and the specified precedence relations are correct. The dummy activity is associated with 0 time for completion. Note that the dummy activity could as well have preceded activity C. Creating the necessary dummy activities is not difficult. When there is need for them, that fact will be apparent, and the appropriate construction can be developed by trial and error.

Activity Cycles

In planning a project, some activities go through a cycle of steps. For example, a test can result in pass or fail. If the product fails the test, rework is required and a retest is scheduled. Looping back and forth between test, rework, and retest is not permitted in PERT networks. They must be depicted in extensive form, as shown in Fig. 3–9.

Many different arrangements of activities and events are possible. Projects of realistic size can have thousands of interrelated activities. Whenever materials, parts, subassemblies, or particular procedures come together for a new activity, an event circle must be used to signify that the previous activity has been completed. Also, the definition of an activity is subjective. The project manager may use few or many activities to represent the same project elements. In good project design, more activities are better than few, so that activities can be controlled.

Estimation of Time

The importance of estimation is often underestimated. A good estimator can save a lot of money by not underestimating the cost of a job. The good estimator can make a lot of money for the organization by not overestimating costs and thereby producing bids that are too high. We are all taught from grade school on to calculate precisely; otherwise, our homework or test problem is marked wrong. Few courses are devoted to improving one's skill in estimating, which means combining rough calculations with judgments based on opinions formed by tentative evaluations.

Management relies upon its ability to estimate. Continually, it must take action before hard data are available. Yet few organizations track the estimating capabilities of their employees. Such tracking is not hard to do if historical records are maintained of

$$\text{Estimate} - \text{actual result} = \text{error}$$

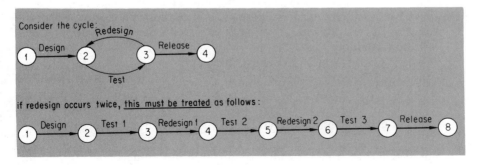

FIGURE 3-9. PERT networks must be developed in extensive form.

104

*Managing
Production and
Operations
Systems Through
Their Life Cycle
Stages*

it would be possible to grade estimators in these terms:

1. How close is the average error to zero?
2. How dispersed are the errors?
3. Do errors tend to be overestimates or underestimates?

There are basically three different methods for obtaining estimates. First is one person's opinion derived from experience. Second is the pooling of several individuals' opinions derived from experience. Many different pooling techniques are available, the most obvious being to use the average value. Third, several parameters of estimation are requested from an individual, and these are combined by a computing formula. Here too, the pooling of several persons' opinions can be achieved. For PERT, the estimation procedure is usually the third kind.

When the PERT system uses three parametric estimates of time for each activity, they are combined by a formula. This formula is used to derive a single estimate of the time that will be required to complete each activity. The project manager is asked to supply:

1. An *optimistic* estimate, called *a*
2. A *pessimistic* estimate, called *b*
3. An estimate of what is *most likely,* called *m*

These three estimates are then combined to give an expected elapsed time, called *te*. The formula for *te* is shown below.

$$t_e = \frac{1}{6}(a + b) + \frac{2}{3}(m)$$

This formula uses more information than a single estimate for activity time, such as *m*. To understand why *m*, "the most likely," is not a sufficient estimate of activity time, consider the following example. If vendor X delivers on time, then two days are required. However, if the vendor cannot deliver on time, then seven days are required. It is most likely that the vendor will deliver on time. Therefore, two days is most likely, but hardly the best estimate of activity time. The range, or spread between shortest and longest times, provides extra insight for the best estimate of activity time.

A possible distribution for these three elapsed time estimates is shown in Fig. 3–10. Because estimates can be checked against actuality, it should be possible to determine what is best for a specific project. At the heart of the issue is the need to develop a reasonably good estimate for the expected elapsed time required for the completion of an activity.

The three values *a, b,* and *m* are used to estimate the **mean** of a **unimodal beta distribution** (this procedure does not apply to a U-shaped beta dis-

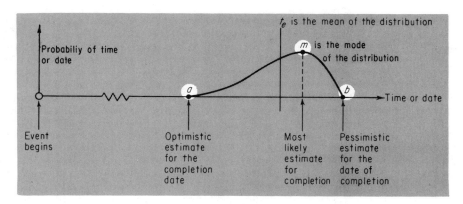

FIGURE 3-10. A *possible* distribution for the elapsed time estimates (There is no assurance that the three estimates a, m, and b, falling at these positions on the time scale of the distribution, will provide a better estimate of the mean than a simple, direct estimate of activity time.)

tribution). For the unimodal beta distribution, if *a* and *b* are equally spaced above and below *m*, then *m* = *te*. That is:

$$t_e = \frac{1}{6}[(m - x = a) + (m + x = b)] + \frac{4}{6}(m) = m.$$

When *a* and *b* are not symmetric around *m*, *te* is moved in the direction of the greatest interval.

An Estimation Dilemma

It is not unusual that two outcomes are both highly probable. A bimodal distribution, as shown in Fig. 3–11, prevails.

We must question whether the mean of the distribution, *te*, is a better estimate than the most likely estimate for completion, *m*. We would choose *m*, and test the effect on our plans of the true time being *m'*. We note also that *m* is a longer period than *m'*. Our preference is to use the least desirable (or worst case) estimate. Consequently, if *m* and *m'* were in reverse positions, we would have yet another dilemma to cope with.

Management must always decide on the best way to deal with such problems. Perhaps the project manager should alter the design of this activity so that the estimation quandary can be removed. The manager should do this only if the distinction between *m* and *m'* seriously affects the project as a whole.

106

*Managing
Production and
Operations
Systems Through
Their Life Cycle
Stages*

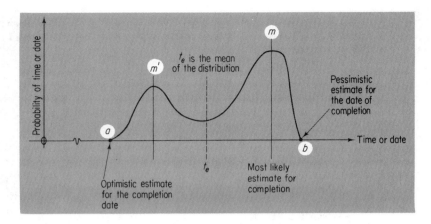

FIGURE 3-11. A bimodal distribution can be the basis for the elapsed time estimate.

An estimate of the variances associated with the expected value of elapsed time is also frequently supplied for the PERT system. **Variance** (denoted by σ^2) is a measure of the spread of a distribution. The spread of a distribution reflects the variability that is being observed. A tall and thin distribution has almost 0 variance. A broad and shallow distribution has a large variance. The square root of variance, called the **standard deviation** (and denoted by σ), also is used to reflect the spread of a probability distribution.

An important statistical fact is that the sum of the variances of a number of consecutive estimates of sequenced independent activities measures the variance of the total sequence. The independence referred to is with respect to activity times—i.e., how long it should take to accomplish each operation—not with respect to starting and finishing times.

For example, if three estimates, te_1, te_2, and te_3 are made, each of them having a particular variance measure σ_1^2, σ_2^2, σ_3^2 then the variance of the sum of these estimates is given by $\sigma_1^2 + \sigma_2^2 + \sigma_3^2$. This relationship is depicted in Fig. 3–12.

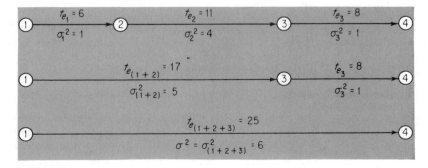

FIGURE 3-12. The variance σ^2 of combined estimates is equal to the sum of the variances of the individual estimates of *independent* activities.

The formula for the variance of the beta distribution (shown in Fig. 3–10) is given by $\sigma^2 = \left[\dfrac{1}{6}(b - a)\right]^2$.

Critical Path Computations

What is the situation for Lensmasters, Inc.? At the outset, it must do three different things. These are:

1. Obtain inputs: materials and skills (activities A_1, A_2, A_3).
2. Construct soft lens production process (activities B_1, B_2).
3. Develop distribution channels (activities C_1, C_2, C_3).

Some constraints exist: A_2 must be completed before either A_3 or B_2 can begin; also A_3, B_2, and C_3 must be completed before product launch (called L) can occur. This network information is illustrated in Fig. 3–13. In addition, the estimates for the duration or elapsed time te of each activity are shown on their respective arcs (in working days).

The network in Fig. 3–13 is not acceptable. The same activity, A_2, appears twice. Therefore, a dummy activity is created, as shown in Fig. 3–14, which solves the problem.

Note that the following unique paths exist in Fig. 3–14's network:

Top path: A_1, A_2, A_3
Dummy path: A_1, A_2, dummy, B_2
Middle path: B_1, B_2
Bottom path: C_1, C_2, C_3

Every event node in the PERT network will be identified with the following two-part scorecard of event calendar dates or clock times.

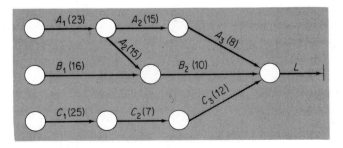

FIGURE 3-13. The network for launching Lensmasters' new soft contact lens (with elapsed time estimates t_e in days). A dummy variable will be required, since A_2 appears twice in the network.

108

*Managing
Production and
Operations
Systems Through
Their Life Cycle
Stages*

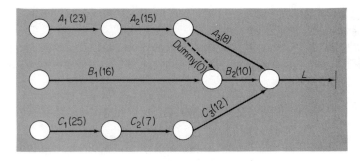

FIGURE 3-14. A dummy activity has been added to the network of Fig. 3-13. The dummy is associated with $t_e = 0$.

T_E	T_L

T_E = earliest possible starting time

T_L = latest allowable starting time

We obtain cumulative total times for each network path, moving along the particular path from the beginning of the project to the end. Call these values T_E. Each cumulative total T_E gives the earliest possible clock time that the next event can begin. In Fig. 3–15, the scorecard of event dates (or times) described above has only the "earliest start up" times entered.

It will be noted that as we sum along different paths, until we arrive at a junction node (e.g., where the dummy activity and B_1 meet before B_2 can start), the joining branches can carry a different cumulative number to that node (in this case, 38 and 16). Whenever this condition arises at a junction node, we accept the largest value of T_E, i.e., 38. All further accumulation proceeds with this larger number, which is the earliest possible starting time for the next event in the network.

The scorecard value of T_E at the last node in the network represents

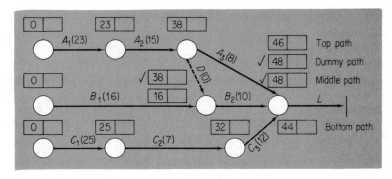

FIGURE 3-15. Lensmasters' network showing the scorecard of event times at each node. Values for T_E (which is the earliest possible clock time that each event can begin) are indicated.

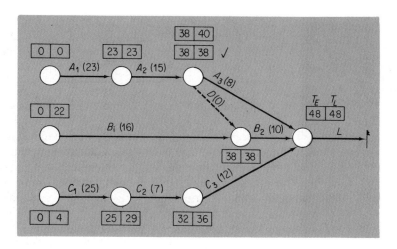

FIGURE 3-16. Lensmasters' network showing the values of T_E and T_L. T_L is the latest possible clock time at which an activity can be started in order for the project to be completed on time.

expected project completion time. It also represents the earliest possible time that the product launch can begin—after 48 working days. This last value of T_E is a measure of the maximum cumulative time of any path in the network—the longest time sequence of activities in the network.

What we want to know is: Which of the four unique paths previously listed accounts for the longest time sequence of activities? That path is called the **critical path.**

To determine the critical path, start with the largest cumulative total. In our case, this is $T_E = 48$, which is the estimated time for project completion. We now move backward through the network. Successively we subtract expected elapsed activity times, *te*. The values derived by subtraction, called T_L (the second box in the scorecard of event times), are assigned to their respective event nodes. Each subtraction ($T_L - te$) is based on the last T_L and the preceding *te*. The starting value of T_L is taken as the largest value of T_E, in this case 48. In Fig. 3–16, the values of T_L are recorded in the scorecard of event times.

In some instances, when moving backward two or more arcs converge on a node such that the values of T_L produced by subtraction are not equal. (For this example, such convergence occurs at A_2's completion node, where T_L can equal either 38 or 40.) Then, we accept the smallest value of T_L, 38, and continue our subtractions with this smallest number. The values of T_L are measures of the latest allowable clock time at which the next activity can be started in order to complete the project in accordance with its critical path time.

The critical path is A_1, A_2, D, B_2, based upon the t_e sums: 23 + 15 + 0 + 10 = 48. This is the longest time path through the network, which is the definition of the critical path. The critical path would be hard to find without this method.

110

*Managing
Production and
Operations
Systems Through
Their Life Cycle
Stages*

A project management algorithm is also available that computes slack time at each node of the network. **Slack time** is the slippage (or wasted time) that can be tolerated in an activity without changing the project completion time.

Measure of Slack Time

The difference, $T_L - T_E$, can be obtained for each event node. It describes the amount of slack that exists at that node in the network. See Fig. 3–17, where the values $T_L - T_E$ are shown in the node circles.

Where slack exists, activities can start later or take longer than planned. Thus, an activity's time estimate can slip by the amount of slack that exists in its part of the network, and yet the total job can still be completed on time. The critical path (or paths) can be recognized by the fact that at every node of the critical path, $T_L - T_E = 0$.

In Fig. 3–17, we observe that $T_L - T_E = 0$ for all of the nodes comprising the path A_1, A_2, D, B_2, which is the critical path. All activities in the bottom path have slack of 4, meaning that any one of them (but only one) can slip behind by 4 days without changing the target time of project completion.

Slack normally applies to an entire path, but sometimes to just one activity. Thus, activity A_3 can slip by its own slack of 2 days[1] and similarly

---

[1]In this example, activity A_3 connects 2 nodes, both on the critical path. As a result, its slack cannot show up on the scorecard, since all nodes along the critical path have 0 slack. The computation of A_3's slack must be computed independently.

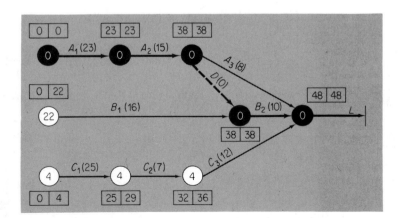

FIGURE 3-17. Lensmasters' network showing the values of $T_L - T_E$ (in the node circles). $(T_L - T_E)$ is the slack time available for the activity that follows. The critical path has $(T_L - T_E = 0)$ for all its activities. In this example the nodes along the path A_1, A_2, D, B_2 are all associated with 0 slack time; therefore, it is the critical path, marked with the darker line.

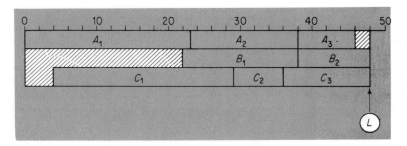

FIGURE 3-18. Lensmasters' project work schedule.

activity B_1 has leeway of 22 days. Remember management's concern in the Lensmasters' situation was that to launch their new product, everything seemed to have to be done at the beginning, and at the same time. Now we know that this is not required. B_1 can wait until the twenty-second day. A_1 must begin on time so that A_2 can be completed before B_2 starts. C_1 can begin 4 days late, followed by B_1 some 18 days later.

Figure 3–18 depicts the project schedule. Note that if the schedule in Fig. 3–18 is followed, three paths through the network have become critical paths. This calls attention to the fact that more than one project path can be critical. Management is hard pressed to handle projects that have a large percentage of critical activities.

Only activity A_3 can be allowed to slip without increasing the time to launch. This is because all slack (except A_3's) has been removed by delaying the start of work for both the B and C branches by the total amount of existing slack. Lensmasters' management might not like that situation, preferring to delay B branch activities by (say) 10 working days and C branch activities by (say) only 1 day.

Knowing which activities have slack is important. Assume that A_1, B_1, and C_1 all begin at the same time. Then, it would be wasteful to do any expediting for activities A_3, B_1, C_1, C_2 and C_3, unless the situation had changed and one or more of them had now joined a critical path. This well-known term (expediting) was first used by Henry Kaiser in connection with maintaining the critical shipbuilding schedules of World War II. The major emphasis of project control should be on critical path activities because they directly affect project completion date.

Distribution of Completion Times

The method we have been using is called PERT/TIME. Time is the only factor under consideration, which is consistent with many planners' objectives. Let us extend the time concept by employing the variance measures shown in parenthesis for each arc in Fig. 3–19.

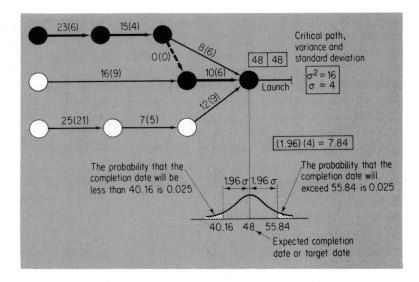

FIGURE 3-19. Lensmasters' Project Network, where the estimates t_e are shown as before but now, in addition, the variance of the estimates are included in parentheses. Also, the distribution of completion times around the expected time of 48 is shown. There is 0.05 probability that the actual completion time will not fall in the range of times 55.84 days to 40.16 days.

We sum the variances, proceeding along the critical path. For the final event that signals completion of the job, we can obtain not only the expected time for project completion, but also an estimate of the variance around this expected value.

Figure 3–19 shows a distribution with both tails cut off at the limit of 1.96 standard deviations (plus and minus from the mean value). Each tail contains the probabilities of an event occurring approximately 25 out of 1000 times.[2] The right-hand tail contains long completion dates. The left-hand tail contains short completion dates.

Thus, moving 1.96 standard deviations (1.96 σ) in either direction gives us a range of times for job completion within which there is a 95 percent

---

[2] This assumes a normal distribution, which would result if many beta distributions were added together to form a single distribution for the project as a whole. Tables of the normal distribution are presented in Appendix B.

Number of Standard Deviations (σ) *± from the Mean*	*Probability that the Actual Time Falls* *Within the Specified Range*
1σ	0.680
1.64σ	0.900
1.96σ	0.950
3σ	0.997

probability that the actual completion date will fall. Stated another way, we have determined, utilizing a 1.96 σ criterion, an earliest and latest project completion date.

The Effect of Estimated Variance

Let us compute the expected completion time of each unique path in the network and its total variance. First, however, we should note that it is statistically correct to sum the variances associated with each activity when the expected activity times are derived from well-behaved distributions such as the normal distribution or the beta distribution.

Path	Expected Completion Time	Total Variance	95% Range (1.96σ)
1 A_1, A_2, A_3	46 days	16	38.16–53.84
2 A_1, A_2, D, B_2 (critical path)	48 days	16	40.16–55.84
3 B_1, B_2	26 days	15	18.40–33.59
4 C_1, C_2, C_3	44 days	35	32.40–55.60

Path 2 is the critical path.

The variance of the fourth path is so large that the upper limit of 55.60 is almost the same as the upper limit of the critical path (55.84). If the activities along the critical path proceed about as expected, but the fourth path activities take excessive times, completion will not occur within 48 working days. Completion, dominated by the new critical path, C_1, C_2, C_3, may require as much as 55.6 days, and this can occur within the 95 percent probability range.

This means that careful managerial attention should be paid to the marketing and distribution activities of the fourth path, since these activities can dominate the present critical path and cause the targeted completion date of the project to be missed.

Why Is Completion Time So Important?

There are three dimensions for assessing projects. These are completion time, total cost, and quality of results. All are important, but it is often the case that the targeted date for finishing the project is the first factor considered. This is not surprising for planetary probes, where a "window" is open at very specific, and often rare, times. The so-called window is defined by such factors as closeness to earth, relative trajec-

114

*Managing
Production and
Operations
Systems Through
Their Life Cycle
Stages*

tories, and so forth. In the same sense, seasonal factors may produce a "window" for the Alaska pipeline, offshore exploratory drilling, or even laying sewer pipes. Even when the window concept does not apply, "as soon as possible" frequently does. Projects usually involve heavy investments that do not start paying off until the project is completed. When viewing project costs against such large investments, managers prefer to spend more now to decrease completion time so that a positive cash flow (or other benefits, e.g., hospital beds) can be obtained "as soon as possible." In bidding situations, project completion time is a major determinant for being awarded the job. Frequently, contract terms include stiff penalty clauses which are incurred if the firm fails to bring the project in on time.

Progress Reports and Schedule Control

At any stage of the project, the manager can ask for a progress report. Each activity should report, on a regular basis, where it stands. Computer printouts indicate activities that are ahead and those that are behind, and by how much. If a shift in the critical path occurs, it is reported. New slack values appear. Control over schedule is excellent. The network is continually updated to reflect project progress.

Project methods have greatly improved the manager's knowledge of what is going on with all project activities, at any time. In the next section, we learn that resource management is yet another benefit derived from PERT and CPM.

PROBLEM
SET

1. Convert Figure 3–20, where activities are labeled as nodes, into an equivalent figure where activities are labeled on arcs.

2. Project management requires many estimates and relies on the quality of these estimates. Discuss the importance of estimation. Why does it count?

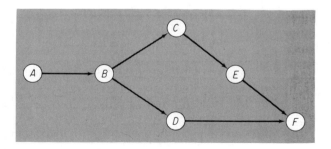

FIGURE 3-20.

3. If an organization wishes to track the estimating capabilities of its employees, how would it go about doing this?

4. What weaknesses of the Gantt project planning technique are overcome by critical path methods?

5. What weaknesses characterize both the Gantt project planning technique and the critical path methods?

6. Draw up an appropriate PERT diagram for the following projects:
   a. A football play
   b. Moving a piano
   c. Dictating a letter
   d. Having a group of three people solve the following problem as rapidly as possible with full accuracy:

$$\frac{(10.314)^4}{(6.501)^2} + \frac{(3.241)^3}{(1.008)^5}$$

Answer: A possible PERT diagram for the arithmetic problem is shown in Fig. 3–21.

We see that up to nodes b and e, 4 individuals could be utilized. After this, only 2 problem solvers would be required, and at node d, the staff requirement is reduced to 1 person. If numerical estimates of required times are associated with these activities, a critical path can be defined. It is interesting to compare actual times against these estimates.

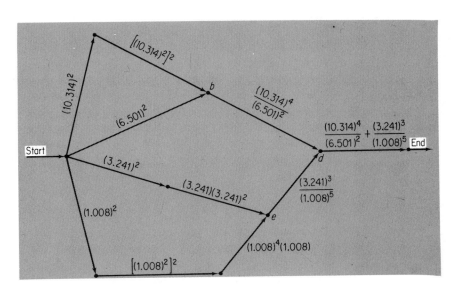

FIGURE 3-21.

116

*Managing
Production and
Operations
Systems Through
Their Life Cycle
Stages*

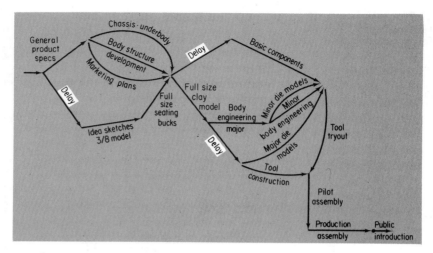

FIGURE 3-22.

Similar networks and analytic procedures can be developed for the other examples specified in this problem.

7. Convert the Gantt project planning chart (Fig. 3–3) into an appropriate critical path diagram. Make whatever assumptions you require. Discuss the advantages of each form of representation.

Answer: It might be said that a PERT diagram has higher dimensionality than a Gantt chart. It requires more detailed information for its construction. Converting a Gantt chart to a PERT chart reveals the significance of this statement far more directly than any set of words. Nevertheless, we can depict the relationship as being somewhat like that of a three-dimensional pyramid as compared to a drawing of the same pyramid.

Good project management practice dictates that a group intimately familiar with the technology of the project construct the critical path diagram. (We can hardly qualify as experts in this regard with respect to Fig. 3–3.) We may, however, attempt to convert the Gantt chart into a PERT diagram by making some approximations concerning the starting and finishing times of an activity. It is frequently useful to introduce delay—that is, an activity having no cost but that takes up a certain amount of time. The PERT diagram might then look something like Fig. 3–22.

Section 3.3 Project Innovations

There are methods for improving the performance of projects. Performance is usually measured in terms of being on target for completion time and budget. Project quality goals cannot be assumed to take care of themselves. Consequently, quality standards must be set as constraints which are monitored throughout the project's life.

Resource Leveling

The fundamental idea of resource leveling is to smooth out the commitment of resources to the project and to balance demand for resources among activities over time. The PERT project method allows us to determine whether a better arrangement of resource utilization might be found. For example, if cash flow to the project is sporadic, the project manager might prefer to smooth this demand for cash over time. Also, if among a set of relatively simultaneous activities, a few are receiving the greatest percentage of project expenditures, it might (or might not) be desirable to level the resource allocations. Once the decision is made to level or smooth resource allocations, tradeoff techniques can be designed to address the specific objectives.

Trading Off Resources over Time

A project that experiences oscillating calls on its resources is hard to manage. For example, if an enormous labor force is required for some work intervals while during other intervals few people are working, an effort should be made to level work force requirements over time. It is costly and disruptive to make major changes in project group size. Also, a facility is designed with specific occupancy in mind, and the task of managing a project is impeded by very uneven resource demand patterns.

To better understand the resource leveling problem over time, refer to Fig. 2–8. The figure illustrates the cash flows of n different products or services and their cumulative total cash flow. Negative cash flows (outflows) most often occur during the startup and R&D stages. The organization must manage its cash flows so that it never runs short of cash to pay employees, buy materials, and so on. If the outflow becomes too large, one or more projects may have to be eliminated or stretched out; consider Fig. 3–17.

Lensmasters could stretch out this project by changing the target interval for completion from 48 to (say) 60 days. The rate of spending for a project of length T can be reduced by stretching T. Leveling can also be achieved by scheduling activities at different times, as allowed by slack conditions. It is always important to make such decisions with the total portfolio of projects that are underway in mind, and to recognize that resources can be traded off between projects, as well as within any specific project.

Trading Off Resources between Activities

The critical path concept is basic to the notion of resource leveling. What is not critical is slack. The existence of slack is an important basis

118

*Managing
Production and
Operations
Systems Through
Their Life Cycle
Stages*

for reallocation of resources and leveling. Shortly, we shall examine a situation where workforce assignments to network activities will be shifted from slack path activities to critical path activities.

This will produce a decrease in the length of the critical path. It will also result in a greater demand for the use of resources, and the demand will tend to be smoother and more constant over time. The resources can include the workforce, materials, equipment, administrative time, and cash to pay both direct and indirect costs.

Trading off resources between activities does not have to result in a shorter critical path. Instead, better resource leveling sometimes might be achieved by moving resources from the critical path to slack paths. This would increase the length of time required to complete the project. The advantage is that there are fewer critical activities to manage. Another option exists: to maintain the critical path activities as they are, but to schedule their work at a slower rate. This has the effect of committing fewer resources per unit of time and lengthening the critical path.

The resource leveling activity is an important P/OM responsibility. Budgetary constraints must be met. Thus, project managers consistently query: Can the budget be met? They also ask from the viewpoint of efficient use of resources: Would there be an advantage in trading slack path resources to the critical path, or vice versa (if either can be done)?

Consider the goal of reducing the length of the critical path. Alteration of the project design that reduces the time of the critical path would either:

1. Decrease the amount of slack that exists in the other branches of the network by trading off their resources to the critical path, or
2. Employ additional resources. The new resources might be obtained by trading them off from other projects or by increasing the total available budget.

We examine the latter alternative below. Therefore, turning to the first option, assume that the length of time it takes to complete each activity is linearly related to the number of workers employed on the job. If the required skills are interchangeable between activities, we could bring the entire network into better balance by shifting workforce resources from slack activities to the critical path. This has been done for a simple example, which is shown in Fig. 3–23.

In Fig. 3–23, the project as originally configured has a completion time of 18. All activities in the upper branch of the project network share a slack of 3. In the lower branch they share a slack of 1. The critical path is the middle branch. Our objective is to trade off resources from slack activities to the critical path, which will reduce the time for completion of the critical path and increase the time of the slack paths, thereby decreasing the amount of slack. This has been accomplished in the modified network of Fig. 3–23, where all the paths are critical.

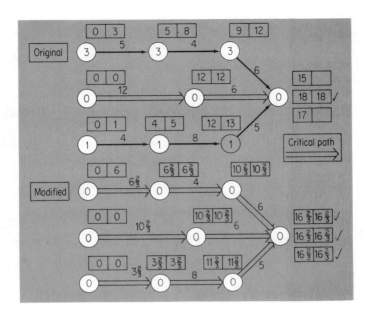

FIGURE 3-23. An example of an original project network which is modified by trading-off resources to remove all slack. A perfectly balanced PERT network is achieved because we have permitted the resources to be fractionated. The target date has been improved by 1-⅓ time units.

In Fig. 3–24 we detail the modification steps that result in all paths being critical. In general, we cannot hope to achieve such perfect balance because workers, machines, and other resources cannot be fractionated at will, and because all skills and facilities are not readily interchangeable between branches. But to the extent that changes can be made, we usually do achieve considerable improvement in the time performance of the system.

Perfect balance may be undesirable. It raises every activity to critical status, imposing enormous burdens on the project manager, who must deal with every instance of slippage as being crucial to project completion. The ability to recognize slack paths, and to trade off resources in the manner we have described above, makes critical path methods significantly more useful than the older methods associated with the Gantt project chart. The paths of greatest slack provide the best opportunities for improving the target date of the project. On the other hand, they also point to places where effort would be wasted in expediting work to meet scheduled deadlines.

Sometimes it is possible to utilize whatever expediting and control facilities exist to improve the variance along the critical path. By doing this, we do not change the target date, but instead reduce the risk of substantially deviating from the target date.

120

*Managing
Production and
Operations
Systems Through
Their Life Cycle
Stages*

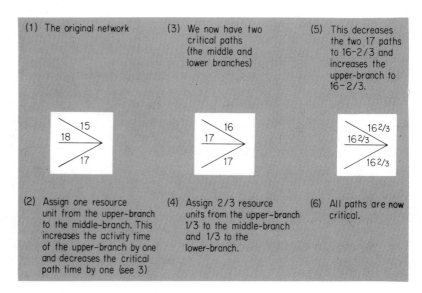

(1) The original network

(3) We now have two critical paths (the middle and lower branches)

(5) This decreases the two 17 paths to 16-2/3 and increases the upper-branch to 16-2/3.

(2) Assign one resource unit from the upper-branch to the middle-branch. This increases the activity time of the upper-branch by one and decreases the critical path time by one (see 3)

(4) Assign 2/3 resource units from the upper-branch 1/3 to the middle-branch and 1/3 to the lower-branch.

(6) All paths are now critical.

FIGURE 3-24. Steps of network modification to decrease slack.

Trading Off Costs and Times

Another way to level resources (or alternatively, to peak their use) is by means of tradeoffs of costs and time. For activities along the critical path, it is often possible to reduce their duration by spending more money. Activities that are not on the critical path can afford to be lengthened in time. The project manager may save money by withdrawing resources from slack activities and funneling the savings to critical path activities of the same project or to other projects.

Let us examine the alternatives of the crash program with peaked resource requirements and the normal program with leveled resource needs. Assume that the project planners desire to run the project on a crash basis—minimum time. This often entails additions to the budget. Another major objective is to minimize cost. This will stretch out project time and relieve budgetary pressures.

The relationships of cost and time have received considerable investigation. Various time-cost systems have been developed to resolve this problem of conflicting multiple objectives.

Trading Off Costs and Times for Quality

Quality (qualities) must be added to the list of multiple objectives. As the *Challenger* tragedy showed, project quality goals cannot be assumed to take care of themselves. Project quality is reflected in long-term performance as well. Bridges that fall, buildings that collapse, and test drug cures that kill are part of a history of project failures no one needs. Less sensational, but quite as dramatic, are project failures in bringing a new product or service to the marketplace. We are not talking about the quality of the product, or the quality of the process used to make the product. We are talking about the *quality of the project* which is responsible for delivering a quality product/process on time. The project has the install and implementation responsibility for the quality of the total system. This aspect of project management is often ignored or overlooked.

PERT/COST/TIME/(QUALITY)

The PERT/COST/TIME system starts in the same way as does PERT/TIME. That is, we construct the representative network of activities and events. However, in this case we have developed two different estimates for each activity. These are:

1. A minimum time estimate and its cost
2. A minimum cost estimate and its time

Figure 3–25 shows the way in which these cost/time tradeoffs might be related for each of the network activities *A, B, C, D*. These activities are illustrated in normal time and crash time networks by Fig. 3–26.

First, the minimum cost estimate (called normal time) is used for each activity, and the critical path is determined for those data. The result will be a completion date based upon minimum cost requirements for com-

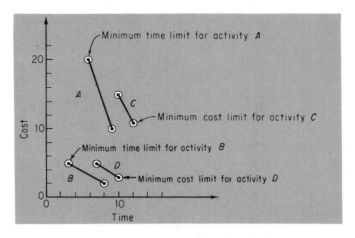

FIGURE 3-25. Some representative COST/TIME relationships where the (weak) assumption is made that linearity prevails over the specified range. The end points are assumed to be limits.

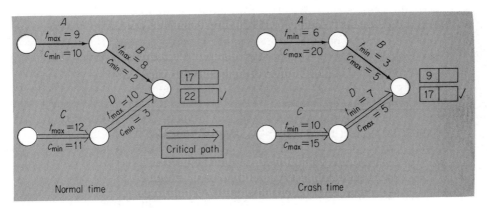

FIGURE 3-26. Comparing normal and crash time networks.

pleting the project. This completion date and the length of time required to complete the project under minimum cost conditions may be too great to be tolerated. Then the minimum (crash) time network can be examined. For the comparison, see Fig. 3–26. For minimum cost and normal time, the bottom path C, D is the critical path, requiring 22 days with a cost of 14. Slack along the upper path A, B is $T_L - T_E = 22 - 17 = 5$ days.

Second, for minimum time (crash program), the bottom path C, D remains critical, but project completion time has been reduced by 5 days to 17 days. The cost has increased by 43 percent to 20. The crash program has not removed slack; it has increased to 8 days. If the top path A, B had not been crashed, then both paths A, B and C, D would be critical at 17 days. By trading off resources between activities (if possible) an even better reduction in total project time might be achieved.

Now, assume that management has stated that total project time should be as close to 20 days as possible. Normal time project planning misses the mark by $+2$ days, and the crash program overshoots the objective by -3 days. Accordingly, alternative times, requiring greater costs, can be substituted for chosen minimum cost activities along the normal time critical path. In this way, the critical path can be shortened until such time that:

1. Another path becomes critical.
2. A satisfactory compromise with the original critical path is achieved.

As a rule of thumb, we make compromises for those activities along the critical path where the ratio of increasing costs for the activity with respect to decreasing time for the activity is smallest. Thus, we select that critical path activity where $|\Delta \text{ cost}| \div |\Delta \text{ time}|$ is smallest. Then the next biggest ratio is used, and so on, until a satisfactory compromise between time and cost is achieved. If the critical path switches, we make our next alterations along the new path.

For our example, the smallest measure of the ratios (of the absolute values) $|\Delta\ \text{COST}| \div |\Delta\ \text{TIME}|$ applying only to the critical path, is associated with activity D. Thus:

Table 3-1

Activity	Increase (Δ Cost)	Decrease (Δ Time)	$|\Delta\ \text{Cost}| \div |\Delta\ \text{Time}|$
C	$+4$	-2	2
D	$+2$	-3	$\frac{2}{3}$

For activity D, $t_{max} = 10$, $t_{min} = 7$. Using the normal time network, set te at 8, which produces the required critical path of 20. What cost ce results? Making the required change for activity D, when $te = 8$, $ce = 4\ \frac{1}{3}$ (see Fig. 3–25). If the graph of Fig. 3–25 is not used, the calculation is:

$$\frac{c_{max} - c_{min}}{t_{max} - t_{min}} = \frac{2}{3} = \frac{c_e - c_{min}}{t_{max} - t_e} = \frac{c_e - 3}{10 - 8} = \frac{c_e - 3}{2}$$

whence:

$$c = \frac{4}{3} + 3 = 4\frac{1}{3}$$

The critical path is now C, D with final $T_E = 20$ and cost = 15 $\frac{1}{3}$. The slack for the upper path A, B is $T_L - T_E = 3$. Figure 3–27 shows this tradeoff solution.

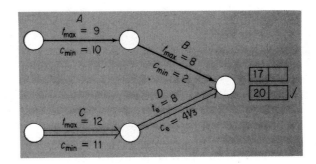

FIGURE 3-27. The tradeoff solution.

124
*Managing
Production and
Operations
Systems Through
Their Life Cycle
Stages*

Maintaining Quality Standards

The PERT/COST/TIME method can be modified to meet the particular requirements of a given project. It can be used to level the demand on financial resources as well as on workforce, facilities, energy, and so on. It is not an optimizing technique; instead, it is a logical attempt to utilize reasonable tradeoffs between cost and time, where they count, in order to obtain an approximation to an optimal result.

Quality issues cannot be ignored. Where quality, cost, and time can be formally related, an extension of these tradeoff notions is not difficult to construct. When quality tradeoffs cannot be formalized, they need to be examined and discussed. This attention is especially applicable to the intangible qualities of project life style and of the system the project delivers. As some examples of these intangibles, consider ergonomics (see Section 8.4), appearance of the delivered system, and quality of life for those working on the project.

Tradeoff models in project planning represent one of the most advanced aspects of P/OM capabilities. Projects are the means by which progress is achieved. The present is altered, hopefully in a constructive fashion. The methods we have discussed do not assure the quality of the future; that remains a social issue.

PROBLEM
SET

1. Explain the difference between resource leveling over time and between activities.

2. Staging a play has been treated by project planning methods. Assume that the network in Fig. 3–28 is a reasonable description of the production and rehearsal activities that must be completed before the play can open.

   We have also made a table showing the estimates for crash and normal times in the network.

Activity	t_{min}	t_{max}	c_{min}	c_{max}
A	5	9	5	12
B	10	12	4	10•
C	3	8	9	15
D	6	7	3	8
E	4	14	12	20
F	5	7	9	12
G	2	3	6	11
H	7	10	2	9
I	3	5	7	9

   a. Find the critical paths for both normal time and crash time.
   b. What slack exists in each case? What are the cost differences?

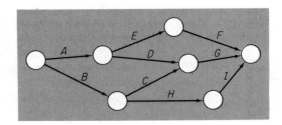

FIGURE 3-28.

c. Assume that the director wants a target date halfway between the required total project times of crash and normal planning. Use resource leveling with cost and time tradeoffs to achieve the objective.

3. How can resource leveling over time and between activities be applied to the project of filming a movie? Note the degrees of freedom that exist for the time order of scenes.

4. Consider a number of projects that are being done together as a portfolio. The portfolio includes a range of risks and expected returns on investment. When examining possibilities for resource leveling, would you tend to concentrate resources on low risk/low return, average risk/average return, or high risk/high return projects? Explain your answer in terms of trading off resources over time, between activities, and between costs and times.

5. The Delta Company manufactures a full line of cosmetics. A competitor has recently brought out a new form of hair spray that shows every sign of sweeping the market and destroying Delta's position in the market. The sales manager asks the production manager what the shortest possible time would be for Delta to reach the market with a new product packed in a redesigned container. The production manager sets down the following PERT structure:

Activity	Initial Event	Terminal Event	Duration
Design product	1	2	
Design package	1	3	
Test market package	3	5	
Distribute to dealers	5	6	
Order package materials	3	4	
Fabricate package	4	5	
Order materials for product	2	4	
Test market product	2	7	
Fabricate product	4	7	
Package product	7	5	

126

*Managing
Production and
Operations
Systems Through
Their Life Cycle
Stages*

a. Construct the PERT diagram.

b. Estimate the durations that you think might apply in a reasonable way. Alternatively, use the hypothetical estimates provided in the answer, part (b).

c. Determine the critical path.

d. Neither the sales manager nor the production manager is satisfied with the way the project is designed, but the production manager insists that because of the pressure of time, the company will be forced to follow this plan. In what ways does this plan violate good practice?

e. By trading off resources, would it be possible to reduce critical path time?

Answer: a. See Figure 3–29.

Answer: b.

Activity	Duration (days)
Design product	30
Design package	15
Test market package	20
Distribute to dealers	20
Order package material	15
Fabricate package	30
Order materials for product	3
Test market product	25
Fabricate product	20
Package product	4

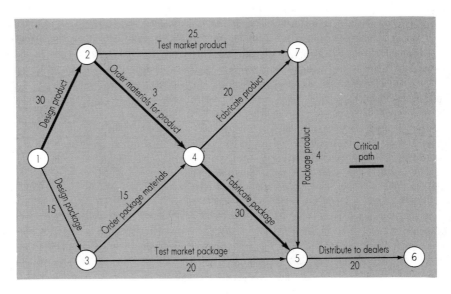

FIGURE 3-29.

c. For the hypothetical expected times in (b), the critical path is shown as a heavier line in the PERT diagram in Figure 3–29.

d. The project has several serious flaws. Materials for both the product and the package are ordered while they are still being individually test marketed. (The notion of separate test markets for the product and the package deserves to be severely criticized. Few marketing situations could justify a procedure that violates the systems concept in such an obvious way.) In addition, fabrication of the product and package is scheduled to begin before the respective test markets have been completed.

This does not permit any improvements suggested by the test market to be incorporated into the product. A further discrepancy arises from the fact that the product is to be packaged before the activity "fabricate package" is completed. This difficulty would have to be cleared up before the project schedule could be approved. It is doubtful that any amount of time pressure could secure the release of this project as it stands.

e. It should, of course, be possible to reduce the critical path time by trading resources from branches with slack to the critical path activities. For instance, the design of the package might be extended so that more effort could be devoted to product design. Other tradeoff possibilities would also be considered, but not until the network design is finalized and approved.

REFERENCES ARCHIBALD, R. D., and R. L. VILLORIA. *Network Based Management Systems (CPM/PERT)*. New York: Wiley, 1967.

BATTERSBY, A. *Network Analysis for Planning and Scheduling,* 2nd ed. New York: St. Martin's Press, 1967.

EVARTS, H. F. *Introduction to PERT*. Boston: Allyn & Bacon, 1964.

IANNONE, A. *Management Program Planning and Control*. Englewood Cliffs, N.J.: Prentice-Hall, 1967.

KELLEY, J. E., JR. "Critical Path Planning and Scheduling: Mathematical Basis," *Operations Research,* 9 (May–June 1961), pp. 296–320.

KERZNER, HAROLD. *Project Management: A Systems Approach to Planning, Scheduling and Controlling,* 2nd ed. New York: Van Nostrand Reinhold, 1984.

LEVIN, R. I., and C. A. KIRKPATRICK. *Management Planning and Control with PERT/CPM*. New York: McGraw-Hill, 1966.

MALCOLM, D. G., J. H. ROSEBOOM, C. E. CLARK, and W. FAZER. "Application of a Technique for Research and Development Program Evaluation." *Operations Research,* 7 (September–October 1959), pp. 646–669.

MILLER, R. W. *Schedule, Cost, and Profit Control with PERT*. New York: McGraw-Hill, 1963.

RADCLIFFE, B. M. et al. *Critical Path Method*. Chicago: Canners Publishing Co., 1967.

STOCKTON, R. STANSBURY. *Introduction to PERT*. Boston: Allyn and Bacon, 1964.

WIEST, J. D., and F. K. LEVY. *A Management Guide to PERT/CPM*. Englewood Cliffs, N. J.: Prentice-Hall, 1969.

PROJECT MANAGEMENT SOFTWARE

There are many PC software packages. We will describe several of them, including QSB, Pac Micro, STORM, and Erikson-Hall (E/H). All of these packages require description of activities and their precedence relations. Consult Appendix A entitled Computer Software that Complements the Text.

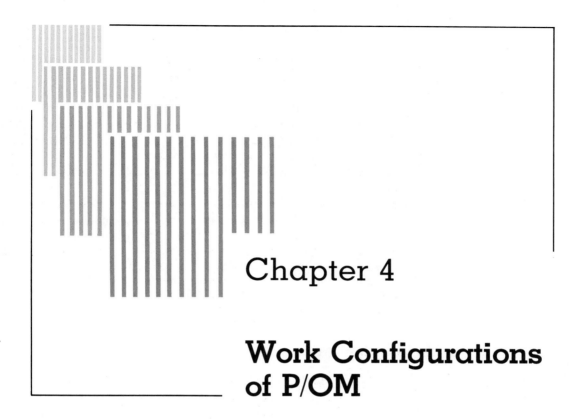

Chapter 4

Work Configurations of P/OM

CHAPTER SUMMARY   There are four basically different ways of doing work—four different kinds of **work configurations (WCs)**. Each kind of **process system** (i.e., work configuration) is best suited to a particular set of conditions. These conditions arise from the character of the product, the process, the market, and the financial situation of the firm. How complex is the product? How many are to be made or serviced? How profitable is the venture?

The four basic work configurations are these:

1. Projects, which are the focus of Chapter 3. Projects are major, one-time undertakings.
2. Flow shops, which are the focus of Chapter 10, are serialized, sequential WCs used to process high-volume outputs at low cost. Continuous production processes represent total commitment to the flow shop concept. Automobile assembly, while less continuous than the chemical industry, represents a high-level commitment to flow shop achievement. Setting up a proper flow shop requires line balancing. This is similar in concept to forcing project resource

130

Managing
Production and
Operations
Systems
Through Their
Life Cycle
Stages

leveling, with the object of converting all project paths to critical status.

3. Job shops (Section 4.2) are batch or lot-size WCs used to process a high variety of low-volume products. When the batch size is large enough, an intermittent flow shop is warranted. This WC has some of the advantages of the flow shop, and the investment in setting up is less. Setup, takedown and changeover costs have to be amortized over the batch size that is run. That is the economic rationale behind the choice of WC, but *quality* considerations play a major role which is harder to measure. Chapter 11 is dedicated to job shop systems.

4. Flexible and Programmable Systems (Section 4.3) are computer-controlled WCs used to produce a variety of low-volume outputs at a low cost. FMS is the popular term for flexible manufacturing systems, which are hybrids of flow shops and job shops. Like agricultural hybrids, the blend produces important new advantages. With flexible systems, changeover costs are composed of all fixed hardware costs and one-time software costs (plus debugging). Chapter 12 is dedicated to examining flexible and programmable systems.

Section 4.1 Flow Shops: High-Productivity WCs

Flow shop management demands carefully preplanning. All aspects of the input/transformation/output process are predesigned with engineering skills. The commitment to equipment investments is often substantial. Usually, the flexibility to change a flow shop process is designed out of the system as a result of the design steps that are taken to increase productivity.

For example, equipment is specially designed to do one particular job and to accept work automatically from a preceding machine that is also specially designed to feed its successor equipment. That is what is meant by sequentially dependent, special-purpose equipment. It is an integrated system; the parts of the process are orchestrated to work together. Specific computer control programs are designed to run such equipment, not to change it from one product to another. What is to be done (the job) can vary from processing mail orders to treating patients; from making pencils to processing film. What is to be done and the way it is to be done must be considered simultaneously.

When a flow shop configuration can be employed, many units can be processed both quickly and cheaply with built-in assurance of stable quality levels. The equipment is in place. The process is predesigned and routinized. The result is a **repetitive process environment.** Because the process is dedicated to repetition, there is ample opportunity to remove "bugs," stabilize performance, and maintain high-quality standards with consistency.

Certain jobs have few options as to how they should be done; other jobs have many. In what manner do specific product characteristics affect the potential for process design? Flow shops satisfy high-demand volume which generally is not seasonal. Most of the time, flow shop output goes into inventory, from which customer demand is satisfied. The quality of flow shop products and services should benefit from capital-intensive rather than labor-intensive process design. Where labor is used, the jobs tend to be repetitive and run contrary to oft-cited demands of labor for job enrichment and an end to boring, repetitive tasks. For flow shop outputs, process decisions have already been made. If knowledge work (decisions, creative insights, and the personal touch) must be exercised during the product or service process, then the flow shop configuration is likely to be inappropriate.

Technological Differentiation

Although no one situation is ever identical to another, P/OM can be applied to diverse sets of operations because certain principles concerning how things can be done are transferable. They are independent of the particular job.

From a technological point of view, major differences exist between the management of the production function in the chemical industry compared to the machine tool industry. The same can be said for comparisons among other industries: between hospital and library management, between different forms of transportation systems, and so on. These differences in physical systems are not trivial; they represent technological differentiation. Knowledge of technology is only partially transferable between industries. Yet from a management point of view, these differences can be subsumed under the four production system classes.

Within each of these headings, there are finer classifications that can be useful. For example, the process of transforming input materials into the output product may require manual or machine operations. Chemical reactions or materials shaping might be involved. Perhaps the process is mining, transport, communications, energy supply, raising livestock, or agriculture. More detailed breakdowns could specify press shop operations, casting, weaving, or harvesting. We can also categorize systems by their specific output: 3.5-inch floppy disks, vitamin B6, digital TVs, running shoes, microwaves, fast food, and MBAs.

Sometimes it is useful to separate technologies in terms of the input materials, such as coffee beans, crude oil, and iron ore. Adequate classification is always a problem because of the highly specialized nature of each industry, and even of companies within an industry. The appropriate body of knowledge that comprises the technology begins with the broadest physical principles, but rapidly encompasses enormous amounts of detail when engineering and production applications are included.

132

Managing
Production and
Operations
Systems
Through Their
Life Cycle
Stages

The study of P/OM must involve technology, but the utility of treating specific technological systems in detail is of dubious value for understanding the management problems. *The one most important distinction affecting the management of processes is the type of work configuration being used.*

The Flow Shop and the Job Shop

The flow shop consists of a set of facilities through which work flows in serial fashion. The operations are performed repeatedly. Flow shops are called serialized because the product flows from one work station to the next adjacent station.

The job shop is not a serially utilized facility. Jobs (in batches) follow spatially different processing patterns while moving through the facilities. Work in process (WIP) waits in line at each of the service (or machine) centers. Figure 4–1 provides a graphic illustration of the difference between flow and job shops.

Items in the flow shop enter the finished goods inventory one after another, whereas they enter in batches for the job shop. The flow shop is caricatured by Charlie Chaplin's portrayal of mass production in the film *Modern Times*. The job shop is called a custom shop when almost no processing patterns are repeated (everything is made to order).

Mostly, the flow shop makes for stock. The job shop makes to order. When high service level with replacement parts is integral to the company's mission, the job shop will make for stock. In this case, many different items will be held in inventory, although in relatively small quantities. This distinction explains why flow shop facilities use special-purpose equipment, designed to deliver the high volume of output needed. Personnel in the flow shop should be highly trained. Even with cross-training in various jobs, the flow shop workforce is composed of specialists. Job shop facilities use general-purpose equipment capable of being fitted with various tools, dies, and fixtures to do a large variety of jobs with the same general-purpose people, at the same facility. The job shop workforce has to be able to do many different kinds of work. Job shop personnel have to be trained as generalists and adapt to continually changing circumstances.

An intermittent flow shop exists when there is a call for high production volumes on a periodic or recurring basis. The concept of serial production must dominate the process. However, the system does not operate all the time. Consequently, a mixture of general- and special-purpose equipment is used. This equipment involves high setup costs. Once set up, however, it should produce high-quality output in a cost-efficient manner. Low production volumes do not justify such expensive setups. For most P/OM purposes, the intermittent flow shop can be treated as a flow shop.

Modular production increases the demand for specific parts to the point where flow shop processing is feasible. Group technology also allows

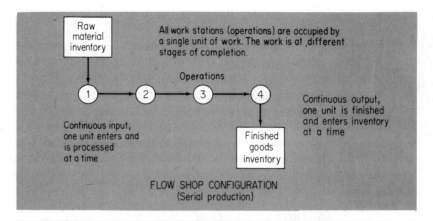

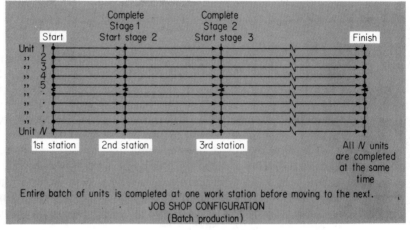

FIGURE 4-1. Serial versus batch processing.

aggregation of demand to permit planning for increased output volumes. Both involve long-term product and process design. The effort is worthwhile because flow shop systems have many benefits. For one thing, they allow for the design and use of specialized machines to relieve workers of stressful and boring tasks. These repetitive tasks used to be justified on the basis of Adam Smith's concept of the division of labor—the efficiencies gained from specialization of work. There are also scale advantages in using special-purpose equipment. Volume production permits highly coordinated promotional, advertising, and marketing activities. Flow shop WIP inventories speed through the system. In the job shop, WIP is high because unfinished batches of items must be stored. Volume purchasing usually earns discounts. Overall, there is a focus to the system that aggregates volume. The Boston Consulting Group portrays this effect by means of an ''experience curve'' (see p. 222).

134

Managing
Production and
Operations
Systems
Through Their
Life Cycle
Stages

When demand permits, the flow shop is used because it is the most efficient configuration. The job shop is less efficient, while being a greater producer of product variety. The movement of each batch of work through the various operations should be carefully planned, although it is difficult to plan well because of the complexity. Batch jobs interact with one another and compete for facilities. The mixture is never the same, and repeated planning is costly. Consequently, the scope and precision of each job shop plan will be less than those for flow shop systems or flexible (FPS) systems, where a one-time major design investment is warranted by the high level of production volume. With respect to FPS, note the difference between economies of scope and economies of scale (pp. 592–594).

What Is Line Balancing?

The main flow shop problem is to attain the required output rate (say of x parts per hour) with the greatest possible efficiency. The output rate goal is determined by anticipated demand. This is both for now (make to order) and for the future (make for stock). Although the problem is one of achieving an efficient process, the effect on costs is so great that the impact is strategic. The **line balancing** solution determines the ability of the flow shop to deliver low unit costs and high profit margin. The solution can be compared with the competitors' situation.

The total job is divided into operations which are then grouped at stations. The product as it is being worked on moves successively from one station to another. Each station is occupied with job components at different stages of completion. If all stations work an equal amount of time, then no stations are idle while others are working. This is the most efficient arrangement.

Figure 4–2 depicts a flow shop with n stations, where the product is processed by moving through work stations from the top of the diagram to the bottom. Two versions are shown. The lefthand version is labeled "Poor balance." The righthand version is labeled "Good balance." The *cycle time, C,* is the length of time the product stays at a station. What is happening at each station is depicted by the length of the bar next to the work station. The open part, to the right of the bar, is the idle time.

This graphic representation permits immediate assessment of the degree to which the line is balanced. On the left, the workload is poorly balanced; there is considerable idle time. On the right, the balance is good. There is almost no idle time in the good balance arrangement. Alternative designs can be studied having a different number of stations (n), or with different cycle times (C), or with different assignments of operations to stations. The goal is to get the right output rate with the smallest amount of idle time, and this is obtained when there is good balance.

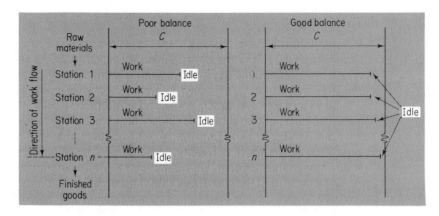

FIGURE 4-2. A flow shop with *n* stations—two versions. C (the cycle time) is the time allotted at each station before the paced-conveyor moves the work along to the next station. Different operations are being performed at each of *n* stations.

Types of Flow Shops

The kind of line balancing that is required will differ according to the type of flow shop that exists. We will examine three independent dimensions for characterizing flow shops.

How Much of a Commitment Can Be Made? Is demand large enough and stable enough over a long period of time to allow writing off the investment while still making a contribution to overhead and profit? If the answer is yes, then a total commitment might be made. (In public systems, instead of contribution to overhead and profit, we require sufficient public benefit to warrant total commitment to a highly productive flow shop hospital or Post Office, for example.) The degree of commitment can range from fully automated, paced flow systems (usually based on the mass production of items carried by a fixed-speed conveyor) to situations in which the demand for a group of similar items is relatively continuous, varying in quantity over time. By similarity of items, we mean that essentially the same production routing and flow are required for each of the items that are run through the system in successive sequences.

Line balancing is a matter of grouping facilities and workers in an efficient pattern. For high-volume production of identical items, costly mathematical studies using linear or·dynamic programming can be justified to achieve line balance. On the other hand, intermittent flow systems are often designed using heuristic procedures and techniques appropriate for partial commitment to flow shop planning.

Mathematical programming methods (such as dynamic programming) exist for examining a great number of alternatives. For example, there

136

Managing
Production and
Operations
Systems
Through Their
Life Cycle
Stages

may be too many different line-balancing arrangements to consider without methodological support. Programming rules can eliminate certain combinations by recognizing that they are dominated by others—for example, their costs can never be lower than other combinations that have already been identified. The algorithm selects the best option. (Such methods are particularly applicable for flexible manufacturing systems where inputs and outputs are constantly changing.)

How Mechanized Is the Process? If the system is labor-intensive (as in many assembly lines), then rest time must be allowed at worker-dominated stations of the conveyor-paced process. If the system is capital-equipment-intensive, then engineering design must provide perfect synchronization between successive stations of the flow shop.

How Much Random Activity Occurs? If workers are trained to do highly specialized tasks, they may work slowly at times and faster at others. Generally they can compensate for deviations so that the paced-line requirements are fully met. When this is not the case, either (1) The line must be stopped (so that all stations except the delinquent one must wait); (2) unfinished work will come off the line which must receive special treatment for completion; (3) a special emergency crew will roam from station to station to remedy problems.

Variation in the time it takes for a person to do a job can account for the need to balance **stochastic systems** (systems where random behaviors occur over time). For example, the time to complete a task may vary with the quality of input materials. Deterministic systems do not possess this random quality, and consequently all times can be specified exactly. In a deterministic system, all operations at each station are assumed to follow predetermined fixed times. Good flow shop design removes as much stochastic behavior from the system as possible.

Synthetic and Analytic Flow Shops

Progressive assembly or production line work is a **synthetic function,** as illustrated in Fig. 4–3. *Synthetic* means that many inputs combine to form a lesser number of outputs. The objective is to achieve a smooth flow. The poorly balanced operations in Fig. 4–2 have been rebalanced so that equal time is spent at each station. Consequently, a paced conveyor belt can be used.

Sometimes an **analytic production function** is the technological requirement. *Analytic* process means that few inputs are treated to produce a greater number of outputs. Analytic systems can result in several flow

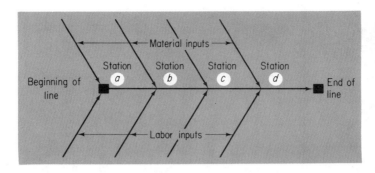

FIGURE 4-3. Synthetic production function.

systems. Usually, the processing is highly mechanized and therefore deterministic schedules prevail. For an example of an analytic production function, see Fig. 4–4, and note the chocolate-processing flow diagram in Fig. 4–5. We see that in the case of the analytic system, the basic raw material is broken down, transformed, and decomposed into various products and by-products. Figure 4–5 pictures the flow of materials as exemplified by a typical analytic industry. In this case, the raw material is the cocoa bean. From it, six different products are derived: cocoa, chocolate-flavored syrup, semi-sweet chocolate chips, semi-sweet chocolate, milk chocolate bars, and milk chocolate kisses.

Flow charts of this type can be helpful for the development of analytic processes. In synthetic operations, on the other hand, various materials and parts are fed into the main stream, where they are joined together to form a basic unit. For example, Fig. 4–6 shows an automobile assembly line. Each component is brought into the production line at the appropriate point, after which it loses its separate identity.

Synthetic processes lend themselves to flow shop assembly systems. Analytic processes usually have a few main products that are handled by continuous refining, such as gasoline and milk chocolate. In addition, there are often outputs that produce low-volume extracts and by-products.

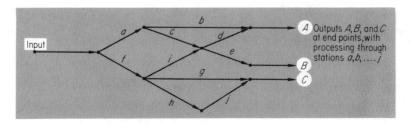

FIGURE 4-4. Analytic production function.

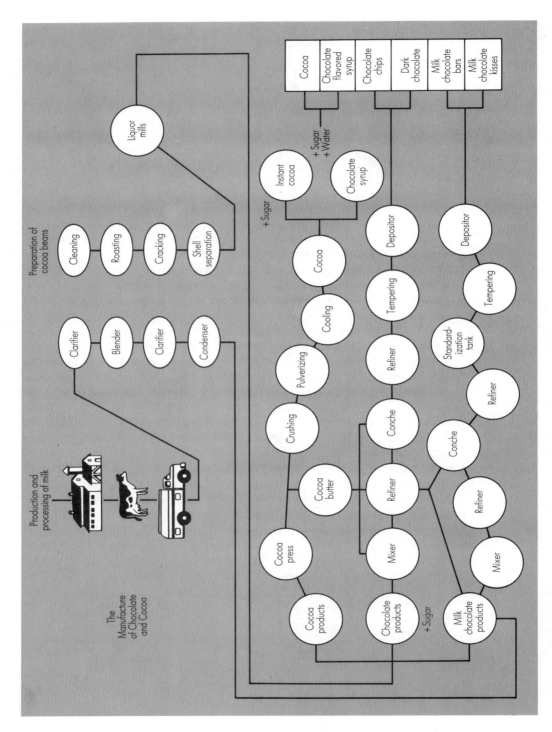

FIGURE 4-5. Chocolate processing [Copyright Hershey Foods Corporation, Hershey Chocolate & Confectionary Division, Hershey, Pa., 17033, U.S.A].

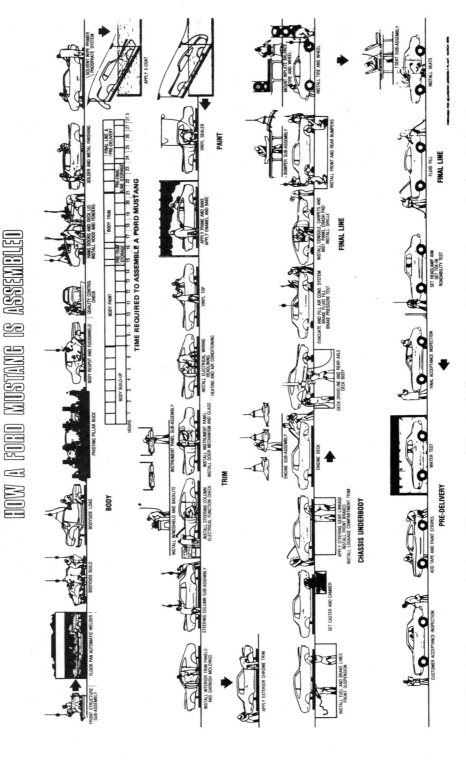

FIGURE 4-6. How an automobile is assembled [Courtesy of Educational Affairs Department, Ford Motor Company, Dearborn, Michigan].

140

Managing
Production and
Operations
Systems
Through Their
Life Cycle
Stages

The latter situations tend to require treatment by job shop or intermittent flow shop configurations.[1]

Most processes combine both analytic and synthetic operations. This would even be true for the examples we have used. However, it is convenient to note the processing differences between what is essentially analytic or synthetic.

The stations through which materials flow have special-purpose facilities designed strictly for the limited product line under continuous flow. (Such configurations present different problems to the planner than those comprised of general-purpose equipment that can accommodate the many different operations of the job shop.) Serial production configurations involve successively differentiated stages (such as a, b, c, and d in Fig. 4–3) based on the division of labor. This arrangement offers at least two advantages:

1. Items produced serially can be shipped continually, thereby reducing inventories.
2. Specialization usually increases efficiency and productivity. There is the economic principle that specialization creates the conditions for trade. According to Kenneth Boulding, if there was specialization without trade, the tailor would starve and the farmer would go naked. Without specialization, trade cannot take place, for there would be nothing to trade. (Kenneth F. Boulding, "The Specialist with a Universal Mind," *Management Science,* 14, 12 [August 1968], B647–B653).

Modular Production (MP) and Group Technology (GT)

Some goods and services lend themselves naturally to flow shop production; others could not be pressed into the flow shop system even if all competitors withdrew from the market, because the life cycle is too short and demand is limited to small runs. Yet there are times when a conversion can be made from job shop operations to intermittent and even permanent flow shop status. The change can take place gradually and partially.

---

[1]The OPT system which was developed about 1980 by Creative Output, Inc., and which stands for optimizing production technique, is a system for removing bottlenecks on the shop floor. This system classifies processes by VAT. A V-process is analytic, starting with a single commodity at the bottom and branching out into refined products at the top. An A-process is synthetic, starting at the bottom with several inputs which are combined to yield a single marketable product. The combination OPT calls a T-process. OPT has focused attention on the fact that each type of process has unique production scheduling characteristics; the A-type process, for example, lends itself most readily to bottleneck scheduling, on which OPT has concentrated.

It is always easier to design toward an ideal when starting from scratch than when attempting to bring about change. On the other hand, when starting up a new system, without the goal of achieving a flow shop, it is more likely that a job shop will result, for at least two reasons: (1) There is a job shop tradition in the United States and Europe. It is based upon pre-1950 technology (which preceded computer-controlled equipment). It is also based upon pre-1960 markets, which were smaller and did not support high-volume production processes. (2) It is easier to settle for a job shop that promises enough profits than to persevere for a flow shop that has potential for even more profits, but with much more risk. Also, not every good and service can be produced by a flow shop, for both economic and technological reasons. We intend to show, however, that opportunities often do exist, but are overlooked.

One approach to achieving flow shop operations is the use of the **modular production** concept. This means specialization in the production of particular parts or activities which can then be included as components of more than one product or service. The roots of such efforts exist in the well-developed concept of standard parts, such as screw threads and lightbulbs. The reason for wanting to achieve such commonality is that one part or operation, if used in several products or services, can accumulate sufficient demand volume to warrant investment in a flow shop. The principle of modularity is to design, develop, and produce the minimum number of parts (or operations) that can be combined in the maximum number of ways to offer the greatest number of products (or services).

The matrix in Table 4–1 illustrates this principle, using products and parts. With N different kinds of parts, a total of M different product configurations is derived. Some of these products require several units of a single part. For instance, PR_4 requires two of PA_2, and PR_j requires two of PA_i. The maximum possible variety, maximum M, that can be obtained with N different parts may be very large. This is especially so when we include both the different possible combinations of the parts and varying numbers of them in combination. Our objective is to have M as large as possible and N as small as possible.

Of course, many of the theoretical possibilities cannot exist and would have no appeal as a product choice for any consumer. But the basic idea of modular design is to have an inventory of parts that can partake in many appealing product configurations. (The same sort of matrix as shown in Table 4–1 must have been designed long ago for the first Erector set. Industry is now taking seriously a fundamental principle long embodied in many children's toys.) A useful measure of the effective degree of modular design might be, therefore, the ratio of the number of products (columns) that can be generated from a given number of parts (rows); that is, objective: MAX M/N.

Group technology is another result of the same concepts; it refers to specialization in families of similar parts. For example, we can develop

142

Managing
Production and
Operations
Systems
Through Their
Life Cycle
Stages

TABLE 4-1 MATRIX OF SPECIFICATIONS FOR THE KIND AND NUMBER OF PARTS TO BE COMBINED FOR EACH OF A GIVEN NUMBER OF DIFFERENT END PRODUCTS

Variety of Parts	Variety of Products							
	PR_1	PR_2	PR_3	PR_4	...	PR_j	...	PR_M
PA_1	1	0	1	1	...	0	...	0
PA_2	0	1	1	2	...	0	...	0
PA_3	0	0	0	0	...	1	...	0
PA_4	0	1	1	0		0		0
.	.	.	.	.		.		.
.	.	.	.	.		.		.
.	.	.	.	.		.		.
PA_i	0	0	1	0	...	2	...	0
.	.	.	.	.		.		.
.	.	.	.	.		.		.
.	.	.	.	.		.		.
PA_N	0	0	0	1	...	1	...	1

PA_i denotes the part identified by the stock number i.
PR_j denotes the product variation listed in the finished goods catalog as j. (As shown above, the product j assembly requires one unit of part 3, two units of part i, and one unit of part N. The sequence of assembly is not indicated.)
PA_N denotes the last part listed in our table.
PR_M denotes the last product variation listed in our table; in this case, it is the product using only one unit of part N.

efficient flow shops for gears, cams, springs, and so on, all of different sizes but of similar design, and having essentially the same production operations. The technology required assures minimum transition costs as the production line shifts from one variant to another.

A company using group technology to improve the profit margin of its line of products or services might become so efficient in this specialized family of operations that it would gradually shift its emphasis from products to parts. Eventually, it would become a parts subcontractor to industry and supply institutions with the output of its most efficient operations.

MP, GT, and the Concept of Interchangeable Parts

Interchangeable parts exist when outputs from a production system can be mixed together in a bin and withdrawn in any order for assembly with other parts that have been similarly produced. This gigantic step (in 1798), which revolutionized the production process, seems to have been inevitable. While Eli Whitney was developing the notion of interchangeable parts in the United States, Leblanc was making the concept operational in France, but neither was aware of the other's work. The growth in use of modular production and group technology partakes of the same sense of inevitability. They are important design concepts.

The traditional idea of interchangeable parts can be interpreted as follows: All units made to the specifications of a particular parts classification can be treated as identical. It does not matter whether a given unit was made at the beginning or end of a production run. Any part can substitute for any other part in its row. Note that this interchangeability exists within each row of the matrix and not between the rows of the table. Interchangeable part modules, on the other hand, are designed to be highly transferable between columns; that is, an interchangeable module enters into many different product configurations. In contrast, production often tends to isolate the columns. Group technology clusters rows together as families. Thus, because of common equipment, materials, and techniques, it becomes feasible to develop flow shop productivity for the family of parts.

It is not enough to plan for and start up a modular production system; it is necessary to preserve it in a changing economic and competitive environment. This can be done only by forecasting possible futures and planning to have sufficient flexibility to bring about necessary changes in product or service design that can sustain the product or service in the mature stage of its life cycle. We will deal with forecasting later in this chapter. Forecasting is essential to the job shop, but it applies here as well, since we have linked the evolutionary changes that affect the flow shop to the consistent changes that characterize the job shop.

PROBLEM
SET

1. It has been said that organizational bureaucracy operates like a badly designed flow shop. Comment on this thought, reflecting on the extent to which it might be true, as well as on those aspects that might be false.

2. How does forecasting apply to the flow shop?

3. Contrast an intermittent flow shop with a regular flow shop. How does it compare with a project?

4. Explain the distinction between analytic and synthetic production processes.

5. Numerically controlled machines (NCMs) can be computer-programmed to do many different jobs. In effect, general-purpose equipment is thus transformed into special-purpose equipment. By relating the programming of adjacent facilities, coordination between stations is achieved. Different items can be turned out from a serialized production process. Explain the relationship of modular production and group technology to NCMs.

6. For what type of products and services does the flow shop appear suited? Answer the same question for flexible process systems. Then

144

Managing
Production and
Operations
Systems
Through Their
Life Cycle
Stages

explain the similarities and differences between the flow shop and the FPS.

7. For what type of products and services does modular design make the most sense? How about group technology?

8. Why does the flow shop provide built-in assurance of stable quality levels? Does the same apply to flexible and programmable systems?

9. The explosion chart shown below is widely used by industry to identify the aggregation of part requirements. How does it relate to modular production and group technology?

Parts	Jobs					Monthly Requirement
	X112	PR5	987	989	TF5	
C32	2	—	—	—	—	120
C325	1	1	1	—	—	180
C45	—	—	4	—	—	320
C47	—	—	1	—	1	100
C549	—	—	1	1	1	130
Monthly Demand	60	40	80	30	20	

10. How does FPS relate to MP and GT?

Section 4.2 Job Shops: Output Variety in Relatively Low Volumes

Job shops are used to produce in batches. The output volume is not large enough to allow a serial line of specialized work to be set up. Using general-purpose equipment, which can do many different things, a substantial variety of output designs can be achieved. The relatively high operating costs are offset by the low initial investment in equipment that can be used for many jobs.

We are surrounded by job shops in everyday life. The kitchen is typical and probably better run than the schoolroom, which is also a job shop. The offices of corporate America are job shops. Most offices are badly managed. Assuming that you have to produce in batches, it is still possible (and increasingly necessary because of competition) to run a good job shop. To get started, you have to be able to obtain a good forecast.

Job shop management is dependent on good forecasting, which in turn is dependent on the backup of an adequate information system. This is not true of the flow shop, where information systems have been predesigned, where demand predictions have been made, and where output volume is fixed. (Chapter 11 treats the job shop in depth and offers basic facts about how to forecast, as well as coverage of the aggregate scheduling model.

Job shop planning starts at the aggregate level. That is, all the different kinds of jobs that might be done in some period of time (forecast needed) are lumped together to determine workforce and equipment requirements. **Shoploading** is the assignment of different kinds of work to various departments or machine centers. This scheduling activity is unique to the job shop. (Many service activities done by job shop process configurations would be difficult to put into flow shop configurations.) Tasks are ultimately assigned in specific order to individuals and machines (this is called **sequencing**).

Throughout this text, the flow shop is advocated for its high productivity. At the same time, we recognize that under many circumstances, especially service situations, the flow shop is not feasible. Accordingly, we stress the powerful techniques that are available for making the job shop as efficient and productive as possible. Aggregate scheduling and the needed forecasting capabilities, as well as shop loading and sequencing, are not applicable to the flow shop. However, in some cases, especially where high volume is required to generate inventory, the use of aggregate scheduling for intermittent flow shop configurations may be justified. For the purposes of aggregate scheduling, the intermittent flow shop can be treated as a job shop when it shares resources with many other kinds of work. However, remember that intermittent flow shops have higher productivity than job shops because their work routines have been serialized; see Fig. 4–1.

Complexity of the Job Shop

The job shop requires managers who know how to juggle production schedules. Often many pressing problems arise, and all must be solved within minutes of one another. As a rule, the job shop manager has direct and immediate contact with customers. This is because the job shop regularly produces to fill specific orders. Some job shops also produce for finished goods inventory where stable and sufficient demand exists, but this must still be fitted into the schedule just as if it were an order from a customer.

A significant difference between goods and services is the inability to build an inventory of "finished" services. Yet even this distinction can lead to innovations. For example, user-friendly programs have an inventory of help menus, and part-time help might be put on call and activated as needed. Contrast these conditions with those of the flow shop, where the process has been predesigned and debugged, where production materials are ordered long in advance in substantial quantities, where requisite skills are fully catalogued and practiced. Although problems can and do arise in the flow shop, they are more orderly, often mechanical, and far better anticipated than those of the job shop.

The flow shop produces inventory that is usually distributed to warehouses first, then to retailers, and finally to the ultimate consumers. Flow

146

Managing
Production and
Operations
Systems
Through Their
Life Cycle
Stages

shop volume often is so large that an organization for distribution of the output is an inherent requirement. If an organization is needed for distribution of the job shop output, it will usually have quite a different form. It will be designed for the distribution of smaller quantities than would apply to flow shop distribution. The job shop produces relatively small amounts of diverse outputs requiring many different materials, skills, setups and takedowns, jigs, fixtures, repair routines, and so forth. In a job shop of any size, hundreds and even thousands of jobs can be going on at the same time. (In some job shops, there are large order sizes and longer production runs. Such shops straddle the flow and job shop, using intermittent flow shop practices in conjunction with job shop techniques.) Products are at different stages and are produced in varying quantities, which means that there is no fixed schedule of equipment utilization, so scheduling work becomes of the greatest importance.

Information management is essential. Bottlenecks removed from the flow shop by design must be kept to a minimum in the job shop by schedule control. The OPT system of managing production uses scheduling rules based on a philosophy of maximizing the throughput at any bottleneck facility. OPT calls these capacity-constrained resources. OPT will be the subject of further discussion in Chapters 5 and 11. Material requirements planning (MRP) is an information system for managing inventories and production scheduling. Material resources planning (MRP II) expanded on the MRP mission by including the capacity-planning problem that precedes inventory planning. The relations among MRP, OPT, and MRP II will be examined in Chapter 7.

In a job shop, each order carries its own delivery date. The salesperson's promised delivery date should not be given without confirmation from the production schedulers. Yet it is not unusual for this to occur, causing conflicts to arise between sales and the production and operations departments. For example, an important customer calls in a rush order, and the general manager gives it the highest priority: "Do it now." What job (or jobs) should be stopped? Decision problems like this occur regularly, yet they are each special and unique with respect to the conflicts that must be resolved. A sudden surge of orders occurs for various products or services. If the workforce is not sufficient, or raw materials are in short supply, or facilities are inadequate, a waiting line develops.

Sales management has good marketing reasons for preferring that certain jobs get done. Operations management has good scheduling reasons for its own recommendations, which may not coincide at all with those of sales. What is to be done? Who is to make the decision? A number of methods allow several parties (such as sales and operations) to represent their concerns in reaching a decision.

Information Management Requirements

With all the different jobs to schedule, materials to stock and dispatch, and so on, the management of information is a necessity for the job shop.

For each job, dozens of kinds of data must be stored, used, checked against, and so forth. Figures 4–7 through 4–10 illustrate the diversity of documents that maintain critical information for the organization. We will consider each of these in turn. Note that Fig. 4–8 applies to a service industry (airlines), whereas Figs. 4–7, 4–9, and 4–10 are relevant to manufacture and assembly.

First, consider the information content of one kind of data required by the job shop—namely, the **blueprint.** There are usually a number of parts that cannot be made without blueprints. Figure 4–7 illustrates the kind and amount of information blueprints contain. While this is not scheduling information, it is related. Only certain machines can be used to make this conveyor takeup unit. Equipment requirements and the quantity to be produced interact with other job requirements in the shop. So blueprint data are essential inputs to the work scheduling decision.

Blueprints are unambiguously detailed descriptions of product output and of special equipment and service facilities required for the process. Note that for the job shop, because there are many different outputs, blueprints of part dimensions and details of tools, dies, fixtures, casting molds, and so on are critically important and continually referenced.

In the flow shop, blueprints are important during the project management phase of bringing the flow shop into being. At that time, they are

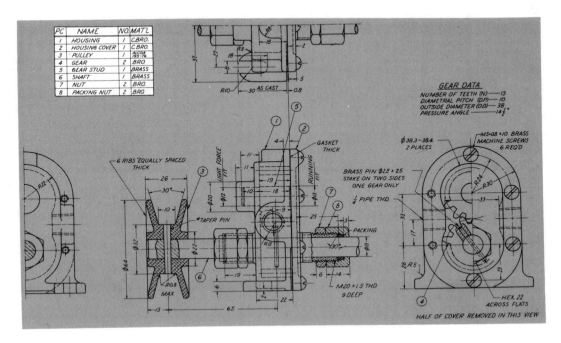

FIGURE 4-7. Blueprint of a gear pump [From Warren J. Luzadder, *Fundamentals of Engineering Drawing,* 9th ed. (Englewood Cliffs, N. J.: Prentice-Hall, Inc., 1986), p. 386.].

148

Managing
Production and
Operations
Systems
Through Their
Life Cycle
Stages

used to coordinate the design of facilities and process specifications with output objectives. For the flow shop, blueprints are referenced and altered with each design engineering change and equipment failure. It is economically feasible to employ highly skilled engineering assistance to obtain the most efficient configurations. Thereafter, use is made of the blueprints only when there is a breakdown. Thus, the project is more like the job shop, requiring frequent reference by technicians to blueprints.

The equivalent of the blueprint in service systems is a carefully detailed statement of methods and procedures—the service to be provided under all conditions that are likely to be experienced. Specific documents and forms that communicate what the job is characterize the information managed by many nonfabricating service systems. Consider, for example,

REPORT NO: SD068   STATION ACTIVITY LIST   RUN DATE 05/21/87
SCHEDULE NBR 7178   PAGE 11
EFFV DATE 06/01/87
                       EQP GROUP EG002 BY EQUIPMENT
                       EQP CATG   EC005

	ARRIVALS							DEPARTURES			
FLT ORG TO	FROM STA	FLT NBR	WKLY FRQY	ARVL TIME	EQUIP TYPE	DPTR TIME	WKLY FRQY	FLT NBR	NEXT STA	TO	FLT TRM
				STATION LAS							
ISP IAD	DFW	567		1928	T S80	*					
CMH CMH	ORD	637		2029	T S80						
PIT PIT	ORD	589		2328	* S80	* 0025		870	ORD		ORD
				STATION LAX							
					S80	0 0700		980	BNA	PHL	PHL
LAS	LAS	31		0711	* S80	* 0756		838	LAD	DFW	BDL
BNA	BNA	961		2037	T S80						
				STATION LGB							
					S80	0 0656		630	ORD	BDL	BDL
					S80	0 0724		504	DFW	ATL	ATL
ATL ATL	DFW	461		1101	* S80	* 1146		284	DFW	LIT	LIT
LIT LIT	DFW	247		1956	T S80						
SYR SYR	ORD	599		2109	T S80						
				STATION LIT							
					S80	0 0700		638	BNA	DCA	DCA
					S80	0 0748		134	DFW	OKC	CMH
PHX PHX	DFW	516		0809	* S80	* 0918		803	DFW	PSP	PSP
DCA DCA	BNA	413		1051	* S80	* 1136		329	BNA	CLE	AUS
BUF CLE	BNA	945		1526	* S80	* 1633		247	DFW	LGB	LGB
SMF SNA	DFW	506		1553	* S80	* 1641		156	BNA	DCA	DCA
LGB LGB	DFW	284		1829	* S80	* 1916		145	DFW		DFW
MSP MSP	BNA	485		2033	T S80						
BFL SBA	DFW	512		2108	T S80						

FIGURE 4-8. American Airlines aircraft routing chart. Courtesy American Airlines.

Post Office procedures, hospital care routines, and airline routing systems (see Fig. 4–8).

A second relevant form of information for the job shop is the bill of materials. This is illustrated for switch Z33 by Fig. 4–9. The **bill of materials** lists all parts required to make the item. It details some important characteristics of each part (materials, costs, and operations). Further, note that switch Z33 is used in only one final assembly of a finished product, the 5-horsepower motor, designated J. With modular production goals, perhaps switch Z33 could be redesigned and used in other assemblies as well as J.

Third, each part listed in the bill of materials has an **operations sheet.** In Fig. 4–10 we show an operations sheet for part no. CH20. It is a fully detailed description of what must be done to make the casing. Let us examine the modular potential of casing CH20. Note how CH20 is used for three different items: switches Z33 and Z34, and an order from an outside organization (T102). This typifies modularity, but can it be further extended? Assume that a new switch Z35 is being designed. Check to see if casing CH20 can do the job. If not, see if a new casing can be designed for the Z35 that also could be substituted for all present applications of CH20. Can the new casing be better, less costly, and so on because of the combined volume? (The same kind of reasoning can be applied to switch Z33.)

In general, operations sheets show:

All departments needed to make the part

All operations and machines (including alternatives when they exist)

All materials, tools, and fixtures required

Part No.	Part name	No./item	Material	Quantity/item	Cost/item	Operations
CH 20	Casing	1	SF 60	0.25 lbs	$0.15	Cast, trim
SJ 64	Drive Sprg.	2	Sprg. St.	....	$0.08	Purchase
RH 82	1" Rod	3	1045 St.	4 in	$0.05	Make
TJ 32	Fitting	1	Ti-6A1-4V	0.10 lbs	$0.85	Forge, anneal

Item Switch Z 33   Sheet No. 1 of 2
Drawings Z 1-Z 6   Assembly 5 hp motor J

FIGURE 4-9. Bill of materials. The item, switch Z33, is used in the assembly of the 5 HP Motor J.

150

Managing
Production and
Operations
Systems
Through Their
Life Cycle
Stages

Part No. CH 20		Economic lot size 500	
Part name Casing		Process time/pce 3.5 h	
Blueprint No.		Set up time 2 h	

Use for   Switch Z 33   Quantity per   1
          Switch Z 34   1
          Sub-contract T 102   50/mo

Material SF 60   Vendor BQV
% Scrap 10   Weight 1/4 lb. per   Cost $0.15 per

Operation No.	Operation	Operation* time	Set up* time	Machine No.	Tool No.	Department
1	Cast			M235 (or M237)	DX103	D6
2	Trim			M81	DX104	D8
3	Drill (2) holes			M631 (or M635)	jig X103	D2
4	Broach			M631 (or M635)	jig X1035	D2
5	Tumble			DR3 24	——————✓	DR3

*Look up on Machine card

Inspection _____✓_____
Authorization _____✓_____

FIGURE 4-10. Operations sheet.

    Operation times and setup times for each operation
    Economic order quantity or economic lot size

The information essential for scheduling is now in our hands. We know what orders are in the shop (item name and quantity). Therefore, we can calculate the total workloads on machines and departments. The loads that result may be unbalanced; then alternative assignments would be tried. Ultimately, some jobs must wait and some facilities must be idle. Schedule decisions will determine which jobs are done first and which facilities work under or overtime.

Contrast the well-balanced, smooth-running line of the flow shop with the multiplicity of decisions that must be made in the job shop and the information that must be kept track of to support these decisions. You begin to perceive why a job shop manager may have to be a very different kind of person (in style and temperament) from the manager of a flow shop. For career planning, students should note that the choice between flow shop, job shop, FPS, and project is likely to have a far more profound influence on success or failure than the choice of company A or company B in the same industry. That is because the character of work in each type of shop is profoundly different, calling for different skills and attitudes, whereas companies in the same industry generally share similar environments.

Managing the Job Shop: A Three-Step Problem

We have stressed the role of information management in running the job shop, because at the heart of the problem is the number of combinations of work/facility assignments that can be made. Some of these combinations are good. Some are terrible; and one or more are best. The computer has altered the organization's capacity to deal with all the data and their combinations, but not enough to allow the entire job shop scheduling problem to be solved in one step.

There are three distinct problem stages that can be managed. They should be solved together as one overall problem, but that cannot be done, because actions that require lead time must be taken before actual orders are in hand. Figure 4–11 shows the three problem stages that comprise the overall problem. (1) We must determine what labor force, raw materials, supplies, and facilities to have on hand for a chosen planning period (say 3 months). This decision, which is based on forecasted demand, is called **aggregate scheduling.** (2) We must assign actual work on hand to facilities (called **shoploading**). This is done for an actionable planning period (say weekly or even daily). If many changes arise regularly, then daily shoploading is probably preferable. Note that work has been assigned to facilities but has not been sequenced. (3) We must sequence the order of work to be done at each facility. (Sequencing might always follow shoploading or be done even more frequently.)

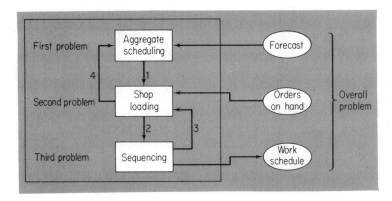

FIGURE 4-11. Three problem stages of the job shop.

152

Managing
Production and
Operations
Systems
Through Their
Life Cycle
Stages

The work schedule is derived in this way: shoploading followed by sequencing. This is not an optimal solution, since interactions abound. To begin with, work can be sequenced at each specific facility efficiently or inefficiently. If the work already assigned could be shifted between the existing facilities, perhaps even better sequences could be arranged. Usually this will not happen because the shop has already been loaded on the basis of criteria other than sequencing efficiency. It is too much work to go back and forth between criteria, so the path marked 3 in Fig. 4–11 will not be followed.

Further, an even better sequence might be found if shoploading and sequencing were treated together (paths 2 and 3 in Fig. 4–11). This could be done by changing the kind and number of facilities used to reach the shoploading solution to get a better sequencing solution. But the decision about facilities was previously made during aggregate scheduling and with enough lead time to bring plans to fruition. Even if the required lead time is short, there are too many computations to permit following an iterative chain of reasoning. Following paths 3 and 4 in Fig. 4–11 would allow aggregate scheduling to be influenced by shoploading, which in turn would be influenced by sequencing. This assumes perfect forecasting ability, since aggregate scheduling is based on forecasting demand and shoploading is based on actual workload.

To explain iterative reasoning, a series of decisions is taken, and then the performance of the system under the new conditions is evaluated. Corrections in the decisions are made to adjust the system so that actual performance comes closer to expectation. The cycle is repeated as many times as necessary. Linear programming (discussed in Chapter 12) exemplifies such iterative procedures.)

Instead of trying to resolve the overall problem, we solve the three problem stages in order. Experience indicates that we get a good enough solution. The difficulty of trying to solve the overall problem is compounded by the interaction between the lead time to alter resources and the degree of uncertainty of demand. When the demand forecast has a high variance and the resource planning lead time is long, aggregate scheduling must be based on risky, long-term forecasts. These can have a very long planning period to allow facilities and workforce plans to be converted to action.

Forecasting on a regular and continuous basis is a particular requirement of the job shop. It is a distinguishing feature not shared by the flow shop or the project.

Forecasts, Predictions, and Estimates

To be unable to foretell anything about the future is a far more mysterious thought than to propose that forecasting can be done to some degree. We know bits and pieces about the nature of matter and the character of time. We gain experience with people's habits, and with the circumstances under which one tends to win or lose a competition. Above all, we know a lot about ourselves, and can generalize this knowledge to predict the behavior of others. Inventory planning and aggregate scheduling are two P/OM areas that are highly dependent upon being able to forecast, predict, and estimate future events.

A series of events that occur over time is called a **time series.** An example of a time series would be: sales demand in three successive months which can be written S_1, S_2, S_3. If the three months are yet to come, we must predict values for the time series $\{S_t\}$. If a believable time series $\{S_t\}$ cannot be derived (so that the predicted time series would have little error when compared to actuality), then no method for aggregate scheduling has any merit.

First, let us distinguish between forecasting, predicting, and estimating. According to the dictionary, **prediction** is associated with prophecy. The definition even suggests augury and divination. **Estimation** is associated with rough or approximate calculations. **Forecasting** assumes that calculations are done beforehand.

In our usage here, analysis done to guess intelligently about future events is called forecasting. If "gut feeling" is used, we call it prediction. While this is not a universal distinction, R. G. Brown states: "I use predict to refer to . . . subjective estimates, and forecast to denote an objective computation." Brown's explanation is reasonably compatible with the use of these terms in this text (see R. G. Brown, *Smoothing, Forecasting and Prediction,* Englewood Cliffs, N.J.: Prentice-Hall, 1962, pp. 2–3). Forecasting and predicting are words we constantly bandy around, so it seemed useful to clarify what distinctions between them we could draw. We still expect that there will be many crossovers in usage.

In decision theory terms, the forecast is chosen as the state that is most likely to happen from among a number of different states that appear to have some likelihood of occurring. For example, we bet on one particular horse in a race. The odds on the board reflect the bets being made for the likelihood of each horse winning. Most individuals bet on the basis of subjective analysis, and thereby make a prediction about which horse will win. In a meteorological example, a forecast is made for tomorrow's weather. At least we hope that the weather report will result from the objective analysis of a probability distribution—that there is a 70 percent probability it will be fair and a 30 percent probability of precipitation.

Aggregate Scheduling

Forecasts of the behavior of aggregations tend to be more accurate than forecasts of the behaviors of the individual components that make up the aggregate. For example, it is easier to forecast next year's (total) aggregate sales level for a department store than next month's aggregate sales level, because the longer period shows less erratic behavior than the short interval. It is easier to forecast aggregate sales for all floors of

154
Managing
Production and
Operations
Systems
Through Their
Life Cycle
Stages

the department store than for any one floor, because fluctuations in individual departments tend to cancel each other out. As shown in Fig. 4–12, trajectories of time series over long intervals tend to be smooth; over short intervals, they are unpredictable. As a result, it is not unusual to study the aggregate system to explain the component systems' behaviors. Thus, the trend from a to b is quite clear in the aggregate system and not as readily apparent from detailed information collected during the short interval t_1 to t_2. Similarly, the department store manager may forecast quarterly sales in aggregate terms and later proportionately divide this gross forecast into estimates of productline sales.

It is usually easier to interpolate or extrapolate on aggregates and later convert to component forecasts through proportioning. **Interpolation** is the process of trying to reconstruct an unknown history between two known points. For example, we know that at t_1 the system was at a and at t_2 it was at b (Fig. 4–13a).

Question: What is likely to have happened at time $t_{1.5}$, which lies between points a and b?

Answer: We cannot say exactly. A likely guess is point c on the straight line. Also, anything greater than point d or less than point e is unlikely. For example, the upper bounds, *pq,* and the lower bounds, *rs,* might express the statistical variation that is believed to apply to 95 percent of all events occurring during the interval of time $t_2 - t_1$.

In short, everything that has been observed, or that can be logically postulated, can be used to estimate the value that might have held at $t_{1.5}$. It might be reasonable, for example, to suggest that adjacent points will be like each other for inertial reasons; that is, the system has a tendency to keep performing in the same way that it has been in the past.

The size of the interval $(t_{1.5} - t_1)$ will restrict how much change could

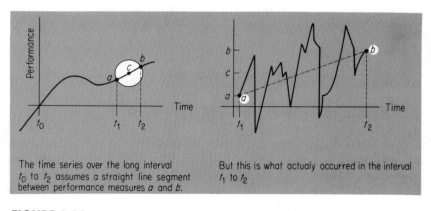

The time series over the long interval t_0 to t_2 assumes a straight line segment between performance measures a and b.

But this is what actually occurred in the interval t_1 to t_2

FIGURE 4-12.

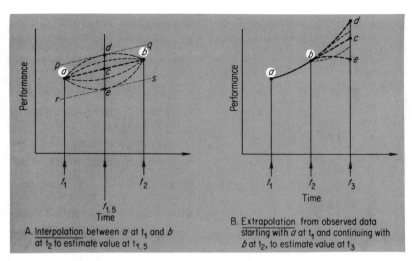

A. Interpolation between a at t_1 and b at t_2 to estimate value at $t_{1.5}$

B. Extrapolation from observed data starting with a at t_1 and continuing with b at t_2, to estimate value at t_3

FIGURE 4–13.

have occurred, given that the system went from a to b during the interval $(t_2 - t_1)$. Proceeding in this fashion, we try to find some reasonable rules for interpolating between a and b.

Extrapolation is the process of moving from observed data (past and present) to the unknown values of future points; see Fig. 4–13b. Extrapolation is typical of many forecasting activities. The same kind of reasoning concerning interval sizes, statistical variation, dynamics of the system, and inertial effect applies as was the case with interpolation.

Given a probability distribution, the mean or mode of that distribution might be the basis for a forecast of a particular event. Fig. 4–14 illustrates a probability distribution and shows how the mean and mode forecasts might differ. The boundary between forecasts and predictions begins to be lost as the use of various techniques requires subjective considerations. The use of expert opinion in place of rigorously derived numbers is not to be outlawed, since there are times when the less rigorous is the more appropriate.

Some forecasts (known as **Bayesian forecasts**) are based on the analytic use of subjective judgments, whereas objective forecasts are derived by counting the number of special events and dividing that number by the total number of all events. For example, if out of 10 letters drawn at random 3 are As, then $p[A] = \frac{3}{10}$. By retaining knowledge of the past, we obtain the historical stream of data known as a **time series.** Contrast this with information that has lost its **time tag.** Information that is bereft of specific time or even time sequence but is known to belong to a given interval of time is called **cross-sectional data.**

The analysis of time series separates out any basic trends in the data that might exist; the analysis also isolates any cyclical variation (perhaps

156

Managing
Production and
Operations
Systems
Through Their
Life Cycle
Stages

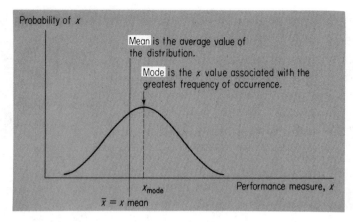

FIGURE 4-14. In the interval $t_3 - t_2$, the performance measure x is believed to be distributed as shown. From this forecast, a prediction for x must be given. Two different rules for prediction that are often used are (1) choose the mean value $\bar{x}$, and (2) choose the mode value x_{mode}.

seasonal). It also identifies and removes a class of information associated with **random variation,** often called **noise.** Many methods exist for filtering out noninforming noise so that ''pure'' trends and ''real'' cycles can be spotted. Difficulty arises because noise often hides fundamental patterns.

Estimation Errors

The history of any system of forecasting can be recorded as a difference between what was expected to happen and what actually happened:

$$\text{Forecast} - \text{actual} = \text{error}$$

For systems of **attributes,** where forecasts take the form of ''yes'' or ''no'' (such as *it is,* or *it is not,* oil-bearing land), we can tally each individual's record to observe who was right most of the time. When forecasters are chosen, preference is given to good forecasters, if you know who they are.

For systems of **variables** (such as estimating next month's sales demand), distributions of forecast error, such as that shown in Fig. 4–15, could be obtained for each individual.

Although B's forecasting errors average out to 0 (because B both over and underestimates equally), A is a better predictor. This is true since we can correct A's bias by adding ϵ to every prediction made by A. Then the A and B distributions are both centered over 0, and A's **variance** is less than B's.

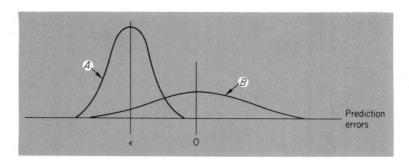

FIGURE 4-15.

Data-based Forecasts

A variety of methods exist for making predictions by extrapolation. We shall discuss a number of these.

Historical and Seasonal Forecasts. When historical information is available, a simple historical forecast can be made based on the assumption that what happened last year will happen again. Thus, for example, if the demand in the previous January was x, then in the coming January it will also be x. This method is effective only if a stable seasonal pattern exists.

If the aggregate level appears to be changing over a period of time but the seasonal pattern remains fixed, then a **base series modification** can be used. For example, assume that in the preceding year the quarterly demands were 40, 20, 30, 10. This gives a yearly demand of 100 units. Now, let us assume that in the current year the yearly demand is expected to increase to 120 units. Then the quarterly forecasts would be $(40/100)120 = 48$; $(20/100) 120 = 24$; $(30/100)120 = 36$; $(10/100)120 = 12$. These quarterly demands total 120 units.

When there is no seasonal pattern and the system is thought to follow a gradual trend, then a **moving average** can be used to advantage.

Moving Averages. This method provides a simple means of obtaining a forecast of future values based on past history. The most recent N successive observations of actual events, such as monthly demand, are recorded. The data are regularly updated to maintain recent information. We shall use $\hat{x}_t$ to represent the forecast value of x in period t, and x_t to represent the actual value that occurred. Then:

$$\hat{x}_{t+1} = (x_t + x_{t-1} + \ldots + x_{t-N+1})/N$$

$$\hat{x}_{t+2} = \hat{x}_{t+1} + (x_{t+1} - x_{t-N+1})/N$$

It will be noted that each next month's forecast is updated by dropping the oldest month of the series x_{t-N+1} and adding the latest observation

158

Managing
Production and
Operations
Systems
Through Their
Life Cycle
Stages

x_{t+1}. This yields the equation for $\hat{x}_{t+2}$, above. In this way, new trends are taken into account, and old information is removed from the system. The moving average method applies to any time period—hours, days, weeks. Here is an example in which a four-period moving average is assumed. We need four values of x_t before we can make a forecast $\hat{x}_t$ and calculate the error.

Month	Actual x_t	Forecast, $\hat{x}_t$	Error
1	1		
2	3		
3	4		
4	4		
5	5	3	−2
6	6	4	−2

The first forecast is 3 ($\hat{x}_5 = (4 + 4 + 3 + 1)/4 = 3$). When the actual demand occurs, it turns out to be 5. The forecast has fallen short by 2. Now a second forecast can be made. We add 5 to the moving average series and drop 1 from the first month. The forecast for the sixth month is 4 [$\hat{x}_6 = (5 + 4 + 4 + 3)/4 = 4$]. Let us say that instead of the forecast of 4 being correct, the actual result is 6. Then, the following period forecast is

$$4.75, \text{ i.e., } \hat{x}_7 = 4 + \left(\frac{6 - 3}{4}\right) = \frac{6 + 5 + 4 + 4}{4} = 4.75$$

The moving average is slowly increasing with the apparent trend. Such slowness of response will be appreciated only if there is a gradual trend. But the manager is beginning to think that demand stability is disappearing. What should be done?

We can handle this situation in a number of ways. One is to decrease the number of observations N in the moving average. This will make the forecasts more responsive to recent events. Try it out with $N = 2$ and see for yourself.

Weighted Moving Averages. A second way to make the forecast more responsive to trends is to use **weighted moving averages.** Let the sum of the weights w_t be 1; thus, $\sum_t w_t = 1$.

Our system of forecast equations becomes

$$\hat{x}_{t+1} = w_t x_t + w_{t-1} x_{t-1} + \ldots + w_{t-N+1} x_{t-N+1}$$

or, specifically,

$$\hat{x}_{t+1} = 0.4x_t + 0.3x_{t-1} + 0.2x_{t-2} + 0.1x_{t-3},$$

for the given weights, 0.4, 0.3, 0.2, 0.1

(Note that the biggest weights are assigned to the most recent observations. This will generally hold true. However, in a rapidly changing system w_t will be much greater ($>>>$) than w_{t-1}, and so on. Thus, $w_t >>> w_{t-1} >>> w_{t-2} \ldots$ etc. This is equivalent to reducing the size of N, which was discussed in the section on moving averages.)

With the previous method of moving averages, all the w_t were treated as being equal—viz., for $t = 5$:

$$\hat{x}_{t+1} = \frac{1}{4}(5) + \frac{1}{4}(4) + \frac{1}{4}(4) + \frac{1}{4}(3) = 4$$

Using the weights (0.4, 0.3, 0.2, 0.1) with the numbers from our previous example, we obtain

$$\hat{x}_{t+1} = 0.4(5) + 0.3(4) + 0.2(4) + 0.1(3)$$
$$= 2 + 1.2 + 0.8 + 0.3 = 4.3$$

This system is responding more rapidly to the (possible) trend (4.3 vs. 4).

Introducing the new value of 6 (as we did before), we again observe an increase in reaction rate, (5.1 vs. 4.75).

$$\hat{x}_{t+2} = 0.4(6) + 0.3(5) + 0.2(4) + 0.1(4)$$
$$= 2.4 + 1.5 + 0.8 + 0.4 = 5.1$$

Thus weighted moving averages can track strong trends more accurately.

Forecasts Using Exponential Smoothing

Often, the use of weighted moving averages is less effective than **exponential smoothing,** which requires less calculation. Many control systems employ exponential smoothing. It has proved effective for such diverse applications as tracking aircraft and forecasting demand levels for inventory systems.

The method of exponential smoothing carries the last average value of actual observations in memory and combines it with the most recent observed value. Thus, $\hat{x}_{t-1}$ is the last forecast made; x_{t-1} is the actual result observed for the period $t - 1$, and $\hat{x}_t$ is the new forecast to be made for period t.

$$\hat{x}_t = \alpha x_{t-1} + (1 - \alpha)\hat{x}_{t-1}$$

160

Managing
Production and
Operations
Systems
Through Their
Life Cycle
Stages

According to the weight α that is used, the response rate of the system can be changed markedly. Thus, using the same data as before, we observe the effect on the forecast $\hat{x}_t$ of different values of α.

$\hat{x}_t$	α
$0.1(6) + 0.9(4) = 4.2$	0.1
$0.2(6) + 0.8(4) = 4.4$	0.2
$0.3(6) + 0.7(4) = 4.6$	0.3
$0.375(6) + 0.625(4) = 4.75$	0.375 ← Moving average result
$0.4(6) + 0.6(4) = 4.8$	0.4
$0.5(6) + 0.5(4) = 5.0$	0.5
$0.55(6) + 0.45(4) = 5.1$	0.550 ← Weighted moving average result
$0.6(6) + 0.4(4) = 5.2$	0.6
.	.
.	.
.	.
$1.0(6) + 0(4) = 6.0$	1.0

This simple updating system requires only one operation. Thus, if $\alpha = 0.1$ and the actual result is $x_t = 4.5$, then $\hat{x}_{t+1} = 0.1(4.5) + 0.9(4.2) = 4.23$.

Small values of α are used for noisy, randomly fluctuating systems that have a basic stability, and larger values are used for emerging and evolving systems, where a goodly amount of weight can only be placed on the last observation. For many aggregate scheduling systems α is kept quite small, in the neighborhood of 0.05 to 0.15, to decrease the system's response to random fluctuations.

Use of Regression Analysis

Another important approach for forecasting is regression analysis. When future outcomes that are to be forecast appear to be related to other factors that lead them (occur first), it is possible to forecast a sequence of future outcomes on the basis of current observations of the other factors.

The **least-squares technique** is a method of regression analysis that can be used to estimate the value of future outcomes, y_{t+k}, if a leading factor x_t can be found. Causality between y_{t+k} and x_t is not assumed. A common causal factor (that is unknown) may be responsible for whatever relationship is found.

**KINDER-
GARTEN
SUPPLIES,
INC.**

Let the sequence of outcomes we wish to forecast be the aggregate demand for kindergarten school supplies. Kindergarten Supplies, Inc. (a job shop company producing a full range of kindergarten supplies and distributing them nationally) assumes that the aggregate demand for kindergarten supplies is related to the number of children born 5 years before. For aggregate planning, Kindergarten Supplies has prepared the information shown in Table 4–2.

TABLE 4-2

Year t	x_t = Number of Children Born in Year t (in millions)	Year $t + 5$	y_{t+5} = Kindergarten Attendance in Year $t + 5$ (in millions)
1	3	6	2
2	4	7	3
3	6	8	5
4	4	9	5
5	8	10	6

It is assumed that the number of children born in a given year leads kindergarten attendance by 5 years, and we have therefore paired the x_ts with the y_{t+5}s that occurred 5 years later. Kindergarten Supplies will use this relationship to determine its aggregate production schedule.

Let us fit a least-squares line to these data. This line will be an estimate of the way in which kindergarten attendance changes as a result of the number of children born 5 years before. It can then be used to extrapolate probable kindergarten attendance in the future for known or estimated numbers of births.

We use what are called **normal equations** (based on the assumption of a linear relationship between x_t and y_{t+5}) to derive the least-squares line. It can be shown that the least-squares line minimizes the total variance of the distances of the observed points from that line. The normal equations achieve this objective.

$$\sum_{t=1}^{t=N} y_{t+5} = aN + b \sum_{t=1}^{t=N} x_t \qquad (4\text{-}1)$$

$$\sum_{t=1}^{t=N} x_t y_{t+5} = a \sum_{t=1}^{t=N} x_t + b \sum_{t=1}^{t=N} x_t^2 \qquad (4\text{-}2)$$

For our example, $N = 5$, which is the total number of pairs of x_t and y_{t+5}. Table 4–3 assembles the data needed for our analysis.

TABLE 4-3

t	x_t	y_{t+5}	$x_t y_{t+5}$	x_t^2
1	3	2	6	9
2	4	3	12	16
3	6	5	30	36
4	4	5	20	16
5	8	6	48	64
Σ	25	21	116	141

162

Managing
Production and
Operations
Systems
Through Their
Life Cycle
Stages

Therefore:

$$21 = a(5) + b(25) \qquad \text{using Eq. (4-1)}$$
$$116 = a(25) + b(141) \qquad \text{using Eq. (4-2)}$$

Solving for a and b, we obtain: $a = 61/80$; $b = 11/16$. These values are introduced in the least-squares line:

$$y_{t+5} = a + bx_t = + \frac{61}{80} + \frac{11}{16} x_t \qquad (4\text{-}3)$$

This least-squares line and the actual scatter of values around it are shown in Fig. 4–16.

To use this line, let us suppose that when $t = 6$, $x_t = 10$. We see that y_{t+5} would be forecast to be 7.6375 million. We would use this line for forecasting only if the observed data appear to fit it well, especially in recent years.

Different forecasts for the same outcomes frequently exist within a single organization. Sometimes, the production manager derives one forecast; the sales manager derives another; branch managers derive still others. Often

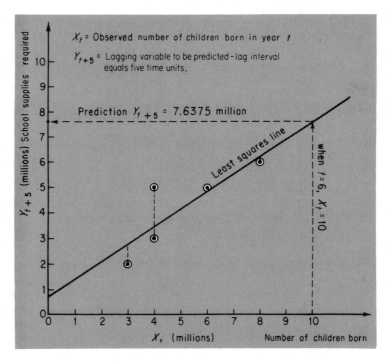

FIGURE 4-16. Least-squares linear relationship between a leading indicator and the variable to be predicted.

a variety of different data bases coexist. Methods for pooling information to provide a stronger forecast should not be ignored. Also, it is of critical importance that all parties share the same forecasts, and usually much stronger forecasts can be obtained if both data and experience are pooled.

Using linear regression, Kindergarten Supplies can prepare an aggregate schedule for its job shop. For aggregate scheduling, many different items are treated as though they were of one kind in terms of demands on resources. (Chapter 11 describes the aggregate scheduling function.)

GLOSSARY
FOR
ANTICIPATING
EVENTS
THAT
CHANGE
OVER TIME

Time series: A succession of values identified with the time of their occurrence.

Forecasting: Using analytic methods to choose a strategy or to identify what event state is the most likely to occur.

Predicting: Using subjective means to name the event that is expected to happen, so that plans can take shape around this event.

Multiple prediction: Using subjective means to name several events that might occur, so that plans and contingency plans can be developed.

Future control: Attempting to modify the future, which would be reflected in altered forecasts and changed predictions.

PROBLEM
SET

1. Contrast the relationship of the job shop and the flow shop with respect to their production of output for finished goods inventory.

2. In a large job shop there are many departments having the same kind of general-purpose equipment, and therefore able to do the same kind of job. Of course, some departments are better for certain kinds of jobs than others. The job shop manager wants to choose the best assignments, but to evaluate all possibilities without a method is generally impossible. To illustrate, assume that 10 jobs are to be assigned to 10 different departments. How many variations must be evaluated, if all possible arrangements are considered?

3. What is the relationship of the bill of materials to the blueprint, and what is the relationship of the operations sheet to the bill of materials?

4. Why is management of the job shop called a single overall problem that must be resolved in three steps? Explain the three subproblems and discuss the effect of solving them in sequential order.

5. The job shop requires a good information management system. Why is this a requirement? Does it apply to the flow shop? Does it apply to projects?

6. Explain the difference between:
   a. Historical and moving average forecasts.
   b. Moving average and weighted moving average forecasts.
   c. Weighted moving average and exponential smoothing forecasts.

164

Managing
Production and
Operations
Systems
Through Their
Life Cycle
Stages

7. The Parks Department has a job shop orientation. Crews of park workers are assigned different tasks, which are completed in batches before another task is tackled. For example, tree care in the previous year required the following number of crew hours.

Month	Crew Hours	Month	Crew Hours
January	110	July	200
February	120	August	220
March	140	September	280
April	180	October	120
May	250	November	100
June	200	December	80

a. Using the moving average method, based on 6 periods, prepare an analysis of prediction error.

Answer:

Month	Total Crew Hours	Prediction	Actual	Error
July	1000	167	200	−33
August	1090	182	220	−38
September	1190	198	280	−82
October	1330	222	120	+102
November	1270	212	100	+112
December	1120	187	80	+107
January	1000	167		

b. Using the moving average method based on 3 periods, prepare an analysis of prediction error. Compare your results with part (a) results above. Discuss.

c. Using the weighted moving average method, based on 6 periods and weights of 0.1, 0.1, 0.1, 0.2, 0.2, 0.3, prepare an analysis of prediction error. Compare your results with those obtained in parts (a) and (b) above. Discuss.

d. Using exponential smoothing, find the x values that would yield the results obtained in parts (a), (b), and (c) above. What α value would you choose? Explain your answer.

8. Draw up an appropriate bill of materials for producing the following items:

a. A table knife.

b. An office stapler.

c. A flashlight.

Answer: The bill of materials for a product should list all parts that are required for its assembly. It is a useful form of information for both the design and control of the production system. A simplified version of the materials for a flashlight might be:

Part No.	Description	Quantity	Cost/Item
10057	Plastic case	1	$0.253
10573	Screw-on battery holder	1	0.029
84638	Switch	1	0.164
74935	Screws to hold switch	2	0.006
67395	Bulb housing	1	0.058
93867	Glass front	1	0.094
12345	Bulb	1	0.132

Similarly, lists can be drawn up for the table knife (simple) and for the stapler (more complex). By assigning part numbers and costs per item, useful bills of materials can be derived.

9. A beach umbrella manufacturer had the following monthly sales in the year just completed:

Month	Sales (Units)
1	500
2	800
3	1,200
4	2,000
5	4,000
6	8,000
7	10,000
8	7,000
9	6,000
10	1,000
11	500
12	300

The company anticipates a growth in next year's sales of 40 percent.

a. Prepare a monthly estimate of sales for the coming year.

b. Why is such a monthly breakdown of sales required?

Answer:

a. Assuming that the seasonal pattern is stable, we need only increase each month's sales (units) by 40 percent.

Month:	1	2	3	4	5	6
Sales:	700	1,120	1,680	2,800	5,600	11,200

Month:	7	8	9	10	11	12
Sales:	14,000	9,800	8,400	1,400	700	420

The prior year's total sales were 41,300 units. With a 40 percent increase, the total sales will be 57,820 units, which is the total of the adjusted, monthly (forecast) figures.

166

Managing
Production and
Operations
Systems
Through Their
Life Cycle
Stages

b. Monthly forecasts are needed to plan production. They are also used to regulate staffing, hiring, and training; to set levels for inventories; and to provide storage facilities for purchased materials and for in-process and finished goods. They are even needed to determine how much cash should be available to meet immediate needs.

10. A manufacturer of kitchen equipment keeps track of new housing starts in his region. He believes that demand for his products follows housing starts by three months. Fit a least-square line to the data below, which are based on the manager's assumptions.

Month	Sales Volume	Housing Starts
1	$45,000	260
2	60,000	250
3	62,000	320
4	30,000	380
5	40,000	500
6	45,000	480
7	68,000	320
8	75,000	400
9	80,000	350
10	45,000	250
11	30,000	100
12	25,000	150

Answer:

Month	Housing Starts (H)	Sales (S) 3 Months Later	H × S	H²
1	260	30,000	7,800,000	67,600
2	250	40,000	10,000,000	62,500
3	320	45,000	14,400,000	102,400
4	380	68,000	25,840,000	144,400
5	500	75,000	37,500,000	250,000
6	480	80,000	38,400,000	230,400
7	320	45,000	14,400,000	102,400
8	400	30,000	12,000,000	160,000
9	350	25,000	8,750,000	122,500
	3,260	438,000	169,090,000	1,242,200

The equation of the least squares line (see pp. 161–162) is:

$$S = a + bH$$

where a and b can be determined by solving:

$$438,000 = a(9) + b(3,260)$$

$$169,090,000 = a(3,260) + b(1,242,200)$$

We find that:

$$S = -12,947.3 + (170.1)H$$

11. Would you prefer a good prediction or a good forecast? Explain your answer.

Answer:

A good forecast will be based on all possible states of nature and their probabilities. Based on this forecast, it is possible to select a strategy that maximizes the expected value. The forecast considers all the various possible outcomes and weights their respective likelihoods. It does not require the specification of a particular state of nature.

A good prediction based on subjective considerations might be preferred either to a weak forecast that reflects lack of pertinent data or to one in which too many factors interact to allow capturing the picture in an analytic way.

It is hard to say that a good forecast is worth more than a good prediction. However, if the manager prefers the quality of the prediction to the quality of the forecast, we assume that the information for good decision-making is better in the prediction than the forecast. Therefore, a good prediction is preferred to a good forecast. There is no such thing as a perfect forecast.

Section 4.3 Flexible and Programmable Systems: Variety with High Quality and Low Cost

In the production of goods, these systems are called flexible manufacturing systems, or FMS. Many information services call them office automation (OA) or integrated office systems (IOS). They go by many names because they are new and changing rapidly over time. To include them all, we use the generic name **flexible programmable systems (FPS).**

These systems apply computer technology to drive all kinds of machines in the office, in the factory, and in the home. FPS can produce a large variety of high-quality goods and services at low unit cost. However, a substantial investment is required.

Characteristics of FPS

The basic elements of flexible systems are the computer-driven work stations which are operated entirely through remote-entry terminals. Transfers of work between work stations also are computerized. The work stations for metalworking are machines using tools such as lathes, drills, and milling machines. The metalworking systems are what is meant by

168

Managing
Production and
Operations
Systems
Through Their
Life Cycle
Stages

flexible manufacturing systems (FMS). Figure 4–17 illustrates an FMS cell with both the machining and the transfers between machines run by software.

There is a hierarchy of groupings of equipment which starts with the single numerically controlled machine (NC). When several NC machines are grouped together but not connected with an automatic transfer system between them, the result is called an **FMS cell.** Such cells are built of related equipment, and that is as far as the integration level of the equipment goes. At the next level of integration, programmable transfer facilities move work from one machine to another without worker assistance. These are called **islands of automation** or **linked NCs.** Figure 4–18 shows the linked NCs or CNCs (computer-controlled).

Computer-controlled equipment can be used for many other jobs than metalworking. For example, laboratory test equipment can be run by software, and the transfers between test stations may also be responsive to program instructions. The processing of film is another good example, but perhaps the best illustration of all is the automobile assembly line. When the level of integration is capable of turning out an entire assembly or subassembly, it is called an **integrated manufacturing system (IMS).**

Integrated Manufacturing Systems (IMS)

Moving through levels of escalating integration, we have gone from the single, stand-alone NC to the dedicated factory. Numerous examples exist at each level. The John Deere Company produces crankshafts on a

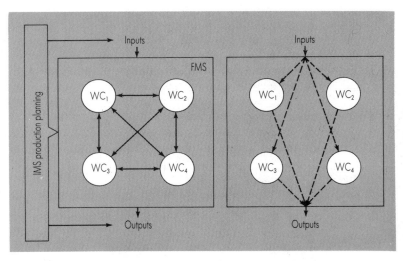

FIGURE 4-17. Essence of FMS/FOS and IMS cells (a manufacturing or office work cell).

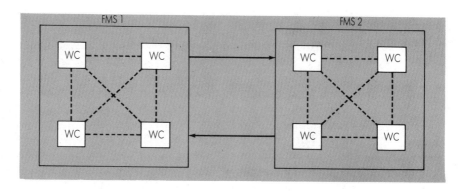

FIGURE 4-18. Islands of automation-linked FMS cells.

flexible basis which qualifies as a fully integrated system. The company has expanded its capabilities by using modular production and group technology concepts. The Illinois Tool Works uses IMS to produce computer keyboards. IBM manufactures electric typewriters at Lexington, Kentucky, with an IMS factory. The U.S. Air Force has involved multiple aerospace companies in a coordinated plan to develop an IMS capable of producing military aircraft. Toyota has an IMS auto plant and Canon has an IMS copier plant in Japan. Many other examples can be cited, each different in scope and level of integration. (In Chapter 12, we discuss the taxonomy of these levels.)

When the IMS is raised to an even higher level, all company planning functions are interconnected. This means that all relevant databases are utilized to do production scheduling, inventory management, and capacity planning. The databases are those of marketing, distribution, human resources, accounting, and so on. Such fully integrated planning systems are called **CIMs (computer-integrated manufacturing systems)**. Chapter 12 explores the development of the CIM.

Integrated Office Systems (IOS)

When the communication systems are integrated, often on an international basis using telecommunication satellites, there is a new technology environment. Databases are connected to provide three levels of information usage. This hierarchy starts with electronic data processing (EDP), which has an established track record. At the next level there is the management information system, which provides information support to managers reaching decisions. Topping the hierarchy are decision support systems, which provide directions to managers. Running these systems is an integrated management function.

Unlike manufacturing examples of FMS, IMS, and CIM, which are well documented, IOS examples are not big news. Probably this is because

170

Managing
Production and
Operations
Systems
Through Their
Life Cycle
Stages

they are partially used in all offices, and their use is not susceptible to easy evaluation. Also, the competitive advantages of IOS are difficult to establish. But this is not always the case. It is well known that American Airlines' Sabre Reservation System has provided great benefits to the company and to many airline customers as well. Merrill Lynch's CMA (Cash Management Accounts) unified cash and stock transactions into a single reporting form for its customers. This IOS gave Merrill Lynch a market share advantage for many years. The American Hospital Corporation put terminals into its clients' hospitals so that they could maintain their inventories in an on-line mode. In effect, this made clients' offices part of the supplier's office system. In summary, IOS is well and thriving, even though it has received less attention than other flexible information processing systems.

How to Evaluate and Justify the New Technology

Using old methods for evaluating the feasibility of new technology has many drawbacks. In fact, many proposals to adapt new technology are doomed to be rejected by the old evaluation methods. The reasons are as follow:

1. Machine purchase decisions are normally reached on a narrow basis which reflects the interests of users of the equipment to be replaced. The lathe user is instrumental in evaluating the replacement lathe proposal. With new equipment, the effects of moving from stand alone to cells, to linked islands, to IMS, transcend the local interests of lathe users.

2. The effects of advanced technology can change as the composition of the plant changes. This runs counter to the traditional expectation that once a new facility is brought on-line, its benefits will be realized. The only expected change is gradual deterioration as the facility ages.

3. Newer technology is becoming available on a continuing basis. Equipment tends to be modular, enhancing the present configurations in ways that may be difficult to forecast. To appreciate this effect, one need only look at the advances that new components and software have made to pc's over time.

4. Present P/OM careers do not include technology assessment of increasingly integrated modular systems.

How to Introduce the New Technology

Potential adopters must understand what the new technologies are able to achieve: These computer-driven systems can change what is being processed from one product to another, almost instantaneously, and at negligible cost. If the process could be endowed with a point of view, it would be that it is consistently engaged in the same activity over time, although the customer views the product it produces as markedly different in the marketplace.

Adoption of the new technology can follow two courses. One is using the incremental approach. This requires careful planning as small steps of change are accumulated to build to higher levels of integration. There are many pitfalls in using incrementalism. Even with careful planning, the pieces do not add together to complete the desired whole. The other approach is to reject incrementalism and go for the whole change. This is like John Deere putting in an entirely new crankshaft manufacturing process. When it is in place, the old one is shut down. This is like Merrill Lynch shifting from the old customer accounting system to the CMA. When the new faucet is opened, the old one is shut down. Change is a major step.

Such big and costly changes are not easy in the usual company environment. There is too much inertia to preserve the status quo. Bureaucracy is designed to protect the company from major alterations in its procedures. To achieve major change, it is useful to have the benefit of a new technology champion. This champion should be a respected member of management who is regarded as an authority on the competitive advantages of technological change. (See Donald Gerwin, ''Do's and Dont's of Computerized Manufacturing,'' Harvard Business Review, March–April 1982.)

The Risks of FPS

Each aspect of the new technologies is undergoing development and change. Applicability of the new technologies is improving all the time. On the other hand, the competitive drive to adopt the new technologies and be first with greater variety advantages and better quality with lower costs is hard to resist. There is the risk of jumping in too soon with major investments, and the risk of not learning the technology soon enough to be wise enough about when to commit major resources. There is the risk of missing out on being first with the conversion of the technological advantages into marketplace advantages. In summary, the risks of being too early or too late provide new opportunities and challenges.

How to Use FPS

The subject of technological development has always been of concern to P/OM. However, until recently it was essentially an engineering evaluation problem. This is because the new equipment was conceptually the same as the old equipment. It was a candidate for replacing the older equipment because it was more efficient, and often, this was just because the old machine had worn out.

172

Managing
Production and
Operations
Systems
Through Their
Life Cycle
Stages

The difference now is that the new technology changes the basic production concept. It is not merely more efficient; it is a different work configuration with the possibility of being more or less effective when interacting with the customer and the marketplace.

International Experiences with FMS

There is a broad base of international users for FMS. This fact reinforces the idea that global competition will be the arena for determining the winners and the losers in the next decade. Since there are substantial differences in the way that FMS is being used in different countries, there is reason to believe that the production and operations leverage of companies operating out of different countries will be different. (This subject receives expanded coverage in Chapter 12.)

Using Linear Programming for FMS Scheduling

Section 12.2 examines the way in which linear programming (a tried and true production model) fits into the no setup cost situation of FMS. Linear programming was developed long before FMS was conceived of as an economic reality. It is therefore pure serendipity to discover that a 1940s mathematical concept is appropriate to a 1990s technology.

PROBLEM
SET

1. What classifications describe different aspects of flexible systems? Why are these classes useful?
2. Do flexible systems apply equally well to the manufacture of goods and the providing of services? Discuss.
3. Say that a company has two plans under consideration: (1) to spend a total of $10 million on a new plant which will use the present equipment; (2) to use the present plant, but install new flexible process equipment at a total cost of $10 million. How should these options be evaluated and compared?

REFERENCES

International Journal of Flexible Manufacturing Systems: Design, Analysis and Operation of Manufacturing and Assembly Systems. Boston: Kluwer Academic Publishers, started in 1987.

Toward a New Era in U.S. Manufacturing: The Need for a National Vision. National Research Council, Washington, D.C.: National Academy Press, 1986.

Managing Automation. New York: Thomas Publishing Company, magazine started in 1986.

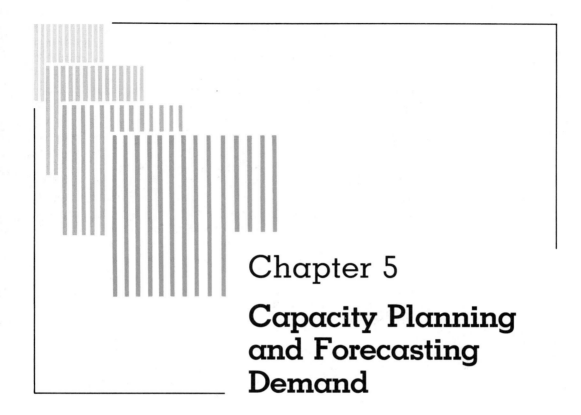

Chapter 5

Capacity Planning and Forecasting Demand

CHAPTER
SUMMARY

The capacity decision is a crucial management responsibility. It sets in motion a scenario for startup and growth which is difficult to alter. Downsizing is demoralizing and costly. The last-minute realization of the need for greater capacity is fraught with difficulties and buys the additional volume at a higher price than would have been incurred from original planning stages. Capacity planning is interwoven with demand forecasting. In some situations, the forecast is less certain than in others. There is higher risk for investment capital. In all situations, there is a balance between risk and return.

Section 5.1 presents two of the basic models of production systems: the input/output model, and the breakeven model. The I/O model epitomizes the production process. What is assumed is that a desired transformation takes place between the input stage and the output stage. The model should be written (I/T/O), but from the inception of the idea, engineers named these systems I/Os. Inputs such as direct labor and direct materials are *transformed* into the outputs which when sold produce the

173

174

Managing
Production and
Operations
Systems
Through Their
Life Cycle
Stages

revenues needed to run the business and needed to reward investors. I/O models relate the costs of inputs and the capital investment in the transformation process to the revenues derived from the outputs of goods or services.

The systems approach is what we call the coordinated and interdependent activities of participants to a decision problem. To solve the problems of: How much capacity? What kind of capacity? (What work configuration?) Where to place that capacity? requires the systems approach. Breakeven analysis facilitates the systems approach. Both linear and nonlinear functions can be used for costs and revenues.

Section 5.2 combines breakeven analysis with a probability distribution to forecast demand by means of a decision matrix. The forecast is likely to be based on market research, or on the judgments of the marketing managers. Share of market reflects customer satisfaction with the quality/price ratio. P/OM and marketing managers need to have a consensus about the relationship of perceived quality and produced quality. At this level of integration, breakeven analysis becomes a significant unifying systems model.

Capacity planning is introduced in Section 5.3 at an even higher level of integrated decision-making. Using price elasticity in conjunction with P/OM economies of scale, we maximize margin contribution. Price elasticity is a form of forecasting in which the primary relationship is the change in demand as the price goes up or down. Since price elasticity is a function of the quality of the productline, the production and operations tie-in with marketing and finance is inescapable.

Section 5.1 The Breakeven Concept and Capacity Planning

Capacity can be installed all at once, or it can be gradually increased. The incremental approach entails low risk, but it can lead to lost opportunities, higher unit costs, and worst of all, poor and inconsistent quality of product.

What size I/O (capacity) does management have in mind? The O is the amount of product that is to be sold. The size of O is determined by projected market share and volume, which in turn dictates the transformation capacity to be installed. But the way in which that capacity is installed (what kind of work configuration) will affect the relationship of input costs to fixed costs. It will also affect the price that can be charged, the quality that can be delivered to the customer, and the profit margins that can be obtained.

The breakeven concept, used properly, forces consideration of the issues raised here. We will try to show this synthesis of functional ideas as we begin to relate the pieces and parts of breakeven analysis by means of the input/output model.

Input/Output Models of Revenues and Costs

Production and **operations** are defined as any process or procedure designed to transform a set of input factors into a specified set of output factors. The system is the set of all such interconnected input/output factors.

A production system can be broken down into the three component parts of inputs, outputs, and process. The diagram shown in Fig. 5–1 illustrates the way in which various factors are brought together and transformed to accomplish the objectives for which the system was designed.

The process can be complicated: Many kinds of inputs can be required. A variety of outputs can emerge. But the idea of transforming a set of inputs so that they yield a set of outputs is straightforward. The design of an actual input/output process for assembling automobiles, delivering tons of gourmet chile con carne, processing millions of insurance premiums, or transporting nuclear waste is another matter. The responsibility for deciding how to do the job is filled with opportunities, challenges, and great risks.

Output and Revenue

Specification of the desired output or outputs is usually the starting point for P/OM planning. Outputs are delivered to the marketplace, where they generate revenue. Financial criteria dictate that the I/O business activity produce a satisfactory return on the invested capital. Some level of return on investment (ROI) is set as a hurdle that must be achieved or bettered. When money is plentiful, investors seek opportunities to increase their supply of it.

Juxtaposed to this is the case where a potentially valuable product has been conceived, but sufficient capital is not available to design and make it. The financial officers of the company have various ways of trying to

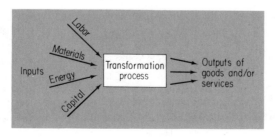

FIGURE 5-1. The transformation system.

176

Managing
Production and
Operations
Systems
Through Their
Life Cycle
Stages

raise the money. If a big investment is required, it is harder to find the capital than if a small investment is needed. The size of the investment required will be determined by the design of the transformation process.

What is a *valuable* product? It is a product that earns a return on investment better than bank interest and better than stocks, bonds, and Treasury notes. That is because the product can be sold to customers for more than it costs to make it. P/OM, marketing, and financial managers are responsible for making the launch successful. Using *competitive analysis,* a sales manager might learn that a competitor has introduced a new formulation of an existing product or service which is receiving strong consumer acceptance. This sales manager should move fast by suggesting actions to counter the competition. Worthwhile ideas can also come from users. Frequently a market survey will uncover a consumer need that is not being satisfied. Where the environment is conducive, a creative employee may just "dream up" a new output that will achieve a successful level of demand.

The starting point can also be traced to input factors and to process factors. If a new material or a new energy source is developed, the discovery may suggest an output that was either overlooked or previously technologically or economically unfeasible. Similarly, a technological discovery can lead to the design of a new process that is capable of producing an entirely new output that could satisfy a public need or an unquenched consumer demand. Numerous cases are on record of a by-product of a process suddenly being recognized as marketable. Here, the existence of one output creates the possibility for another.

Because of the dynamic character of the marketplace, new public and private output opportunities are continually developing. A previously unwanted product or service can unexpectedly shift into a situation where it is under substantial demand. Of course, the reverse is also true. An accepted product or service can lose popularity, and its share of market can take a nosedive. Sometimes, the fall from grace can be traced to the activities of a competitor, but it can also be explained as a life cycle shift in consumer wants. It is the essence of the life cycle management problem that the transformation process could turn out one day to be producing something that nobody wants anymore.

Interfunctional Models

When considering how much production capacity is needed, all managers must pool their knowledge. The managers of production, marketing, personnel, finance, and so on should consider simultaneously:

1. The productline and the process
2. The demand volumes that can be generated in the marketplace for a reasonable range of prices

3. The costs and qualities that various feasible work configurations can deliver

Chapter 4 highlighted how work configuration choice affects product quality and per unit product cost. Choosing the appropriate work configuration requires understanding the alternatives. Some of the issues that underlie the capacity planning alternatives are these:

How the productline was developed by R&D
How the productline can change as a result of future R&D
How well R&D works with Engineering
How Engineering gets along with Production

How Marketing decided what price to charge for the product
What volumes those prices will generate
What effect specific quality standards have on price
What effect existing competition has on quality standards
How any and all of the above are likely to change

What process alternatives (WCs) exist
What fixed and variable production costs each will have
What range of output volumes makes sense for each process
What other unit costs apply, including distribution costs
What output qualities each process alternative can deliver

What depreciation applies to each work configuration
How fixed costs are determined from the depreciation
How the variable costs (per unit) are determined
Whether the variable costs can be improved with learning over time

Since capacity planning requires good communications between the functions, we turn to the question of who does well in achieving such interfunctional systems. During the late 1980s it became apparent that the Japanese excelled at interfunctional cooperation. By studying the Japanese model, we can improve our ability to engage in interfunctional discussions. Western industries do not readily achieve a cooperative internal dialogue. In fact, there are a number of criticisms of MBA programs for not providing training in and awareness of interfunctional systems within companies.

Figure 5–2 portrays the idea of quality being shared by all the functions of the firm. Successful U.S. firms such as Xerox and Ford have embraced

178
Managing
Production and
Operations
Systems
Through Their
Life Cycle
Stages

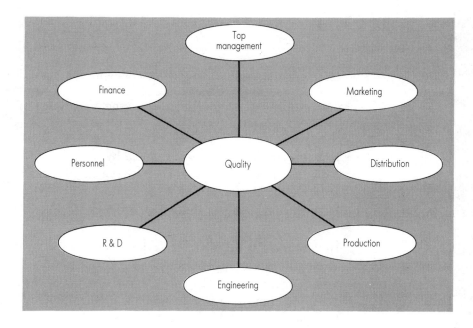

FIGURE 5-2. Inter-functional cooperation.

the notion that quality is the mediating channel through which all managers in the organization can relate to all the others. Therefore, when referring to I/Os and their cost and revenue structures, and to breakeven analyses, we should try to keep in mind that adherence to the precepts of Fig. 5–2 will enhance the effectiveness of our methods.

The Process and Fixed Costs

The output of an economic process is expected to have greater value than the combined costs of the inputs and the depreciated investment in the process. As revenues are earned, the firm starts to recover what it has expended. Then, after cost recovery is completed, the profit begins to be made. If full cost recovery is never achieved, then a loss is sustained.

This notion of input/output is different from the engineering expectations for physical systems. A theoretically perfect engine has output equal to input. Because of friction and heat losses, the usable output in the physical world is less than the sum of the input energies. The efficiency of a process η in engineering terms is:

$$\eta = \frac{\text{useful output}}{\text{input}} \leq 1$$

Such inefficiency would produce bankruptcy in the economic world. The efficiency of a firm is measurable in these terms, but the team of managers is expected to create wealth, not reduce it. In economic systems, the efficiency η must be greater than 1, indicating that a benefit can be had or a profit can be made. P/OM understands and integrates both the engineering and the economic points of view in its planning activities.

A **transformation process** consists of production factors that are paid for by fixed costs. These are costs that do not vary as a function of output rates. What kinds of costs are these? Although an accounting convention does apply here, nevertheless a good deal of interpretation is possible in the assignment of costs to the fixed cost category. For example, depreciation allowances that result from the ageing of machines are invariant to the amount of use the equipment receives. Consequently, it is appropriate to include such expenses as part of fixed costs. (On the other hand, depreciation that results from use of the machines violates this concept.) Another fixed cost might be municipal taxes that are independent of the company's revenue. Fixed power and light charges and basic insurance charges also belong to the fixed cost category. For the most part, fixed costs arising as a result of investment in plant and facilities are depreciated as a function of time and not as a function of output volume.

Service organizations can have substantial fixed costs from computer systems, delivery systems, and buildings and facilities. The view that services are labor-intensive and have low capital requirements has become increasingly inaccurate as information technology has developed satellites and telecommunication networks to connect in-house computers. The Federal Express delivery system, which uses aircraft to and from a sorting hub, is another example of a capital-intensive service operation.

Inputs and Variable Costs

Inputs are variable-cost P/OM factors. Variable costs are paid out on a per unit (of volume) basis. Direct labor and direct material costs are typical. They can be charged directly to each unit of production. Variable costs also create certain anomalies of classification. There are, for example, indirect labor charges associated with office work. Such costs are difficult to attribute to a particular unit of output or on a cost-per-piece basis. Normally they are assigned to the accounting category of (fixed) overhead costs. Similarly, salaries paid to supervisors fall outside the definition of variable costs. In general, if a cost cannot be assigned on a per unit basis, it gets treated as a fixed cost.

Materials, labor, and energy constitute the inputs. Plant and facilities make up the process. By means of scheduling inputs to the production process, management exercises most of its day-to-day control over the outputs.

180

Managing
Production and
Operations
Systems
Through Their
Life Cycle
Stages

Functional Areas and Revenues and Costs

Management exercises operating control over the production system in two different ways:

1. By controlling the inputs with respect to input rates, cost, quality, and so on, it controls the variable costs.
2. By altering the process (or procedure)—that is, by rearranging the process elements—it controls the fixed systemic costs.

Managers of the various functional areas participate in reaching capacity decisions in three different ways.

1. **Fixed-cost Systems.** P/OM and Engineering management share the responsibility for recommending plant types and work configuration designs. Financial management plays the ultimate role of accepting or rejecting the recommendations. The CFO (chief financial officer) is the person who usually signs off on the facilities.
2. **Variable-cost Systems.** P/OM has the major operating responsibilities, given the plant and work configuration decision in 1 above. Finance provides the operating budget. P/OM has much discretion in how to spend the budget.
3. **Revenue.** Marketing has the major responsibilities for setting prices and determining customer quality expectations (which lead to design specifications). Marketing analyzes competition, plans advertising and promotion strategies, and estimates demand. While such activities are considered to fall outside the P/OM domain, they affect output volumes and capacity plans.

Variable-cost systems are traditionally treated as being the major concern of P/OMs. With technology providing many work configuration options, it has become increasingly apparent that fixed cost systems decisions may be difficult to justify by using traditional financial criteria. The management team (including P/OM) has to make known its concerns for nontraditional criteria that must be accounted for in reaching fixed cost plant decisions. Decisions concerning facilities investments require considering future competitive capabilities along with technology and company survival. Such issues demand cooperative consideration by marketing and financial managers, engineers and P/OMs.

Revenue considerations are derived from customer perceptions of quality and price. It is also essential to factor in what is competitively substitutable. Since quality, cost, and therefore price, product availability, and variety are completely related to demand, marketing inputs play a major role in capacity planning. Demand affects production volumes and thereby output cost per unit. In spite of these obvious interdependencies, marketing and production divisions seldom achieve the level of cooperation that is necessary for coordinated decision-making.

The Breakeven Chart

The breakeven model is an extension of the fundamental input/output model. It associates costs and revenues with the input/output factors. Breakeven was developed in the 1930s by Walter Rautenstrauch, an industrial engineer and professor at Columbia University. (See W. Rautenstrauch and R. Villers, *The Economics of Industrial Management,* New York: Funk & Wagnalls, 1949). It is a fundamental model of P/OM and provides important insights about production systems.

Breakeven analysis can be presented in mathematical terms or in graphic form. It is easier to understand the concept using the graphic approach first. A breakeven chart is shown in Figure 5–3. The rapid acceptance and application of the breakeven chart by the P/OM field illustrates the concern of production and operations management with the three factors of revenues, fixed costs, and variable costs.

The y axis of the chart (called the ordinate) represents dollars. The x axis (called the abscissa) represents volume. The ordinate is used to graph dollars of fixed costs, variable costs, and revenues. The abscissa can be dimensioned in terms of the production volume—that is, the number of units made by the company in a given period of time. Alternatively, the abscissa can be dimensioned as a percentage of the total production capacity the company has available. All these dimensions are shown in Fig. 5–3.

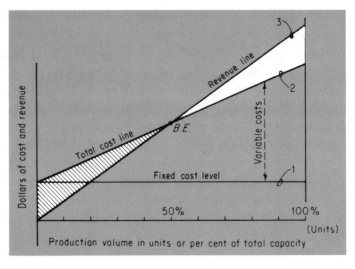

FIGURE 5-3. The breakeven chart. (B.E. is the breakeven point.)

182
Managing
Production and
Operations
Systems
Through Their
Life Cycle
Stages

Three lines have been marked on the chart. Line number 1 is a fixed cost function which applies to a specific period of time. The fixed charges behave as expected; that is, they do not change as a function of increased volume or increased capacity utilization. We previously defined fixed costs by this particular characteristic. The fixed costs for a one-year chart would be different from the fixed costs for a three-year chart. The latter would have to carry three years of depreciation and other overhead charges. Line number 2 is called the total cost line. It is a linear function that increases as production volume gets larger. In actuality perfect linearity may not hold, but the approximation is good enough. Also, linear relationships do adequately describe many situations. The P/OM field accepts this assumption for many cases. Line 2 graphs the sum of fixed and variable costs. The latter by definition increase with additional volume. Variable costs do not begin at the zero level. They are added to the fixed costs, which exist even at a zero production level. Vertical distances across the triangular area lying between fixed costs and total costs measure the variable costs that are obtained at specific production volumes.

For example, to make a unit of a particular item requires a certain amount of labor and materials. If the sum of the labor and materials used for 1 unit cost $0.10, then the total variable costs (vc) for 100 units would be $10, and the total vc for 1,000 units would be $100. That is what we mean by a linear variable cost function. Recalling our earlier discussion of the structure of fixed costs, we should add to the vc depreciation that is applicable to machine utilization. Taxes that are levied on the basis of units produced or revenue obtained would also be appropriate to add to the variable cost. Some power and light charges, heating charges, storage charges, and insurance charges would be included if they fit the definition of variable costs.

The categorization of costs into fixed, variable, and total costs is appropriate to the analysis of the P/OM function. It fits the basic assumptions of an input/output system. The graphic model is readily understood by production people, and it constitutes an important bridge between them and other functional managers with respect to the most basic question of how much capacity is best.

Line 3 in Fig. 5–3 is the revenue line. It is also a linear function that increases with greater production volume. Much of the time, we can accept the assumption of linearity. This implies that our company is operating at a low enough share of the total market that free competition can adequately describe its situation. Often that assumption is satisfactory. But at what volume does linearity no longer apply? As the company produces greater quantities of a product, it gets harder to sell them. At some point, the total revenue will not increase at the same rate. Variable costs per unit may decrease while sales costs per unit increase because the market for the item becomes saturated. It may be necessary for the company to lower its price to obtain a greater share of the total market.

The extent to which demand increases as the price is reduced is known as the price/demand elasticity. This elasticity can be a mysterious and ill-defined area. Although we can generalize that demand is negatively correlated with price, this is not always the case. There are instances where a company obtains increased demand as a result of raising price. In this case, we are dealing with the psychology of the consumer and the fact that a market may not exist for a low-priced product because it does not carry sufficient prestige value to the consumer.

In Fig. 5–3, the cross-hatched area between the total cost line and the revenue line represents loss to the company—i.e., the area to the left of the breakeven point (BEP). The white area between the same lines represents profit to the company and lies to the right of this point. Therein lies the definition of the *BEP*. At the breakeven point, there is no profit and no loss. Profit starts to the right of it; losses lie to the left of it.

In breakeven models, cost recovery is improving as volume increases up to the breakeven point. At breakeven, cost recovery is completed. The *BEP* occurs at a specific volume of production (in units) or a given percent utilization of plant capacity. Figure 5–4 shows the relationship of profit and loss to production volume. In this figure, the *y* axis measures amount of profit or loss. Here we observe the character of the linear system. The line begins at negative profit (or loss). With volume growth, the loss decreases until it reaches zero at the *BEP*. Then it increases linearly throughout the range of positive profits until max profit is achieved at 100 percent of capacity.

Analysis of the Linear Breakeven Model

Two factors must be considered in reaching conclusions about any specific breakeven situation. The first is the production volume position of the BEP. The second is the rate at which profit increases for each additional unit of capacity that can be sold. This second point is repre-

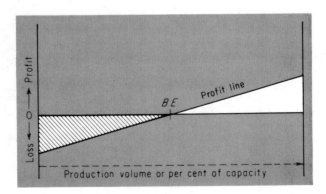

FIGURE 5-4. Profit vs. production volume. (B.E. is the breakeven point.)

184

Managing
Production and
Operations
Systems
Through Their
Life Cycle
Stages

sented by the slope of the line in Fig. 5–4. If the profit line shown in Fig. 5–4 were rotated clockwise so that it fell almost on top of the x axis, very little profit would be obtained as a result of increased use of plant capacity. If the slope of this line were increased, then greater returns could be obtained once demand exceeded the *BEP*. In terms of the figure, this means mechanically rotating it counterclockwise about the *BEP*. At the same time it should be noted that, because of the assumption of linearity, the losses or penalties for operating under the *BEP* also become proportionately greater as we move farther away from the *BEP*. This is more or less true in most practical situations.

Our first concern has to do with the position of the *BEP*. If it is moved to the right, then the organization must operate at a higher level of capacity before it is worthwhile to make the product. Conversely, by reducing the breakeven point volume (moving it to the left), the pressure to secure a larger demand volume is decreased. Decisions with respect to these two criteria can be complex. Notice that in Fig. 5–5 two profit lines are drawn. Each is meant to be descriptive of a result obtained from different production configurations. Alternative A has a lower BEP than alternative B. This makes A more desirable than B with respect to this single criterion (*BEP* volume). But the profit function B has a greater rate of return once the *BEP* has been reached. Alternative B is preferred with respect to this other criterion (slope).

If the volume represented by point a can be generated, then both alternatives yield equal profit. If we can operate at a volume in excess of point a, then alternative B is preferred. If we cannot, then our choice would be alternative A. Fig. 5–6 shows the four different situations that can arise.

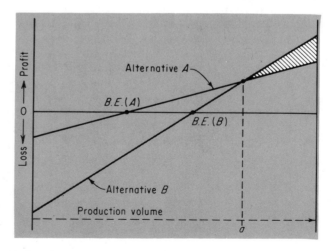

FIGURE 5-5. Profit vs production volume for alternative production configurations A and B. B.E. (A) is the breakeven point for A. B.E. (B) is the breakeven point for B.

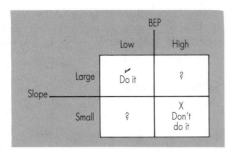

FIGURE 5-6.

Two of the boxes lead to clear-cut decisions. An alternative with a lower *BEP* and higher rate of return slope is the winner. The loser has the reverse set of attributes. What happens when an alternative has a preferred *BEP* coupled with a lower rate of return? The answer can only be obtained by combining the profit and loss function with a probability distribution of demand. This is done by using a decision matrix (see Section 5.2).

The interrelationships of fixed and variable costs, sales volumes, revenues, and profits give rise to situations similar to the ones described above, and shown in Fig. 5–5. Thus, one plan may require a smaller investment than another but produce a product or service of poorer quality, resulting in lower sales volume. In this case, the lower *BEP* is preferred and the rate of return is less critical.

As an alternative, we could decrease the selling price to achieve increased sales volume, but this might decrease the rate of return to an unacceptable point. Also, there are tradeoffs. Often, lower investment processes operate with higher variable costs. We invest in facility improvement to achieve lower variable costs, improve quality, and derive greater market share. Each alternative has its own patterns of interconnected expenditures, costs, and benefits.

**CASE: PER-
SONALIZED
HAND-
HELD
CALCU-
LATORS**

A second-year MBA is convinced that he can help pay for his schooling in the following way. Expensive calculators are brought to class by students. There is perpetual fear of leaving it by mistake and returning to find it gone. The student reasoned that if the calculators had the owner's name engraved on the back, other students would not feel free to take it. Having saved enough money, he is willing to invest it in an engraving machine designed for just such a purpose. He believes he has a good chance of being profitable the first year. Is this reasonable?

DATA:

He intends to be able to process 400 units per month. However, he estimates that expected demand will be 250 units per month. The fixed costs per month for equipment rental is $200. Space rental is $100 per month.

The variable processing costs include materials, which cost 15 cents per unit of work, and labor (his charge) costing 35 cents per unit of work. He intends to charge $2 to personalize a calculator.

QUESTION At what percentage of capacity is the breakeven point achieved? We construct the breakeven chart (see Fig. 5–7).

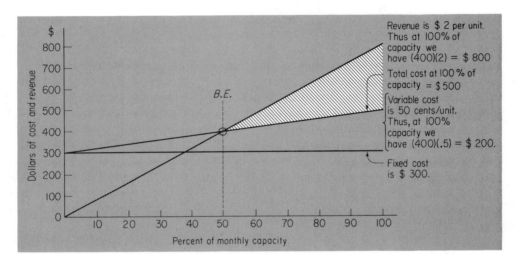

FIGURE 5-7. An example of breakeven analysis for the MBA entrepreneur.

ANSWER Breakeven occurs at 50 percent of capacity, or 200 units. The expected demand was 250 per month. Thus, he expects to make $75 per month personalizing calculators. This is based on:

$$\text{Profit} = (\text{price} - vc)\ \text{volume} - \text{fixed costs}$$
$$\$75 = (\$2 - \$0.5)250 - \$300$$

In addition, the student is charging 35 cents per unit for his labor. This provides him with $87.50 = (250)($0.35) per month, for a total of $162.50 per month. Whether this is enough to warrant his going into business will depend on the quality of his estimates, his expenses, and his other alternatives for earning money.

Breakeven Related to Work Configurations

Much useful perspective about P/OM is available through study of the breakeven chart. Additional factors will appear when we consider the potentials of the flow shop, the job shop, flexible work systems, and projects.

At the outset, we know that the fixed costs associated with designing and setting up a flow shop are much higher than the fixed costs of a job shop (where general-purpose rather than special-purpose equipment prevails). General-purpose equipment is commercially available, whereas special-purpose equipment must be designed to specifications. Also, the movement of materials between equipment is mechanized for the flow shop, whereas it is done mostly by hand in the job shop.

For the higher fixed costs of the flow shop, the manager expects to obtain lower variable costs. The job shop manager must do everything possible to keep the high variable costs under control. If there is sufficient stable demand to warrant investment in flow shop design and if technology exists to deliver low variable costs at the required quality level, then the manager will invest in flow shop design.

The decision to employ flow shop design requires careful analysis of all relevant factors. For example, assume that expensive materials are required per part and that these are the same for either the flow shop or the job shop. Unless the decrease in labor costs per part (as a result of using the flow shop) more than compensates for the greater fixed costs required, the decision will be in favor of the job shop. As another example, say that demand is very elastic with respect to price, and that flow shop design cuts total costs per unit dramatically for relatively high volumes of output. If it can be shown that sufficient demand can be realized and sustained in the face of both existing and potential competition, the flow shop will be chosen.

Flexible systems offer a third choice. The fixed costs are high, but the equipment is not special-purpose. Since linked automation can be operated remotely 24 hours a day and 7 days a week, the high fixed costs can be amortized across a broad productline. This is conditional upon being able to generate demand that will keep the equipment occupied. Flexible equipment is not general-purpose either; it is an association of interrelated equipment with some purpose in mind, like crankshafts, pistons, fast food, or check processing. Once the appropriate software has been written, it can be modified more easily to make or do like things. Therefore, flexible systems are constrained by their focus on a family of activities.

FPS benefit from not having to set up each new task by hand, as in the job shop. The computer takes charge of the changeovers, and this is done without producing defectives, which typically occur during changeover in the job shop. Setup and takedown costs have to be factored into the job shop cost structure; either they have to be amortized and treated as fixed costs, or included as part of the variable costs. These costs do not exist with the flow shop or the FPS.

Breakeven analysis is of use when starting to examine what form of work configuration to employ. To reach capacity decisions, it is also necessary to understand how demand elasticity changes with price and

188

Managing
Production and
Operations
Systems
Through Their
Life Cycle
Stages

quality. Japanese industry started to specialize in flow shops following the MacArthur initiative to rebuild the Japanese economy after World War II. This concentration on flow shops allowed Japaneses export industries the cost advantages gained from great productivity. They also emphasized quality and thereby earned relative price inelasticity (meaning that customers remained loyal in the face of price increases). By reducing prices and spending more than competitors for marketing, Japanese industry was able to capture very large shares of world markets. Yet when petroleum prices skyrocketed (circa 1974), the variable cost advantages began to deteriorate. This cut into the significant fixed cost benefits of flow shop specialization. The Japanese did not pull out of the market, but continued to improve their flow shop configurations.

As a general rule, the flow shop is the preferred production configuration, but special constraints on its use must always be taken into consideration. When the decision is made to use the job shop, the most efficient possible job shop is desired. In Chapters 10 and 11, we discuss the design of flow shops and job shops. We spend more time on job shops, because the skills and knowledge of engineering specialists are needed (and can be justified) in designing the flow shop. However, we do not ignore the design of the flow shop, because the situation often arises where a flow shop design can be put into place for a period of time—the intermittent flow shop. Although it does not have the productivity of a permanent flow shop, it still provides cost leverage when compared to the job shop.

Life cycle planning uses breakeven analysis to study the best startup alternatives. The application requires demand forecasts at given price, promotion, and advertising levels. For the flow shop, long-range forecasts are required; for the job shop, shorter-range forecasts are in order. Most projects are based on contracts, yet estimates are needed to specify completion dates and costs. Breakeven analysis is appropriate for the project to the extent that job shop activities are used to furnish goods and services for various phases of the project.

Linear Breakeven Equations

It is straightforward to translate the graphic breakeven chart into its algebraic equivalent. Some individuals prefer the graphic form; others prefer the mathematical statement. The choice depends upon the use that is to be made of such analyses. When communication with P/OM personnel is required, the graphic approach is generally more effective.

Both methods provide the same solutions to any specific problem— the output volume or percent of capacity used at the *BEP*. The capacity measure is frequently used with the flow shop, which is always designed with a maximum capacity. Capital-intensive industries (such as steel) relate their performance to the percentage of capacity that is utilized. On the other hand, labor-intensive industries (such as check processing) are more likely to use measures of production volume than capacity.

To write the equations, we assign symbol equivalents to the relevant factors:

R = gross revenue per time period T
p = price per unit with the assumption that the market will absorb everything that can be made at the same price
V = number of units made in time period T and therefore sales volume in time period T
FC = fixed costs per period T
vc = variable costs per unit of production
TC = total costs per period T
PR = total profit per period T

The revenue line for period T is given by:

$$R = (p)V$$

The total cost line for period T is equal to:

$$TC = FC + (vc)V$$

Total profit for the interval T is (in terms of volume):

$$PR = R - TC$$
$$= (p)V - FC - (vc)V$$
$$= (p - vc)V - FC$$

EXAMPLE 1. Should we install a conveyor belt? We will use break-even analysis, where the time period T = 1 year.

	Alternative 1 No Conveyor	Alternative 2 Install Conveyor
V	18,000 units per year	18,000 units per year
FC	$10,000 per year	$12,000 per year
vc	$0.50 per unit	$0.45 per unit
p	$2.00 per unit	$2.00 per unit

For alternative 1: (at 100 percent of volume)

Profit = $(2 - 0.50)(18,000) - 10,000 = \$17,000$ per year

For alternative 2: (at 100 percent of volume)

Profit = $(2 - 0.45)(18,000) - 12,000 = \$15,900$ per year

190

Managing
Production and
Operations
Systems
Through Their
Life Cycle
Stages

The breakeven point is easily calculated by setting profit = 0; then [1]

$$V \text{ (breakeven point)} = \frac{FC}{\text{price} - vc}$$

For alternative 1:

$$V \text{ (breakeven point)} = 10,000/(1.5) = 6667 \text{ units}$$

For alternative 2:

$$V \text{ (breakeven point)} = 12,000/(1.55) = 7742 \text{ units}$$

It is a simple matter to convert from units of volume to percentage or fraction of capacity. For example, *BEP* as a fraction of total capacity for alternative 1 is 6667/18,000 = 0.37; for alternative 2, it is 7742/18,000 = 0.43. We note that the profit at full capacity utilization for alternative 1 promises $1,100 more profit than alternative 2. Also, in terms of the *BEP,* we prefer alternative 1 because it has a lower value. So there is no doubt that we should select Alternative 1.

EXAMPLE 2. Should we buy machine A or machine B? We employ breakeven analysis where the time period T = 3 months or 1 quarter.

	Alternative 1 Machine A	Alternative 2 Machine B
V	5000 units per quarter	5000 units per quarter
FC	$2500.00 per quarter	$3500.00 per quarter
vc	$0.50 per unit	$0.10 per unit
p	$2.00 per unit	$2.00 per unit

First, we test the profit for each alternative at an estimated 3,000 units per quarter, which is 60 percent utilization of capacity. For alternative 1:

$$\text{Profit} = (2 - 0.50)(3,000) - 2,500 = \$2,000 \text{ per quarter}$$

and for alternative 2:

$$\text{Profit} = (2 - 0.10)(3,000) - 3,500 = \$2,200 \text{ per quarter}$$

---

[1]This relationship is valid only when price $- vc \geq 0$, i.e. when price $\geq vc$. Ordinarily, it is assumed that pricing follows an analysis of costs and therefore no competent manager would accept a price that does not cover the variable costs with room to spare. Consider, however, the plight of even partially regulated industries, such as transportation and utilities, where operating costs could grow faster than changes in rate structure. The worst possible breakeven value would be infinite, arising when price = vc. Negative breakeven volumes have no meaning.

Next, for full-capacity utilization, for alternative 1:

$$\text{Profit} = (2 - 0.50)(5,000) - 2,500 = \$5,000 \text{ per quarter}$$

and for alternative 2:

$$\text{Profit} = (2 - 0.10)(5,000) - 2,500 = \$6,000 \text{ per quarter}$$

Thus, alternative 2's profit is preferred both at the point of 60 percent estimated utilization and at full utilization. The breakeven points are as follows:

for alternative 1:

$$V \text{ (breakeven point)} = \frac{2,500}{1.5} = 1,667 \text{ units or } \frac{1,667}{5,000} = 0.333$$

for alternative 2:

$$V \text{ (breakeven point)} = \frac{3,500}{1.9} = 1,842 \text{ units or } \frac{1,842}{5,000} = 0.370$$

Alternative 1 has a superior breakeven point, but it does not have better profit, even at 60 percent utilization. The conflict between expected profit and *BEP* advantage must be resolved by the decision model approach, discussed in Section 5.2.

Analysis of Nonlinear Breakeven Model

The anticipated volume of operations is critical in the determination of a production system's design. If the market is such that at a certain price unlimited demand exists, then for these linear systems we would always operate as far to the right as our plant capacity permits.

In reality, at some point linearity ceases to be a reasonable description of the market's responses. Increased volume can be obtained only by a decrease in price or by an increase in promotional and selling costs. These two situations are shown in Figs. 5–8 and 5–9. The combination of these effects is illustrated in Fig. 5–10.

There is another effect that might have to be taken into account—namely, the decreasing per unit costs of production which The Boston Consulting Group has found with increasing output experience. Part of the cost advantage is derived from economies of scale. Another part is derived from the learning phenomenon, where productivity increases with experience. But there is an overall systems effect as well, such that marketing, distribution, and production efficiencies benefit one another. The result reported by The Boston Consulting Group is approximately a 25 percent decrease in unit costs for each doubling of production output. If such an effect is present, the shape of the total cost curve in Fig. 5–10

192

Managing
Production and
Operations
Systems
Through Their
Life Cycle
Stages

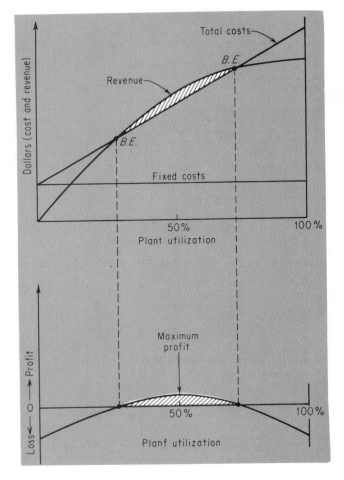

FIGURE 5-8. Breakeven chart with the assumption of a decelerating revenue as product price is lowered to achieve full plant utilization.

will be altered, perhaps enough to look like the revenue curve shown in Fig. 5–11. It is then possible to derive a situation with the same breakeven consequences as strictly linear functions: Produce as much as you can, since there is only one breakeven point.

In each of these cases, there is an operating volume where profit is maximized. (Fig. 5–11 represents a situation where maximum profit could occur at or above 100 percent capacity utilization.)

It is P/OM's responsibility to design and run a work configuration that will yield maximum profit. However, the problem of doing this successfully is complicated far beyond anything that a breakeven chart can show.

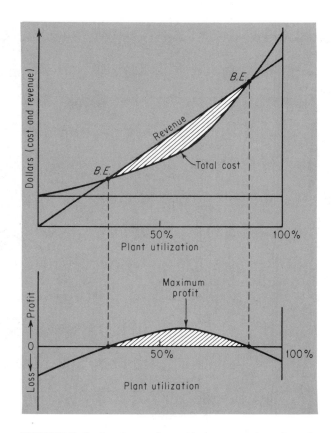

FIGURE 5-9. Breakeven chart with the assumption of accelerating promotional costs required to achieve full plant utilization. Note that the maximum profit point has shifted from 50 percent utilization (Fig. 5-8) to a higher value of plant utilization.

A danger of simple abstractions is that they tend to hide major difficulties. Hence, we warn ourselves to proceed with caution.

First of all, the breakeven chart, even when couched in nonlinear form, represents only one product. Most companies have mixed-model and product-mix decisions. The line consists of a number of different items or services. These must share resources, including capital and management time. The breakeven chart is difficult to apply when such complications are introduced. In addition, a specific period of time is embodied in each breakeven chart. If we assume that the company can sell 5 million units over a five-year period but only 10,000 in the first year, then the result of a five-year analysis may be quite appealing. But on the basis of a one-year analysis, the product would be rejected. But cost estimates applied to a five-year period might not be sufficiently believable to allow management to act on them. Other unexpected costs can arise. For ex-

194
Managing
Production and
Operations
Systems
Through Their
Life Cycle
Stages

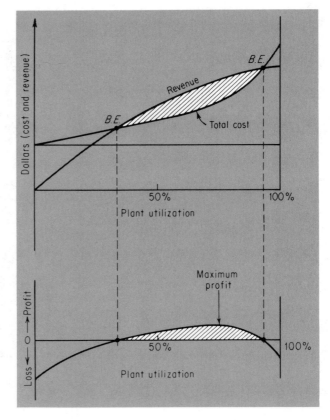

FIGURE 5-10. Breakeven chart with both assumptions—that is, decelerating revenue and accelerating costs.

ample, if the company overproduces, overstock units could be sold only by reducing price. If the unsold units are held in inventory, they will create additional costs, such as storage, insurance, and carrying costs.

For each situation some maximum profit (optimal) situation exists. Whether it can be found or not is another matter. But only with the nonlinear breakeven chart does this fundamental optimization objective of management appear. The traditional breakeven approach overlooks this particular aspect of the problem.

PROBLEM
SET

1. With reference to Fig. 1–5, a breakeven chart cannot be constructed for product *B* based on a price of $0.58 per unit and a maximum production volume of 8 million units. Describe what is feasible.

2. Discuss the following observation: The breakeven chart can represent only one product at a time. For most companies, decisions must include the fact that a product mix is involved. The line consists of a number

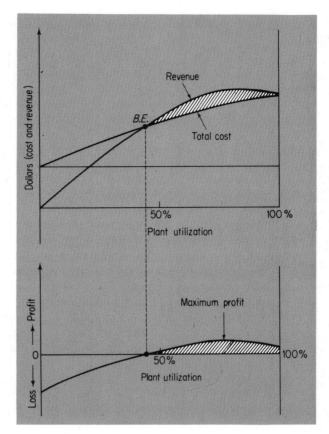

FIGURE 5-11. Breakeven chart with decelerating revenue and costs.

of different items or services. These must share resources, including capital and management time. The breakeven chart is difficult to utilize when such additional complications are encountered.

Answer: The problem of assigning fixed costs among different items in the product line is at the root of this difficulty. Accounting for fixed costs must be done whether or not breakeven analysis is used. The application of breakeven for one product at a time will provide results that are partially consistent with management's view of fixed-cost allocations; but it violates the system's view.

3. Discuss the following observation: A specific period of time is embodied in each breakeven chart. If we assume that a company can sell 5 million units over a five-year period but only 10,000 in the first year, then the result of a five-year analysis may be quite appealing. On the basis of a one-year analysis, the product would be rejected. But cost

196

Managing
Production and
Operations
Systems
Through Their
Life Cycle
Stages

estimates applied to a five-year period might not be sufficiently believable to allow management to act on them. Further, unexpected costs can arise. For example, if the company overproduces, overstock units could be sold only by reducing the price. If the unsold units are held in inventory, they will create additional costs, such as storage, insurance, and carrying costs.

4. Describe situations in which nonlinear analysis might be required for the breakeven chart.

Answer: It is rare that the per unit profit of an item can be held constant over a wide range in demand. If it is considered desirable to increase sales beyond a certain point, it becomes necessary to incur some additional expenses. This creates nonlinearity in the variable-cost sector. Sometimes it is more advantageous to achieve the same effect by lowering prices, thus creating a nonlinear revenue line. Demand-stimulating devices such as quantity discounts or advertising allowances are other frequent causes of nonlinearity in the system. A less obvious cause of nonlinear relations in the breakeven chart arises as a result of a change in the fixed costs of the process. As an example, assume that the demand for the product increases sharply. At first it is necessary only to increase total expenditures for labor and raw materials, while holding per unit expenditures constant; the variable costs associated with increased production are unchanged. However, as full capacity is approached, a decrease in efficiency occurs. Such factors as overtime premiums and overutilization of machinery create an increase in per unit variable costs. If still more production is required, a new machine may be purchased or a new plant must be constructed. This will alter the fixed-cost component and produce nonlinear discontinuities. For a system without nonlinearities, rational management would attempt to increase production without limit, since increased production would always mean increased profit.

5. The Gamma Company has engaged a management consultant to analyze and improve its operations. Her major recommendation is to conveyorize the production floor. This would represent a sizable investment for the Gamma Company. In order to determine whether or not the idea is feasible, a breakeven analysis will be utilized. The situation is as follows: The cost of the conveyor will be $200,000, to be depreciated on a straight-line basis over a 10-year period—that is, $20,000 per year. The reduction in operating cost is estimated at $0.25 per unit. Each unit sells for $2.00. The sales manager estimates that, on the basis of previous years, Gamma can expect a sales volume of 100,000 units. This represents 100 percent of capacity. Present yearly contribution to fixed costs is $100,000. Present variable-cost rate is $0.50. Should Gamma install this conveyor?

6. The Omega Corporation is considering the advantages of automating a part of its production line. The company's financial statement follows.

Omega Corporation

Total Sales		$40,000,000
Direct labor	$12,000,000	
Indirect labor	2,000,000	
Direct materials	8,000,000	
Depreciation	1,000,000	
Taxes	500,000	
Insurance	400,000	
Sales costs	1,500,000	
Total expenses		$25,400,000
Net profit		$14,600,000

The report is based on the production and sale of 100,000 units. The operations manager believes that with an additional investment of $5 million the variable costs can be reduced by 30 percent. The same output levels and qualities would be maintained. Using five-year, straight-line depreciation ($1,000,000) per year, construct a breakeven chart. If the company insists on a 20 percent return on investment, should Omega use flexible systems? (Discuss all costs.)

7. a. List as many variable costs as you can.
   b. List as many fixed costs as you can.
   c. To what extent are accounting data available in various organizations with respect to such items?
   d. What is overhead cost or burden? How should it be treated in a breakeven analysis?

Section 5.2 The Breakeven Decision Model

We know what breakeven analysis is about, but what is a **decision model**? It is a basic model that helps a manager decide what to do and it is applicable to all managerial decision problems. It is the product of the intensely studied field of decision theory. In this section we tie together breakeven analysis and decision theory. Capacity planning when demand is uncertain is the purpose of bringing these two subjects together.

Decision Theory

Every decision situation is composed of five basic elements.

1. Strategies or plans constructed of controllable variables. Variables are problem factors that can take on different values. Some variables have only two states; for example, a switch is either on or off. This is called a binary variable. Other variables exist within a closed range, such as time of day, which runs from 00: 01 to 24: 00. Some

198

Managing
Production and
Operations
Systems
Through Their
Life Cycle
Stages

variables cannot take on negative values—for example, age or hardness. Profit is positive and loss is negative profit. Certain variables are limited to discrete scales (only integer values can occur); for example, the number of students in a class. Others, such as temperature and weight, are continuous. Independent and dependent variables are defined on p. 202.

2. States of nature composed of noncontrollable variables.

3. Outcomes, which are observations of results that occur when a specific strategy is employed and a particular state of nature exists. Outcomes are dependent variables; their costs and qualities are dependent on what the other (independent) variables are doing.

4. Forecasts of the probabilities (likelihood) that each state of nature will occur.

5. The decision criterion that dictates the way in which the information derived in items 1 through 4 above will be used to select a single plan to follow.

Decision theory applies to all types of situations, including P/OM decisions. It was recognized long ago that P/OM decisions often are treated as being deterministic, although they are affected by variability. The decision matrix allows probability distributions to be used when warranted.

Further, lacking a comprehensive framework for the consolidation and organization of information, the tendency was to pile fact upon fact, and method upon method. The result was fragmentation (analysis) and not integration (synthesis). Present-day practitioners recognize the role that decision theory can play in relating the parts to each other.

Analysis and Synthesis

The key word is *synthesis*. Over the course of many years, the multitude of decision problems that comprise P/OM have been identified and their special characteristics have been analyzed. Analysis is the process of breaking down a system into parts that can be more easily examined. Synthesis is the reverse procedure; the parts are integrated to form the whole. Both procedures are essential if the solution to a problem is to be obtained and implemented. We know a lot about analysis, but less about synthesis. The decision model brings all of the decision elements (the five listed above) together and provides synthesis.

Strategies

Strategies are alternative plans for achieving outcomes or objectives, such as more profit, higher output rate, and lower cost. Strategies are often called actions because they are composed of steps that can be taken by management. For example, either install a conveyor belt or maintain the present materials handling system. Strategies must be constructed of controllable variables, or they will not serve management.

States of Nature

States of nature describe those factors in a situation that affect the expected results of a strategy. It is assumed that these variables are not under the manager's control, although good management finds ways to assume control in certain instances. Weather, political events, and the state of the economy are three situations where it is difficult to assume control. Management has more responsibility with such states of nature as machine failure, percent of defectives, price changes by suppliers, invention of new materials, process innovations, shifts in consumer demand levels, labor turnover rates, and absenteeism. For example, alter failure rates by selecting reliable equipment, or by using preventive maintenance. Both are strategic functions that provide some control over failure rates. Similarly, salary level (a strategic variable) can alter turnover and absenteeism, but the control is indirect and incomplete.

A **probability distribution** is the only way to forecast which state of nature will occur in a given situation. There is an observed or estimated likelihood that each state will occur, say, x times in one hundred trials. That likelihood is measured as the probability of occurrence of the state of nature. There is a 0.50 probability that the state of nature "heads" will occur with each toss of a true coin. [We can represent this as p (heads) $= 0.50$.] The meteorologist just announced a 30 percent probability of precipitation tomorrow—i.e., p (rain) $= 0.30$. Figure 5–12 illustrates a five-state probability distribution where state of nature, A, has only one chance in a hundred trials of appearing—$p_A = 0.01$—whereas state of nature C has the highest probability $p_C = 0.40$. The sum of these probabilities will be 1.00, indicating that one of these states of nature must occur, thus: $p_A + p_B + p_C + p_D + p_E = 1$.

When we are able to ignore states of nature, we call this class of decision problem **decision making under certainty (DMUC)**. Some typical examples of production systems models based on the assumption of certainty are these:

1. Machine loading models which assign various jobs to different machine centers
2. Sequencing these jobs through specific facilities
3. Determining an optimal product mix
4. Optimal assignment of people to jobs
5. Optimal traffic plan for shipping goods
6. Optimal production runs; that is, how many units to produce at one time

200
Managing
Production and
Operations
Systems
Through Their
Life Cycle
Stages

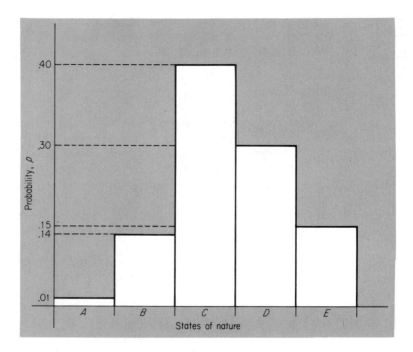

FIGURE 5-12. A *forecast* for the likelihoods of states of nature *A* through *E*.

Exceptions exist for each of the five situations listed above, but the majority of cases are solved without considering uncontrollable variables and therefore states of nature. Even though many problems seem to fall into the DMUC category, the assumption of certainty cannot be taken for granted. Cataloguing the uncontrollable features of a problem may be vital to the success of the decision-maker.

For problems where uncertainty exists, the planner must try to determine the relevant states of nature. Groupthink can help. Unless some kind of objective, formal procedure is used, there is no opportunity for group participation. Oversights can be costly. Capacity planning, where demand is uncertain, is one such problem.

Setting Up the Decision Matrix

Strategies are symbolically represented by S_i, where i can take on any value 1 through n. Thus, if $n = 2$, we have only two strategies; if $n = 5$, we have five strategies. States of nature are represented by N_j, where j can take on any values 1 through m. When $m = 1$, each company strategy produces a unique result; that is, DMUC. It is equivalent to saying that no matter what happens in the environment, the same outcome will result from using a specific strategy. When the variables (noncontrollable) can combine in two different ways, then $m = 2$. A particular strategy and a specific state of nature produce a unique set of results called an outcome, O_{ij}. This is the outcome for the ith strategy and the jth state of nature. We observe, measure, and record only those results that are of interest.

P/OM objectives determine what is of interest. For example, a product design S_1 operating under a given set of environmental conditions N_1 will fail after a stated number of hours. If we wish to select the design that has the longest life, then "time to failure" is the outcome of interest. Other possible outcomes include quality of performance; amount of maintenance; number of returns; plant capacity used; amount of materials, labor, and energy consumed; and contribution to profit.

Below, we present an example of an outcome matrix where four design strategies are being evaluated under five different type-of-use conditions. The generality of the matrix is apparent. In the form that it is written, the strategies could just as well describe such diverse situations as the best way to lay out the office or the choice of an optimal code system for a catalogue. The states of nature would describe relevant noncontrollable factors applicable to each case. For every intersection, an outcome measure must be obtained that describes the performance of the chosen strategy.

	N_1	N_2	N_3	N_4	N_5
S_1	3	5	4	2	8
S_2	5	3	2	4	6
S_3	4	4	4	4	4
S_4	4	5	4	2	8

Assume the objective is to choose that design which promises the longest expected lifetime of use. The (4×5) matrix produces 20 cells or intersections. At every intersection an entry will be made that describes the average lifetime of the particular design, operating under specific conditions. Outcomes are obtained in three different ways:

1. By means of estimates and guesses
2. By observation, laboratory experimentation, engineering data, and so on
3. By a knowledge of relationships that have previously been observed to apply (i.e., a theory)

All three methods are common, and combinations can be used. (We are not discussing the means by which a choice is to be made between strategies.) Outcomes relate only to what will happen when a particular strategy is used and a specific state of nature has occurred.

The controllable variables of a strategy may be representable in numerical terms. The same applies to the noncontrollable variables. A math-

202

Managing
Production and
Operations
Systems
Through Their
Life Cycle
Stages

ematical function is used to relate these two kinds of variables and to derive the outcomes they will produce. In mathematical terminology, outcomes are called **dependent variables**. The controllable and noncontrollable variables are called **independent variables**. As before, the outcomes are represented by O_{ij}, where i is the particular strategy used and j is one of the states of nature that can occur. Let us write this symbolically:

$$O_{ij} = f(S_i, N_j)$$

We read this as follows: The dependent variable O_{ij} is a function of the independent variables S_i and N_j. A critical question concerns the nature of the actual function (f). To explain it requires a specific model. For example, a hypothetical relationship might be as follows:

$$O_{ij} = S_j N_j$$

If S_i were a variable length and N_j a variable width, then O_{ij} is a measure of area.

The profit or market share values of alternative strategies for product or service plans are not easily measured. Neither are plant location plans, process design plans, or most of the other long-term P/OM problems. Engineering, inventory, and scheduling problems, on the other hand, do fit this pattern. A great number of decision situations can be resolved within a mathematical framework. For example, we use the mathematical description of the breakeven decision model.

Adding Forecasts to the Decision Matrix

To begin, we identify all the relevant states of nature. Then we forecast the likelihood of occurrence for each of the states of nature. The forecast completes the decision matrix.

Assume, for example, that the manager is concerned with the costs of four possible ways of scheduling production (strategies 1, 2, 3, 4). The costs relate to how a number of different items are sequenced through machine centers and how the size of the production runs used affect the efficiency of these operations. States of nature N_1 through N_5 are five different patterns of demand for the various items which include all demand patterns that could possibly arise. The forecast $\{P_j\}$ for each demand pattern has also been supplied. The decision matrix might be like that shown in Table 5–1.

It appears that a complex relationship describes the way in which the controllable variables interact with the noncontrollable variables to produce outcomes. The costs of overstock, carrying stock, understock, setting up equipment, and idle facilities would be interacting in a variety of ways.

TABLE 5-1 DECISION MATRIX OF WEEKLY COSTS FOR ALTERNATIVE SCHEDULING STRATEGIES (in thousands of dollars)

State of nature:	N_i	N_1	N_2	N_3	N_4	N_5
Forecast:	p_i	0.1	0.2	0.1	0.4	0.2
Strategy	1	10	12	14	12	8
Strategy	2	8	12	16	14	10
Strategy	3	16	14	12	14	15
Strategy	4	14	14	14	14	14

Twenty different computations were required to produce this matrix. In addition, the forecast for the five states of nature had to be derived. The first forecasting step would be to identify the states of nature by specifying the range of demand levels that might occur for each item.

What is the probability of each demand level? Study of what has happened in the past may help. Should observations be taken over the total year, a particular season, or a particular month? Assume that 50 weeks of observations are available, and have been sorted into their appropriate classes, as follows:

Demand Pattern	Observed Frequency	Probability
N_1	5	0.1
N_2	10	0.2
N_3	5	0.1
N_4	20	0.4
N_5	10	0.2
	50	1.0

How believable are these probabilities? We have a high degree of confidence in our forecast if we know that the system that causes the occurrence of the states of nature is unchanging, and that our sample provides a good description of the relative frequencies of the states of nature. Both conditions are required. We could have an accurate description of what happened in the past, but the past may not be indicative of the future. Assuming that the fundamental conditions from which the forecast is derived remain unchanged, that system is stable. Stability is a vital concept for all management decision making that uses a forecast. Stability is more likely to exist for a short rather than a long time interval.

Statistical quality control (SQC) is one of the most powerful P/OM tools. It can inform the manager of the fact that a once stable system has become unstable. It can be used to find out if a startup system is initially stable. When the system is stable, the manager knows what range of demands, performances, behaviors or output qualities to expect. The stable system cannot be improved without changing the system itself; that is, the causal factors that drive it must be altered. (See pp. 268–269).

204

Managing
Production and
Operations
Systems
Through Their
Life Cycle
Stages

What should we know about states of nature? The main considerations are these:

1. How many states of nature (N_j) are relevant?
2. Can we identify all relevant N_j's?
3. Can we estimate the N_j's probabilities of occurrence?
4. Are these probabilities stable?

We now have the information needed to proceed with the final step of the decision process. With strategies, states of nature, outcomes, and forecast assembled in a decision matrix, what do we do?

Decision-Making under Risk (DMUR)

If two or more N_j's are relevant, and if all these relevant N_j's can be identified, and if the forecast is believed, then decision-making under risk (DMUR) exists. Each state N_j has a probability p_j of occurring. Then the sum of all p_js must be 1. In notation, we write:

$$p_1 + p_2 + p_3 + p_4 + p_5 + \ldots + p_j + \ldots + p_m = 1.00$$

If there are five relevant states of nature, then $m = 5$.

When a problem conforms to the specifications of DMUR it must be resolved by using averages or expected values. This satisfies the fact that over a period of time, the ups and downs of the system will average out to produce the result given by the expected value. Let us use the information presented in the decision matrix on p. 203 to reach a decision. We obtain the expected value, EV_j, for each strategy, i, as follows:

$$EV_i = p_1 O_{i1} + p_2 O_{i2} + \ldots + p_j O_{ij} + \ldots + p_m O_{im}$$

For example, $p_1 O_{11} + p_2 O_{12} + p_3 O_{13} + p_4 O_{14} + p_5 O_{15}$ equals the expected value for the first strategy. Thus, we are saying that the average value of the ith strategy will be equal to the sum of the products of each row entry multiplied by its appropriate p_j. In this way, we derive:

$$EV_1 = 1.0 + 2.4 + 1.4 + 4.8 + 1.6 = 11.2$$

$$EV_2 = 0.8 + 2.4 + 1.6 + 5.6 + 2.0 = 12.4$$

$$EV_3 = 1.6 + 2.8 + 1.2 + 5.6 + 3.0 = 14.2$$

$$EV_4 = 1.4 + 2.8 + 1.4 + 5.6 + 2.8 = 14.0$$

The scheduling strategy S_4 is invariant (insensitive) to demand patterns; the same outcome (14) results for each state of nature. By studying the abstract decision matrix, we do not find out why this is so. We need an explanation of what constitutes S_4. The answer could be as simple as letting the foreman and his dispatchers determine schedule, subject to a budget limit of $14,000. If our objective is to use the plan that provides the lowest total weekly cost, then S_1 is the choice to make.

Examples of DMUR-type problems are machine breakdowns and process failures, rates of producing defectives, frequency of complaints, distribution of delivery intervals (lead times), variations of worker productivity, and the analysis of stable consumer demand systems. DMUR methods are not to be used when volatility and instability characterize the occurrence of the events you want to forecast. This might apply to consumer demand for a new service, new product consumer demand (where the new product represents a substantial innovation and there is nothing comparable to utilize as a guide), speculative real estate ventures, developments in architectural style and available building materials, technological changes, stock market indexes, wage rate demands and union attitudes, and the state of the economy.

Decision Matrix and the Breakeven Chart

Now we can tie together the decision matrix and the breakeven model. We use a service industry for illustration: airline transport. What kind of plane should we choose? The problem involves capacity planning, cost analysis, and demand analysis. The latter is based on prices charged and qualities perceived by airline customers. This is a legitimate and challenging P/OM problem, and one in which forecasting has tended to be neglected. Until the mid-1970s, airlines tended to make equipment decisions based on the supposed competitive advantage of being first with the newest technology. The assumption that with newer, faster, and bigger equipment demand would always rise to exceed the breakeven point turned out to be incorrect. The supply of seats began to grow faster than the demand for them. A sharp rise in petroleum prices made the airlines acutely conscious of the need to invest in technology that could be operated at low cost per passenger mile flown.

CASE: ALPHA AIRLINES

Various equipment capacity strategies exist for the airlines. Suppose that Alpha Airlines wants to determine whether it should convert from jumbo jets (like the 747, flown in the 1980s) to more economical wide-body planes, which are available in the 1990s.

The Alpha Airlines operations manager draws up break even charts for these alternatives. Fig. 5–13 holds for 1980 jet planes. With the conversion to a 1990 fleet of jet aircraft, Fig. 5–14 applies. Table 5–2 presents hypothetical data used to construct Figs. 5–13 and 5–14. The time period is assumed to be one year.

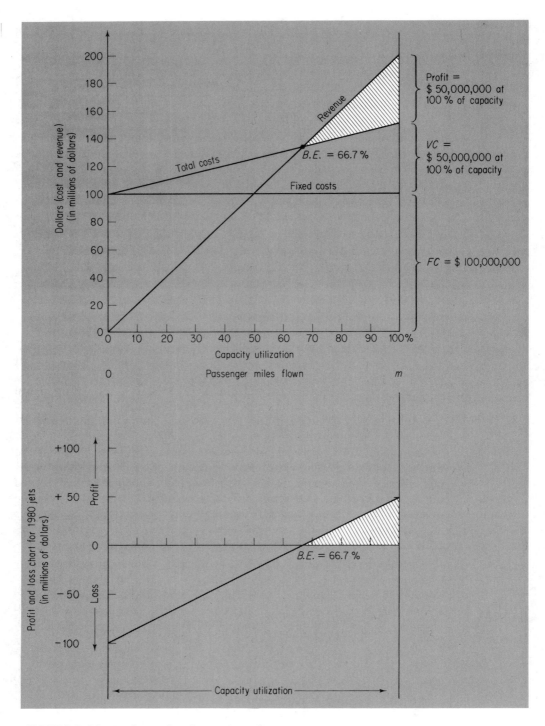

FIGURE 5-13. Breakeven chart for 1980's jet fleet.

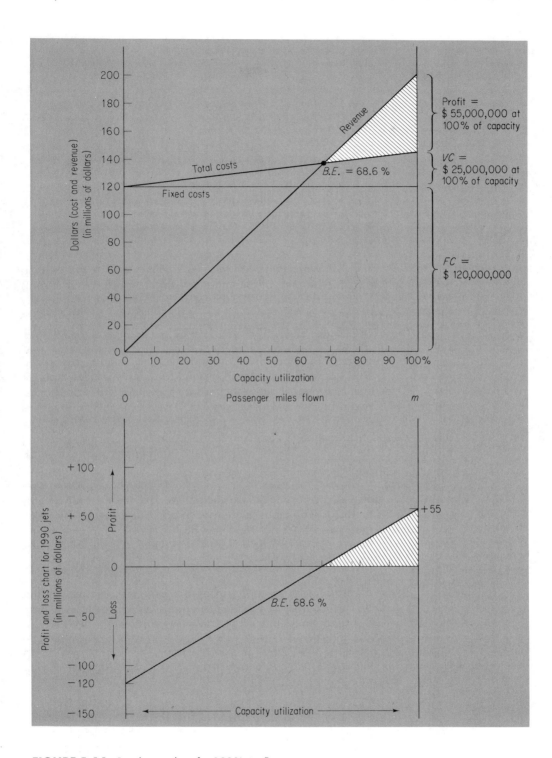

FIGURE 5-14. Breakeven chart for 1990's jet fleet.

208

Managing
Production and
Operations
Systems
Through Their
Life Cycle
Stages

TABLE 5-2

	1980s Jet Fleet	1990s Jet Fleet
Fixed costs*	$100,000,000	$120,000,000
Variable costs†	500,000	250,000
Unit revenue† (or price)	2,000,000	2,000,000

*Fixed costs include ground installations and are depreciated on an annual basis.

†Based on 1 percent (a unit) of capacity utilization, where capacity is measured in terms of passenger miles flown in a year. *Note:* It is assumed that both jet fleet configurations have the same total capacity and unit revenues. If customers prefer one plane to another, demand level would be affected rather than price.

From Fig. 5–13, we observe that the breakeven point for the existing 1980 jet fleet is 66.7 percent of full-capacity usage. Figure 5–14 reveals that the breakeven point for the 1990 jet fleet is 68.6 percent of full-capacity utilization. We emphasize that these are hypothetical constructs. The airlines run at much lower breakeven percentages ranging from 30 to 45 percent. (See Problem 10 at the end of this section.)

Figure 5–13, and the table data, show that Alpha Airlines' amortized investment in 1980 aircraft and related ground facilities is smaller than for the 1990 jet fleet. However, its variable costs of operating flights are higher with the 1980 jets than it would be with the 1990 equipment. By converting to a 1990 fleet (Fig. 5–14), Alpha Airlines will increase its fixed costs, but it will reduce its variable costs. As an additional point, we are not considering mixtures of 1980 and 1990 jets, although such combinations make sense and would ordinarily be analyzed.

We have shown that the present 1980s jet fleet achieves a lower breakeven point than the proposed 1990s equipment. This means that a satisfactory "load factor" will be higher if the conversion is approved. This result would disturb most executives in the airline industry. *Load factor* is the airline industry term for percent of capacity flown by paying passengers. A well-managed airline has a ratio of load factor to *BEP* that is well above 1.

At the same time, note that as compensation for this poorer *BEP*, the 1990 jet aircraft produce larger marginal returns on profit. This means that if Alpha Airlines can operate at higher passenger (and cargo) loads than the *BEP*, greater profit can be made by converting the fleet to 1990 equipment. The reason that the new equipment raised the *BEP* is that the total cost line for 1980 was lower than that for 1990, in spite of the 1990 operating cost advantages. The 1980 fixed costs were sufficiently lower than the 1990 fixed costs.

The example has been purposely set up to create a conflict (see Fig. 5–6). Which should be chosen, the lower *BEP* or the higher rate of return? We cannot answer this question because something is still missing from this analysis. A forecast is required for the various levels of demand for seats and for aircraft miles to be flown. Forecasts are almost always needed to make good capacity decisions—for example, to provide estimates of public demand for a service such as health care or to estimate sales volume in the private sector for a new laser printer. Both cases are related to decisions about optimal production capacities and the kinds of process configurations (1980 vs. 1990 planes) to be used.

With some care, we determine that the probability of annual customer demand is as shown in Table 5–3.

We have assumed that the demand probabilities are independent of the type of plane flown. If preferences exist, the higher levels of capacity utilization would be favored by larger probabilities. We shall apply the same probability distribution to both 1980 and 1990 aircraft. This assumption might not stand up in reality (see Problem 11 at the end of this section). We will consider its effect below.

A different amount of profit is associated with each level of demand. This amount of profit can be read from the breakeven charts (revenue minus total costs) or directly from the accompanying profit and loss charts. Thus, from Fig. 5–13 at 0 percent demand, there is a loss of $100 million. At 100 percent capacity, there is a profit of $50 million. Relate the probability distribution to the profit at each demand level D by multiplying profit at D times the probability of D. Adding up these products for all demand levels, we obtain the average (or expected) profit for the given strategy. As derived in Table 5–4, the expected profit for Alpha's 1980 fleet of jets is $9.5 million.

We know that the *BEP* for 1980 jets is 66.7 percent. By multiplying columns (1) and (3), we can determine the expected (or average) demand that the probability distribution implies. Ignoring the values of demand associated with 0 probability, we calculate the expected value of this irregular distribution to be equal to a load factor of about 73 percent, i.e., 0.05(40%) + 0.10(50%) + 0.15(60%) + 0.20(70%) + 0.25(80%) + 0.20(90%) + 0.05(100%) = 73 percent. Consulting the breakeven chart for 1980 jets (Fig. 5–13), we can measure the profit at 73 percent capacity utilization and determine that it is $9.5 million.

TABLE 5-3

Demand Level D	Probability of Demand Level D
40% of capacity	0.05
50% of capacity	0.10
60% of capacity	0.15
70% of capacity	0.20
80% of capacity	0.25
90% of capacity	0.20
100% of capacity	0.05
	1.00

210

Managing
Production and
Operations
Systems
Through Their
Life Cycle
Stages

TABLE 5-4 COMPUTATION OF EXPECTED PROFIT FOR 1980 JETS

(1) Demand D	(2) Profit at Level D (in millions of dollars)	(3) Probability of D	(2) × (3) (Profit)(Probability)
0%	−100	0	0
10	−85	0	0
20	−70	0	0
30	−55	0	0
40	−40	0.05	−2
50	−25	0.10	−2.5
60	−10	0.15	−1.5
70	+5	0.20	+1.0
80	+20	0.25	+5.0
90	+35	0.20	+7.0
100	+50	0.05	+2.5
		1.00	+9.5

Expected profit = $9,500,000

Turning to 1990 jets, we perform the same kind of calculations. Consulting the breakeven chart for the 1990 jet fleet (Fig. 5–14), we measure the profit at 73 percent capacity utilization and determine that it is $7.75 million. This expected profit is calculated in Table 5–5.

Based on this analysis, we recommend that Alpha Airlines retain its fleet of 1980 jets. The expected profit with 1980 jets is greater than the expected profit with 1990 jets. Management should note, however, that this decision is sensitive to the probability of demand. If 1990 jets are more attractive to enough customers, the results can change dramatically. For example, see

TABLE 5-5 COMPUTATION OF EXPECTED PROFIT FOR 1990 JETS

(1) Demand (D)	(2) Profit at Level D (in millions of dollars)	(3) Probability of D	(2) × (3) (Profit) × (Probability)	(1) × (3) (Demand) × (Probability)
0%	−120	0	0	0
10	−102.5	0	0	0
20	−85	0	0	0
30	−67.5	0	0	0
40	−50	0.05	−2.50	2
50	−32.5	0.10	−3.25	5
60	−15	0.15	−2.25	9
70	+2.5	0.20	+0.50	14
80	+20	0.25	+5.00	20
90	+37.5	0.20	+7.50	18
100	+55	0.05	+2.75	5
		1.00	+7.75	73

Expected profit = $7,750,000
Expected demand = 73 percent

Table 5–6. The probability of 40 percent demand has been decreased by 0.05, and the probability of 100 percent demand has been increased by that amount. As a result of this change, the expected profit of the 1990 jet fleet rises to $13 million even though the expected demand has increased to only 76 percent. Alpha Airlines choice is now to change over to the 1990 jets.

Management should be on the lookout for other changes in conditions that might alter the decision. For example, there could be shifts in total customer demand or in route preferences, or in technology which could lower fixed costs, thereby changing the recommendation.

A breakeven chart such as that in Fig. 5–15 can provide useful comparative insights about the interaction of factors that lead to the selection of one strategy over another. These insights reflect the classifications of fixed costs, variable costs, revenues and demand probabilities. With the addition of forecasting, the breakeven model has become a unifying decision model.

This approach overrides the problem of what to do when one strategy has a better *BEP*, but a poorer marginal rate of return, than another strategy (see Fig. 5–6). Flow shop conditions can be tested against job shop conditions to determine which work configuration should be used. The forecast removes the need for traditional breakeven analysis. This is true because all decision-makers have in mind an estimate of the likelihood that the company will operate above or below that point. Without this

TABLE 5-6   COMPUTATION OF EXPECTED PROFIT FOR 1990 JETS (With Modified Probability Distribution)

(1) Demand (D)	(2) Profit at Level D (millions of dollars)	(3) Probability of D	(2) × (3) (Profit) × (Probability)	(1) × (3) (Demand) × (Probability)
0%	−120	0	0	0
10	−102.5	0	0	0
20	− 85	0	0	0
30	− 67.5	0	0	0
40	− 50	0.00	0	0
50	− 32.5	0.10	− 3.25	5
60	− 15	0.15	− 2.25	9
70	+ 2.5	0.20	+ 0.50	14
80	+ 20	0.25	+ 5.00	20
90	+ 37.5	0.20	+ 7.50	18
100	+ 55	0.10	+ 5.50	10
		1.00	+ 13.00	76

Expected profit = $13,000,000
Expected demand = 76 percent

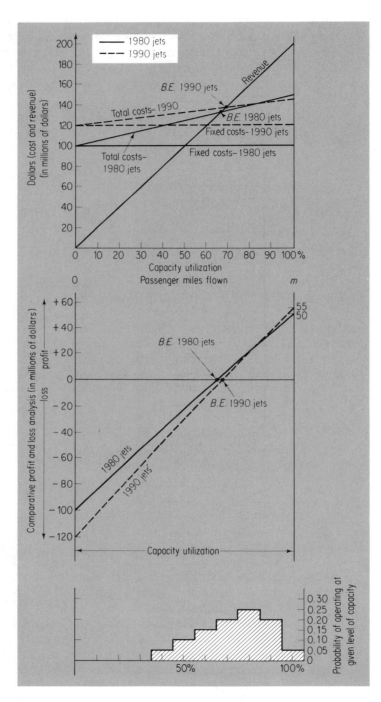

FIGURE 5-15. A comparative breakeven chart for 1980 jets versus 1990 jets.

estimate, the breakeven point is meaningless. Our method has merged the *BEP* and the marginal rate of return into a single problem.

Flow Shop Air Travel: An Example

What constitutes a flow shop in the airline situation? The ideal would be a conveyor belt that takes the passenger to a capsule which takes off immediately for the required destination. Less ideal, but still in the right direction, is the requirement for large planes, so that the number of take-offs and landings (setups and takedowns) can be minimized. Another requirement is totally booked aircraft (planes depart only when all seats are filled). This might mean that customers either wait for service until a plane is filled or else commit themselves to the kinds of regulations that apply to shuttle or charter flights. Planes might not fly on fixed schedules. Competition for seats among airlines would be eliminated. Even relaxed government regulations concerning flight schedules would be changed. These conditions for flow shop airline activities may be politically un-acceptable. They may be rejected by the public, even though they could reduce airline fares. Assume that you have been summoned as an expert (P/OM) witness by a congressional committee. What questions should committee members ask? What answers will you give?

PROBLEM SET

1. Why is it useful for P/OM to differentiate between decision-making under certainty and under risk?

2. What is the significance of a breakeven strategy compared to other kinds of strategies?

3. With respect to strategy invention, it has been suggested that a methodological discovery can have as marked an effect as a technological breakthrough. Discuss this idea. Is there any precedent for the statement?

   Answer: Methodological advances can bring about great changes in P/OM systems. They may not seem as spectacular as technological breakthroughs. Nevertheless, the development of modern inventory control techniques has created important new methods for mail-order retail companies, manufacturing companies, and department stores that have clearly had a major impact. Blending petroleum crudes by linear programming methods and scheduling work using network algorithms are two other examples of methods that have revolutionized P/OM systems. The impact of new methods increases as computer software models become more sophisticated.

4. Why is it important to differentiate between analysis and synthesis?

5. Solve the decision problem posed on p. 201 (where the objective is to choose that design which promises to maximize the expected life of the product), under the following four probability conditions:

214

Managing
Production and
Operations
Systems
Through Their
Life Cycle
Stages

			Values of p_j		
	N_1	N_2	N_3	N_4	N_5
Condition 1	0	1.00	0	0	0
Condition 2	0.20	0.30	0.50	0	0
Condition 3	0	0	0.30	0.30	0.40
Condition 4	0.20	0.20	0.20	0.20	0.20

Comment on the character of these conditions and their effects on the results.

6. How do catastrophic events, such as earthquakes and floods, relate to states of nature?

7. Explain to a group of ecologists how states of nature apply to their area of concern.

8. Develop an appropriate decision matrix for each of the problems below. This requires describing specific strategies and relevant states of nature. Load the cells of the matrix with reasonable estimates for the outcomes. Assign sensible probabilities. Solve the problem you have designed. The generality of the decision matrix approach for resolving problems should be evident from the ubiquitousness of these situations.

I Strategies: Equipment alternatives for a fire company

   States of nature: Equipment failure rates
   Outcomes: Measures of downtime
   Objective: Minimize downtime

II Strategies: Alternative hospital layouts

   States of nature: Varying demand levels for different treatments in the hospital's service mix
   Outcomes: Measures of bottlenecks and delay
   Objective: Minimize delay

III Strategies: Different production materials

   States of nature: Varying costs for these materials and different levels of consumer demand
   Outcomes: Profit measures
   Objective: Maximize profit

IV Strategies: Varying number of repairmen

   States of nature: Probabilities of machine breakdowns
   Outcomes: Measures of the cost of downtime
   Objective: Minimize cost

V Strategies: Different computer systems

States of nature: Varying data loads on the department
Outcomes: Measures of the age of information
Objective: Minimize age of information in the system

VI Strategies: Different numbers of toll booths

States of nature: Varying numbers of arrivals
Outcomes: Measures of customer waiting time
Objective: Minimize customer waiting time

VII Strategies: Supermarket checkout counter arrangements

States of nature: Number of customers with small and large orders
Outcomes: Measures of idle time of checkout clerks and customer waiting time
Objective: Minimize total cost of checkout clerks' idle time and waiting time of customers

VIII Strategies: Different catalog numbering systems

States of nature: Various users of the catalog
Outcomes: Measure of errors in ordering
Objective: Minimize ordering errors

Answer: This problem is intended to encourage discussion and to permit consideration of various P/OM situations. Many other problems can be set up in addition to these eight.

Choosing case V as an example, examine four different hypothetical computer systems. The data load may be light, medium, or heavy. Some corresponding estimates have been developed and are shown in the decision matrix of Table 5–7.

The minimum expected age of information occurs with computer system 4. Perhaps, however, the fourth system is too costly, as compared to system 1, or it may be less able in performance.

TABLE 5-7 MATRIX OF THE AGE OF INFORMATION (IN HOURS)

	States of Nature			
Strategies	Light	Medium	Heavy	
p_i	0.2	0.7	0.1	EV_i
System 1	1.0	2.1	4.0	2.07
System 2	0.7	2.5	4.3	2.32
System 3	1.2	2.8	2.7	2.47
System 4	1.1	2.0	3.7	1.99

216

Managing
Production and
Operations
Systems
Through Their
Life Cycle
Stages

**TABLE 5-8   MATRIX OF THE AGE OF
INFORMATION (IN HOURS)**

Strategies p_i	State of Nature			
	Light 0.2	Medium 0.6	Heavy 0.2	EV_i
System 1	1.0	2.1	4.0	2.26
System 2	0.7	2.5	4.3	2.50
System 3	1.2	2.8	2.7	2.46
System 4	1.1	2.0	3.7	2.16

With thoughtful discussion, such examples can show the general applicability of the decision matrix to operations management problems. Carry the example one step further. We test the sensitivity of the problem solution to changes in the data. In Table 5–8, we have changed the values of the p_js, but only slightly. This is called **sensitivity analysis.**

The result is unchanged in that the fourth system will provide the minimum expected age of information. However, we observe that the change in the p_j values has raised the expected age for all but one of the systems. This is shown in Table 5–9.

Relatively speaking, systems 1, 2, and 4 are invariant to the type of change that is suggested, whereas system 3 appears to be highly sensitive.

9. Explain this statement: The problem of achieving synthesis is too complex to permit the exclusive use of judgment. It is too large for a purely methodological treatment. Properly used, the combination of objective and subjective methods can be synergistic. (*Synergistic* means that the effect of the whole system is greater than the sum of the individual effects of the parts of the system operating independently.)

Answer: The exclusive use of (subjective) judgment, as a means of selecting an optimal strategy for a complex P/OM system, is virtually impossible, because the relevant problem detail is too great for individual perception, human memory, and cerebral calculation. Similarly, (objective) methodology cannot reflect the scope of interacting subsystems. A combination of the two approaches is essential.

TABLE 5-9

System	1	2	3	4
After change	2.26	2.50	2.46	2.16
Before change	2.07	2.32	2.47	1.99
Difference	+0.19	+0.18	−0.01	+0.17

Thus, design of alternatives accepts intuition. Evaluation depends heavily on objective, analytic methods. By combining subjective and objective methods, the total benefits usually will exceed the sum of the benefits derived from each method's being used alone. Therefore, an appropriate combination is said to be synergistic. To achieve such advantages, the combination must be coordinated by management.

10. For the case of Alpha Airlines, if the 1990 jets are purchased, assume that the new fleet has twice the capacity of the old fleet of 1980 jets. This means that twice the number of passenger miles can be flown. Does this affect the analysis? Explain.

Answer: As can be seen from Fig. 5–16, with the above assumption, the *BEP* drops to 34 percent from 68 percent. The probability distribution used in the text should no longer apply, but if it does, that means that Alpha Airlines has invested in a lot of useless capacity. If there are significant probabilities for flying at capacities that are more than 100 percent of 1980s jet capacity, then the 1990 jets look attractive.

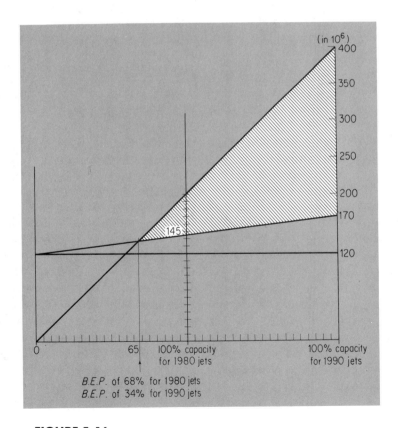

FIGURE 5-16

11. If the demand probabilities are dependent on the type of plane that is flown, what different steps would you take in analyzing Alpha Airline's choice situation?

Section 5.3 Capacity Planning: Combining Economies of Scale and Price/Demand Elasticities

This capacity planning model merges two basic concepts. First, we make use of the notion of economies of scale, as reflected by the Boston Consulting Group's experience curve. Second, the price elasticity of demand is related to the output volumes of the experience curve. Quality considerations are relatively easy to include as elasticity decreases with quality improvement.

Price Elasticity and Substitutability

We discussed price/demand elasticity on pp. 7–10. The relationship is a forecast in which price affects demand volume. Figure 5–17 shows some of the complexities of the situation. The line, or curve, can have different slopes. The smaller the slope, the more inelastic the relationship between price and demand volume. A rubber band is highly elastic; it stretches when it is pulled. When demand is elastic, it stretches when price pulls it. An elastic demand curve has a high slope.

Why do some products have high and others low elasticity? The explanation is that products for which customers can readily find substitutes are price elastic. The degree of substitutability of margerine for butter,

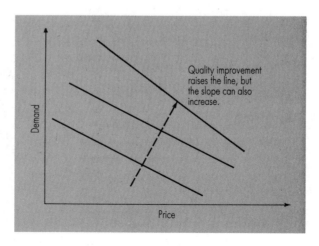

FIGURE 5-17. Price elasticity relations.

one VCR for another, one kind of service for another, determines customers' willingness to pay more for a specific product.

Substitutability is a reflection of customer loyalty to a product. A loyal customer is one who keeps on returning to the company for goods or services not easily found elsewhere. That is the customer's perception, and it is worth a lot to the company. But loyalty is not a simple subject. Brand loyalty is not the same as company loyalty. The customer may want General Electric for all appliances or just for lightbulbs. Most customers do not even know they could buy a diesel locomotive from GE.

In addition to slope differentials, price/demand lines can lie higher or lower on the chart (look again at Fig. 5–17). The higher the line, overall, the stronger the product. At any given price, the higher line obtains a larger demand volume and a greater market share. Customer-perceived superior product quality raises the price/demand line. The added volume can be worth a lot to the company. If quality can be achieved with benefits outweighing costs, that is the way to go. For almost all cases, much quality improvement is free, and thereafter the returns for improved quality far outweigh the costs of achievement.

The Economies of Scale Model

According to the production function of economic theory, product can be delivered at lower unit costs when the output volume increases. The Boston Consulting Group (BCG) has done many empirical studies of this phenomenon. Their results confirm that decreasing costs result from larger production volumes. Figure 5–18 shows the general shape of this function,

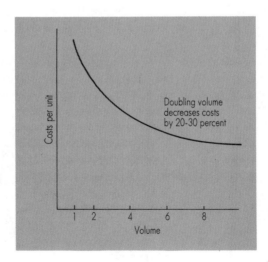

FIGURE 5-18. Costs decrease with volume.

220

Managing
Production and
Operations
Systems
Through Their
Life Cycle
Stages

which the BCG calls the experience curve. The rate of decrease falls between 20 percent and 30 percent for each doubling of volume, where volume is a surrogate for experience.

What accounts for the improvement in costs? For a given work configuration, as the output volume gets larger, many factors operate to make the process more efficient. Workers learn their jobs better. It takes less time to do the jobs. In part, this is the learning curve phenomenon, which is described below.

The Learning Curve

Worker productivity rates improve with practice. (Rates of output deteriorate between practice intervals.) Learning is responsible for the observed improvement. This applies to individuals as well as groups. After a while, with continued practice, learning reaches a productivity plateau where the time to produce a unit is about constant. Always applicable when the worker stops the job and then starts up again, learning is especially applicable to start-ups.[2] The learning effect is shown in Figure 5–19.

The equation, $T(n) = kn^{(1 - \lambda)}$ is read as follows:

$T(n)$ = cumulative time to make n units, consecutively
k = time required to make the first unit $n = 1$
n = trial number (the number of units made)
h = the learning coefficient, $0 < \lambda < 1$.

---

[2]Nicholas Baloff, "Estimating the Parameters of the Startup Model—An Empirical Approach," *The Journal of Industrial Engineering,* 18, 4 (April 1967), 248–53.

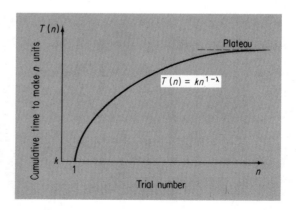

FIGURE 5-19.

We observe that when $\lambda = 0$, the cumulative time $T(n)$ increases linearly (kn), and there is no plateau. As $\lambda \to 1$, the plateau effect becomes accentuated. With learning, leveling off is always expected. The value of λ, therefore, reflects the speed with which the plateau effect is felt.

Often, average time measures are used to describe learning.

$$\overline{T}(n) = \frac{T(n)}{n} = kn^{-\lambda}$$

The same terms apply, as before. When $\lambda = 0$, $\overline{T}(n) = k$, which is the condition for nonlearning. Figure 5–20 illustrates $\overline{T}(n)$.

Attempts such as these to describe learning in quantitative terms has been shown to work with some reasonable level of predictive success.[3] In labor-intensive situations especially, the results can be useful. Many refinements exist, including S-curves and learning functions that include variables to describe the character of the job to be done.

When workers are used in the flow shop, the effect of learning is pronounced. For example, assembly line startup times will decrease and running times will stabilize as the workers repeat the same operations. The learning effect is less marked for the job shop. If orders for work are too small, then the advantages of learning (lowering the cost per piece) will hardly be achieved before a new job is started. Cost bids for product must take learning into account by pricing jobs at the average productivity rate. Time study begins after the worker stabilizes at the plateau level. In some instances there are multiple plateaus; learning starts again after a stable interval of continued practice.

Learning models suffer from some serious flaws. The learning function that is used must be matched to the specific situation. Forgetting as a

---

[3]C. C. Pegels, ''On Startup or Learning Curves: An Expanded View,'' in *Management of Production,* ed. Martin K. Starr (London: Penguin Books Ltd., 1970), pp. 183–95.

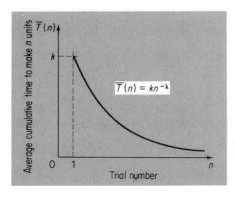

FIGURE 5-20

222

Managing
Production and
Operations
Systems
Through Their
Life Cycle
Stages

function of the pattern of intervals between trials deserves serious attention, and little is known about this aspect of learning. Still, in project planning, the learning model has introduced predictive ability.

What effect does job enrichment have on learning rates? What is the significance, in time studies, of the assumption that a worker can be tested at a stable point of "normal" activity? What part does learning play in the empirically observed decrease in per unit costs called the experience curve by The Boston Consulting Group?

In addition to worker learning, the experience curve includes refinement of materials used by both product and process. When a formal process is used to improve materials, it is called **value analysis.** There is always technological change taking place. Most of the time, technology brings about minor alterations in material capabilities, but these changes translate into major product alterations (see value analysis, pp. 315–316).

Concurrent with the minor changes, broad shifts in material usage occur gradually, but pervasively. For example, the shift from metals to plastics has been taking place over fifty years. The metal industries' share of the product and construction market has been gradually falling over this period of time, but total volume did not start to contract severely until about ten years ago. New materials are used by producers because of many different advantages that are not always obvious. For example, plastics are used by auto manufacturers because they are light and decrease the weight of the car. The decreased weight improves gas mileage, allows a smaller engine to provide better pickup, and makes it easier to satisfy government emission regulations. The price of plastics versus metals, on a per car basis, has improved over the years to complete the rationale for switching materials. The same kind of reasoning could be used to explain the shifts from the Stone Age to the Bronze Age to the Iron Age to the Plastic Age and in the future to the Ceramics Age. (Ceramics now appear to be the next material.)

Also, cost advantages accruing from discounts given for volume purchases support the experience curve. Pressing to consolidate suppliers, ultimately seeking single-supplier systems, many firms are able to generate substantial savings in materials and components.

Merging the Models

The experience curve and the price elasticity model can be combined as shown in Figure 5–21. For a given price (p), the demand it will produce (x) is found in the right-hand quadrant of the graph. At that volume of demand (x), the *BCG* curve yields the variable cost (vc). These terms combine as margin contribution.

$$\text{Margin contribution} = (p - vc)x$$

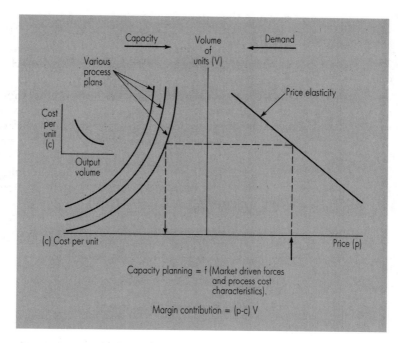

FIGURE 5-21. Marketing/production planning interface.

Maximizing Margin Contribution

The ability to determine margin contribution and to maximize it is best illustrated by an example. We will analyze the Ace Rahm Company case. First, linear breakeven analysis and then nonlinear breakeven analysis are used (in variants A, B and C) to explore the situation. In variant D, the merged *BCG* and price elasticity model is explored. It is called price elasticity—capacity planning.

CASE: ACE RAHM COMPANY

In this case you can use the data of the hypothetical business called ACE RAHM COMPANY to run through various kinds of capacity analyses. A PC diskette enables all the computations to be made and graphed on-line. It is called Capacity Planning and is listed in appendix A, where a variety of P/OM software is described. After doing these exercises, you can input other company data (from cases and actual situations) and resolve real capacity-planning problems.

**VARIANT
A: LINEAR
TOTAL
COST (*TC*)
AND
REVENUE
(*R*)**

Ace is studying the upgrading of its current CD-ROM which stands for *compact disk read-only memory*. It has the conventional 4.72-inch diameter of CDs used for playing music. However, when designed to serve as a computer peripheral, 550 megabytes of data can be stored on it (equivalent to 1,500 floppy disks). The current CD-ROM is called D1. The upgraded version (called D2) requires new process technology. The disks from the new process would have fewer defectives (disks that do not track properly). Also, disks can be produced at a lower cost if there is sufficient volume to warrant investing in the new process. General specs are standardized for all CD-ROM disks.

Ace believes that linear breakeven analysis is appropriate for comparing processes D1 and D2. The information for both systems is listed below (where x = production volume):

	Disk (D1)	Disk (D2)
TC	10x + 4500	9x + 3800
R	30x + 10	32x + 8
x*	500 units/month	500 units/month

x* = Volume at 100% capacity

Determine breakeven points and profits at 100 percent capacity for both the D1 and the D2 strategies.

Note: If a conflict exists in reaching a decision, such as better profit slope and poorer breakeven point, then the expected value criterion should be used.

Contrast the result of assuming a uniform probability distribution (all probabilities are equal) with the following one called the skewed distribution.

CAPACITIES (%)

0–10	10–20	20–30	30–40	40–50	50–60	60–70	70–80	80–90	90–100

PROBABILITIES

0.10	0.20	0.60	0.10	0.00	0.00	0.00	0.00	0.00	0.00

ANSWERS:

	EQUATION	BREAKEVEN X	MAX PROFIT @ X = 500
VARIANT A:	D1 Profit = 20x − 4490	BE D1 = 224.50	D1 Profit = $5510
	D2 Profit = 23x − 3792	BE D2 = 164.87	D2 Profit = $7708

UNIFORM DISTRIBUTION

% Cap	x	Prob.	D1 Profit	D2 Profit	D1 EV.	D2 EV.
0.05	25	0.1	−3990	−3217	−399	−321.7
0.15	75	0.1	−2990	−2067	−299	−206.7
0.25	125	0.1	−1990	−917	−199	−91.7
0.35	175	0.1	−990	233	−99	23.3
0.45	225	0.1	10	1383	1	138.3

(Continued)

UNIFORM DISTRIBUTION			D1	D2		
% Cap	x	Prob.	Profit	Profit	D1 EV.	D2 EV.
0.55	275	0.1	1010	2533	101	253.3
0.65	325	0.1	2010	3683	201	368.3
0.75	375	0.1	3010	4833	301	483.3
0.85	425	0.1	4010	5983	401	598.3
0.95	475	0.1	5010	7133	501	713.3
		Uniform Dist. Expected Values =			$510.00	$1958.00

SKEWED DISTRIBUTION						
% Cap	x	Prob.	Profit	Profit	D1 EV.	D2 EV.
0.05	25	0.1	−3990	−3217	−399	−321.7
0.15	75	0.2	−2990	−2067	−598	−413.4
0.25	125	0.6	−1990	−917	−1194	−550.2
0.35	175	0.1	−990	233	−99	23.3
		Skewed Dist. Expected Values =			−$2290.00	−$1262.00

VARIANT B: LINEAR *TC* AND NONLINEAR *R*

Ace changes the assumption about a linear revenue curve when it is learned that competition will be greater than had been anticipated. This new assumption is called D3. The information, is as follows:

	OLD ASSUMPTION (D2) All Linear Functions	NEW ASSUMPTION (D3) Nonlinear Revenue
TC	$9x + 3800$	$9x + 3800$
R	$32x + 8$	$-0.40x^2 + 180x + 100$

Describe the effect of introducing the nonlinear revenue function on breakeven points. What is the maximum profit?

What expected values occur when the probability distributions introduced in part A of the case are used?

ANSWERS:

VARIANT B: D3 Profit $= -.4x^2 + 171x - 3700$

BE(1) = 22.86
BE(2) = 404.64
x (Max. Profit) = 213.75
Max. Profit = $14,575.62

UNIFORM DISTRIBUTION				
% Cap.	x	Prob.	D3 Profit	D3 EV.
0.05	25	0.1	325	32.5
0.15	75	0.1	6875	687.5
0.25	125	0.1	11425	1142.5
0.35	175	0.1	13975	1397.5
0.45	225	0.1	14525	1452.5
0.55	275	0.1	13075	1307.5
0.65	325	0.1	9625	962.5
0.75	375	0.1	4175	417.5
0.85	425	0.1	−3275	−327.5
0.95	475	0.1	−12725	−1272.5
		Uniform Dist. Expected Values =		$5800.00

% Cap.	x	Prob.	D3 Profit	D3 EV.
0.05	25	0.1	325	32.50
0.15	75	0.2	6875	1375.0
0.25	125	0.6	11425	6855.0
0.35	175	0.1	13975	1397.5
			Skewed Dist. Expected Values =	$9660.00

VARIANT C: NONLINEAR TC AND R

Ace now recognizes that the new production process for D2 will result in some added costs as the volume of output increases. This assumption is called D4. The appropriate relationships are these:

	OLD ASSUMPTION (D3) Only Nonlinear Revenue	NEW ASSUMPTION (D4) All Nonlinear Functions
TC	$9x + 3800$	$0.10x^2 + 6x + 8000$
R	$-0.40x^2 + 180x + 100$	$-0.40x^2 + 180x + 100$

Describe the effect of introducing the nonlinear total cost function on breakeven points. What is the maximum profit?

What expected values occur when the probability distributions in part A of the case are used?

ANSWERS:

VARIANT C: D4 Profit $= -.5x^2 + 17.4x - 7900$ BE(1) $=$ 53.68
                                                                  BE(2) $= 294.32$
                                                                  x (Max. Profit) $= 174$
                                                                 Max Profit $= 7238.00

UNIFORM DISTRIBUTION

% Cap.	x	Prob.	D4 Profit	D4 EV.
0.05	25	0.1	−3862.5	−386.25
0.15	75	0.1	2337.5	233.75
0.25	125	0.1	6037.5	603.75
0.35	175	0.1	7237.5	723.75
0.45	225	0.1	5937.5	593.75
0.55	275	0.1	2137.5	213.75
0.65	325	0.1	−4162.5	−416.25
0.75	375	0.1	−12962.5	−1296.25
0.85	425	0.1	−24262.5	−2426.25
0.95	475	0.1	−38062.5	−3806.25
			Uniform Dist. Expected Values =	$−5962.50

SKEWED DISTRIBUTION

% Cap.	x	Prob.	D3 Profit	D3 EV.
0.05	25	0.1	−3862.5	−386.25
0.15	75	0.2	2337.5	467.50
0.25	125	0.6	6037.5	3622.50
0.35	175	0.1	7237.5	723.75
			Skewed Dist. Expected Values =	$4427.50

VARIANT D: PRICE ELASTICITY/ CAPACITY ANALYSIS

Rather than spend a lot of money on a better process for making CD-ROM disks, it has been suggested that Ace management should offer bonuses to employees for producing fewer defectives and put quality circles into practice. Price and quality (especially reliability) are key variables for sales of CDs. The price elasticity equation has been estimated as:

$$p = -100x + 1,200 \qquad \text{(x is in units of 1000 and valid up to 10,000 units/month)}$$

CD-ROM disks could be produced by a serialized flow shop process which is cost-sensitive to output rates. The variable cost relationship is assumed to be as follows:

$$vc = 10x - 20 + 2000/x \qquad \text{(x is in units of 1000 and valid up to 10,000 units/month)}$$

Note: There are three methods for solution. The first is solving the equations—what values will maximize $(p - vc)x$. The second is to graph the results and approach the optimum by trial and error. The third is to use the analysis on the diskette mentioned above. With the diskette, call up ANALY2 to determine the output volume for optimal margin contribution.

Ace's process designers have suggested a modification to the flow shop configuration that would produce a more reliable tracking disk. This change makes the product less price elastic, and alters the price/volume relationship as follows:

$$p = -100x + 1,300$$

At the same time, the variable cost to volume relationship increases:

$$vc = 11x - 20 + 2,100/x$$

What has happened to the margin contribution?

ANSWERS:

VARIANT D		
(1) Contribution		
Margin $= -110x^2 + 1220x - 2000$	MC BE(1) = 2.00	
	MC BE(2) = 9.09	
	X (Max. MC) = 5.54545	
	Number of Units = 5545.45	
	Max. MC = \$1382.73	
(2) Contribution		
Margin $= -111x^2 + 1320x - 2100$	MC BE(1) = 1.89	
	MC BE(2) = 10.00	
	X (Max. MC) = 5.94595	
	Number of Units = 5945.95	
	Max. MC = \$1824.32	

(x in 000's)

REFERENCES   ACKOFF, R. A., ed. *Progress in Operations Research,* Vol. I. New York: Wiley, 1961.

BAUMOL, WILLIAM J. *Economic Theory and Operations Analysis,* 2nd ed. Englewood Cliffs, N.J.: Prentice-Hall, 1965.

BROOKS, L. D., *Financial Management Decision Game* (FINGAME) Homewood, IL, Irwin, 1982.

CHURCHMAN, C. W., R. A. ACKOFF, and E. L. ARNOFF. *Introduction to Operations Research.* New York: Wiley, 1957.

CHURCHMAN, C. WEST. *Prediction and Optimal Decision.* Englewood Cliffs, N.J.: Prentice-Hall, 1961.

————. *Theory of Experimental Inference.* New York: Macmillan, 1948.

DANNENBRING, D. and M. K. STARR, *Management Science,* McGraw-Hill, Inc., NY, 1983.

DEAN, JOEL. *Managerial Economics.* Englewood Cliffs, N.J.: Prentice-Hall, 1951.

DOOLEY, A. et al. *Basic Problems, Concepts, and Techniques; Casebooks in Production Management.* New York: Wiley, 1968.

FABRICANT, SOLOMON. *A Primer on Productivity.* New York: Random House, 1969.

FORRESTER, J. W. *Industrial Dynamics.* New York: Wiley, 1961.

GOLD, BELA. *Foundations of Productivity Analysis.* Pittsburgh: University of Pittsburgh Press, 1955.

HARE, VAN COURT, JR. *Systems Analysis: A Diagnostic Approach.* New York: Harcourt Brace Jovanovich, 1967.

HERTZ, D. B., and R. T. EDDISON, eds. *Progress in Operations Research,* Vol. II. New York: Wiley, 1964.

KASNER, EDWARD, and JAMES NEWMAN. *Mathematics and the Imagination.* New York: Simon and Schuster, 1963.

LUCE, R. DUNCAN, and HOWARD RAIFFA. *Games and Decision.* New York: Wiley, 1958.

MILLER, D. W., and M. K. STARR. *Executive Decisions and Operations Research,* 2nd ed. Englewood Cliffs, N.J.: Prentice-Hall, 1969.

OPTNER, S. L. *Systems Analysis for Business Management,* 2nd ed. Englewood Cliffs, N.J.: Prentice-Hall, 1968.

SASIENI, M., A. YASPAN, and L. FRIEDMAN. *Operations Research Methods, and Problems.* New York: Wiley, 1959.

SCHELLENBERGER, R. E. and L. A. MASTERS, MANSYM IV: A Dynamic Management Simulation with Decision Support Systems. NY, John Wiley, 1986.

SCHLAIFER, R. ROBERT. *Analysis of Decisions under Uncertainty.* New York: McGraw-Hill, 1967.

SIMON, H. A. *The New Science of Management Decision.* New York: Harper & Row, 1960.

STARR, MARTIN K. *Systems Management of Operations.* Englewood Cliffs, N.J.: Prentice-Hall, 1971.

WAGNER, H. M. *Principles of Management Science.* Englewood Cliffs, N.J.: Prentice-Hall, 1970.

WALD, A. *Statistical Decision Functions.* New York: Wiley, 1950.

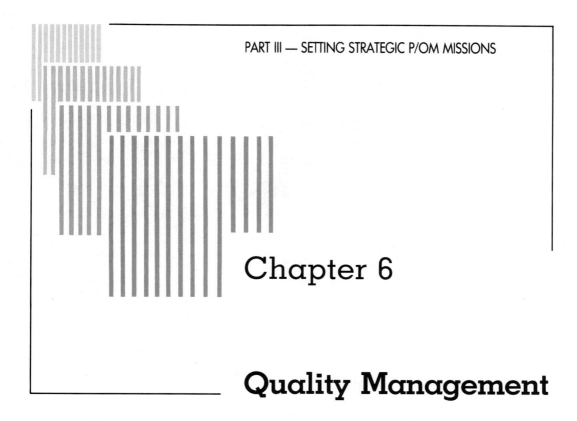

Chapter 6

Quality Management

PART
SUMMARY

The managers of all functional areas should share in choosing company strategies and in setting its standards. For example, managers of production and operations, marketing and finance must agree upon their common purposes. Agreement centers on the selection of strategic missions for the firm, and the answers to such questions as these: Is the prime objective to be the lowest unit cost producer? Is it to be the highest quality producer? Is the customer's special attraction to excellence in service, including no wait for spare parts? (Caterpillar, Inc., promises free parts and service if a needed spare part is not available within 48 hours.) The management team is unlikely to ignore the successful prescription followed by many global companies, namely: Simultaneously, be the highest quality and the lowest unit cost producer. The figure presents a matrix showing the interactions of the various strategic missions. The matrix provides a way of illustrating such joint strategic missions as these: high quality and low unit costs, high quality and moderate service, high variety and strong warranties.

229

(+ IS POSITIVE CORRELATION; − IS NEGATIVE CORRELATION)
(ENTRIES ARE A FUNCTION OF WORK CONFIGURATION, SITUATION, ETC.)

Missions	LUC	HQ	HSL	WL	CS	PI	RTΔ	G	CON	STM
LUC	x	+	−	−	−	+/−	+/−	+	+/−	+/−
HQ	x	x	+/−	−	+	+	+	+	−	−
HSL	x	x	x	−	−	−	−	+	−	+
WL	x	x	x	x	−	+	+	+	+	−
CS	x	x	x	x	x	+	+	−	+	−
PI	x	x	x	x	x	x	+	+	+	−
RTΔ	x	x	x	x	x	x	x	+	+	+
G	x	x	x	x	x	x	x	x	+	−
CON	x	x	x	x	x	x	x	x	x	+
STM	x	x	x	x	x	x	x	x	x	x

KEY
LUC — Low unit costs
HQ — High quality
HSL — High service level
WL — Wide line (product-mix)
CS — Custom service
PI — Product innovation
RTΔ — Response to change
G — Growth
CON — Convertibility
STM — Speed to market

USE INVENTION
TO CONVERT −'s
TO +'s

Matrix of trade-offs between strategic missions.

First, the company's strategy must be determined. Then, supplier selection, technological change, and workforce policies can be linked to customer needs and the strategic missions of the firm. Chapter 6 covers quality management. Chapter 7 treats materials management. Chapter 8 addresses human resource management, and Chapter 9 is devoted to facilities management.

In terms of the input-output model, Chapter 6 represents output quality achievement. Chapters 7, 8, and 9 reflect the input costs required to achieve superb output performance.

CHAPTER SUMMARY

The exploration of quality management for both goods and services includes consideration of the dimensions needed to describe quality. Section 6.1 examines the functional and nonfunctional aspects of defining quality, and the tradeoffs that exist between cost and quality.

Quality management requires methods to assure that specified qualities are delivered to customers. Section 6.2 describes how such assurance of product quality is obtained by means of inspection of suppliers' inputs as well as the company's own outputs. Often, inspecting each unit is either not economical or practical. Consequently, the use of acceptance sampling procedures are described.

Section 6.3 addresses the control of process characteristics by means of statistical quality control (SQC). The way to create and use control charts (called the x bar, the R, and the p charts) to monitor the process is described. The SQC methods are detailed so that they can be implemented in a real situation.

Section 6.4 examines the broadly inclusive category of total quality control (known as TQC). The Japanese emphasis on quality created an organizational impact which led to everyone in the company participating in the quest for continuous quality improvement. The section describes how organizations with TQC use quality circles, zero-defects programs and Taguchi methods in their pervasive search for perfection of quality.

When Is Quality Free and When Is It Costly?

Quality and cost tradeoffs must be explored. Figure 6–1 shows that sometimes quality improvements are accompanied by cost decreases. The usual conception of the quality/cost relationship is that improvements in quality can be gained only at a higher cost (also shown in Figure 6–1).

***When is quality free?*[1]**　When the number of defectives produced is decreased, cost is reduced and quality is improved. To reduce the number of defectives may require no out of pocket expense. If there is an initial investment, then the per unit cost of quality improvement decreases as the output volume goes up. With flexible process technology, high variety and output volume can be achieved at a negligible unit cost.

Building quality into the product in the first place can remove the need for as much inspection. Reduction in the number of inspectors provides an immediate saving. Building quality in, rather than removing defectives by inspection, may require nothing more than thinking carefully about the job that has to be done, or coming up with a clever idea about how to hold or position the work piece, or it may necessitate changing suppliers and/or reducing the number of suppliers. These are examples of the kind of quality-improving, cost-reducing relationships which underlie the concept that quality is free.

When is quality costly?　When the work system, made up of people and equipment, is being used consistently in the best way possible, then the system is said to be stable. The quality level of the output cannot be improved, except by fundamentally altering the system. To improve quality may require substantial investment in new equipment and retraining

---

[1]Philip B. Crosby, *Quality Is Free (The Art of Making Quality Certain)*, New York: McGraw-Hill, 1979.

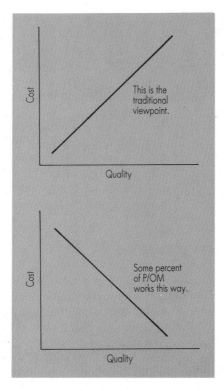

FIGURE 6-1. Quality cost relations.

the workforce. In other words, you can't do better with what you've got. It can become costly to improve upon the quality that an existing well-run system can produce. Quality improvement is costly when it requires changing the system with better materials, facilities, training, and skills.

The total costs of quality achievement are often broken down into the costs of failures, the costs of appraisal, and the costs of prevention. Creative design of product and process can decrease the number of failures while eliminating the costs of preventing defectives and the need for inspection to detect them. Initial investment for prevention of failures by design is responsible for eliminating most of the ongoing costs.

Let us break down the ongoing quality costs as follows:

1. The costs of failures, including product repairs, part and product replacements, and loss of customer goodwill.
2. The costs of prevention, including stopping the process to correct it; the costs of altering work-in-process and also reworking finished goods. (Note that initial process design costs are not included here.)
3. The costs of appraisal, including inspecting work-in-process, finished goods, and incoming materials from suppliers.

Section 6.1 The Dimensions of Quality

The definition of quality is the first job to be completed before a quality achievement program can be introduced. Definition usually involves many variables. Figure 6–2 shows a list of candidate variables needed to describe the quality of an automobile. It is a list prepared by a person who has never really thought about the problem of defining product quality.

The categories (taxonomy) can be better organized. Section 6.1 will provide a means of redrafting Figure 6–2. We suggest that you develop a better organized form of Figure 6–2 in the Problem Set following this section.

Market research might be able to assist in the development of a list of variables that fully describe the qualities that count. It may have to use in-depth interviews because survey instruments might miss some factors that count. For example, if the survey designer does not know that some people use laundry detergents to clean floors and walls, then quality questions concerning this aspect of usage will be missed.

How do you define the QUALITY of a car?
List all variables that could be relevant to any potential customer.

1. Safety
2. Mechanical reliability
3. Heating
4. Ventilation
5. Air Conditioning
6. Controls
7. Displays (ease of viewing)
8. Trunk
9. Ease of servicing
10. Routine handling
11. Emergency handling
12. Braking / Typical distance
13. Comfort of ride
14. Noise
15. Driving position
16. Front seating room
17. Rear seating room
18. Fuel economy
19. Starting
20. Engine running smoothly

21. Acceleration
22. Transmission (type, reliability)
23. Turning radius
24. Horsepower
25. Protection of driver in a crash
26. Tires (type e.g. radial, steel belted)
27. Cost
28. Available options
29. Availability of spare parts
30. Availability of qualified service
31. Turbocharging?
32. Fuel injection vs. carburation?
33. Corrosion resistance.
34. Type of brakes
35. Type of suspension
36. Cruising range
37. Anti-swerge, anti-lock braking system
38. Seats (leather, cloth)
39. Adjustability of seats
40. Adjustability of steering column

(add additional sheets, as needed).

FIGURE 6-2. List of quality variables for autos (student resource).

Another consideration is that qualities are often ignored until variation from some accustomed standard is perceived. For example, the height of the car seat might be ignored until it becomes either too high or too low. Also, what is too high for one person might not be high enough for another. The list of qualities must include those factors that become relevant when they take on values some customers may deem abnormal. The list should also include qualities that may be important for only some customers. This is the basis of **niche** marketing.

Market research is hard pressed to supply information about quality variables for products that are new to the market. For example, when Sony first introduced the videocassette recorder (VCR), the list of qualities that might count was short and uncertain. It is doubtful that such properties as freeze-frame or multiprogramming over as many weeks as possible, or digital technology, were influencing the choice of qualities on the list.

Quality definition is crucial to installing successful methods and practices for achieving quality goals. The list of quality variables blueprints what is needed for measuring qualities as an inspection function. The list details the quality target and an acceptable range. That information is needed to ensure that quality standards are being met. The complete definitions are required for monitoring process outputs. The P/OM area must have complete awareness and specification of all qualities before starting up an SQC (statistical quality control) system. The same must be said with respect to installing TQC (total quality control) as an integral part of corporate procedures and of the corporate culture. The Xerox Corporation has done this by making quality everybody's responsibility. At Xerox, the program to educate and implement TQC started in 1980, and is still going strong to date.

Two Different Quality Viewpoints

P/OMs conceive of their job as requiring the development and operation of a process for getting work done. They believe the organization has entrusted them with the responsibility of transforming input resources into a specific set of outputs. The transformation process is designed to deliver product compatible with the company's quality goals. The P/OM interprets this to mean that the outputs should be of some assured level of quality, produced at a minimum cost for that quality level.

Quality has two different interpretations, depending on whose viewpoint is being used. One is the consumers' view of the value of qualities desired and qualities received. This view of quality is value-driven and marketing-oriented. It should be noted that each manufacturing or service provision stage has its own set of suppliers and consumers. When this orientation is promoted by management, then everyone has the consumers' viewpoint (above) and the producers' viewpoint (below).

The producers' viewpoint of quality is what we call the P/OM-oriented view of quality. A close approximation to this use of the term is consistency. A set of standards is defined, and all units of production must consistently meet those standards. The consumer may consider such standards to be evidence of low or high quality depending upon what was expected. The consumer's concern is service, performance, appearance, and so on. The P/OM's concern is that specifications be met, whatever they may be.

To achieve specified output quality, two basic factors must be treated. The first is that the quality of input materials (often received from suppliers, but also internal transfers between departments) must be maintained at designed levels. This subject is a major concern of Section 6.2. Second, the process must be controlled to deliver the desired output quality. Section 6.3 addresses the problems of controlling output quality. Section 6.4 puts the entire systems objective in focus using TQC: Quality is dependent upon total commitment, total communication, and total coordination.

To the consumer, quality and "high quality" are the same thing. The P/OM has a problem here. As an individual, the manager wishes to produce an output that possesses "high quality." But the job calls for the delivery of an output of "specified quality" that is in line with the investment in the process and the budget for operating costs.

In the P/OM sense, quality is an agreed-upon set of standards and tolerance limits. These specifications are operational terms, not value judgments. To consider quality in operational terms, it is an absolute necessity that dimensions of quality be expressed in measurable terms. Every manager would like to minimize costs and maximize "high quality." Sometimes these objectives cannot be achieved simultaneously. At other times, they march to the same drummer. In either case, it is better to maximize quality subject to cost constraints than to minimize costs subject to quality constraints.

What are the categories for describing the attributes (or dimensions) of output quality?

Functional Qualities

1. Utility of purpose
2. Reliability of function
   A. Conformance to standards in use over time
   B. Deterioration of function over time (durability)
   C. Failure characteristics and expected lifetime
   D. Cost of maintenance (preventive and remedial)
   E. Repairability (quality, cost, and time)
   F. Guarantees and warranties

3. Human Factors
   A. Safety
   B. Comfort
   C. Convenience

Nonfunctional Qualities

1. Style and appearance
2. Self-image of user
   A. Price
   B. Prestige
3. Timeliness of design
4. Style and variety

Functional Qualities

Purpose utilities are usually the most fundamental product qualities. They are associated with specific, functional classes of use, such as soap to wash the face or tires to keep wheels rolling. The same applies to services. We know what the purpose of a credit card is, why we pay telephone bills, and what purpose a college education is supposed to serve. We could devise measures of service quality for all these cases. Often, purposes are clear. At other times, they are intrinsically difficult to state. In either case, the measurement of how well a product or service performs its intended function is necessary if standards are to be set.

Physical and consumer evaluations are ways to measure quality. For example, can we measure how good a food product tastes, how comfortable a chair is, or how convenient to use a hammer is? We can measure the sweetness of the food, or ask people if they like the taste. We can count the number of springs used in the chair, or ask people if it is comfortable. We can measure the power the hammer's user can wield, or ask people if they prefer one handle to another. Assumptions can always be made about the way in which the measurable, physical factors relate to consumer evaluations of the utility of functions. The control of quality is directly related to specified standards of measurable physical factors.

Reliability is a critical functional quality. It concerns the ability of the output to perform according to specifications over a given period of time. This attribute of functional quality raises some interesting problems. P/OM is responsible for controlling the quality of a product while it is being created or manufactured. Thereafter, each unit of product has a history of its own. Observations, measurements, and specifications of quality must include the variety of possible histories for each unit that is sold. It is on such a basis that warranties and guarantees are determined and set.

There are different ways of describing reliability. For example, durability refers to reliability over time. When we discuss the durability of a product, we are referring to the fact that the functional utility attributes will continue to perform within some set of limits over a given period of time. The width of the limits represents an important aspect of the definition of quality for the design. We expect that parts of the product will become worn with use, whereas other characteristics will age independent of use. Furthermore, chance events can affect performance characteristics. Generally, the expected performance will increasingly deviate from the initial design standard over a period of time, as shown in Fig. 6–3.

This phenomenon, which we call **drift,** is characteristic of a great many functional attributes of mechanical, chemical, and electrical products. Consider a simple electric lightbulb. When first used, it will generate some given number of lumens. Then, as it ages and as a function of both hours of use and the number of times that it is turned on and off, the output of the bulb will vary. It will produce less and less light. At some point in time, the bulb will fail entirely.

Complete or total failure is easy to define. However, if we can no longer use our light source once its output falls below a certain threshold, then for all functional purposes the lightbulb has failed and must be replaced. Our ordinary definition of failure for the lightbulb specifies a zero output threshold. A more sophisticated definition requires the specification of a given level of light below which the unit cannot be said to be performing satisfactorily. Thus, performance specification in terms of operational limits is equivalent to failure specification. When talking about quality, the manager must think in these more complex terms, because the output will be tested in terms of them.

A unit can exhibit erratic performance before it reaches the failure threshold. For example, the lightbulb might alternately get brighter and

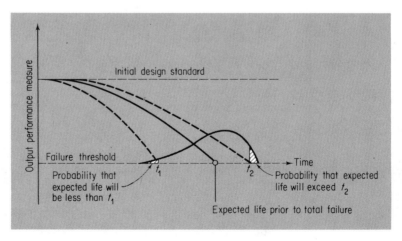

FIGURE 6-3. Expected performance over time exhibits increasing deviation from the initial design standard.

dimmer. This constitutes still another measure of reliability; that is, the specification of allowable variability of performance. Reliability is not a simple dimension. Both reliability and failure can be described successfully only by using statistical terms because, at best, we can make a prediction of how long the unit can be expected to continue to function satisfactorily.

There are many reasons why failure and reliability, as definitions of quality, play an extremely important role. Some types of failure do not permit repair, whereas others do. The definition and specification of quality is concerned with ease of maintenance and the cost of replacement parts. These factors affect the consumer's judgment of quality. A multicomponent unit usually has different replacement characteristics for each of its parts. Generally, there are some parts which, when they fail, represent an irremedial breakdown. Should a unit be designed in this way, or should the development of replaceable parts be encouraged? Replacement requires that a service function be developed. How good must such a sales, engineering, and service function be and how accessible to customers? Automobile manufacturers often stress this aspect of product quality. Service organizations also stress reliability; for example, airlines advertise that they are on time. Employment agencies advertise that they have bonded personnel. Electrical and telephone failures create serious hardships. Voltage drops (drift) cause major inconvenience.

Management must know the reliability of its products or services to come up with the specification of guarantee period. How long should this period be? What terms are reasonable? How many different components should be covered? The essence of quality control and quality assurance is embodied in a realistic evaluation of the way in which the product performs over its lifetime. It is only scratching the surface to measure quality dimensions without tying such measurements into the complete evaluation of product quality and performance.

In Chapter 8 we discuss the importance of human factors such as safety, comfort, and convenience. The human factors area relates equally well to product and service management. All the aspects of quality discussed in Section 8.4 apply here.

Nonfunctional Qualities (II)

Nonfunctional qualities play an important part in the consumer's judgment of quality. They are difficult to measure. Nevertheless, the role of these attributes is as important to the definition of quality as any in the functional category. We are dealing with questions related to the appearance of the product or the style of the service. We are concerned with the way in which the consumer interprets the intangible qualities of the output. This involves us with sociological and psychological implications of quality. To think in such terms requires a turn of mind that cannot easily be associated with the usual production department. This is why industrial designers have come to play an important role in the development of the nonfunctional attributes of successful products.

The consumer's self-image concerning the use of a specific brand in a given product class raises many questions concerning this intangible aspect of quality specification. There has always been a belief in the marketing field that consumers are motivated, to some extent, by the symbolic relationships of the product to their own personal life. One can find references to Freud, Adler, Jung, and related schools of analysis in the literature of the motivational market researcher. In theory, at any rate, the designer is able to communicate with consumers on the different levels of their needs as consumers and thereby to produce a product or service that receives acceptance both in concept and in form.

For the complete specification of quality, still other attributes play a part. These include the package, the label, and even the instructions to the consumer for using the product properly. Another factor is the variety of choice. Section 4.1 pointed to the marketing implications of modularity as a means of providing a broad selection base for the consumer. In Chapter 12, we discuss the product mix aspect of variety.

All these factors taken together establish a frame of reference that is sufficiently psychoanalytic to make the P/OM wonder how to specify standards of quality. Typical of these difficulties are questions concerning the visual appearance and styling of a design. Style changes are a function of time. What is in style today can be out of style tomorrow. The way in which one style replaces a previous style should follow some logical pattern, although not necessarily a predictable one. Various studies confirm the fact that some form of stability does exist concerning changes in style. Consumer acceptance turns out to be not as erratic as one might suppose. In some cases, style cycles have been found—for example, in the clothing industry, in hair styles, and in millinery styles.[2]

Architects play a primary role in influencing the accepted styles of a particular culture at any point in time. This relationship has intrigued many designers and architects.[3] To the extent that product design follows architecture, reasonable predictions can be made about the evaluation of nonfunctional design characteristics of products. At the same time, we should not lose sight of the basic principles which, because they underlie

---

[2]See, for example, Agnes Brook Young, *Recurring Cycles of Fashion (1760–1937)* (New York: Harper & Row, 1937).

[3]See, for example: Henry Dreyfuss, *Designing for People* (New York: Simon and Schuster, 1955); Le Corbusier, *Toward a New Architecture* (London: Architectural Press, 1948); Raymond Loewy, *Never Leave Well Enough Alone* (New York: Simon and Schuster, 1951); Eliel Saarinen, *Search for Form* (New York: Reinhold, 1948); Walter Dorwin Teague, *Design This Day* (New York: Harcourt, Brace & World, 1940).

all matters of shape and form, relate architecture, engineering, and industrial design.[4]

Each case of product design management demands its own analysis, but certain fundamentals of **innovation** appear to play a part whether we are talking about the ultimate consumer or an industrial consumer. Also, it is uncertain to what extent an industrial consumer is concerned with the nonfunctional category of quality specification.

1. There is a historical basis for the evolution of design forms. Thus, timeliness of a design can be critical. There are well-documented cases of designs that have been rejected because they appeared too soon.

2. There is need for complete specification of quality. It can be accomplished only if a coordinated effort is made by both operations and marketing management (see further discussion below concerning quality function deployment).

3. There is a technological basis which is predicated on available materials and process knowhow.

With respect to the third point, some significant knowledge about technological change is available. It has no specific guidelines to offer product management, but it does have important conceptual ones. Service systems evolve with predictable styles. Changes in social attitudes alter the nonfunctional dimensions of service quality far more rapidly than those of product quality. It is not easy to measure the success of a health care delivery system or of a change in postal procedures, but it is possible, and it must be done if quality control is to be established.

Quality Function Deployment and Companywide Quality Control

Companywide quality control (CWQC) has three characteristics: (1) One philosophy ties the various organizational levels and functions together with a common set of values. This is a company culture in which

---

[4]See, for example: George D. Birkhoff, *Aesthetic Measure* (Cambridge, Mass.: Harvard University Press, 1933); Samuel Coleman, *Nature's Harmonic Unity* (New York: The Knickerbocker Press, 1912); *Proportional Form* (New York: The Knickerbocker Press, 1920); Ozenfant, *Foundations of Modern Art,* trans. J. Rodker (New York: Dover Publications, 1952); J. Schillinger, *The Mathematical Basis of the Arts* (New York: Philosophical Library, 1948); D'Arcy W. Thompson, *On Growth and Form,* Vols. I and II, 2nd ed. (Cambridge, Eng.: University Press, 1959 reprint); L. L. Whyte, ed., *Aspects of Form* (Bloomington: Indiana University Press, 1961).

It is noteworthy that in the United States attention to industrial design began to diminish after the 1950's. At the same time, the application of statistical quality control was disappearing. Publications of research relating architecture, engineering and industrial design stopped.

quality achievement plays a dominant role. (2) There are industrywide standards. The Japan Industrial Standard, Z8101-1981, is widely accepted by Japanese industry. (3) The prime goal of the company is to launch new products with lowest costs and highest quality before any competitors can reach the market with the winning combination.

The quality deployment function (QDF) is part of the CWQC effort. It is the means by which the customers' requirements are spread throughout the organization and made understandable to all participants in the achievement of the company's goals. Matrices play an important part in the communication of customers' needs, both vertically and horizontally, to those involved in all aspects of product development and production. These are listed by L. P. Sullivan as: marketing strategies, planning, product design and engineering, prototype evaluation, production process development, production, and sales. He describes various steps and matrices for conscious deployment of customer requirements throughout the organization.[5]

The Tradeoffs of Cost and Quality

Cost and quality are critical tradeoff dimensions. As shown in Figure 6–1, sometimes achieving better quality requires increasing costs. These costs are usually incurred at process startup or changeover. The capital investment in equipment and facilities can be positively correlated with the quality that can be delivered by those facilities. Positive correlation occurs only if there is awareness of how to use the investment to promote quality.

There are costs involved in taking an existing process investment and improving it so that superior quality is produced. For example, better training of workers is a cost that will be more than offset by reduction in defectives. In this case, the net change in cost is a saving realized in conjunction with a quality improvement. By using the process more efficiently quality can be improved and, at the same time, lead to decreased costs. The net saving involves a larger decrease in failure cost offset by a smaller increase in prevention cost. Appraisal cost changes will probably be small and tend to balance out.

The interaction between specific cost and quality dimensions is complex, but generally we can state:

Service or product qualities = f(capital investments, management methods, supplier relations, and worker motivation) Investments include equipment and facilities.

---

[5] L. P. Sullivan, ''Quality Function Deployment,'' *QUALITY PROGRESS*, June 1986, pp. 39–50.

Costs = f(production costs, sales promotion costs, sales volume, perceived quality)

Sales volume (in units) = f(price, perceived quality, sales promotion costs)

Dollar volume = revenue = (price)(sales volume)

Profit = dollar volume − total costs

This formulation may seem to ignore competitors, but on closer inspection we realize that sales volume (in units) and revenue reflect the market shares of competitors. Relative product quality effects price-demand elasticity. If there is only one place to get the product (as in a monopoly), the customers seem to be entirely loyal. As a larger number of competitors vie for the same market, nonloyal customers become increasingly scarce. Consistently high product qualities may be necessary to stay the course.

In the economists' view, both dollar volume and total costs will increase with improved quality. In Figure 6–4, the curve of dollar volume is shown

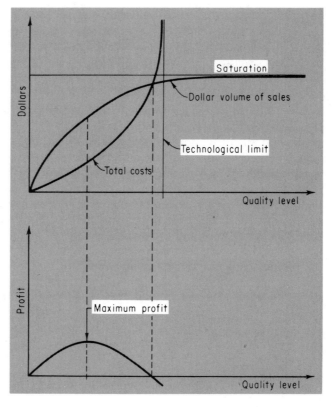

FIGURE 6-4. There is a level of quality that will maximize profits.

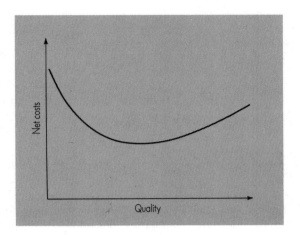

FIGURE 6-5. Net costs reach a minimum at some quality level.

as a decelerating function because at some point, market saturation begins to take effect. The curve of total costs is assumed to be an accelerating function, because it becomes increasingly difficult to improve quality (like a golf score). Therefore, as shown in Figure 6–4, there is a level of quality that will maximize profits. There is an upper limit to the level of quality that can be achieved within a given technological framework.

The economists' view has been shown to be correct for certain situations and not for others. First, the effect of quality on market share can be substantial. Against all odds, the Japanese auto companies secured 30 percent of the U.S. domestic market. The secret marketing weapon was quality. Second, with appropriate knowledge about the importance of understanding the causes of variation, quality improvement can reduce costs. Figure 6–5 shows a situation where net costs decrease with increasing quality.

To understand the measurement, or scoring, of overall quality (which consists of the product's bundle of attributes), see the discussion of dimensional analysis, pp. 437–441. In that case, the overall quality (or value) of option A is measured relative to that of B by means of a ratio comparing the products (multiplications) of the quality factors raised to exponential powers. The exponents represented the individual assessments of the importance of each (quality) attribute. Thus, overall quality level is a multi-attribute description of quality that reflects managerial estimates of the relative importance of the different attributes that contribute to the judgment of overall quality level.

PROBLEM
SET

1. Develop a taxonomy for the quality of an automobile that replaces a list of qualities with a classification system that sheds light on the types of qualities.

2. Why does a taxonomy of quality improve understanding of management's responsibility for competitiveness?

3. Explain the measurement or scoring of quality. Can such procedures cost more than they are worth?

4. The term "robust quality" has been used with increasing frequency by students of quality as a competitive issue. Consult the dictionary for "robust;" what explanation can be given for this distinction?

Section 6.2 Inspection and Acceptance Sampling

To establish quality controls, we must describe the dimensions of quality so that they can be measured. In all discussions that follow, we shall assume that managerial agreement exists concerning the dimensions and standards for defining quality.

Let us focus on input quality and the function of inspecting incoming materials. We use the generic term **materials** to include everything purchased from outside, or produced by another department of the same firm, including components, subassemblies, maintenance materials, and housekeeping supplies. Service inputs (such as those from knowledge workers) can be more difficult to evaluate. Nevertheless, often they can be treated successfully by measuring speed of delivery and quality of the delivered product. For example, how many typing errors were there, how crisp were the french fries, and how satisfied is the customer with the repair service? With a little imagination, the same methods work for describing the qualities of goods and services.

Input material standards must be stated explicitly to make certain that they conform to quality specifications. These specifications are set to meet the needs of the process for workable materials which can be transformed into process outputs that satisfy market expectations and create loyal customers.

Costs of Defective Inputs

Inferior materials create many kinds of costs. For example, the cost of unusable items (generally refunded), or the cost of not having a part when it is needed. This could be called the cost of emergency orders. It is often associated with engineering design changes. The item is thought to be in stock, but it is not. This cost can be severe. For example, assume that a generator part, known to fail occasionally, is carried in stock at a quantity level in excess of expected usage. The high inventory level is geared to the fact that if no spare is on hand, the generator is shut down. So a large buffer stock is maintained. When a failure of this part occurs, the repair team discovers that all the spares are faulty and cannot be used. They should have been inspected when they were received. Or they may have spoiled after being added to stock.

In the same way, if a company manufactures a product that requires a raw material, or a subcontracted subassembly which has been put into stock but found to be unusable when it is needed, production is stopped until a usable supply can be obtained (see the inventory model on pp. 312–315).

There is also the cost of disgruntled customers. In this case, we assume that the quality of the purchased items does not affect the production process but does affect the quality of the final unit. It is the consumer who perceives the difference in quality. It is the producer of the final unit who receives and deserves full blame (with consequent losses) for having passed the inferior material along to the consumer. The vendor of the inferior items enjoys relative anonymity. Inspection of the purchased item could have avoided this cost—but then there would be an inspection cost. Proper management of the inspection function is based on the need to balance various costs. We spend as much on the inspection process as would be required to offset penalties of the types described above. One part of the total costs in Fig. 6–4 is the cost of inspection. We isolate this inspection system and attempt to minimize its total costs.

One Hundred Percent Inspection

Total, or 100 percent inspection, often has higher costs than inspecting some portion (a sample) of all items. Such higher costs might be justified if increased accuracy is derived as a result of using 100 percent inspection and the penalty for being inaccurate is great. However, total inspection is seldom the most accurate method that can be followed. It has been found that 100 percent inspection tends to produce carelessness and error due to fatigue. The inspector's human frailties become apparent when there are many items to be inspected, quickly and with no relief.

Furthermore, 100 percent inspection is out of the question where destructive testing is required. A manufacturer of firecrackers, bullets, a food product, or soap flakes cannot destroy (eat, taste, make into suds) a total shipment in order to find out if each item comes up to the standards. So 100 percent inspection, whether it be done by person or machine, is slow, costly, and frequently unreliable—even when it is possible. On the other hand, for a few truly critical items (where performance is a matter of life and death), 200 or 300 percent inspection might be insufficient. In the project shop especially, repeated inspection with crosschecks is essential.

Acceptance Sampling Terminology

At Western Electric Company in the 1920s, a growing body of statistical theory was used to develop sampling plans that could be employed as substitutes for 100 percent inspection. These sampling inspection techniques were applied to purchased and subcontracted parts, raw materials, office supplies, and maintenance parts. They could also be used by producers to conduct sample tests of their own output. At the same time, the sequential test methods of statistical quality control were being developed. These are more frequently used by producers who have sufficient run sizes to evaluate and control their own output.

The only kinds of sampling procedures that had been used before this were proportional sampling methods, which are wrong (though often intuitively appealing). Before we can explain why this is so, let us develop the terms and symbols necessary for discussing sampling plans.

$$N = \text{the lot size}$$

This is usually the total number of items produced by the vendor within a single shipment. More generally, it can be the total production run of the producer for which the conditions of the system remained essentially unchanged. Thus, it is assumed that the quality of items within a lot is homogeneous. This means that the average number of defectives produced by the process does not change from the beginning to the end of the run.

Every time there is a change of conditions, such as startup each day or one worker relieving another, it should be assumed that a new lot has begun. Where this information is not known, a reasonable number of shipping units should be termed a lot.

The average fraction or percent of defective parts is called the *process average* and symbolized by $\bar{p}$. It must be estimated from the process behavior. The fraction defective or percent defective in a lot is called p. It is usually unknown.

$$n = \text{the sample size}$$

The items to be inspected should be a representative sample drawn at random from the lot. We do not just inspect material that happens to be at the top of the box. Housewives have always known this when they buy strawberries; managers have not always been so astute.

$$c = \text{the sample criterion}$$

This criterion is defined so that when n items are drawn from a lot size of N, and k items are found to be defective, then if $k > c$, we reject the entire lot. If $k \leq c$, we accept the lot. Therefore, c is called the *acceptance number of the sampling plan*.

For example, if 5 items (n) are drawn from a lot size (N) of 20, and the acceptance number (c) is set at 2, if 3 items are found to be defective ($k = 3$), we reject the entire lot because $k > c$. However, if 2 or less items are found to be defective ($k \leq 2$), we accept the lot (minus the defectives we have found) because $k \leq c$. With the acceptance number $c = 0$, one defective item results in rejection of the lot.

**CASE:
PROPOR-
TIONAL
SAMPLING
AT
FARMERS'
BANK**

The underlying assumption of proportional sampling is that if we had 2 lots, A and B, and A was twice as large as B, then we should draw twice as large a sample from A as from B.

Farmers' Bank is branching out. It engages a market research firm to find out how its present customers feel about the bank's services. The bank has 4 different kinds of accounts, including:

No-interest checking accounts
Day of deposit to day of withdrawal savings at 5 percent
2-year 6 percent savings certificates
4-year 7 percent savings certificates

Also, it classifies its customers according to whether they are rural, suburban, or city dwellers. Thus, 12 categories of customers will be sampled, and they are each of different sizes. The bank manager learns that the market research firm intends to mail the survey to 20 percent of the customers in each of the 12 categories. This procedure upsets the manager. Does it upset you?

Let us take a close look at proportional sampling. The percentage of a lot to be inspected is fixed at $n/N = K$. In this case, there are 12 lots and 20 percent of each is to be inspected. An unhappy customer is classified as a defective item. If $c = 0$ is the acceptance number being used, the total lot will be rejected if any defectives are found. The bank will interpret a rejected lot as an entire category of customers who are unhappy with the services it renders to that category.

Figure 6–6 illustrates three different 20 percent sampling plans. Once we explain how to read them, it will be evident why the bank manager has every reason to be concerned.

Operating characteristic curves (called OC curves), which are shown in Fig. 6–6, clearly demonstrate that the proportional sampling concept is wrong. The horizontal axis is the actual fraction defective in the lot, called p. The OC curve shows how P_A, the probability of accepting the lot, changes with respect to p for a number of different sampling plans, all of which utilize the same sampling proportion of $n/N = 0.20$ and the same acceptance number, $c = 0$. Thus, these plans, all of which are based on the policy of proportional sampling, produce significantly different results. The probability of accepting a lot of 20 items is much higher than the probability of accepting a lot of 50 items, and both have higher P_As than for 100 items—when proportional sampling is used. This is not an acceptable condition for inspection. We can note the effect of changing the value of c by looking at Figure 6–8. The comparison can be made between $n = 20$, $c = 0$, and $n = 20$, $c = 1$. There is a significant decrease in the discriminating ability of the plan when the acceptance number, c, is increased from zero to one. Consequently, there is a great deal of control over the robustness of the sampling test through the manipulation of the acceptance number. The classic case is $c = 0$.

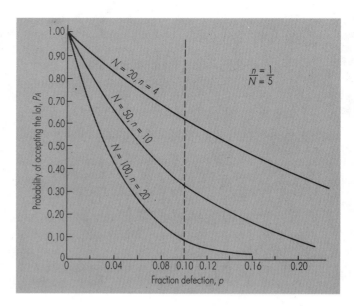

FIGURE 6-6. Operating characteristic (OC) curves for several proportional sampling plans
In all these cases $c = 0$ and the proportion sampled is 20 percent. Farmers' Bank will change its policy for any category of customer in which one or more of the customers are unhappy with the bank's practices.

Assume that if 10 percent (or more) of the bank's customers in any category are markedly unhappy with the bank's practices, the bank intends to change its present policies with respect to that category as it expands to new locations. (*Note:* The bank's definition of a defective is an unhappy customer as measured by some explicit set of answers to the survey questionnaire. Since the acceptance number c is zero, if one or more defectives appear in the sample, the bank will reject the lot; i.e., change its policies.)

In one category, there are 20 accounts ($N = 20$). Four questionnaires will be sent ($n = 4$). If one or more replies is a defective (unhappy customer), the policies for that category will be changed. The probability of accepting the lot (no change in policy) is more than 60 percent (P_A), given that the true degree of unhappiness is $p = 0.10$ (see Fig. 6–6).

How is P_A derived? See p. 253 for the equation $P_A = (1 - p)^n$. With $p = .10$, then $1 - p = .90$, and this number raised to the fourth power is $.9 \times .9 \times .9 \times .9 = .66$, which is an approximation to the value of $60+$ percent for P_A, as stated above. The formula that we have used assumed that N was larger than 20. The hypergeometric formula (p. 259) would have used $N = 20$ for a better estimate.)

In the second category, $N = 50$, $n = 10$, $c = 0$, and the probability of making no change is greater than 30 percent. In the third category, $N =$

$100, n = 20, c = 0$. Here, the probability of making no change is slightly under 10 percent, given that the actual degree of unhappiness is $p = 0.10$.

The bank manager has good reason to be distressed. Proportional sampling results in different and arbitrary criteria for determining what policies to follow. We have developed the case of Farmers' Bank in order to demonstrate several things. First, proportional sampling does not work. Second, the definition of acceptable quality and of defectives does not have to conform to the usual manufacturing application of these terms. Now let us return to the notion of a buyer's wanting to inspect the input shipments from a supplier or vendor.

What sampling method should be used to manage input qualities? The answer is that by choosing appropriate values for n and c, we can develop an *OC* curve that should be acceptable to both vendor and buyer. (We will use the terms suppliers and vendors interchangeably.) The definition of what is acceptable cannot be the decision of the buyer alone. The situation calls for compromise and negotiation between the vendor and the purchaser. (Purchasers and buyers are also interchangeable terms.) Fig. 6–7 shows what is involved.

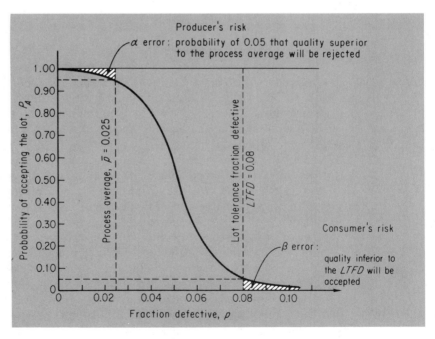

FIGURE 6-7. Consumer's and producer's risks, shown in this OC curve, are determined by negoiation.

The two shaded areas marked alpha and beta in Fig. 6–7 are two
different kinds of risk. The alpha area is called the **producer's risk.** It
gives the probability that acceptable lots will be rejected by the sampling
plan that is shown. Acceptable lots are those which have a smaller fraction
of defectives than are normally produced by the process (i.e., the process
average, $\bar{p}$). This limit is also called the **average quality limit (AQL).**

On the other hand, the beta area represents the probability that unacceptable levels of defectives will be accepted by the sampling plan. This
is called the consumer's risk. The limiting value, defined by the consumer,
is called the **lot tolerance fraction defective, LTFD.** If percentage defective
is used instead of fraction defective, the limit is called LTPD. It is also
known as the **reject quality limit (RQL).** LTFD, LTPD, or RQL are the
lowest quality limits the consumer is willing to tolerate in each lot. To
the right of this point on the x axis of Figure 6–7, the buyer would like
to reject all lots. But this is impossible if inspection by sampling methods
is to be used. Therefore, the buyer compromises by saying that no more
than beta percent of the time should such quality be accepted by the
sampling procedure.

The Cost of Inspection

Given the process average, $\bar{p}$, alpha, and the consumer's specification
of LTFD and beta, a sampling plan can be found that minimizes the cost
of inspection. In this cost we include the expense of **detailing,** which is
the operation of inspecting 100 percent of the items in all rejected lots to
remove the defective pieces.

Such a sampling plan imputes a dollar value to the probability of falsely
rejecting lots of acceptable quality (alpha). If the producer wishes to
decrease the alpha-type risk, it can do so by improving the process average
$\bar{p}$. But an improvement of this kind may be costly. It is likely that the
consumer would be forced to accept part of this increased cost in the
form of higher prices. Whether it is the producer or the consumer who
bears the cost of inspection (or if they share it), they must agree that the
only rational procedure to be followed is to minimize inspection costs and
negotiate about the values for LTFD and beta. Under some circumstances, they might also consider improvements that can be made in $\bar{p}$.

It is important to observe that any sampling plan, of a specific c and
n, completely specifies the alpha and beta risks for given levels of $\bar{p}$ and
LTFD. In turn, the sampling plan requires n inspections for every lot. If
the process average, $\bar{p}$, is the true state of affairs, then alpha percent of
the time the remainder of the lot will be inspected. Thus, the average

number of pieces inspected will be $n + (N - n)$ (alpha). This number is also called the **average sample number (ASN)**.

As n gets large, approaching N, with all other factors remaining constant, the plan becomes increasingly discriminating and alpha approaches 1. The effect is illustrated in Fig. 6–8. This results in the average number of pieces to be inspected approximating N. We have $n + (N - n)$ $1 = N$.

On the other hand, we observe that as n gets small, approaching 1, beta increases rapidly and approaches 1, while alpha tends to become 0. In this case, the average number of pieces that will be inspected will be close to 1, but the consumer's risk will be high. Between these extremes, there exist appropriate values of c and n that will minimize the average number of pieces to be inspected for some specified level of consumer protection. Thus, in Fig. 6–8, Plan A requires that (on average) $[20 + 80(0.06)] = 24.8$ pieces be inspected. Plan B requires $[10 + 90(0.21)] = 28.9$ pieces to be inspected (given $N = 100$). Both plans provide the same consumer risk.

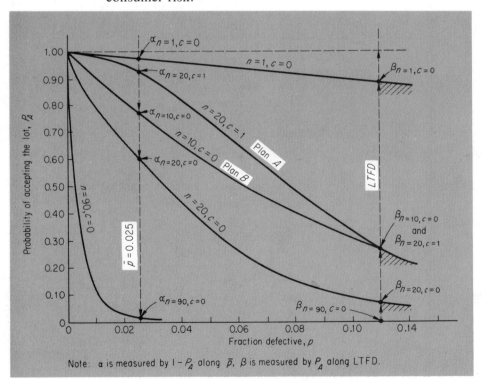

Note: α is measured by $1 - P_A$ along $\bar{p}$, β is measured by P_A along LTFD.

FIGURE 6-8. As the sample size increases, all other factors remaining constant, the plan becomes increasingly discriminating from the point of view of the consumer; that is, β approaches zero, but the cost of inspection increases rapidly as α approaches one. For a given level of β protection there is a sampling plan that minimizes the cost of inspection. Thus, for LTFD = 0.12 and β equals 0.26, Plan A has a lower cost of inspection than Plan B.

Design of Operating Characteristic (OC) Curves

How are the kinds of plans we have been discussing constructed? One of the most direct approaches is to utilize tables that have been designed for this purpose.[6] On the other hand, *OC* curves can be derived directly from appropriate mathematical statements.

Hypergeometric Distribution

The **hypergeometric distribution** is used when the lot size N is small, so that the effect of successive sampling, which reduces the number of unsampled units remaining in the lot (i.e., N units, $N - 1$ units, $N - 2$ units), can be taken into account.

When N is large enough so that the effects of diminishing sample size are negligible, the binomial distribution can be used. Neither the binomial nor the Poisson distributions require specification of N, since in both cases, N is assumed to be infinitely large. These distributions are discussed below.

Figure 6–9 illustrates the fact that when N equals 1,000, the assumption

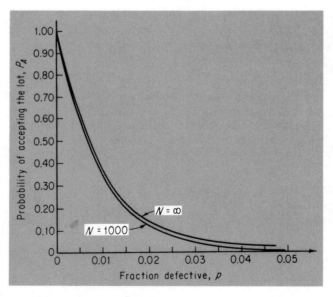

FIGURE 6-9. When the lot size N is reasonably large, say approximately 1000, the assumption of an infinite lot size does not introduce great inaccuracy into the sampling plan. The binomial and Poisson methods for deriving OC curves assume that $N = \infty$.

---

[6]Harold F. Dodge and Harry G. Romig, *Sampling Inspection Tables, Single and Double Sampling* (New York: Wiley, 1951).

of an infinite N does not introduce much inaccuracy into the sampling plan. It is usually reasonable to employ the binomial or Poisson distributions when N is equal to much less than 1,000—say N = 100, or even less.

Consider the following simple hypergeometric formula for a sampling plan with acceptance number $c = 0$.

$$P_A = \frac{(N - x)!(N - n)!}{(N - x - n)!N!}$$

where x = the number of defectives actually in the lot and x/N is therefore the actual fraction defective of the lot, p.

As we vary x from 0 to N, we determine the different values of P_A that are associated with each level of fraction defectives. Thus, in the case where $N = 4$, $n = 1$, and $c = 0$, the formula for P_A would be:

$$P_A = \frac{(4 - x)!3!}{(3 - x)!4!} = \frac{(4 - x)!}{4(3 - x)!} = \frac{4 - x}{4}$$

Then, for the different values of x we would get:

TABLE 6-1

x	$x/N = p$	P_A
0	0.00	1.00
1	0.25	0.75
2	0.50	0.50
3	0.75	0.25
4	1.00	0.00

We can illustrate the binomial computation of the OC curve quite readily. For the situation where $c = 0$, the binomial formulation becomes:

$$P_A = (1 - p)^n$$

As previously noted,[7] there is no provision for specifying the lot size, N. Then, when $n = 1$, we obtain $P_A = (1 - p)$. In this case, the results are identical with those derived for the hypergeometric distribution above.

---

[7] On pp. 259–260 we give the general form of the hypergeometric distribution (for cases where $c > 0$). Then, on pages 260–263, the use of the binomial and Poisson distributions to derive OC curves is explained. The capability to construct OC charts is of benefit, but it is not essential for the user who has handbooks of sampling plans available in the library. See MIL STD 105D, and Dodge and Romig, referenced in the prior footnote. The more recent standards are known as ANSI/ASQC Z 1.4—1981.

Product quality is established by an expensive testing procedure that does not harm the product. One hundred percent inspection is considered too expensive, so hypergeometric sampling is used.

The company's OC curve is the one derived in Table 6–1. Four diamonds are made at a time, and one of them is selected for testing. If a defect is found, the remaining three diamonds are tested. The process average for defectives is $\bar{p} = 0.25$. What is the average number of pieces inspected? Following the reasoning on pp. 250–251, if the process average, $\bar{p} = 0.25$, is the true state of affairs, then $P_A = 0.75$, and alpha $= 1 - P_A = 0.25$, or 25 percent of the time the remainder of the lot will be inspected. Thus, the average number of pieces inspected will be: $1 + (4 - 1)0.25 = 1.75$ diamonds.

Average Outgoing Quality Limit (AOQL)

Quality management is assisted by the idea of an **average outgoing quality (AOQ).** This is a measure of the average or expected percentage of defective items that the producer will ship to the consumer under different conditions. First, every sampled lot is divided into n units to be inspected, and the remaining $(N - n)$ units. The probable number of defectives in the unsampled portion $(N - n)$ is $\bar{p}(N - n)$. Out of every 100 samples taken we expect that P_A will be the fraction of samples that is passed without any further examination. These are the only units that cannot be tagged as defectives and replaced (in the sense of detailing). Note that $1 - P_A$ of the 100 samples will be rejected and fully detailed, which will identify all other defectives. Consequently, $P_A\bar{p}(N - n)$ is the expected number of defectives that will be passed without having been identified for every N units processed.

As another approach, the ratio $P_A p(N - n)/N$ is used. This fraction is called the AOQ (average outgoing quality), and it changes value as p does.

$$AOQ = P_A p(N - n)/N$$

Note that the value of P_A changes with p in accordance with the specifics of the sampling plan, which are based on the values of n and c that are chosen. Thus, AOQ is a function of all the elements of a sampling plan and can therefore be used as a means of evaluating a sampling plan. Specifically, for each value of p an AOQ measure is derived. It is the expected value of the percent defectives that would be passed without detection if the process were operating at the value p. The AOQ measure reaches a maximum level for some particular value of p. The maximum level is termed the average outgoing quality limit (AOQL).

For example, consider the following computations using our previous hypergeometric and binomial results

TABLE 6-2

p	P_A	$(N - n)/N$	AOQ
0	1	3/4	0
1/4	3/4	3/4	9/64
1/2	1/2	3/4	12/64 (AOQL)
3/4	1/4	3/4	9/64
1	0	3/4	0

Perhaps another example, based on a more refined hypergeometric *OC* curve, would help. In this case $N = 50$, $n = 10$, and $c = 0$. (See Plan 1 on pages 259–260.)

TABLE 6-3

x	x/N = p	P_A
0	0.00	1.00
1	0.25	0.75
2	0.50	0.50
3	0.75	0.25
4	1.00	0.00

The maximum value of AOQ has been calculated as 0.02541. It is the AOQL also shown in Fig. 6–10. The average outgoing quality limit (AOQL) describes the worst case of percent defectives that can be shipped, if it is assumed that the defectives of rejected lots are replaced with acceptable

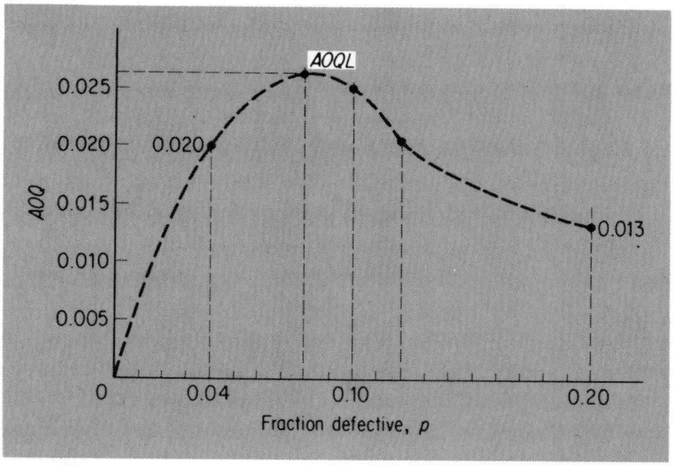

FIGURE 6-10. The average outgoing quality as a function of process defective rate *p* with the limit *AOQL* equal to 0.02541, occurring at $p = 0.08$.

product and that all lots are thoroughly mixed so that shipments have a homogeneous quality.

Multiple Sampling

Other types of sampling plans are utilized when the amount of inspection required by the single sampling plan appears to be too great. By **single-sampling plan,** we mean that the acceptance decision must be made on the basis of the first sample drawn. If **double sampling** is used, a second sample can be drawn, if needed. In general, with double sampling, inspection costs can be lowered.

The double sampling plan requires two acceptance numbers c_1 and c_2 such that $c_2 > c_1$. Then, if the observed number of defectives in the first sample of size n_1 is k_1:

1. We accept the lot if $k_1 \leq c_1$.
2. We reject the lot if $k_1 > c_2$.
3. If $c_1 < k_1 \leq c_2$, we draw an additional sample of size n_2. The total sample is now of size $n_1 + n_2$.

If the number of defectives in the total sample is $k_1 + k_2$, then:
4. We accept the lot if $(k_1 + k_2) \leq c_2$.
5. We reject the lot if $(k_1 + k_2) > c_2$.

Figure 6–11 illustrates the way in which double sampling divides the graph space into unique acceptance and rejection regions.

There are also multiple sampling plans and sequential sampling plans. Tables exist which enable a manager to choose an appropriate plan without having to engage in onerous numerical calculations. Best cost remains the criterion for choosing a plan.

The inspection cost per piece can vary greatly, depending upon the nature of the item and the definition of a defective, which may not be a straightforward matter. Given such a definition, it might require days of testing to determine whether an item is acceptable. For example, a defective might be defined as a unit possessing any three flaws where 100 different kinds of flaws could occur.

It is instructive to see how so many different factors come together in a discussion of this kind. We observe that the process average, the quality expectations, the inspection cost, and the market's acceptance of the product are tightly interwoven and that any approach to management decision-making which bypasses a synthesis of these issues is bound to be counterproductive.

CASE: CITY WASTE DISPOSAL

A double sampling plan is used to inspect the quality of work of sanitation teams. The plan is that out of 1,000 streets, 36 are chosen randomly and inspected. If all 36 are satisfactory, then inspection is discontinued for that

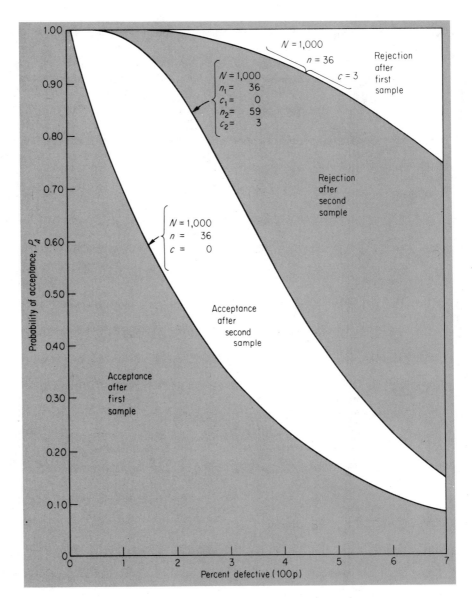

FIGURE 6-11. Characteristics of a double sampling plan [From Eugene L. Grant, *Statistical Quality Control*, 5th ed. (New York: McGraw-Hill Book Company, Inc., 1979), p. 376.]

day. If more than 3 of the 36 are unsatisfactory, all streets are inspected, and the sanitation teams are required to return and clean up all unsatisfactory conditions.

If at least 1 and not more than 3 defective cleanups are found, another 59 streets are chosen randomly and inspected. The number of unsatisfactory conditions found in the first sample is added to those found in the second sample. If the total number of defective cleanups is 3 or less, inspection is discontinued. Otherwise, 100 percent inspection is required.

Assume that the average number of defective cleanups is 30 streets out of 1,000. Using Fig. 6–11, note that for 3 percent defective, the probability of discontinuing inspection after the first sample is about 34 percent (36 streets inspected). The probability of having to inspect 1,000 − 36 = 964 streets is about 2 percent (1.00 − 0.98 on the chart). The probability of discontinuing inspection after the second sample is approximately 70 − 34 = 36 percent (36 + 59 = 95 streets inspected). The probability of having to inspect 1,000 − 36 − 59 = 905 streets is 0.98 − 0.70 = 0.28, or 28 percent. We can summarize these results as follows:

(1) Number of Streets Inspected	(2) Probability of Occurrence	Product (1) × (2)
36	0.34	12.24
964	0.02	19.28
95	0.36 ⎱ 0.64*	34.20
905	0.28 ⎰	253.40
	Expected number of streets inspected =	319.12

*The probability of having to take a second sample is: 1.00 − 0.34 − 0.02 = 0.64, or 64 percent.

This result is unsatisfactory to the manager of City Waste Disposal. Not only is the expected number of streets to be inspected too high, but the impossibility of inspecting 1,000 streets at one time makes the plan unfeasible. Instead, the manager suggests that the city be divided into 5 zones of 200 streets. Each day, one zone will be chosen randomly and a double sampling plan based on N = 200 will be used. In that way, the maximum number of streets to be inspected will never exceed 200, and the expected number will be well below the maximum. Everyone agrees.

Acceptance Sampling for Job Shop and FPS Output

In a job shop or a flexible processing system, where small batches of items are produced, there is insufficient output to use statistical quality control (SQC) methods. (These are described in the next section.) Therefore, acceptance sampling (AS) of small-batch production runs must be used to monitor quality. SQC requires large batch sizes and is ideally suited to continuous sampling of the serial production of flow shops and intermittent flow shops.

The control of quality for FPS product is under development. FPS presents new challenges for measuring and monitoring output. The lot sizes can be so small as to prohibit the use of AS. Because of the non-repetitive nature of the output but the repetitive focus of the process, efforts are being made to utilize measurements of the accuracy of the process settings. As the software drives the equipment, monitors determine whether the equipment functions as intended by the CAD/CAM designers. The scenario then relates equipment motions and positions with an in-depth analysis of the product's quality.

OC Curves for the Hypergeometric Distribution

For sampling without replacement, the hypergeometric distribution should be used. We cannot assume that each item drawn for the sample of size n is then replaced before the next unit is drawn. The lot size N is finite and small enough to allow such depletion to affect the results. If we replaced items, to keep N of constant size, we might by chance keep sampling exactly the same item over and over. Also, with destructive testing, we cannot replace sampled items that must be destroyed to ascertain their quality.

The number of defectives in the lot is specified as the variable x. Then, x/N is the actual fraction defective of the lot. When we draw the first unit for the sample, the probability of drawing a defective will be x/N. We do not replace this unit after recording its state, and therefore when the second unit of the sample is drawn, the probabilities are a function of $(N - 1)$. This is true whether the first sample drawn was defective or not. Thus, when the difference between N and $(N - 1)$ is significant, we use the combinatorial formulation:

$$P_j = C_{n-j}^{N-x}C_j^x/C_n^N = \frac{(N - x)!x!n!(N - n)!}{(n - j)!(N - x - n + j)!j!(x - j)!N!}$$

All variables are described above, except j, which equals the number of defectives in the sample.

TABLE 6-4 EXAMPLE OF THE DETERMINATION* OF OC CURVES FOR $c = 0$ AND $c = 1$, $N = 50$; $n = 10$

Abscissa Value	Plan 1 For $c = 0$ $j = 0$		$j = 1$	Plan 2 For $c = 1$ $j = 0 + 1$
$p = \dfrac{x}{N} = 0$; $x = 0$	$P_{A,j=0} = \dfrac{50!10!40!}{10!40!50!}$ $= 1.000$	$P_{A,j=1} = 0.000$		$P_{A,j=0+1} = 1.000$
$p = \dfrac{x}{N} = 0.04$; $x = 2$	$P_{A,j=0} = \dfrac{48!2!10!40!}{10!38!2!50!}$ $= 0.637$		$P_{A,j=1} = \dfrac{48!2!10!40!}{9!39!50!}$ $= 0.326$	$P_{A,j=0+1} = 0.963$
$p = \dfrac{x}{N} = 0.10$; $x = 5$	$P_{A,j=0} = \dfrac{45!5!10!40!}{10!35!5!50!}$ $= 0.311$		$P_{A,j=1} = \dfrac{45!5!10!40!}{9!36!4!50!}$ $= 0.432$	$P_{A,j=0+1} = 0.743$
$p = \dfrac{x}{N} = 0.20$; $x = 10$	$P_{A,j=0} = \dfrac{40!10!10!40!}{10!30!10!50!}$ $= 0.083$		$P_{A,j=1} = \dfrac{40!10!10!40!}{9!31!9!50!}$ $= 0.268$	$P_{A,j=0+1} = 0.351$

*Note: These computations can be facilitated by using a log table of factorials, for example, E. L. Grant and R. S. Leavenworth, *Statistical Quality Control*, 5th ed. (New York: McGraw-Hill Book Company, Inc., 1979).

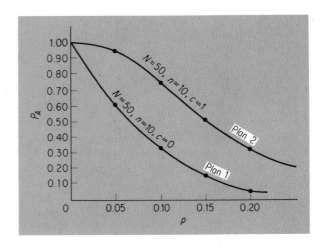

FIGURE 6-12.

The curves are drawn in Fig. 6–12 for both of the hypergeometric plans derived in Table 6–4. Note that the second column gives the probabilities for values of x when $j = 0$. This is equivalent to the $c = 0$ plan. However, the third column, which gives the probabilities for values of x when $j = 1$, must be added to the second column, resulting in the fourth column, which is the plan for $c = 1$. The reason is that the $c = 1$ plan must include both $j = 0$ and $j = 1$ events.

OC Curves Based on the Binomial and Poisson Distributions

When the system is insensitive to lot size, N, then either the binomial distribution or the Poisson distribution can be used. Both assume that the lot size is infinite, and require far less computation than the hypergeometric distribution. We stated that when N gets reasonably large (say, 1,000), the assumption of an infinite N does not introduce distortion. In many applications, even when N is as small as 100 the infinite assumption is satisfactory.

Binomial Distribution

The binomial distribution is represented by:

$$\text{Prob } (j; n, p) = \left[\frac{n!}{j!(n - j)!} \right] p^j q^{n-j}$$

where

$$p + q = 1.$$

When $j = 0$, the probabilities are calculated for the $c = 0$ plan.
    To obtain the OC curve for $n = 100$, $c = 0$, we have:

$$P_A = \text{Prob} (0; 100, p) = \left[\frac{100!}{0!(100 - 0)!} \right] p^0 q^{100} = q^{100} = (1 - p)^{100}$$

Table 6–5 is derived by substituting values of p between 0 and 1 into the binomial formulation. Note that $0! = 1! = 1$.

TABLE 6-5

Fraction Defective, p	1 − p	$(1 - p)^{100} = P_A$
0.00	1.00	1.000
0.01	0.99	0.366
0.02	0.98	0.133
0.04	0.96	0.017
.	.	.
.	.	.
.	.	.
1.00	0.00	0.000

For the acceptance number $c = 1$, we require the same kind of addition as was the case for the hypergeometric. Thus, obtain the sum:

$$P_A = \text{Prob} (0; 100, p) + \text{Prob} (1; 100, p)$$

for values of p.
    To derive the OC curve for $n = 100$, $c = 1$, using the binomial formulation, we compute:

$$\text{Prob} (1; 100, p) = \left[\frac{100!}{1!(100 - 1)!} \right] p^1 (1 - p)^{100-1} = 100p(1 - p)^{99}$$

Table 6–6 follows.

TABLE 6-6

Fraction Defective, p	1 − p	$100p(1 - p)^{99}$
0.00	1.00	0.000
0.01	0.99	0.370
0.02	0.98	0.271
0.04	0.96	0.070
.	.	.
.	.	.
.	.	.
1.00	0.00	0.000

By adding the third columns of Tables 6–5 and 6–6, we achieve the $c = 1$ plan, shown in the fourth column of Table 6–7.

TABLE 6-7

Fraction Defective, p	$j = 0$ $(1 - p)^{100}$ $P_A(c = 0)$	$j = 1$ $100p(1 - p)^{99}$	$P_A(c = 1)$
0.00	1.000	0.000	1.000
0.01	0.366	0.370	0.736
0.02	0.133	0.271	0.404
0.04	0.017	0.070	0.087
.	.	.	.
.	.	.	.
.	.	.	.
1.00	0.000	0.000	0.000

As expected, the *OC* curve for $c = 0$ is far more stringent than for $c = 1$.

Poisson Distribution

It is even simpler to use the **Poisson distribution.** Like the binomial, it assumes sampling with replacement (i.e., N can be treated as infinite). Also, p should be small.

$$\text{Prob } (j; \text{m}) = \frac{m^j e^{-m}}{j!}$$

Let $j = 0$, which is equivalent to $c = 0$, and let $n = 100$. Then, since $m = np$, we have $m = 100p$.

TABLE 6-8 **Prob $(0; 100p) = e^{-np} = e^{-100p}$**

Fraction Defective, p	$100p = m$	Prob $(j; m) = P_A$
0.00	0	1.000
0.01	1	0.368
0.02	2	0.135
0.04	4	0.018
.	.	.
.	.	.
.	.	.
1.00	100	0.000

We observe that this result is essentially the same as that obtained by using the binomial distribution. It should be remembered that a sampling plan where $c = 1$ requires computations of P_A for $j = 0$, which are then added to those of P_A for $j = 1$ to obtain the sampling plan for $c = 1$. Thus, we have Tables 6–9 and 6–10.

TABLE 6-9   Prob (1; 100p) = (100p)e^{-100p}

Fraction Defective, p	100p = m	Prob (j; m)
0.00	0	0.000
0.01	1	0.368
0.02	2	0.271
0.04	4	0.073
.	.	.
.	.	.
.	.	.
1.00	100	0.000

TABLE 6-10   COLUMN 3 SUMS OF TABLES 6-8 AND 6-9

Fraction Defective, p	j = 0	j = 1	P$_A$
0.00	1.000	0.000	1.000
0.01	0.368	0.368	0.736
0.02	0.135	0.271	0.406
0.04	0.018	0.073	0.091
.	.	.	.
.	.	.	.
.	.	.	.
1.00	0.000	0.000	0.000

The Poisson approximation of the binomial is good for small values of p. Comparing Tables 6–10 and 6–7, through the range of $p = 0.00$ to 0.04, we see that the OC curves are sufficiently similar to use either approach. How small p should be is determined by the acceptability of the results; does the range $0.00 - 0.04$ provide sufficient accuracy?

Let us compare one larger value (for $c = 0$ and $p = 0.10$):

$$\text{Binomial } P_A = (1 - 0.10)^{100} = 0.000027$$
$$\text{Poisson } P_A = e^{-100(0.10)} = 0.000045$$

Poisson approximation yields an error of 67 percent when $p = 0.10$, in this case. The fit will depend upon the specifics. It can easily be checked for any situation.

1. "Quality" has two quite different interpretations. One is the consumer's. The other is the producer's. What are the differences, and why do they matter?

2. What inputs to the process require quality management?

3. Distinguish between functional and nonfunctional qualities. For example, are all the functional attributes and none of the nonfunctional attributes measurable?

4. Describe the purpose utilities of food. Since there are multiple purposes, the question arises as to whether certain purposes consistently have greater utility than others. Also, do all foods follow the same pattern? Do patterns shift over time? Discuss these specific questions and then draw generalizations about the concept of purpose utility.

5. Differentiate between services and products with respect to the dimensions of quality.

6. Explain what is meant by the "tradeoffs of cost and quality." When does this concept apply and when does it not apply? When is there a level of quality that will maximize profits? Does this apply to both goods and services?

7. Can the quality of service inputs be managed by the methods of acceptance sampling? Explain your answer.

8. Why is 100 percent inspection unacceptable in most cases? When is it necessary, and what must be done then to make it feasible?

9. Are proportional sampling methods always wrong? Explain.

10. With reference to Fig. 6–4, how is quality level defined?

11. In acceptance sampling, lot size N must be known. What implications does this fact have for the job shop as compared to the flow shop?

12. Quality is a P/OM responsibility. What is meant by this statement?

13. Discuss the concept of reliability as a measure of quality. What does it mean in the case of:

    a. A bar of soap?

    b. A laser printer?

    c. Truck tires?

    d. A filing system?

    e: Steel girders?

    f. A sprinkler system for fire protection?

    g. The handle of a suitcase?

    h. Check processing?

    i. A vaccination program?

    j. The screen of an 8-pound portable PC?

    k. Treatment at a fast food restaurant?

14. As a manufacturer of automobile batteries, you wish to offer the longest possible warranty period. Your policy is based on the belief

that a guarantee period which is longer than your competitors' will increase your sales volume and provide a larger market share. For this reason, you specify that the cost of replacements should use up whatever additional profits you receive as a result of the increased sales volume.

a. What information do you need?

b. How do you propose to handle this problem?

15. What role does (can or should) the industrial designer play in the P/OM's operations? Try to answer all three questions.

16. CREDITCARTER produces credit card blanks which are furnished to various organizations that offer credit to customers. PETROGAS buys the card blanks in lots of 20,000 and inspects each shipment with acceptance sampling. Through negotiations, it has been agreed to set the consumer's risk, beta, at 0.06, and the producer's risk, alpha, at 0.08. CREDITCARTER'S process average for defectives is 0.003. If $c = 0$, what sample size n should be used, and what will be the value of the lot tolerance fraction defective?

Answer: First, we use the equation

$$P_A = (1 - p)^n$$

The value of P_A on the *OC* curve at the process average will be

$$(1 - \alpha) = 0.92 = (1 - \bar{p})^n = (1 - 0.003)^n$$

or

$$0.92 = (0.997)^n$$

In log form:

$$\log 0.92 = n \log 0.997$$

or

$$-0.0362122 = n(-0.0013048)$$

so

$$n = 27.75, \text{ or } 28$$

Again, we use the binomial equation to determine the value of p_{LTFD}. Thus,

$$\beta = (1 - p_{LTFD})^n \text{ or } 0.06 = (1 - p_{LTFD})^{27.75}$$

With logs, we have

$$\log 0.06 = 27.75 \log (1 - p_{LTFD})$$

or

$$\frac{-1.22184}{27.75} = -0.04403 = \log (1 - p_{LTFD})$$

whence

$$(1 - p_{LTFD}) = 0.90359$$

and

$$p_{LTFD} = 0.096$$

17. Omega Electronics uses flow shop methods to manufacture large, integrated semiconductor circuitry which must be highly resistant to vibration and heat. Only destructive testing can be used to check the acceptability of an integrated circuit package. Each unit is costly. The application of the circuit is such that a failure endangers lives. What inspection procedure should be used?

18. The Yukon Company requires a destructive test to determine the quality of the firecrackers it manufactures. Assume that five giant firecrackers compose a lot. The company tests one and ships four, if the test is successful. If the test is not successful, the remaining four are sold as seconds.

   a. Specify the characteristics of this single sampling plan and derive the *OC* curve.

   b. What do you think of this plan?

   Answer: a. This is a sampling plan where $N = 5$, $n = 1$, and $c = 0$. If the process average, $\bar{p} = 2/5$, then the probability of selecting a defective firecracker for the test is 0.40. This means that there is a 2/5 chance of rejecting the lot, or a $1 - 2/5 = 3/5$ chance of accepting it. Following this line of reasoning, the *OC* curve can be quickly derived (see Fig. 6–13).

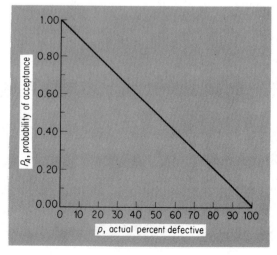

FIGURE 6-13.

b. This plan does not provide a sensitive test (with $p = 3/5$ there is still a 2/5 chance of passing the lot), but the nature and cost of the product do not warrant too much fuss. There is a large producer's risk here (with $p = 1/5$ there is a 1/5 chance of rejecting the lot), but this fault is partially overcome by selling the remaining 4 as seconds, if a reasonable price can be charged for such items.

19. The fast food chain Fingerlickin Jones wants to apply QC methods, such as acceptance sampling, for all the foods it buys from suppliers. It wants to start with the biggest purchases, namely, potatoes for french fries and chopped meat for burgers. Fingerlickin uses six sources for potatoes and ten meat suppliers. Please advise the chain's CEO, Annette Jones.

Section 6.3 Statistical Quality Control of the Outputs

Statistical quality control was developed by Walter Shewhart during the 1920s. SQC was quickly recognized by industry as a crucial addition to the theory of production and operations. Dr. W. E. Deming has referred to this as the theory of variations. The theory took hold in Japan, and was adopted as a basic part of P/OM practice. It applies equally well to goods and services.

Managing the Quality of Process Outputs

By using statistical quality control (SQC), we get to fathom what we are doing. By fathom, we mean to understand deeply and thoroughly. Such learning is applicable and necessary for all products, both goods and services. Dr. Deming calls this "profound knowledge."

Inputs and transformation processes are more or less invisible to the market. The impressions of an organization that customers form are basically dependent on the outputs, including products and advertising. Some companies allow customers to visit their plants or research labs, but that is a disappearing community service.

When output quality is perceived as excellent, consumer response is loyalty. This can take the form of quick repurchase if the product's purchase cycle allows. It can also take the form of "word of mouth" praise or criticism about a particular organization's goods or services. Different degrees of loyalty are needed by the company in line with the life cycle stage of the productline. Automobiles are a mature market, and here it is essential for the competitive company to win and hold customers. Stereos, electronic music systems, and TVs are more volatile; their life cycle stages are startup and growth, with no mature stage. Although loyalty is less important in such markets, companies like Sony and Mitsubishi have developed loyal customer bases. Loyal customers accord special functional and nonfunctional qualities to their choices, which have a lower degree of substitutability as a result.

What is visible in the output? What is the reason that consumers choose different brands? Quality is difficult to measure, and must be defined correctly to be managed. Market research may help to provide operational guidelines. The research must include utility functions, appearance, service offered by the company, coverage and period of guarantee, repair and maintenance requirements, and the "not so obvious" many other factors that often count.

The second consideration concerns how output volume changes over time and where this output is directed. Included are such distribution factors as delivery date, product availability, and the treatment of back orders. The P/OM is responsible for the control of all these kinds of quality, not just schedule control.

The Output Quality Monitor

Walter Shewhart[8] developed a quality control model that altered the organization's understanding of work. Also, it enabled managers to control the quality of output. The primary component of this model is a **monitor,** which determines whether or not a **stable system** exists. The model monitors a process to determine whether or not the system is regularly meeting expectations: delivering the specified outcome within the expected range of variation and achieving the manager's objectives while maintaining a stable process.

The monitor distinguishes between the many small, random factors that perturb but cannot be removed from a system and the relatively large causal factors, which are called **assignable causes of variation.** Something can and must be done about assignable causes, since they are both unwanted and identifiable. The monitor, using the methodology of statistical quality control (SQC), can tell us that something seems to be changing; that the system no longer appears to be following an established (stable) pattern. This is important information. Figure 6–14 locates the SQC monitor (which makes comparisons of actual quality to predetermined standards) within the information flows of the control system. Feedback is an essential function. The information that is fed back from the monitor to the control system identifies the possible existence of assignable causes of variation, if they exist.

Assignable and Chance Causes of Variation

Assignable causes of variation are disturbances that can enter the system at any time. They can be there when the process is started, and can

---

[8]W. A. Shewhart, *Statistical Method from the Viewpoint of Quality Control,* W. E. Deming, ed. (Washington, D.C.: Department of Agriculture, 1939).

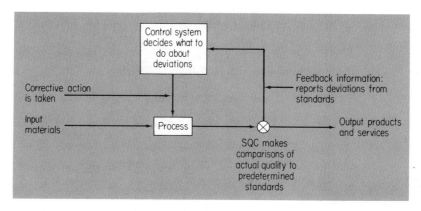

FIGURE 6-14. The general structure of a statistical quality control (SQC) system for an input/output process.

remain undetected until large penalties have to be paid for the poor quality of production. The SQC control monitor is designed to recognize that such assignable disturbances exist. Once spotted, assignable causes ordinarily can be removed.

Other causes of variation which are inherent properties can be found in all systems, and nothing can be done about them. They are called **chance causes of variation.** They can neither be identified nor removed. Chance causes arise from so many sources that even if a few were found and something done about them, the overall effect would be negligible. For example, chance causes arise from variations in the temperature of every moving part of a machine, and from dust particles that land on a worker's glasses.

It is vital that the manager be able to separate the two types of causes of variation. The SQC model establishes a procedure for doing this. It helps focus on removing assignable causes of variation. What is left is the least necessary variation; only chance cause factors remain. The SQC monitor provides differentiation between types of disturbances. If a process is already stable, it is expected that output will remain stable. But various things can happen. A tool can shift position. The quality of material that is being worked on can change. The worker can make a mistake. Shewhart proposed that by measuring a sequence of outputs in terms of a specified characteristic, it would be possible to derive **control limits.** The control limits describe the range of output measures to be expected if the process were stable (see Figure 6–15). As long as the observed values fall within the control limits and do so randomly (without special patterns), no change in the system is believed to have occurred. Thus, as long as the measurements of outputs produced by the system fall between the limits and give evidence of purely random behavior, the process is called stable. When the observed results do not appear to be random (one test of which is that they fall outside the limits) the system is "out of control." Managerial action is called for, and process corrections are made.

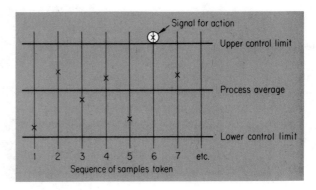

FIGURE 6-15. Prototype of a control chart.

Inspection Standards

There is change in the technology of inspection. Optical sensors coupled with computers have been altering the precision and consistency of physical inspection systems. The first issue that must be resolved is what standards to use.

It is our purpose to design product and process together in such a way that the smallest number of defectives will occur when the process is stable. We say we will build in quality instead of inspecting out defectives in order to exercise quality control. We build quality into the product in line with the specifications and inspection standards. Then the inspection function will be removing defectives that arise from a stable process producing goods or providing services.

The P/OM is primarily involved with the concept of specifications, although in practice this will be translated into a large variety of detailed technical specifications, such as hardness, tensile strength, color, and surface finish. To measure these characteristics, the departments are provided with inspection instruments such as gauges, micrometers, optical comparators, and devices for measuring hardness, tensile strength, and surface finish. These physical outputs are visible and can be measured. It is expected that they will conform to some set of specifications such as those communicated by a blueprint. In some production areas, however, the specification of output quality is a far more elusive matter. The problem of providing exact and measurable quality specifications for the taste of food or the odor of perfume is an example. (For an interesting discussion with respect to these problems of taste and smell, see *Flavor Research and Food Acceptance,* sponsored by Arthur D. Little, Inc., New York: Reinhold, 1958.)

We need to set correct standards that reflect high quality. Then we can inspect for quality. For example, the Food and Drug Administration (FDA) is required to develop and enforce standards that protect the consumer from hazards that could not otherwise be perceived. Setting such standards is difficult, but once they are set, food and drug samples can be tested to see whether they meet the selected standards. It is not unusual for these standards to be changed as additional laboratory or usage information is acquired. In a somewhat different sense, we have standard yards, standard meters, standard footcandles, and standard colors. Standard intervals between standardized maintenance procedures are specified by the FAA (Federal Aviation Administration) for aircraft. Standards of the FAA for on-time airline departure are also set and could be monitored as a dimension of quality by SQC.

Quality standards can exist only when design standards are met. The fact that more than one company subscribes to a set of design standards accounts for the fact that company C can use a bolt manufactured by company A and a nut manufactured by company B. Standard designs for gauges have been generally accepted and are described as American Gauge Design Standards. Standard bulb sizes, screw threads, radio tubes, and flashlight batteries are related to the interchangeability of parts between companies and across industries. The acceptance of such design standards has had a crucial effect on the growth of industry. Manufacturing is presently involved in great debate about how to set standards for computer-assisted equipment. General Motors has introduced MAP (Machine Automation Protocol), which is an attempt to derive and set industry standards.

Sequenced Inspection

How should we monitor and control an organization's repetitive output to assure consistent achievement of quality standards? How is the SQC model used to control quality? We do not draw samples at random from a homogeneous lot, as we did for AS. Instead, we monitor the output, keeping intact the sequence. For AS, we assumed homogeneity of the vendor's output. For our own production process, we no longer make this assumption. On the contrary, we ask ourselves:

Does our process exhibit homogeneity? (Yes)
Is our product meeting quality standards? (Yes)
Then how can we guarantee that it will continue to be homogeneous and of specified quality?

Quality control is an ongoing inspection procedure. It is a sequential sampling method that is more powerful than 300 percent inspection. The reason is that it does much more than spot defectives and remove them. It diagnoses the problems of a process in delivering the specified qualities, and allows them to be corrected. The user of control charts is the process doctor. Like a doctor, he or she must be familiar with the history of the process, with the process charts, and with the probable causes of certain patterns. Nevertheless, problems may be missed, and even when detected, their causes cannot always be identified.

To ensure control, the feedback link shown in Fig. 6–14 is required. The inspection operation costs money. The gain to be derived from this expense must at least offset the costs incurred. Two basically different types of inspection exist, and each has different costs and abilities. Not unexpectedly, the more expensive procedures promise greater responsiveness and control. The added costs occur because greater amounts of more refined information are required.

1. **Classification by attributes.** This is achieved by sorting the output by type. Thus, for example, we might divide our output into rejects and nonrejects, good and bad, "go" or "no go," or some other binary division. We followed this procedure with acceptance sampling. The definition used to define a defective unit of output may be very complex. Nevertheless, the eventual label placed on each unit is limited to either accepted or defective.

2. **Classification by variables.** In this case, exact scaled measurements are made of particular variables such as length, hardness, weight, electrical resistivity, impact strength, dielectrical strength, melting point, modulus of elasticity, high temperature superconductivity, pounds shipped, miles flown, food consumed, cases heard, and a variety of other physically measurable quantities for which some standard measures are available.

SQC Range and Quality Target Value

No matter how well designed a process is, there will always be some variation from a standard level of performance. Consequently, it is logical to set the standard as a range. (In Section 6.4 we will consider replacing the range with a target value. This is in line with the work of Dr. Taguchi. See pp. 299–300.) With the range, we accept all product that falls within the limits as meeting the specified standards. With the target, we assume a cost (or loss) for any deviation from the target (which has a zero loss).

On blueprints, tolerance ranges are stated for specific dimensions—for example, the length of the bolt is 2.41 ± 0.03. It is expected that the produced length of the bolt will fall within the specified range most of the time—between 2.38 and 2.44. The process may be able to make bolts that fall within the range 99.99 percent of the time. On the other hand, the process may not be suited to produce within the specified range.

Confusion frequently exists regarding the relationship of the engineer's specifications of tolerance and the characteristics of the production process used to produce the part. The engineer's specifications cannot demand more than the process is able to deliver.

There are also tolerance limits for services; the weight of the hamburger should be a quarter-pounder plus or minus w. The hamburger-making process may fall under the lower tolerance limit too often, and a better process for weighing out the burger should be found. The tolerance limits on the number of spelling errors a typing pool is permitted is 3 per 100 letters plus 2 and minus 3. This means that the acceptable range is 0 to 5 per 100 letters. Working on a word processor with a spellchecker would alter the tolerances. What would be an acceptable range? Spellchecker programs are not perfect.

To be reasonable, tolerance limits must be adjusted to the abilities of the process. Every process has a characteristic output variability that can be translated into a product quality range. For example, if it is desired to fill a bottle to a given weight, w, then it is expected that variation measured as a distribution of values will occur between $w - a$ and $w + b$. An engineer or a manager can specify tolerances that cannot be met. Unless there is a machine or facility capable of providing parts that fall within the tolerance range, the objective cannot be achieved. Only by means of a new system, which might include a fundamental technological change, can such specifications be met.

SQC Fundamentals

Statistical quality control (SQC) is able to differentiate between chance cause factors, which are fundamental to all processes, and assignable cause factors, which can be isolated and removed from the process. Using the range of acceptability, it is possible to determine when a process is stable (operating without assignable causes).

A control chart such as the one in Fig. 6–15 is the graphic monitor of the production system. The control chart is based on samples taken of the output. The sample values are averaged, yielding sample means. The samples are tagged by their place in the sequence of production. Sample means in sequence is the key to making control charts work.

Control charts are used for several purposes: First, to determine the fundamental or inherent variation level of a process, and second, to determine whether the process is stable at startup and whether it continues to be so during the ongoing production process. Since stability is defined as the condition of a process in which only inherent chance cause factors are at work, the yield from such a process is the best that can be obtained.

Standard Error of the Mean

Statistical control procedure is based on the fact that the observed variation within each sample of size n can be directly related to the variation between the means of all of the samples that are taken in sequential order.

The variance measure associated with each subgroup's sample size is

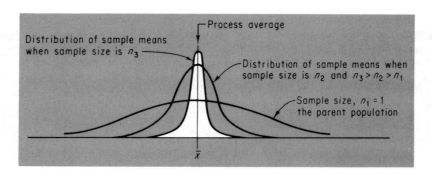

FIGURE 6-16. The standard deviation of sample means (measured from the process average) decreases in inverse proportion to the square root of the sample size.

represented by $\sigma_{\bar{x}_n}^2$, where n is the subgroup size. The standard deviation is simply the square root of this term, that is $\sigma_{\bar{x}_n}$. The standard error of the mean is:

$$\sigma_{\bar{x}_n} = \frac{\sigma}{\sqrt{n}}$$

where σ is the standard deviation of the population from which the sample means are being drawn. The $\sigma_{\bar{x}_n}$'s are called the **standard error of the mean.** These standard deviations are measures of the variability of the distributions of the sample means. The degree of variability is directly affected by the sample size used.

Figure 6–16 illustrates several distributions, each of which is based on a different sample subgroup size, and compares these distributions of means to the population distribution. The population distribution can be thought of as a distribution of sample means for which the subgroup size is one. In other words, if we set the subgroup size of n equal to 1, we obtain the relationship:

$$\sigma_{\bar{x}_1} = \sigma$$

which is as it should be. The population distribution is the unit-by-unit output of the production process.

**CASE:
BUTTON-
MAKERS**

Buttonmakers produces a variety of sizes, types, and colors of buttons, but the biggest seller is the fancy pearl shirtsleeve button, standard on men's shirts. A new high-speed process has been activated, and the company, following its consultant's advice, has instituted a statistical quality control program.

One of the key qualities to monitor is the outside diameter (OD) of the button. It is supposed to be 1.10 cm (approximately 7/16 inch). The tolerance range for the button is generally stated as 1.10 ± 0.08 cm. If it is bigger than 1.18 cm, it passes with difficulty through the buttonhole. If it is smaller than 1.02, the shirt sleeve tends to slip open.

The data in Table 6–11 have been obtained during startup. The question to answer is whether the output is stable by statistical quality control standards.

$$\text{Process average: } \bar{\bar{x}} = \frac{11.058}{10} = 1.106$$

$$\text{Average range: } \bar{R} = \frac{0.30}{10} = 0.03$$

For each subgroup, using the associated observations, we calculate the sample average, or sample mean value $\bar{x}$. Then we add up all our sample mean values and divide that total by the number of samples taken. This gives us the process average.

For Buttonmakers, the sum of the sample means is 11.058, and the number of subgroup samples is 10. Therefore, we calculate the process average to be $\bar{\bar{x}} = 1.106$ cm (using 3 decimal places).

Next, in addition to the mean value, we obtain for each subgroup the difference between the largest observation and the smallest observation. This is the measure of the *range*, called R. We add together all the sample range measures, R. We divide this total by the number of samples taken, and obtain the average range, R. For Buttonmakers, the sum of the sample ranges is 0.30, and the number of subgroup samples is 10. Therefore, we calculate the average range to be $R = 0.03$.

We have obtained the expected value for each subgroup as well as a convenient measure of the variation that appeared in the subgroup. These samples represent a sequence of observations, made over a period of time

TABLE 6-11   BUTTONMAKERS—SQC DATA SHEET FOR THE OD OF MENS FANCY PEARL SHIRTSLEEVE BUTTON

Subgroup Sample Number	Observation Number				Sample* Mean $\bar{x}$	Sample* Range R
	1	2	3	4		
1	1.14	1.12	1.13	1.12	1.1275	0.02
2	1.06	1.09	1.07	1.08	1.0750	0.03
3	1.09	1.10	1.11	1.09	1.0975	0.02
4	1.12	1.13	1.12	1.10	1.1175	0.03
5	1.10	1.14	1.10	1.09	1.1075	0.05
6	1.09	1.10	1.10	1.08	1.0925	0.02
7	1.10	1.12	1.13	1.11	1.1150	0.03
8	1.09	1.11	1.12	1.09	1.1025	0.03
9	1.10	1.10	1.10	1.15	1.1125	0.05
10	1.11	1.11	1.10	1.12	1.1100	0.02
.	.	.	.	.	.	.
.	.	.	.	.	.	.
.	.	.	.	.	.	.

*Sum of sample mean column = 11.0575; sum of sample range column = 0.30.

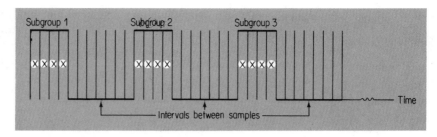

FIGURE 6-17. Subgroup size and the intervals between samples are critical determinants of control chart methodology.

(see Fig. 6–17). Each sample is called a subgroup; each subgroup, composed of 4 observations, is obtained by securing 4 measures in successive order, without permitting intervening periods to occur.

Then an interval of time is allowed to elapse. The next subgroup sample is taken at a later point in time. It is vital that we preserve the order of these samples, though observations can be mixed within samples. Thus, observations taken for subgroup 2 must not be confused with observations taken for subgroup 3. The preservation of order is crucial to the use of statistical quality control.

Buttonmakers intends to take a sample of 4 consecutively made buttons once every 15 minutes. This will yield 32 subgroup samples per day. If a change occurs in the process, at most 15 minutes of production will be spoiled.

Choosing the Sample Subgroup Size

How is the subgroup size chosen? (Why did Buttonmakers choose $n = 4$?) How does the interval between samples get set? To start: The interval between samples usually is fixed and unchanging. However, methods do exist that decrease the between-sample interval when the value of a subgroup mean approaches one of the control limits. Similarly, if a run seems to be developing, the interval would decrease.

The point is that in the face of evidence that the system may be going out of control, the subgroup size should tend to increase and the interval between samples should definitely decrease until 100 percent inspection would be used during the emergency. Cost balance is involved, and so are specific system properties. Let us examine Fig. 6–18.[9] There is a point, N_o, at which minimum total cost occurs. As more observations are taken (say in a day) there is an almost linearly increasing cost, line A. As fewer observations are taken, there is a greater chance that the system will go out of control and start producing defective items without its being

---

[9]Note the similar inventory model on p. 333.

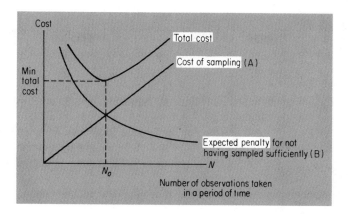

FIGURE 6-18. Determining the optimal number of observations N_o to be made in a given interval.

noticed so that immediate remedial action can be taken. The expected penalty for defective output decreases as N gets larger, because it is expected that the system will be malfunctioning for a shorter time (see curve B).

The question remains: how do we choose subgroup sizes and intervals between samples. If N_o is selected at $32 \times 4 = 128$ observations per day by Buttonmakers, should this be $n = 2$ repeated 64 times with appropriate intervals between, or $n = 4$ repeated 32 times, or $n = 64$ once in the morning and once in the afternoon?

The criterion is that the successive observations within the subgroup should be close enough together to insure that they are relatively homogeneous and that no change is likely to have occurred in the process. We then space successive subgroups in such a way that any lack of homogeneity that might occur over time is likely to be picked up. In general practice, subgroup sizes of 4, 5, and 6 can be readily used. The spacing between subgroups will depend on the production rate and the inertial nature of the process—the speed with which change can take place.

Startup in the Flow Shop

A pertinent aspect of SQC is the fact that many processes, when they are first translated from design to practice and monitored by the SQC control model, are revealed to be out of control. By making judicious changes in the process, it can be brought under control. Thereafter, it can be monitored for new disturbances that might enter the system.

How many values are required before it is possible to set up a control chart? That is, how many subgroups should be collected? In the Buttonmakers' example, we used only 10 subgroup samples. Usually, this is far too few; Shewhart said that 25 subgroup observations should be made before drawing up and interpreting the control chart.

Repetitive Process Environments

The SQC model is most applicable to the flow shop. Although we could invent examples of how it might be used for a project, the repetitive nature of work, to which SQC is addressed, is seldom found in projects. For sizable job shop orders, SQC might be used effectively, but in this case to justify the startup costs, the job shop would be employing intermittent flow shop methods.

SQC is a powerful model that provides economic leverage by relating consumer expectations with production capabilities. The fact that the flow shop is the major beneficiary, uniquely profiting from the application of SQC, is yet another economic advantage of the higher-volume processing configurations.

Deriving Control Limits for the $\bar{x}$ Chart

The range R is a statistical measure of the observed variability within each sample subgroup. It is, in fact, directly related to the standard deviation σ that could be derived for each sample group by statistical analysis. $\bar{R}$ is the average range of the subgroups; it describes the average within-group variability. To focus on between-group variability, we track the sequence of sample means $\bar{x}$ on the control chart. To construct the control chart, we derive the control limits (see Fig. 6–15). The control limits are based on the distribution of the sample means, since we will be plotting means $\bar{x}$ and not observations x. The control limits are placed a distance from the process average, $\bar{\bar{x}}$, such that the area in the tails of the distribution describes the percent of time that an observation $\bar{x}$ will fall above and below the control limits, even though nothing has happened to the process stability.

Figure 6–19 shows this relation for a spread of ± 3 standard deviations of the sample mean distribution (called s.d. of s.m.d.). With ± 3 s.d. of s.m.d., each tail has an area of 0.00135. For this setting of control limits, it is expected that 2.7 out of 1,000 sample means will fall outside the limits, 1.35 above and 1.35 below. It may be easier to understand 27 out of 10,000, and for each tail 135 out of 100,000. If, instead, 1.96 s.d. of s.m.d. had been used, then 95 percent of all sample means would fall within the control limits (see p. 112 for additional data concerning the probabilities of tail areas associated with different values of sigma).

How are the s.d. of s.m.d. obtained? First, note that sample means must be distributed with less variation than the observed values of x (see Fig. 6–20). Means average out extreme values to produce in-between values. It has been previously shown (Figure 6–16) that as the sample

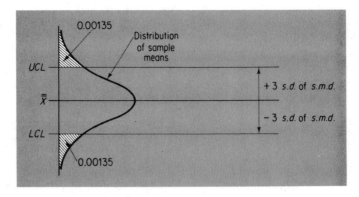

FIGURE 6-19. The construction of the control chart is based on control limits placed around the mean some given number of s.d. of s.m.d. In this case, three s.d. of s.m.d. are used. The unshaded area = 0.9973.

size n gets larger, the sample mean distribution gets narrower. Accordingly, our derivation of control limits is as follows:

1. Obtain a set of range values R (measure of within-group variation).
2. Calculate the average $\bar{R}$ (average of within-group variation).
3. $\bar{R}$ must be modified to describe the variability of sample means, where the sample size is n. Table 23-2 is based upon the known relationship between the range and the standard deviation. It provides a 3-sigma (s.d. of s.m.d.) protection level. Then, for the appropriate value of n, find the coefficient A_2, and multiply it by $\bar{R}$.
4. For the $\bar{x}$ chart: Upper control limit for $\bar{x} = \bar{\bar{x}} + A_2\bar{R}$
   Lower control limit for $\bar{x} = \bar{\bar{x}} - A_2\bar{R}$

Note that $\pm A_2\bar{R}$ represents ± 3 standard deviations of the sample mean distribution *as inferred from average within-group* variability. If the actual

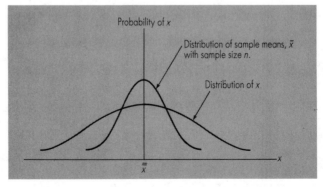

FIGURE 6-20. The distribution of sample means $\bar{x}$ has less variability than the distribution of observations x.

sample mean variability is the same as the inferred variability, then $\bar{x}$ values will fall outside the control limits with the expected frequency of 0.00270.

TABLE 6-12
COEFFICIENTS FOR
DERIVING 3-SIGMA
CONTROL LIMITS FOR $\bar{x}$
CHART (COEFFICIENTS ARE
BASED ON THE NORMAL
DISTRIBUTION)

Number of Observations in Subgroup n	Factor for $\bar{x}$ Chart A_2
2	1.88
3	1.02
4	0.73
5	0.58
6	0.48
7	0.42
8	0.37
9	0.34
10	0.31
11	0.29
12	0.27
13	0.25
14	0.24
15	0.22
16	0.21
17	0.20
18	0.19
19	0.19
20	0.18

Texts on SQC present tables of coefficients for other than 3-sigma protection levels.

Using the x Bar Chart for Variables

Figure 6–21 shows an x bar ($\bar{x}$) control chart on which we have marked the upper limit, the lower limit, and the process average, $\bar{\bar{x}}$. We know that the distance between the process average and the two limits is a function of $\bar{R}$. The value $\bar{R}$, in turn, is the average range obtained for the subgroup samples of size n. Thus, the distance between the process average and the control limits is a function of the average variability associated with subgroups of size n.

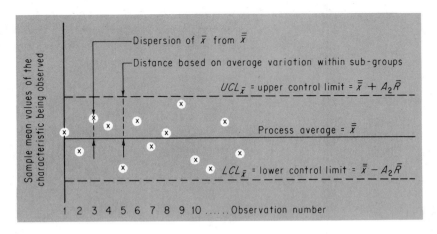

FIGURE 6-21. Control chart for variables—$\bar{x}$.

The Range Measure

When calculations are not computerized, it is a lot more convenient to measure the range than to go through the calculation of the standard deviation. Tables give the relationship of the expected range to the population standard deviation for varying sample sizes assumed to be drawn from a normal universe.[10] This ratio factor is designated as d_2.

$$d_2 = \frac{\bar{R}}{\sigma}$$

Let us introduce this relationship into our previous equation for the standard error of the mean, and thereby derive

$$\sigma_{\bar{x}_n} = \frac{\bar{R}}{d_2\sqrt{n}}$$

It is usual to position control limits at some specified number of standard deviations away from the expected value of the process. We use three sigma control limits, which is a commonly selected value for technological systems. Consequently, we can then write:

$$3\sigma_{\bar{x}_n} = \frac{3\bar{R}}{d_2\sqrt{n}} = A_2\bar{R}$$

---

[10]See the tables in Eugene L. Grant and Richard S. Leavenworth, *Statistical Quality Control,* 5th ed. (New York: McGraw-Hill, 1979), pp. 73, 644.

The A_2 factor is available in table form (see p. 280), where $A_2 = 3/d_2\sqrt{n}$. The upper control limit and the lower control limit, where the process average is $\bar{\bar{x}}$, are given by

$$\text{Upper-control limit for } \bar{x}: \text{UCL}_{\bar{x}} = \bar{\bar{x}} + A_2\bar{R}$$

$$\text{Lower-control limit for } \bar{x}: \text{LCL}_{\bar{x}} = \bar{\bar{x}} - A_2\bar{R}$$

And,

$$A_2\bar{R} = \frac{3\bar{R}}{d_2\sqrt{n}} = \frac{3\bar{R}}{\dfrac{\bar{R}}{\sigma}\sqrt{n}} = \frac{3\sigma}{\sqrt{n}} = 3\sigma_{\bar{x}_n}.$$

On our control chart, in proper sequence, we enter the x bar values, which are the subgroup averages. Statistical theory tells us that if the process is stable, then the successive, observed values of the sample means will fall between the control limits 99.73 percent of the time. This is true because three-sigma limits were used. If we had utilized limits other than three-sigma, we would have obtained different probabilities of exceeding the control limits.

Let us construct the x bar chart for Buttonmakers using the data in Table 6–11.

The process average $\bar{\bar{x}} = 1.106$ cm
The average range $\bar{R} = 0.03$
The sample size $n = 4$
The coefficient $A_2 = 0.73$ (see Table 6–12)
The upper control limit $UCL_{\bar{x}} = 1.106 + 0.73(0.03) = 1.128$
The lower control limit $LCL_{\bar{x}} = 1.106 - 0.73(0.03) = 1.084$

Figure 6–22 shows the $\bar{x}$ chart with all of the subgroup mean values being plotted. One point is well below the *LCL* (subgroup sample number 2). Another reading is almost at the *UCL* (subgroup sample number 1). These two points occur at the very beginning of the startup period. Because of this, we will not worry about them. In fact, we should remove early out-of-control points (say any occurring within the first 25 observations). It is to be hoped that we can account for the causes of these outage signals, but if not, we can assume that they are part of learning the job. (Problem 14 on p. 293 requests the recalculation of the control chart minus subgroup samples number 1 and 2.)

As things stand, Buttonmakers' stated objective of 1.10 cm is not being met by the process average of 1.106 cm (which rounds off to 1.11). Yet all of the values of x (in Table 6–11) fall within the tolerance range of 1.10 ± 0.08. On the basis of these too few subgroup samples, the but-

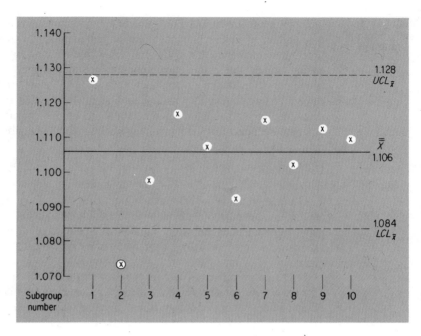

FIGURE 6-22. $\bar{x}$ control chart for the outside diameter (OD) of Buttonmakers' men's fancy pearl shirtsleeve button.

tonmaking process appears to be stable. More observations are needed, but at least as far as the $\bar{x}$ chart is concerned, we are off to a good start.

If the character of the process changes because assignable causes enter the system, this should become apparent when some values of $\bar{x}$ fall outside the control limits. Another characteristic of an unstable system is that a run of values all above or all below the process average may occur. (The longest run in Buttonmakers' startup, Fig. 6–22, is of length two.) Runs are often symptomatic that a process is trending in a particular direction.

For comparison purposes, examine the probabilities with which certain control emergency signals will appear when the process is stable. First, the probability of a point's falling outside the three-sigma limits is approximately 1/370 (*Note:* 87/10,000 = 1/370). Second, the probability that 9 points in a row will lie on one side of the process average is 1/256. The probability that 10 points in a row will fall on a particular side of the process average is 1/512. See Problem 13, p. 293, for these calculations.

For most manufacturing processes it is assumed that the output dimensions conform to the normal distribution. Tables 6–12 and 6–13 are based on the normal distribution. What happens when the population is not normally distributed? Ideally, we would like the control system to operate in much the same way. That is, as long as the distribution of the output quality measure remains stable, no matter what shape it has, we would like to be able to use the SQC criterion to tell us that no change has occurred in the process. It is a gift of nature (known as the central limit theorem) that distributions of sample means will tend to be normal even though the population from which the samples are drawn is not normally distributed. Shewhart showed that even though samples are drawn from rectangular, triangular, and other types of distributions, the distributions of the sample means tend to be normal. It is sufficiently true so that we need not concern ourselves with this problem.

Using the R Chart for Variables

Having measured quality variables, the x bar chart monitors the process average. The same numbers lend themselves to construct a chart to monitor the process dispersion. This chart is called an R chart. It is based on the same range measures that had to be derived to construct the x bar chart.

The reasoning involved in the development of the upper and lower control limits for the R chart parallels our previous discussion for the $\bar{x}$ chart. The appropriate equations for three-sigma limits are:

$$\text{The upper control limit for } R = \text{UCL}_R = D_4\bar{R}$$

$$\text{The lower control limit for } R = \text{LCL}_R = D_3\bar{R}$$

Table 6–13 presents the respective D_3 and D_4 values that must be used to determine three-sigma, R-chart control limits (just as A_2 was required for the $\bar{x}$ chart). Utilizing the appropriate D_3 and D_4 coefficients obtained from Table 6–13, we construct the R chart for our example. For Buttonmakers' data:

$$\text{UCL}_R = D_4\bar{R} = 2.28(0.03) = 0.0684$$

$$\text{LCL}_R = D_3\bar{R} = 0(0.03) = 0$$

Figure 6–23 presents the R chart for startup observations 1 to 10. The pattern is stable. There are no out-of-control subgroup observations, and no runs appear. Diagnosing symptoms, as read on the pair of $\bar{x}$ and R charts, we see that the process is stable, delivering the output quality that Buttonmakers desires, even though the process average (1.106 cm) does not exactly match the specifications (1.100 cm).

Symptoms and Diagnosis

The interpretation of the $\bar{x}$ and R charts is of crucial importance. If a change occurs in the process character, it can be of the following types: (1) The process average may change; (2) the process dispersion may change; or (3) both changes may take place. We can add a fourth type of

**TABLE 6-13 COEFFICIENTS FOR
DETERMINING FROM $\bar{R}$ THE 3-SIGMA
CONTROL LIMITS FOR R CHARTS
(COEFFICIENTS ARE BASED ON THE
NORMAL DISTRIBUTION)**

Number of Observations in Subgroup n	Factors for R Chart	
	Lower Control Limit D_3	Upper Control Limit D_4
2	0	3.27
3	0	2.57
4	0	2.28
5	0	2.11
6	0	2.00
7	0.08	1.92
8	0.14	1.86
9	0.18	1.82
10	0.22	1.78
11	0.26	1.74
12	0.28	1.72
13	0.31	1.69
14	0.33	1.67
15	0.35	1.65
16	0.36	1.64
17	0.38	1.62
18	0.39	1.61
19	0.40	1.60
20	0.41	1.59

Texts on SQC present tables of coefficients for other than 3-sigma protection levels.

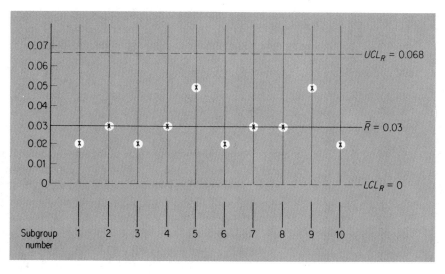

FIGURE 6-23. R control chart for the outside diameter (OD) of Buttonmakers' men's fancy pearl shirtsleeve button.

change—namely, other fundamental characteristics of the distribution can change, such as its skew or symmetry. However, these changes are more subtle and less useful for the interpretation of symptoms and diagnosis of causes.

If only the process average changes, this fact will probably be picked up by the $\bar{x}$ chart and not by the R chart. The situation might occur, for example, if a machine setting shifts permanently. That is, the change is of a sustained type.

Alternatively, the process average may remain unchanged, but the dispersion of the process shifts. For example, an operator may be able to control output at the mean level, but does this by working fast at certain times and slow at other times to compensate. Balancing extremes creates a pattern of instability that is likely to be detected on the R chart and not on the $\bar{x}$ chart.

Various change combinations can occur when sporadic elements enter and leave the system in some unknown fashion. These sporadic assignable causes are more difficult to detect than the sustained types discussed above. Other kinds of changes can also occur—for example, a gradual shift in the mean. Tool wear could account for such trend shifts. Worker carelessness can produce oscillatory behavior in which both limits may be repeatedly violated. Runs will appear for a variety of reasons and can usually be associated with trend factors, such as tool or gauge wear.

It should be noted that the process is not always the guilty party; the inspectors and/or their tools might account for a signal of instability. To assist management, the entire relevant system must be identified so that useful process conclusions can be drawn. It is worth noting that 100 or 200 percent inspection does not provide analytic assistance for the diagnosis of causes of change.

The "zero-defects" programs, urged by many companies on their employees, can be interpreted in the light of control theory as setting unobtainable goals for psychological reasons rather than for technological ones. Because the zero-defects goal is unobtainable, the eventual psychological effect may be worker frustration.

Using the p Chart for Attributes

Now consider a less elaborate control method, called the p chart. It is less expensive to utilize than the $\bar{x}$ and R charts because only a single chart is used. The required computations are less onerous than those required for the $\bar{x}$ and R charts. The p chart is called the **control chart for fraction defectives.** It is based on sampling by attributes, which was previously described.

The key, as was the case for acceptance sampling, is the ability to define a defective. Although the p chart is less expensive to use than control charts for variables, it is not as sensitive as the combination of the $\bar{x}$ and the R chart. It is not as good a diagnostic tool, because it uses less information. Even the $\bar{x}$ chart alone is a more powerful tool. However, the p chart will indicate the existence of assignable causes when they occur, and it does this at a lower cost than monitors based on variables. The lower cost of using the p chart might be offset by a slower reaction time.

If the measurement of quality *as a variable* is difficult, costly, or impossible, then the measurement of quality as an attribute is worth considering. For example, a good candidate for p charts is the wine-tasting situation, where acceptable quality is based on judgment involving criteria never made explicit. The data must be collected in the same way as was previously explained for monitoring variables. That is to say, homogeneous subgroups are chosen, and a period of time is allowed to elapse between the subgroup observations. The same kind of reasoning applies to the determination of subgroup sizes and between sample intervals as was true for the $\bar{x}$ and R charts. The sequential character of the control chart is as much in evidence as it was before, and the preservation of the order of observation is as crucial.

CASE: HOLIDAY NOVELTIES, INC.

Consider the following brief case as an example of the use of a p chart. Holiday Novelties, Inc., has received an order to make 1,800 sets of Christmas tree decorative lights. Management has decided to check the production defect rate to see what the level is, and to determine if it is stable. A p chart is to be used with 6 sample subgroups. The subgroup sizes can vary because of interference with other jobs which diverts or withholds required equipment and personnel. The SQC operator knows that one of the side benefits of the p chart is the fact that sample size can vary without impairing the construction or use of the chart. Thus, the data presented in Table 6–14 are collected.

The number of observed defectives is recorded for each subgroup. The total number of inspected items is now divided into the total number of

TABLE 6-14 HOLIDAY NOVELTIES—CHRISTMAS TREE LIGHTS

Subgroup Sample	Number Inspected, n	Number Defective, d	Fraction Defective (d/n)
1	25	1	0.040
2	25	2	0.080
3	36	3	0.083
4	64	4	0.063
5	25	3	0.120
6	25	2	0.080
	200	15	

One hundred percent inspection of each subgroup is used for this test.

observed defectives. This gives the process average $\bar{p}$. For our example $\bar{p}$ is equal to 0.075.

$$\bar{p} = \frac{15}{200} = 0.075$$

To determine the control limits, use the binomial description of the standard error of the mean. Then, to determine sigma (σ):

$$\sigma = \sqrt{\frac{\bar{p}(1 - \bar{p})}{n}} = \sqrt{\frac{(0.075)(0.925)}{n}} = 0.263 \sqrt{\frac{1}{n}}$$

This is a function of the subgroup sample size n. Because the upper and lower control limits are specified in terms of sigma, the limits vary as a function of n.

For this example we have chosen one-sigma limits, which means that 32 percent of the time a point can be expected to appear above or below the control limits, even though the process is stable. Because this out-of-control signal will occur often, the user might take one such event as a sign for alertness and two such events within a short interval as a signal that something is wrong. There is a lot of room for such inventiveness in quality control practices.

TABLE 6-15 HOLIDAY NOVELTIES—CHRISTMAS TREE LIGHTS

	Observations		Computations			Plot
Subgroup Sample	Number Inspected, n	Number Defective	σ	UCL $\bar{p} + \sigma$	LCL $\bar{p} - \sigma$	Fraction Defective
1	25	1	0.053	0.128	0.022	0.040
2	25	2	0.053	0.128	0.022	0.080
3	36	3	0.044	0.119	0.031	0.083
4	64	4	0.033	0.108	0.042	0.063
5	25	3	0.053	0.128	0.022	0.120
6	25	2	0.053	0.128	0.022	0.080
	200	15				

The complete computations for Holiday Novelties are shown in Table 6–15, and the results are plotted in Fig. 6–24. Note the variation in the spread between the control limits. When the subgroup size is constant, the computations are even more simplified. Only 1 upper and 1 lower control limit need be drawn on the p chart. The advantage of illustrating variable subgroup sizes is that, in practice, it is not always possible to draw samples of constant sizes.

Holiday Novelties appears to have a stable process. The fifth subgroup value approaches the upper limit, but the "alert" is called off when the sixth subgroup values approach the mean. The defective rate of 7.5 in a hundred might be improved, and probably will be as the job is "learned."

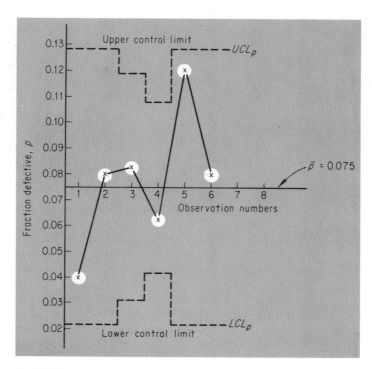

FIGURE 6-24. Control chart for attributes—p for data given in Table 6-15.

Using the p Chart for Some Job Shops

The *p* chart is not only less costly to use than the *x̄* and *R* charts; it is also constructed more rapidly. For these two reasons, it can be employed with smaller order sizes than the *x̄* and *R* charts. Still, it is not feasible to use the *p* chart with the really small order sizes that characterize many job shops and flexible processing systems. Holiday Novelties' Christmas tree lights, with 1,800 sets ordered, can check enough subgroups to make the effort worthwhile.

Design of Limits

Figure 6–25 illustrates a system in which a lack of control exists. Observe that a point has gone out of control. This usually is taken as a signal that something is wrong and that corrective action should be taken. It is always possible that the "out" point occurred by chance. The run lends credence to the notion that a real change might be taking place and provides supporting evidence for the belief that the observation is not spurious.

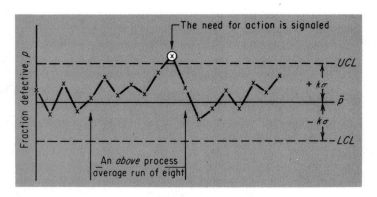

FIGURE 6-25. The control chart indicates that the system may be unstable.

Buttonmakers used three-sigma limits. Holiday Novelties used one-sigma limits. The choice of $k = 1$, 2, or 3 sigma control limits, or some value in between, is a management policy decision. It is hard to defend a choice of one or another control limit, but the characteristics of the decision are such that if the penalty is high for not recognizing when the process is out of control, then it becomes more desirable to utilize less than three sigma limits. The distance between the limits decreases as the size of k decreases. This means that more events are likely to fall outside the control limits.

The choice of k is a matter of balancing costs. Pertinent costs include the expense that occurs when a signal is received requiring search for assignable cause. There is the cost of a false alarm, when no assignable causes is found. An opposing cost is that of inaction when instability occurs but is not spotted. Missing the potential for a major breakdown carries a heavy penalty. With this guide in mind, the P/OM should choose control limit values that will balance the costs.

Control chart settings for averages and limits must be regularly reviewed. Changes detected in averages can, in turn, affect the sigma value that is computed and utilized. In all SQC methodology it is essential to review and update the system's parameters so that decisions can be based on "what is," and not on "what was." After an assignable cause has been detected and removed from the system, it is necessary to readjust the control limits. Sometimes another 25 subgroup observations are required before it is again possible to apply the control criterion.

Other Applications and Conclusions

Another control chart applicable for goods and services is called the c chart. This control chart can be applied to situations where it is desirable to record the frequency of occurrence of a number of different types of defects that are found for a particular item. For example, we can examine telescope lenses for different kinds of defects and flaws. Then, we might list the observed frequency of the different kinds of defects that occur in every inspected unit. When using the c chart, it is most common to have a subgroup size of 1, although this is not a requirement. It is necessary, however, that defects of each type occur independently of each other. If they are dependent, the underlying assumptions of the c chart will not be met.

Behavioral applications for SQC are not as well known as those applied to manufacturing.[11] Worker productivity, including group performance, can be stabilized and monitored for stability with this methodology. We can appreciate why the p chart has been used for monitoring observations obtained from work sampling methods; see pp. 368–373.

Startup processes should be checked for stability. Often they will not be stable, and they must be made so before full-scale production runs are undertaken. Output rate should be stabilized for the flow shop. Otherwise, the solutions to inventory problems, line-balancing systems, and sequencing problems will be incorrect. We must avoid applying solutions to a system that is shifting.

The subject of statistical control is not one that can be taught in depth in a matter of minutes. Experience with the process and with the use of the charts is essential. Theoretical interpretations gloss over the kind of penetrating insights that an experienced practitioner can obtain from control charts. SQC has been of enormous significance to the P/OM field, but its full potential has been tapped only by the Japanese. Reliability problems become increasingly important as equipment becomes more automated and processes become more complex. Quality assurance for the customer is the P/OM's obligation.

Tolerance Limits and Control Limits

Figure 6-26 indicates the way in which output tolerance limits and statistical process control limits are related. We have modified control limits so that they apply to the parent population. This modification was accomplished by means of the equation for the standard error of the mean. The tolerance limits do not require alteration, because they already apply to the parent population distribution.

---

[11]See J. A. Fitzsimons and R. S. Sullivan, *Service Operations Management*, NY, McGraw-Hill, 1982.

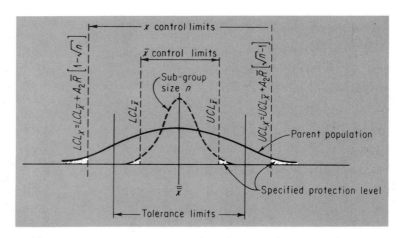

FIGURE 6-26. The relationship of tolerance limits and control limits. ($\bar{x}$ values can fall within tolerance limits, although x values will fall outside with greater frequency than the specified level of protection.) *Note:* tolerance limits are specified by engineers in line with product design; control limits characterize the particular production process that has been assigned to do the job. Management strives to achieve minimum costs in matching product requirements with process abilities.

PROBLEM
SET

1. A job shop that seldom produces lot sizes greater than 20 units cannot employ the $\bar{x}$ and R charts of SQC. Why is this so? What can be done to enable it to use quality management?

2. A flow shop with a high-volume serial production line makes cardboard boxes. An important quality is impact resistance, which requires destructive testing. Can SQC methods be used with destructive testing? What quality control method(s) do you recommend? Discuss.

3. How can the consumer tell that an organization employs statistical quality control? How can he or she tell if it does not?

4. What role does SQC play in life cycle management?

5. Differentiate between assignable and chance causes of variation. Give some examples of each kind of variation. How can you tell when an assignable cause of variation has arisen in a system?

6. What is a stable system? Why is the condition of stability so relevant to the activities of P/OM?

7. Why is the use of statistical quality control by drug and food manufacturers imperative? Would you recommend two-sigma or three-sigma control limits for food and drug applications of SQC?

8. How might SQC be used by the airlines to monitor on-time arrival and departure (service qualities highly valued by their customers)?

9. One of the major reasons that statistical quality control is such a powerful method is its use of sequenced inspection. Explain why this is so.

10. How should the subgroup size and the interval between samples be chosen?

11. Differentiate between the construction of the $\bar{x}$, R, and p charts. Also distinguish between the applications of these charts.

12. What is meant by "between-group" and "within-group" variability? Explain how these two types of variability constitute the fundamental basis of statistical quality control.

13. It is sometimes possible to detect an unstable system when a run of values all above or below the process average occurs. What is the probability that a run of ten values, all above the process average, will occur?

    Answer: The probability that the first value will be greater than the process average is 1/2; that the first two values will be greater than the process average is 1/4. In general, the probability that the first n values will be greater than the process average is $1/2^n$. Similarly, the probability that the first n values will be less than the process average is $1/2^n$. Consequently, the probability that the first n values will all be either greater than or less than the process average is:

$$\frac{1}{2^n} + \frac{1}{2^n} = 2\left(\frac{1}{2^n}\right) = \frac{1}{2^{n-1}}$$

    The numerical answer to the question is $1/2^{10} = 1/1024$.

14. Consultant's note to the quality control engineer: Request recalculation of the $\bar{x}$ chart for Buttonmakers's men's fancy pearl shirtsleeve button on p. 283. Remove subgroup sample data for points 1 and 2. Please furnish comments on results and further recommendations.

15. Can quality control exist without feedback? How about quantity control? Explain your answer.

16. A shampoo manufacturer specifies that the contents of a bottle of shampoo should weigh 6 ± 0.10 ounces net. A statistical quality control operation is established and the following data are obtained:

Sample Number				
1	6.06	6.20	6.04	6.10
2	6.10	5.95	5.98	6.05
3	6.03	5.90	5.95	6.00
4	6.03	6.05	6.10	5.94
5	6.12	6.40	6.20	6.00

   a. Construct an $\bar{x}$ chart based on these five samples.

   b. Construct an R chart based on these five samples.

   c. What points, if any, have gone out of control?

d. Comment on your results and briefly discuss the role of SQC in production and operations management. Include such factors as management's choice of tolerance limits, subgroup size, and sample size.

Answer: Utilizing the discussion on pp. 275–276, we first determine the sample means and ranges as follows:

Sample No.	Mean, $\bar{x}$	Range, R
1	6.10	0.16
2	6.02	0.15
3	5.97	0.13
4	6.03	0.16
5	6.18	0.40

$$\bar{\bar{x}} = 6.06 \qquad \bar{R} = 0.20$$

a. The $\bar{x}$ chart is constructed from the equations

$$\text{UCL}_{\bar{x}} = \bar{\bar{x}} + A_2\bar{R}$$

$$\text{LCL}_{\bar{x}} = \bar{\bar{x}} - A_2\bar{R}$$

where for a sample subgroup size of 4, $A_2 = 0.73$ (Table 6–12). Thus:

$$\text{UCL}_{\bar{x}} = 6.06 + (0.73)(0.20) = 6.206$$

$$\text{LCL}_{\bar{x}} = 6.06 - (0.73)(0.20) = 5.914$$

The appropriate control chart is shown in Fig. 6–27.

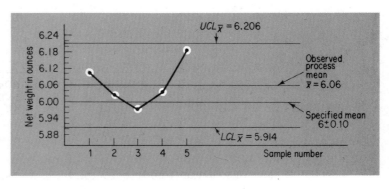

FIGURE 6-27.

b. For the R chart: $UCL_R = D_4\bar{R}$ and $LCL_R = D_3\bar{R}$, from Table 6–13, for $n = 4$:

$$UCL_R = (2.28)(0.20) = 0.456$$

$$LCL_R = (0.0)(0.20) = 0.000$$

The appropriate control chart is shown in Fig. 6–28.

c. No points have fallen outside of the control limits for either the $\bar{x}$ or R charts, so we can assume that the process is a stable one. (Of course, the sample is of absurdly small size.)

d. Statistical quality control is a vitally important mathematical tool capable of monitoring the output of a production process. It is able to provide the P/OM with reliable observations concerning the stability of the production process. In this way it performs a control function, because it keeps management aware of changes in the system's pattern.

In this example, management has requested tolerance limits of ± 0.10 oz. These obviously cannot be satisfied even though the specified mean value of 6.00 is close to the observed process average of 6.06. Of the 20 individual values that are shown, none is less than the lower tolerance limit specification—but 4, or 20 percent, are above the upper tolerance limit specification. We note that the process gives no sign of being out of control. It is not, however, able to deliver the goods with respect to tolerance limits.

The stability of a system is a separate issue from its technological characteristics. In this case, the production system has not been (or cannot be) designed to meet engineering requirements.

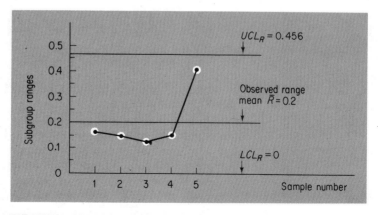

FIGURE 6-28. Ishikawa causes of defects diagram.

The subgroup size of 4 may be unsatisfactory based on the fact that an unreasonable degree of variability is evident within each subgroup. The fact that there is variability between the averages of the subgroups would lead us to believe that adequate spacing has been provided between subgroups. We know, however, that since such variability exists, the sample size of 5 subgroups is far too small to base any real conclusions on it. Our objective has been to provide insight into issues such as those discussed above and to illuminate the importance of SQC as a fundamental operations management technique.

17. A food processor specified that the contents of a jar of jam should weigh 14 ± 0.10 ounces net. A statistical quality control operation is set up, and the following data are obtained:

Sample Number				
1	14.02	14.04	14.08	14.06
2	14.10	14.24	14.00	14.90
3	14.80	14.75	14.70	14.51
4	14.59	14.90	14.01	14.02
5	14.96	14.26	14.81	14.17
6	14.40	14.83	14.68	14.93
7	14.86	14.32	14.90	14.04
8	14.56	14.96	14.69	14.63
9	14.85	14.71	14.05	14.91
10	14.75	14.19	14.05	14.09

   a. Construct an $\bar{x}$ chart based on these 10 samples.
   b. Construct an R chart based on these 10 samples.
   c. What points, if any, have gone out of control?
   d. What reasons could be given for the appearance of an assignable cause at some time in the future?
   e. What can be surmised from the shapes of the curves on these charts?

Section 6.4 TQC = Total Quality Control

Total quality control was developed in the 1970s by the Japanese. The name stands for a broad philosophy of quality which is tied into the present-day, highly developed theory of production and operations. TQC involves the quality of the P/OM process as well as the quality of the product. Here we try to put SQC and TQC into the P/OM context. It should be noted that since 1980, great interest has developed in the achievement of quality by companies. As a result, many different systems have appeared. TQC is more fundamental than most of the newer systems.

It represents the quality concepts that were developed by the Japanese using the fundamental foundations of quality control established by Shewhart.

Development of TQC

Using notions developed by Western Electric and the Bell Labs, the Japanese economic recovery plan, following the end of World War II, concentrated on high-volume flow shop configurations. The plan was to obtain low unit costs with the best possible quality. The assistance of such masters of quality as Dr. Deming and Dr. Juran led to a reversal of goals—namely, obtain the highest quality level, subject to existing cost structures. The goal reversal put the central focus on quality, with the objective of striving for continual improvement.

Quality as a function of reducing variance came naturally to the Japanese. The Japan Productivity Center acted as a clearinghouse. Great contributors to the theory included Drs. Deming, Ishikawa, and Juran.

Integration of Many Factors

The idea of TQC grew out of the notion that everything plays a part in the achievement of quality. If any link in the chain is weak, the chain breaks. First, there is the supplier-producer-customer link. The producer must do everything possible to root out the sources of poor quality. For any given system, no matter how complete the list of sources seems to be, it can never include every factor that could produce an assignable cause of variation. So each person responsible in any way for the goods and services is on guard for problems. Meanwhile, management designs and installs a system. By improving that system, additional quality is achieved.

Innovative Product/Process Qualities

Innovation of product qualities to improve competitiveness is a constant goal of the Japanese. A Japanese word, *dantotsu,* means striving to be the ''best of the best.'' When we connect that term with *kaizan,* which means ''always improving,'' we can understand the constancy of effort that is made to improve the product to be the best competitor.

Quality function deployment (QFD), previously mentioned, provides a paper trail of responsibilities for product qualities as they fan out throughout the organization. Suppliers are also involved. This approach to deploying quality was started by Toyota in 1973. QDF has both positive and negative aspects associated with its influence on innovation. Paperwork, which routinizes procedures and assigns responsibilities, can inhibit creativity while it improves control.

There are many examples of successful innovative thinking in firms where employees are urged to use suggestion systems. Mazda reported an annual average of 70 + suggestions per worker, with a high percentage of acceptances. At TRW, the philosophy has been developed that:

Quality is to Product
as
Accounting is to Finance

The emphasis is on the fact that quality is the organization's problem, and that ownership of responsibility is required. Awareness without motivation will not contribute to the continuous long-term enhancement of quality that is required to be a winner.

Quality Circles

Since the early 1970s, various U.S. companies have reported establishment of **Quality Circles** (also known as **QC Circles**). These are teams composed of workers who are related to common process interests. For example, at Lockheed facilitators were trained to help group formation, problem identification, and problem-solving.

The members of the Quality Circle generally meet on a regular basis to discuss problems that exist with the process. Often they receive training in the process functions and in statistical process control (SPC). In Japan, this training includes statistical quality control (SQC). The difference between SPC and SQC is one of breadth, the SPC is technological and functional and embraces the more focused SQC. It is important to note that in Japan many hours of training are the norm, whereas in the United States a great deal of time is devoted to gripe sessions. U.S. workers often enjoy these so-called rap sessions, but lacking the training a great record of accomplishment is not evident.

There has been a fad in the United States to copy the QC Circles initiated in Japan. Because the copies have been incomplete, the success rates have been less than spectacular. It is to be noted that a failed QC Circle effort is less beneficial than none at all, because it represents another half-hearted management commitment. In some companies, such as General Motors, the gripe session aspects of the teams was acknowledged at the start, and the groups were called Quality of Work Life. By acknowledging the real purpose of the groups, the probability of continuation and success was increased.

When training is used, the subjects covered usually include these:

1. Pareto diagrams (See Figure 6–29)
2. Ishikawa causal diagrams (See Figure 6–30)
3. Deming's PDCA cycle (See Figure 6–31)

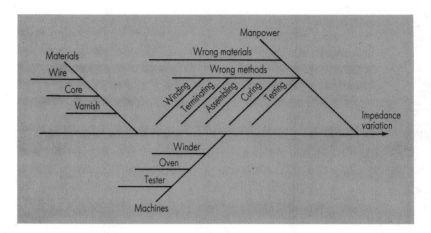

FIGURE 6-29. Pareto diagram for quality analysis.

Taguchi Loss Function

An alternative to using the control limit concept of control charts was set forth in 1960 by Genichi Taguchi. The method is based on the idea that any deviation from the target has a cost associated with it. Deming states that "Loss is leaving the optimum," and the Taguchi loss function, which is shown in Figure 6–32, clearly agrees with this notion.

Using the design of experiments, it is possible to design products and the processes that make them so that failures can be minimized. Table 6–16 illustrates the stages at which countermeasures can be taken to reduce sources of variation.

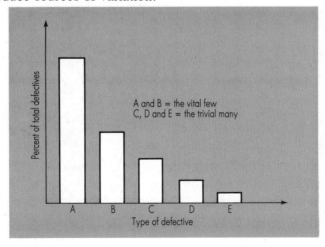

FIGURE 6-30. Ishikawa casual diagram showing sources of impedance variation.

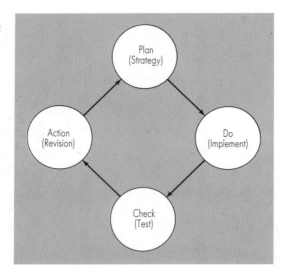

FIGURE 6-31. PDCA corrective cycle.

Zero Defects, Zero Inventory, JIT and Process Flows

The fundamentals of continuous process flows require that no defectives occur. Thus, there is a connection between JIT which implies zero inventory and the concept of zero defects. In their QC Circles, workers

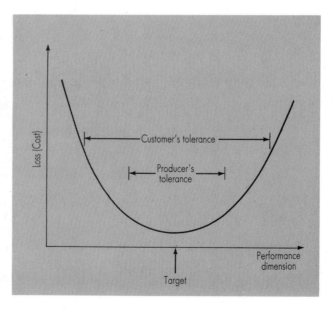

FIGURE 6-32. Taguchi loss function.

TABLE 6-16 Product Development Stages at Which Countermeasures Against Various Sources of Variation can be Built into the Product

Product Development Stages	Sources of Variation		
	Environmental Variables	Product Deterioration	Manufacturing Variations
Product design	O	O	O
Process design	X	X	O
Manufacturing	X	X	O

O—Countermeasures possible.
X—Countermeasures impossible.
Source: Raghu N. Kackar, "Off-Line Quality Control, Parameter Design, and the Taguchi Method," *Journal of Quality Technology*, Vol. 17, No. 4, Oct. 1985, p. 177.

talk about zero defect goals and never attain them. Unless zero defects is known by all to be an unattainble goal, its existence can demoralize the work force. Near-zero defects goals are an alternative that some companies prefer.

PROBLEM SET

1. How do SQC and TQC relate within the P/OM context?
2. What is the connection between the costs of doing business and TQC?
3. Explain how preventive and remedial maintenance support the achievement of TQC.
4. What is meant by the statement: "In the TQC environment, everyone is responsible for surpassing standards and for calling immediate attention to any deviation from the quest for perfection"?
5. Explain how the Japanese words *dantotsu* and *kaizan* describe conditions that are needed for innovation.
6. What does innovation have to do with TQC?
7. What is Quality Function Deployment? Who started it and why?
8. Explain the statement: "Quality is to product as accounting is to finance"?
9. Contrast QC Circles and groups dedicated to Quality of Work Life.
10. How do suggestion systems relate to TQC?
11. Explain, illustrate and exemplify Pareto Diagrams, Ishikawa Causal Diagrams and Deming's PDCA Cycle.
12. How do the Taguchi Loss Function and the control charts of SQC relate?
13. Visit the library to obtain a book that deals with the design of experiments. Write a page length report explaining this subject. Then explain why Taguchi recommends using the design of experiments for product/process design.
14. Explain the benefits of the "near-zero defects" concept.

REFERENCES   CROSBY, P. E. *Quality Is Free.* New York: McGraw-Hill, 1979.

DEMING, W. E. *Out of the Crisis.* Boston: MIT Center for Advanced Engineering Studies, 1986.

DODGE, HAROLD F., and HARRY G. ROMIG. *Sampling Inspection Tables,* 2nd ed. New York: Wiley, 1944.

DUNCAN, A. J. *Quality Control and Industrial Statistics,* 5th ed. Homewood, Ill.: Richard D. Irwin, 1986.

FEIGENBAUM, A. V. *Total Quality Control,* 3rd. ed. New York: McGraw-Hill, 1983.

FITZSIMONS, J. A., and R. S. SULLIVAN. *Service Operations Management.* New York: McGraw-Hill, 1982.

GRANT, F. L., and R. S. LEAVENWORTH. *Statistical Quality Control,* 5th ed. New York: McGraw-Hill, 1979.

GRIFFITH, GARY. *Quality Technician's Handbook.* New York: Wiley, 1986.

HANSEN, B. L., and P. M. GHARE. *Quality Control & Applications.* Englewood Cliffs, N.J.: Prentice-Hall, 1987.

ISHIKAWA, K. *What Is Total Quality Control? The Japanese Way.* Englewood Cliffs, N.J.: Prentice-Hall, 1985.

JURAN, JOSEPH M. *Quality Control Handbook,* 3rd ed. New York: McGraw-Hill, 1974.

LANDERS, RICHARD R. *Reliability and Product Assurance.* Englewood Cliffs, N.J.: Prentice-Hall, 1963.

SHEWHART, WALTER A. *Economic Control of Quality of Manufactured Product.* Princeton, N.J.: D. Van Nostrand, 1931.

STOUT, KEN. *Quality Control in Automation.* Englewood Cliffs, N.J.: Prentice-Hall, 1985.

TAGUCHI, GENICHI. Introduction to Quality Engineering. Asian Productivity Organization, Tokyo, 1986.

WADSWORTH, H., K. STEPHENS, and A. GODFREY. *Modern Methods for Quality Control and Improvement.* New York: Wiley, 1986.

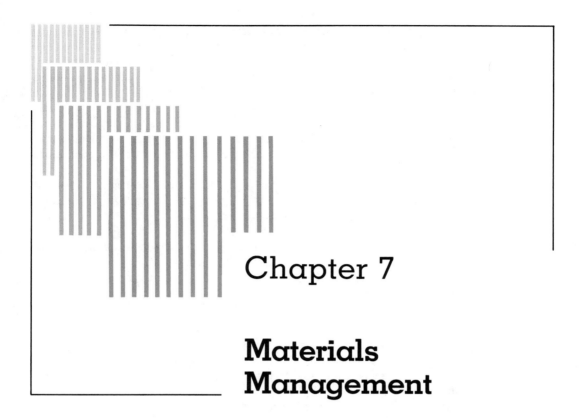

Chapter 7

Materials Management

CHAPTER
SUMMARY

Materials planning is different for the flow shop, the job shop, projects, and flexible processing systems. Section 7.1 addresses the purchasing function: receiving, inspecting, and storing. It is concerned with the materials management functions, including value analysis and inventories of critical parts. Section 7.2, Inventory Problems, starts out with ABC problem categorization. It looks at the difference between material requirements planning (MRP) and order point policies (OPP), and then goes on to describe and classify costs. Material requirements planning (MRP) is the subject of Section 7.3. Order point policies (OPP) is the subject of Section 7.4. MRP is most often appropriate for the job shop and for projects. OPP is most often appropriate for the flow shop. Neither approach to materials planning is exclusively reserved for any form of process configuration. Consequently, it remains for us to explain why one system would be preferred over another. Further, Section 7.3 examines the management information system (MIS) that unifies the materials management function.

Section 7.5 discusses supplier selection and relations. This topic is increasingly important because of the large percentage of operating costs that are due to materials. Various surveys indicate that between 40 and 60 percent of factory costs are attributable to outside purchases. By judicious supplier selection and relations, it is possible to reduce the total cost of outside purchases. What makes a selection judicious is not clear: Some firms argue for single supplier sourcing to reduce variation, while others claim the need for many suppliers to guarantee delivery of crucial items that could otherwise be interrupted by strikes, weather, and competitive pressures.

Material costs are a large percentage not only of factory costs, but also of the operating costs of services. Many service organizations require substantial materiel support. The spelling of the word *materiel* with an *e* often signifies military weapons and supplies. The military establishment is a very large service organization that needs lots of inside and outside supplies: room and board, shelter and clothing, weapon systems, ammunition, and so on. Materials management has had more influence as the costs of raw materials, components, and subassemblies has risen.

Section 7.1 Materials Management Functions

Purchasing is a major function related to P/OM. Receiving inventories, inspecting them to see if their qualities meet specifications, determining when and how much to order, and from which suppliers, are other functions of materials management. Engineering design changes (EDCs) and startups can affect all of these functions in a variety of special ways that should be considered as part of the life cycle management problem.

Materials of many kinds are inputs to all process configurations for both products and services. Consequently, materials planning is essential for high productivity and cost advantages. Not only do purchases from suppliers represent a large percent of price, but they represent an increasing portion of the cost that must be recovered before the company can start to make a profit. Another way of looking at this issue is as follows: If either direct labor costs or materials costs could be reduced by the same percentage, the average firm would save twice as much by choosing the materials cost reductions.

The ordering of materials should be as correct as possible in every aspect. Mistakes are more costly in some situations than in others, but in all cases they are to be avoided. The worst case is likely to be for the mature flow shop. The least worst case is likely to be for the job shop and/or startups. Flexible and programmable systems have some built-in advantages of being able to shift from one product to another, with minimum penalty, when a materials problem is encountered. There will be more discussion later about the effects of life cycle stages and work configurations on materials management.

Materials specifications must be defined exactly. They must be priced right, delivered on time, and inspected for faults. Information about materials must be managed with skill. Stock outages can delay or even halt production of both goods and services. This seems so obvious for manufacturing needs that the application to services is frequently overlooked. Consider the hospital that runs out of blood, the aircraft carrier at sea that runs out of water, the office without paper clips or staples, the printer without paper, or the fast food restaurant that is out of stock on french fries.

The costs of mistakes can be exorbitant. A refinery once needed a replacement gasket costing $85. Several gaskets were listed as being in stock, but they turned out to be the wrong size. The cost to the refinery was substantial, since it had to cut production and send a chartered plane 700 miles to get the proper gasket. The importance depends on the kind of product, the life cycle stage in the market, and the nature of the process configuration that is being used.

Materials Management for the Flow Shop, the Job Shop, Projects, and Flexible Processing Systems

The management of materials requires different rules (and decision models) for different markets, life cycle stages, and production configurations. That is, certain kinds of problems posed by the materials requirements of flow shops are not the same for job shops, projects, and flexible processing systems.

Flow Shop. The flow shop needs a continuous supply of a limited and unchanging set of materials. The line has to be shut down if stock outages occur. On the other hand, carrying large amounts of inventory can be costly and require more storage space than should be available. Pilferage, obsolescence, and deterioration are the banes of large inventories. However, one benefit of large order quantities placed long in advance of delivery is that substantial discounts can usually be obtained.

Knowing when to order and how much to order is the managerial imperative. Therefore, an **order point policy (OPP)** that specifies when and how much to order for each item, independent of what is happening to other items, makes sense. Order point planning is discussed in Section 7.4.

For new flow shop lines, much vendor (and supplier) competition can be expected. Vendors (and suppliers) actively compete to supply the materials requirements of high-volume demand systems.

Job Shop. The job shop has a varied and changing set of material requirements. These may include certain materials, the uses of which are repeated with some degree of regularity, and others that are unique or infrequent orders. (See the discussion of the ABC characteristics of the job shop, pp. 316–318.) Generally, the job shop involves many smaller order quantities of far more kinds of materials than the flow shop. Consequently, smaller discounts can be obtained, and tracking stock levels creates a serious information management problem. With respect to materials management, the job shop can be viewed as having a continuing stream of projects and startups which lack the major impact associated with projects and startups.

The use of material requirements planning (MRP) involves having a good information system to track the components needed for each job in the shop. Also, the time when those components are needed must be specified and acted upon with sufficient lead time. MRP will be discussed in Section 7.3.

For the job shop, many vendors can be involved, and changes from one to another are not unusual. A single decision that deviates from optimal materials planning cannot do much harm; only the cumulative effects of repeated divergences from acceptable results can impose severe penalties over a period of time. Occasionally, a job can be delayed while corrections are made. Especially for small jobs, the consequences of delay are slight. This is not true of the flow shop, and it is seldom true of the project, where delays usually impose severe penalties. It is true of the FMS, where a large variety of products on the menu permit flexible shifting to other work while materials errors are corrected. It is also true of the service-oriented job shop, where flexible processing routines enable switching to alternative tasks while corrective procedures are undertaken with suppliers.

Projects. Projects such as building ships or buildings have stages when certain materials are used that will not be used again. Since the activity stages are nonrepetitive, the majority of orders are placed only once. Nevertheless, material requirements planning can be used successfully to track the timing of materials needed for specific activities. The order point concept would apply only to those materials that are used consistently and uniformly throughout the project. Order point policies would be appropriate when demands are independent of the specific project activities, such as lubricants for machines, food for workers, and lightbulbs. In contrast, if MRP logic is used, the right amount of cement can be ordered, to be delivered on time, for a specific construction job of known dimensions.

Often, much work on project materials is subcontracted to suppliers who are familiar with aspects of the materials requirements of particular project stages. Cost of materials may be less critical than on-time delivery. Frequently, the materials required are unique, and there is little experience in producing them. Discounts for quantity purchases are rare, and special setup charges are not unusual. Careful follow-up with suppliers is essential when experience with vendors is limited. Also, if the vendors have minimum familiarity with the fabrications they are supplying, this can lead to production difficulties in the vendors' shops. As an example, the supplier of the stage sets for a Broadway play may have never before dealt with some of the special effects that are to be used. Without follow-up, the play's director may be in for some surprises when the dress rehearsal begins.

Materials management requirements are affected by working experience with vendors. There is increasing belief in a materials system with fewer suppliers and a greater trust relationship. This subject is addressed in Section 7.5.

The materials management function is a two-way street. Both the supplier and the supplied must have knowledge of the products and services that are supplied and how they are used. Quantities that are needed over time should be matched as much as possible to shipments that are made over time, which is an approach to **Just in Time (JIT)**. Expectations of buyers for performance by suppliers change when there is continuity in the supply and demand relationship. Although each situation is unique, the variables that should be considered can be generalized (see Section 7.5).

The Materials Information System

Material inputs produce direct costs (which means they apply to each unit of work that is done). Therefore, they are also called variable costs and they are associated with the variable-cost line of the breakeven chart (Chapter 5). As previously noted, these costs often constitute a major share of operating costs. Consequently, the breakeven aspect of materials cost control is critical to P/OM.

U.S. companies have been moving toward an organizational integration of the information required for materials control. In the past, a variety of materials management activities existed as individual operations, each run by managers who seldom communicated with each other. Eventually, in the search for greater effectiveness, a single, central materials control department has appeared in numerous organizations.

Today, many organizations have a vice president in charge of materials control. The responsibilities vested in a materials control department include at least four subfunctions:

Purchasing and vendor relations
Inventory stock control
Acceptance sampling for quality control
Accounting to pay the bills

Each function interfaces with the others and with many other departments within the organization. Coordination of activities is essential, which is why information management is stressed.

Figure 7–1 is a flow diagram which depicts the various communications that unite the materials management area. Observe the many forms of communication that must flow between the organizational units in order to achieve an integrated materials control department. In addition, the materials control department communicates with research and development, with the P/OM department, with other operating divisions of the company, and with outside organizations, including the vendor's R&D department.

The Purchasing Function

Purchasing agents and their supporting organizations have a traditional role of great importance. This role is changing, becoming more integrated within the organization, and more important as well. Through its procurement function, the organization operates as a customer. Accordingly, it is responsive to the marketing strategies of the various vendors from whom it obtains the required materials. The traditional role of purchasing is to push vendors on price by shopping around. As described in Section 7.5, many companies are altering this approach in favor of a long-term relationship with few suppliers.

The importance of the buying function depends upon the extent to which the company requires outside suppliers. This is the **make or buy** problem, discussed in Section 7.5. If the P/OM cannot make the product, the importance of the buying function increases. A mail-order company, for example, produces a small fraction of the materials that it offers for sale. Mail-order buyers are important people. They are responsible, in large measure, for the success of their companies. However, they must accept the risk of making errors such as overestimating demand or paying too high a price. The penalties of being wrong are high.

The purchasing function is involved with negotiating abilities and the psychology of bargaining. Relations with vendors cannot be pinned down to a formula. They can affect "deals" that are made and favors rendered. Buyers can succeed in achieving special arrangements because of friendly relationships. These are not dishonorable relationships, because they include the evaluation of both buyer and supplier of the long-term stability and goodwill value of the relationship for both companies.

However, in the American business environment, personal relationships are not considered a reasonable basis for enterprise decisions. In other cultures, for example in Latin America and the Middle East, personal friendships are considered business assets that reduce risk and have monetary value. Part of this cultural difference can be traced to the importance placed upon legal contracts in the United States. Because of the growth of global business, these factors can play a major role in determining management's success in handling the affairs of subsidiaries outside the United States. For a useful discussion of these points, see

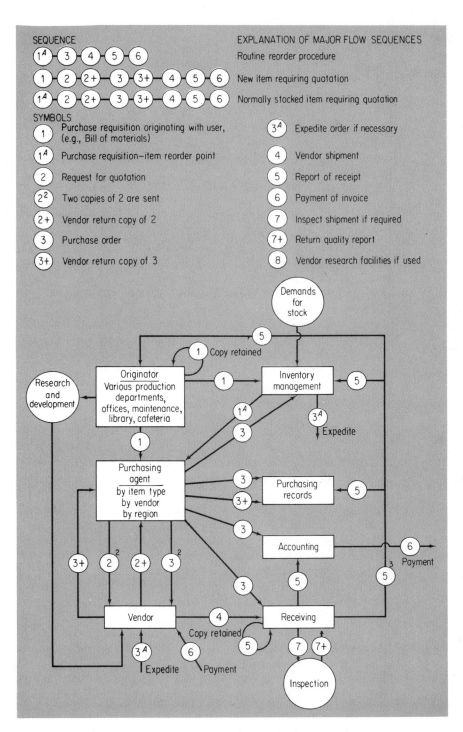

SEQUENCE

EXPLANATION OF MAJOR FLOW SEQUENCES

(1^A)—(3)—(4)—(5)—(6)   Routine reorder procedure

(1)—(2)—(2+)—(3)—(3+)—(4)—(5)—(6)   New item requiring quotation

(1^A)—(2)—(2+)—(3)—(3+)—(4)—(5)—(6)   Normally stocked item requiring quotation

SYMBOLS

(1) Purchase requisition originating with user, (e.g., Bill of materials)

(1^A) Purchase requisition—item reorder point

(2) Request for quotation

(2^2) Two copies of 2 are sent

(2+) Vendor return copy of 2

(3) Purchase order

(3+) Vendor return copy of 3

(3^A) Expedite order if necessary

(4) Vendor shipment

(5) Report of receipt

(6) Payment of invoice

(7) Inspect shipment if required

(7+) Return quality report

(8) Vendor research facilities if used

FIGURE 7-1. A detailed flow diagram of materials management.

309

Edward T. Hall, "The Silent Language in Overseas Business," *Harvard Business Review,* 38, 3 (May–June 1960), pp. 87–96.

Purchasing records provide a history of what has been done in the past, what costs were involved, who the major suppliers were, as well as the costs, discounts, quality levels, and delivery periods for specific items. But the purchasing function is not the same in many different companies. Different skills emphasize types of materials and vendor purchasing traditions. It would be impossible to discuss all the intricate relationships that have been developed by buyers and vendors in order to achieve maximum satisfaction for both parties.

Vendor Releasing and JIT. One important procedure should be mentioned. It is called **vendor releasing.** In this case, a buyer contracts for a substantial number of units and thereby obtains discount prices. The vendor agrees to ship fixed or varying amounts of the purchased material at stated intervals. Often, only the approximate shipping quantities for each time period are agreed upon. Generally, the buyer is in a position to change the quantities, from time to time, if it is done with sufficient notice. We can observe how an arrangement such as vendor releasing depends upon a good forecast of demand and an accurate specification of the vendor's lead time.[1] It requires a fairly long-term commitment to obtain the benefits of quantity discounts. Job shops that use large quantities of certain basic materials can employ vendor releasing to obtain discounts approximating those of the flow shop.

Vendor releasing characterizes one aspect of just in time (JIT) scheduling. It reduces the amount of stock that the buyer must hold as inventory. When JIT is mentioned, we tend to conjure up the delivery of units one at a time to the production line. But such an extreme view is not realistic. JIT is working when frequent small deliveries are being made, and storage space for purchased supplies is minimized and/or shared with the supplier. Therefore, vendor releasing, which is an old inventory procedure, anticipated managements' broad acceptance of JIT.

Internal transfers between departments in the same company should be viewed as materials that are sent by suppliers. The criteria for evaluating suppliers can be applied to internal transfers as readily as outside purchases. What are the run sizes, and who holds the inventories? The internal departments can negotiate the terms just as if they were buyer and supplier.

Receiving, Inspection, and Storage (RI&S). An important part of the materials management job is receiving suppliers' shipments. There must be some kind of facility that will allow the supplies to be unloaded from trucks, freight cars, hopper cars, and so on. This is often called the

---

[1]**Lead time,** or **lag time,** is the interval that elapses between the placement of an order with the vendor or supplier and the receipt (into the warehouse) of the products.

receiving dock. It is not unusual for freight cars or hopper cars to be used as storage facilities, with materials being unloaded as needed.

The supplies should be inspected to see if they are what was ordered and to make sure they are undamaged. Specific quality checks can be made using acceptance sampling methods. If the materials are acceptable they are moved to the storage facility, which is often the company warehouse. If they are not acceptable, the actions taken should have been thought out beforehand. This is not a time to panic, and the scenario of wrong shipments, bad parts, and so on is not rare. The appropriate management style is to have worked out this scenario beforehand with the suppliers.

The important points are that RI&S take time and cost money. RI&S also affect quality by adding more handling and by increasing the exposure of the supplies to damage, loss, and theft.

Bidding. Sometimes many vendors are asked to submit a bid for the cost of supplying their product. The bids will include delivery dates and various quality specifications, so there is more than one criterion upon which to rate the competing vendors.

The bid system is commonly associated with government purchasing, but it is also familiar in situations where industrial firms have no prior vendor arrangements and in which costly purchases (such as for engineering and construction jobs) are to be made. Bidding is applicable only when a competitive market exists for the goods or services that are to be acquired. One of the most familiar service bidding situations where quality counts first and foremost is when advertising agencies vie for an account.

Some bidding models indicate that as the number of competitors increases, the size of the winning bid decreases. The reason is that different costing systems, capacity and load conditions, skills, and facilities exist for each bidder. As a result, the range of bids will increase. On the basis of this reasoning, the procurement manager would want as many bidders as possible.[2]

But there is an opposing force at work. As the number of bidders increases, the cost of ordering rises, since each bid must be evaluated not only for costs, but for many intangible factors that affect the ordering decision. For example, the lowest bidder promises to meet a delivery schedule that historical evaluation indicates is unlikely to be fulfilled. Too many bidders may drive the expected profit so low that qualified suppliers refuse to join the bidding, leaving the field open to the less qualified.

A company may not choose to buy from the organization presenting the lowest bid. Price is seldom the only factor that should be taken into consideration when awarding a contract. Among other things, it is necessary to consider the guarantees of quality, the experience of the vendor,

---

[2]See David W. Miller and Martin K. Starr, *Executive Decisions and Operations Research,* 2nd ed. (Englewood Cliffs, N.J.: Prentice-Hall, 1969), pp. 425–437.

the certainty of delivery, and the kind of long-term supplier-producer relationship that is likely to develop. Transportation costs are another factor. A high bid received from a vendor 2 miles away may be less costly, after transportation, than a lower bid from a potential supplier located 13,000 miles away. It is not enough to compare bids on an FOB point of origin basis.[3]

Bidding is applicable for project procurement policies and for startup purchase arrangements for the flow shop. It is less relevant for the job shop, although it may make sense when costly components are involved. Bidding is always useful when there is suspicion that special deals are being made between suppliers and company personnel.

Inventories of Critical Parts. In the flow shop and for projects, the failure of certain parts will shut down the line or seriously delay project completion. An entire refinery can be shut down, and the cost of lost production may well run into millions of dollars. Should spares of all critical parts be kept in stock? If so, how many of each kind? How likely is it that a spare part kept in stock for an emergency is, in fact, a faulty part that will fail upon use? Often, severe technical problems are involved in purchasing critical parts for the maintenance of complex technological systems. Only buyers familiar with production equipment and its requirements are able to evaluate the failure characteristics of their acquisitions.

Inventory policies for critical parts are a function of the type of maintenance that is used—preventive or remedial maintenance, or a combination of the two. In many systems, the technical basis used for purchasing decisions is critical. When reliability and failure are of major importance, the purchasing function is frequently assigned to a scientifically trained individual. This is particularly necessary when technical engineering specifications are used.

CASE: CITY HOSPITAL'S CRITICAL PARTS IN-VENTORIES

For an important class of maintenance inventories, critical spare parts can be obtained inexpensively only at the startup of the facility that will be needing the spare parts. If it turns out later on that an insufficient supply of these critical parts was acquired, the cost of obtaining additional spares is much higher. (By critical, we mean that if the part fails, the facility ceases to function in an acceptable fashion.)

Assume that City Hospital is purchasing an emergency generator for the operating room in its new wing. Engineering data indicate that a particular critical part has a probability of i failures (pi) over the lifetime of the machine. There is a cost c for each spare part purchased at the time the generator is acquired. When a spare part must be purchased at a later time because

---

[3]*FOB Detroit:* This familiar expression is read "freight on board, Detroit." It means that the price is quoted without shipping charges from Detroit to whatever point of destination is involved.

not enough were purchased at the startup, the cost is estimated to be c' (which includes renting a generator as a temporary replacement and the large cost per replacement part charged by the vendor, who must treat the spare part request as a special order).

For a simple example of this model, let $i = 1, 2, 3$, meaning that at least 1 failure must occur and that no more than 3 failures can occur over the lifetime of the generator. Also, assume that the probability of failure is distributed as follows:

1 failure	$p_1 = \frac{1}{2}$
2 failures	$p_2 = \frac{1}{3}$
3 failures	$p_3 = \frac{1}{6}$

The sum of these probabilities must equal 1. Let $c = \$5$ and $c' = \$400$. The question we wish to answer is: How many spare parts, k, should be ordered at the time of the original purchase? Note that the spare part is inexpensive if purchased initially. However, the failure of the part without a replacement is a critical event, costing 80 times the price of the spare.

A decision matrix can be constructed to represent this problem (see Table 7–1).

The minimum expected cost is obtained by ordering 3 spares. This result was anticipated. At least 1 failure will occur (in line with the given probability distribution), so at least 1 spare must be ordered. Further, the cost of obtaining a spare after the initial order is so much greater than with the initial order that City Hospital will order 3 spares with the generator.

Let us review the steps required to obtain the expected values in the table above. The outcome entries in the matrix are computed with two different relationships. First, when the number of failures equals or is less than the number of parts originally ordered with the generator, the cost is simply kc. Second, when the number of failures is greater than the number of parts originally ordered, the cost is $kc + (i - k)c'$. For example, if three failures occur ($i = 3$) and only two parts were originally ordered ($k = 2$), then the cost is $(2 \times 5) + (3 - 2)400 = 410$. After the matrix of total costs is completed, the expected values are obtained in the usual fashion.

TABLE 7-1   FAILURE COST MATRIX FOR THE CITY HOSPITAL GENERATOR

		Number of Failures Occurring During Generator's Lifetime			
		1	*2*	*3*	
	p_i	$\frac{1}{2}$	$\frac{1}{3}$	$\frac{1}{6}$	Expected Cost
Initial number of	1	5	5 + 400	5 + 800	271.67
spare parts k	2	10	10	10 + 400	76.67
ordered	3	15	15	15	15.00 (min.)

Expected cost for $k = 1$: $5(1/2) + 405(1/3) + 805(1/6) = 271.67$

Expected cost for $k = 2$: $10(1/2) + 10(1/3) + 410(1/6) = 76.67$

Expected cost for $k = 3$: $15(1/2) + 15(1/3) + 15(1/6) = 15.00$

For realism, assume that all numbers are in thousands. With an expected cost of $15,000, City Hospital should order 3 spare parts with the generator. This is more than $60,000 cheaper than ordering 2, and more than $250,000 cheaper than ordering only 1 spare with the generator.

When the 3 parts arrive with the generator, they should be inspected carefully to make certain that they will do the job, if and when they are called upon. We could complicate the problem considerably by adding a charge for carrying a part in stock, by changing the probabilities of failure according to when a failure occurred, or by allowing more than 1 spare to be reordered after failure. All such issues, and others as well, can be treated in a realistic, but more complicated model. For City Hospital, we assumed that whenever a failure occurred, the probabilities of additional failures remain unchanged.

Question: What would the decision be if zero failures are expected with 0.97 probability and the other failure rates are all 0.01?

Answer: The matrix would now be:

		0	1	2	3	
p_i		0.97	0.01	0.01	0.01	Expected Cost
	0	0	400	800	1200	24
k	1	5	5	405	805	17
	2	10	10	10	410	14 (min.)
	3	15	15	15	15	15

which means that City Hospital would shift from ordering 3 spares to 2. Observe that the differentials between the strategies are no longer so large. The decision can save as much as $10,000, but only by comparing a no spare strategy to the $k = 2$ strategy.

Question: If $c = 5$, $c' = 20$, and $p_1 = 1/2$, $p_2 = 1/3$, $p_3 = 1/6$, how many spares should be ordered? Note that the initial acquisition cost remains the same, but is now only 1/4 the failure replacement cost.

Answer: The failure cost matrix is:

		1	2	3	
p_i		1/2	1/3	1/6	Expected Cost
	1	5	25	45	$18\frac{1}{3}$
k	2	10	10	30	$13\frac{1}{3}$ (min.)
	3	15	15	15	15

which signifies a change wherein 2 spares should be ordered instead of 3.

The decision matrix lends itself nicely to representing this static form of inventory problem where there is a one-time purchase. This is not a flow shop inventory model, but is applicable to the job shop and to the project manager. Variability of demand (in this case, the spare parts failure distribution) is only one way in which uncertainty about the order size can arise. Other causes are defectives (requiring additional parts to be made to fill the order), spoilage, and pilferage. All such factors can be accounted for with probability estimates and the decision matrix methodology.

Value Analysis (Alternative Materials Analysis)

The use of value analysis is a part of materials management. The idea behind **value analysis** is that the quality of the product must be enhanced, or at least maintained, while at the same time, the cost of the product should be as low as possible. Value analysis is applied to all materials used by the process or for the product (hospital materials, restaurant foods and silverware, auto dashboard and steering wheel).

Value analysis and methods analysis are often considered together. **Methods analysis** is the systematic examination of all operations in any process in search of a better way of doing things, such as combining operations, eliminating unnecessary operations, making work easier. Method analysts are widely employed by both government and industry.

Methods analysis is primarily concerned with process improvement and only incidentally with materials. We could describe value analysis as "the analysis of the value of alternative materials." It is inevitable that value and methods analysis must share some common ground. They tackle the same kinds of problems and they provide similar kinds of problem resolutions.

Undoubtedly, the growth of interest in value analysis can be explained by the fact that materials technology has been undergoing rapid and dramatic changes. Major changes in new materials seem to appear in waves. At the present time, we are moving out of the metals into plastics and ceramics. Research efforts to develop new materials will bring new breakthroughs in the 1990s.

On another front, materials shortages can be experienced by organizations. For example, the petroleum shortage of the 1970s led to major P/OM distortions. Companies were faced with the need to make swift alterations in the composition of their products, both goods and services. Other temporary shortages that have occurred during the last twenty years include yellow fats, paper products, lumber, and water. Companies have met the shortages in different ways. For example, alternate formulations may be prepared by R&D and kept ready for anticipated contingencies. Material shortages can hit particularly hard at the flow shop, which is least flexible in adapting to change.

With growing frequency, government agencies prohibit the use of well-established materials. The food industry has experienced bans on sac-

charine, cyclamates, food dyes, and preservatives. The detergent industry
has been forced to reformulate its products several times because of the
ecological effects of phosphorous and enzyme additives. And government
restrictions will continue to grow in number.

If value analyses of alternative materials have been done, then alternatives do not have to be hastily sought when shortages occur or government edicts forbid the use of specific items. The procedures of value
analysis are applied to established products during the mature life cycle
stage, as well as to new ones during the startup and growth stages.

Successful value analysis requires a well-structured approach. This is
reflected by the consistent application of a set of relevant questions. For
example:

1. What is this product or service intended to do?
2. How much does it cost to provide this product or service?
3. What materials are used, and how do they affect items 1 and 2?
4. What other materials could be used?
5. How do the alternative materials affect items 1 and 2?

Questions 1, 3, and 5 focus on quality. The discussion about quality
on pp. 233–240 showed that defining what a product or service is intended
to do is complex and difficult. Accordingly, the utility of value analysis
will depend upon the knowledge and creative insight that the individuals
who are doing these studies can bring to bear. The value analysis approach
has been designed to release such insights by providing a structural framework to encourage the development of alternative strategies.

The starting point is the examination of an existing output. The purposes or functions of this output are divided into primary and secondary
classes. Significant functions are then related by analogy to other items
and then to materials that are thought to provide similar properties.

It is by means of analogies that material alternatives are derived. For
example, we develop comparisons between different joining methods,
which include adhesion, cohesion, welding, brazing, and mechanical fas-
tenings such as screws, nuts and bolts, lock washers, cotter pins, and
nails. Both methods analysis and value analysis are used to discover new
alternatives. But we must always guard against investments in efficiency
studies before effectiveness issues have been thoroughly considered.

Section 7.2 Inventory Problems: Types and Costs

The distinction between different kinds of inventory situations must
be understood if materials management is to be effective. The costs that
underlie the choice of inventory strategies are examined in a systems
context (referred to as ABC). This is a way of choosing to solve the
problems (designated A) that really count; solutions to them provide savings significantly larger than the costs of providing the solutions.

ABC Classification of Inventory Systems

Many significant distinctions between types of inventories need to be made. First, as in the case of City Hospital, some items are functionally critical to operations, no matter how much or how little they cost. The lack of one spare engine part could ground an aircraft. The need for a gasket might close down a continuous petrochemical process.

Second, there are items that are important because their dollar volume (dollars per unit × number of units) is high. These can be a few expensive items, many inexpensive ones, or mixtures of both. A significant division of all items under materials management is based on the recognition that a few items have high dollar volumes and many others have substantially lower dollar volumes.

Figure 7–2 portrays the usual case where 20 to 30 percent of all items carried in the inventory account for as much as 70 to 80 percent of the company's total dollar volume. As an example, say that a hotel carries an inventory of 1,000 different items for which it spends $1 million annually. In the average case, about 25 percent of these items would cost approximately $750,000. This is called the A class of inventory items, as shown in Figure 7–2. These items are obtained as follows: All items are rank-ordered by dollar volume. Then the top-ranked items are chosen one by one, in descending order of contribution, until 75 percent of the total dollar volume is aggregated.

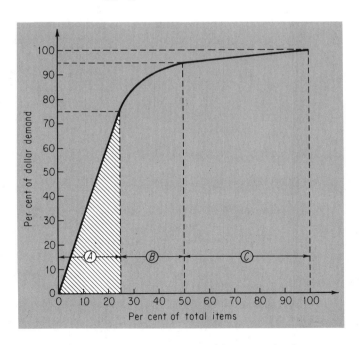

FIGURE 7-2. General representation of the A-B-C classification. The lion's share of dollar demand is produced by a small percentage of items.

Reduction of inventory costs (savings) relates directly to dollar volume. Therefore, potential savings available as a result of better inventory policies will be far greater in the A class than in the B or C classes. This is particularly apparent when it is pointed out that the cost of inventory studies tends to be proportional to the number of items under consideration.

The B class (another 25 percent of all items) may account for 15 or 20 percent of dollar volume. Thus, for the hotel, another 250 items might account for $200,000. The C class often deals with no more than 5 to 10 percent of the company's total dollar volume, although 50 percent of all items belong in that group. Therefore, 500 hotel items involve about $50,000 of the total dollar volume.

There is no commitment to provide class breaks at 25 and 50 percent of all items, nor a need to use three classes. It is essential, however, that the P/OM recognize the unequal contributions of different items in the inventory. We call this a **disproportionate effect.** Equivalent effort should not be spent on improving the inventory policies of all items.

Another important classification is based on the difference between static and dynamic situations. In the static case, only one purchase decision can be made. City Hospital's spare parts model is such a case. A well-known problem that is often cited to explain the static situation is the "Christmas tree problem." The Christmas tree dealer can place only a single order for trees. Then, on Christmas Day, the dealer learns whether the order size estimation was exactly right, or over or under. In the case of overestimated demand, salvage value is sometimes available. For example, a department store that overbuys on toys shipped from abroad in time for the holiday season can often sell those toys at a discount after the selling season is finished. Dynamic situations require different considerations because the demand for such items is continuous. The problem becomes one of adjusting inventory levels to balance the various costs so that total variable costs are minimized. Variable means that these costs change with order size.

Inventory Costs

The heart of inventory analysis lies in the identification of relevant costs. There are many kinds of inventory costs. We will itemize some of those that are most frequently encountered.

1. Cost of Ordering. Each time a purchase is made, both fixed and variable costs are incurred. The fixed costs of ordering include the salaries of the permanent staff of the order department. Also counted as fixed costs are investments in equipment and overhead charges. Fixed costs are not changed by order size or frequency of ordering, so they are not included in the inventory policy model.

The variable cost component consists of drawing up the purchase requisition form, the cost of sending this purchase requisition to the vendor, and any costs that increase as the number of purchase requisitions increases. Not to be overlooked are opportunity costs associated with alternative uses of both time and equipment. Thus, the ordering cost for a self-employed shopkeeper must take into account the fact that the owner could be redecorating windows, talking with a customer, or using the time in some other profitable manner.

As the number of orders increases, the fixed costs remain constant and the variable costs increase. For example, City Hospital now processes 100 orders per week. A new inventory policy requires that 150 purchase requisitions be processed in a week. It is agreed that the ordering department must be enlarged. The increase in labor costs, equipment, and overhead is considered to be additional variable cost. In this way, the ordering cost is determined on top of a base ordering system.

2. *The Cost of Carrying Inventory*. Organizations strive to maintain minimum inventories. In times of slack demand and uncertainty, companies often begin to cut back on inventory. Why is this so? The answer is that inventory is a form of investment. Company capital is tied up in materials and goods. If the capital were free, alternative uses might be found for it. The company could take this liberated capital and put it in the savings bank, thereby earning interest on the money.

It should be noted that the interest income is a variable cost which depends upon the number of units stocked, the price per unit, and the interest rate applicable. More speculative investments could be made in the stock market. The company could purchase additional equipment and expand capacity, or even use this money to diversify. These are the so-called opportunities which when ignored incur the cost of not doing that much better with the investment. By holding inventory, the company foregoes investing its capital in alternative ways. *Opportunity costs account for a large part of the costs of carrying inventory.*

Inventory carrying costs must also include the expense of storing inventory. As was the case for the ordering department, costs should be measured from a fixed base. We must consider only the variable cost component associated with storage. These are the costs over which the P/OM can exercise control using inventory policies. Thus, if a company has shelf space for 1,000 units but can get a discount if it stocks at least 2,000 units, to get this discount it must expand storage capacity or rent additional space. An appropriate inventory cost analysis can determine whether or not the discount should be taken. The extra costs incurred are a variable cost component associated with holding inventory.

Items that are carried in stock are subject to pilferage losses, obsolescence, and deterioration. These costs represent real losses in the value of inventory. Pilferage is particularly characteristic of certain items. Small items, for example, are more likely to disappear than large ones. Tool cribs are provided with attendants and frequently kept locked when the plant is shut down for the night and over the weekend. Tools have general appeal and almost universal utility. They are small enough to filch; ergo the tool crib concept. Department stores suffer enormous pilferage losses; hotels lose ashtrays and towels; pencils and stamps disappear in offices. Pilferage losses add substantially to the carrying costs of many organizations.

Obsolescence can occur quite suddenly because of technological change, or it can be the kind of loss that is associated with style goods, toys, and Christmas trees. Out of season and out of style, these items lose value and must be sold at a special reduced rate. The problem of determining how much inventory to carry will be affected by the nature of the inventories and the way in which units lose value over time.

An additional component of the carrying cost includes both taxes and insurance. If insurance rates and taxes are determined on a per unit basis, the amount of inventory stocked will directly determine the insurance and tax components of the carrying costs.

A Sample Determination of Carrying Cost. The following table is furnished only as a guide. Hypothetical figures have been entered that are similar to the carrying cost computations of many companies in the United States. Each situation is different, so accountants and operating managers must assess those costs that apply to their particular situation.

Category	Percent (High)	Percent (Low)
Loss due to inability to invest funds in profit-making ventures, including loss of interest	14.00	10.00
Obsolescence	3.00	1.00
Deterioration	3.00	1.00
Transportation, handling, distribution	2.00	1.00
Taxes	0.25	0.10
Storage cost	0.25	0.10
Insurance	0.25	0.10
Miscellaneous	0.25	0.10
Pilferage	Highly variable	
C_c = Carrying cost expressed as a percentage of the product's cost, per year	23.00	13.40

3. Cost of Out of Stock. If a company cannot fill an order, there is usually some penalty to be paid. Sometimes the customer goes elsewhere, and the penalty is the value of the order that is lost. If this customer is annoyed because of having to do without or needing to find a new supplier, and if this customer continues to hold a grudge against the company, then the loss of a sale plus the loss of goodwill must be translated into a cost.

If the buyer is willing to wait to have the order filled, then the company treats this situation as a **back order.** Back orders cost money. They can alienate customers. To avoid this, some companies fill customers' orders with a more expensive substitute. The cost factor is not difficult to determine in this case. Whatever the system—back ordering, the use of material substitutions, **fill or kill** (which means no back orders allowed), and so on—some costs of being out of stock will occur. The **lost goodwill cost** is considered to be one of the most significant and one of the most difficult to evaluate.

4. Other Costs. The above costs are usually considered most relevant in determining inventory policy, but many other costs also play a part in specific cases. For example, there are systemic costs associated with running the inventory system, costs of delays in processing orders, costs of discounts not realized, setup costs, costs of production interruptions, salvage costs, and expediting costs. In some instances, one or more of these costs will dominate the inventory policy evaluation.

Differentiation of Costs for Flow Shops, Job Shops, Projects, and FPS

For the flow shop, the cost of ordering is low, because orders for the same items are placed with regularity. On the other hand, the carrying cost of inventory tends to reflect the profitability of the industry. The reason for this relationship is that the carrying cost rate C_c is larger where reinvestments in the process or in marketing and distribution can continue to bring excellent profitability and ROI (return on investment). Out-of-stock costs are generally severe. The line may have to shut down or run at some fraction of total capacity. For this reason, large safety stocks are usually held in the inventory, no matter how high the carrying costs. Depending on the particular kind of flow shop, pilferage costs will vary. Because materials at different stages of completion are moved from station to station, only the last station has access to the finished goods. Consequently, flow shop pilferage can be controlled to a great extent.

For the job shop, the cost of ordering is often high. The right vendors have to be located for various jobs that call for special materials, new components, and so on. The carrying costs will tend to be lower than those of the flow shop to the degree that the job shop is less profitable. But over-ordering to provide protection against defectives leaves an increasing accumulation of small amounts of materials and components that eventually can be sold as salvage. This increases the costs of obsolescence. Pilferage costs also can turn out to be quite high because of the lesser degree of control that can be exercised over smaller amounts of many items. Out-of-stock costs are more or less significant (depending on the situation), but far less so than for the flow shop.

For the project, the cost of ordering can be extremely high. Bidding, which is expensive, is often used. Project managers must buy from a variety of vendors with which they have had little experience. For small items that are essentially one-shot purchases, minimum effort is made to bring efficiency and control to the purchasing function. Carrying costs are relatively unimportant, because the inventory is quickly used up. Where this is not the case, items are sold for salvage without being held as obsolete inventory. Pilferage may be a significant cost. Out-of-stock costs can be large, especially if the outages apply to activities along the critical path. The importance of being on time with the project has led to the development of critical path methods that permit a great deal of control over out-of-stocks. Though these project control methods are costly, they are warranted by the high out-of-stock costs. They help minimize (or eliminate) the number of outages to which the high out-of-stock costs can be applied.

For the FPS, the cost of ordering tends to be low because there is a focus on product/process materials that more nearly matches the flow shop than the job shop. Carrying cost rates are high because of the large capital investment and the profitability of the technology when it is properly managed. Out-of-stock costs are not as significant as for the flow shop, since small batches are run and shifts can be made to other products while waiting for rapid delivery of enough materials to keep the waiting customers happy. Lot sizes are small enough so that air delivery can be used. Pilferage and obsolescence of small amounts of inventory are less likely than for the job shop, since materials are monitored by computer. The FPS situation is partly a cross between the flow shop and the job shop, but it has additional unique advantages that are directly attributable to the flexibility of FPS technology. This seems to permit better cost control than is available for the more traditional work configurations.

Section 7.3 Material Requirements Planning (MRP)

MRP is an inventory management information system. It uses forecasts of uneven, sporadic, lumpy demand as inputs to the planning process for inventory levels. Demand is aggregated across common parts in the productline. For example, if the same motor is used for a blender, a slicer, and a serving robot, aggregate the demand for the motor over all three products over time (see modular production and group technology, pp. 140–143). A key attribute of MRP is that it is appropriate when most of the parts to which it is applied are used sporadically but repetitively over time. It can apply when parts are needed only once, but it does not apply when usage is steady, smooth, and continuous. Then, OPP (see Section 7.4) applies.

How MRP relates to CIM

MRP is a management information system that is needed by the large, multiproduct job shop. It is also ideal for FPS, where information control is equivalent to the central nervous system of the human body. FPS is a form of **CIM (computer integrated manufacturing).** The middle I of CIM should really stand for information. MRP and CIM are interdependent.

The MRP Approach

MRP has been around for three decades, but it has drawn broad national attention and support for less than half that time. Orlicky indicates that he and others began its development around 1960. Also, he states: "The number of MRP systems used in American industry gradually grew to about 150 in 1971, when the growth curve began a steep rise as a result of the 'MRP Crusade,' a national program of publicity and education sponsored by the American Production and Inventory Control Society (APICS)."[4]

The MRP approach to materials planning makes good sense when demand is infrequent for many different end products. Since MRP is an MIS (management information system), it can keep track of many items. MRP is also applicable when demand, over time, changes size—i.e. when demand is not smooth but is lumpy. These descriptions of demand are typical of job shop experience, and include the intermittent flow shop.

In addition, MRP should be used for items and ingredients that are components of the end product. "Material requirements planning calculates requirements for new materials, semi-finished materials or components (parts, subassemblies) based on plans to make the item that these materials go into."[5] We have made reference on a number of occasions to the part composition of end products. For example, see p. 142 for the matrix of modular production and p. 144 for the (parts) explosion chart. The Gozinto chart (see p. 476) is another illustration of the P/OM concern for cascades of end products from components, components from subcomponents, and so on.

Let us start with the BOM (bill of materials), which is shown in Fig. 7–3. The BOM lists all the parts which go into a specific end product. To apply MRP, consider switch: Z33, which is part of the end product: 5-HP motor J.

---

[4] See Joseph Orlicky, *Material Requirements Planning* (New York: McGraw-Hill, 1975), p. ix.

[5] G. W. Plossl and O. W. Wight, "Designing and Implementing a Material Requirements Planning System." Presentations at APICS 13th International Conference by J. A. Orlicky, G. W. Plossl, and O. W. Wight, Cincinnati, Ohio, October 8, 1970.

```
Item  Switch Z 33                          Sheet No.  1  of  2
Drawings  Z 1-Z 6                          Assembly  5 hp motor  J

Part No.   Part name   No./item   Material    Quantity/item   Cost/item   Operations

CH 20      Casing      1          SF 60       0.25 lbs        $0.15       Cast, trim
SJ 64      Drive Sprg. 2          Sprg. St.   ............    $0.08       Purchase
RH 82      1" Rod      3          1045 St.    4 in            $0.05       Make

TJ 32      Fitting     1          Ti-6A1-4V   0.10 lbs        $0.85       Forge, anneal
```

FIGURE 7-3. Bill of materials.
The item, switch Z33, is used in the assembly of the 5 HP Motor J.

First, we draw up the end product master schedule, entering the required production quantities as shown in Table 7–2. For each part, we draw up the appropriate component materials plan (see Table 7–3). Our immediate interest is switch Z33, one unit of which is required for each 5-HP motor J. Note that the time between order and delivery (called lead time) is 2 weeks.

TABLE 7-2 MASTER SCHEDULE FOR 5-HP MOTOR J

Past Due	Week									
	1	2	3	4	5	6	7	8	9	10
	—	60	—	—	—	80	—	—	40	—

TABLE 7-3 COMPONENT MATERIALS PLAN FOR SWITCH Z33

Lead Time = 2 Weeks	Past Due	Week									
		1	2	3	4	5	6	7	8	9	10
Gross requirements		—	60	—	—	—	80	—	—	40	—
Stock on hand (SOH)		80	20	20	20	20	—	—	—	—	—
Net requirements		—	—	—	—	—	60	—	—	40	—
Planned order release		—	—	—	60	—	—	40	—	—	—

The production schedule calls for 60 5-HP motor Js in week 2, 80 in week 6, and 40 in week 9. We have 80 units of switch Z33 on hand in week 1. Because 60 J-type motors are scheduled for week 2, the stock on hand (SOH) for switch Z33 will decrease to 20 in week 2. That level of SOH will continue through week 5, when it will be used up, leaving a net requirement of 60 units.

Lot Sizing Policies

We can plan ahead, ordering the 60 units of switch Z33 2 weeks in advance in week 4 (called planned order release). Similarly, we must place an order for 40 units of switch Z33 in week 7 to accommodate the production schedule of week 9. Our ordering policy is lot for lot. That is, when the gross requirement for the 5-HP motor J is X, order X units of switch Z33 two weeks in advance.

We should, in fact, call this policy lot for lot with corrections for errors. (This policy, without errors, has zero carrying costs. If setup costs are low, it is a preferred lot sizing policy.) Without errors, we should never have any SOH. But in week 1, the record begins with 80 units of SOH. The reason is that in a prior period the actual gross requirements fell short of expectations. As a result, excess stock exists which takes 5 weeks to dissipate. Carrying charges for this inventory may be high if the cost per unit for switch Z33 is large.

The planned order release policy we have just described tracked net requirements. No attention was paid to the setup costs of each new production run, or to the carrying costs of excessive inventory when the expected gross requirements exceed the actual gross requirements. We can design a lot sizing policy (called minimum total cost policy) that balances setup (or ordering) costs and carrying costs. When setup (or ordering) costs are equal to carrying costs, total cost is minimized.

The unit cost of switch Z33 equals $10. The carrying cost rate is 1 percent per month, and setup cost to produce switch Z33 is $15. In Table 7–4, we list monthly net requirements. Then we sum these in the column titled "cumulative lot size." Thus, if we produce enough for the first month only, the lot size is 20 units. If we produce enough for the first 4 months, then the lot size will be 150 units. For each policy, we determine the carrying cost. If we produce enough for only the first month, there are no carrying costs. Producing for 2 months entails no carrying charges for the first 20 units consumed in month 1, and $4 for the second month. Thus:

$$20 \text{ units } \times \$10/\text{unit} \times (0.01) \times 0 \text{ months carried} = \$0$$

$$40 \text{ units } \times \$10/\text{unit} \times (0.01) \times 1 \text{ month carried} = \underline{\$4}$$

$$\text{Total} = \$4$$

Producing 120 units for three months requires:

$$20 \text{ units} \times \$10/\text{unit} \times (0.01) \times 0 \text{ months carried} = \$ \ 0$$

$$40 \text{ units} \times \$10/\text{unit} \times (0.01) \times 1 \text{ month carried} = \$ \ 4$$

$$60 \text{ units} \times \$10/\text{unit} \times (0.01) \times 2 \text{ months carried} = \underline{\$12}$$

$$\text{Total} = \$16$$

To determine the carrying cost of producing 150 units for 4 months' requirements, we simply add the 3-month total to the carrying cost of the fourth month's net requirements.

$$30 \text{ units} \times \$10/\text{unit} \times (0.01) \times 3 \text{ months carried} = \$ \ 9$$

$$\text{Carried forward from 3-month lot size policy} = \underline{\$16}$$

$$\$25$$

The setup cost of $15 is closest to the carrying charges of $16 for a lot size of 3 months' requirements. Consequently, we would produce 120 units at this time. Future computations and results might differ markedly. If this approach is used, both the ordering interval and the quantity ordered will vary over time.

TABLE 7-4

Month	Net Requirements	Cumulative Lot Size	Months Carried	Carrying Cost	Policy: Order for Months
1	20	20	0	0	1
2	40	60	1	$4	1 + 2
3	60	120	2	$16	1 + 2 + 3
4	30	150	3	$25	1 + 2 + 3 + 4

Another possible lot sizing policy is to determine a fixed order quantity. This is done by using the EOQ model, which is discussed in Section 7.4. The ordering interval then varies according to net requirements. Nine alternatives are treated by Orlicky (see pp. 120–133 of his book). None of the nine alternatives is clearly superior to all others.

MRP as a Management Information System (MIS)

Codes for Part Numbers. Identical parts are used in different products. If the parts are identified with similar numbers, including as a prefix or a suffix the product number, then the overall need for each part can be determined by a computer sort. The parts also belong to families which can be made with quick alterations on the same machine. These can be grouped by sorting if the code numbers reflect the similarities. For service systems, forms, interviews, maintenance steps, and food ingredients can be coded for sorting to determine aggregate demands for common needs.

The appeal of MRP is that its logic extends down the tree of components and subcomponents. For our switch Z33, we now develop net requirements for casing CH/20, drive spring SJ/64 (2 units required per switch), and 1-in. rod RH/82 (three units required per switch). When a change occurs in the aggregated gross requirements for 5-HP motor J, the effect cascades all the way down the materials planning tree. Computer support of this information system is based on coding connections so that the linkages can be spotted.

An organized information system will spot the fact that switch Z33 is also used in other end products than 5-HP motor J. The net requirements for switch Z33 should represent all uses, and the planned order release should reflect the merged net requirements statement.

Updating and Correcting. The master schedule for end products and the component materials plan are updated regularly by a time shift. Accordingly, in a weekly schedule the past week would be dropped and the next week added. As this is done, the computer revises all planned order release dates that have been reached for which orders are to be placed. Deliveries are recorded as increases to stock on hand (SOH). Changes in gross requirements are made according to the latest information.

There are two options for updating. The first of these is called **regeneration.** In effect, an entirely new master plan is set up and the old one is discarded. The second approach, called **net change,** modifies the existing plan. In a large job shop, both approaches demand highly systematic information management. Each has advantages and disadvantages, but overall the net change system has greater appeal, because it identifies the effects of specific changes.

MRP or OPP

We have identified the situations in which MRP is most likely to be the best materials planning route. Equivalent generalizations can be made about when not to use MRP and to apply order point planning (OPP) techniques, described in Section 7.4.

1. When demand is independent of the production schedule, as it often is for finished goods of flow shops, maintenance supplies, and so on, OPP should be used.
2. With serial production, where process materials must be on hand at all times, OPP should be used.

3. When demand is fairly regular and continuous, as opposed to being lumpy and sporadic, OPP and MRP should be compared to decide which to use. If there are many interdependent components, the probability is good that some form of MRP will be beneficial.

Also, it should be noted that various combinations of MRP and OPP are possible. The advantage of bringing them together is that order point planning accents cost minimization, while material requirements planning focuses on the forecasts and the interdependencies of components and end products. Materials management that uses both tracks of reasoning is apt to benefit.

PROBLEM
SET

1. How does materials planning differ for the flow shop, the job shop, and the project?

2. What is meant by time-phased requirements planning for MRP?

3. With respect to MRP, what is the difference between updating by regeneration compared to the net change method? Discuss the pros and cons of each.

4. The master schedule for end product P is as follows:

Week	Gross Requirements
1	400
2	200
3	200
4	300
5	500
6	100
7	600
8	400

Stock on hand for p_1, a component of P, is 700.

  a. Develop the planned order release schedule for p_1, assuming a lot for lot sizing policy (with corrections for stock on hand).

  b. The cost of a unit of p_1 is $12. The carrying cost rate is 0.25 percent per week. The setup cost to produce p_1 is $48. Lead time is 2 weeks. Using the minimum total cost policy, determine the appropriate planned order release schedule.

5. Contrast goods and services with respect to "in-process" and "finished" inventories.

6. With what lines of the breakeven chart are material inputs associated?

7. Should your company get a computer before or after you organize to introduce material requirements planning? Discuss.

8. List some of the items inventoried by the administration of your school. Do you think they employ the concept of an ABC-type distribution?

9. Assuming that your company has a long history of bidding for jobs, prepare a study that would be useful in evaluating the results to date and in achieving improvements in bidding.

Answer: A table of the bids offered for all jobs can be compiled. The individuals responsible for the bid should be listed along with a column for pertinent remarks. A column should be left for entry of the company's actual performance on all jobs that have been received, undertaken, and completed. For those cases where our company has not been awarded the job, estimates should be made of the winning bidder's actual costs. This table, when a sufficient sample has been taken, can be very useful for the analysis of the company's bidding procedures.

10. For the spare-part failure model on p. 313, assume that a salvage value of $2 now exists. Would this alter the solution to the problem?

11. Let us return to City Hospital's problem of how many spares to order with the emergency generator, when $c = 5$ and $c' = 20$. What set of probabilities for $i = 1, 2,$ and 3 failures will produce equal expected costs for all three strategies $k = 1, 2,$ and 3?

Answer: Solve the four equations:

$$5x_1 + 25x_2 + 45x_3 = V$$

$$10x_1 + 10x_2 + 30x_3 = V$$

$$15x_1 + 15x_2 + 15x_3 = V$$

$$x_1 + x_2 + x_3 = 1$$

and you will derive $x_1 = \frac{1}{4}$, $x_2 = 0$, $x_3 = \frac{3}{4}$, and V(the expected value) $= 15$. This last point is obvious from the bottom row of the decision matrix.

12. As the P/OM of a large company producing copying machines, how do you react to the announcement that the vice president in charge of materials management has set up a value analysis group under the head purchasing agent?

Section 7.4 Order Point Policies (OPP)

Order point planning (OPP) has been in use for at least fifty years. The concepts were developed in the 1920s, and the calculations could be done without a computer. MRP, on the other hand, which requires the information processing capacity of large computers, did not appear until the 1960s.

The **economic order quantity (EOQ) model** (also called the **square root model**) goes back to early industrial engineering efforts. See, for example, Benjamin Cooper, "How to Determine Economical Manufacturing Quantities," *Industrial Management,* 72, 4 (1926), pp. 229–233; and Raymond E. Fairfield, *Quantity and Economy in Manufacture* (Princeton, N.J.: D. Van Nostrand, 1931). The mathematical work that underlies present order point models was developed in the 1940s and 1950s. See, for example, Aryeh Dvoretsky, J. Kiefer, and Jacob Wolfowitz, "The Inventory Problem," *Econometrica,* 20 (1952), pp. 187–222, 450–466, and Kenneth J. Arrow, Theodore E. Harris, and Jacob Marschak, "Optimal Inventory Policy," *Econometrica,* 19 (1951), pp. 250–272. At first the field emphasized the mathematical aspects of inventory models at the expense of the real inventory problems themselves. However, since 1960, a great deal of effort has gone into making the mathematical methods applicable to real situations.

Japanese inventory methods stress cost reduction of ordering and setting up jobs. In effect, they bypassed the applicability of OPP models. They also emphasized supplier relationships to accomplish goals which are not represented by the inventory models—namely, high product quality, communication of impending problems, short lead times and delivery reliability.

The Economic Order Quantity Model (EOQ) for Batch Delivery

How do the costs defined in Section 7.2 operate in an inventory system where deliveries of purchased supplies are made at regular intervals? The quantities will be delivered in batches of x units (the order quantity). Also, we assume that the production system uses up the inventory at a constant rate and that there is no variability in this rate or in the delivery intervals. Because of the assumptions we have made, all units ordered will be used up. There will be no salvage costs for excess units, and no stock outages. (Later we will allow for variability in the rate of inventory usage and in the length of the delivery interval.)

The proposed conditions apply to many P/OM systems. They are applicable to the flow shop and to FPSs, which receive materials in batches that can be small and delivered just-in-time (JIT). They are also relevant for the job shop or the project or the intermittent flow shop where the question arises: Should all the inventory that will be needed to meet the demand be purchased at one time or in several lots, over time?

This is not like City Hospital's static inventory problem, because demand is certain for this inventory. All inventory purchased will be used up, and no shortage of supplies can occur. Although it is assumed that consumption occurs at a uniform, continuous rate, it is seldom a serious problem if the conditions are not met precisely. The objective is to balance the time stream of opposing costs so that an optimal inventory procedure can be designed.

Figure 7–4 shows the relationship of the order quantity x with variable ordering costs and carrying costs. Let x equal the number of units pur-

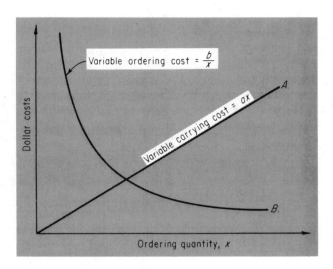

FIGURE 7-4. Variable ordering costs and carrying costs as a function of the order quantity x.

chased per order. We see that as the number of units purchased at one time increases, the carrying costs rise. This is line A. On the other hand, as the number of units per order increases, the number of orders that must be placed in a year will decrease. This declining ordering cost is line B. If the demand for a particular item amounts to 500 units per year, we could order all 500 units at one time. Only one order would have to be placed per year. The 500 units would gradually decrease from the beginning to the end of the year so that an average of approximately 250 units would be carried in stock for that year. For the job shop or the project, the time interval can be consistent with the activity schedule— 1 month, 10 days, or 1 week. Figure 7–5 indicates the withdrawal pattern. The carrying cost rate must be applied to the 250 average number of units.

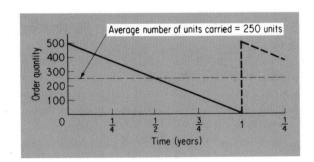

FIGURE 7-5. Continuous withdrawal pattern when x = 500 and only one order is placed per year.
The demand is 500 units per year.

Only one order is to be made, so the ordering cost would be incurred once.

Now consider the policy of ordering twice a year. There would be 250 units ordered with each of two purchase requisitions. These 250 units get used up regularly until nothing is left. At that point, the next order of 250 units arrives. The stock level moves back up to a full bin of 250 units. Then the decline begins again until, at the end of the year, nothing is left. We now have half of the 250 units as the measure of the average number of units of inventory—125 units. The ordering cost is incurred twice, but the carrying cost is applied to the smaller average inventory of only 125 units. Figure 7–6 illustrates this, and it also shows what would happen with five orders per year. Each purchase requisition consists of a request for 100 units. The average number of units on hand would now be 50, and the variable cost per order is incurred five times.

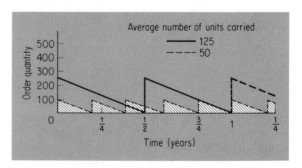

FIGURE 7-6. Continuous withdrawal pattern when $x = 250$ and two orders are placed each year; also when $x = 100$ and five orders are placed each year.

In each case, the total variable cost is the sum of the total variable ordering cost component and the total variable carrying cost component. Thus:

Total variable cost = total variable carrying cost
+ total variable ordering cost

The goal is to write an appropriate cost equation which includes all relevant variable costs, such as obsolescence, pilferage, and so on. Then we proceed to minimize this total variable cost equation with respect to the order size x. It is quite clear that different costs result from different ordering policies. The smallest possible carrying charges would occur when we placed 500 orders for one unit at a time. On the other hand, a small ordering cost could be achieved by ordering only once.

Figure 7–7 shows the plot of the total variable cost equation. It is the sum of the two cost factors, ordering cost B and carrying cost A. This equation has a minimum (total variable cost is minimized) when $x = x_O$, which is called x optimal.

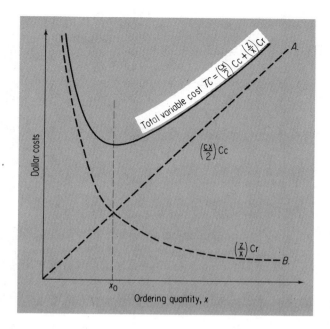

FIGURE 7-7. The total cost resulting from different ordering policies, x, is the sum of the carrying costs, line A, and the ordering costs, line B.

Let us write the explicit equation for total variable cost.

1. The average number of units carried in stock is $x/2$, where x is the number of units purchased per order.
2. The average dollar inventory carried is $cx/2$, where c is the unit cost of the item.
3. The total carrying cost per year would be $(cx/2)C_c$, where C_c is the carrying cost rate, applied as a percentage of the product's cost per year. This is the first term of the total-cost equation.
4. The number of orders placed per year is z/x, where z is the total demand per year, and x is as defined previously.
5. The total ordering cost per year will then be $(z/x)C_r$, where C_r is the variable cost per order. This is the second term of the total-cost equation.
6. The time interval can always be adjusted to be consistent with the activity schedule.

Then the total variable cost TC is described as follows:

$$TC = \left(\frac{cx}{2}\right) C_c + \left(\frac{z}{x}\right) C_r$$

We can minimize this equation by plotting the points for each cost component and then adding them together (see Fig. 7–7). Also, we could use trial and error methods by substituting different values of x into the total variable cost equation until the minimum value of TC is obtained. Both approaches are cumbersome and usually unnecessary.

Using one simple fact, we can find the value of x_O. That fact is this: *The minimum total cost always occurs at the crosspoint of lines A and B.* This statement applies to all equations of the form $y = ax + b/x$.

Therefore, set $(cx/2)C_c = (z/x)C_r$, and solve for x to obtain the economic order quantity:

$$x_O = \sqrt{\frac{2zC_r}{cC_c}}$$

This model, which applies to flow shops, job shops, FPS, and projects, signals the square-root relationship between the optimal order size and all the factors that influence what is optimal, and how far from optimal we may wander. The EOQ inventory model has great applicability by itself; it can also be extended and used with other concepts. It is the most fundamental equation in inventory theory. Upon it is built a variety of models that reflect the interplay of additional relevant factors.

Even when risk exists in the system, a version of the EOQ model can be developed in which a reserve stock level is added. Other modifications of this model permit stock outages to occur at some fixed level. Discounts can be examined to see whether the company should take advantage of them. When the inventory is self-supplied by the production system rather than purchased from an external vendor, the model can be converted to indicate optimal run size. This variant is called the economic lot size model. The point to remember in all applications is that the value of x_O that will produce a minimum cost can be readily determined by equation and *not by intuition*. The human brain is not a square-root thinker.

CASE: THE LION'S DEN

This famous student lounge is managed by a business student who learned about the EOQ model in a P/OM course. The manager decided to try out EOQ on one item, with the idea of extending its use to other items if satisfied. Accordingly, the following estimates for determining the optimal order quantity for napkins were derived.

$$\text{Carrying cost rate} = C_c = 0.06 \text{ per year}$$

$$\text{Price} = c = \$0.005 \text{ per napkin}$$

$$\text{Demand} = z = 3000 \text{ napkins per month}$$

$$= 36{,}000 \text{ napkins per year}$$

$$\text{Cost per order} = C_r = \$2 \text{ per order}$$

Then, the total variable cost equation could be written and simplified.

$$TC = \left(\frac{0.005x}{2}\right) 0.06 + \left(\frac{36,000}{x}\right) 2 = 0.00015x + \frac{72,000}{x}$$

The manager used the EOQ formulation

$$x_O = \sqrt{\frac{2zC_r}{cC_c}} = \sqrt{\frac{2(36,000)(2)}{(0.005)(0.06)}} = \sqrt{480,000,000} = 21,909$$

and determined that 21,909 napkins should be ordered at one time (actually 22,000, since orders must be placed in units of 1,000). This represents about 7⅓ months' supply. The present policy is to order 3,000 napkins on a monthly basis.

Since there was such a great difference in policy indicated, the manager decided to compare the total variable costs for each.

$$x = 3,000 \quad TC = 0.00015(3000) + \frac{72,000}{3000} = \$24.45$$

$$x_O = 22,000 \quad TC_O = 0.00015(22,000) + \frac{72,000}{22,000} = \$6.57$$

Indeed, there is a big difference, but such small sums were involved that the manager wondered whether EOQ was worth the bother. Then he thought, "I spend 36,000(0.005) = $180.00 a year on napkins. By using the EOQ policy, I save $24.45 − 6.57 = $17.88, which is almost like a 10 percent discount on the purchase price. If I can do as well on many other purchased items, it will add up to a substantial overall saving." (Still, there was a nagging thought: "Where am I going to store a seven months' supply of napkins?")

The Economic Lot Size Model (ELS) for Continuous Delivery (Not Continuous Production)

Having investigated the relationship that describes the optimal order quantity when purchase orders are delivered (by an outside vendor or one's own shop) in batches, let us now consider a comparable problem. It is identical in all respects, except that the supplier provides continuous JIT-like delivery, or as often occurs, the company is its own supplier, providing continuous delivery. Figure 7–8 illustrates the difference between batch-type and continuous delivery systems.

Figure 7–9 depicts the variations in stock level over time for the continuous delivery situation. We call this formulation the **economic lot-size model (ELS)** because the production run quantity is called a *lot*.

The sharp sawtooth form that applied to the EOQ case, where a total

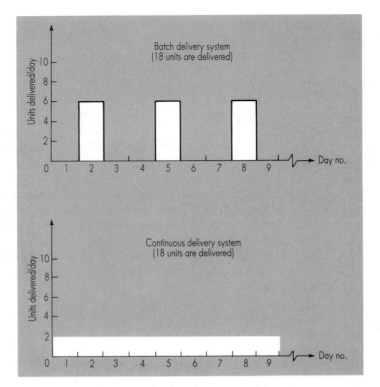

FIGURE 7-8. Contrasting batch and continuous delivery systems.

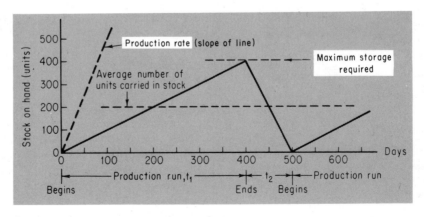

FIGURE 7-9. The economic lot size model, ELS, used to determine the optimal production run.
It also can be used to study the effect of varying the production rate.

shipment of stock was delivered at one point in time, has been replaced by a gradual stock buildup. There is continuous withdrawal, so the stock level reaches a maximum and then begins to decline. We can see why the ELS model (which determines production run size) is of primary interest to a supplier or self-supplier, whereas the EOQ model (which determines the order quantity) captures the interest of the purchaser.

The key to understanding the role of the ELS model is that it provides continuous delivery with discontinuous production. It epitomizes the behavior of FPS, and of intermittent flow shops which are designed to run one item and then change over to run another item using the same or similar equipment, the same work stations, and the same workers. The ELS problem is increasingly encountered in the job shop as flexible NC and CNC equipment (see p. 168) is installed. Because of the ability to change over rapidly and at low cost, the ELS can be small.

The ELS model can run the gamut from the continuous production of the flow shop to very short production runs. When the vendor delivers the economic order quantity to the buyer, the production of the required batch can be thought of as instantaneous. Let us develop the model so that we can examine these relationships.

The cost of an order is no longer relevant. In its place we substitute C_s, which is the setup cost. Usually it is much larger than the order cost. For FPS it is almost negligible. The setup cost is composed of at least two parts: (1) the cost of labor required to prepare the facility for the new production run, and (2) the cost of lost production occasioned by the facility's being down while being prepared for the new job. In addition, there are two other variables:

$$p = \text{production rate in units per day}$$
$$d = \text{demand rate in units per day.}$$

The optimal run size is derived in a manner similar to the derivation of the economic order quantity.

Our total variable cost equation is

$$TC = \left(\frac{cx}{2}\right)\left(\frac{p-d}{p}\right)C_c + \left(\frac{z}{x}\right)C_s$$

where $\left(\dfrac{p-d}{p}\right)\dfrac{x}{2}$ can be shown to be the average number of units carried in the inventory. Setting the two terms of the equation for total variable cost equal to each other (because minimum total variable cost occurs at the x value, where the two lines in Fig. 7–7 cross), we obtain the value for x_O.

$$x_O{}^2 = \left(\frac{2zC_s}{cC_c}\right)\left(\frac{p}{p-d}\right)$$

and

$$x_O = \sqrt{\frac{2zC_s}{cC_c}\left(\frac{p}{p-d}\right)}$$

Furthermore, the production run x_O must equal pt_1 (where $t_1 =$ the length of time of the production run). Since $x_O = pt_1$, we can solve for t_1 as follows:

$$t_1 = \frac{x_O}{p}$$

We know that the period of each cycle $t = t_1 + t_2 = x_O/d$ (where $t_2 =$ the length of time between production runs). For a graphical explanation of t_1 and t_2 see Fig. 7–9. The explanation of this equation follows from the fact that

$$x_O = dt$$

which means that the optimal run size must satisfy the demand per day times the number of days of the cycle. Then,

$$t_2 = t - t_1 = \frac{x_O}{d} - \frac{x_O}{p} = x_O\left(\frac{p-d}{pd}\right)$$

so we are now able to compute production run time t_1 and the time between production runs t_2.

CASE: PENMAKERS, AN EXAMPLE OF THE ELS MODEL

This company produces inexpensive ballpoint pens using a flow shop configuration. The ink cartridges are made in an intermittent flow shop where different colors are run successively. Blue ink is the major color, having by far the largest share of sales. Penmakers has obtained new equipment for producing the ink cartridges and wishes to recalculate the optimal production run size for blue cartridges.

The following data have been assembled:

Yearly demand $= z = 200,000$ per year $= 250d$

Daily demand $= d = 800$ per day $= z/250$

(*Note:* We are assuming 250 working days per year. Consequently, daily demand d multiplied by 250 days is equal to yearly demand. From this we can determine the value of d.)

Daily production $= p = 1800$ per day

Setup cost $= C_s = \$20$ per setup

Carrying cost rate $= C_s = 0.15$ of the unit cost per year

Unit cost $= c = \$0.06$ per cartridge

The optimal lot size x_O would be

$$x_O = \sqrt{\frac{(2)(200,000)(20)(1800)}{(0.06)(0.15)(1000)}} = \sqrt{\frac{(144)(10^8)}{9}} = \frac{(12)(10^4)}{3}$$

$$= 40,000 \text{ cartridges}$$

The production run time is

$$t_1 = \frac{x_O}{p} = \frac{40,000}{1800} = 22.22 \text{ days}$$

The cycle period is determined:

$$t = t_1 + t_2 = \frac{x_O}{d} = \frac{40,000}{800} = 50 \text{ days}$$

and so the period between runs is

$$t_2 = x_O \left(\frac{p - d}{pd} \right) = 40,000 \left(\frac{1000}{800 \times 1800} \right) = 27.78 \text{ days}$$

This means that Penmakers will have about 28 days to run all other color cartridges. Fitting them onto the line will not be an easy task. One approach that can be used to determine the optimal run sizes for a sequence of items produced serially on the same facility is described below.

Multi-Item ELS Intermittent Flow Shop Systems

It is not unusual for a variety of different items to follow one another in serial fashion through the system. This is an intermittent flow shop. All items are produced on the same equipment, in the same order of processing, but requiring some new setups as each different item begins production.

Given that a best sequence of items is known (or if the order of processing is not relevant to cost), then a simple formulation has been suggested concerning the amount of each item to run.[6]

There are n different products that are all made on the same equipment,

---

[6]See J. F. Magee and D, M. Boodman, *Production Planning and Inventory Control*, 2nd ed. (New York: McGraw-Hill, 1967), pp. 354–356.

and each product is made only once in the cycle. Using i to denote specific products, we find that the optimal run sizes would be:

$$x_{O_i} = \sqrt{\frac{2z_i^2 \sum\limits_i^n C_{s_i}}{\sum\limits_i^n (cC_c)_i z_i \left(1 - \dfrac{d_i}{p_i}\right)}}$$

Let us use the Penmakers' case, where blue, red, and green ink cartridges are to be made in the sequence blue, red, green. Red has a high setup cost, since it follows blue, which stains the equipment more than the other colors.

	Blue	Red	Green
z	200,000	150,000	100,000
d	800	600	400
p	1,800	1,800	1,800
C_s	20	100	40
C_c	0.15	0.15	0.15
c	0.06	0.06	0.06

Then:

$$x(blue)_O = \sqrt{\frac{2(4 \times 10^{10})160}{2600}} = 70{,}164.64 \begin{cases} t = 87.70 \\ t_1 = 38.98 \\ t_2 = 48.72 \end{cases}$$

$$x(red)_O = \sqrt{\frac{2(2.25 \times 10^{10})160}{2600}} = 52{,}623.48 \begin{cases} t = 87.70 \\ t_1 = 29.23 \\ t_2 = 58.47 \end{cases}$$

$$x(green)_O = \sqrt{\frac{2(1 \times 10^{10})160}{2600}} = 35{,}082.32 \begin{cases} t = 87.70 \\ t_1 = 19.49 \\ t_2 = 68.21 \end{cases}$$

Our previous optimal solution for blue cartridges (see p. 339) has now been altered by the constraints of the red and green cartridges, which must be able to run on the same equipment when the blue cartridges are not running. This matching of run/nonrun time has been accomplished:

$$t_2(blue) = 48.72 = t_1(red) + t_1(green) = 29.23 + 19.49$$

$$t_2(red) = 58.47 = t_1(blue) + t_1(green) = 38.98 + 19.49$$

$$t_2(green) = 68.21 = t_1(blue) + t_1(red) = 38.98 + 29.23$$

To accomplish this, Penmakers is paying a higher total variable cost, but the serial production, intermittent flow shop is fully utilized.

The Range of Inventory Systems

Consider the ELS equation for optimal run size.

$$x_O = \sqrt{\frac{2zC_s}{cC_c}\left(\frac{p}{p-d}\right)}$$

If d is almost equal to p, then $(p - d)$ approaches 0. This means that x_O becomes very large, approaching infinity as the difference between d and p approaches 0. This result makes sense. It states: If the demand rate is as great as the production rate, then run the process continuously. There is no inventory buildup, and the line in Fig. 7–9 showing stock on hand runs flat against the x axis.

On the other hand, if p is much greater than d ($p > > > d$), then x_O equals EOQ. The increasing stock on hand line rises almost perpendicularly, as in Fig. 7–5 and 7–6. The producer is literally able to supply the order quantity on demand, much as is the case when delivery is received from an outside vendor. This result is also reasonable: The condition that is given approximates the state of being able to receive total replenishment upon request.

Lead Time Length and Variability

For both economic order quantity (EOQ) and the economic lot size (ELS) systems, the lead time required to supply items for inventory must be known. In Fig. 7–10, the lead time or replenishment time is called LT; the reorder point (RP) is the stock level at which a new order should be placed.

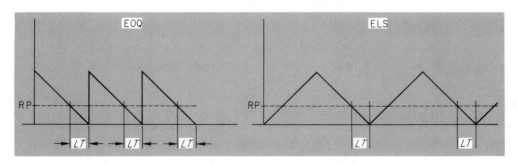

FIGURE 7-10. When lead time (LT) is known, at a specific level of stock (RP), a new order is placed.

Consider the EOQ case. The components of lead time include:

- The period for recognition of the fact that it is time to reorder
- The interval for doing whatever clerical work is needed
- Mail or telephone intervals for communicating with the vendor
- Recognition of the order by the vendor, who will see whether the requested items are in stock, and if not, will set up to make them
- Delivery time while the vendor ships the items
- Processing of delivered items by the receiving department, which may require inspection
- Time needed to enter items on the warehouse stock cards

Similar descriptions could be given for the ELS case, where the sometimes illusory advantages of dealing within your own firm, and thereby having greater control, appear. Note too that when the EOQ model is applied to self-supply with batch production, appropriate lead times should be included in the schedule.

Lead times can be variable. When they are, estimates must be made of the variability, and appropriate steps must be taken to include the effects of variability in the analyses. Usually, a larger estimate of lead time than the expected value is used, such as $(1.5)LT$.

Perpetual Inventory Systems

The economic lot size model and the economic order quantity model do not allow for variability in demand. Often in practical instances this assumption is unreasonable. As a result, a class of inventory models has been designed to cope with situations where demand level fluctuates.

These models apply to the intermittent flow shop, the paced-flow shop, and FPS as well. In the latter case, variability of demand can arise from changes in the number of defectives since this affects order shipments. It can also occur if the conveyor rate is changed from time to time.

In general, these models do not apply to job shops, where there is no continuity of demand. The same can be said about projects. Static inventory models do apply. When there is continuous but lumpy demand for the job shop, the methods of MRP should be used.

A department store provides an excellent example of a mixture of inventory situations. *Some items are ordered once.* For example, Christmas toys are ordered the previous July and shipped by sea. What is left over (after Christmas) is discounted and **remaindered** (sold at a discount, also called **salvage**). Shortages cannot be made up, since there is only one order. Other items are stocked regularly, and the demands for them can vary greatly. The buyer orders the economic order quantity, but has on hand some extra stock (called **reserve stock** or **buffer stock**) so that when demand is heavier than expected, orders can still be filled. How much reserve stock should be kept on hand? The answer involves balancing the added carrying costs against the costs of running out of stock. As one cost goes up, the other goes down.

The department store can design a **perpetual inventory system.** The *perpetual* in the name means that such a system is on-line, tracking the stock on hand (SOH) inventory level at each transaction of withdrawal or stock entry. The design parameters include answers to the following three questions:

1. How much reserve stock should be carried?
2. When should an order be placed?
3. How many units should be ordered?

Many companies use perpetual inventory systems to determine when they should order next. The system works as follows: Withdrawal quantities are entered on the stock card each time a unit is withdrawn from stock. The withdrawal quantity is subtracted from the previous stock level to determine the present quantity of stock on hand.

A minimum level is designated as the **reorder point quantity** for each item. This level is marked on the respective stock card. When the minimum level has been reached, an order is placed for the economic order quantity, x_O. The level of stock represented by the reorder point (RP) is equal to the expected demand in the lead time (LT) period, plus what is called the reserve stock or buffer stock (BS).[7]

The buffer has been designed to absorb a certain percentage of the fluctuations in demand that are likely to occur for each particular item. The buffer stock is geared to provide some chosen level of protection against stock outages. The level that is chosen is based on the balance of out of stock costs and carrying costs associated with the buffer stock. Figure 7–11 illustrates the way in which a perpetual inventory system operates. Note that when demand is heavy, the RP is reached quickly.

---

[7]This rule always applies when the lead time is equal to or less than the optimal period between reorders (t_O), i.e., $LT < (x_O/z = t_O)$. However, a rule that covers all situations, including the cases where $LT > t_O$, is now given. The reorder point RP should be calculated as follows: $RP = BS +$ fractional part of $[LT/t_O]x_O$. The fractional part of $[LT/t_O]x_O$ is equivalent to the expected demand in the lead time period, less deliveries that occur in the lead time period. Deliveries are represented by integer values of $[LT/t_O]$.

Perhaps the best way to explain the equation above is by an example. Assume that the lead time LT is two days, and the optimal period between reorders is $t_O = x_O/z = 110/60 = 1.83$ days. Thus:

$$t_O = 1.83 \text{ days} < LT = 2 \text{ days}$$

Buffer stock is specified as $BS = 20$ and $x_O = 110$ has also been given. Therefore:

$$RP = 20 + \text{fractional part of } [LT/t_O]110.$$

The fractional part of $[LT/t_O] = 1.09$ is 0.09, whence

$$RP = 20 + 0.09(110) = 29.9, \text{ or } 30 \text{ units}$$

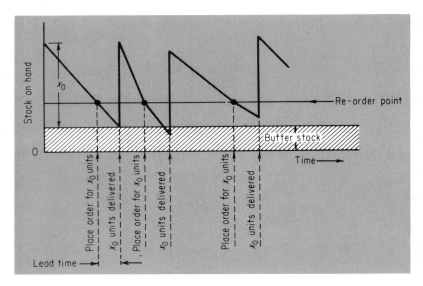

FIGURE 7-11. A perpetual inventory system where stock on hand is recomputed with each withdrawal.

The calculation of the reorder point is not difficult. First, as has been noted, stock must be provided to cover the expected demand in the lead time period. Call this S. Then, additional buffer stock is to be provided which gives some specified level of protection against going out of stock in the same lead time interval. Call this additional inventory BS. Figure 7–12 shows the situation for the probability distribution of demand in the lead time period.

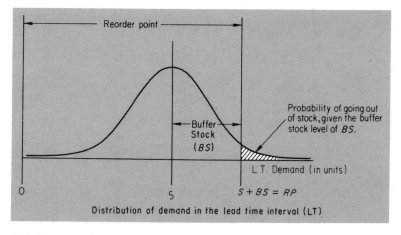

FIGURE 7-12. Determination of the reorder point (RP).
It is $S + BS$ units where S is expected demand in the lead time interval.

This department store chain intends to install computerized perpetual inventory control for all A-type items in its inventory. For a trial run, it has decided to use a high-volume face cream sold in the cosmetics department. This face cream has an expected demand of 20 jars per day; sometimes the demand goes as high as 30 or as low as 10 jars.

The lead time between placing an order with the supplier and receiving the replenishment stock is regular, since the supplier's warehouse is nearby and this face cream is in continuous production. Lead time is 2 days. Accordingly, we know that the expected demand in the lead time interval is 40 jars.

To this number 40 (which matches expected demand in the interval elapsing between placing the order and receiving it, inspecting it, and putting it in stock) we add buffer stock to protect against outages caused by greater than expected demand. By keeping appropriate records, it is determined that the demand in any 2-day period exceeds 60 jars only once out of every hundred 2-day periods that we have studied.

Storemasters has decided that it is desirable to be protected at this level. That is, only once in a hundred lead time periods (of 2 days) will Storemasters be unable to fill a customer's order for face cream. Thus, it has been determined that the reorder point will be $40 + 20 = 60$ jars. Further, buffer (or reserve) stock is 20 jars.

Notice that the reorder point analysis is independent of the calculation of the economic order quantity. This is true because out of stock protection is solely a function of expected demand in the lead time period and the variability of extra demand in the lead time period.

This statement does not strictly apply to the case where $LT > t_O$ (see footnote 7). Whenever the lead time period includes a delivery, we subtract the delivered number of units x_O from the reorder point RP. Thus, the economic order quantity does affect the reorder point analysis, but only because a delivery of this amount has been made. The fractional part of LT/t_O remains independent of the calculation of EOQ.

Storemasters has determined the reserve stock without using estimates of real costs for being out of stock. It is better to use real costs, but if we lack them, it is entirely feasible to estimate how often we are willing to allow stock outages.

It is also useful to point out that, in practice, lead time varies. If the variation is small, it can be neglected. (We have held it constant.) With variable lead time, we would increase the lead time period by some percent, and this would automatically increase the size of the reserve stock.

**SIMULATION
OF THE
PERPETUAL
INVENTORY
MODEL**

To illustrate how the perpetual inventory system works, we now simulate daily demand and track the stock level to determine when to place an order. Suppose the economic order quantity has been determined to be $x_O = 110$ jars. Assume that an order has just been received, so we have 110 jars on hand.

Look at Table 7–5. The column marked simulated demand is derived by using random numbers to sample the normal distribution of daily demand, which ranges between 10 and 30 with a mean level of 20. (Discussion of simulation with random numbers appears on pp. 528–531.)

TABLE 7-5

Day	(Beginning of Day) Stock on Hand	Simulated Demand	Units Ordered at Reorder Point	Order Received
1	110	25		
2	85	30		
3	55	20	110	
4	35	15		
5	20 + 110 = 130	36		110
6	94	18		
7	76	22		
8	54	25	110	
9	29	17		
10	12 + 110 = 122	19		110
11	103	25		
12	78	32		
etc.	etc.	etc.		

In this simulation, the average daily demand is 23.67 (the expected value is 20). Two orders have been placed in 12 days [the expected value is $(12 \times 20)/110 = 2.18$]. (*Note:* For this calculation, expected demand for 12 days is divided by x_O.) Stock on hand dropped as low as 12 on the tenth day, but this was immediately replenished by the receipt of the second order. Although simple, the simulation does reveal to Storemasters' management how this particular perpetual inventory policy ($x_O = 110$, $BS = 40$) will operate.

The Two-Bin System for Perpetual Inventory Control

The two-bin system provides a clever way of continuously monitoring the order point in a perpetual inventory system. Figure 7–13 is almost self-explanatory. There are two bins marked 1 and 2. Assume that they are filled with titanium bolts. Withdrawals are made from Bin 2 first. When Bin 2 is empty, start using Bin 1, and place a replenishment order. When the replenishment order is received, Bin 1 is filled to the reorder point level. The remainder of the order is placed in Bin 2. If Bin 1 is at the reorder point level, all of the incoming items are placed in Bin 2. Each time Bin 2 is emptied, a new order is placed because it is equivalent to reaching the reorder point.

The two-bin system is not feasible for many kinds of items, but when applicable, much clerical work is eliminated. It is particularly well suited

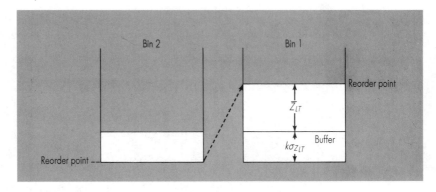

FIGURE 7-13. A two-bin perpetual inventory system.
When Bin 2 is depleted, an order is placed for the EOQ.

to small items like nuts, bolts, and fasteners. These are things that are too small and too numerous to make a withdrawal entry on a stock card for each transaction. The same applies to measuring out and recording withdrawals of liquids.

Periodic Inventory Systems

Periodic systems are based on determination of a fixed and regular review period. Some items may be reviewed once a week, others once a month, semi-annually, or yearly. The optimal period is determined by $x_O/z = t_O$. For example, if $x_O = 110$ units and demand $z = 220$ units per year, then $t_O = .5$ years $= 26$ weeks. Items with small x_O and large z have short review periods.

Although t_O is most often a fraction of a year, it may be greater than a year. Such a long period would characterize items with small demands and large optimal run sizes. Thus:

$$t_O = \frac{x_O}{z} = \frac{1}{z}\sqrt{\frac{2zC_r}{cC_c}} = \sqrt{\frac{2C_r}{cC_cz}}$$

However, even if the demand level is relatively high, the time between reviews may be short—because, for example, the cost per unit c is high.

At each review, the stock on hand is determined. An order is then placed for a variable quantity. This quantity is larger than usual when demand has been greater than expected. It is smaller than usual when demand has been less than expected. Thus, in the case of the periodic inventory model, the review period is fixed, but the order quantity is variable. Figure 7–14 illustrates the way in which a periodic order system functions.

The target level M is determined by calculating the expected demand in a review period plus one lead time interval. To this is added buffer stock, which offers protection against excessive demand in a review pe-

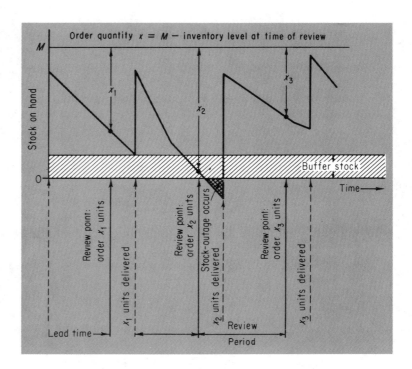

FIGURE 7-14. A periodic inventory system where stock on hand is computed only at fixed intervals. At that time, an order x of variable size is placed.

riod plus one lead time interval. The same kind of reasoning applies in this case as was explained when Figure 7–12 was introduced.

When the optimal order quantity x_O is subtracted from the target level M, the remaining stock size is somewhat larger than the reorder point of the perpetual inventory model. It is greater because the planning period for M must be one review period plus one lead time interval. Extra inventory has to be carried, and this is an added cost of using the periodic inventory system.

On the other hand, the clerical costs of the perpetual model are higher than those of the periodic model. The use of the two-bin system, when it is feasible, can reduce the clerical cost of operating a perpetual inventory system, because the reorder point signal is automatic. Many items, however, cannot be stored in bins and do not lend themselves to this arrangement.

The clerical cost advantage of the periodic model diminishes when online, real-time computer systems produce the calculations required to operate the perpetual inventory model. As a result, there has been a long-term trend toward perpetual systems and away from periodic ones. But some industries prefer the regularity of the periodic method, which often ties in with changeover intervals for production processes.

1. Explain why the two-bin perpetual inventory system is particularly appropriate for small items such as nuts and bolts. Does it need anything special for liquids?

2. Develop the arguments pro and con for order point models.

3. The Bureau of Water Testing uses a chemical reagent that costs $500 per gallon. Use is regular at ⅓ gallon per week. Carrying cost rate is considered to be 12 percent per year, and the cost of an order is $125.

   a. What is the optimal order quantity?
   The Department of Maintenance Supplies could make this reagent at the rate of ⅛ gallon per day, at a cost of $300 per gallon. The setup cost is $150.

   b. How has your answer changed? What course of action do you recommend now?

4. Modify the Storemasters' perpetual inventory model as follows: Face cream has an expected demand of 15,000 jars per year (or 60 jars per day). Lead time is 3 days. It has been determined that demand in any 3-day period exceeds 200 jars only once out of every hundred 3-day periods. This outage level (of 1 in 100 LT periods) is considered acceptable by P/OM. The economic order quantity has been derived as 2,820 jars. Set up the perpetual inventory system.

5. Use the information given in Problem 4, plus the fact that it has been determined that demand in any 50-day period exceeds 4,000 jars only once out of every hundred 50-day periods. This outage level (of 1 in 100 LT periods) is considered acceptable by the P/OM. Set up the periodic inventory system.

6. Compare the results derived in Problems 4 and 5. What are your recommendations, taking into account all the characteristics of perpetual and periodic inventory systems?

7. If, in a dynamic inventory problem under certainty, the costs are

$$c = \$10 \text{ per item}$$

$$C_c = 16 \text{ percent per year}$$

$$z = 5000 \text{ units per year}$$

$$C_r = \$10 \text{ per order}$$

What is the optimal order quantity? Now, assume that you are going to make this same item with equipment that is estimated to produce $p = 30$ units per day. Also, c then equals $6 per item and $C_s = \$150$ per setup. How has your answer changed? What would you do?

Answer: The optimal order quantity is

$$x_O = \sqrt{\frac{2zC_r}{cC_c}} = \sqrt{\frac{2(5000)10}{10(0.16)}} = 250$$

To compare this result with self-supply, given the decreased cost per item and the increased setup cost as compared to order cost, we have

$$\sqrt{\frac{2zC_s}{cC_c}\left(\frac{p}{p-d}\right)} = \sqrt{\frac{2(5000)150}{6(0.16)}\left(\frac{30}{30-\frac{5000}{250}}\right)}$$

$$= 2165$$

The optimal run size with self-supply is more than 8 times the optimal order quantity. The run time would be: $t_1 = 2165/30 = 72.17$ days. Average inventory under self-supply conditions is

$$\frac{y}{2} = \frac{(p-d)t_1}{2} = \frac{10(72.17)}{2} = 360.85 \text{ units}$$

If the item is ordered from a vendor, the average inventory is 125 units. Average dollar inventory for the self-supply situation is $2165.10, whereas for the outside purchase it is $1250. When we compare yearly total costs TC, we find that with outside suppliers, total cost is $400 + 5000(10) = $50,400; with self-supply, the total cost is $693 + 5000(6) = $30,693.

On the face of it, we should use self-supply. However, many other factors are important that are not included in these equations—for example, skills and abilities that are available within the company, the existing demand levels with respect to existing capacity, and so on.

8. The C & B Food Company bottles instant coffee, which it purchases periodically in quantities of 120,000 pounds. The coffee mixture costs C & B $2.40 per lb. The company ships 1,200,000 one-pound bottles of instant coffee per year to its distributors. The demand is constant and continuous over time. What carrying cost (in percent per year) is implied by this policy if an order costs $100 on the average? Discuss your result.

Answer: From the economic order quantity inventory model we know:

$$x_O = \sqrt{\frac{2zC_r}{cC_c}}$$

where in this case:

$x_O = 120,000\,\text{lb (Assuming optimal procedures to impute } C_c.)$

$z = 1,200,000\,\text{lb}$

$C_r = \$100$

$c = \$2.40$

Substituting and solving for C_c, we obtain

$$C_c = \frac{1}{144} = 0.7 \text{ percent per year}$$

This implied carrying cost does not consider possible fluctuations in coffee market prices which may determine C & B's buying pattern during the year. In any case, the percentage is far too low. It is obvious that C & B is not following an optimal ordering policy.

9. What production run lengths would you recommend for the following items?:

i	z_i (per year)	C_{si}	c_i	p_i (per day)
1	200	100	6	10
2	400	50	10	12
3	600	20	15	14
4	800	80	9	20

where $C_c = 0.24$ per year and $z_i = 250d_i$.

Could all these items be scheduled to run on the same equipment? Discuss.

10. Under what circumstances would you prefer a periodic inventory system to a perpetual system?

11. For Storemasters' use of the perpetual inventory system, it has been decided to run an additional 12 days of simulated demand. The numbers to be used are:

Day	13	14	15	16	17	18	19	20	21	22	23	24
Demand	32	25	19	17	25	22	18	36	15	20	30	25

Describe your results.

12. Cardmakers' manager of the greeting card production department has been buying two rolls of acetate at a time. They cost $200 each. Card production requires 10 rolls per year. Ordering cost is estimated to be $4 per order. What carrying cost rate is imputed?

Answer:

$$2 = \sqrt{\frac{2(10)4}{200C_c}}$$

$$4 = \frac{2(10)4}{200C_c}$$

$$C_c = 0.10$$

which seems reasonable.

13. Using the data in Problem 9, determine the production run lengths necessary for all items to be scheduled on the same equipment. Compare your results with those obtained in Problem 9.

Section 7.5 Supplier Selection and Relations

It is critical to know how to select suppliers and what to expect of them. Methods for vendor selection and relations with these suppliers have been changing. Many organizations have been adopting single sourcing or the use of a limited number of vendors. Particular conditions, including special trust relations, are fundamental to the success of these arrangements.

The first consideration is make or buy. When the decision is to buy, the situation must be examined carefully. Will there be a requirement to use bidding? Which vendor or supplier can deliver the quality ranges that fit the tolerances? What are the prices and delivery schedules? Such questions are viewed with the following perspective.

In understanding supplier relations, it is useful to turn to conventional wisdom about the difference between vendors and suppliers. The company has considerable experience and familiarity with its suppliers. It has a working relationship with its suppliers. Suppliers are involved in long-term relationships. This could reflect contractual relations that include the agreement to be involved in product improvements together.

Vendor is a more impersonal term connoting dealers, an open marketplace, and a "take it or leave it" attitude based on price. As commonly used by U.S. companies, *vendor* is the term used when there is no working relationship. Many vendors are encouraged to bid on each job.

Supplier Relationships

The are many reasons why a company uses suppliers instead of making a product or performing a service itself. The need to keep focused is paramount. Many parts or services are necessary to complete the productline, but they are minor factors in defining the product. Some parts are the specialty of other firms that sell a better product than the company could make at a lower cost. Outsourcing for cost advantages is a common explanation.

The number of suppliers a firm uses can fluctuate, rising during periods of slow sales. Then, the company tries to achieve cost reductions by downsizing. This is done by substituting suppliers for existing departments.

Criteria for Selecting Suppliers

The basic criteria by which U.S. firms judge the suitability of suppliers is changing. It is moving from:

Approach A: 1 price, 2 delivery, 3 quality, to
Approach B: 1 quality, 2 value per dollar, 3 JIT delivery

Companies that use Approach A tend to be looking for suppliers continuously. These companies are always reevaluating the price differentials. Occasionally, they are dissatisfied with delivery or quality.

Companies that use Approach B tend to be looking for long-term relationships with suppliers. They want as much information as possible about the supplier's processes and quality competence. They consider the size of suppliers' organizations as well as the supplier's customers. Some companies evaluate the supplier's ability to survive the loss of their purchase orders. They do not want to be in the position of bankrupting a supplier, because that threat will distort the working relationship. This follows IBM's policy to limit the importance of IBM to any vendor.

As shown in Figure 7–15, a scoring model can be used to evaluate a set of vendors. Much deeper insights would be generated for setting up the long-term relationships with suppliers. The use of scoring models

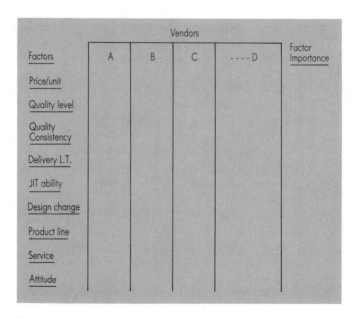

FIGURE 7-15. Vendor scoring model.

requires evaluating each vendor for each of the factors on a scale of 1 to 10. Figure 7–15 demonstrates the procedure, which is also described in Chapter 8.

Single Sourcing with JIT and TQC

Many organizations have been working toward just-in-time (JIT) delivery. This requires including suppliers in the definition of their own TQC system. The risk exposure of single sourcing to achieve JIT is high. If the supplier's organization goes on strike or gets a better customer, the worst possible scenario has occurred. To avoid this situation requires patient negotiation which assures that each party has a long-term interest in maintaining the association. The supplier must believe that the buyer will not cancel the stream of orders. The buyer must believe that the supplier will be steady and dependable in quality. Both parties must know their joint requirements and expectations, including all criteria for quality improvement and cost control.

REFERENCES

AHITUV, N., and S. NEUMANN. Principles of Information Systems for Management, 2nd Ed., Wm. C. Brown, Dubuque, Iowa, 1986.

ALFANDRY-ALEXANDER, MARK. *An Inquiry into Some Models of Inventory Systems.* Pittsburgh: University of Pittsburgh Press, 1962.

ALIAN, GEORGE W., ed. *Purchasing Handbook.* New York: McGraw-Hill, 1958.

AMERICAN MANAGEMENT ASSOCIATION. *Managing the Materials Function.* Report No. 35, Mfg. Division. New York: AMA, 1959.

AMMER, DEAN S. *Materials Management.* Homewood, Ill.: Richard D. Irwin, 1962.

ARROW, K., S. KARLIN, and H. SCARF. *Studies in the Mathematical Theory of Inventory and Production.* Stanford, Calif.: Stanford University Press, 1958.

BROWN, R. G. *Decision Rules for Inventory Management.* New York: Wiley, 1965.

———. *Statistical Forecasting for Inventory Control.* New York: McGraw-Hill, 1961.

BUFFA, E. S. *Operations Management—Problems and Models,* 2nd ed. New York: Wiley, 1968.

CADY, E. L. *Industrial Purchasing.* New York: Wiley, 1945.

COOK, T. M., and R. A. RUSSELL. *Introduction to Management Science.* Englewood Cliffs, N.J.: Prentice-Hall, 1977.

ENGLAND, WILBUR B. *Procurement,* 4th ed. Homewood, Ill.: Richard D. Irwin, 1962.

FETTER, ROBERT B., and WINSTON C. DALLECK. *Decision Models for Inventory Management.* Homewood, Ill.: Richard D. Irwin, 1961.

GAVETT, J. W. *Production and Operations Management.* New York: Harcourt Brace Jovanovich, 1968.

HADLEY, G., and T. WHITIN. *Analysis of Inventory Systems.* Englewood Cliffs, N.J.: Prentice-Hall, 1963.

HANSSMANN, F. *Operations Research in Production and Inventory Control.* New York: Wiley, 1961.

HEINRITZ, S. F., and P. V. FARRELL. *Purchasing: Principles and Applications,* 5th ed. Englewood Cliffs, N.J.: Prentice-Hall, 1971.

HILLIER, F. S., and G. J. LIESERMAN. *Introduction to Operations Research.* San Francisco: Holden-Day, 1987.

HOLT, C., F. MODIGLIANI, J. MUTH, and H. SIMON. *Planning Production, Inventory and Work Force.* Englewood Cliffs, N.J.: Prentice-Hall, 1960.

HOTTENSTEIN, M. P. *Models and Analysis for Production Management.* Scranton, Pa.: International Textbook Co., 1968.

McGARRAH, R. E. *Production and Logistics Management.* New York: Wiley, 1963.

MAGEE, JOHN F., and DAVID M. BOODMAN. *Production Planning and Inventory Control.* New York: McGraw-Hill, 1967.

MASSE, P. *Les Reserves à la Regulation de I'Avenir dans la Vie Economique,* 2 vols. Paris: Hermann, 1946.

MILES, L. D. *Techniques of Value Analysis.* New York: McGraw-Hill, 1961.

MORAN, P. A. *The Theory of Storage.* London: Methuen, 1959.

MORSE, P. M. *Queues, Inventories, and Maintenance.* New York: Wiley, 1958.

NILAND, POWELL. *Production Planning, Scheduiling, and Inventory Control.* New York: Macmillan, 1970.

ORLICKY, JOSEPH. *Material Requirements Planning.* New York: McGraw-Hill, 1975.

PLOSSL, G. W., and O. W. WIGHT. *Production and Inventory Control.* Englewood Cliffs, N.J.: Prentice-Hall, 1967.

PRICHARD, J., and R. H. EAGLE. *Modern Inventory Management.* New York: Wiley, 1965.

SCHONBERGER, R. J., *Japanese Manufacturing Techniques.* New York: The Free Press/Macmillan, 1982.

———. *World Class Manufacturing.* New York: The Free Press/Macmillan, 1986.

SPRAGUE, R. H., JR., and E. D. CARLSON. *Building Effective Decision Support Systems.* Englewood Cliffs, NJ: Prentice-Hall, Inc., 1982.

STARR, MARTIN K., and DAVID W. MILLER. *Inventory Control—Theory and Practice.* Englewood Cliffs, N.J.: Prentice-Hall, 1962.

WAGNER, H. M. *Statistical Management of Inventory Systems.* New York: Wiley, 1962.

WELSH, W. F. *Tested Scientific Inventory Control.* Greenwich, Conn.: Management Publishing Co., 1961.

WHITIN, THOMSON M. *The Theory of Inventory Management,* 2nd ed. Princeton N.J.: Princeton University Press, 1953.

WIGHT, OLIVER W. *Production and Inventory Management in the Computer Age.* Boston: Cahners Books, 1974.

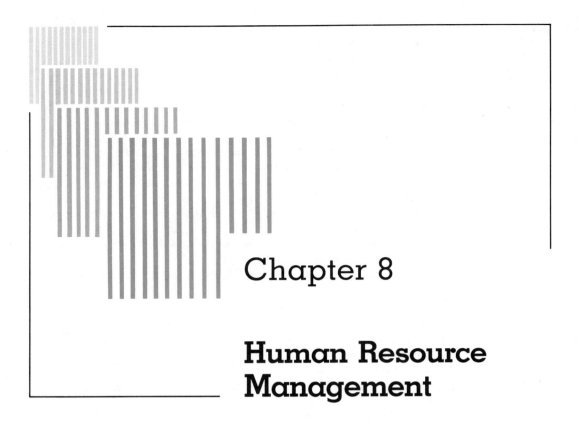

Chapter 8

Human Resource Management

CHAPTER
SUMMARY
The most demanding problem that P/OM has faced since Frederick W. Taylor studied how work should be done has been the question of how managers should relate to and deal with employees. Production and operations managers want to know how to foster competence, how to obtain commitment, how to develop and maintain motivation, and how to secure the loyalty of people who work in the system. In many companies, adversarial relationships abound between management and workers and their unions.

Section 8.1 examines the measurement of worker productivity in the job shop, flow shop, FPS, and project. (The subject is called productivity evaluation, or more traditionally, worker evaluation).

Section 8.2 examines job improvement, job evaluation, and wage determination. (Capturing the most recent approaches to this subject, the section is titled "Jobs Viewed as Systems of Work.")

There are different opinions about the effect of using the traditional methods described in Section 8.2. Consequently, in Section 8.3 we present some recent approaches to improving quality and productivity.

In addition to economic considerations, the management of human resources concerns a variety of human factors that do not lend themselves to quantification. Yet they are not less important. Section 8.4 deals with the safety, comfort, and efficiency of human beings at their workplace. The study of human factors starts with workers who are the consumers of workplace facilities and equipment and extends to customers who use products and services.

While the manufacturing workforce in the United States is getting smaller, its importance in achieving competitive performance is increasing. The service workforce continues to expand, but its low productivity is the topic of much concern. Non-adversarial relationships between managers and workers are the hallmark of global competitors who export to the United States, as well as those who manufacture and provide services domestically. In many successful domestic firms, management and workers are a team. Some companies use participative management; others share decision-making responsibilities.

Closer harmony with unions is evident in such plants as Bridgestone Tire, as well as in U.S. firms such as Ford and GM. On the floor, workers are making important creative contributions. The HR component is increasingly recognized as a part of successful competitive strategies, with emphasis on selection, training, motivation, and commitment to excellence.

Section 8.1 Productivity Evaluation

Productivity measurement is necessary but not easy to achieve. There has been much discussion about the measurement of individual performance being counterproductive. Some measurement systems (like those generally used in Japan) focus on group performance. Evaluation of workers is apt to decrease productivity if it is not done in the right way.

Measuring of Worker Productivity

The evaluation of worker performance starts with knowing how to measure output. Then a standard is needed to compare with the actual output. Engineers can define expected outputs for machines, but managers find definition elusive for employees.[1]

The contribution of human resources to the total cost of goods and service outputs is usually sizable. This is particularly so in the service

---

[1]See, for example, A. Abruzzi, "Formulating a Theory of Work Measurement," *Management Science,* 2, 2 (January 1956), pp. 114–130; also S. B. Littauer and A. Abruzzi, "Experimental Criteria for Evaluating Workers and Operations," *Industrial Labor Relations Review,* 2, 4 (July 1949), pp. 502–526; and R. Henderson, *Performance Appraisal* (Reston, Va.: Reston Publishing, 1980).

sector, which has been growing at an extremely fast rate, but it also remains true in the production of goods. The direct labor component for manufacturing is not as large as it used to be, and it has been decreasing. However, the cost of human resources involved in management and staff functions is significant. These show up as overhead costs. The cost of labor and human resources also appears in the cost of materials purchased from suppliers.

Because the direct labor cost as a percentage of factory costs is different in various industries, the desire to measure and control it will vary from one situation to another. For example, in the banking industry, check processing remains labor-intensive.

The problem of measuring human resource (labor) costs has received widespread and continuous attention over many years, and it will continue to interest many companies. By and large, the problem of measuring worker performance remains critical whenever people play a significant part in the system. There is difficulty in measuring productivity and some reason to believe that the measurement process itself affects productivity. As a result, union-management relations have developed in an atmosphere of confrontation stemming from the uncertainty of all parties concerning the parameters for measuring the performance of the workforce.

Measuring Worker Performance

The material which follows is in accord with the traditional point of view concerning the benefits of work standards. Section 8.3 presents a different point of view.

The search for a measure of worker performance and its value has led to production standards. A **production standard** is a criterion specifying the amount of work to be accomplished in a given period of time. These standards state specifically what the expected productivity is for a particular job. However, the output rate for any one worker is variable; no two workers are alike. How, then, are these standards established? Which individual is the standard worker? Before we examine alternative approaches for the resolution of such problems, let us question why standards are needed. The answer is that management would like to be able to compute the real costs of production efforts. Measurement of costs is necessary to provide estimates of the cost of goods and services. Let us list some production activities that require reasonable estimates of labor costs.

1. The breakeven chart needs believable estimates. Direct labor is part of the variable cost component. Indirect labor, administration, and creative endeavors, such as research, are part of the fixed cost component. See pp. 181–186.

2. For the decision matrix, labor estimates are required to determine a minimum cost strategy or for the purpose of defining a maximum profit strategy. See pp. 200–205.

3. The plant selection problem requires estimates of labor costs in different areas of the country. See pp. 429–430.

4. Labor costs are needed for aggregate scheduling and shoploading. See pp. 541–547.

5. In Chapter 12, the question of an optimal product mix is related to FPS (see pp. 607–612). To find such a mix we are required to estimate the profitabilities of various items that compete for production capacity. For a sensitive system, small errors in estimating labor costs can produce sufficiently different estimates of profit per piece to change entire aspects of the company's product mix.

6. When new product and service alternatives are evaluated, estimated labor costs are reflected in proposed price levels, estimated sales volume, and estimated profitability. How can we choose between alternative new products unless it is possible to estimate the labor cost per part and thereby the expected profitability? See pp. 612–616.

7. One major decision involves the extent to which a company should mechanize its operations and move toward FPS or the flow shop configuration. This problem boils down to a comparison between labor costs and machine costs for approximately the same services (see pp. 599–600). Without reasonably good estimates of the respective costs per part, decisions to employ FPS, or a flow shop, or a job shop cannot be based on a sound foundation.

8. Many organizations are in business areas that traditionally bid for new jobs (see pp. 311–312). With increased government spending, the use of bidding has grown. More companies utilize subcontracting than ever before. Bidding systems frequently require estimates that predate experience with the process. If the company hopes to remain solvent, let alone make sufficient profit, it must be able to estimate with a high degree of precision what the labor cost component will be for the job. If it is unable to do this, it is usually not advisable to enter a bid.

9. The capacity planning problem (see pp. 177–179, 218) involves good estimates of the variable costs for different work configurations, and at different volumes.

These are just a few examples of the way in which labor costs affect company performance. Why do we make such a special case for labor costs? Because they are among the least certain elements in the system. We are able to predetermine the costs of purchased materials, power, insurance, and machine and equipment costs. These factors do not introduce the same kind of uncertainty as labor cost estimates. The problem of estimating how much labor will be required to turn out a given volume of output is involved with behavioral factors, as is the complex problem of determining consumer demand levels. Behavioral elements are not well understood. The language of behavioral modeling is tentative and vague.

As the production configuration becomes more like a flow shop, the importance of the labor estimation problem is reduced. To reduce variability and achieve increased levels of certainty, P/OMs tend to choose machines in place of labor, subject to about equal tradeoff costs. However, as if in compensation, new problems have arisen. There has been growth in the wage rates of indirect labor such as administrative, sales promotional, and creative personnel. (The computer has helped offset some of these.)

The problem of assigning such overhead costs to output has not been satisfactorily resolved. In addition, uncertainties in consumer demand exact a greater toll when automatic processes are utilized. Mistakes are costly because these facilities demand high investment and are relatively inflexible. In any case, the problem of how to measure the productive capacity and related costs of the labor component remains a major issue. Let us consider some of the ways in which this problem can be approached.

CASE: TIME STUDIES — THE RAZOR-MAKER CORPO-RATION

Jobs differ from one another, and so do people. In order to find a common ground for setting standards and evaluating the efforts and outputs of workers, it is necessary to begin the analysis on a very elementary level. Originally, **production studies** were used. These represented situations where the worker was observed constantly over a long period of time. The approach can be compared to 100 percent inspection. Both the job and the worker were studied with patient detail. This method has such shortcomings that it is now seldom used. The primary weaknesses are high cost, unreliable results, and belligerent subjects.

The 100 percent sample gave way to sampling procedures. Present-day time studies are based on sampling methods derived from developments begun in the 1920s. Work sampling procedures led to **time and motion studies.** Instead of tracking the worker continuously, time and motion studies obtained a sufficient sample of observations to answer such questions as how long it takes to do a job, and the expected daily output of a worker.

First, the person doing the time study observes the overall job. Next, the job is broken down into basic elements. These, when added together, form the **job cycle.** This cycle should be relatively short and used repetitively. It will constitute the major portion of the worker's job. Time study methods are difficult to apply for long-cycle jobs. The character of a short-cycle, repetitive job is illustrated by the razor-packing operation of the Razormaker Corporation (see Fig. 8–1).

A stopwatch is employed to time the cycle elements. A number of different kinds of such watches are available. Each is designed for particular types

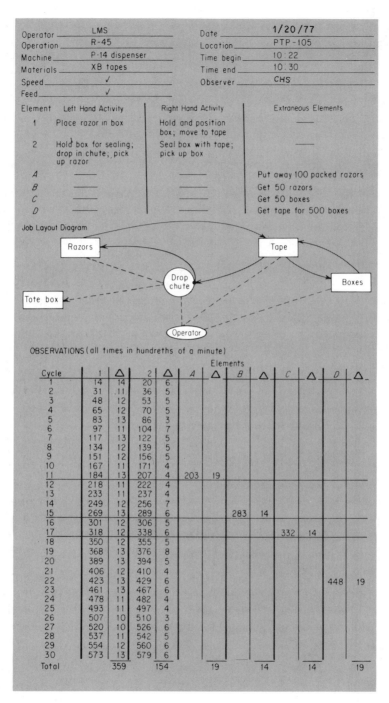

FIGURE 8-1. A time study sheet with 30 cycles The operation (R-45) is to package razors.

of applications as well as to satisfy personal preference. We differentiate only between the continuous and snap-back methods for using stopwatches. The snap-back approach is used to time each work element directly (see the columns headed △ in Fig. 8–1). When an element is completed, the watch hand is returned to 0 to begin timing the next element. Continuous readings are cumulative and require subtraction to determine element times (see the columns headed 1, 2, A, B, C, and D in Fig. 8–1). The snap-back system usually requires a larger sample for the same precision that can be obtained from the continuous method.

Usually, the stopwatch is attached to a time study board, which holds an observation, or **time study sheet.** Such a time study sheet is shown in Fig. 8–1. The illustration presents a completed time sheet that lists the kinds of information usually obtained. There is as much information as possible about the operation being observed: the work elements of the job, as well as a diagram of the razor packing layout; the name of the operator, the machine being used, the setup being used, the materials, the speed and feed rates, and whatever other information characterizes the total job.

The need for all these data follows from the point that a time study done under one set of conditions may not apply to another set. Thus, if the job is being done on a type A facility, it cannot be assumed that a similar production standard will apply to a type B facility. Change of materials, location, and a host of other factors can mean different results. Further, to check on a study by replication it is necessary to set up conditions as similar to those of the initial study as possible. When time study results are contested, the variability of study conditions and/or their variance with actual conditions are frequently introduced to win the argument.

The job in Fig. 8–1 has been broken down into two elements. The activities of the left and right hands are described for each element. Element 1 requires that the left hand should be placing a razor in a box while the right hand holds and positions the box so that the razor can be inserted. Presumably, the hand operations are coordinated. Element 2 finds the left hand holding the box for the right hand, which must seal the box with tape. Then the left hand releases the box over a chute, which carries the box away. The layout for this job, as pictured on the time sheet, does not show distances of the operator from the work place and materials. Often the exact layout with distances is supplied.

The time study begins as the observation for element 1 in the first cycle is entered in the first column; the observation for element 2 in the first cycle is recorded next. Then, cycle 2 begins, and so forth. These element values are continuously timed. The sample size is 30 cycles, all of which are listed on the sheet.

After the observations have been made, computations are begun. The initial cycle required 0.20 min. Of this, element 1 consumed 0.14 min and element 2 took the remaining 0.06 min. The second cycle ends at 0.36 min. This means that the second cycle consumed 0.36 − 0.20 = 0.16 min. For the second cycle, element 1 required 0.11 min and element 2 used the remaining 0.05 min. The rest of the values are obtained in the same way, by subtraction. (The stopwatch used is a decimal-minute type. It is read directly in hundredths of a minute.)

In addition to the basic cycle, the time sheet lists extraneous elements. These are operations which must be done every now and then. For example, the extraneous element A is the requirement that after 100 razors have been packed and dropped into the chute, the tote box they fall into must be taken away. Element B concerns the fact that the worker must interrupt the basic work cycle every 50 razors to get a new supply of razors. The other extraneous elements are equally easy to figure out. We see that the extraneous elements will break into the short-cycle system regularly. Therefore, when we include them, the total job is really of longer duration. Elements 1 and 2 constitute the major subcycle within this system.

The longest cycle is element D, which occurs once every 500 boxes. It is therefore the *shortest common-cycle time for all elements in the system*. This point is significant; even the shortest-cycle, repetitive jobs usually include very long-cycle, extraneous elements. The time study inspector must catch these longer-cycle elements and include them in the study. Thus, we have included observations that are relevant to the extraneous elements in our data. (As we will see shortly, work sampling is an effective method for coping with the problem of the long-cycle factors.)

Productivity Standards

Using time study data, we can develop a productivity standard for job shop operations and for worker performance in the line-balanced flow shop. There is limited applicability for the FPS.

There is a difference in the degree of measurement effort that makes sense for these three cases. The job shop worker might spend several days with a particular job and then move to another. A time study would be made to determine productivity standards for each job. The razor packer is part of an assembly operation for the Razormaker Corporation, which manufactures razors on a flow shop basis. Usually, a number of workers are doing the same operation, so the productivity standard is set to represent the expected output of all workers similarly engaged. The productivity standard is needed to determine the expected output rate of each worker. Then we know how many workers are required, and we can estimate the labor cost component of the finished products or services.

Let us examine Table 8–1, which is a summary of the information previously collected for Razormaker.

All the elements—1, 2, A, B, C, and D—are listed. Total times are collected for each element as they appeared in the 30-cycle period. Those are the column sums for each element, including the extraneous factors. The total time for element 1 is 359; for element 2 it is 154; it is 19, 14, 14, and 19, respectively, for the extraneous elements A, B, C, and D.

TABLE 8-1 RAZORMAKER CORPORATION—TIME STUDY SUMMARY

Element	1	2	A	B	C	D	
Total time observed	359	154	19	14	14	19	
Number of observations	30	30	1	1	1	1	
Expected cycles per observation	1	1	1/100	1/50	1/50	1/500	
Average time or selected time*	11.97	5.13	0.19	0.28	0.28	0.04	
Allowances or leveling factors	0.95	1.00	1.00	1.00	1.00	1.00	
Adjusted time or normal time*	11.37	5.13	0.19	0.28	0.28	0.04	
Correction for rest and delay	110%	110%	110%	110%	110%	110%	TOTAL
Standard time*	12.51	5.64	0.21	0.31	0.31	0.04	19.02

*In hundredths of a minute.

The number of observations for each element is recorded. There are 30 such observations for elements 1 and 2. By chance, during this period of time, each extraneous element occurs once. The third row of the summary sheet lists the number of occurrences that can be expected per cycle. We divide the first row by the second and multiply this quotient by the third row. In this way, an average time, or selected time, is developed for each of the operations that constitute the job. For example, dividing 359 by (30) and then multiplying by 1, we obtain 11.97 hundredths of a minute, or 0.1197 min for element 1. For element 2, we obtain 0.0513 min, and so forth.

Now we come to one of the toughest jobs in the time study system. This is the choice of an allowance or leveling factor.[2] Whom should the time study inspector observe? Generally, an average worker is chosen, operating under standard conditions, using presumably routinized methods. But if the subject appears to work at something more or less than an average rate, a **leveling factor,** or **allowance,** must be applied. The allowance is applied to the average or selected time to obtain **adjusted time,** or **normal time.** This is simply the product of the average time and the allowance.

If the leveling factor is 110 percent, meaning that the observed worker is faster than normal, the adjusted time will be larger than the average time, meaning that the normal (slower) worker can be expected to take longer than the observed time. In the case of the operator who is working at 95 percent of normal in the judgment of the time study inspector,

---

[2]Training in leveling is accomplished in many ways. One of the most used is motion pictures, given a projector with a variable speed control.

multiplication produces a normal time that is less than the selected time, meaning that the average worker can go faster. For the average worker, the leveling factor is 100 percent. This leaves the resulting system of numbers unchanged. In Table 8–1, only element 1 diverges from average. On this aspect of the job, the worker is rated as slower than average. The leveling factor 0.95 is multiplied by the selected time 11.97 to obtain the adjusted time of 11.37.

Because of leveling, our efforts to achieve precise measures and our hopes for precision may seem to be a waste of time. But this is not exactly the case. The leveling estimate introduces a different kind of measurement error than do the time study errors. Clearly, we would prefer neither type of error, but these two types of errors tend to cancel each other.

On what basis does the time study inspector decide whether a worker is performing above, below, or exactly at the normal level? The answer is that time study inspectors, after much practice, can agree among themselves about the ratings, even though the concept of a standard basis for allowances is undefined and subjective.

Even if we could accept leveling with no qualms, we must now add another rough correction. This is the **rest and delay correction factor.** Usually, it is assigned values that range from 5 to 15 percent, depending upon the character of the job, the degree of personal needs, and so on. The adjusted, or normal, time is multiplied by the rest and delay factor. In this way we derive the **standard time,** which is the basis of the production standard. Note that the standard times are listed along the bottom row of the summary box. Each element, including the extraneous elements, has its standard time. The sum of all the elemental standard times is the standard time of the operation. In our example, this is 0.1902 min.

The Expected Cost of the Operation

$$\text{Productivity standard} = \frac{60 \text{ min}}{\text{hour}} \times \frac{100 \text{ boxes}}{19.02 \text{ min}} \cong 316 \text{ boxes per hour}$$

Divide 60 minutes per hour by the operation's total standard time. This tells us that approximately 316 boxes per hour is the expected output rate for the job. That is, 60/0.1902 equals a productivity measure of 316 boxes per hour. If the wage rate for this class of job is $2 per hour, the labor cost component for the operation would be $2/316 = $0.006, or the expected cost of the operation is a little more than a half-cent apiece.

The primary weaknesses of time study are the definition of an average worker, applying the leveling factor, applying the rest and delay correction, and not recognizing influential extraneous elements. Advocates of time study methods claim that satisfactory answers have been found for these problems.

Everyone admits that time study is a skill, not a science. To begin with, the use of the stopwatch requires training and practice. The same applies to leveling. Time study practitioners seldom break down elements into less than 0.04 min, because less than this interval is difficult to observe. The major criticism of time study centers around leveling, but another problem worthy of consideration is the fact that the worker's performance may not be stable in the Shewhart sense (see pp. 268–269). Also, when workers begin a job they have not done for a while (even overnight), they improve their productivity through repetition. This phenomenon, called "learning," is discussed on pp. 220–222. The time study should not begin until the worker's learning ceases and performance has stabilized.

Also, the fact that the worker is seldom interested in participating in the study and may have no desire to provide an accurate production standard of performance is another criticism. The expert time study inspector is supposed to sense this and make appropriate changes in the leveling factor. One can question who will win such a contest—the observer or the observed? Another issue of importance to the time study field is the sample size, or many cycles should be observed.

Sample Size

Time study methods are based on sampling. Therefore, a statistical question arises concerning how large a sample should be taken. The formula given below is predicated on the assumption of a degree of accuracy in time studies that is not warranted by the requirements for leveling and rest and delay factors. However, statistical measurement error is of a different sort, and it can be controlled. Therefore, on this basis we have at least some means for setting a proper sample size. Thus:

$$N' = \left[\frac{40 \sqrt{N \sum\limits_{i=1}^{i=N} x_i^2 - \left(\sum\limits_{i=1}^{i=N} x_i \right)^2}}{\sum\limits_{i=1}^{i=N} x_i} \right]^2$$

where x_i is the ith observation for a particular element, N is the number of cycles observed up to this point, $\sum\limits_{i=1}^{i=N} x_i$ is the sum of all N of the x_i measures, and N' is the number of cycles that *should* be observed. Specifically N' is the required number of cycles to be observed so that we obtain 95 percent confidence that the true element time lies within the range $\bar{x} \pm 0.05\bar{x}$, which is $\pm$ 5 percent of the observed average time.

Because the job is composed of many different elements, we must use the element that will dominate the sample size by requiring the largest value of N'. The largest N' derived from Table 8–2 is $N'(2) = 66.7$.

TABLE 8-2

Reading i	Element 1 $x_i(1)$	2 $x_i(2)$	1 $x_i^2(1)$	2 $x_i^2(2)$
1	14	6	196	36
2	11	5	121	25
3	12	5	144	25
4	12	5	144	25
5	13	3	169	9
	62	24	774	120

$$\bar{x}_1 = \frac{62}{5} = 12.4 \quad \bar{x}_2 = \frac{24}{5} = 4.8$$

$$\text{For element 1: } N'(1) = \left(\frac{40\sqrt{5(774) - (62)^2}}{62}\right)^2 = 10.8$$

$$\text{For element 2: } N'(2) = \left(\frac{40\sqrt{5(120) - (24)^2}}{24}\right)^2 = 66.7$$

Having completed a partial study, the time study inspector will check to find out how much further to go. If a value for N' is obtained that is larger than N, observations must continue to be taken. This sample size evaluation procedure is repeated until the largest value of N' is equal to or less than the actual number of observations made, that is, max $N' \leq N$.

Our example begins with $N = 5$ observations of the two elements. We find that N' for element 2 dominates the sample size. It specifies 66.7 readings. Because we have taken only 5 readings, we must enlarge the sample size. We take another 5 readings and then test again. See Table 8–3. In this way, we keep collecting observations until we find that max N' is equal to or less than N.

$$\bar{x}_1 = 12.6 \qquad \bar{x}_2 = 4.7$$

$$N'(1) = \left(\frac{40\sqrt{10(1596) - (126)^2}}{126}\right)^2 = 8.5$$

$$N'(2) = \left(\frac{40\sqrt{10(227) - (47)^2}}{47}\right)^2 = 6.6$$

Since max $N' = 8.5$, which is equal to or less than $N = 10$, we may stop taking samples.

Time study methods are used in spite of their inherent problems because the need for cost information is fundamental. At the same time, for many applications, such as long-cycle systems and for estimating jobs

TABLE 8-3

Reading i	Element 1 $x_i(1)$	Element 2 $x_i(2)$	Element 1 $x_i^2(1)$	Element 2 $x_i^2(2)$
1	14	6	196	36
2	11	5	121	25
3	12	5	144	25
4	12	5	144	25
5	13	3	169	9
6	13	4	169	16
7	12	5	144	25
8	12	5	144	25
9	14	4	196	16
10	13	5	169	25
	126	47	1596	227

that do not yet exist, other methods have been developed. We now consider some of these.

It may seem strange that certain kinds of workers cannot account for the way in which they spend their time. This applies, for example, to office-workers, research personnel, creative staff, and managers themselves. Recognition of this problem led the manager of TSCH (The State Court House) to employ **work sampling,** also called **operations sampling.** This is a method for determining, with reasonable accuracy, the percentage of time that workers are engaged in different tasks.

The state legislature has slashed TSCH budget by 30 percent. This measure was not directed only against TSCH; financial difficulties afflict the entire state government. The manager of TSCH has decided to use a P/OM technique called work sampling to resolve the problem. The alternative is a political solution—namely, to dismiss all those hired in the last six months. That policy would produce the fewest repercussions. However, the manager believes that the problem is longer term and that productivity is the issue. Among the people hired within the last six months, many are highly productive and others are not. At the same time, many employees with years of service are unproductive.

The manager decides to study the efficiency of TSCH by means of work sampling. No one is to be dismissed unless he or she is clearly nonproductive. (The manager believes that a certain percentage of individuals meet that description.) Meanwhile, normal attrition will gradually reduce the payroll. At the same time, all outside help is to be discontinued. The manager projects that first-year performance will break even with budget. Thereafter, TSCH will have budget to build up inventories that were depleted, to invest in capital improvements, and so on.

How does one apply the work sampling method? The ideas that are fundamental to work sampling were derived at about the same time as techniques for sampling the quality of materials. In the 1930s, Tippett reported on his experiments with work sampling in English textile factories.[3] At about the same time, Morrow was utilizing the same type of technique in factories in the USA.[4]

As was true of materials sampling, the observations taken of workers' activities represent less than a 100 percent study. Therefore, the observations must be randomly made in time and of sufficient number that an accurate picture can be constructed to show what is going on in the system.

TSCH will divide its day into 450 intervals, each of which is a working minute. The manager agrees to randomly select 54 of these 450 intervals. These will constitute the sample. Then, 450 chips numbered consecutively from 1 to 450 are thrown into a bowl. By drawing 54 chips at random from the bowl, we determine a set of assignments for observations to be made each day. A simpler method than the bowl of chips requires tables of random numbers and Monte Carlo number assignments.

A random number table has the important property that there is no pattern whatever to the numbers listed in the table. The numbers are generated by a process comparable to withdrawing numbered chips from the bowl. This is true if the procedure of drawing numbers from the bowl is completely unbiased—if every number has an equal chance of being picked at each selection. A comprehensive discussion of Monte Carlo procedures is given on pp. 528–534.

The Monte Carlo assignments could be made as follows. We wish to sample 54 out of 450 minute intervals. This is 0.12 of the total number of daily intervals. Let:

Monte Carlo numbers 00–11 stand for Take an Observation,
Monte Carlo numbers 12–99 stand for No Observation

We now draw 450 pairs of random numbers in succession. As we read successive numbers from the table, we determine whether we are supposed to take an observation. Thus, assume the following random numbers:

62831   04609   83826   57106   38640

Reading these off in pairs from left to right, we find the information in Table 8–4. A table of random numbers can be read in any direction, including along table diagonals, as long as it is done consistently,

[3]Tippett, L. H. C., ''Statistical Methods in Textile Research'', Journal of the Textile Institute Transactions, Vol. 26, pp. 51–55, February, 1935. Also, Technological Applications of Statistics, John Wiley & Sons, NY, 1950.

[4]Morrow, R. L., Motion Economy and Work Measurement, Ronald Press Co., NY, 1957.

Because all random numbers are equally likely, on the average, 12 out of 100 (or 1.2 out of 10) random numbers will signify that an observation should be made. The sample we have drawn has delivered 3 out of 10, but this is in the nature of statistical systems. Sometimes they will be high, sometimes low; in the long run, the results will average out.

The purpose of this method is to insure that a good sample is drawn—one which neither observer nor worker can anticipate. Only in this way can the observations be unexpected and the situation that is observed be known to be unpremeditated and representative. Thus, a good approximation of what takes place in TSCH will be available. Following the directives of the random numbers, the observer makes an appearance at the workplace at the third, fifth, tenth, and so on, intervals. The observer makes the observations, records them, and departs.

TABLE 8-4

Time Interval	Random Number	Monte Carlo Interpretation	Working	Idle
1	62	No observation		
2	83	No observation		
3	10	Observation	x	
4	46	No observation		
5	09	Observation	x	
6	83	No observation		
7	82	No observation		
8	65	No observation		
9	71	No observation		
10	06	Observation		x
.	.	.	.	.
.	.	.	.	.
.	.	.	.	.
etc.	etc.	etc.		

The purpose of the observations for The State Court House has been to determine how much of the time workers are engaged or idle. If a particular project or operation were the observation base, then categories of what was being done might be used. When a sufficient sample has been taken, ratios can be formed as descriptive measures of what goes on in the system. For example, assume that for a particular day, 45 observations have been made. Forty times, the individual was found to be busy. Then $40/45$, or $8/9$, of the time the operator can be assumed to have been engaged in a productive task.

The manager's use of work sampling should not be to catch the workers off guard. Rather, it is to map out their activities and to help them utilize their time more fully. A more elaborate study than the one we have just described will help TSCH manager to make this point. Rather than just observing whether workers are idle or busy, the expanded analysis notes how the workforce spends its time. This type of study is more appropriately called operations sampling than work sampling.

	Filing	Phoning	Typing	Other	Total
Number of times observed	60	182	30	28	300
Percent of total	20	61	10	9	100

TSCH manager has discovered that 61 percent of the time the state workers are on the telephone and thinks it is unlikely that this heavy commitment to the telephone is strictly business. The manager decides to remove the telephone from each person's desk. A central switchboard, with controls on incoming and outgoing calls, is to be installed. This is one of the manager's decisions. Another one is to centralize filing, appoint a file maintenance supervisor, and allow only file clerks access to the files. These decisions may be wrong. They are based on the manager's assessment of workload requirements and attitude toward workers. There are other ways to resolve what the manager deems to be misuse of the telephone. At least, as a start, he or she should talk to the workers and communicate management's perceptions. Restricting access to the files also seems counterproductive. The workers might have some good ideas about how to cut down on filing time.

Work Sampling: Advantages and Disadvantages

Many variations can be made on this basic theme. The operations or work sampling study is designed to reveal what many workers and executives cannot tell—namely, how they spend their time. A 100 percent sample could not provide as reliable a picture, because the constant pressure of observers creates bias and distortion that sampling methods eliminate. We have tried to show how work sampling can be of real value when properly utilized. The State Court House manager will increase the productivity of the operation if he or she rejects the political solution in favor of the economic solution.

TSCH manager has not dealt with time studies of the specific jobs. Time studies are of little help when noncyclical jobs or long-cycle jobs are involved. In these cases, it is difficult to measure, or even approximate, productive outputs. For those situations where work sampling or time studies can be used, work sampling offers attractive advantages, such as the fact that time study requires skills, whereas the work sampling observer can be relatively unskilled.

Further, all extraneous elements that can enter the short-cycle job are not always picked up by time study. A properly designed work sampling study will frequently prove to be a more effective way of dealing with special extraneous factors that characterize the job shop. To apply work sampling for the determination of time standards (see Problem 5 at the end of this section), we ask, first, what the job should be like—what percent of time is spent in filing, phoning, typing, and so on?

From the work sampling study, we know what the job is like now. By redesigning the job—getting a switchboard, buying faster filing systems, setting new policies—the observed work is brought closer to the time standard objectives set by management. Also, for later job evaluation, it is important that the jobs should accomplish what management needs.

Work sampling should not be used to punish or withhold. It should be used to make everyone aware of unnoticed behaviors. The manager should try to solve problems through cooperation.

Work Sample Size

Designing a study that will reveal needed information with measurable reliability that cannot be obtained in a less expensive way is the essence of work sampling. But how large a sample is needed?

The same question was asked previously with respect to time studies. The answer is also similar. We have:

$$N = \left(\frac{k}{s}\right)^2 p(1 - p)$$

where

N = The number of observations to be taken to provide a sufficient sample. A sufficient sample is defined by management in terms of k and s.

k = The number of normal standard deviations required to give a confidence measure of α. When $k = 1$, $\alpha = 68$ percent; when $k = 2$, $\alpha = 95$ percent; when $k = 3$, $\alpha = 99.7$ percent. (See p. 112.)

α = The likelihood that the true value of p falls within the range $p \pm s$.

s = The accuracy range specified by management such that the true value of p falls within the range $p \pm s$.

p = The fraction of total observations that an activity is observed to occur. When using this formula, we need only compute N for the one activity that dominates the sample size requirements.[5] This will be the activity whose observed p is closest to $1/2$.

---

[5] It should be noted that the sample formula given on p. 366 was based on an interval of the type $p \pm sp$. If we had used that relationship here, our sample size formula would be

$$N = \left(\frac{k}{s}\right)^2\left(\frac{1 - p}{p}\right)$$

The dominating activity, in this case, will be the one with the smallest p value. This is smaller than the actual sample of 400. Therefore, the sample size is sufficient and we can stop.

An example is the most direct way to reinforce the above explanation. We shall use The State Court House office sampling figures given on p. 371. The phoning activity has a value of p that is closest to $\frac{1}{2}$; $p = 0.61$. Let $k = 2$ and $s = 0.05$. Then

$$N = \left(\frac{2}{0.05}\right)^2 (0.61)(0.39) = 381$$

Because only 300 observations were made, it is necessary that an addition be made to the sample. We shall presume that 100 more observations are taken and that p(phoning) $= 240/400 = 0.60$. Then

$$N = \left(\frac{2}{0.05}\right)^2 (0.6)(0.4) = 384$$

Synthetic Time Standards

It is difficult to obtain accurate measures of a fair day's output under many circumstances. There is also the problem of preparing estimates for jobs that have not been physically realized. Both motives led to the development of **synthetic** or **predetermined time standards.**

The basis of synthetic time standards is the fact that every job is composed of a set of elements that are common to all jobs. The unique feature of a particular job is the way in which this common alphabet of elements is used and the way in which the elements are arranged. Frank Gilbreth was one of the first management pioneers to describe such an alphabet of job elements or modules. He called these modules **therbligs** and named 17 of them.[6]

For example: *Grasp* begins when hand or body member touches an object. Consists of gaining control of an object. Ends when control is gained. *Position* begins when hand or body member causes part to begin to line up or locate; consists of hand or body member causing part to line up, orient, or change position. *Assemble* begins when the hand or body member causes parts to begin to go together; Consists of actual assembly of parts, and ends when hand or body member has caused parts to go together. *Hold* begins when movement of part or object, which hand or body member has under control, ceases; consists of holding an object in a fixed position and location, and ends with any movement.

From this beginning, A. B. Segur, who had worked with Gilbreth, developed his system of **Motion-Time-Analysis (MTA),** which was a work measurement procedure utilizing predetermined, standard, work element

[6]Marvin E. Mundel, *Motion and Time Study, Principles and Practices,* 4th ed. (Englewood Cliffs, N.J.: Prentice-Hall, 1970), pp. 243–248.

times. MTA was based upon the fundamental notion that "Within practical limits the times required of all expert workers to perform true fundamental motions are constant."[7]

Once the standard modules, or work elements, were named, it was possible to study thousands of different operations in which each of these elements appeared. Motion pictures were made of many different kinds of jobs, and these in turn were analyzed to determine the appropriate statistical distribution of element times. Expected standard times were obtained in this way. Tables of such standard times for various work elements are shown in Fig. 8–2. This is the system of synthetic standards known as **MTM**, the **methods-time-measurement system.**[8]

Another well-known system is that of **Work-Factor,** for which tables of standards are also available.[9] Various options of the Work-Factor system can be used. The abbreviated Work-Factor system for estimating, and for long-cycle operations. The Detailed Work-Factor System for short-cycle highly repetitive work. Under the name WOCOM, it has been computerized, which eliminates a great deal of the work required to establish production standards with predetermined times. The system also permits a reduction in the effort required to design motion patterns for the simplification of work (see pp. 384–89).

Using predetermined standards, we can derive a standard time for a job. The time measurement units, TMU for MTM, are given in terms of 0.00001 hr; for work-factor, the time unit is 0.0001 min.

1. Describe the job completely and isolate the work elements.
2. Determine the appropriate times for each element as specified by the system being used.
3. Add the times together. This requires that the isolated work elements be independent of each other, or that any existing interactions be taken into account so that the sum truly reflects the total time for the job.

An example of how synthetic times are used to determine production standards, to develop estimates, and to compare alternatives is shown in Fig. 8–3. Some advantages of synthetic time standards, as compared to those derived from conventional time study methods, are these:

1. The leveling factor problem is bypassed. It is already included in the synthetic time standard, because rating differences are averaged

---

[7]J. H. Quick, J. H. Duncan, and J. A. Malcolm, Jr., *Work-Factor Time Standards, Measurement of Manual and Mental Work* (New York: McGraw-Hill, 1962), p. 4.

[8]Harold B. Maynard, G. J. Stegemerten, and John L. Schwab, *Methods-Time-Measurement* (New York: McGraw-Hill, 1948).

[9]Quick et al., *Work-Factor Time Standards, Measurement of Manual and Mental Work,* pp. 435–446. Also *A Synopsis of the Detailed Work-Factor System of Labor Measurement,* Wofac Co., Division of Science Management Corporation, 140 Allen Road, Liberty Corner, NJ 07938, 1982.

METHODS-TIME MEASUREMENT
MTM-I APPLICATION DATA

1 TMU	= .00001	hour	1 hour	= 100,000.0 TMU
	= .0006	minute	1 minute	= 1,666.7 TMU
	= .036	seconds	1 second	= 27.8 TMU

Do not attempt to use this chart or apply Methods-Time Measurement in any way unless you understand the proper application of the data. This statement is included as a word of caution to prevent difficulties resulting from mis-application of the data.

MTM ASSOCIATION FOR STANDARDS AND RESEARCH
9-10 Saddle River Road
Fair Lawn, N.J. 07410

TABLE I – REACH – R

Distance Moved Inches	Time TMU				Hand In Motion		CASE AND DESCRIPTION
	A	B	C or D	E	A	B	
3/4 or less	2.0	2.0	2.0	2.0	1.6	1.6	**A** Reach to object in fixed location, or to object in other hand or on which other hand rests.
1	2.5	2.5	3.6	2.4	2.3	2.3	
2	4.0	4.0	5.9	3.8	3.5	2.7	
3	5.3	5.3	7.3	5.3	4.5	3.6	**B** Reach to single object in location which may vary slightly from cycle to cycle.
4	6.1	6.4	8.4	6.8	4.9	4.3	
5	6.5	7.8	9.4	7.4	5.3	5.0	
6	7.0	8.6	10.1	8.0	5.7	5.7	
7	7.4	9.3	10.8	8.7	6.1	6.5	**C** Reach to object jumbled with other objects in a group so that search and select occur.
8	7.9	10.1	11.5	9.3	6.5	7.2	
9	8.3	10.8	12.2	9.9	6.9	7.9	
10	8.7	11.5	12.9	10.5	7.3	8.6	
12	9.6	12.9	14.2	11.8	8.1	10.1	
14	10.5	14.4	15.6	13.0	8.9	11.5	**D** Reach to a very small object or where accurate grasp is required.
16	11.4	15.8	17.0	14.2	9.7	12.9	
18	12.3	17.2	18.4	15.5	10.5	14.4	
20	13.1	18.6	19.8	16.7	11.3	15.8	
22	14.0	20.1	21.2	18.0	12.1	17.3	**E** Reach to indefinite location to get hand in position for body balance or next motion or out of way.
24	14.9	21.5	22.5	19.2	12.9	18.8	
26	15.8	22.9	23.9	20.4	13.7	20.2	
28	16.7	24.4	25.3	21.7	14.5	21.7	
30	17.5	25.8	26.7	22.9	15.3	23.2	
Additional	0.4	0.7	0.7	0.6			TMU per inch over 30 inches

TABLE II – MOVE – M

Distance Moved Inches	Time TMU			Hand In Motion B	Wt. Allowance			CASE AND DESCRIPTION
	A	B	C		Wt. (lb.) Up to	Dynamic Factor	Static Constant TMU	
3/4 or less	2.0	2.0	2.0	1.7				
1	2.5	2.9	3.4	2.3	2.5	1.00	0	**A** Move object to other hand or against stop.
2	3.6	4.6	5.2	2.9				
3	4.9	5.7	6.7	3.6	7.5	1.06	2.2	
4	6.1	6.9	8.0	4.3				
5	7.3	8.0	9.2	5.0	12.5	1.11	3.9	
6	8.1	8.9	10.3	5.7				
7	8.9	9.7	11.1	6.5	17.5	1.17	5.6	
8	9.7	10.6	11.8	7.2				**B** Move object to approximate or indefinite location.
9	10.5	11.5	12.7	7.9	22.5	1.22	7.4	
10	11.3	12.2	13.5	8.6				
12	12.9	13.4	15.2	10.0	27.5	1.28	9.1	
14	14.4	14.6	16.9	11.4				
16	16.0	15.8	18.7	12.8	32.5	1.33	10.8	
18	17.6	17.0	20.4	14.2				
20	19.2	18.2	22.1	15.6	37.5	1.39	12.5	
22	20.8	19.4	23.8	17.0				
24	22.4	20.6	25.5	18.4	42.5	1.44	14.3	**C** Move object to exact location.
26	24.0	21.8	27.3	19.8				
28	25.5	23.1	29.0	21.2	47.5	1.50	16.0	
30	27.1	24.3	30.7	22.7				
Additional	0.8	0.6	0.85				TMU per inch over 30 inches	

TABLE III A – TURN – T

Weight	Time TMU for Degrees Turned											
	30°	45°	60°	75°	90°	105°	120°	135°	150°	165°	180°	
Small – 0 to 2 Pounds	2.8	3.5	4.1	4.8	5.4	6.1	6.8	7.4	8.1	8.7	9.4	
Medium – 2.1 to 10 Pounds	4.4	5.5	6.5	7.5	8.5	9.6	10.6	11.6	12.7	13.7	14.8	
Large – 10.1 to 35 Pounds	8.4	10.5	12.3	14.4	16.2	18.3	20.4	22.2	24.3	26.1	28.2	

TABLE III B – APPLY PRESSURE – AP

FULL CYCLE			COMPONENTS		
SYMBOL	TMU	DESCRIPTION	SYMBOL	TMU	DESCRIPTION
APA	10.6	AF + DM + RLF	AF	3.4	Apply Force
APB	16.2	APA + G2	DM	4.2	Dwell, Minimum
			RLF	3.0	Release Force

MTMA 101
PRINTED IN U.S.A.

FIGURE 8-2. Time values for various classifications of motions [Copyrighted by the MTM Association for Standards and Research. No reprint permission without written consent from the MTM Association, 9-10 Saddle River Road, Fair Lawn, New Jersey 07410].

TABLE IV – GRASP – G

TYPE OF GRASP	Case	Time TMU	DESCRIPTION	
PICK-UP	1A	2.0	Any size object by itself, easily grasped	
	1B	3.5	Object very small or lying close against a flat surface	
	1C1	7.3	Diameter larger than 1/2"	Interference with Grasp on bottom and one side of nearly cylindrical object.
	1C2	8.7	Diameter 1/4" to 1/2"	
	1C3	10.8	Diameter less than 1/4"	
REGRASP	2	5.6	Change grasp without relinquishing control	
TRANSFER	3	5.6	Control transferred from one hand to the other.	
SELECT	4A	7.3	Larger than 1" x 1" x 1"	Object jumbled with other objects so that search and select occur.
	4B	9.1	1/4" x 1/4" x 1/8" to 1" x 1" x 1"	
	4C	12.9	Smaller than 1/4" x 1/4" x 1/8"	
CONTACT	5	0	Contact, Sliding, or Hook Grasp.	

EFFECTIVE NET WEIGHT

Effective Net Weight (ENW)	No. of Hands	Spatial	Sliding
	1	W	W x F_c
	2	W/2	W/2 x F_c

W = Weight in pounds
F_c = Coefficient of Friction

TABLE V – POSITION* – P

CLASS OF FIT		Symmetry	Easy To Handle	Difficult To Handle
1—Loose	No pressure required	S	5.6	11.2
		SS	9.1	14.7
		NS	10.4	16.0
2—Close	Light pressure required	S	16.2	21.8
		SS	19.7	25.3
		NS	21.0	26.6
3—Exact	Heavy pressure required.	S	43.0	48.6
		SS	46.5	52.1
		NS	47.8	53.4

SUPPLEMENTARY RULE FOR SURFACE ALIGNMENT

P1SE per alignment: >1/16 ≤1/4"	P2SE per alignment: ≤1/16"

*Distance moved to engage—1" or less.

TABLE VI – RELEASE – RL

Case	Time TMU	DESCRIPTION
1	2.0	Normal release performed by opening fingers as independent motion.
2	0	Contact Release

TABLE VII – DISENGAGE – D

CLASS OF FIT	HEIGHT OF RECOIL	EASY TO HANDLE	DIFFICULT TO HANDLE
1—LOOSE—Very slight effort, blends with subsequent move.	Up to 1"	4.0	5.7
2—CLOSE—Normal effort, slight recoil.	Over 1" to 5"	7.5	11.8
3—TIGHT—Considerable effort, hand recoils markedly.	Over 5" to 12"	22.9	34.7

SUPPLEMENTARY

CLASS OF FIT	CARE IN HANDLING	BINDING
1— LOOSE	Allow Class 2	
2— CLOSE	Allow Class 3	One G2 per Bind
3— TIGHT	Change Method	One APB per Bind

TABLE VIII – EYE TRAVEL AND EYE FOCUS – ET AND EF

Eye Travel Time = 15.2 x $\frac{T}{D}$ TMU, with a maximum value of 20 TMU.

where T = the distance between points from and to which the eye travels.
D = the perpendicular distance from the eye to the line of travel T.

Eye Focus Time = 7.3 TMU.

SUPPLEMENTARY INFORMATION

— Area of Normal Vision = Circle 4" in Diameter 16" from Eyes

— Reading Formula = 5.05 N Where N = The Number of Words.

TABLE IX – BODY, LEG, AND FOOT MOTIONS

TYPE		SYMBOL	TMU	DISTANCE	DESCRIPTION
LEG—FOOT MOTION		FM	8.5	To 4"	Hinged at ankle.
		FMP	19.1	To 4"	With heavy pressure.
		LM_	7.1	To 6"	Hinged at knee or hip in any direction.
			1.2	Ea. add'l inch	
HORIZONTAL MOTION	SIDE STEP	SS__C1	*	<12"	Use Reach or Move time when less than 12". Complete when leading leg contacts floor.
			17.0	12"	
			0.6	Ea. add'l inch	
		SS__C2	34.1	12"	Lagging leg must contact floor before next motion can be made.
			1.1	Ea. add'l inch	
	TURN BODY	TBC1	18.6	——	Complete when leading leg contacts floor.
		TBC2	37.2	——	Lagging leg must contact floor before next motion can be made
	WALK	W__FT	5.3	Per Foot	Unobstructed.
		W__P	15.0	Per Pace	Unobstructed.
		W__PO	17.0	Per Pace	When obstructed or with weight.
VERTICAL MOTION		SIT	34.7	——	From standing position.
		STD	43.4	——	From sitting position.
		B,S,KOK	29.0	——	Bend, Stoop, Kneel on One Knee.
		AB,AS,AKOK	31.9	——	Arise from Bend, Stoop, Kneel on One Knee
		KBK	69.4	——	Kneel on Both Knees.
		AKBK	76.7	——	Arise from Kneel on Both Knees.

TABLE X – SIMULTANEOUS MOTIONS

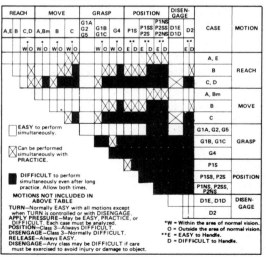

☐ EASY to perform simultaneously.

▨ Can be performed simultaneously with PRACTICE.

■ DIFFICULT to perform simultaneously even after long practice. Allow both times.

MOTIONS NOT INCLUDED IN ABOVE TABLE

TURN—Normally EASY with all motions except when TURN is controlled or with DISENGAGE.
APPLY PRESSURE—May be EASY, PRACTICE, or DIFFICULT. Each case must be analyzed.
POSITION—Class 3—Always DIFFICULT.
DISENGAGE—Class 3—Normally DIFFICULT.
RELEASE—Always EASY.
DISENGAGE—Any class may be DIFFICULT if care must be exercised to avoid injury or damage to object.

*W = Within the area of normal vision.
O = Outside the area of normal vision.
**E = EASY to Handle.
D = DIFFICULT to Handle.

FIGURE 8-2. *Cont.*

TABLE 1 — POSITION — P

Class of Fit and Clearance	Case of † Symmetry	Align Only	Depth of Insertion (per ¼")			
			0 >0≤1/8"	2 >1/8≤¾	4 >¾≤1¼	6 >1¼≤1¾
21 .150" — .350"	S	3.0	3.4	6.6	7.7	8.8
	SS	3.0	10.3	13.5	14.6	15.7
	NS	4.8	15.5	18.7	19.8	20.9
22 .025" — .149"	S	7.2	7.2	11.9	13.0	14.2
	SS	8.0	14.9	19.6	20.7	21.9
	NS	9.5	20.2	24.9	26.0	27.2
23* .005" — .024"	S	9.5	9.5	16.3	18.7	21.0
	SS	10.4	17.3	24.1	26.5	28.8
	NS	12.2	22.9	29.7	32.1	34.4

*BINDING—Add observed number of Apply Pressures.
DIFFICULT HANDLING—Add observed number of G2's.

†Determine symmetry by geometric properties, except use S case when object is oriented prior to preceding Move.

TABLE 1A — SECONDARY ENGAGE — E2

CLASS OF FIT	DEPTH OF INSERTION (PER 1/4")		
	2	4	6
21	3.2	4.3	5.4
22	4.7	5.8	7.0
23	6.8	9.2	11.5

TABLE 2 — CRANK (LIGHT RESISTANCE) — C

DIAMETER OF CRANKING (INCHES)	TMU (T) PER REVOLUTION	DIAMETER OF CRANKING (INCHES)	TMU (T) PER REVOLUTION
1	8.5	9	14.0
2	9.7	10	14.4
3	10.6	11	14.7
4	11.4	12	15.0
5	12.1	14	15.5
6	12.7	16	16.0
7	13.2	18	16.4
8	13.6	20	16.7

FORMULAS:
A.   CONTINUOUS CRANKING (Start at beginning and stop at end of cycle only)

TMU = [(N×T)+5.2]•F+C

B.   INTERMITTENT CRANKING (Start at beginning and stop at end of each revolution

TMU = [(T+5.2) F+C]•N

C	=	Static component TMU weight allowance constant from move table
F	=	Dynamic component weight allowance factor from move table
N	=	Number of revolutions
T	=	TMU per revolution (Type III Motion)
5.2	=	TMU for start and stop

FIGURE 8-2. *Cont.*

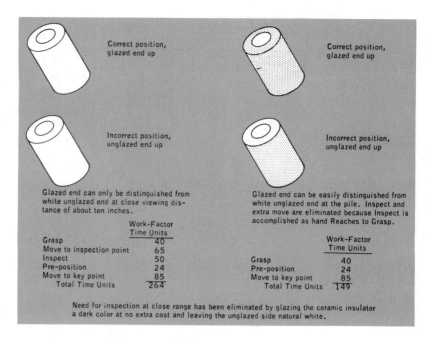

FIGURE 8-3. Time reduction through elimination of visual inspection [From J. H. Quick, J. H. Duncan, and J. A. Malcolm, *Work-Factor Time Standards* (New York: McGraw-Hill, Inc., 1962), p. 417].

out across many jobs and many operators. In short, *no rating factor is required with these systems.*

2. Distortions that arise because of observer bias and interaction between the observer and the worker can be controlled and removed from the synthetic times. This is not the case for time studies.

3. Time studies are normally based on an established job. For all new jobs there is a learning period for the worker. During this period, observations are unreliable. Even on established jobs, workers improve productivity after startup. The problems of using time studies where learning occurs are bypassed through the use of predetermined time standards.

4. The cost of determining production standards is reduced.

5. The synthetic production standard is founded upon element times derived from very large samples of observations. This increased reliability of the standard time cannot be obtained with time studies, because it is out of the question to utilize such large samples for studying any one particular job.

6. The speed of preparing cost estimates, as well as their reliability for new jobs, new products, and so on, is improved. Production schedules can be quickly determined and modified. Product-mix analyses can be expedited.

The Work-Factor system includes time values and techniques for measuring microminiature assembly operations, and Mento-Factor is used to develop standards for operations which consist primarily of mental work.

Synthetic time standards are not applicable to *creative* mental functions. Also, process technology is now far smaller than microminiature. For example, semiconductor chip manufacture deals with thicknesses measured in atoms. Computer-aided design (CAD) and computer-aided manufacture (CAM) bypass human operators as much as possible, since they are a source of contamination, which lowers yields. As a result, direct labor plays an ever-smaller part in factory operating costs.

New jobs occur regularly in the job shop, but at different frequencies, according to the character of the shop. So, for the job shop, synthetic time standards are needed to prepare estimates and bids. At best, synthetic time methods have occasional application to the flow shop. The productivity of the flow shop is better measured in terms of its line balance and cycle time. The synthetic methods are too refined for projects, and have limited applicability for FPS.

To categorize the work-measurement field, we can generalize as follows:

1. Time study is applicable for short-cycle, repetitive operations that are presently being performed and can therefore be observed.
2. Work sampling can be used for long-cycle, repetitive operations that are presently being performed so that they can be observed. The cycle must be stable, or else the sample has no meaning.
3. Synthetic (or predetermined) time studies can treat nonrepetitive, noncyclical jobs as well as jobs that are not yet being done, so that they cannot be observed.

PROBLEM
SET

1. Frederick W. Taylor thought that the relationship between the well-designed job, the best worker, and the reasonable wage scale could be determined by logical analysis and intelligent experiment. The concept of the well-designed (specialized and efficient) job has been attacked. The same is true of the notion of best workers and worst workers. A guaranteed wage and pay not related to individual productivity have been suggested as the only reasonable wage scale. Discuss.

2. Output volume determines wages. Wages are a major factor of worker motivation. Motivation conditions worker performance with respect to output volume. Figure 8–4 illustrates this feedback relationship. However, additional inputs (arrows) have been added to the figure to indicate that other factors also affect output volume, wages, and worker motivation. Describe these "other" factors.

3. We have been commissioned to study the activities of a research laboratory. It has been decided that work sampling should be used because

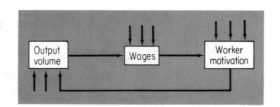

FIGURE 8-4.

the continued presence of an observer would alter the behavior patterns of the research teams. Do you agree? Discuss.

4. For the study described in Problem 3, what categories of activities might apply? How often should observations be made? Would you use random sampling or make your observations at set times that are known to the researchers?

5. The following data have been collected by the Razormaker Corporation, using operations sampling to study Operation R-45 (see Fig. 8–1).

Activity	Description	No. of Times Observed
1	Place razor in box	212
2	Seal box, etc.	90
A	Put away 100 boxes	10
B	Get 50 razors	8
C	Get 50 boxes	7
D	Get tape	12

How do these results compare with those derived by the time study (see p. 360–365)? Discuss.

6. What is meant by the following statement: Time studies can be used for purposes of estimation and bidding, but they are unacceptable as a means of setting work standards for the amount of output that each employee is expected to produce.

7. Foodpackers, Inc., packs figs in syrup in jars. The imported figs are weighed out in lots of 1 pound. There are 12 figs to the pound, on the average. The figs must be inserted in a jar to which a portion of fig syrup is added. Then the jar is sealed with a twist cap.

   a. Analyze the job. Develop what you consider to be a good sequence of work elements.

   b. Sketch the process flow and layout.

   c. Use an operation chart to detail the work involved.

   d. Prepare a time sheet.

   e. Assume that the time study has been taken and supply your own hypothetical data for these observations. Then determine the standard time for the job (use at least 10 cycles).

Answer: The purpose of this question is to permit the development of a relatively thorough analysis of time study methods. An adequate answer would be far too involved to present here. Nevertheless, the fundamental structure is shown.

a. The basic components of the job are: Get the figs to the scale; weigh the figs; get the jar; put the figs in the jar; get the syrup; add the syrup; get the cap; seal the jar with a twist; remove the jar.

b. The process flow chart might be something like the one shown in Fig. 8–5. The flow can then be adapted to a specific floor plan layout.

c. A simplified operation chart might be:

	Left Hand	Right Hand
Element 1	Get figs and put them on scale until correct weight is achieved	Get a jar
Element 2	Put figs in jar	Clamp jar and get syrup
Element 3	Get cap	Add syrup
Element 4	Screw on cap	Unclamp jar
Element 5	Move toward figs	Put jar on conveyor

d. & e. A time chart is a convenient form for recording the elapsed time of each of the 5 elements of the process during successive cycles (see Table 8–5). Pertinent information concerning who is being observed, who is observing, where, when, and so forth should also be noted.

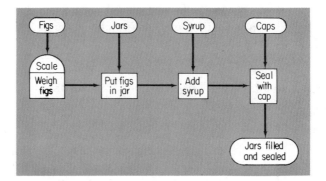

FIGURE 8-5.

**TABLE 8-5   FIG PACKING TIMES (IN HUNDREDTHS
OF A MINUTE)**

		Element				
		1	2	3	4	5
Cycle	1	15	8	7	10	10
	2	13	8	8	11	10
	3	15	7	8	12	10
	4	17	9	9	11	11
	5	12	9	6	10	10
	6	14	7	7	10	9
	7	14	8	6	9	9
	8	13	8	6	9	10
	9	15	7	8	9	11
	10	16	9	7	10	9
Total time		144	80	72	101	99
No. of obs.		10	10	10	10	10
Exp. cycles		1	1	1	1	1
Average time		14.4	8.0	7.2	10.1	9.9
Allowance		1	1	1	1	1
Normal time		14.4	8.0	7.2	10.1	9.9
R&D Correction		1	1	1	1	1
Standard time		14.4	8.0	7.2	10.1	9.9

Far more complex data can be employed. The method we use follows the one developed in Fig. 8–1 and Table 8–1. Then, the total standard time for the job would be:

$$14.4 + 8.0 + 7.2 + 10.1 + 9.9 = 49.6 \text{ hundredths minutes}$$
$$= 0.496 \text{ minute per jar}$$

So: $\dfrac{60}{0.496} \approx 2(60) = 120$ jars per hour—standard output.

8. The President of Foodpackers learns about predetermined time standards. He calls you in and asks for a report on the applicability of synthetic time methods to check the above times. Develop the appropriate report.

Section 8.2 Jobs Linked Together as Systems of Work

Is the process used by people in their work system as good as it can be? That means working smarter, not harder. It means that a common goal is shared by all to produce a quality product. It means that managers are there to help workers overcome problems and improve the system, not to act as authority figures.

Major efforts to improve the system of work, which is composed of subunits called jobs, can pay off handsomely and continuously. There is an established track record for companies worldwide that follow the principles which drive out all employees' fear of losing their jobs. These principles emphasize training, learning, and job improvement. Firms that use these principles[10] have world-class management and outperform competitors.

Job Improvement, Job Evaluation, and Wage Determination

There is benefit to be gained by viewing the entire set of jobs as a system involving all employees, both workers and managers. Working together as a team, their outputs are the revenue earners. **Job improvement** will result in a blend of effects, including lower costs, increased output rates, better deliveries, greater variety, and above all else, better quality.

Job evaluation is a term often used to describe analyzing a job and improving it. It is more valuable to consider job evaluation as system evaluation, in which sets of interrelated jobs are analyzed and improved as an entire network. Traditional job evaluation looked upon each job as a separate and independent part of the workplace. This view is not as powerful as the system view.

Wage determination for production workers is based upon the difficulty of jobs performed, the amount of training and skill required, and their presumed value to the company. As can be observed from this one sentence, there are problems in defining an unambiguous basis for establishing wages. For example, the difficulty of a job and its value to the company may not be correlated. Skill required and value to the company may be inversely related. There is a logical flaw in the old approach to wage determination that cannot be remedied by reasoning. This fact is apparent in reading about legal efforts to prove wage discrimination—say, between women and men.

The traditional approaches to wage determination are still practiced by many organizations. They are covered here, along with an effort to point out their inadequacies and to highlight the fact that the old ways of determining wages are being replaced by a systems approach in world-class organizations. The systems approach is based on a common pay rate for team members working together. To the extent that the group is successful in generating profit for the company, they are rewarded as a group by bonuses. There is **cross-training,** so that many people do different jobs at different times. The old system would have trouble sorting out what each person should be getting paid. Accounting is far easier with the new approach. Everyone in the group receives the same pay, and all work for

---

[10]W. Edwards Deming, *Out of the Crisis* (Cambridge, Mass.: M.I.T. Center for Advanced Engineering Study (CAES), 1986).

the same system. Some companies call the bonus system by the name **gainsharing.** More unions are allowing cross-training. There is more emphasis on training, including the use of quality circles, quality of work life groups, and participation groups.

Often, job improvement results from time study, when it is done for the right reasons and in the right spirit. However, it is counterproductive to develop time standards for work that is known to be badly designed. Instead, work simplification should be used first to develop as good a job as possible. This takes into account the systems view of each job as a service to the next worker in the sequence. When this thinking has been done, the application of time studies and productivity measures may lead to real improvement.

Work Simplification (Methods Study)

The notion that work patterns could be studied and improved was the core from which modern P/OM evolved. Frederick Taylor, Henry Gantt, Frank Gilbreth, Lillian Gilbreth, and others recognized that intuitive and judgmental methods of managing could be assisted by ''scientific'' analysis. The form the analysis took was based on the premise that if the parts were improved, then the whole must be better. We now know that analysis can go just so far, and that, in fact, it can mislead us. We talk about the system, and wherever we use analysis we subsequently require synthesis. We reject efficiency without the simultaneous consideration of effectiveness. *We should avoid doing better and better what we shouldn't be doing at all.*

This caution does not, however, reduce the utility of work simplification when properly applied. After all, efforts to improve efficiency represent investments. Like all investment alternatives, the burden of proof that an efficiency study is the best possible way to proceed falls upon those who would use it. But it must also be remembered that diminishing utility is likely to set in when what is already quite efficient is pushed to be more so. The desire for ''efficiency'' and ''perfection'' is frequently more a matter of personal values than of rationality. When this is not the case, work simplification, job evaluation, value analysis, and methods analysis are legitimate and desirable investments for company resources.

We can identify **work simplification** as an important part of methods study. The latter term is widely used (see pp. 315–316) to describe engineering efforts to improve productivity, decrease costs, and increase worker satisfaction with the job. However, methods study encompasses a broader range of techniques than work simplification. Much of the material in this chapter would be considered part of the methods engineer's work.

While traditional work simplification is known to look at one thing at a time, present-day methods emphasize the systems approach. If the systems approach is allowed to encompass the strategic levels of corporate planning, then work simplification is a powerful force for improving the process and the quality of output. It was from a basic urge to improve "things" that production management methodology began to search for new ways to look at the process. It was recognized that the process was composed of operations and that the operations could be broken down until such micromotion units as therbligs were created as the ultimate in microcategorization.

Micromotion units are very small divisions of work—for example, wrist movements in grasping, finger motions in releasing, eye movement to search without head motion, head movement in searching. Micromotions were identified as the components of all work, and they could be put together in different ways to create different operations. As previously mentioned on page 373, the Gilbreths developed 17 such job elements, calling them "therbligs."[11]

On the one hand, classification was a fundamental tool of the work simplification analyst. On the other hand, a means to organize and sequence these data was required. The fundamental method used was the visual representation of work flows. Such schematics typify the contributions of the early scientific management pioneers. Many of these charting techniques are still used in preference to computer simulations, because they are the easiest way to cope quickly with the complexities of work. As in any method that relies heavily on categorization, an important decision is how fine or how broad to make the categories. The choice was made to develop analytic tools for each of the various levels that would be encountered. Thus, the process chart was relatively macro in its view of the system (see Figs. 8–6 and 8–7). Essentially, it charted the spatial sequence in which materials flow through the various stages of the production transformation process. These methods are applied to serialized work flows and large enough batch operations to warrant the attention. Some degree of repetitive production is required. On the other hand, the methods are too crude for substantial flow shops such as automobile assembly. There has been no utilization for FPS systems, nor is any use likely.

At the next level of detail come **operation charts,** where observation is concentrated on a specific worker and the particular work station. Frequently, the level of analysis is in accord with the element interval requirements of time study methods. An example of this schematic is shown in Fig. 8–8. The right and left hand movements could be traced in terms of as fine a breakdown as the therblig classes, or with equal facility at grosser levels. Various symbols were developed to facilitate visual orientation and communication. There is nothing unalterable about these

---

[11]F. B. Gilbreth, *Primer of Scientific Management* (New York: D. Van Nostrand, 1914).

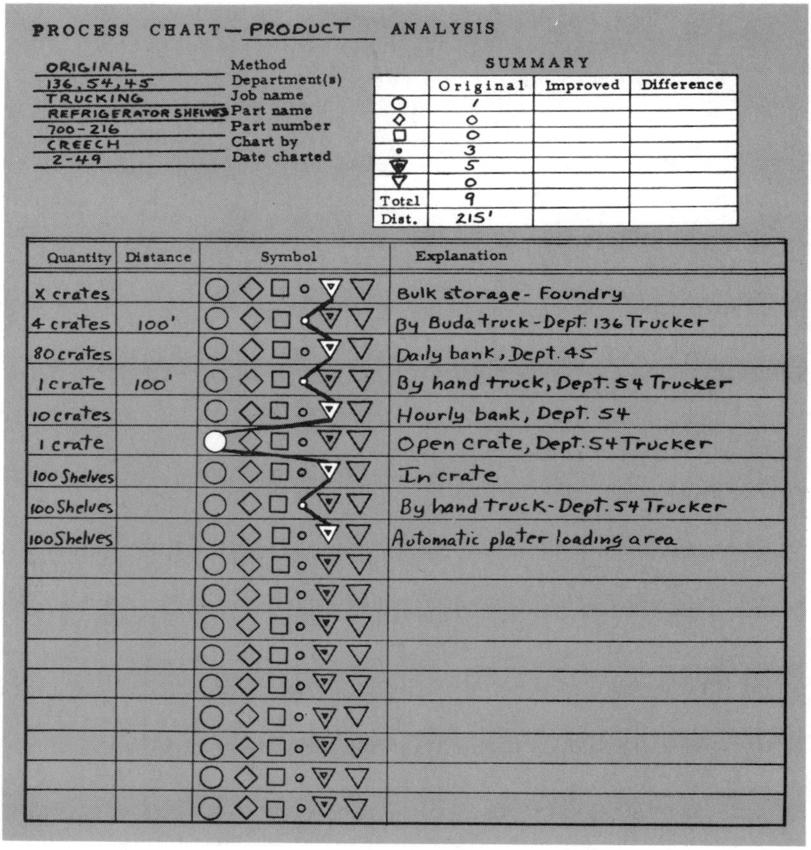

FIGURE 8-6. Process chart-product analysis for original method of handling refrigerator food shelves from bulk storage to plating department [From Marvin E. Mundel, *Motion and Time Study*, 5th ed. (Englewood Cliffs, N.J.: Prentice-Hall, Inc., 1978), p. 61].

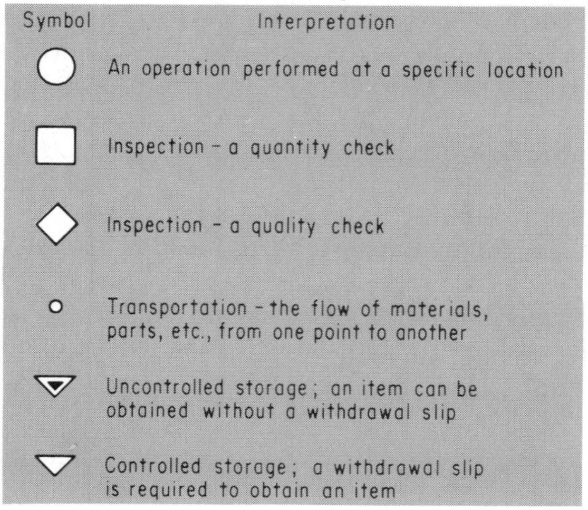

FIGURE 8-6 continued. Symbol key for flow process chart.

PROCESS CHART — PRODUCT ANALYSIS

PROPOSED _____ Method
136, 54 _____ Department(s)
TRUCKING _____ Job name
REFRIGERATOR SHELVES ____ Part name
700-216 _____ Part number
CREECH _____ Chart by
2-49 _____ Date charted

SUMMARY

	Original	Improved	Difference
○	1	1	0
◇	0	0	0
□	0	0	0
○	3	2	-1
▽	5	3	-2
▽	0	0	0
Total	9	6	-3
Dist.	215'	75'	-140'

Quantity	Distance	Symbol	Explanation
X crates		○ ◇ □ ○ ▽ ▽	Bulk storage - Foundry
1 crate	15'	○ ◇ □ ○ ▽ ▽	By hand truck - Dept. 54 trucker
1 crate		○ ◇ □ ○ ▽ ▽	Open crate - Dept. 54 trucker
100 Shelves		○ ◇ □ ○ ▽ ▽	In crate
100 Shelves	60'	○ ◇ □ ○ ▽ ▽	By hand truck - Dept. 54 trucker
100 Shelves		○ ◇ □ ○ ▽ ▽	Automatic plate - loading area

FIGURE 8-7. Process chart-product analysis for proposed method of handling refrigerator food shelves from bulk storage to plating department [From Marvin E. Mundel, *Motion and Time Study*, 5th ed. (Englewood Cliffs, N.J.: Prentice-Hall, Inc., 1978), p. 61].

charts and the symbols used: Practice has yielded the standard form shown here, but modifications can be made according to requirements.

The charts are intended to be data organizers to permit intelligent evaluation of the situation so that reasonable alternative arrangements can be achieved. A chart that portrays present conditions is compared with charts for one or more competing alternative plans.

Another familiar work simplification chart is concerned with the operating characteristics of the man-machine system. It is **the man-machine time chart,** which encourages visual analysis of the way in which people and machines interact. It permits their joint operations to be coordinated. In Fig. 8–9 we observe that both the operator and the machine are idle 50 percent of the time. The problem seems to stem from the fact that the machine cannot be used during the make ready or put away operations. In other words, the primary machine function must be interrupted both to prepare and to remove successive parts. If this were not true, then the

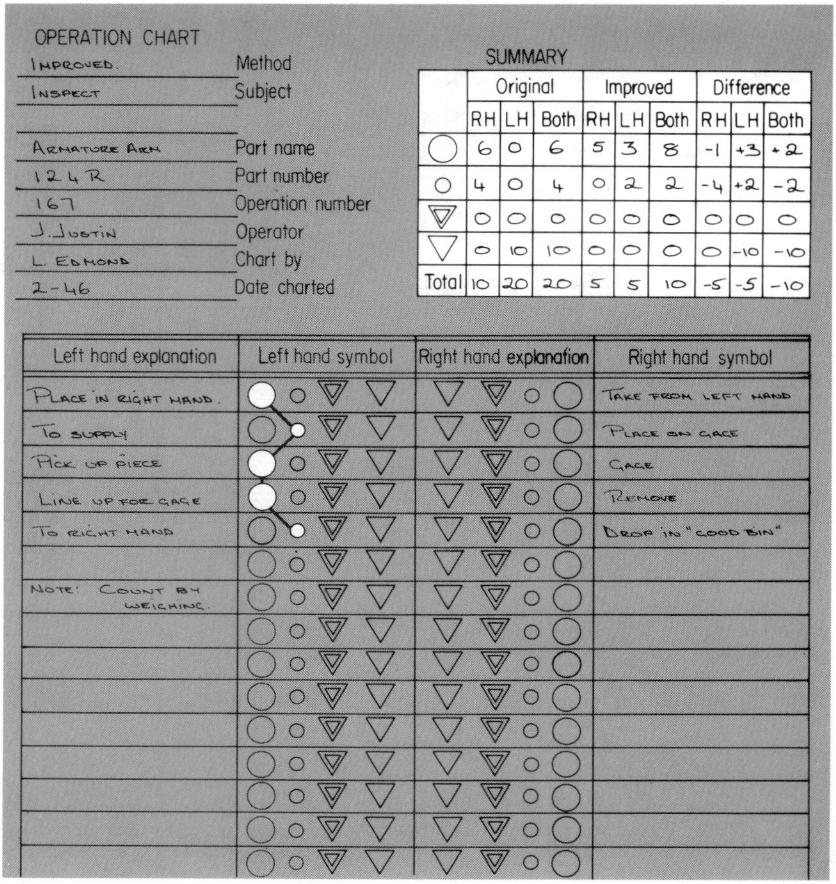

FIGURE 8-8a. Operation chart for inspect relay armature arm (improved method) using form with preprinted chart symbols [From Marvin E. Mundel, *Motion and Time Study*, 3rd ed. (Englewood Cliffs, N.J.: Prentice-Hall, Inc., 1968), p. 204].

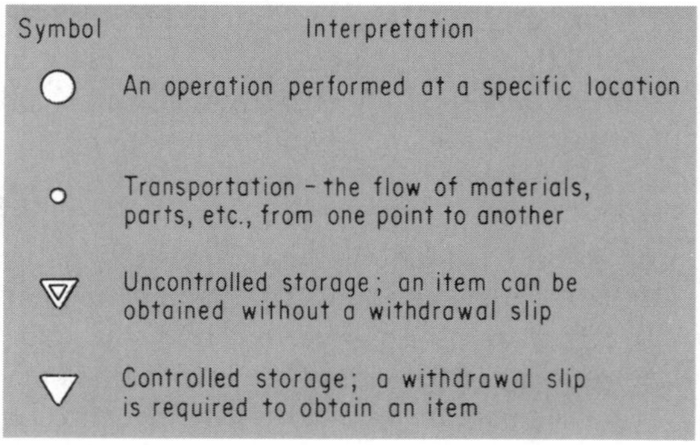

FIGURE 8-8b. Symbol key for operation chart (Figure 8-8a).

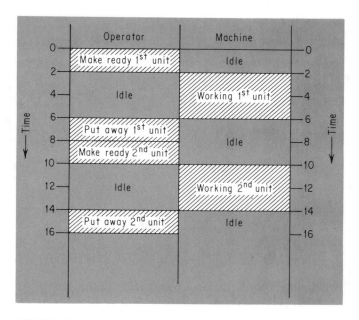

FIGURE 8-9. Man-machine time chart—Machine A, Plan 1, see p. 391.

more efficient arrangement shown in Fig. 8–10 could be used. Here, after the first cycle, both worker and machine are 100 percent utilized.

Now assume that machine B can be used where make ready and put away idle the facility but can be done at the same time. Then, if the operator is supplied with a helper, machine utilization can be increased from ½ to ⅔. Both operator and helper have only ⅓ utilization factors, as shown in Fig. 8–11. Let us examine the use of these charts in the context of an example.

**CASE:
FOOD-
PACKERS,
INC.**

Foodpackers runs an efficient job shop, canning and packing foods that change according to season, market prices, and so on. The cans, jars, and boxes span a broad range of shapes and sizes. Consequently, general-purpose packing equipment characterizes the process.

The company derives its profit margin by setting up the most efficient job shop routines possible. Many times, the operational sequences approach the productivity of an intermittent flow shop. The balancing of workers with simple machine functions lies at the heart of Foodpackers' success.

A bulk shipment of figs has arrived from Tunisia. Two plans are being considered for packing figs in 1-pound boxes. Consult Figs. 8–9 and 8–11 for Plans 1 and 2, which are detailed below. The relevant costs are:

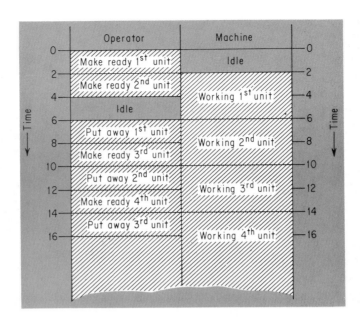

FIGURE 8-10. Man-machine time chart—Machine A is modified to permit 100 percent utilization of both operator and machine.

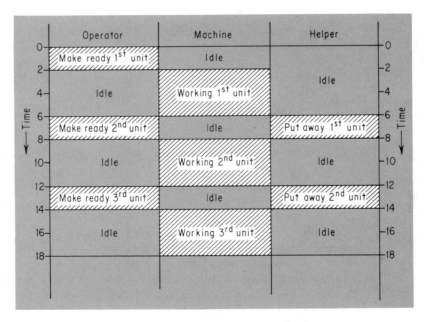

FIGURE 8-11. Man-machine time chart—Machine B, Plan 2.

Operator's wage = $6.00 per hour

Helper's wage = $3.50 per hour

Machine A's cost = $10.00 per hour

Machine B's cost = $14.50 per hour

Value of output = $3.00 per box

We analyze the situation in the following way:

PLAN 1   Machine A is utilized 50 percent of the time. It takes 4 minutes to pack a box, so 7.5 boxes are packed per hour (30 working minutes of machine time per hour ÷ 4 minutes per box = 7.5 boxes per hour). These are sold for $22.50. From this revenue we subtract the sum of machine A's hourly cost and the hourly wage of the operator; that is, $22.50 − $16.00 = $6.50. This is a measure of gross profit per hour for plan 1.

PLAN 2   Machine B is utilized 66⅔ percent of the time. Therefore, 10 boxes can be packed per hour. These are valued at $30. We subtract machine B's hourly cost and the hourly wages of both operator and helper. This gives $30 − $24 = $6 of gross profit per hour.

DECISION   Select plan 1. Foodpackers must persistently use such planning because its profit margin is tight. After subtracting the costs of figs, boxes, and fillers, there is not much profit. Efficiency of operations spells the difference between profit and loss.

We can see how closely related work simplification is to time study analysis. Before production standards are agreed upon as a basis for planning, jobs should be studied as a system and brought to a point where common sense and good judgment can no longer be readily used to improve the entire operation.

The success of suggestion systems in companies where employees are not driven by work standards and where there is little fear of losing one's job indicates the extent to which improvement can be continuous. Good suggestions are rare in companies where the suggestion might result in someone being fired because a job is no longer necessary.

In recent years, there has been deemphasis on work simplification in many industries. This is because job shop lots are decreasing in size; line changeovers to new and modified outputs are becoming more frequent; computer-integrated flexible manufacturing systems and adaptive automation require intense preplanning that obviates the need for ongoing improvement of operations; and more elaborate methodologies of operations research and management science such as simulation have appeared, which compete for investment study dollars with the older methods.

Job Enrichment

The operator is working constantly in Fig. 8–10. The only relationship the operator has is with the machine. On the other hand, in Fig. 8–11, operator and helper are idle at the same time and can communicate with each other, if the machine is not too noisy. It is also possible that operator and helper could talk with other operators and helpers who are idle at the same time. Still, the job is repetitive, and the individuals tend to be isolated by the need to tend the machine.

A great deal has been written which contends that such isolation runs counter to people's desires to work with other people on nonroutine tasks or, if routine, on tasks that are complex enough not to repeat every few minutes. Because of the economic benefits of specialization, organizations have designed many jobs that are highly repetitive and very narrow in scope. Workers have complained about the dehumanizing quality of such work.

There is also contrary research evidence that a significant number of workers prefer simple, highly repetitive tasks. Some like it hot, and some like it cold, so there is an opportunity for management to explore preferences with each worker. Work assignments can be made according to worker preference in many work systems, because both types of work exist.

The flow shop can be particularly tedious for workers who like variety. As more stations are added, productivity rises. However, cycle time gets shorter, placing an increasing burden on station workers, who have shorter jobs to do with greater frequency. The quality of work can deteriorate under such circumstances. Worker dissatisfaction can increase. For example, the Vega plant of General Motors at Lordstown suffered a long and difficult strike shortly after it was built because of worker dissatisfaction with the flow-shop pace.

During the 1970s, organizations started to redesign their production lines so that workers would be required to do many different jobs. For example, Volvo of Sweden began experimenting with teams that built an entire car. Other organizations decreased the level of specialization in their line-balanced systems. This increased the size of each work station and the work content per employee. By the late 1980s, General Motors set up lines where teams worked at different stations and the car was transferred by conveyor from one station to another. Again, the work content per employee is larger. Overall, with cross-training and employee involvement in quality, the work content per employee continues to increase.

Most of the complaints center around the paced-conveyor flow shop as well as its intermittent forms rather than the job shop, but there are tedious aspects about the job shop as well. The project is usually immune to such complaints. If there is any criticism on the part of project workers, it is the continual crises that afflict their nonroutinized workdays. There may be complaints for FPS, since human support teams can perform dull tasks to service their computer masters.

Cross-training for job rotation (where workers exchange jobs) has become increasingly acceptable. Job enlargement (with its larger work content) has also taken hold. Greater worker participation in decision-making has been endorsed by both public and private organizations. Certainly, suggestion making has caught on in well-managed organizations. The ultimate criterion is whether the objectives of the organization can be met with less specialization and with less authority over workers.

Wage Plans and Incentives

Tradition has it that the problem of determining human resource costs has two parts. First, what is a reasonable output? That is, how much service should be rendered or how many pieces should be expected per unit of time? The second problem deals with this question: What is a fair wage for reasonable output?

How difficult it is to answer this question is underscored by further queries: How can we equate the work done by a secretary and a punch press operator? What is a fair salary for the research director compared to the operations manager? If two people work equally hard but one turns out 10 fine pieces while the second turns out 20 good pieces, should we pay them equal salaries? Should a person be paid for time or for physical output? How is quality rewarded?

These two questions hinge on two points that seem able to be studied rationally. First, what value does the company derive from its human resources? Second, considering the factor of supply and demand for the kind of services the organization requires, how much should it pay? It may not be possible to determine the value of any individual to the company. This applies to the president as well as the worker on the line and in the office. It is a team that plays together and forms a support net that may make it possible for one of them to hit home runs while the others are hidden in the shadows. But without the support system of the shadow people, there would be no more home runs from the star.

Also, variation between workers' outputs are often best explained as statistical variability from a stable system. We would not want to reward chance cause, and even less would we want to punish it.

Now let us turn to the second aspect of the two-part problem. With respect to a ''fair'' wage, the manager is concerned with the motivational forces that affect creativity and productivity. The fact that behavior can be influenced by various inducements (for example, monetary incentives), whereas machines cannot be, points up a major difference between the two and is still another aspect of man-machine relations.

A startling case history was obtained in the 1930s by a study group from Harvard at the Hawthorne Works of the Western Electric Company in Chicago. The original study concerned levels of illumination and their effect on productivity. It was discovered that whether the illumination was raised or lowered, productivity was improved. The key discovery (known as the Hawthorne effect)[12] was that employees responded positively to management's interest and attention. This response level overrode the functional effects of the illumination level. Such complex behavior is one important difference between people and machines.

Some critics of this study claim that the result was a self-fulfilling prophecy. Even if this is true, it still appears reasonable to expect positive reactions from workers to care and attention.

Motivation can be both positive and negative. We usually associate the latter with poor employee morale. When discussing incentives and motivation, the major difficulty is the measurement problem. Nevertheless, accepting the lack of precision involved, we know that incentives are a real causal factor that can affect worker behavior. Incentives include wages, job title, office size and floor, organizational importance, ability to participate in decisions, vacations, leisure time, and variety of tasks assigned. For the most part, these categories represent intangible qualities that escape definition and measurement. For example, we speak of leadership, knowing that an undefinable characteristic is involved. It is a characteristic intimately involved with the subject of motivation and incentive, yet we lack a yardstick by which to measure it. One of the ways to try to set an objective standard for the control of incentives is through wage plans.[13]

What is a fair wage? Do we measure real wages in terms of the cost of living, or do we compare monetary wages as they are found in different parts of the country? Is it reasonable to compare, for a given industry, rural with urban wages? There has been a continuing attempt to relate monetary wages to real wages. For this reason, the minimum wage as fixed by law has been steadily increased over the years in order to keep pace with a rising cost of living. From each company's point of view, there is some level of wages that is optimal. High wages remove dollars that could otherwise be invested in expansion. Salary increases might cause dollars to be withheld from stockholders. This action produces predictable results in the stock market. It generally lowers the credit ratings banks will offer. But low wages discourage highly skilled and able personnel. They produce negative motivation, increase turnover rates,

---

[12]Roethlisberger, F. J., and W. J. Dickson, Management and the Worker, Harvard Univ. Press, Cambridge, Mass., 1939.

[13]Wage plans have not helped the U.S. achieve success as a global competitor. Wage incentives may be effective in obtaining large quantities of output. They do not assist in raising the quality of outputs.

and increase recruitment costs. (This can be related to the costs associated with $W_t - W_{t-1}$ in aggregate scheduling. See pages 541–550.) From the company's point of view, neither high nor low wages are desirable. Rather, a wage rate that produces a balanced system of costs is desired.

Each wage rate is part of a set of wage rates that apply to different jobs. Balance is necessary here as well in the relationship of jobs to one another and the wage rates they earn. This brings us to job evaluation as a necessary first step in the determination of an equitable wage.

Approaches to Job Evaluation

Several different approaches have been used to job evaluation. One way is to use purely qualitative evaluations. A second possibility calls for the ranking of jobs in terms of contribution to the organization. A third approach is based upon an explicit point system. The purely qualitative approach is said to be susceptible to personal bias. Because of this, it is disappearing from use. But that may be a mistake. The quantitative approaches are also biased, but in the guise of numbers do not seem as susceptible to subjectivity.

Ranking is used even though it does not indicate how much one job differs from another. The most quantitative approach is the point system. Each job is classified in terms of a number of factors required for the job. At least, this has the benefit of bringing to management's attention the character of each job.

Job Factors

1. Intelligence
2. Physical skill
3. Physical effort
4. Responsibility that must be assumed in order to accomplish the job
5. Working conditions, including the environment and other human factors relevant to job accomplishment

A job can be described in terms of these attributes, but there is a lot of ambiguity in measuring them. Each job requires a varying amount of each factor. By assigning point values to each factor, it is possible to derive a total score for any job. The score is equivalent to a monetary wage rate. It is intended to reflect the requirements of the job in terms of the significant factors. Presumably, in this way an approach is made to the problem of determining true worth to the company. After all, the real issue is: What is a particular job, or set of operations, worth to the organization?

For machines, the costs are easily derived, but the worth of the machines to the company is not readily understood. For people, the problem is worse. Both what you should pay them and what they will contribute is hazy. For this reason, the approach that says pay the same wage to all members of the team is appealing to many companies.

From Evaluation to Wage Rate

To convert job point levels into appropriate wage rates, the **key job concept** is often used. Certain key positions are commonly found in the industry. These might include the position of secretary, foreman, and skilled tool and diemaker in a metalworking firm; or secretary, flight attendant, and pilot for an airline. The key jobs are studied in terms of the factors listed above. Then a job rating is assigned.

Based upon an industrywide geographic analysis of the going wage rates for key positions, a curve can be drawn such as that shown in Fig. 8–12. We see that first the key jobs are located on this graph. Then a curve is put through the key job points. All other jobs are assigned appropriate wage rates by estimating their positions on the curve between the key job points.

To illustrate the use of the point system and the key job concept, assume that four key positions are identified in hospital management. Call these four jobs A, B, C, and D. Each job has been evaluated and given the number of points shown in Table 8–6. The ratings are based on job requirements for intelligence (1), physical skill (2), physical effort (3), responsibility (4), and working conditions (5).

A maximum of 220 points is available to be assigned to any position. A job demanding the utmost intelligence can receive 50 points. A job that is done under the worst possible working conditions would be assigned 20 points. The assignment of the maximum number of points available from each job factor is a management judgment of the contribution each

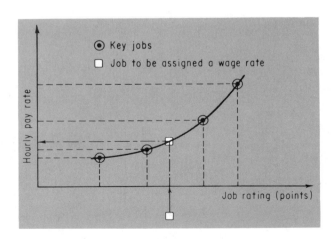

FIGURE 8-12. The key-job curve where hourly pay rate is related to the job's rating.

**TABLE 8-6   POINT ASSIGNMENTS AND AVERAGE WAGE RATES
FOR KEY POSITIONS**

| Key Jobs | Maximum Number of Points Available, Shown Above Each Category | | | | | Total Points of Job | Average Hospital Wage Rate/Week for Key Position |
	50 1	40 2	30 3	80 4	20 5		
A	20	20	30	10	20	100	$200
B	50	10	10	60	0	130	$400
C	40	40	10	70	15	175	$700
D	25	20	10	10	10	75	$150

factor makes to the achievement of organizational objectives. The assignment of a given number of points from each factor to a particular job is also a management judgment based on the job evaluation. The key job curve derived from Table 8–6 is shown in Fig. 8–13. Consider non-key job E, which has been rated with 150 points. Consulting Fig. 8–13, we see that job E would be associated (by interpolation) with a weekly wage of $500.

Although this seems to be a relatively straightforward method for pricing jobs, many additional factors intervene. These include the use of incentive plans, merit rating systems, the importance of seniority, the effect of cost-of-living factors, the supply and demand both regionally and nationally for certain skills, and the notion of a guaranteed annual wage.

Let's recapitulate the steps required to establish a wage rate structure:

1. Develop relevant job factors, and assign each one its maximum point value.

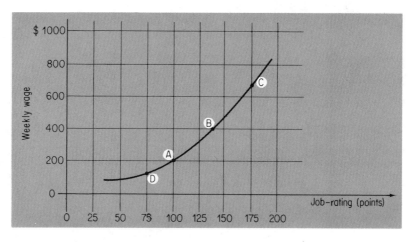

FIGURE 8-13. Key-job curve for the hospital positions.

2. Classify jobs in terms of the relevant factors, and assign each job its point allocation.
3. Select key jobs and determine appropriate wage rates from industry data.
4. Draw the key job curve.
5. Assign wage rates to nonkey jobs by interpolation and extrapolation.
6. Take special factors into account, such as seniority, merit ratings, and incentive plans.

Wages Based on Output Rate

Many jobs, such as executive and administrative positions, cannot be assigned a wage based on output rates. It is also true of creative and research jobs, and clerical operations. Indirect labor, by definition, cannot be paid on the basis of production output. Various models that tie pay to employee motivation have been developed. The history of incentive plans goes back to the beginning of the industrial movement in the United States. Frederick W. Taylor, Henry Towne, Henri Fayol, and others were concerned with incentive, profit sharing, work definition, work division, authority and responsibility, and the questions of satisfactory pay. Each incentive model was intended to obtain maximum worker participation. Each was designed to provide an equitable distinction between workers who expend different amounts of energy and contribute different benefits to the company and to provide a balanced system of wages for the company. With respect to the first point, they may have succeeded in maximizing output at the cost of quality. If this is the case, then they did not succeed in creating a balanced system of wages for the company. The models are straight piecework, piecework with a guaranteed base, and the general incentive model.

Straight Piecework Model.

$$W = HA\left(\frac{O_A}{O_S}\right)$$

where

H = hourly rate in dollars per hour.

A = actual time worked in hours per week.

O_A = actual output per hour in pieces per hour.

O_S = standard output per hour in expected number of pieces per hour.

W = weekly wage rate in dollars per week.

H/OS is the rate in dollars per piece of completed work and is derived in terms of an output standard (from time studies) and a wage standard (from job evaluation). The worker has no security with this wage plan. Weekly wages decrease proportionally as actual work output falls.

2. Piecework Model with a Guaranteed Base.

$$\text{for } O_A \le O_S \qquad W = HA$$

$$\text{for } O_A > O_S \qquad W = HA \left(\frac{O_A}{O_S} \right)$$

In this case, the worker is guaranteed at least a weekly wage rate of $W = HA$. And, as in model 1, when actual output becomes greater than standard output, take-home pay increases above the base level HA.

3. General Incentive Model.

$$\text{for } O_A \le O_S \qquad W = HA$$

$$\text{for } O_A > O_S \qquad W = HA \left[1 + k \left(\frac{O_A}{O_S} - 1 \right) \right]$$

Here again, the minimum is established at $W = HA$. Now, however, we observe that the incentive given is proportional to the size of the coefficient k. For OA greater than $OS,$ some fraction of the value of the extra production of the worker is paid, both as reward and incentive. The value of k depends upon the plan that is used. For example, with the Halsey 50-50 plan, $k = \frac{1}{2}$. In the 100 percent bonus plan, $k = 1$. This is equivalent to the piecework model with a guaranteed base.

In the Bedaux plan, $k = \frac{3}{4}$. Many other plans also have been tried. The history of these plans and their results leads us to the belief that they work for volume and not for quality. Other approaches must be used to provide workers with incentives to produce high-quality products. Wage incentives based on volume are motivators for volume, but that is hardly surprising. Volume motivators do not appear to be positively correlated with quality achievement. Quality motivators are the subject of the next section.

PROBLEM
SET

1. How do the micromotion divisions of work, such as therbligs, relate to the basic motions of synthetic time standards such as MTM?
2. What is the relationship of work simplification to methods study?
3. Compare the purpose of process charts with that of operation charts and discuss the differences.

4. The Volvo Company of Sweden has utilized job enlargement for the production of some of its automobiles. What does this mean? How does the Volvo assembly differ from that of a standard paced-conveyor flow shop?

5. How does the concept of job enrichment affect the economic advantages to be gained from specialization through division of labor? What other factors might influence productivity?

6. What was learned from the Hawthorne experiment? How does it apply, in general, to human resource management? Why have some critics faulted the study of AT&T's Hawthorne Works?

7. Job improvement can lower the costs of output. This may enable an organization to drop its prices and/or increase the quality of its productline or service mix. The managers of other organizations must ask themselves why their costs are not competitive. However, especially in the job shop, the cost of studying the job and the workplace may offset the economic advantages to be gained from improvement. This is less likely with respect to the intermittent flow shop. Explain.

8. Airborne, Inc., has decided to use the point-based, key job curve system to set employees' wages. Four key jobs were identified and rated with points (see the table below).

Job	Job Point Rating	Industry Wage (Annual) for Key Jobs
Secretary	10	$ 24,576
Flight attendant	15	$ 40,480
Engineer	30	$ 88,192
Pilot	40	$120,000

a. Derive the wages for ground crew with a 25-point job rating.

b. Derive the wages for ticket office personnel with a 12-point job rating.

9. Assume that the man-machine situation on pp. 387–91 is now as follows: Both make ready and put away can be accomplished only when the machine is idle. These operations cannot be performed simultaneously. Two machines are used and are to be tended by a single operator. The element times are unchanged. Use a man-machine time chart to find the best way of handling this situation.

Answer: The man-machine time chart depicting the optimum configuration under the given condition would be:

	Machine 1	Operator	Machine 2
0			
	Idle	Make ready 1	
2			
	Work	Idle	Idle
4			
	1	Make ready 2	
6			
		Put away 1	Work
8	Idle		
		Make ready 3	2
10			
	Work	Put away 2	
12			Idle
	3	Make ready 4	
14			
		Put away 3	Work
16	Idle		
		Make ready 5	4
18			

If this configuration is used, each machine will be idle one-half of the time (the operations of make ready and put away are being performed at these times). On the other hand, the operator is being utilized 100 percent of the time. The arrangement is optimal if the worker's wage is much greater than the cost of idle machine time.

10. Company X is about to undertake a program to encourage employees to suggest new products and revisions of present design. A strong incentive is provided. The company employs 5,000 workers, and it is expected that the number of suggestions per year will average about one per person. If the average working year is 250 days, there will be about 20 suggestions per day to be screened. The suggestions are to be sorted by the sales division; only marketable ideas will be forwarded to the P/OM. It is decided that an initial screening process will be used to eliminate unworkable suggestions. Those ideas that pass the screening will then be subjected to a more intensive feasibility study.

   a. Develop a logical procedure P/OM can follow to achieve its objectives. Make sure to include all questions required by the decision process.

   b. Estimate the number of employees required to administer such a program.

   Answer: Form an interfunctional committee. The size of the committee that will be able to cope with the workload will be a function of the expected number of suggestions the sales division will consider to be marketable and therefore pass back to the production department. If the sales division really does its job, the large number of ideas that must be reviewed by the P/OM will be carefully reduced.

On the other hand, if real cooperation does not exist, sales may just pass most of the ideas along to production in order to avoid investing a great deal of time in the suggestion procedure. Then, at a later stage, after P/OM has done the initial filtering, the sales division could veto ideas that would not be marketable. This approach would overburden production and waste its time.

Someone has to do the initial filtering. On the other hand, if the sales division has been appointed to serve as the initial filter in the system, the sales division could erroneously reject good ideas, figuring that too many ideas superficially accepted and sent along to the P/OM would lead to complaints that might reach top management. This high rejection procedure has its flaws too. It is likely to anger the workers who have submitted suggestions, leading to an increased number of grievances and generally poor morale. Both costs would be experienced by the production division alone. Here we see an example of how divisional boundaries can produce unexpected distortions unless a systems point of view prevails so that cooperation and understanding can flow across the boundaries. Also, employee training will improve the quality of suggestions.

a. Specifically, P/OM would begin by asking questions to check the technological feasibility of the various projects suggested. Once it is established that a specific product can be made or a specific service can be offered, or a specific process improvement is feasible, a production study that relates costs to qualities could be undertaken. The economic feasibility of the production process would have to be assessed in terms of the market potential for various price and quality combinations. (An elaborate answer to this question can be framed in terms of PERT diagrams.)

b. Let us assume that the following table applies:

Period of time = 100 days

Number of Suggestions	Level of Activity	Average Time Spent per Suggestion	Total Time
2000	Sales division	$\frac{1}{5}$ hour	400 hours
1000	Production—1st Level	$\frac{1}{2}$ hour	500 hours
100	Production—2nd Level	10 hours	1000 hours
1	Production—3rd Level	40 hours	40 hours

According to this set of estimates, one idea emerges every 100 days for serious consideration by the engineering, production, and sales departments. To achieve this, the sales division must contribute 4 hours per day, whereas the production department must use almost two men on this function to achieve the required 15.4 hours per day.

11. Two man-machine plans are compared in the text (pp. 391). For what value of output would these plans be equal?

Answer:

$$7.5p - 16.00 = 10p - 24$$

$$p = \$3.20 \text{ satisfies the conditions}$$

12. In Razormakers' cafeteria, the tables are packed together. This was done, given the limited available space, to allow 90 percent of all employees to eat at the same time. Now, an employee complaint has been filed. How should this matter be handled?

13. An employee group has petitioned Razormakers' management to introduce flexitime. Flexitime is one of several names used to describe a plan whereby workers can start and finish work (almost whenever they want) so long as they work, say, 40 hours a week. You have been asked to give management a brief summary of the pros and cons.

14. What are the pros and cons of wage incentive plans? Examine the options described on pp. 398–399, and explain why you might prefer one or another.

Section 8.3 Productivity and Quality Achievement

Employee Involvement Groups

At the Ford Motor Company, they are called Employee Involvement Groups. At General Motors, they are called Quality of Work Life. These worker groups meet to improve the performance of the company. If that means increasing output volume, they will work on it. There may be a delivery crisis that must be overcome. These groups will address any problem. But the one mission each group is always responsible for is continuous quality improvement.

Facilitators are individuals who help organize these groups. By training facilitators, it is possible to use limited resources to create many groups, each of which is focused on particular aspects of the production function. Group members are often the source of suggestions for improvement. Various forms of individual appreciation and admiration and group rewards of the same kind turn out to be effective incentives for the groups to work at making real contributions. In some companies, monetary incentives are also available, usually these are distributed on a group basis.

Training Counts

Some of the groups undergo training in statistical methods that can be applied to understanding and controlling the variation all work processes entail. Even where statistical training is not used, attention is paid to how the job should be done. Training is a group responsibility, and it is utilized in a serious way.

One of the best examples of intense training is the NUMMI case. More than eight months were spent by Toyota management in training for the startup of this GM/Toyota joint venture. Training involves contingency planning. For example, the employees speculate about what can go wrong. They then develop scenarios about how to handle the contingency. The emphasis is on the system as a whole, and all of the details that can emerge from that system.

A Ford Motor manager responsible for changing the company's quality awareness stated: "We try to push micro-management." He said that the farther away you get from the process manager, the more dangerous it is. This attention to the plant floor, or the kitchen in the restaurant, or the office, must be balanced by the blessing for these activities from the top. The organization must provide an infrastructure that supports productivity and quality achievement.

Also, it must be noted that many management reporting systems emphasize measures that can be counterproductive. For example, if machine utilization is decreased when employees take time to meet in groups, management must be able to add up the whole equation: reduced machine utilization + increased group time = time well-spent.

A different approach to training is required when dealing with project productivity during the life cycle stages of startup and growth.

Project Productivity

The productivity of indirect labor, including that of clerical, administrative, and supervisory positions, is difficult to define and measure. And it is even more difficult to measure the productive output of a project team. Yet this is a crucial measurement, because large quantities of money are spent on projects. Quality achievement for projects is directly related to productivity. The reason is that there is a smooth transition from plans to reality; the quality standards are built into the plan.

Let us define productivity as some number of units of project accomplishment per period of time. We assume that environmental and workforce conditions remain relatively stable over each particular interval. Productivity is measured per phase rather than in the aggregate. An average measure of productivity can then be obtained for the total project. Underlying this definition is the belief that project tasks can be divided into unit phases or accomplishment units.

We would like to maximize the productivity of the project team in each phase so that the total job can be completed in the minimum possible time. A short development time is often crucial for competitive reasons. To minimize completion time, we must employ just the right number of workers. Another basic objective is to achieve project completion at a reasonable, if not a minimum, cost. It has been observed that the most efficient team size with respect to cost will frequently require a smaller group of research workers than would be needed for maximum group productivity. In other words, group size for minimum cost is smaller than for minimum project development time. Thus the definition of an optimal group size depends on the manager's objectives.

Fig. 8–14 illustrates the point. The horizontal axis represents the number of workers engaged in any particular phase of project development. For the entire project, consisting of various phases, manpower commitments can be regulated to control progress and performance. The vertical axis is measured in two ways: productivity (the solid line) and cost (the dashed line). Minimum cost occurs before the point of maximum productivity is reached. Cost is determined by the number of workers and the time required to complete the job.

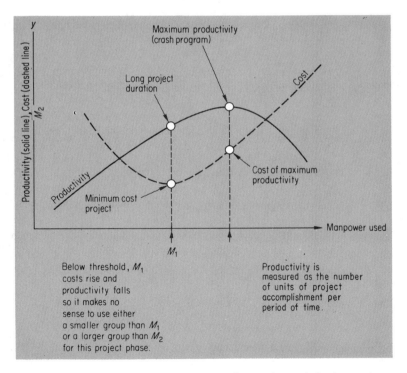

FIGURE 8-14. Cost and productivity interrelations that underlie the cost/time analysis of any project phase.

If we have two workers earning $12,000 per year and it takes them six months to complete this development phase, the total cost of this phase of the project is $12,000. On the other hand, if four workers are employed, each earning $12,000 per year, and it takes them four months to complete the project phase, the cost of doing this job is $16,000. Minimum cost in this example occurs when two workers are used instead of four. How is productivity affected? Because four workers complete the project phase in four months, their efforts place them higher on the productivity curve than the two-person group. Assume that four workers produce the maximum number of accomplishments per hour. This is the team size that can finish the job first. More or less than four workers will have a somewhat lower overall team productivity. With this in mind, it is not surprising that two workers might have something more than half the productivity of four. So for our specific example, the four-person team can accomplish the job in the minimum amount of time but at a higher total cost, as compared to the two-person team.

Which result do we want? If our objective is to minimize time, then four are indicated. If our objective is to strike some efficient balance between the cost of doing the job and the time for completion, something less than the maximum productivity group size is indicated. This result is important when we are dealing with sizable projects and development programs consisting of many phases, each of which requires substantial team sizes. Frequently, because of marketplace competition, great urgency is attached to obtaining maximum productivity and minimizing the total time to accomplish the job. This also provides more time and more people to achieve the quality goals.

Overstaffed Projects

There is a natural tendency to overestimate project workforce requirements. The result can be detrimental to quality. Productivity drops off when more than an optimal number of individuals are involved on the job. This can be explained in a number of ways, including use of the old adage: "Too many cooks spoil the broth." For those who prefer a logical explanation: Productivity falls off above a certain group size because of communication and supervision problems. Under new management approaches, supervisors of projects (as well as of job shops, flow shops, and FPS), are trainers and helpers rather than observers and auditors.

Overstaffing is a consequence of many basic urges of management. It is only natural to think that a "massive" effort can produce results faster. As we have seen, it is frequently true that minimum cost will not coincide with minimum completion time. But the "massive" effort is likely to overshoot the mark and result in project delay, quality problems, and additional costs.

What can happen if management overestimates workforce requirements? Assume that the group size chosen that is somewhat larger than would be required for maximum productivity. As a result of this choice, project costs are greater than was expected and the job takes longer than the required time. The result is paradoxical. The project manager believes that workforce requirements have been underestimated. The manager attributes the additional cost to the additional time required to complete the project. The next time a similar job must be undertaken on a tight schedule, the manager will employ even more people. This pushes the results farther to the right on our curve in Fig. 8–14. Productivity drops even lower. A longer time is required to accomplish the job. Costs are greater than ever. Quality achievement is at risk. Instead of correcting the error, the manager is led further astray.

Cost and time estimates are predicated on historical records. Thus, over time, project budgets increase. More and more workers are allocated to each job. We see that a special form of Parkinson's law is in operation. Parkinson observed that work expands to fill up time available for its completion, which is another way of saying that people create work that would not otherwise be done.[14]

In turn, we require more people to handle the jobs that have been created. The process is self-perpetuating. When we couple this with the productivity paradox we have just described, we can understand why many organizations have experienced great difficulty in controlling expenditures on new product and service development.

PROBLEM SET

1. Figure 3–25 shows the cost/time tradeoffs for PERT network activities. Compare these relationships with the one shown in Fig. 8–14 describing the cost and productivity interrelations that underlie the cost/time analysis of any project phase. Are the relationships consistent? Are they the same? Explain your answer.

2. New street lights are to be installed along Parker Avenue. A team of 5 workers can complete the job in six months. On the other hand, with 10 workers completion can be achieved in three months. The workers are paid $1,000 per month. For maximum productivity, which team arrangement will you choose? For minimum cost, which arrangement is preferred? What is your recommendation?

3. Why is there a tendency to overestimate project manpower requirements? What can be done about it?

Section 8.4 Ergonomics and Human Factors

Many considerations must be taken into account by the P/OM when determining how to employ the human mind and body in the production process. The study of such problems has given rise to the development

---

[14]C. N. Parkinson, *Parkinson's Law* (Boston: Houghton Mifflin, 1957).

of **human factor models.** They are concerned with the way in which people fit into the working environment. What control can be exercised over it? How should the worker's tools be designed? What is known about the design of the products and services people require? Such studies are called by a number of different names. We have used the label "human factors", but we could have called this subject "human engineering" or "biomechanics," or used a British term, "ergonomics." Text material on the life cycle management of goods and services (see pp. 30–46) should be reexamined by the reader within the context of this section.

Design of the Job and the Workplace

The productivity of a motivated worker can be poor if the assigned job is badly designed. Part of the design of the job is the layout of the process. Human factors pertain to workers or consumers with equal applicability. The worker is a consumer of facilities and equipment at the workplace. It is a managerial responsibility to recognize this interaction and to provide the worker with a safe and efficient job environment.

This responsibility is harder to fulfill for the job shop than the flow shop. This is because new jobs characterize the job shop. If the worker does not feel safe, one basic human need is not being satisfied. But lack of safety does not always act as a disincentive. The worker, feeling compelled to earn as much money as possible, may disregard safety. Management has been known to look the other way when the pressure is great to deliver on time or to increase production output. After an accident, neither the worker nor management can find any way to rationalize the tragedy.

Safety

Acceptable levels of safety are difficult to specify. We know that the ideal situation is "perfect" safety, but like zero defects, perfect safety is an unobtainable state. So-called "safety factors" are designed into bridges, ships, and planes. This is done to raise safety to as near-perfect levels as possible.

Sometimes we speak about "fail-safe" systems. By this we mean that the system is immune to crucial accidents or disastrous fortuitous events except where the probabilities of such occurrences are so small that they can be ignored. According to Borel, these might be events associated with probabilities in the neighborhood of one in a million (0.000001).[15]

---

[15]Emile Borel, "Valeur Pratique et Philosophie des Probabilities," *Traite du Cacul des Probabilities et de ses Applications*, Tome IV, Fascicule 3, ed. Emile Borel (Paris: Gautier-Villars, 1950).

To achieve this, high-level safety factors must be incorporated into the basic design of the system for all its vulnerabilities.

Safety poses a curious problem. We cannot really evaluate the value of an arm, or a leg, or a life. If faced with the question, we would state unequivocally that a life is of enormous value, but we do not act as though this were so, nor could we if we tried. It would mean that every swimmer would have a personal retinue of lifeguards. That after each flight, a plane would be completely overhauled and new parts installed to replace all the old ones. The fact that we do not behave in this manner does not lessen our concern for safety. If anything, our concern increases as a direct result of the fact that we cannot act in accord with our moral values; rather, we act in terms of an obscure compromise between moral and economic values.

Bypassing the complicated philosophical and ethical problems involved in this subject, we can all readily agree that safety is a major consideration. Although we cannot find a behavioral model to determine the value of life and limb, we can attempt to minimize accident rates subject to a reasonable set of system constraints. Machine designs must assure a reasonable level of safety to machine operators. Here, differences between people play a part. A satisfactory machine design for a male worker may not prove to be equally safe or productive for a female operator. During World War II, a famous movie actress started a fad for long hair that was worn partially over the face. Machine design did not protect workers with such hairdos, and a number of serious accidents occurred. Various government agencies requested the actress (Veronica Lake) to change her hairstyle. She did, and the situation improved.

In certain cases, humans are susceptible to damage where the source of trouble lies beyond the capabilities of their own sensory protection. This is true, for example, where odorless toxic gases find their way into the air supply. Another case is where workers are inadvertently exposed to radioactive materials that cause radiation poisoning before detection is possible. Positive steps must be taken to prevent these conditions from arising, and to correct them immediately if they occur. Processes that produce toxic gases must be isolated so that they cannot contaminate the air supply. Nontoxic impurities can be kept out of the air by utilizing exhaust hoods close to the source of such impurities. For this vacuum-cleaner-type action to be effective, the through-put rate of air intake must be regulated according to the weight of the contaminent particles. Radioactive substances cannot be detected readily. For radiation hazards, proper shielding is a necessity. Where this is not possible, machines are substituted and controlled at safe distances from the radioactive materials. Geiger counters and other protective devices are used to provide a warning if some dangerous malfunction occurs.

Many safety problems arise because of laziness or corner-cutting. In these cases, the danger is apparent to all concerned, but somewhere along the line adequate measures are not taken. It is not enough to supply goggles to workers where, either because of intense light or flying particles, eye impairment might result if they are not used. It is necessary to make certain that they are used. Problems of safety also involve a proneness to accidents which seems to arise from psychological factors triggered by an initial chance occurrence. The problem of accident proneness has been researched, but no antidote has been found.

Safety problems for workers also arise because of the complex equipment and processes found in the production area. It is the P/OM's obligation to insure worker safety. The model of the human shows a hardy soul but a vulnerable body. Fundamentally, the best way to ensure safety is to design a total system of products, tools, facilities, and services that adequately considers the range of hazardous conditions that can occur. Safety models constitute an area of total interaction between individuals and physical elements of the production system. Often, preventive measures may be more effective than remedial ones.

The Man-Machine Interface

The Industrial Revolution was based on the fact that for certain kinds of operations, machines can do things that people cannot. Over a period of time there has been an increasing level of sophistication with respect to the design of mechanisms using electronics. This has led to many instances of the replacement of people by machines that has brought improved quality and profits. Initially, repetitive physical jobs were particularly susceptible to improvement by utilizing machines instead of workers. Now we find that mechanical and electronic control systems can be substituted for many mental activities formerly done by people. At the heart of this latter change is the computer.

For most complex activities, well-coordinated combinations of people and machines are ideal. We speak of the way in which people and machines are coordinated as the **man-machine interface.** For example, eyesight is considerably augmented by both microscopes and telescopes. Hearing is extended by amplification. Fully automatic recognition systems are becoming available as optical scanners and for voice recognition.

The lever and the pulley served to enlarge the feats of strength people could perform. Machines are better than muscles for producing enormous forces. On the cerebral side of the ledger (just as is the case with the sensory system), a coordinated effort is usually rewarding. Books, films, tapes, and records provide mechanical storage of memory. But human memory is basically different from computer memory. The two types of memory can be combined to produce a superior, coordinated memory. Memory is only one aspect of the thinking process. No one knows how humans think, but we have learned a great deal about the nature of thinking as a result of the computer. For some thinking jobs, people are better than computers. The interface problem is to find the optimal utilization pattern for both kinds of systems components. This requires a knowledge of behavioral models and computer control models. Let us therefore make a brief comparison between human and computer abilities.

1. The organization of human memory allows creative thinking that has not yet been duplicated by computers. An important characteristic of human memory is that it is highly selective. It rejects repetitious data, and it forgets easily. Perhaps the most important liability of the human memory, aside from the forgetting characteristic, is the fact that it can so easily distort information without realizing that this distortion has taken place.

2. Perseverance is an area where humans cannot compete with the computer. The brain fatigues rapidly when repetitive, routine operations are required. The computer, on the other hand, is indifferent to the number of repetitions that must be furnished. However, the computer is awkward at handling situations where no prior pattern has been discovered. Recent work in artificial intelligence (AI) and expert systems (ES) holds much hope that the computer can become creative.

3. Humans are able to devise intricate rules of logic and program these rules for use by the computer. This is so even though humans are unable consistently to apply the logical rules they have devised.

4. For speed of computation with complex but routine operations, the computer wins. However, a substantial amount of time can be required to preplan the procedures and steps that will be followed by the computer system. For all CIM-type systems, a great deal of preplanning time is required to achieve a relevant man-machine interface analysis.

5. Variability is one of the most important factors. The essence of process management is recognition and control of variability. Humans do not work at a constant rate. The distribution of times required by a human operator has substantially greater variance (variability) than would apply to a machine or a computer-driven machine. The same applies to the quality of the output.

6. Analysis of the interface (or boundary) across which man and machine communicate reveals that the human senses are related to the monitoring function in control systems. The use of physical devices is growing, but there are some cases where the combination of people and machines is superior. A particular advantage of mechanical and electronic sensing equipment is that it can handle cross-talk situations. Cross-talk occurs when several sensory perceptors are simultaneously called upon to receive input data. Because machines can be designed to operate efficiently with cross-talk, the design of the man-machine interface of a particular situation will depend upon the monitoring requirements for the system.

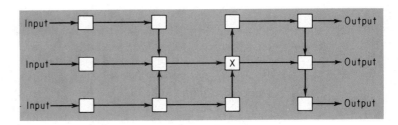

FIGURE 8-15. The failure of one mechanical component can produce the equivalence of failure in other mechanical components. There is only one mechanical unit in this diagram, which when broken down, will shut off the entire system.

When control devices are too sensitive because they do continuous monitoring, sample-data designs can be substituted. The essence of the sample-data system is the fact that it will monitor each sensory channel at intervals. Where cross-talk exists, it can sample what is going on at various places in the system simultaneously. Man inherently acts as a sample-data system, being unable continuously to monitor the behavior of any system. Good systems design calls for proper scheduling of the sample periods.

Humans are subject to sensory illusions. Many examples can be found in psychological literature of physical relationships that are distorted by the human sensory mechanism. Machine sensing fallibility also occurs. Machines tend to misinterpret different kinds of physical relations than do human senses. Interface design takes advantage of this difference, using each where best applied.

Another topic of importance to job and workplace design is the reliability of system components. For human machines, failures of physical and mental health are treated by the class of repair people known as medical doctors and psychiatrists. Health is affected by various kinds of overloads. In addition, failings in one human component are frequently contagious. Machine failures are often (but not always) independent of the condition of other machine units in the system. Humans can repair failed machines. At the present time, machine repair of itself or other machines, by means of AI or ES, is in early stages of development.

Fig. 8–15 shows how the failure of one machine can result in the shutting down of other machines. The doctor in this case is the repair-person. Interface design requires full consideration of such factors and must allow for the possibility of a speck of dust getting in the operator's eye, or a piece of grit getting into a gear train.

Human Factors and the Information System

All activities are forms of information to be managed. Every operation has its counterpart in data form and is transformable into data. Plans are information maps. Controls are information regulators. The job, as planned and produced, is fully described by information. This realization has an important effect: It focuses attention on the necessity of managing information.

Both workers and machines require information to accomplish work. Each have characteristic ways of transmitting, receiving, channeling, and storing information. However, the use of electronic and mechanical storage systems is needed to augment the limited and fallible human memory system. Libraries, file drawers, microfilm records, and computer memories are important components of the total system. The machine elements must be viewed in terms of their relationship to the human components of the system.

Information continually flows back and forth across the man-machine interface. People and machines can operate together only when there is adequate communication. Language translation must be taken into account. The syntax and grammar of the machine are far more precise, and the vocabulary far smaller, than that of the people in the system.

Extensive mechanical storage of information creates serious problems. Significant costs must be incurred to maintain it as well as to search it to obtain the required information. The cost of both storage and searching rises as the volume of information that is stored increases. The Dewey Decimal System of categorization developed for information retrieval from library storage has provided a model information storage system. However, the amount of information available for conducting business has increased at an exponential rate. Far more sophisticated schemes for retrieving information are now required.

When the job and the workplace (for a continuous stream of job shop operations) are being designed, duplication of efforts is not unusual. However, the time required to avoid duplicative efforts—by surveying all relevant databases to determine whether or not a similar job has previously been designed—may cost a greater amount than would be needed to recalculate or redevelop the same information. When the cost of searching equals or exceeds the cost of development, we choose to duplicate efforts. There is only one other potential course of action, and that is to reduce the cost of searching. This can be accomplished by designing adequate computer systems for information retrieval.

We have been experiencing a technological revolution of information capabilities. Incredible advances in hardware, software, and the flexible equipment it controls are announced on a daily basis. Telecommunication networks are connecting plants and offices worldwide. As these new data systems are developed, the cost of sharing information is substantially reduced. Meanwhile, the value of information is increasing (in the sense that it is a purer grade of ore); and the probability of locating vital information quickly is being significantly improved. As a result, the optimum volume of information to search through is growing exponentially. Figure 8–16 shows the nature of the change.

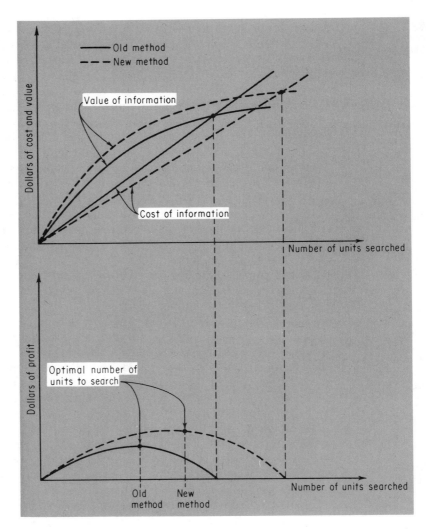

FIGURE 8-16. With improved information retrieval methods, it is possible to search more effectively, less expensively, and more rapidly. Consequently, the optimum number of units to search increases.

Another aspect of information searching is that it takes a given length of time to recover the information that is needed. The age of information can inflict severe penalties if it becomes excessive.

Each situation dictates its own time scale for measuring the age of information. At some age control is lost, an emergency has developed, or the information has become worthless. Relatively continuous control is an important factor when the system's performance is sensitive to the age of information. Quality control requires maintaining the sequence of information. If the process is continuously changing, as with FPS, then sample-data intervals must be small.

Another example of the detrimental effect of overly delayed or overage information is in the inventory area. Here, the critical age of information is a function of various factors, such as the demand rate for items, the reserve stock policy (the extra units carried to meet unexpectedly high demand), and the length of time required to get a replenishment order filled. Consider perpetual inventory systems. Assume that the specified reorder level is reached for an item and that this information is not sent by the stock clerk to the purchasing department immediately. While the information that will trigger a purchase order is aging, further withdrawals can reduce the stock level and create a stock outage before a new order can be placed, let alone filled.

Information recovery treats the problem of how to design the information transference characteristics of a system. It is concerned with directing various kinds of information to workers and machines at appropriate points in time. It is a critical determinant of control, safety, and other job factors of basic importance.

Design of Equipment: Another Aspect of Quality Definition

The design of facilities and the working environment is a form of industrial architecture. In many ways, it represents the same kinds of approaches and the same set of human factors objectives as those of industrial designers. As a concrete example, look at the design for the foot pedal of an industrial lift truck (Fig. 8–17). The Henry Dreyfuss design group believed that the foot pedal should serve as an extension of the foot. Foot pressure studies were made, and the dimensions of workers' feet were taken into account. This kind of workplace design maximizes safety and productivity.

The human factors area treats both the physiological and psychological characteristics of people. It attempts to provide high levels of safety and comfort. It is concerned with the appearances of things, and the way they affect efficiency. All the senses and the interrelationships of the senses to both motor and mental responses are part of the fabric of these factors, which describe the interactions of the worker and the workplace, the plant and the office.

Not just sight, illumination, and color concern the designer; hearing, noise, taste, smells, temperature and temperature changes, and body orientation are other factors that condition the performance and attitudes of the workers in a system.

The physical structure of human beings affects workplace design in many ways. What is not immediately apparent is the flaw in logic of an individual using himself or herself as a physical model of what other people need or want. Self is not a sufficient design guide for the consumer product design or for employee workplace considerations.

This is a point of importance. The design of the job, the workplace,

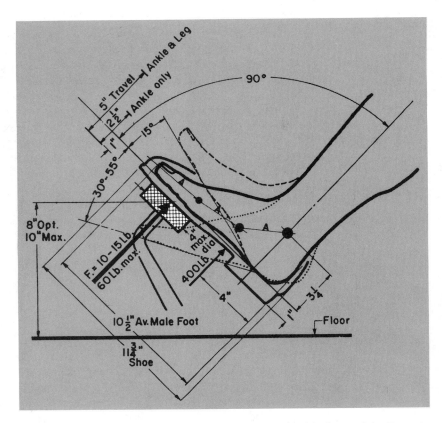

FIGURE 8-17. Detailed studies and drawings were made of the foot pedal to determine its final placement. The Henry Dreyfuss design group believes that the foot pedal should serve as an extension of the foot. Foot pressure studies were extremely important for the early development of Monotrol Control. [From William F. H. Purcell, A.S.I.D., *Designing for Heavy Duty,* Chilton Company, Automotive Industries, 1962].

the product, and/or the service is frequently based on personal interpolations or extrapolations that are erroneously assumed to apply to a majority of other people. This text recommends the use of statistical survey techniques to evaluate the needs and preferences of people, rather than to assume the designer's preferences are the best estimates of what is satisfactory for most people. The statistical survey is part of the methodology of human engineering.

Because people come in different shapes and sizes, it is necessary to study their relevant characteristics with respect to the objectives of the system's design. The statistical analysis of physical differences between individuals has proved to be of great benefit in all areas where people operate on or interact with the physical environment. Our first example was the foot pedal in Fig. 8–17. Now consider how many jobs entail much telephone work. Yet all workers are not equally comfortable (productive) with a given set of design dimensions. These include the spacing between cap centers, angle of receiver cap, weight, and so on (see Fig. 8–18). Because of the differences between people, we want to answer the question, comfortable for whom? It is operational to select a design that satisfies a statistical criterion relative to the distribution of pertinent human characteristics.

The requirements of a representative distribution of people can be determined. A design based on statistical knowledge regarding these dimensions would satisfy the minimum requirements for a majority of potential users. We know that an ideal handset for a small person could not, at the same time, be ideal for a large one. Design problems can be resolved only by determining the requirements of a representative cross-section of potential users. The final design cannot provide equal satisfaction for all people, but it can be sufficiently satisfactory for an appropriate number of users.

Another example can be derived in terms of the search for comfortable shoes. Suppose that a department store, recognizing that its employees

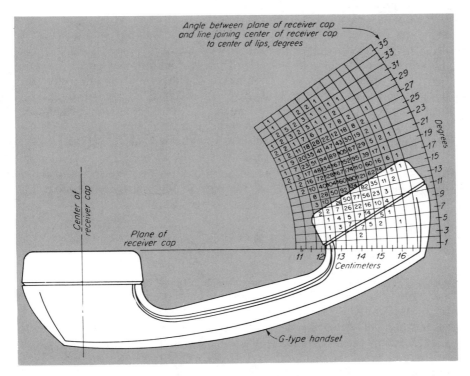

FIGURE 8-18. Summary of face dimensions used in design of telephone handset. The chart indicates the number of people for whom specific distances and orientations were found to be suitable. [From Ernest J. McCormick, *Human Engineering* (New York: McGraw-Hill, Inc., 1976); based on the work of W. C. Jones and A. H. Inglis, "Development of a Handset for Telephone Stations," *Bell System Technical Journal*, Vol. XI, 1932, p. 262. Reprinted with permission from *The Bell System Technical Journal*, Copyright 1932, The American Telephone and Telegraph Company].

are on their feet all the time, decides to supply them with a new line of shoes. The objective is to keep the same level of variety, but to alter the sizes and shapes of shoes with the intention of improving the level of comfort. To achieve this objective, it is necessary to obtain statistical distributions of foot measurements. These would describe the various foot characteristics of the population of potential shoe users (in this case, department store personnel). The characteristics of feet chosen to be studied would be those that are relevant to the comfort of users. The appropriate set of dimensions have to be determined before an empirical study could be conducted. Then, with a sufficiently large sample of people properly measured for the appropriate dimensions, reasonable job and workplace design decisions can be made.

Consider another example. Assume that our objective is to design a chair that would be standard equipment in an office. Many different body forms, heights, and weights would have to be considered if we are to offer a reasonable level of comfort to the greatest number of potential users. Toward this end, we would measure a representative sample of users of these chairs. Again, first we must determine of what measurable dimensions comfort is a function. We note that the sample would be quite different if the office is to be staffed with men only, or women only, or a combination of men and women. (Chairs for a kindergarten would pose another problem.) Generally, the larger the diversity among users, the less the satisfaction that can be obtained for any one user. Although this is an argument for uniqueness among designs, it must be counterbalanced against the added costs of providing greater satisfaction to a smaller number of users.

As we consider the design of the workplace, we are struck by the great number of factors that account for the qualities of comfort and convenience. Shoes, telephones, typewriters, floors, chairs all contribute to the comfort, safety, and convenience of workers doing their jobs.

Sensory Systems and Quality

Another aspect of human factor models concerns the sensory abilities of humans. Again, differences between individuals must be taken into account. For example, a certain combination of colors may produce higher attention levels for one type of viewer than for another. Color relates to the quality of the workplace and worker productivity. Color also relates to the quality of the product, as perceived by different customers and in terms of safe use of the product.

One practical problem is the determination of what colors to use to signal danger. Color-blind people cannot sense red. How should we color the various parts of machines, the office, the company library, a plant cafeteria? Color affects the behavior of an individual in various ways—for example, the degree to which fatigue occurs, general alertness, mood, and attitude. The superiority of a certain color combination for a specific purpose must be predicated on the fact that differences exist among people. Design utility is statistically determined, just as it was in the case of the telephone handset.

Individual preferences vary with respect to the amount of light that is both comfortable and satisfactory for accomplishing a given job. The range can be quite large, as shown by the following distribution for the amount of light preferred for reading.[16]

Footcandles	Number of People
0–50	none
50–100	4
100–150	38
150–200	46
200–250	62
250–300	89
300–350	45
350–400	22
400+	3

During World War II, many studies were undertaken to determine superior designs for aircraft controls such as dials, gauges, tracking devices, gunsights, and the like. Since that time, a great deal of work has been done by various organizations and institutions. As a result, a large body of literature concerning the visual sensory system is now available.

The sense of hearing has been studied with equal fervor. Many production operations are quiet, but others produce extremely high noise levels. Two questions arise with respect to this noise factor. First, how does it affect workers' performance and second, to what extent can it damage hearing? The appropriate answers are that within reasonable limits, noise does not decrease the performance of an individual. However, varying degrees of hearing loss are associated with exposure to a noisy environment. Noise levels are measured in decibels. This is a logarithmic transformation of the ratio of a given sound level to a standard value which is the standard of just audible sound. Fig. 8–19 presents a chart of some representative noise levels as they are generated by different sources. Because workers suffer a degree of hearing loss when repeatedly exposed to certain types of sound, it behooves management to provide adequate protection for all individuals exposed to such hazards. Appropriate materials and structures can be used to achieve noise control or abatement when it appears that the process is not susceptible to design changes that will decrease the noise levels.

---

[16]These results are reported by W. S. Fisher, General Electric Company, Large Lamp Department, Nela Park, Cleveland, Ohio, in a private correspondence with Sylvester K. Guth, Manager, Radiant Energy Effects Laboratory, General Electric Company. The sample of 309 individuals was given the visual task of reading from the pages of a telephone book.

Sound–power ratio | Decibels | Environmental noises | Specific noise sources | Decibels

Sound–power ratio	Decibels	Environmental noises	Specific noise sources	Decibels
100,000,000,000,000	140			140
10,000,000,000,000	130		50 hp siren (100 ft)	130
1,000,000,000,000	120		Jet takeoff (200 ft)	120
100,000,000,000	110	Casting shakeout area	Riveting machine*	110
10,000,000,000	100	Electric furnace area	Cutoff saw* / Pneumatic peen hammer*	100
1,000,000,000	90	Boiler room / Printing press plant	Textile weaving plant* / Subway train (20 ft)	90
100,000,000	80	Tabulating room / Inside sports car (50 mph)	Pneumatic drill (50 ft)	80
10,000,000	70		Freight train (100 ft) / Vacuum cleaner (10 ft) / Speech (1 ft)	70
1,000,000	60	Near freeway (auto traffic) / Large store / Accounting office		60
100,000	50	Private business office / Light traffic (100 ft) / Average residence	Large transformer (200 ft)	50
10,000	40	Minimum levels, residential areas in Chicago at night		40
1000	30	Studio (speech)	Soft whisper (5 ft)	30
100	20	Studio for sound pictures		20
10	10			10
1	0		*Operator's position	0

FIGURE 8-19. Noise level of typical noises. This figure also shows the ratio of sound energies for various decibel levels. [From Ernest J. McCormick, *Human Engineering* (New York: McGraw-Hill Book Co., Inc., 1976)].

Another issue concerns the nuisance effect of noise. If there is inherent, high-level noise associated with a particular production process, this fact should be taken into account when the plant is geographically situated—for example, airport location in the case of jet aircraft. Community good-will can be rapidly alienated if this point is overlooked. Noise abatement can be achieved in a number of different ways. This is the job of the acoustical engineer, and we will not attempt to delve into the technology relevant to noise control. But it might be useful to distinguish among three major ways of coping with noise:

1. Eliminate or reduce it by introducing technological (design) change.
2. Isolate it by moving the source to a remote or protected location.
3. Dampen or absorb it by using specially designed materials such as fiberglas.

Human sensory systems have the ability to receive many other stimuli besides light and sound. As a beginning, include such sensations as smell, touch, and taste; the perception of body orientation; temperature and humidity; vibration; and the sense of passing time. Pain is an additional factor produced by external conditions. Human factor models have been developed, and are being developed, to measure such sensory characteristics not only for averages, but also for differences between individuals. Thus, comfort and pain share the same dimensional continuum. What is comfort for one may be less comfort for another and perhaps pain for a third. The key in all these considerations is the fact that most design, in the past, has proceeded on the basis of the designer's own personal set of sensory, anatomical, motor, and mental characteristics. Such egocentric design produces an amount of penalty that is proportional to the divergence between the designer's preferences and the statistical distribution of population preferences.

PROBLEM
SET

1. The British call the human-factors area ergonomics. What is the derivation of this word? (*Hint:* you will find in the dictionary that *ergon* is the Greek word for work.)
2. What can be done to improve the design of the workplace?
3. What is meant by a fail-safe system?
4. Certain workers have a history of numerous accidents, whereas most workers have few accidents. What can be done for those who exhibit accident-proneness?
5. What role does the computer play at the man-machine interface? Discuss the kinds of interactions that can take place.
6. In the text it is stated: "Analysis of the interface (or boundary) across which man and machine communicate reveals that the human senses are related to the monitoring function in control systems." Explain this statement. Under what circumstances would you recommend a machine monitor rather than a human monitor?
7. How do air traffic control problems relate to the age of information?
8. What factors would ordinarily be considered when a proposed plan calls for replacing a worker with a machine? What criteria would apply to the decision?

Answer: The nature of the job that must be done is the basic determinant. Some jobs cannot be done by machines, except at an extremely high cost. As often, a variety of jobs cannot be performed by a human operator. Aside from obvious physical constraints, we must consider the minimization of cost, given that both a person and a machine can suitably perform the required tasks. We could begin by comparing the costs of a list of human factors. Thus, the cost of memory should reflect the fact that machine memories are smaller but more reliable than those of people. The cost of dexterity should be considered. Machines possess great advantages both in the speed and fineness of prescribed movements. Where movements cannot be specified exactly (e.g., the surgeon), then the machine costs rise rapidly, approaching infinity for the present state of technology. Learning ability costs can be included. Machines have new artificial intelligence. We must also characterize the statistical properties of the people and the machines in the system. People contribute high variance to activities, while the performance of machines insures low variance, approaching 0. By taking all such factors into account, we are able to provide the appropriate man-machine configuration.

9. Prepare a human factors analysis, treating all variables that might be relevant with respect to the following situations:

   a. The design and manufacture of a belt

   b. The redesign of an automobile

   c. The design of an electric circuit fuse

   d. The design of a hearing aid

   e. The arrangement of high-noise equipment in a plant

   Answer: In situations characterized by *a* through *e*, human factors analysis deals with questions such as the distributions of various anatomical proportions in the population. Thus, for example, we would consider waist sizes for the belt design, leg lengths for automobile seat design, hand sizes for installing and handling electric fuses, and ear shapes with respect to the design of the hearing aid. Other physiological factors also pertain, such as dexterity, reaction time, nature of hearing loss, and safety from electric shock. In addition, psychological considerations related to the feeling of safety, reliability, prestige, and embarrassment conveyed by the object are of the utmost importance, although they are usually harder to quantify and therefore more difficult to analyze in an objective fashion.

10. There is a visual phenomenon known as the Purkinje effect: The fact that a great decrease in the intensity of illumination darkens red, orange, and yellow much more than blue and green, so that the point of maximum brilliance in the spectrum is shifted from the yellow into the green. A suggested explanation is that the rods that give vision in faint light are tuned to shorter wavelengths than the cones that

dominate vision in bright light. Under what circumstances might this human factor be of importance?

Answer: This effect could have great significance with respect to the output of a factory where color matching is important and where there is reliance on external illumination. On a more individual level, the Purkinje effect is responsible for the difficulty in distinguishing whether a traffic light is red or green during twilight hours. It demonstrates the relevance of this human factor to the design of man-machine systems. (A well-designed red-green traffic signal could have different shapes in addition to different positions (red normally over green) to indicate positively—even to the color blind—a stop or go signal.)

11. How would you go about taking into consideration the percentage and distributional characteristics of color blindness? When might this factor be significant?

12. Describe the characteristics of the man-machine interface with respect to the following:

    a. A pinball machine
    b. A dictionary
    c. A pencil
    d. A computer programmed to prepare invoices
    e. A continuous conveyor
    f. A television set
    g. A 35-mm camera

    Answer: This question is intended to encourage discussion concerning the relevant system of variables that is shared by the man in the system with the facilities that he uses, as well as the total environment that surrounds them both. Thus, for example, the dictionary is one form of memory. Access to it requires a corresponding human memory for the appearance of the word. The individual who does not know the exact spelling can then undertake a search procedure to locate the sought-after word based on memory of the sounds of the word and the various rules that are known for translating sounds into spelling. Since conflicting rules exist in English, we must frequently use trial and error. Other rules would apply to different languages. This would be an environmental factor. The individual can use the dictionary to locate meaning if the precise spelling is known. One can also obtain correct pronunciation under these circumstances. Yet frequently the dictionary is used for discovering or checking on the *spelling* of a word. The question of whether this is the best possible systems design resides in the nature of the man-machine interface and also leads to the consideration of the role of a thesaurus. Similar consideration can be given to each of the facilities listed for this question.

REFERENCES   ATTNEAVE, F. *Applications of Information Theory to Psychology*. New York: Holt, Rinehart & Winston, 1959.

BARNES, R. N. *Motion and Time Study,* 7th ed. New York: Wiley, 1980.

BELCHER, D. W. *Wage and Salary Administration,* 2nd ed. Englewood Cliffs, N.J.: Prentice-Hall, 1962.

BITHER, S. W. *Personality as a Factor in Management Team Decision Making*. University Park: The Pennsylvania State University Press, 1971.

CHAPANIS, A., W. R. GARNER, and C. T. MORGAN. *Applied Experimental Psychology*. New York: Wiley, 1949.

CHAPANIS, ALPHONSE. *Man-Machine Engineering*. Belmont, Calif.: Wadsworth, 1965.

W. EDWARDS DEMING, *Out of the Crisis* (Cambridge, Mass.: M.I.T. Center for Advanced Engineering Study (CAES), 1986).

FLETCHER, HARVEY. *Speech and Hearing*. Princeton, N.J.: Van Nostrand, 1950.

HALL, EDWARD T. and MILDRED REED HALL, *Hidden Differences: Doing Business with the Japanese*. Anchor Press/Doubleday, Garden City, NY, 1987.

HANSEN, B. L. *Work Sampling.: For Modern Management*. Englewood Cliffs, N.J.: Prentice-Hall, 1960.

KIDDER, TRACY, *The Soul of a New Machine,* Little Brown & Co., 1981

KRICK, EDWARD V. *Methods Engineering*. New York: Wiley, 1962.

LEHRER, R. N. *Work Simplification*. Englewood Cliffs, N.J.: Prentice-Hall, 1957.

LOUDEN, J. K., and J. W. DEECAN. *Wage Incentives*. New York: Wiley, 1959.

MCCORMICK, E. J. *Human Factors in Engineering and Design,* 4th ed. New York: McGraw-Hill, 1976.

MAYNARD, H. B., G. J. STEGEMERTEN, and J. L. SCHWAB. *Methods-Time Measurement*. New York: McGraw-Hill, 1973.

MUNDEL, MARVIN E. *Motion and Time Study: Principles and Practice,* 5th ed. Englewood Cliffs, N.J.: Prentice-Hall, 1978.

QUICK, J. H., J. H. DUNCAN, and J. A. MALCOLM. *Work-Factor Time Standards*. New York: McGraw-Hill, 1962.

ROETHLISBERGER, F. J., and W. J. DICKSON. *Management and the Worker*. Cambridge, Mass.: Harvard University Press, 1939.

SALVENDY, GAVRIEL, ed. *Handbook of Human Factors*. New York: Wiley, 1987.

SAYLES, LEONARD R., and GEORGE STRAUSS. *Personnel: The Human Problems of Management,* 3rd ed. Englewood Cliffs, N.J.: Prentice-Hall, 1972.

SIMON, H. A. *Models of Man*. New York: Wiley, 1957.

SPECIAL DEVICES CENTER. *Handbook of Human Engineering Data,* 2nd ed. Office of Naval Research, Technical Report SDC 199-1-2, NavExos P-643, Project Designation NR-783—001, 1951.

TEEVAN, RICHARD C., and ROSERT C. BIRNEY, eds. *Color Vision*. Princeton, N.J.: Van Nostrand, 1961.

TICHAUER, E. R. "Biomechanics Sustains Occupational Safety and Health." *Industrial Engineering,* February 1976, pp. 46–56.

VROOM, VICTOR. *Work and Motivation*. New York: Wiley, 1964.

WOFAC CO., Division of Science Management Corp., *A Synopsis of the Detailed Work-Factor System of Labor Measurement,* Liberty Corner, NJ, 1982.

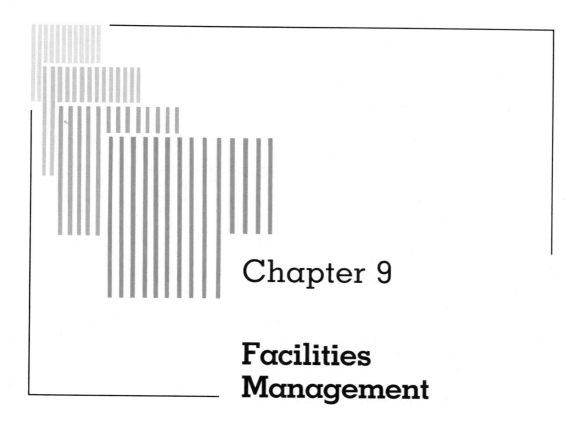

Chapter 9

Facilities Management

CHAPTER
SUMMARY

This chapter focuses on facilities for production and operations. Depending on the type of process, the buildings may be office buildings, factories and production plants, hospitals, airline terminals, laboratories, libraries, warehouses, and schools. The buildings contain equipment such as typewriters, machines, computers, and furniture. In other words, facilities are the structures and their contents located and arranged to promote the objectives of P/OM. Facilities management is needed to support the operations and activities of projects, job shops, flexible systems, and flow shops.

Facilities management is focused on housing the process and its equipment during the startup and growth period of the life cycle stages. This is like buying the company's first home, or renting its first apartment. Then come changeovers (as the family grows), and the plant or office moves into quarters more fitting for the mature stages of the life cycle.

Investments in facilities are generally sizable. Consequently, much attention has been devoted to improving decision-making capabilities with regard to facilities management. But these decision areas are complicated

425

and resistant to quantitative description. Approaches that estimate expected return on investment (ROI) are among the most applicable techniques in use for facilities decisions. Cost minimization might be the policy followed by not-for-profit institutions subject to constraints guaranteeing adequate service levels. Such institutions might prefer to maximize the benefits they offer, subject to cost constraints, but this is difficult to formulate, because benefits are often intangible and hard to quantify. Still, some systematic approaches have been developed, and they are discussed here.

The location/site facility selection problem is the broadest problem in the facilities management area. It is a problem composed of two parts that interact. First is the facility location problem and second, the specific facility (site) that is chosen. The discussion in Section 9.1 includes the selection of facilities by means of both qualitative and quantitative reasoning. All facilities house equipment that is used to make goods or to provide services. Equipment needed for the factory differs from what is needed for the office, the hospital, or the restaurant. But selection decisions, for all cases, share common properties that enable us to set down generic considerations (see Section 9.2).

How should facilities be arranged? This is often called the plant layout problem. Since interest in service organization layout problems is as keen as in manufacturing layout problems, the idea of generalizing the term by refering to "facilities" to encompass both has been accepted. There are qualitative and quantitative approaches available for resolving facility layout problems, as Section 9.3 shows.

Section 9.1 Facilities Selection

The facility selection process consists of two related decision problems. What is the right general location for the kind of facility that is being sought? For example, which region, or even better, which state? It could be resource-specific: near water or timber; near skills; and so on. The second issue is to choose the specific building or site that satisfies the first constraint.

Location to Enhance Service Contact

Service industries must locate close to customers to achieve the contact that characterizes their service. Bank tellers or ATMs (automatic teller machines) are the **contact points** in making deposits or withdrawals. Branch banks, gas stations, fast food outlets, and public phones are scattered all around town, since "close to me" is one of main choice criteria used by the customer. Shopping malls are located so that many people find it convenient to drive to them. For all retail businesses, the location decision is determined by ability to generate high customer contact frequency.

An exception to the advantage of proximity for contact is services rendered to vacationers. This service is twofold. First the airline provides transport, and then the hotel or resort offers food, shelter, sports, and entertainment. The facilities management problem is the key to success in the hotel and resort business.

Government service institutions locate close to their clients, the citizens. Municipal governments provide service to those who live within the municipality; they do not extend police and fire protection beyond the tax-paying boundary. Federal service often requires regional offices to be effective.

A refinery can be located at the oil fields close to its raw material sources. It could also be located adjacent to its market. Fig. 9–1 shows that petroleum refining is an analytic process. The raw material is crude oil from the well, which is refined into a number of finished products. Flow charts of this type can be helpful for process development of analytic systems. Quite different cost structures result, depending upon how far the refinery is from the wells and, in turn, how distant the customers are from the finished product.

The Just-in-Time Orientation for Facilities Management

Supplier factories (such as automobile suppliers) where parts are made for later assembly can be located close to their source of process inputs, such as metals, plastics, or energy. The manufacturing operations can be separated from customers' assembly operations. But increasingly, such suppliers locate their facilities close to customers' assembly lines. That allows the suppliers to deliver on a just-in-time basis.

The advantages are that the suppliers must be given enough volume to justify locating so close to a customer. Also, the decision to be a just-in-time supplier requires mutual trust and loyalty. Just-in-time suppliers benefit from the proximity by being a single source (or one of very few sources) to their customer. Communication can be face-to-face and frequent. The customer benefits from reduction of inventory levels and the mutual advantages of trust and loyalty.

The assembly operation is often located close to the markets that purchase the process outputs. Multiple facilities lead to additional questions concerning the division of functions between several facilities. Although such problems are complex, we know that there is some optimal locational arrangement of facilities. The question is: How do we go about determining this optimal arrangement?

The location decision is an **interfunctional** decision. As will be noted from the considerations discussed below, many factors are in the territory of finance, marketing, transportation and distribution, purchasing (nearness to suppliers for JIT), CEOs (for corporate headquarters decisions). P/OMs are involved from A to Z.

Petroleum Refining

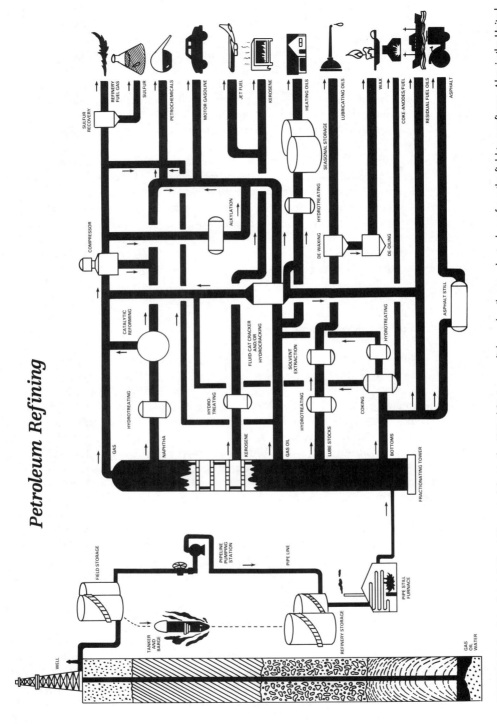

FIGURE 9-1. Oil refining. It should be noted that in the United States very little crude oil moves by tank car from the field to a refinery. Also, in the United States, naphtha from a fractionating tower is generally separated into two fractions—one that goes directly to motor gasoline after chemical treatment and the other that is reformed for octane improvement prior to blending into motor gasoline. [Courtesy of Exxon USA's Refining Department]

Decisions regarding the location of facilities require consideration of many factors. Sometimes, however, one major factor overrides the others. Frequently, the overriding factor is the desire to qualify as a just-in-time supplier. When many factors count, they are part of an interactive, multiple-criteria, facility-selection decision problem.

Location Factors

The following six factors normally play a significant role in location decisions:

1. Process inputs
2. Process outputs
3. Process requirements
4. Personal preferences
5. Tax and legal factors
6. Site and plant availabilities

With respect to the first two factors, we are primarily concerned with shipping and transportation costs.

Process Inputs. Such dependency is the case where bulky or heavy raw materials are major inputs for the production process. It is why analytic-type industries try to locate near the source of their materials. In this way they can minimize their overall transportation costs. These overall transportation costs include shipping inputs to the facilities and shipping outputs from them.

In Chapter 4 we examined the characteristics of analytic and synthetic systems from the viewpoint of batch versus flow processes. Now we consider the facility-location decision in the same terms. In the analytic system, the basic raw material is broken down, transformed, and decomposed into various products and by-products. If there is one location from which inputs arrive and many widely separated destinations to which they are shipped, it is likely that a location near the input source will turn out to have economic advantages. In synthetic operations, various materials and parts are fed into the mainstream process, where they are joined together to form a single basic unit (see Fig. 4–6, for auto production and assembly as an example of a synthetic industry).

In addition to materials that are process inputs, we also have human resource inputs, which were discussed in Chapter 8. Workforce costs are one of the most important factors in the determination of a suitable plant location for certain labor-intensive industries. Service industries are particularly sensitive to this factor. Companies that employ large workforces have been known to change locations to take advantage of a lower wage scale. This motive impelled New England textile firms to close up shop in the North and move to the South. However, with increasing use of robots and automation, the labor problem has been alleviated for most industries. There has also been a reduction in differential wage rates by regions of the country and between national and foreign locations.

Taken together, these changes have reduced the dependency of the location decision on the cost of labor. Wage differentials between countries are closing. Even where they are significant, they present something of an illusion. This is because tariffs, cost of materials, international exchange rates, taxes, and other factors tend to balance out over time what appear to be immediate substantial labor wage rate advantages.

In addition, there are more subtle costs of human resources. Foremost is the availability of various skills within a particular region. Movement from a high-skill, high-wage area to a low-skill, low-wage area can be accomplished only when sufficient process mechanization and/or automation is achieved. The computer has altered the skill requirements of both blue and white collar functions. Technological progress with computer-controlled machines of all kinds permit a company to trade off higher machine investments for lower wages and less workforce skills. A tradeoff potential is created between worker power and machine power, which makes the location decision less dependent on the expense of both indirect and direct labor. Workforce cost evaluation also includes consideration of turnover rates, absenteeism, and employee reliability, as well as costs of hiring and training workers. Some of these considerations are discussed in Chapter 11, where aggregate scheduling is treated. Different production schedules will be used according to the costs we have just discussed.

Facilities location (a system problem) interacts with the management of operations. The size of a labor market and the attitudes of workers and their unions can figure heavily in some location decisions. These considerations are likely to affect location decisions with respect to urban labor markets as compared to suburban and rural markets. From various sources, demographic information by area (such as population size, education, and income) can be pooled with industrial data concerning hourly earnings, right-to-work laws, and so forth. Such a database allows the manager to be informed when reaching a location decision.

Process Outputs. The location of the company's markets can be a significant factor, under certain circumstances. For example, service industries must be near their markets. The assembly functions of synthetic industries frequently locate near markets, because many raw materials must be gathered together from diverse locations and assembled into large-scale single units.

Process Requirements. Many processes require special environments. When the technology of the process requires large amounts of water, then only locations where such water resources are available can be considered. Another common process requirement is the need for substantial amounts of power. Not too many locations can supply such power. Accordingly, the location problem is cut down in size.

Certain processes produce disagreeable odors and in other ways disturb the environment. For such cases, both urban and suburban locations are ruled out. Pollution control laws differ by regions. Noise and other community irritants should be considered even if not covered by law.

Sometimes a process is responsive to factors such as temperature, humidity, and other weather conditions. To an extent, internal weather conditioning obviates such factors. But this is not always the case. Coastal locations must be avoided when a saline atmosphere adversely affects materials and equipment. Another example of the relevance of weather conditions is frequently overlooked. If a process requires highly skilled individuals to perform certain operations, then absenteeism can be a significant problem. It would be sensible to locate in a climate where illnesses due to weather are less common.

Space factories will orbit earth, providing weightless and particle-free environments. Clean-room environments with contamination controls and cool rooms to enable superconductivity are process requirements that might be better met in one location than another.

Personal Preferences. CEO's and owner/entrepreneurs may prefer a specific location for entirely personal reasons. Logical arguments for other locations are not likely to prevail. Once it has been decided to relocate an operating facility, strong monetary incentives must be used to encourage company personnel to relocate with the company. The cost of moving people and inducing them to do so must be added to the cost of losing talented workers and managers. These costs should be balanced against the costs of building a new group with the same level of skills and company loyalty in the new location.

Tax and Legal Factors. Because of high corporate taxes, personal income taxes, and sales taxes, desirable locations with respect to other variables may be bypassed. A favorable tax structure provides such basic motivation that many decisions are made to locate a new plant or to relocate a going operation solely for this reason. Many states provide tax and regulatory advantages which attract new companies. The regulatory advantages result in shifts of company headquarters to the more favorable locations.

In addition to tax advantages, communities attempt to attract industries by providing industrial parks or properly zoned land at advantageous rates. Cities offer tax abatement, financing, and even joint investment to attract business. Although some communities want industrial growth, most attempt to attract only certain types of industries. Others have been reluctant and even hostile toward industrial development. Companies that fail to perceive community attitudes frequently rue this oversight.

Site and Plant Availabilities. At any point in time, a list of available sites can be compiled. A complex problem exists; namely, when should we make the decision to buy or rent one of them? Some sites already have structures built on them. Other sites require building.

Assume that the desirability of each site could be evaluated with a single measure and that a rank-ordered list of sites has been developed. Figure 9–2 illustrates such a list, where E_1 is considered to be best, E_2 is next best, and so on. At any time, a new opportunity can arise. Thus, E_k is shown as a new arrival. The quality of E_k can be measured, and it will be placed in its proper rank-order in the list.

Sites must be removed from the list when some other organization rents or buys them—for example, E_j. Then the question is, when is E_1 good enough so that it can be chosen as a location? If the manager waits, the best choice may disappear. If the manager does not wait, the day after committing the company to a new location, a better one may appear.

This decision problem can be modeled, but the probability estimates that a new opportunity will arise or an existing opportunity disappear are hard to obtain. The quality criteria for ranking E_1, E_2, . . . , can be developed. Although the manager may not be able to achieve a real application of this model, he or she gains insight by thinking of the problem in this way.

Work Configuration and Facility Selection

In many flow-shop situations there is little ambiguity concerning the shape and form of buildings and basic facilities. There is heavy investment in the design of the process, and it is clear what kind and shape of structure will be needed to house that process. The same considerations apply to FPS. Project design also tends to constrain the kind of facilities that can be used. Building rather than renting may be required for all these cases.

Job shops have greater flexibility and more choices available. Therefore, FPS, flow shops, and projects tend to be located without consideration of the rental opportunities and their costs, whereas job shop locations may well be determined by the list of available rentals.

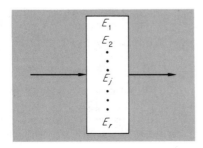

FIGURE 9-2.

Specific product and service industries are often associated with particular kinds and shapes of structures. A great deal of technological information and understanding of real process details is required to reach a decision.

Facility Factors

The manager must be able to define the type of structure that is desired to house the product's or service's process. Sometimes the choice of building and the choice of location are related. Often they are not. Dependency occurs when there is a need to rent specialized and unique structural configurations that exist only in certain places. Building one's own facility removes much of the pressure, as does the requirement for a general facility configuration rather than a highly individualized one.

In general terms, when renting, building, or buying, one must consider many elements. Expert assistance from architects and building engineers should be obtained to insure the proper evaluation of an existing facility or the proper plan for a new structure. Among the elements to be considered are these.

Is There Enough Floor Space? Is the space open, with wide bays, so that machines, workers, and materials handling equipment can be effectively arranged and utilized?

How Many Stories Are There? Early factories were multistoried. With the development of improved transportation, particularly the automobile, plants could be located outside the central city on less expensive land. The one-story building followed. It is usually preferred unless sufficient reason can be found to justify multistory buildings, which are more expensive to construct, especially when floor loads are high because heavy equipment must be supported. In certain industries, gravity feed conveyors are used. In such cases, multistory buildings are necessary.

What Kind of Roof Is Used? This was an important question at one time (pre-1950). Thereafter, heat, air conditioning, and lighting technologies advanced to the point where an assist from roof design seemed unnecessary. Roof shapes permit at least a degree of control over illumination, temperature, and ventilation. For example, the sawtooth roof construction was used extensively in the 1930s to provide even illumination of workspaces. Irrigation of flat rooftops was used for temperature control. Architectural factors again became important for temperature control in the 1970s when fuel shortages developed, energy prices soared, and all organizations became conscious of light, power, and heat bills.

Apart from such considerations, if the process requires hoists and cranes, then high roofs and ceilings are needed. Gravity conveyors operate best with either multifloors or high ceilings.

What Type of Construction Should Be Used? The answer will, in large measure, determine the feasibility of converting an old building to conform to a new set of specifications. This answer will be the major determinant of both new construction costs and the speed of construction. Building codes must always be observed. Industrial parks usually require a degree of conformity with respect to construction and appearance.

Such factors as foundations, floors, walls, and windows are part of the architectural design of a building. They affect layout flexibility and building convertibility. In addition, insurance rates will be dependent upon the type of construction used. The considerations mentioned concerning light, power, and heat bills also are relevant to the type of construction chosen.

What Kind of Maintenance Requirements Will There Be? The immediate maintenance of flow shop facilities is critical and costly. For the job shop, maintenance is less demanding. Older buildings will usually require maintenance more often than newer ones, and entail greater costs. Equipment housed within old buildings have a greater risk of being down because of old pipes, wiring, and so on.

What Determines Resale Value? The resale value of a facility may be important. In general, special-purpose facilities designed for a unique process make special structural demands and create a lower resale value than general-purpose facilities. The latter accept process requirements that are not unique but fit a pattern that is satisfactory for many different kinds of processes.

What Conveniences Should the Building Have? If the building is located at a distance from the city, it might be essential to provide a parking lot as well as cafeteria facilities. Many companies require a medical room or a plant hospital on the premises. There must be adequate rest rooms. In some instances an auditorium is included in the plans. Railroad sidings or docking facilities may be of major importance. If this is the case, the construction or rental plan must take such factors into account.

What Appearance Should the Building Have? Different architectural styles appear at different points in time. Attitudes and policies of management strongly influence these decisions. Some executives consider appearance to be a frill, whereas others take it so seriously that they insist on illumination of the building at night and the provision for an impressive view from the air.

There is no question that a beautiful building increases employee pride in the company. It is less certain how it influences the consumer's evaluation of the company. On the other hand, how these truisms affect productivity and profit remains an intangible factor. In any case, a clean and neat appearance is correlated with good morale and business success.

Should We Rent, Buy, or Build?   The answer to this question depends upon what is available. If a suitable building exists, its cost can be compared with costs that would be incurred if a new building were constructed. Rent or buy alternatives depend upon what is offered.

How long should we wait to see what buildings become available? If no suitable structure exists, then an appropriate facility must be constructed. Airline terminals are built for this reason. In the communications field, radio and TV stations are built to specifications. Unused power generating plants are not found in rentable condition. When there is nothing available to meet the need, it must be built. On the other hand, when the process requirements are not unique, many suitable facilities usually can be found. This would apply to office space, which is commonly rented. The problem of buying, renting, or building can be clarified by a comparison of costs based on present worth analysis.

Cost Determinants   A facility selection decision represents an attempt to minimize costs, including opportunity costs. For example, there is a cost of staying put and not moving to a new location. The investigation required to choose a new facility has a cost all its own that should be considered explicit, rather than being taken for granted. The collection of relevant data is facilitated through the cooperation of regional Chambers of Commerce. They are able to provide good information, usually without cost. But location studies are not free, and the costs rise as the number of locations investigated increases.

The facility selection problem involves long-term, nonrepetitive commitments. Many of the risk factors are difficult to analyze properly. The decision requires a sizable investment and creates heavy sunk, or nonrecoverable, costs. It involves other costs as well.

Consider two kinds of fundamental cost factors: tangible costs and intangible costs. The latter are distinguished by the fact that it is almost impossible to measure them. They can only be judged intuitively. Although it is difficult to measure many of the tangible costs, nevertheless, to some extent, they can all be measured. Among the tangible costs are these:

The cost of land. This is often thought of as an investment.

The cost of renting, buying, or building. Discount analysis, such as that shown on pp. 70–74, can be helpful.

Incoming and outgoing transportation costs. Charges for bringing raw materials and fuels to the facility and for moving finished goods to the market. Using different means of transport affects lead times. For example, air, rail, and trucking delivery times differ. Transportation costs affect decisions concerning the size of reserve stocks, economic order quantities, and discounts taken or foregone. Also, these costs should be included in the determination of market price, which affects demand volume and consequently shipping quantities.

Power and water costs. The fuel shortage of the 1970s has not been forgotten. Energy consumers, such as airlines, agriculture, and petro-chemicals are sensitive to fuel prices. Water costs often include purification.

The cost of taxes and insurance. Return on investment (ROI) should be calculated after taxes.

Labor costs. The tradeoff costs for different man-machine configurations should be investigated.

The cost of moving. This includes production stoppage costs incurred during relocation. Inventory buildups can help offset the effects of production stoppages for the intermittent and paced-flow shop. Work in the job shop and project would be delayed.

In determining an optimal facility selection, intangible costs place a severe burden on the manager. Consider some of these:

Costs for scarce labor. Competition for labor (blue and white collar), where there are shortages, creates costs that change over time. These costs vary as a function of the attractiveness of a particular region for all industries. When an attractive location is recognized, many companies move to this area to take advantage of regional opportunities. Saturation occurs, and at some point competition for available labor resources can become a serious hardship.

Costs of adversarial relations with unions. Union attitudes are critical but difficult to assess. Militant unions develop reputations, but a change of leadership or policy within the union can alter the stereotype. Shifts in the economy and changes in the fortunes of a particular industry will shift union attitudes.

Costs of community antagonism. Community attitudes are not measurable. Enclaves of resistance to industrial development can be significant, particularly when such groups are led by individuals who are influential members of the community. It is possible to document specific instances where companies have developed plans to move into a new community, only to discover that a powerful group is prepared to resist the move. Because of its investment in planning the move, and because some executives become enraged at being thwarted, some companies have attempted to fight this battle. Even if the company succeeds legally, the anger aroused can prove to be a lasting penalty. For example, bus service may be suspended on routes from the city to the plant location. A community board is offended and rezones the plant location so that fire protection is denied. This causes a rise in insurance rates, so the company develops its own fire protection unit. Other possible adversarial scenarios include the municipality's withholding adequate sewage facilities and the passage of new zoning laws that prevent company expansion.

Costs of regulations. Local and state ordinances must be taken into account. There is no direct way to attach costs to such rulings. Legal advice, which is costly, especially for small firms, is usually required. Each locale has its own economic considerations in terms of such costs as workmen's compensation payments, unemployment insurance, waste disposal laws, pollution and smoke control requirements, noise abatement rules, and other nuisance regulations.

Costs of the environment. The costs of weather and other natural phenomena should not be overlooked. Such events as hurricanes, earthquakes, and floods can produce heavy penalties. Although these are acts of nature, some locations are more prone to them than others. Companies in low-lying areas near rivers have higher probabilities of being flooded. Similarly, known earthquake and hurricane zones exist. Normal weather conditions also produce costs that can be associated with specific locations. Companies locating in the North must be prepared to pay for heating equipment and costly fuel bills. Industries locating in the South may find larger investments in air conditioners, as well as higher power bills. Other costs related to weather concern the maintenance of plant and deterioration of equipment.

How can all these factors be related? Scoring models, the next topic, provide a start.

Facility Selection Using Scoring Models

If the costs were measureable, then we could write an equation of the general form:

Total costs $= f$(tangible, intangible, and opportunity cost factors)

and we would minimize the equation.

We cannot write the mathematical equation, but we can approach the problem in a quantitative way. The intangibles are tough to deal with, but not impossible. There are many factors that interact with the facility selection decision. We cannot name them all, but we can try to capture the essential ones. We do this with a multiple-criteria method for simultaneously evaluating tangible and intangible costs. The comparison among strategic alternatives is akin to measuring the opportunity costs of choosing one thing which thereby prohibits doing the other.

Opportunity costs give us a way of dealing with benefits, since they measure the costs of not doing the best possible thing. For a hypothetical example, say that Orlando, Florida, has the best community attitude (call best a 1) for the ABC Company. ABC is comparing Englewood Cliffs,

New Jersey (which it rates a 3 for community attitude) with Orlando. The opportunity cost is obtained by subtracting the alternative's value from the best $(1 - 3)$. That is how we derive the opportunity cost of 2.

Decisions related to intangible cost systems present some difficulties. Several means of resolving these problems can be suggested.

1. Entirely subjective decisions can be made. Decisions are often made in this way, but if you can move to 2, you are better off.

2. A quasi-objective approach can be utilized which requires that preference measures be stated for various factors that describe different aspects of the system's performance. Weights or index numbers can be used to express preference. These measures are then used to make a comparison in some objective manner, so that a choice can be made.

Tangible costs can be measured, but to mix them with intangible costs, we must place weights of relative importance on both kinds of costs. Then we combine them all, treating measured values as though they were also preferences. The major difficulty in evaluating alternative facilities is the fact that conflicting objectives, having quite different dimensions, must somehow be combined to provide a reasonable basis for evaluation.

A scoring model provides a method that will organize the information relevant to the decision. One or more managers can study what is known, what is agreed upon and what is not, what appears to require additional research, what is considered important, whether consensus exists about what is important, and so on. Further, this method provides a solution that can be accepted or rejected by the managers concerned. The decision may be to accept a solution rejected by the method. This is acceptable, because it is an informed decision.

First, we develop an example; then we apply the method to that example.

CASE: LASER-MAKERS, INC.

Lasermakers is searching for a new plant location. This medium-size laser manufacturer develops two plans based on six factors. Three factors are tangible (directly measurable), and the other three factors are intangible. With respect to the latter, at best they can be assigned a scale position between 1 (best) and 6 (worst). (The discussion could have included many more of the factors previously discussed without changing the methodological significance.)

Let Plan 1 specify building a plant in Boston, while Plan 2 specifies building a plant in Camden, New Jersey. Assume that the proposals have been evaluated as shown in Table 9–1.

Dollars must be added together. By using discounting methods, we can make dollars apply to the same period of time. Companies will have different measures for the relative importance of dollars, depending upon their assets.

TABLE 9-1   A COMPARISON BETWEEN ALTERNATIVE PLANT LOCATIONS FOR LASERMAKERS

Factors	Boston Plan 1	Camden Plan 2	Weight*
Building costs and equipment costs—yearly depreciated value	$500,000	$300,000	4
Taxes (per year)	$ 50,000	$ 20,000	4
Power cost (per year)	$ 20,000	$ 30,000	4
Community attitude	1	2	1
Product quality as a function of worker morale and skill	2	3	5
Flexibility to adapt to situations that are likely to occur	1	6	3

*The larger the weight, the more important the factor is considered to be relative to the other factors.

Thus, Lasermakers' management evaluates dollars with a weight of 4, which indicates more importance than any other factor—except product quality—as a function of worker morale and skill (which is weighted 5).

The weighting is arbitrary, but it is not random. The executive committee, composed of five top executives, agreed on the evaluation in Table 9–1. Such agreement lends support to the use of these particular numbers. If factors such as community attitude, product quality, and flexibility could be associated with a dollar value, there would not be a dimensional problem to resolve. Everything could be measured in dollars, and there would be no need for weights. However, we must recognize that the latter elements represent intangible costs. The attempt to estimate such costs in dollars would prove arduous with little conviction that the results are satisfactory. On the other hand, it is possible for the manager to rank the relative merits of the two plans for each intangible factor.

The example utilizes a scale from 1 to 10 to measure factor outcomes (the value of 1 represents the best possible result and the value of 10, the least desirable). This is because the table is written in terms of costs. (The value of 10 would be optimal if the table had been constructed in terms of profit.) Thus, with respect to community attitude, Plan 1 is preferred to Plan 2. On the whole, both seem to be considered desirable. With respect to flexibility, Plan 2 is inferior to Plan 1.

Let us turn to the third column in the table, "Weight." These weighting factors (or index numbers) represent the relative importances of the set of outcome objectives being analyzed. According to the weights that have been assigned, product quality is the most important consideration, whereas community attitude is least important. Flexibility is rated as being slightly less important than costs. This arrangement of weighting values would change if the company's capitalization were altered or if the planning objectives were modified. The numbers we have used represent assignments for a particular set of individuals and circumstances.

Various approaches can be used for obtaining the weights. These include: (1) Using the estimates of that individual who is responsible for this decision. (2) Using an average value obtained by pooling the opinions of Lasermakers' top executives, who have different responsibilities with respect to the decision. (3) Employing an informal blending of the opinions of Lasermakers' executives to develop a set of estimates and weights that are agreeable to all parties.

A noteworthy characteristic of the third approach is that it creates an interfunctional opportunity for project participants to communicate about the facility decision. They can do this: First, with respect to which factors are likely to be critical determinants of the decision. Second, concerning the estimates of the outcomes for each of the factors, a set of which must be supplied for each of the alternative plans. Third, with respect to the selection of the weights which indicate the relative importance in each executive's mind for the critical factors required to evaluate the system. For problems of this kind, the scoring model's multiplication method of evaluating alternatives by means of weighting factors is reasonable and frequently used.[1]

This approach, which Lasermakers' management has decided to employ, was chosen because it is the best one that is suitable for dealing with intangible factors. The company's profits are not good. In better years, the profit and loss statement pleased stockholders and the investment bankers. Now, the company's performance has been marginal. As the controller points out, the problem has not been with the hard numbers relating to production quality. Lasermakers uses flow shop production, and the lines have been well balanced. It has been the inefficiencies of intangibles that have eroded profits. Perhaps, just because of the rigorous line design, worker morale has been poor. In turn, the community has not been supportive.

This approach requires that location preference be expressed as a ratio of the products of the outcomes raised to powers for each plan. We compare the plans in ratio with each other. The comparison measure is R.

$$R = \frac{\text{preference for location 1}}{\text{preference for location 2}}$$

$$= \left(\frac{O_{11}}{O_{21}}\right)^{w_1} \left(\frac{O_{12}}{O_{22}}\right)^{w_2} (\cdots) \left(\frac{O_{1j}}{O_{2j}}\right)^{w_i} (\cdots) \left(\frac{O_{1n}}{O_{2n}}\right)^{w_n}$$

Estimates are supplied to describe the values of the various outcomes each location will produce. For the ith location we would measure each

---

[1]See, for example, the use of this method to evaluate alternative aircraft designs as used by a major aircraft manufacturer. L. Ivan Epstein, "A Proposed Measure for Determining the Value of a Design," *The Journal of the Operations Research Society of America*, 5, 2 (April 1957), pp. 297–299. Also, C. Radhakrishna Rao, *Advanced Statistical Methods in Biometric Research* (New York: Wiley, 1952), p. 103; also, see Walter R. Stahl, "Similarity and Dimensional Methods in Biology," *Science*, 137, 20 (July 1962), pp. 205–212, and P. W. Bridgman, *Dimensional Analysis* (New Haven, Conn.: Yale University Press, 1922); this is also available in paperbound edition, 1963.

factor outcome: $O_{i1}, O_{i2}, \ldots, O_{ij}, \ldots, O_{in}$. Each outcome is then weighted for its relative importance. Call the weighting factors $w_1, w_2, \ldots, w_j, \ldots, w_n$.

The ratio R is a pure number, meaning that it has no dimensions. For example:

$$\frac{(\$)^{w_1}(\text{quality})^{w_2}}{(\$)^{w_1}(\text{quality})^{w_2}} = \text{pure number}$$

If all outcomes are measured in the same dimension (e.g., dollars), this approach would incorrectly treat a single dimension as though it were many outcomes having a variety of dimensional properties.

In Lasermakers' numerical example, presented in Table 9–1, all costs are based on a one-year period, so we can add them together. This yields $570,000 and $350,000, respectively, for alternatives 1 and 2. Accordingly, the comparison is:

$$R = \frac{\text{preference for location 1}}{\text{preference for location 2}} = \left(\frac{570,000}{350,000}\right)^4 \left(\frac{1}{2}\right)^1 \left(\frac{2}{3}\right)^5 \left(\frac{1}{6}\right)^3 = 0.002$$

$$= \frac{1}{500} = \frac{\text{costs of Plan 1}}{\text{costs of Plan 2}}$$

With this result, Lasermakers will choose location 1 because the ratio is less than 1. The costs of location 2 (in the denominator) are greater than the costs of location 1 (in the numerator). Accordingly, the choice is the alternative in the numerator.

The method of evaluation that has been employed here is useful for a wide range of project-type decisions. It would be appropriate for product-design decisions, process- and service-design decisions, equipment selection, and plant-location plans. Lasermakers' executive committee accepted the Boston location. If it had not, there should be good explanations as to why that solution was rejected.

Facility Selection Using the Transportation Model

Now we will develop a transportation model to resolve the location decision in a different way. This model uses established costs of transportation. It determines optimal shipping patterns, where optimal is defined as the minimum total cost of transportation. When transportation costs dominate the facility location problem, a straightforward approach exists for analyzing this situation. By **transportation costs,** we mean the combined costs of moving raw materials to the plant and of transporting finished goods from the plant to one or more warehouses. To develop and illustrate the model, let us return to the Lasermakers situation. In Table 9–1 we did not consider transport costs. Now we do so.

It is determined that, on the average, the cost of moving raw materials to the Boston location is $6 per production unit. It is $3 to Camden. The cost of shipping from the Boston location to the distributor's warehouse is $2 per unit; from Camden, it is $4 per unit. These data are shown in Fig. 9–3. Total transportation costs for the Boston location are $8 per unit; for Camden, they are $7. Therefore, Lasermakers would choose Camden.

We can complicate the problem by creating two distributors' warehouses (called markets) and by allowing the possibility of multiple facilities. Figure 9–4 illustrates this situation, which fits the pattern of a simple distribution problem. The question is this: Which facilities should ship how much to which warehouses? The problem can be resolved by means of the generalized transportation algorithm, which is described below. At this time, we solve the problem by means of trial and error methods.

Using the costs specified in Fig. 9–4, we can prepare a transportation matrix (Table 9–2). The matrix cell entries are the costs of transporting finished goods from factory i to market j. (*Note:* Factories are distinguished by rows, $i = 1, 2$. Markets are represented by columns, $j = 1, 2$.) In the case of Lasermakers, $i = 1$ stands for Boston location and $i = 2$ represents Camden. Also, we have added the description of supply and demand. Thus, each market demands 40 units per day to be shipped from either F1 or F2, or a combination. Both factories can be designed so that they will have a maximum productive capacity of 90 units per day. Which

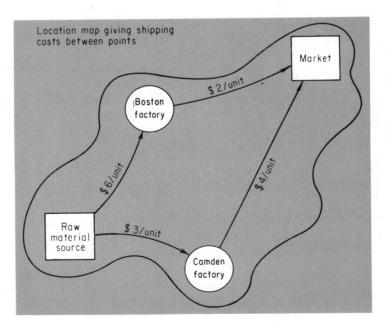

FIGURE 9-3. Plant-location problem (where only one market and one raw material source exist).

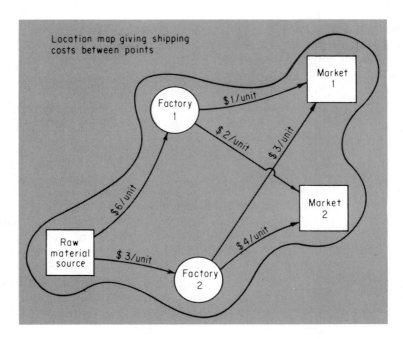

FIGURE 9-4. Plant-location problem—factory 1, factory 2, or both? (where two markets and one raw material source exist).

location should be chosen for Lasermakers' factory? We allow the possibility of choosing both.

In the first place, note that total daily supply potential exceeds total daily demand by 100 units, assuming that both factories operate at full capacity. (We will not permit this to occur.) To correct the theoretical imbalance between supply and demand, we create a slack, or dummy market (DM), to absorb 100 units per day. The market does not really exist. Therefore, whichever factory is assigned the job of supplying the dummy market is, in effect, eliminated as a location.[2]

A possible pattern of shipments is shown in Table 9–3. If this were the optimal solution, we would interpret this matrix as stating that F_2 is the

TABLE 9.2

Factory (F_i)	Raw Material Transport Costs	Market (M_i)		Supply
		M_1	M_2	
F_1	$6/unit	$1/unit	$2/unit	90 units/day
F_2	$3/unit	$3/unit	$4/unit	90 units/day
	Demand	40 units/day	40 units/day	

---

[2]Dummies are used to balance supply and demand in Chapters 11 and 12.

TABLE 9-3

Factory	M₁	Market M₂	DM	Supply
F_1			90	90
F_2	40	40	10	90
Demand	40	40	100	180

best location because it supplies the real markets, M_1 and M_2. Further, F_1 should be eliminated because it has been assigned the task of supplying the dummy market, which does not exist. We also note that the excess capacity of F_2 has been allocated to the dummy, which means that F_2 will work at ⁸⁄₉ of capacity, supplying only real demand.

Is this result really the best solution? The best numerical solution will result in minimum total transportation costs, so we must find out if there is any better arrangement. The matrix of total transportation costs would be as shown in Table 9–4. The raw material transportation costs have been added to the finished goods transportation costs. Any shipments to the dummy market cost $0, because it does not exist.

Total Cost Procedures for Solving the Transportation Problem

Step 1. Start with any solution that balances supply and demand (we have done this in Table 9–3 above).

Question: What is the total cost of the shipping plan described in Table 9–3? There are 40 units shipped from F_2 to M_1 at $6 per unit, or $240, and an additional 40 units are shipped from F_2 to M_2 at $7 per unit, or $280. The total cost is $240 + $280, which equals $520 per day.

Step 2. Choose the lowest-cost nonassigned cell, and find out what the effect of moving 1 unit to that cell will be. That is, will total shipment costs increase or decrease? Make sure that the supply and demand totals are unchanged. This requires subtracting one unit and adding one unit at

TABLE 9-4   TOTAL TRANSPORT COSTS PER UNIT

Factory	M₁	Market M₂	DM
F_1	6 + 1 = $7	6 + 2 = $8	$0
F_2	3 + 3 = $6	3 + 4 = $7	$0

TABLE 9-5

Factory	M₁	Market M₂	DM	Supply
F_1	1		89	90
F_2	39	40	11	90
Demand	40	40	100	

appropriate places in the matrix. If no saving is obtained, go to the next lower cost cell and do the same. Test every nonassigned cell.

Question: Can we lower the cost of $520 by shipping one unit from F_1 to M_1? If we ship one unit from F_1 to M_1, we must rearrange the total shipping schedule, as shown in Table 9–5. The total cost of this shipping arrangement is:

$$(\$7 \times 1) + (\$6 \times 39) + (\$7 \times 40) = \$521 \text{ per day}$$

Because 1 unit shipped from F_1 to M_1 produces a greater total cost, more than 1 unit shipped in this way will be even worse.

Can we lower the total cost by shipping 1 unit from F_1 to M_2? See Table 9–6.
The total cost result is:

$$(\$8 \times 1) + (\$6 \times 40) + (\$7 \times 39) = \$521 \text{ per day}$$

Again, no decrease in total cost has been found. Because no other possibilities exist for alternate shipping routes, we conclude that the original solution was optimal. The location to be chosen is factory 2 in Camden.

Step 3. If a decrease in total cost is obtained, then ship as many units as possible to the location where one unit produced a decrease.

An Illustration. Assume that a starting assignment pattern (Step 1) has been selected as shown in Table 9–7.

TABLE 9-6

Factory	M₁	Market M₂	DM	Supply
F_1		1	89	90
F_2	40	39	11	90
Demand	40	40	100	

Step 1.

TABLE 9-7

	Market			
Factory	M_1	M_2	DM	Supply
F_1	40		50	90
F_2		40	50	90
Demand	40	40	100	180

Question: What is the total cost of the shipping plan described in Table 9–7? The total cost is:

$$(\$7 \times 40) + (\$7 \times 40) = \$560 \text{ per day}$$

Step 2. The lowest nonassigned cost is $6 at F_2, M_1. Table 9–8 illustrates the pattern for testing one unit at the $6 location.
The new total cost is:

$$(\$7 \times 39) + (\$6 \times 1) + (\$7 \times 40) = \$559$$

Step 3. We have decreased total cost. Therefore, move as many units as possible to the new location. We can move 39 units from F_1, M_1 to F_2, M_1. Then we must increase F_1, DM by 39 and decrease F_2, DM by 39. Table 9–9 shows the resulting shipping assignment. As we know from our previous tests of the matrix, we cannot improve upon this result. If we did not know this fact, we would continue testing.

Northwest Corner Method. Now we consider a slightly more elaborate example, where up to three factories might supply two markets. The cost entries in Table 9–9 are total transportation costs per unit. Assume that Lasermakers has an actual operating factory F_1, which has a maximum capacity of 50 units per day. The demand for the product is greater than the supply, 80 units per day. The locations F_2 and F_3 are under serious consideration. Whichever is chosen, it has been decided to install a production capacity of 90 units per day. As before, we assume that transportation costs dominate the plant location decision.

TABLE 9-8

	Market			
Factory	M_1	M_2	DM	Supply
F_1	39		51	90
F_2	1	40	49	90
Demand	40	40	100	

TABLE 9-9

Factory	Market M_1	M_2	DM	Supply
F_1	$7/unit	$8/unit	$0/unit	50 units/day
F_2	$6/unit	$7/unit	$0/unit	90 units/day
F_3	$8/unit	$10/unit	$0/unit	90 units/day
Demand	40 units per day	40 units per day	150 units per day	230 units per day

Let us make our initial assignment pattern conform to the northwest corner method described below (see Table 9–10). Again, supply and demand are balanced with a dummy market, DM.

To use the northwest corner method, we begin in the upper lefthand corner of the matrix and allocate as many units as possible to F_1, M_1. This is 40 units. More than 40 units would exceed demand. We assign as many units as are allowed by whichever constraint dominates, the row constraint of 50 units or the column constraint of 40. In this case, it is the column constraint, so 40 units are entered at F_1, M_1. But F_1 still has 10 units of unassigned supply. These 10 units can be assigned at F_1, M_2. All of F_1's supply is now allocated. However, M_2 still requires 30 units. These are assigned from F_2 (we move down in the matrix and to the right). F_2 then has 60 unallocated units remaining. These are assigned to DM (and therefore they will not be made or shipped). To complete the matrix, F_3's supply of 90 units must be allocated. We place them in the F_3, DM cell.

The northwest corner method will always satisfy the requirement for an initial feasible solution, but so would a procedure that starts at any corner. Whatever method is used to obtain an initial feasible solution, it must produce:

$$M + N - 1 \text{ assignments}$$

given a matrix with N rows and M columns. This number does not apply only to initial solutions; it applies to all intermediate solutions, and to the final and optimal solution as well.

TABLE 9-10

Factory	Market M_1	M_2	DM	Supply
F_1	40	10		50
F_2		30	60	90
F_3			90	90
Demand	40	40	150	230

The number of shipments used should never exceed $M + N - 1$, where:

$$M = \text{the number of markets}$$

$$N = \text{the number of factories}$$

For the example above, we have $3 + 3 - 1 = 5$, which is the number of shipments derived by means of the northwest corner rule. We can never obtain a better solution with more than five shipments, and usually we would obtain a worse one. Although the logic of this point is indisputable, the most convincing demonstrations can be derived by working through a few simple examples, such as one factory and many markets or two factories and many markets.[3]

Marginal Cost Procedures for the Transportation Problem

We now test to find out whether a cost reduction can be achieved. There are four possible changes that could be made in the shipping pattern of Table 9–10.

1. We could shift 10 units from F_1, M_2 to F_1, DM (see Table 9–11). If more than 10 units were shifted, this would create a negative shipment at the intersection of F_1, M_2, a situation that could not be tolerated. Similar restrictions exist with respect to other changes.
2. We can shift 30 units from F_2, M_2 to F_2, M_1.
3. We can shift 30 units from F_2, M_2 to F_3, M_1.
4. We can shift 30 units from F_2, M_2 to F_3, M_2.

Let us evaluate the change in marginal cost that will result from shipping one unit from F_1 to DM.

1. Ship 1 unit from F_1 to DM: + \$0
2. Ship 1 less unit from F_1 to M_2:   − \$8
3. Ship 1 more unit from F_2 to M_2: + \$7
4. Ship 1 less unit from F_2 to DM: − \$0
                                Total: − \$1

---

[3]There is an exception which results in less than $M + N - 1$ assignments, called the state of **degeneracy**. This condition is a purely technical problem, which can always be resolved by adding a negligible amount to an appropriate row or column total. There is no exception that results in more than $M + N - 1$ assignments.

TABLE 9-11

| Factory | Market | | | Supply |
	M_1	M_2	DM	
F_1	40		10	50
F_2		40	50	90
F_3			90	90
Demand	40	40	150	230

The total cost can be reduced one dollar by making this change. Each of 10 units can be shipped for $1 less per unit. This is a total cost reduction of $110. Proceeding in the same fashion, we find the change in marginal cost for the other three options discussed above.

1. Shipping 1 unit from F_2 to M_1 produces zero change.
2. Shipping 1 unit from F_3 to M_1 would result in extra expense of $2 per unit.
3. Shipping 1 unit from F_3 to M_2 would result in extra expense of $3 per unit.

Accordingly, we choose the first option and shift 10 units from F_1, M_2 to F_1, DM. The new transportation matrix has already been shown in Table 9–11.

We have tested this arrangement to see if any other savings can be made (Table 9–12). The marginal cost changes that would result from further modification of the shipping pattern are shown in the circles of the matrix in Table 9–12. Additional improvement is possible. Forty units can be shifted from F_1, M_1 to F_2, M_1. As Table 9–13 shows, we would then have:

TABLE 9-12

| Factory | Market | | | Supply |
	M_1	M_2	DM	
F_1	40	(+1)	10	50
F_2	(−1)	40	50	90
F_3	(+1)	(+3)	90	90
Demand	40	40	150	230

The marginal cost analysis shows that no further improvements can be obtained. Because factories 1 and 3 ship only to the dummy, they will be eliminated. The solution also states that factory 2 will operate at 8/9 of capacity.

TABLE 9-13

Factory	Market M$_1$	M$_2$	DM	Supply
F$_1$	(+1)	(+1)	50	50
F$_2$	40	40	10	90
F$_3$	(+2)	(+3)	90	90
Demand	40	40	150	

We can see how the transportation method can be of real help to companies such as Lasermakers. Say there were production differentials at the various locations; for example, low taxes or high worker productivity at one location may result in a lower per unit production cost. This can be added in with shipping costs, making each row's costs higher by the per unit production costs of the supplier.

In Table 9–14, per unit production costs of the three facilities differ. This is a modification of Table 9–9, where the production costs are equal and therefore ignored. (Note that the dummy market's costs remain zero because we do not want to bias assignments to the dummy with costs that never actually appear.) Lasermakers could analyze alternative warehouse (market) locations. It could also study the effects of using different modes of transportation for the same route, such as train vs. plane vs. truck. The production cost differentials will play their parts.

The limitations of the transportation method should also be understood by management. The model is linear and does not reflect the many other factors that influence location decisions. Intangible factors have been ignored. When the intangibles are critical, the transportation cost differentials of the various alternatives can be combined with other costs and used with the intangible factors in a dimensional scoring model analysis. The trial and error procedure we have been using consists of evaluating the change in total costs that results from alternative shipping patterns for one unit. If a savings can be made by changing the pattern, then we put as many units as possible into the preferred location, creating a new shipment pattern. If per unit profits are available, then the calculations

TABLE 9-14

Factory Costs ($/Unit)	Factory	Market M$_1$ ($/Unit)	M$_2$ ($/Unit)	DM	Supply (units/day)
20	F$_1$	27	28	0	50
28	F$_2$	34	35	0	90
12	F$_3$	20	22	0	90
Demand (units/day)		40	40	150	230

can be reversed to determine total profits. Each empty cell is evaluated to learn whether a shipment of one unit to it would increase profit. In this way, locations can be found that will maximize total profit. There is no problem identifying the optimal assignment. When every empty cell is evaluated, and none of them produces a decrease in total cost, or increase in total profit, then the optimal solution has been found.

With a large matrix, this approach would take forever. Instead, we can call on a number of methods for finding the optimum assignments. They are based on algorithms that have been programmed for personal computers. See, for example, STORM—Transportation Programs, in Appendix A. Some of the algorithms use linear programming to solve the transportation problem. Others use network methods which evaluate the opportunity costs of making one assignment rather than another. The stepping-stone method, described below, is a network method. We also present the generalized transportation method as a means of deciding on locations of factories, plants, offices, warehouses, and so on.

The Stepping-Stone Method

Given that an initial feasible assignment of shipments has been made, two questions arise.

1. How do we use an algorithm to evaluate the effect on the costs of shipping 1 unit to a nonassigned location of the transportation matrix?
2. How do we use an algorithm to determine the maximum number of units that can be shifted to a better assignment?

The stepping-stone approach is most easily described by example. Using the northwest corner approach we obtain the following initial assignment, where cost per unit of shipping is indicated within the box in the upper right-hand corner of every shipping assignment possibility. We can reverse the algorithm to maximize profits if the data for per unit profits is substituted for cost per unit.

	M_1	M_2	DM	Supply
F_1	7 40	8 10	0	50
F_2	6	7 30	0 60	90
F_3	8	10	0 90	90
Demand	40	40	150	230

To evaluate the effect on costs of reassigning shipments (question 1), choose any nonassigned cell and:

1. Move horizontally (along that row) until an assigned shipment is located that has another assignment in its same column. Thus, to evaluate the effect on costs of shipping one unit to F_3, M_1, move to F_3, DM (90).

2. Move vertically until an assigned shipment is located that has another assignment in its same row. Continuing with our example, move from F_3, DM (90) to F_2, DM (60).

3. Repeat step 1. In this case, move from F_2, DM (60) to F_2, M_2 (30).

4. Repeat step 2. In this case, move from F_2, M_2 (30) to F_1, M_2 (10).

5. Repeat step 1. In this case, move from F_1, M_2 (10) to F_1, M_1 (40).

6. We continue this pattern until we return to the starting point. In this case, the starting point was F_3, M_1 (no entry, but testing). We move from F_1, M_1 (40) to F_3, M_1 (to be evaluated).

The specific cost evaluation for 1 unit is as follows:

Add 1 unit to F_3, M_1	Added cost $8
Remove 1 unit from F_3, DM	Subtracted cost 0
Add 1 unit to F_2, DM	Added cost 0
Remove 1 unit from F_2, M_2	Subtracted cost $7
Add 1 unit to F_1, M_2	Added cost $8
Remove 1 unit from F_1, M_1	Subtracted cost $7

The net change is $+\$16 - \$14 = +\$2$, which would increase costs. Therefore, no shipment will be made to F_3, M_1. The pattern of change is shown in Fig. 9–5.

This is called the stepping-stone method, because assigned shipments are the only "stones" that can be counted as part of the path, and only horizontal and vertical paths are permitted. There is always 1 path, and only 1 path, that will complete a circuit.

This statement is valid for any shipment pattern that conforms to the $M + N - 1$ requirement of the (linear) transportation model. Occasionally, a degenerate shipping pattern arises, where the number of assignments is less than $M + N - 1$. In this case, the symbol epsilon (ϵ) should be added to the missing stepping stone. Epsilon is evaluated as so close

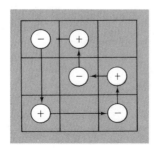

FIGURE 9-5.

to zero that it will not affect the final solution, but will allow the path circuit to be completed (see Problem 5, p. 461).

We now turn to question 2. How do we determine the maximum number of units that can be shifted from one assignment to another? We are talking now about shipping amounts and not costs. The smallest number of units, associated with the subtracted costs $\ominus$, is the maximum number of units that can be shifted. Thus, in our example, these are (90 at F_3 DM), (30 at F_2, M_2), and (40 at F_1, M_1). Consequently, no more than 30 units can be entered at F_3, M_1. If more than this number of units were assigned to F_3, M_1, then a negative shipment assignment would occur at F_2, M_2, which is infeasible.

The Generalized Transportation Method

Many forms of problems, including the location decision, can be represented by the transportation model. Therefore, it is worthwhile to become familiar with an alternative method. This generalized method provides insight into the nature of the cost structure of the transportation model, and especially the role of opportunity costs in a solution. A side benefit is that the generalized method is faster for obtaining solutions by hand or computer.

Let us review the basic idea of the transportation method, namely: A supply of resources is to be allocated to users of those resources in such a way as to find a pattern of allocation that minimizes costs or maximizes profits. Each source, shipper, or producer can split its allocations among users. The output of several sources can be assigned to a single user. These relations are reflected in the matrix below, where the cost of shipping one unit from a particular producer P_i to a specific consumer C_j is stated as c_{ij}:

Consumers

		C_1	C_2	C_3	$\cdots$	C_j	$\cdots$	C_m	Supply
	P_1	c_{11}	c_{12}	c_{13}		c_{1j}		c_{1m}	s_1
	P_2	c_{21}	c_{22}	c_{23}		c_{2j}		c_{2m}	s_2
	P_3	c_{31}	c_{32}	c_{33}		c_{3j}		c_{j3m}	s_3
	.								.
	.								.
Producers	.								.
	P_i	c_{i1}	c_{i2}	c_{i3}		c_{ij}		c_{im}	s_i
	.								.
	.								.
	.								.
	P_n	c_{n1}	c_{n2}	c_{n3}		c_{nj}		c_{nm}	s_n
	Demand	d_1	d_2	d_3	$\cdots$	d_j	$\cdots$	d_m	

Constraints on producers' supplies (in a given time period) are indicated by s_i values and consumers' demands are shown by d_j values.

First, let us consider a 2×2 transportation matrix, with the given values for supplies and demands for the period, and unit costs of allocation, as shown:

	C_1	C_2	Supply
P_1	4	6	600
P_2	2	5	400
Demand	300	700	1000

The minimum cost allocations can be determined by: First, finding any feasible allocation pattern (i.e., a pattern that properly matches supply and demand totals); second, examining the effects of making changes in that pattern; third, making changes that assure improvement; and fourth, stopping when no further improvement can be obtained. The similarity to linear programming rules (see pp. 620–621) is hardly accidental. Transportation models can always be solved by LP methods.

A. How do we quickly derive a jumping-off solution?
B. How can the patterns of reassignment be evaluated rapidly?
C. How do we find the maximum amount that can be reassigned?

Let us consider each of these questions. We will use a larger example (Matrix I) as our basis for discussion.

MATRIX 1

	C_1	C_2	C_3	Supply
P_1	4 50	6	3	50
P_2	2 50	5 110	8	160
P_3	7	3 190	2 60	250
P_4	4	5	6 140	140
Demand	100	300	200	600

Total cost $= 50(4) + 50(2) + 110(5) + 190(3) + 60(2) + 140(6)$
$= 2380$

To answer question A, we use the northwest corner method. Thus, starting in the upper left-hand corner, as many units are assigned to P_1C_1 as is allowed by whichever constraint dominates, the row constraint of 50 or the column constraint of 100. In this case, it is the row constraint, so 50 units are entered at P_1C_1, but the C_1 column still has 50 units of unfilled demand. These can be assigned at P_2C_1. However, all of P_2's supply is not yet assigned. In fact, 110 units can be assigned at P_2C_2, which leaves 190 units of C_2 demand unfilled. Continuing in this way, we complete the total matrix of assignments.

For question B, the net costs of all assignments that have not been made can be determined by the stepping-stone method.

Now let's focus on the generalized transportation method (also called the modified, or MODI, method).

Step 1. Write the matrix of actual costs, (c_{ij}) called (Matrix II).

Step 2. Create a new matrix (Matrix III) where only those costs are entered that represent assignments, as in Matrix I with its northwest corner assignments. Circle each assignment's cost.

MATRIX II

	C_1	C_2	C_3
P_1	4	6	3
P_2	2	5	8
P_3	7	3	2
P_4	4	5	6

MATRIX III

	C_1	C_2	C_3
P_1	④		
P_2	②	⑤	
P_3		③	②
P_4			⑥

Step 3. Develop row and column costs for Matrix III, such that every circled entry equals the sum of its row cost plus its column cost. The first cost we choose is 0. It can be entered for any row or column (Matrix IV). Thereafter, all other row and column costs are determined by the numbers in the matrix.

MATRIX IV

	C_1	C_2	C_3	Row Costs
P_1	④			0
P_2	②	⑤		-2
P_3		③	②	-4
P_4			⑥	0
Column Costs	4	7	6	

Next:

1. Arbitrarily, we assign the 0 cost to row P_i.
2. Then the cost assigned to column C_i must be 4, since $0 + 4$ must equal ④ at P_1, C_1.
3. The cost assigned to row P_2 must be -2, since $-2 + 4$ must equal ② at P_2, C_1.
4. The cost assigned to column C_2 must be 7, since $-2 + 7$ must equal ⑤ at P_2, C_2.
5. The cost assigned to row P_3 must be -4, since $-4 + 7$ must equal ③ at P_3, C_2.
6. The cost assigned to column C_3 must be 6, since $-4 + 6$ must equal ② at P_3, C_3.
7. The cost assigned to row P_4 must be 0, since $0 + 6$ must equal ⑥ at P_4, C_3.

Step 4. Complete Matrix IV by entering calculated costs in all empty matrix cells. Each entry equals the sum of the row cost plus the column cost. For example, the cost at P_2, C_3 is equal to $-2 + 6 = 4$. This yields Matrix V.

Step 5. From Matrix II, cell by cell, subtract Matrix V. Zeros will occur at every circled entry. This produces Matrix VI, which is the opportunity cost matrix that would have been derived from calculations of every stepping-stone path in Matrix I.

FIRST ITERATION

MATRIX V

	C_1	C_2	C_3	Row Costs
P_1	④	7	6	0
P_2	②	⑤	4	-2
P_3	0	③	②	-4
P_4	4	7	⑥	0
Column Costs	4	7	6	

MATRIX VI   THE OPPORTUNITY COST MATRIX

	C_1	C_2	C_3
P_1	0	-1	-3
P_2	0	0	$+4$
P_3	$+7$	0	0
P_4	0	-2	0

Step 6. Change Matrix I assignments by selecting the largest negative value in Matrix VI (this is -3 at P_1, C_3) and assigning as many units as possible to it. The biggest per unit cost saving can be made in this manner— a net decrease of \$3 for each unit shipped to P_1, C_3. Matrix VII presents the new assignment pattern.

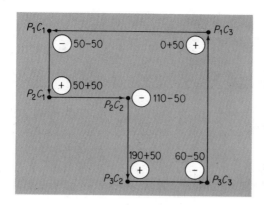

FIGURE 9-6. The pattern for transferring units to $P_1 C_3$.

FIRST ITERATION

MATRIX VII

	C_1	C_2	C_3	Supply
P_1			50	50
P_2	100	60		160
P_3		240	10	250
P_4			140	140
Demand	100	300	200	600

Total Cost

$50 \times 3 = 150$

$100 \times 2 = 200$

$60 \times 5 = 300$

$240 \times 3 = 720$

$10 \times 2 = 20$

$140 \times 6 = \underline{840}$

2230

Now, to answer question C: How do we determine the maximum amount that can be shifted? This is answered in the stepping-stone material. Fig. 9–6 shows the pattern of units shifted; below, we describe the specific operations.

How many units can be entered at $P_1 C_3$? The pattern for unit changes must be examined in terms of how many units are presently assigned to each "take out" position (indicated by negative signs in Fig. 9–6's network). The smallest such number with a negative sign is the answer. Otherwise, some assignments would become negative, which violates the feasibility condition. Thus, no more than 50 units (at $P_1 C_1$) can be reassigned.

Having completed the reassignment of 50 units to $P_1 C_3$, we now go through steps 1 to 6 again. We continue reassigning until no more negative numbers appear in Matrix VI; no further improvement is possible. This is shown in the following Matrices.

MATRIX V'

	C_1	C_2	C_3	Row Costs
P_1	1	4	③	3
P_2	②	⑤	4	4
P_3	0	③	②	2
P_4	4	7	⑥	6
Column Costs	−2	1	0	

MATRIX VI'

	C_1	C_2	C_3
P_1	+3	+2	0
P_2	0	0	+4
P_3	+7	0	0
P_4	0	−2	0

This time, we began our computations for Matrix V' by placing the zero in column 3. From Matrix VI', we see that as many units as possible should be shipped to P_4, C_2, where an opportunity cost of − 2 exists.

From Matrix VII, we derive Matrix VII' based on shifting 140 units from P_4, C_3 to P_4, C_2. Thus:

SECOND ITERATION

Total Cost

$50 \times 3 = 150$

$100 \times 2 = 200$

$60 \times 5 = 300$

$100 \times 3 = 300$

$150 \times 2 = 300$

$140 \times 5 = \underline{700}$

1950

MATRIX VII'

	C_1	C_2	C_3	Supply
P_1			50	50
P_2	100	60		160
P_3		100	150	250
P_4		140		140
Demand	100	300	200	600

We evaluate this pattern with a third iteration to see if any further improvement is possible.

THIRD ITERATION

MATRIX V''

	C_1	C_2	C_3	
P_1	1	4	③	4
P_2	②	⑤	4	5
P_3	0	③	②	3
P_4	2	⑤	4	5
	−3	0	−1	

MATRIX VI''

	C_1	C_2	C_3
P_1	+3	+2	0
P_2	0	0	+4
P_3	+7	0	0
P_4	+2	0	+2

The answer is No. *All opportunity cost evaluations are positive.* Total cost has decreased with each new iteration:

From a northwest corner assignment total cost of $2,380
To a first iteration total cost of $2,230
To a second iteration total cost of $1,950
To a third iteration—STOP

We have reached the final solution. The total cost cannot be less than $1,950. Had a zero opportunity cost appeared in the cost evaluations of Matrix VI″ (other than the assigned zeros), this would have signified that alternatives existed. The P/OM decides which of the minimum cost alternatives is preferred. Note that the final solution has six assignments. Thus, it meets the condition $M + N - 1 = 4 + 3 - 1 = 6$. When supply and demand are not equal, a dummy slack variable having all zero unit costs can be created to take care of this situation. The dummy, whether it be needed for the rows or columns, is meant to take up the slack. Whatever is assigned to it is not done.

Finally, if we wish to use the transportation model to achieve profit maximization rather than cost minimization, the rule concerning which new assignment is preferred is reversed. The largest possible plus-valued opportunity cost evaluation is chosen to be entered in the network. The procedure stops when all evaluations are negative.

The transportation model is well-suited for location analysis. It does not require a square matrix, and the solutions require relatively little time to compute. On the other hand, it is linear, since unit costs or profits are not able to be changed as a function of volume. Also, since each matrix applies to a specific period, no allowance is made for interdependencies over time.

The generalized transportation method works by setting a zero opportunity cost on all entries in the assignment that is being evaluated. Then row and column opportunity costs are developed to determine the per unit opportunity costs of all possible shipment entries that are not in the assignment. If any of the nonassigned possibilities reveals a negative opportunity cost the largest of these is entered, and a new assignment pattern is developed and tested for further possible improvement. The basis of the solution for any transportation problem is the minimization of opportunity costs realized by shifting assignments between rows and columns, or suppliers and producers.

PROBLEM
SET

1. How do the total cost and marginal cost procedures differ from the stepping-stone and generalized transportation methods?

2. For the matrix below, use trial and error methods to answer questions b, c, and d. (For parts b, c, and d, show the revised shipping assignment.)

a. Ignoring the boxes marked with x, what kind of shipping assignment has been made?

b. What is the maximum number of units that can be shipped to x_1?

c. What is the maximum number of units that can be shipped to x_2?

d. What is the maximum number of units that can be shipped to x_3?

		1	2	3	4	
	A	30	x_1		x_2	30
	B	40				40
	C	10	40			50
From	D		20	10		30
	E			20	40	60
	F				20	20
	G	x_3			10	10
		80	60	30	70	240

(To, columns 1 2 3 4)

3.

MATRIX 1

	1	2	3
A	10	6	
B		12	2
C			12

MATRIX 2

	1	2	3
A	10		6
B		12	2
C		6	6

To evaluate different shipping assignment patterns, Matrix 1 was changed to Matrix 2 by adding 6 units at A_3. As a result, three cells have been altered.

a. What problem does this suggest?

b. If instead 2 units had been put in at A_3, what shipping pattern would have resulted?

c. How many cells would have been altered?

d. Why is the shipping pattern suggested in (b) preferred?

4. Based on trial and error reasoning, what is the optimal assignment for the transportation problem below?

MATRIX OF SHIPMENTS
(with northwest corner assignments)

	1	2	3	Supply
A	10	6		16
B		12	2	14
C			12	12
Demand	10	18	14	42

MATRIX OF SHIPPING
COSTS

	1	2	3
A	6	10	5
B	8	3	7
C	9	4	2

5. In the shipping matrix below, the manager wishes to shift 6 units from A_1 to A_2.

	1	2	Supply
A	6		6
B	12	6	18
Demand	18	6	24

a. What happens to the shipping matrix as a result of this move? What is that condition called?

b. To use the stepping-stone method, what must the manager do to the matrix?

6. The industries listed below tend to form high-density clusters in specific geographic areas. Is there a rational explanation for the specific clusters?

a. Financial services

b. Automobiles

c. Stockyards

d. Textiles

e. Semiconductors

f. Aerospace

g. Resort hotels

h. Motion pictures

i. Publishing

j. Cigarettes

k. Steel

l. Petroleum

Answers: Many factors operate to create geographic clustering. Obvious answers may not be correct or may be only partial explanations of complex, multidimensional systems of factors. First, there are historical reasons that may be lost in time. For example, canals offered cheap water transport to the New England factories. A second possible variable is that of "follow the leader." A company might assume that, since a competitor is operating successfully in a given area, it too can move there with less risk because of the precedent and empirical evidence that the area is at least satisfactory. The next company in this industry faced with a location problem now sees two companies operating in this area and moves in with even less trepidation. For the fifth company, the decision to move anywhere but to this same region is fraught with danger, because it runs contrary to practice. People with certain skills begin to cluster. Further, suppliers cluster around their customers, especially as just-in-time practice expands. Area advantages can change, improving or deteriorating as a result of clustering. For example, an entire region can suffer from aging plant. This accounted for the New England textile industry moving to the South. Answers for specific industry clustering are left to student research. The benefits of industry-specific analyses for the study of P/OM are significant.

7. The Omicron Company has two factories, A and B, located in Wilmington, Delaware, and San Francisco, California, respectively. Each has a production capacity of 550 units per week. Omicron's markets are Los Angeles, Chicago, and New York. The demands of these markets are for 150, 350, and 400 units, respectively, in the coming week. A matrix of shipping distances is prepared, and the shipping schedule is determined to minimize total shipping distance. Estimate the distances and solve this problem on that basis.

Answer: Using the approach outlined on pp. 448–451, we first estimate the shipping distances (in thousands of miles) as follows:

	Los Angeles	Chicago	New York
(A) Wilmington	3.0	1.0	0.3
(B) San Francisco	0.4	2.0	3.0

An initial solution is determined by the northwest corner rule. (Note that the use of a dummy market is required to compensate for the fact that supply exceeds demand. Also, the distances assigned to the dummy are zero.)

	Los Angeles	Chicago	New York	Dummy	Supply
(A) Wilmington	150	350	50	0	550
(B) San Francisco	0	0	350	200	550
Demand	150	350	400	200	1100

This northwest corner allocation produces a shipping schedule with a total distance of:

$$1000 [150(3) + 350(1) + 50(0.3) + 350(3) + 200(0)]$$
$$= 1,865,000 \text{ miles}$$

If we modify the northwest corner allocation, we could, for example, ship 350 units from San Francisco to Chicago. This eliminates the 350 units to be shipped from San Francisco to New York, as well as the 350 units from Wilmington to Chicago. We now have 400 units going from Wilmington to New York. The change in total distance would be:

$$1000 [350(2) - 350(3) + 350(0.3) - 350(1)] = -595,000 \text{ miles}$$

which is a substantial improvement. The new matrix is then:

	Los Angeles	Chicago	New York	Dummy	Supply
(A) Wilmington	150	0	400	0	550
(B) San Francisco	0	350	0	200	550
Demand	150	350	400	200	1100

In the same way, a further saving can be made by shifting 150 San Francisco units from Chicago to Los Angeles. Thus:

	Los Angeles	Chicago	New York	Dummy	Supply
(A) Wilmington	0	150	400	0	550
(B) San Francisco	150	200	0	200	550
Demand	150	350	400	200	1100

A check of the matrix will reveal that no further distance savings can be obtained by shifting any units, so this must be the optimal arrangement. The minimum total distance is:

$$1000 [150(0.4) + 150(1) + 200(2) + 400(0.3)] = 730,000 \text{ miles}$$

8. Omicron decides to build a third plant. The best locations are Chicago, Illinois, and Cleveland, Ohio. The new plant would have a productive capacity of 400 units. Keeping the market demands unchanged from Problem 7 above, what should Omicron do?

9. Use the dimensional scoring method described on pp. 437–441 to resolve the following long-term decision problem. An equipment choice is to be made between two alternative computer designs, and the following data have been obtained:

	Design 1	Design 2
Cost	$0.5 million	$0.6 million
Speed	2	1
Memory	3	2
Flexibility	4	5
Size	50 square feet	40 square feet

Characteristics are scaled so that large numbers are less desirable than small numbers. Establish your own weighting factors for each of the cases below, and comment on the way that the choice changes as a function of the particular point of view that is employed.

a. The computer manufacturer in terms of the potential market.

b. A mail-order company where the unit will control inventory.

c. A NASA systems manufacturer operating under government contract, where the unit will be used for scientific calculations.

Answer: For a mail-order company, memory size and cost are very important. Speed is relatively important (depending upon the specific circumstances). Physical size and flexibility play secondary roles. An appropriate set of weighting factors might be:

Item	Factor
Cost	5
Speed	3
Memory size	6
Flexibility	1
Size	1

Using the methods of pp. 440–441, we can write:

$$\frac{\text{Preference for design 1}}{\text{Preference for design 2}} = \left(\frac{0.5}{0.6}\right)^5 \left(\frac{2}{1}\right)^3 \left(\frac{3}{2}\right)^6 \left(\frac{4}{5}\right)^1 \left(\frac{50}{40}\right)^1$$

$$= \frac{9375}{256} > 1$$

We would therefore choose design 2 in this case.

Similar analysis applies to the other examples. Here too, assigning values and estimating weights can lead to interesting discussions, which ultimately produce results similar to the one above. The computer manufacturer might stress flexibility, or size, or memory, depending upon its marketing philosophy. Actual company product lines exist that represent such differences in market segmentation. The NASA-system manufacturer will care less about cost, but is likely to emphasize size and flexibility.

10. For the supply and demand situation, shown with costs in the matrix below, what is the optimal transportation pattern?

	C_1	C_2	Supply
	4	6	
P_1	100	500	600
	2	5	
P_2	200	200	400
Demand	300	700	1000

Note: Problems 3, 4, 5, 7, 8, and 10 can be solved by the stepping-stone method or the generalized transportation method.

Section 9.2 Equipment Selection

Without the proper tools and equipment, even a skilled and motivated worker is hard pressed to do more than a mediocre job. The design of work stations was discussed in Chapter 8, as well as the pros and cons of measuring worker performance. This section tries to capture the qualitative and quantitative interactions of equipment selection and equipment performance. Being able to estimate equipment performance is essential for the selection procedure. The estimates of performance cannot be naive. They must be used to explain expected variation in the qualities of the product.

Variance and Volume

Two major differences exist between equipment that can do essentially the same kind of work. First is the volume of transactions or production rate that each alternative can handle; second is the inherent variation of qualities associated with the equipment. Process variations must be compatible with tolerances that have been specified for product qualities (see Chapter 6).

For example, the cutting abilities of all lathes are not identical. Some can deliver product that is $\pm .01$, others can deliver product that is $\pm .0001$. We have already pointed out (above) the differences in their output volumes. For another example, all secretaries are not identical. Some can deliver 100 words per minute with one error per 10 pages, others can deliver 40 words per minute with 10 errors per page.

Interactions: Equipment Selection with Facility
Selection and Layout

The selection of equipment necessary to do the job precedes facility layout (discussed in Section 9.3). Ideally, facility layout would then precede facility selection. This chapter began with facility selection (Section 9.1) because the location problem is so important. However, the specific facility cannot be selected without considering the equipment it will house.

The equipment to be used has size and weight and height, and it causes certain things to happen, such as vibrations and noise. As a result, equipment dictates the facility design that can be used, but it does not influence facility location, except when the right kind of building happens to exist in a specific location. Many times, however, the facility selected is not perfect for the equipment and the flows between equipment. Then the facility layout must be arranged and rearranged to make a specific process fit a particular structure management has selected.

P/OMs have a pretty good idea of the equipment that will be required at the chosen facility, and therefore of the general adequacy of a particular structure. The process of deciding what to do is interactive going back and forth between facility selection, equipment selection and facility layout. For example, it is not unusual to find that equipment selection must bend to fit a selected facility.

Effects of Work Configurations and Life Cycle Stages

There are equipment selection methods that apply to the job shop or the project which enable the manager to choose between alternative equipment, machine, or work centers that do essentially the same job. But they do the jobs at different costs and output rates, and with different qualities of work. The differences can be significant. For example, the differences between:

A simple machine lathe to make a few similar pieces
A turret lathe to make a couple of dozen similar pieces
An automatic screw machine to make thousands of similar pieces

For another example, the differences between:

A single PC work station for a few calculations
A couple of PCs networked for many calculations
A mainframe computer for many more calculations
A supercomputer for an extremely large number of calculations

The methods for choosing between such equipment alternatives are discussed in Chapter 10.

For the carefully pre-engineered equipment systems which are characteristically found in the flow shop, or an FPS, or in a continuous processing system, equipment selection is much more intricately bound up with technology. Consequently, decision-making about these more capital-intensive systems requires the direct participation of technological experts in cooperation with financial analysts. We begin shortly with the application of discounted cash flow analysis. Our methods are general and do not get involved with specific technology, although relevant estimates about both present and proposed equipment performance are required from engineers and equipment manufacturers.

The effect of life cycle stages is significant. Equipment selection is related to proposed output volumes. Note the two examples given above. The first indicates different volumes for different lathes and the second shows variation in the number of calculations each computer setup is designed to handle. Over a product's life cycle, be it the lathe output rate or the computer output calculations, the volume of transactions is expected to change a great deal. Consequently, what is appropriate equipment for startup may have to be replaced for maturity. Planning is required to have used up or resold the equipment that is to be phased out when a transition in the life cycle stage occurs. Change takes place over time with the gradual deterioration in the performance of equipment. The effects of change must be factored into the life cycle considerations.

Discounting Analysis: Selecting among Equipment Alternatives

In Chapter 2, pp. 70–74, we developed a buy or rent analysis and a make or buy analysis. Now, we look at the question of how to choose equipment on an economic basis through financial analysis. We use **discounted cash flow (DCF) analysis.**

It is assumed that the technological features of the equipment are identical and that they will produce the same output qualities. This is a poor assumption which has to be changed at a later stage of the analysis. But, for the moment, we are just looking at the dollar estimates of costs and revenues. If this assumption is not acceptable, then it is necessary to employ a scoring model to perform a dimensional analysis for equipment selection, much in the same way it was previously used for facility selection. Money was only one of the factors used in the scoring model to make a facility selection. There was product quality, community attitude, and flexibility to adapt.

Let us determine the cost of equipment alternatives when several relevant factors change over time. For example, if we want to compare alternative facilities that have different expected service lifetimes and/or different operating costs that change as a function of usage and age, we apply discounting functions at all the appropriate points in the time streams of payments.

CASE: TIRE-MASTERS, INC.

To illustrate, Tiremasters, Inc., is planning to install an entirely new computer-controlled materials-handling system. The company has received two proposals for different arrangements of hand trucks, fork-lift trucks, cranes, and computerized conveyors. Each alternative represents an integrated materials handling system.

Operating costs in Table 9–15 must be related to optimal run sizes for the equipment served by the materials-handling facilities. Comparisons are sometimes made where the costs for one alternative are based on an efficient system, while the costs for the second alternative are based on an inefficient system.

TABLE 9-15

	Materials Handling System A	Materials Handling System B
Estimated service life	3 years	2 years
Investment	$25,000	$20,000
Discount factor	6 percent per year	6 percent per year
Operating cost per year	$2,000	$1,000

Equipment manufacturers have been known to use the following kind of argument when trying to sell their products: "You have nothing to lose in buying this equipment. If the savings obtained as a result of using the new equipment are not sufficient to pay for it, then we will gladly take it back and make a full refund." A manufacturer's representative can base this offer on the observation (not stated to the customer) that the operations on the present equipment are inefficient.

When the new equipment is installed, a thorough study will be made of how to utilize it. This will include efficient work routines and optimal production runs. Then, the advantage of the new equipment, at least in part, is connected with the development of optimal work routines rather than with the superiority of the new equipment derived from fundamental technological advances. If a study of the use of the present equipment is made, savings can also be realized. It is only on the basis of equally efficient use of equipment that an intelligent comparison of alternative facilities can be made.

The required comparison of the alternative materials-handling plans, A and B, is given below. The smallest common period for systems A and B is 6 years. During that period of time, system A will turn over twice, and system B will turn over 3 times. Then, using the discounting data (p. 79), for system A (2 cycles), we derive Table 9–16:

TABLE 9-16

End of Year	Investment A	Discounted Operating Costs	Total Discounted Cost	Average Cost per Year
0	$25,000 × 1.000 = $25,000		$25,000	
1		$2000 × 0.943 = $1886	26,886	$26,886
2		2000 × 0.890 = 1780	28,666	14,333
3	$25,000 × 0.840 = $21,000	2000 × 0.840 = 1680	51,346	17,115
4		2000 × 0.792 = 1584	52,930	13,233
5		2000 × 0.747 = 1494	54,424	10,885
6		2000 × 0.705 = 1410	55,834	9,306

And for system B (3 cycles), we obtain Table 9–17:

TABLE 9-17

End of Year	Investment B	Discounted Operating Costs	Total Discounted Cost	Average Cost per Year
0	$20,000 × 1.000 = $20,000		$20,000	
1		$1000 × 0.943 = $943	20,943	$20,943
2	$20,000 × 0.890 = $17,800	1000 × 0.890 = 890	39,633	19,817
3		1000 × 0.840 = 840	40,473	13,491
4	$20,000 × 0.792 = $15,840	1000 × 0.792 = 792	57,035	14,259
5		1000 × 0.747 = 747	57,782	11,556
6		1000 × 0.705 = 705	58,487	9,748

We have discounted both investment sums and operating costs. Year by year these costs have been added together to give total discounted cost. Tiremasters can now make a comparison of alternatives A and B with these figures.

At the end of 6 years, system A has accumulated total discounted costs of $55,834, which is $2,653 less than system B's total. It should be noted that when the facilities under consideration have different estimated service lives, we must always use the smallest common cycle of these lifetimes.

Average costs are frequently used as the basis for comparison. These are the total costs divided by the number of years of the cost accumulation. Using either the total discounted costs or the average yearly determination of cost, Tiremasters would select materials-handling system A.

The steps that have been followed are straightforward. System A requires an initial investment of $25,000. Because it is paid at the beginning of the first year, it is already at present value. At the end of the first year $2,000 has been paid out in operating costs. The $2,000 is discounted to a value of $1,886. In fact, the operating costs are paid out over the period of a year. Therefore, a more accurate computation might be based on monthly operating charges which are appropriately discounted with the monthly discount factor. We observe that at the conclusion of the first year the average yearly costs for system A are $26,886. This is equal to the total costs for a one-year period.

Next, we add the second year's operating costs, properly discounted, and again as though the costs were incurred at the end of the second year. These amount to $1,780. The second year's operating costs are then added to the previous year's total costs, giving a figure of $28,666. For average yearly costs (over a two-year period), we divide by 2. This results in a figure of $14,333.

We continue our computations in the same way until the total cycle period of 6 years is covered. If the equipment has salvage value at the time it is replaced, then the salvage amount, properly discounted, is subtracted from the total accumulated cost.

Other techniques can also be used for determining an optimal selection of equipment and facilities. Among such techniques we should include the breakeven chart (especially when it is applied in its decision matrix form) and the scoring model approach.

A note of caution! All intangibles should be considered. For example, if one of the materials handling systems will reduce the number of defectives, then a cost reduction should be factored into the time stream. Better yet, the DCF should be couched in terms of revenues. The intangibles affect both costs and revenues. For example, how do the new systems affect flexibility to change, downtime, the number of varieties that can be run, lead times and cycle times, throughput, and quality?

Scoring Models for Equipment Replacement

Refer to pp. 437–441 where a scoring model was developed for the facility location problem. In this equipment-selection problem the choice could be made between an existing machine and a proposed one. It could also be made between three or more machines, where several are being considered to replace an existing machine. The scoring model is also applicable for startup situations.

The relevant variables would be different costs of operating the equipment, different rates of output, different qualities of output, different levels of variety that can be produced. The main differences between the scoring model approach and that of discounting cash flows are these:

1. The scoring model is capable of dealing with attributes that are not measured in dollars.
2. It is not necessary to assume technological equivalence between the equipment alternatives. Allowance can be made for differences in quality, productivity, and variety—factors which relate to changes in revenue.
3. Discounting highlights the effects of different payment rates over time. The scoring model concentrates on some specific period of time, such as one year or five years.

Section 9.3 Facility Layout

The facility layout problem is well known as the plant layout problem to manufacturers. No matter what it is called, the methodology is equally applicable to service products. Good layouts require the combined insights and talents of good engineers, fine architects, and creative interior directors. In other words, there are fundamental analysis problems, structural systems requirements and constraints, and many artistic opportunities.

Facility choice is constrained by the process being used. Once the process has been specified and the appropriate types of equipment have been selected, it is necessary to arrange all the system components in an optimal (or satisfactory) layout. In some job shop cases, the plant may have already been selected. For many flow shops and some projects, the plant location choice is affected by layout considerations, and vice versa.

For every kind of system, careful thought has been given to the selection of specific machines, desks, computer work stations, and so on. The same care is given to specifying the number of such work stations needed to provide adequate capacity (see the discussion of capacity planning, pp. 174, 218). The possible paths for material flows between the work stations have been surveyed. The sensible placement of operators and the number of operators have also been discussed. Usually, however, equipment alternatives exist. When the equipment alternatives affect layout decisions, they must be studied together. This can also alter facility selection. For these reasons, the layout problem, even with fixed equipment selections, is still extremely complex.

Trial and Error Approach to Layout with Graphics

Decisions concerning the arrangement of specific work elements are what we refer to as the **layout problem.** For the flow shop, the solution to the line-balancing problem provides direct guidelines and constraints for layout. Essentially one job flows through the system. For the job shop, specific equipment is often grouped into work centers of common flow patterns. There are several major flow patterns through the system. This concept helps the P/OM by creating fewer work elements to think about. Although physical models of the work space and the selected equipment are frequently helpful in guiding arrangement, intuition underlies their use (see Fig. 9–7).

Models can be two- or three-dimensional. Often, two-dimensional floor plans with cutouts or templates representing the various pieces of equipment are used. CAD-type computer software plays an increasingly important role.

When conveyors are employed, overhead space requirements may be important, and three-dimensional models are preferred. These techniques are useful for approaching a satisfactory layout, but they do not hold out any promise of finding an optimal layout. Can an optimal layout really be found? For the job shop, it is not productive to seek an optimal arrangement. There are too many possible layout variables and combinations of facilities and work spaces. There is no way to search through them all. Figure 9–7 illustrates the kind of complexity we are addressing.

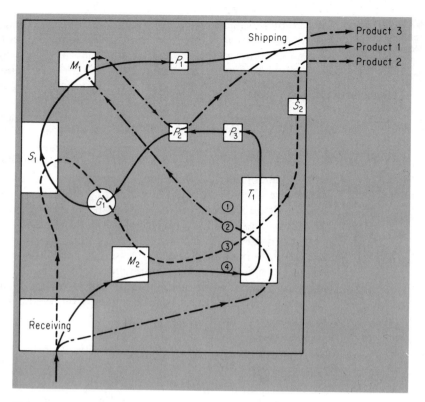

FIGURE 9-7. Flow process layout diagram for a system with multiple product-mix requirements.

As the production process approaches total mechanization and, ultimately, complete automation, technological constraints operate. The flow shop configuration warrants large study investments, so the notion of an optimal layout becomes more tenable. For the general case, however, it is desirable to talk about obtaining a satisfactory layout. What is a satisfactory layout? Some possible measures of a layout's effectiveness are these:

1. More capacity, or better yet, more throughput of the system under different arrangements. For flow and project shops, it is essential to balance the output rates of consecutive operations. This is the line-balancing problem. Such balance is not expected for the job shop, nor is it characteristic of FPS.

2. Less investment and lower operating costs of various production configurations.

3. More flexibility to change a layout, as required.

4. The amount of work-in-process (WIP) to be as small as possible.

The layout problem is complicated by the question of whether we make do with an existing plant or build a new one to our specifications. Frequently, when a rental arrangement is used, basic structural changes are prohibited or are not economically sensible. When an existing structure has been purchased, it may not be economically feasible to knock down walls, add sections, and make other structural changes. Such alterations require investment in plant, and such investments must be justified in terms of alternative uses of these funds. The relative permanence desired for any physical arrangement of components is a matter of importance. If a continuous production line is to be set up, it obviously presents different conditions than would be encountered with a job shop system.

Given some knowledge of the facility construction, a well-known basic approach to the layout problem makes use of hand-drawn schematics or computer-graphics. For example, there are process charts and operation charts, shown by Figures 8–6, 8–7, and 8–8. All decisions that follow the use of these schematics are clearly dominated by intuition. It is also reasonable to work with flow process layout diagrams (Fig. 9–7). Thus, for example, an initial layout and system is conceived (e.g., Fig. 9–8). Then, various changes are proposed as challengers. Figure 9–9 is representative of a proposed improvement.

In general, a satisfactory resolution of the facility layout problem is considerably expedited by the use of flow process layout diagrams, as shown in Figs. 9–8 and 9–9. These diagrams describe the flow of food shelves for a refrigerator manufacturer. The flow path is superimposed on the floor plan. Alternative layout arrangements produce different flow patterns. Changes in layout are normally made until a satisfactory flow pattern is achieved. Appropriate process charts are developed to describe those characteristics of the system's flow that do not lend themselves to visual representation, as in Figs. 8–6, 8–7, and 8–8. Note that special symbols are used to indicate different categories of system behaviors. Figure 8–6 presents the key for interpreting these symbols. There is no totally uniform convention with respect to such symbols, and in practice, many variations will be found.

The summary box of the flow process chart permits rapid comparison of various layout plans. Fig. 8–7 illustrates a proposed revision. The summary box of the proposed method reveals that two kinds of improvements will result if the original layout arrangement is changed. These include 1 less transport and 2 less uncontrolled storage stages. The travel distance has been decreased by 140 feet. If the first layout is in actual use, then it is necessary to compare the cost of making the change with the reduction in operating costs that can be achieved. The comparison requires the use of an appropriate discounting formula so that the stream of savings can be properly evaluated.

It is frequently more practical to begin the layout plan in an environment totally divorced from the spatial constraints of reality. An assembly diagram, also called a **Gozinto (goes-into) chart,** is a flow diagram concerned

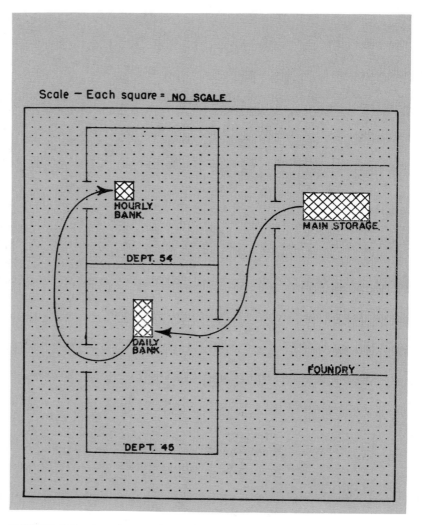

FIGURE 9-8. Flow diagram for original method of handling refrigerator food shelves from bulk storage to plating department [From Marvin E. Mundel, *Motion and Time Study*, 5th ed. (Englewood Cliffs, N.J.: Prentice-Hall, Inc., 1978), p. 60].

neither with real time nor real space; only sequence is presented (see Fig. 9–10). Generally, service activities such as transportation and storage are excluded. Using the chart in Fig. 9–10, one can determine an intelligent arrangement of facilities based on the essential sequential requirements of the process. This chart details which parts (e.g., base, arm, plunger) are made and which are purchased (only the rubber pad is purchased). Following the lines, from left to right, we learn which parts enter into each subassembly, and where, for example, subassembly *X* in department 2, *Y* in department 3, and *Z* in department 8. Then, *X* and *Y* are joined

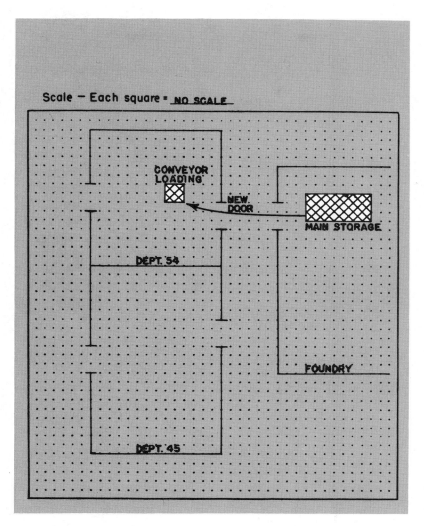

FIGURE 9-9. Flow diagram for the proposed method of handling refrigerator food shelves. Note that a wall has been broken through to yield direct access to the conveyor. [From Marvin E. Mundel, *Motion and Time Study,* 5th ed. (Englewood Cliffs, N.J.: Prentice-Hall, Inc., 1978), p. 62].

together in department 3 and painted in department 5. After heat treating in department 6, subassembly Z is welded to subassembly $(X + Y)$ in department 8, cleaned in department 12, and inspected in department 1. The relevance of MRP is underscored by the cascade of interdependent components shown in Fig. 9–10. Also, we observe the job-shop nature of this work, wherein batches of components and subassemblies move through seven different departments.

The layout problem is much more complicated when a common set of

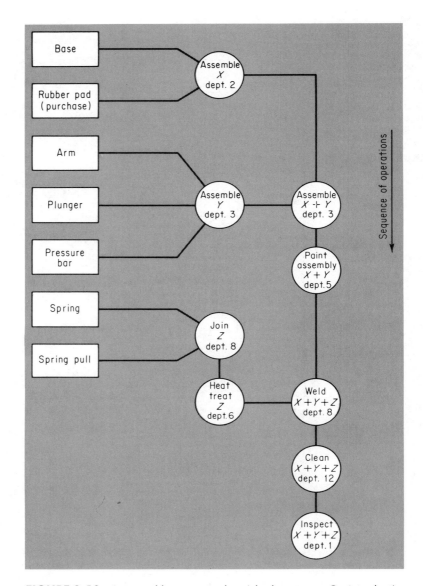

FIGURE 9-10. An assembly sequence chart (also known as a Gozinto chart).

facilities must be shared by multiple products that require different flow paths and sequences through the system. For example, Fig. 9–7 portrays a flow process layout diagram where alternate routes must be followed by the several products in the company's product mix.

To find layout plans that are satisfactory for such cases requires considerable juggling of the facilities. As a rule, the product that contributes the greatest percentage to total profit is given preferential treatment, and the others less so in accordance with their value to the company. At least, this heuristic simplifies the problem. When there is only one major product being processed in an approximation of the flow shop configuration, it is reasonable to route that product on a minimum cost path.

Case: The Mayor's Office—The Minimum Cost Path Layout

The layout problem is surprisingly large and complex in mathematical terms. This is true even when we dismiss many of the intangible factors that ordinarily are reserved for intuition. The layout problem for an average size job shop, strictly in cost terms, is recognized to involve consideration of billions or trillions of alternatives.

This explains why the intuitive approach has been so widely used for job shop layout decisions. It is always possible (even probable) that intuition will overlook some excellent solutions. But one thing is certain: while optimality may be missed, the manager will not accept an illogical and inappropriate solution. Let us see why the formal analysis of the layout problem for the job shop is so demanding.

The layout problem of a flow shop or a project shop would be different from a job shop. The layout, in these cases, would actually interact with the line-balancing solution and the project tradeoff solution. So it is most often the job shop layout problem to which we address ourselves. The mayor's office is an excellent example of a job shop. The office is composed of work centers that are responsible for different functions, such as typing, filing, phoning, copying, and so forth. Work flows back and forth between centers. Although there is a pattern, it is one rich with combinations and variations.

The mayor has brought in a management consulting firm to study the layout problem. The head consultant explains to the 160 individuals who work in the mayor's office—at different civil service levels with an assortment of job descriptions—that the layout study will include tangible and intangible factors, but the first crack at the problem will be to determine which work paths are used the most, and what distances work has to travel. It has been stated by the mayor that time savings will be given back to the workers in different forms. Part of it can be used for training to higher grades, strictly on a voluntary basis. The rest of the saved time is available for relaxation. Ultimately, a set of locations will be chosen to which the work centers will be assigned so as to minimize the costs of shuffling work around.

Here is how the mayor's consultants view the problem:

Define the *job shop* as consisting of N work centers, $WC_j (j = 1, 2, \cdots, N)$, and N locations, $L_i (i = A, B, \cdots, N)$. Each work center has a fundamentally different activity, and each location is clearly defined.

There is a distance $d_{ii'}$ between any 2 locations and a work flow rate of $F_{jj'}$ between any 2 work centers. Also, there is a cost $C_{jj'}$ for handling work between centers. (It is the cost per unit of flow per unit of distance moved.)

As an example, let us assign work centers 1 and 2 to locations A and B, respectively. The distance between A and B is 10 feet in either direction, i.e., $d_{AB} = d_{BA} = 10$ feet (see Matrix 1). The work flow rate between centers 1 and 2 is 100 (1 → 2) plus 40 (2 → 1). (See Matrix 2.) Thus, $F_{12} + F_{21} = 140$. Assume that all handling costs (including C_{12} and C_{21}) are equal to 1 per unit of flow per unit of distance moved.

The cost of locating work centers 1 and 2 at locations A and B, with respect to each other, is

$$FC_{12} = C_{12}(d_{AB}F_{12}) + C_{21}(d_{BA}F_{21})$$

where $FC_{jj'}$ is the total work flow cost between work centers j and j'. For our illustration

$$FC_{12} + FC_{21} = 1(10 \times 100) + 1(10 \times 40) = 1400$$

After assigning all work centers to locations, we determine the sum of all total flow costs for that configuration, i.e., $\sum_{i}\sum_{i'} FC_{jj'}$. This is the grand total of handling costs for the specific layout. Our objective is: *Minimize materials-handling costs.*

We will use this case as an example in our discussion of layout methods.

Assume that five office spaces are designated. The question is, how to assign five work centers to these locations? Figure 9–11 portrays a floor layout with five work centers assigned to specific locations. More complex illustrations would involve several floors of an office building, or materials handling in a large manufacturing job shop. The office is a job shop with many flow patterns. Its layout problem is complicated, because different kinds of work flow through a common set of facilities, as in Fig. 9–8. The material being handled by the mayor's office is mostly information in different forms.

Matrix of Distances

Divide the mayor's office into locations (see Figure 9–11). Next, measure either the time or distance required to transport work from one location to another. It is now possible to construct a matrix that shows the appropriate time or distance for transporting work between any two locations of the office. An example is Matrix 1.

MATRIX 1   DISTANCES $d_{jj'}$ BETWEEN LOCATIONS L_i OF THE OFFICE (IN FEET)

		To Location				
		A	B	C	D	E
	A	0	10	20	32	40
	B	10	0	16	18	20
From location	C	20	16	0	12	15
	D	32	18	12	0	10
	E	40	20	15	10	0

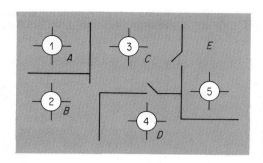

FIGURE 9-11. The floor layout of the mayor's office with 5 work centers 1, 2, 3, 4, and 5 (e.g., filing, typing pool, reproduction equipment, etc.) assigned to 5 office locations A, B, C, D, and E.

Given a specific office, its configuration will constrain the way in which work centers can be assigned to office space. For example, there are security constraints for the computer center, usage constraints for the copy machine, and privacy requirements for the filing center. The telephone center should be isolated from the typing pool. Similar constraints exist in other layout situations. For manufacturing, machinery can be assigned only to certain areas. Cranes may require special height clearance. Upper floors are needed for gravity conveyors. Press shops cannot be located near offices because of noise. Receiving and shipping should logically be close to truck docks and rail spurs.

The diagonal of the matrix is 0, because it is assumed that within a location no travel is required. Also, as a general rule, the matrix will be symmetrical; that is, the distance from *A* to *B* will be equal to the distance from *B* to *A*. This is not always the case—for example, if an "up" escalator connects two floors while stairs are used to go down; or in a factory, if unidirectional (gravity) conveyor systems connect some of the plant locations.

Work Flow Rates

Although the distances between locations may be small, the frequency with which work travels between stations is high. Therefore, an efficient layout, which assigns work centers to office locations in a near-optimal fashion, can produce substantial savings when compared with an arbitrary assignment method. The workers have incentives to complete this study, since they benefit through training and increased relaxation time.

For the mayor's office, measures of work flows between stations yields Matrix 2. Matrix 2 is seldom symmetrical. For example, there is no reason to expect as much work to move from the filing center to the typing pool, as vice versa. The diagonal of Matrix 2 is blocked because although the rate of work transfers within each center can be measured, such work is assumed to travel zero distance. Since a cost is associated with moving a unit of work a given distance, internal transactions will have zero cost. Consequently, they will not affect our solution.

MATRIX 2   WORK FLOW RATES $F_{ij'}$ BETWEEN WORK CENTERS WC_i AND $WC_{j'}$ (IN NUMBER OF UNITS PER DAY)

		To Work Center				
		1	2	3	4	5
	1	x	100	60	80	20
From	2	40	x	50	10	90
Work	3	80	90	x	60	30
Center	4	120	10	40	x	70
	5	110	5	5	30	x

The mayor's consultants decide to evaluate the present configuration first. The work centers are presently assigned to the office locations as follows: 1A, 2B, 3C, 4D, 5E (see Fig. 9–11). Matrix 3 represents the total daily work flows (number of units times distance traveled) for the present configuration. It is obtained by multiplying the distance between the assigned work centers by the work flow rates between them.

MATRIX 3   TOTAL DAILY WORK FLOWS ($F_{ij'} \times d_{ij'}$) BETWEEN WORK CENTERS j AT PRESENTLY ASSIGNED LOCATIONS i (IN TOTAL UNIT FEET TRAVELED PER DAY)

		To Work Center				
		1	2	3	4	5
	1	0	1000	1200	2560	800
From	2	400	0	800	180	1800
Work	3	1600	1440	0	720	450
Center	4	3840	180	480	0	700
	5	4400	100	75	300	0

Because we have been told to consider all costs to be $1 per unit foot traveled, Matrix 3 is also a matrix of total work flow costs. Bearing this in mind, we now have a picture of what the present assignment configuration means. The mayor's office is paying heavily for work flows from centers 5 and 4 to center 1, as well as from center 1 to center 4. Perhaps there is no better arrangement, but that fact is hardly certain. There are 5! ways (120) to assign 5 work centers to 5 locations, and we have just looked at one of these.

Costs for Distance Traveled

We need one more matrix to complete our analysis (namely, the costs per unit for distance traveled). It could be that all work flows have the same handling costs. We have assumed a unit cost to this point. If, however, cost differentials do exist, then the matrix of costs (per unit of flow per unit of distance moved) must be multiplied cell by cell with the matrix of total daily work flows.

Matrix 4 presents an example of a matrix with cost differentials, and Matrix 5 (the result of multiplication with Matrix 3) is the matrix of total work flow costs.

MATRIX 4   COSTS PER UNIT OF FLOW PER UNIT OF DISTANCE TRAVELED BETWEEN WORK CENTERS j AT PRESENTLY ASSIGNED LOCATIONS i (IN DOLLARS PER WORK UNIT PER FOOT MOVED)

		To Work Center				
		1	2	3	4	5
	1	x	0.8	1	0.5	0.5
From	2	0.8	x	1	1	1
Work	3	1	1	x	0.8	0.8
Center	4	0.5	1	0.8	x	1
	5	0.5	1	0.8	1	x

MATRIX 5   TOTAL DAILY WORK FLOW COSTS $FC_{ij'}$ (IN DOLLARS)

		To Work Center					
		1	2	3	4	5	
	1	0	800	1200	1280	400	
From	2	320	0	800	180	1800	Total Costs
Work	3	1600	1440	0	576	360	= \$16,600
Center	4	1920	180	384	0	700	
	5	2200	100	60	300	0	

The large costs associated with work flows from centers 5 and 4 to center 1, and from center 1 to center 4 have been reduced, but they still appear formidable. Relocation analysis would still appear to be worthwhile.

Let us return to Matrix 3 and, assuming that equal unit flow costs are appropriate, determine the total costs for this case. Matrix 6 presents this information and, in addition, shows the total costs that originate with a center (row sums) and total costs that culminate with a center (column sums). It is striking that work center 1 completes almost 45 percent of all transactions ($10,240/23,025 = 0.44$). Perhaps some basic redesign is called for—a point that will hardly be lost on the mayor's consultants.

MATRIX 6 TOTAL DAILY COST OF WORK FLOWS BETWEEN CENTERS, $FC_{ii'}$

		To Work Center					
		1	2	3	4	5	
	1	0	1000	1200	2560	800	5560
From	2	400	0	800	180	1800	3180
Work	3	1600	1440	0	720	450	4210
Center	4	3840	180	480	0	700	5200
	5	4400	100	75	300	0	4875
		10,240	2720	2555	3760	3750	23,025

Total costs = \$23,025

Also, the mayor will be surprised to learn that the total costs of handling work between centers 1 and 4:

$$(\$3840 + \$2560 = \$6400)$$

and between centers 1 and 5:

$$(\$4400 + \$800 = \$5200)$$

are so large (see Matrix 7). The office layout should be changed.

Improving Layouts

Two heuristics come to mind when one is searching for rules by which to improve the office (or plant) layout.

1. Assign the centers with large work flow rates between them to locations as close as possible.
2. Assign the centers with small work flow rates between them to locations as distant as possible.

The mayor's consultants try to apply these rules. First, in Matrix 7, they have summed all the costs of each pair of work centers.

MATRIX 7 SUMS OF DAILY PAIRED WORK CENTER FLOW COSTS $FC_{ii'} + FC_{i'i}$

		To and from Work Center				
	1	2	3	4	5	
1	0	1400	2800	6400	5200	
2		0	2240	360	1900	
3			0	1200	525	
4				0	1000	
5					0	

Total costs = \$23,025

The biggest number in Matrix 7 relates work centers 1 and 4. Accordingly, work center 1 is placed at location A and work center 4 is placed at location B. Note in Matrix 1 that 10 is the shortest distance between any two locations, but it is also available at *D* and *E*. That alternative should be tried, as should others which seem to merit analysis. We should bear in mind that our approach is heuristic and therefore could bypass a clue that might yield a superior solution.

Centers 1 and 5 have large flow costs. Thus, work center 5 is placed at location *C*. Similar reasoning assigns work center 3 to location *D*. This forces work center 2 to location *E*. However, we would have placed work center 2 as far from center 4 as possible, because the work flows between them are the smallest in the matrix, so we achieve the benefits of both heuristics with this move.

The assignment is *1A, 2E, 3D, 4B, 5C*. Matrix 1 times Matrix 2 now becomes Matrix 8. Thus:

MATRIX 8

	Location Distances					Work Flow Rates					Total between Center Work Flows				
	A	*B*	*C*	*D*	*E*	*1*	*4*	*5*	*3*	*2*	*A* *1*	*B* *4*	*C* *5*	*D* *3*	*E* *2*
A	0	10	20	32	40	1	x	80	20	60	100	0	800	400	1920	4000
B	10	0	16	18	20	4	120	x	70	40	10	1200	0	1120	720	200
C	20	16	0	12	15	5	110	30	x	5	5	2200	480	0	60	75
D	32	18	12	0	10	3	80	60	30	x	90	2560	1080	360	0	900
E	40	20	15	10	0	2	40	10	90	50	x	1600	200	1350	500	0

Assuming that equal unit flow costs apply, we derive Matrix 9, which is similar in concept to Matrix 7.

MATRIX 9 TOTAL DAILY COST OF COMBINED WORK FLOWS BETWEEN CENTERS

	Work Center					
	1	*2*	*3*	*4*	*5*	
1	0	5600	4480	2000	2600	
2		0	1400	400	1425	Total costs
3			0	1800	420	= $21,725
4				0	1600	
5					0	

There has been a substantial decrease in cost ($1,300, or almost 6 percent) but it is possible that greater decreases could be achieved. We have tried only two configurations out of 120 possibilities. Of course, our improved version was based on a reasonable heuristic, so it should be better than an alternative picked at random. Yet other layouts exist which conform with the general idea of the heuristic, and these should be tried.

The CRAFT Layout Heuristic

The simple heuristics we have used up to this point are not sufficiently powerful to cope with a big problem. Total enumeration is out of the question for a big problem. However, a strong heuristic approach exists. It was developed by G. C. Armour and E. S. Buffa. It is called CRAFT (Computerized Relative Allocation of Facilities Technique).[3]

The improvement algorithm is based on exchanging the locations of pairs of work centers, and for each exchange computing the alteration in materials handling costs. This is demonstrated for the case of Olympic Studios that follows. There are $n(n - 1)/2$ such pairs, starting with any one machine center. The best exchange is made, and then the procedure continues, starting with a different work center.

For example, with 4 centers 1, 2, 3, and 4 (starting with 1), the first iteration of $n(n - 1)/2 = 4(3)/2 = 6$ pair exchanges would be:

Exchange Number	①	2	3	4	Exchange Pair
1	2	1	3	4	1,2
2	3	2	1	4	1,3
3	4	2	3	1	1,4
4	1	3	2	4[(*)]	2,3
5	1	4	3	2	2,4
6	1	2	4	3	3,4

Say that the fourth exchange 1 3 2 4 is best (*). Then the second iteration begins with any center except 1, which has been used already. Arbitrarily, let us choose 2:

Exchange Number	1	3	②	4[(**)]	Exchange Pair
1	2	3	1	4	2,1
2	1	2	3	4	2,3
3	1	3	4	2	2,4
4	3	1	2	4	1,3
5	4	3	2	1	1,4
6	1	4	2	3	3,4

---

[3]Gordon C. Armour and Elwood S. Buffa, "A Heuristic Algorithm and Simulation Approach to the Relative Location of Facilities," *Management Science,* 9, 2 (January 1963), pp. 294–309. Also, see Elwood S. Buffa, Gordon C. Armour, and Thomas E. Vollmann, "Allocating Facilities with CRAFT," *Harvard Business Review,* 42, 2 (March–April 1964), pp. 136–5B. An actual, successful application of CRAFT to a movie studio layout is cited in the *Harvard Business Review* article.

Say that the best (**) is still 1 3 2 4. We must now begin the third iteration with either center 3 or 4. Arbitrarily, let us choose 4. The best arrangement found by the third iteration is the starting point of the fourth and final iteration, which tests all pairs in terms of center number 3.

As an upper limit $n^2/2$ computations are required with each of n iterations (which also is a reasonable upper limit), whereas total enumeration requires $n!$ computations. At $n = 4$, the breakeven point is reached. Thereafter $n!$ grows far more rapidly than $n[n(n - 1)/2]$. As reported in the articles cited in the footnote, the algorithm is effective and provides substantial savings over an intuition-based layout.

**CASE:
OLYMPIC
STUDIOS—
A
SIMPLIFIED
APPLICATION
OF CRAFT**

Olympic is a well-known film studio that moves sets and personnel between locations regularly. The moves are costly but necessary, since at each location a different kind of work center operates: space available, camera setups, supporting props, and so on.

Olympic's management wants to determine the best layout, invest in it, and stick with it. Assume that three locations (A, B, and C) exist with distances (in feet) between them as shown in Display 1.

DISPLAY 1

		To		
		A	B	C
	A	0	4000	2000
From	B	4000	0	3000
	C	2000	3000	0

Filming activities are sequenced through 3 work centers (1, 2, and 3) with monthly flow costs per unit distance, as shown in Display 2.

DISPLAY 2

		To		
		1	2	3
	1	x	$50	$70
From	2	$20	x	$40
	3	$30	$80	x

With these data, we may be able to improve upon the existing assignment, which is 1A, 2B, 3C. The total monthly flow cost matrix (in thousands) for the existing layout is derived by multiplication (Display 3).

DISPLAY 3

	A 1	B 2	C 3
1	0	200	140
2	80	0	120
3	60	240	0

Total monthly cost = $840,000

Using CRAFT for our heuristic, start with work center 1 and exchange locations, as shown in Display 4.

DISPLAY 4

Variation	Location A B C	Total Monthly Flow Costs* (in thousands)
Original	① 2 3	$840
First exchange	2 1 3	820 ←
Second exchange	3 2 1	890
Third exchange	1 3 2	900

*These flow costs are computed in the same way Display 3 was derived.

We take the best of these results ($820,000, which occurred with the first exchange) and start the series of exchanges with work center 2. This is shown in Display 5:

DISPLAY 5

Variation	Location A B C	Total Monthly Flow Costs* (in thousands)
Start	② 1 3	$820 ←
First exchange	1 2 3	840
Second exchange	3 1 2	850
Third exchange	2 3 1	920

We can stop. Because of the small number of work centers and locations ($n = 3$), we have ended up enumerating all $n!$ possible arrangements of work centers and locations. With values of n larger than 4, this will not occur. CRAFT has been of great help to Olympic Studios. The heuristic technique produces $20,000 of savings a month ($840,000 − 820,000 = $20,000). Note also how bad a solution might have been achieved by chance: the worst case is 2A, 3B, 1C with total monthly flow costs of $920,000.

Work Sheet for CRAFT Computations

$$
\begin{array}{ccc}
\boxed{\begin{array}{ccc} A & B & C \\ 2 & 1 & 3 \end{array}}
\end{array}
$$

$$
\begin{vmatrix} 0 & 4 & 2 \\ 4 & 0 & 3 \\ 2 & 3 & 0 \end{vmatrix} \times
\begin{vmatrix} \text{x} & 20 & 40 \\ 50 & \text{x} & 70 \\ 80 & 30 & \text{x} \end{vmatrix} =
\begin{vmatrix} \text{x} & 80 & 80 \\ 200 & \text{x} & 210 \\ 160 & 90 & \text{x} \end{vmatrix} = 820
$$

$$
\boxed{\begin{array}{ccc} A & B & C \\ 3 & 2 & 1 \end{array}}
$$

$$
\begin{vmatrix} 0 & 4 & 2 \\ 4 & 0 & 3 \\ 2 & 3 & 0 \end{vmatrix} \times
\begin{vmatrix} \text{x} & 80 & 30 \\ 40 & \text{x} & 20 \\ 70 & 50 & \text{x} \end{vmatrix} =
\begin{vmatrix} \text{x} & 320 & 60 \\ 160 & \text{x} & 60 \\ 140 & 150 & \text{x} \end{vmatrix} = 890
$$

$$
\boxed{\begin{array}{ccc} A & B & C \\ 1 & 3 & 2 \end{array}}
$$

$$
\begin{vmatrix} 0 & 4 & 2 \\ 4 & 0 & 3 \\ 2 & 3 & 0 \end{vmatrix} \times
\begin{vmatrix} \text{x} & 70 & 50 \\ 30 & \text{x} & 80 \\ 20 & 40 & \text{x} \end{vmatrix} =
\begin{vmatrix} \text{x} & 280 & 100 \\ 120 & \text{x} & 240 \\ 40 & 120 & \text{x} \end{vmatrix} = 900
$$

$$
\boxed{\begin{array}{ccc} A & B & C \\ 3 & 1 & 2 \end{array}}
$$

$$
\begin{vmatrix} 0 & 4 & 2 \\ 4 & 0 & 3 \\ 2 & 3 & 0 \end{vmatrix} \times
\begin{vmatrix} \text{x} & 30 & 80 \\ 70 & \text{x} & 50 \\ 40 & 20 & \text{x} \end{vmatrix} =
\begin{vmatrix} \text{x} & 120 & 160 \\ 280 & \text{x} & 150 \\ 80 & 60 & \text{x} \end{vmatrix} = 850
$$

$$
\boxed{\begin{array}{ccc} A & B & C \\ 2 & 3 & 1 \end{array}}
$$

$$
\begin{vmatrix} 0 & 4 & 2 \\ 4 & 0 & 3 \\ 2 & 3 & 0 \end{vmatrix} \times
\begin{vmatrix} \text{x} & 40 & 20 \\ 80 & \text{x} & 30 \\ 50 & 70 & \text{x} \end{vmatrix} =
\begin{vmatrix} \text{x} & 160 & 40 \\ 320 & \text{x} & 90 \\ 100 & 210 & \text{x} \end{vmatrix} = 920
$$

PROBLEM
SET

1. Discount analysis is suggested as a means of comparing alternative equipment that is equivalent technologically.

   a. What does technological equivalence mean?

   b. If the equipment being compared is not technologically equivalent, what two methods might be used as a basis for making the selection?

2. Smokestack output contamination has been regulated by local ordinance. The cost of Company A's electronic precipitator is $8,000. It will last 5 years. Maintenance costs are $1,000 per year. The alternative is Company B's chemical filtering system, which costs $12,000,

lasts 10 years, and has operating cost of $500 per year and maintenance charges of $100 per year. Both systems meet the ordinance requirements. Which system do you recommend for the Northwest Paper Company, which uses a conservative 6 percent discount factor for all present value analyses?

3. A small drill press is valued at $1,000. It is expected to last 2 years. It costs $4,000 per year to operate. A larger drill press can be purchased for $3,000. It will last 4 years. It costs $3,000 per year to operate. Which drill press should we purchase? (Use a 6 percent discount factor.) Comment on your result.

4. At City Hospital, 2 miniaturized insertable cameras are under consideration for surgical support. Camera A costs $800 and has operating costs of $0.10 per picture. Camera B costs $1200 and has operating costs of $0.08 per picture. The forecast (in pictures demanded per year) is:

1st Year	2nd Year	3rd Year	4th Year	5th Year
5000	6000	8000	8000	10,000

City Hospital estimates its return on available funds at 6 percent per year.

a. Approximately at what point in time are the 2 cameras equivalent in value?

b. What is the average cost per year of each camera at the end of the fifth year?

Answer: An analysis similar to that in Problem 3 applies to this problem, except that the yearly operating cost must be computed on the basis of the projected use of the camera. Thus:

End of Year	Camera A	Discounted Operating Cost	Total Cost	Average Cost
0	800(1.000) = 800		800	
1		500(0.943) = 472	1272	1272
2		600(0.890) = 534	1806	903
3		800(0.840) = 672	2478	826
4		800(0.792) = 634	3112	778
5		1000(0.747) = 747	3859	772

End of Year	Camera B	Discounted Operating Cost	Total Cost	Average Cost
0	1200(1.000) = 1200		1200	
1		400(0.943) = 377	1577	1577
2		480(0.890) = 427	2004	1002
3		640(0.840) = 538	2542	847
4		640(0.792) = 507	3049	762
5		800(0.747) = 598	3647	729

a. After 3 ½ years, both cameras have a total cost of about $2,795. After that, camera B has lower average costs.

b. The average cost per year of camera A = $772; of camera B, $729.

5. **a.** Using the CRAFT heuristic, how many assignments of 4 work centers to floor locations can be made with a 4-story building? (No splitting of work centers is allowed.)

Answer: 4! = 24

b. How many CRAFT exchanges can be made each time that a new work center is selected as the basis for exchanging?

Answer: 4 × 3 ÷ 2 = 6

c. Develop a scenario of exchanges to include at least 2 iterations. The matrix of distances between locations is:

	A	B	C	D
A	0	1	2	3
B	1	0	1	2
C	2	1	0	1
D	3	2	1	0

And the matrix of total daily flow costs, per unit distance traveled, between work centers is:

	1	2	3	4
1	0	8	10	5
2	8	0	10	10
3	10	10	0	8
4	5	10	8	0

How many of the 24 possibilities did you obtain? Our scenarios follow:

	A	B	C	D		Total Costs
START	(1)	2	3	4		162
1	2	1	3	4		172
2	3	2	1	4		174
3	4	2	3	1		
4	1	4	3	2		
5	1	3	2	4	← one of the best	154
6	1	2	4	3		
START	1	3	(2)	4		
1	2	3	1	4		
2	1	2	3	4		
3	1	3	4	2		
4	4	3	2	1		
5	1	4	2	3		
6	3	1	2	4		

Answer: In these scenarios, there are 12 unique layouts. Work out the costs for these.

6. Using the cost data of Matrix 4 (p. 000), try to find the layout for the mayor's office that has the lowest total daily flow cost.

7. Tree Top Nurseries has found an ideal greenhouse. The owner has offered to rent or sell it under the following conditions: (a) Rent of $6000 per year; (b) buy immediately for $48,000. Tree Top's management has decided that a 9-year comparison of the alternatives is reasonable. They estimate the worth of the greenhouse at the end of 9 years to be $8,000. The interest rate of 6 percent is used to evaluate all Tree Top investments. What should be done?

8. Complete the total enumeration of all possible arrangements for the 3 × 3 layout problem described by the 2 matrices below. Work out a few examples of total daily flow cost.

	Location Distances				Work Flow Rates		
	A	B	C		1	2	3
A	—	25	40	1	—	2	5
B	25	—	10	2	1	—	3
C	40	10	—	3	6	4	—

(Assume unit costs.)

9. Finding the best locations for police and fire stations is a pressing urban problem. Discuss the nature of this problem and what variables are likely to be important. How does this compare to the facility layout problem?

10. Explain why, in a job shop, the matrix $[F_{jj'}]$ might have few 0 entries, whereas in a flow shop the matrix might have 1 entry per row.

Answer: The job shop is based on the existence of flexible routines between all work centers. In other words, a well-designed job shop can be identified by its utilization of many flow paths for jobs. In the flow shop, on the other hand, specific routines are emphasized and, where possible, unidirectional flows between locations such as A → B → C → D → etc., are not confounded with flow potentials such as B → A and A → C. Special-purpose machines underscore these flow shop designs.

REFERENCES

APPLE, JAMES M. *Plant Layout and Materials Handling,* 2nd ed. New York: Ronald Press, 1963.

COOK, T. M., and R. A. RUSSELL. *Introduction to Management Science.* Englewood Cliffs, N.J.: Prentice-Hall, 1977.

DEAN, JOEL. *Managerial Economics.* Englewood Cliffs, N.J.: Prentice-Hall, 1951.

ISARD, WALTER. *Location and Space-Economy.* New York: Wiley, 1956.

KARASKA, G. J., and D. F. BRAMHALL. *Location Analysis for Manufacturing.: A Selection of Readings*. Cambridge, Mass.: M.I.T. Press, 1969.

MAGEE, JOHN F. *Physical Distribution Systems*. New York: McGraw-Hill, 1967.

MASSE, PIERRE. *Optimal Investment Decisions*. Englewood Cliffs, N.J.: Prentice-Hall, 1962.

MILLER, RICHARD B. *Plant Location Factors, United States*. Monograph, Noyes Development Corporation, 188 Mill Road, Park Ridge, N.J. 07656, 1966.

MOORE, JAMES M. *Plant Layout and Design*. New York: Macmillan, 1962.

MUTHER, RICHARD. *Practical Plant Layout*. New York: McGraw-Hill, 1955.

REED, RUDDELL, Jr. *Plant Layout*. Homewood, Ill.: Richard D. Irwin, 1961.

STARR, M. K. *Systems Management of Operations*. Englewood Cliffs, N.J.: Prentice-Hall, 1970.

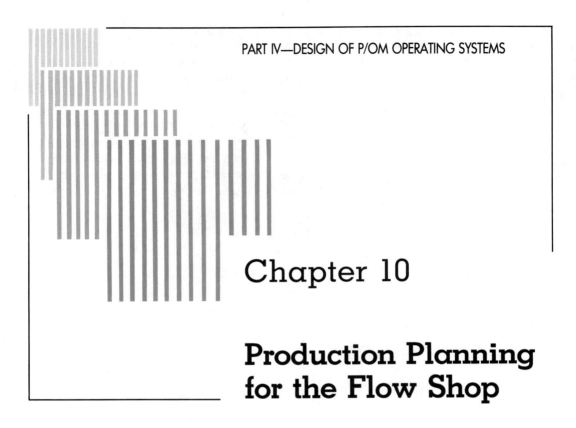

Chapter 10

Production Planning for the Flow Shop

CHAPTER SUMMARY
The line balancing problem arises in the flow shop because operations must be partitioned into nearly equal work assignments to avoid idle time at specialized facilities. This applies to labor-intensive systems as well as to mechanized systems. Much line balancing work has been focused on assembly line balancing, where workers and their equipment are paced by the conveyor belt. In this chapter we expand upon the concept of the flow shop as a high-productivity system. In Chapter 4 we discussed modular production systems and the application of group technology to families of parts. Both modular production and group technology are means of achieving the large volume of production required to justify the flow shop as a high-productivity system.

We begin in Section 10.1 the problem of deterministic line balancing. An example is built around the precedence diagram of Filmasters', Inc., and its situation. The calculation of cycle time is established. It is equal to total work content time divided by the number of stations. The limits on cycle time are also established. Cycle time can be no less than the longest operation time, and no more than total work content time. We show how productivity and cycle time relate. The concepts of perfect balance and balance delay are dovetailed with the development of station layouts.

In Section 10.2 we discuss various heuristic methods for achieving line balance. Heuristic methods employ "rules of thumb," common sense, and experience to find near-optimal solutions to problems. Heuristic models are based on applying logical rules to the solution of problems. They are used when strictly mathematical approaches cannot succeed or are too costly. The line balancing problem provides a good example of when it makes sense to use heuristics.

The stochastic line balancing problem is introduced in Section 10.3. Its relationship to queueing models is examined with sufficient detail to allow an analytical maximum profit solution to the choice between alternative bulk-mail-sorting, flow shop configurations. Simulation is explored as a line balancing method, and with an example.

PC programs have been developed which permit simulations of flow shop processes. There is also software that can do line balancing (Section 10.1) and queueing analyses (Section 10.2). These and other commercial software applicable to the flow shop are discussed in Appendix A.

Section 10.1 Line Balancing Methods

All other things being equal, the high-volume, properly balanced flow shop is the best route to lowest costs and finest quality. This is true unless an FPS or FMS (Chapter 12) can be justified, in which case excellent levels of variety are also obtainable. The smooth-running flow shop, with a continuous stream of product and very low WIP levels, epitomizes a system with **economies of scale.**

Juxtaposed to this is the push-type production system, which does not have a continuous stream of product. It does have bottlenecks which cause disruptive backups of costly WIP to form. Various methods which support JIT have been developed to help reduce and remove such WIP queues from the process.

The flow shop is often introduced at the mature stage of the product life cycle; the job shop is used for output during startup and growth. As the growth of volume passes the point where investments in flow shop equipment can be justified, the job shop is replaced by the flow shop. Startup flow shops move to garner the greater margin contributions at the outset of product launch. The risk is greater, and to offset that risk, marketing plans must be developed and supported to achieve volume levels that are economically sufficient as soon as possible.

The need for a line balancing method arises because many activities are required to fashion the goods and services that constitute the flow shop's output. Activities are comprised of operations, which must be assigned to work stations. For balance, the stations will be equally loaded with work; total operation times at each station should be about the same. But equal work assignments at stations are not easily achieved because:

1. Most of the operations must be done in specific sequences.
2. Operation times follow production necessities, and there is only minimum flexibility to alter these times.
3. The productive capabilities of people and equipment differ. They do not work at the same rate, and they do not make the same kind or number of mistakes.

The Precedence Relations of Work Stations

The flow shop is a balanced sequence of operations. For example, raw materials enter station 1 at 9 A.M. Stations 2, 3, 4 are idle. Between 9:00 and 9:03 the raw materials are worked on at station 1; they move to station 2 at 9:03. At the same time, new raw materials enter station 1. Then at 9:06 station 3 begins to operate. We continue in this way until all stations are actively engaged. Every 3 minutes raw materials enter at station 1 and finished goods leave the final station. We have started up the flow shop.

How do we determine the order of stations? Sometimes it is easy to specify which operation must follow another. For example, we must first prepare a surface before we paint it. At other times, different orderings can be used. An example is the repetitive "job" of preparing a patient for a specific hospital treatment. Certain operations must precede others, but many parts of the sequence are flexible.

CASE: HEART SURGERY

Figure 10–1 might illustrate a precedence diagram for a generalized open heart surgery procedure. This procedure utilizes 45 operations. The hospital intends to set up the procedure on a flow shop basis so that patients are sequentially processed, with different teams engaged in specialized activities along the line. (This flow shop idea is in actual use in the United States, so designers can expect to improve upon known arrangements.)

There are three teams of doctors, technicians, and nurses. They are called I, II, and III. There are three operating rooms and one patient in each at different stages (I, II, and III) of the procedure. Each team moves from one room to the next. I is prep and start procedure, and III is finish up procedure. The diagram can be read as follows: Operation 1 (performed by team 1) is followed by operations 3 and 7 (same team). Operation 7 is followed by operation 9 (performed by the third team in the operating room). Operation 9 is followed by operation 41 (same team), and so on.

The medical teams tell us that this "job" can be accomplished in alternate ways. The decision of how to sequence these steps should be the result of careful consultation with those who have experience with similar procedures.

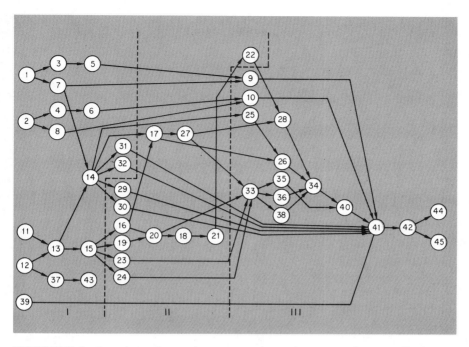

FIGURE 10-1. Precedence diagram for a repetitive hospital treatment administered by three medical teams.

But they must also take advantage of technology that did not exist when the prior processes were designed.

Like any flow shop, once decisions are made, they are difficult and costly to change. There are psychological commitments as well as investments in facilities that can lock routines into place. That is why the system should be carefully examined before a final design sequence is selected. To assign activities to each team, this precedence diagram has been partitioned into three sections, each of which can be considered as a station.

Is it realistic to use a flow shop for heart surgery? If each operation takes 6 hours, how many patients can be treated in a 10-hour day? What kind of charges per operation would be needed to break even? Compare "normal" surgery with the flow shop system. How is quality likely to be affected? How about cost?

We can try to answer these questions with approximations (see Problem 8, p. 506). We are not going to be able to resolve all the issues. Even if we had the data, it would take too much time and obscure the basic concepts in a welter of detail. The problem has been introduced to illustrate the kind of problems we are concerned with and with which we can cope. We will look next at a much smaller problem. Real line balancing problems are seldom so small.

**TABLE 10-1 FILMASTERS'
OPERATION TIMES**

Operation (i)	Operation Time (ti), Minutes
1	0.4
2	0.5
3	0.6
4	0.7
5	0.5
6	1.0
7	0.6
8	0.1
9	0.4

**CASE:
FILMASTERS,
INC.**

This mail-order film processor has developed a new, computer-controlled color process that promises to improve the quality of work while speeding up film developing and printing time. The company executive committee has agreed to run a flow shop operation starting with the receipt of films in the mail to the return of finished work by mail. It has had the plant manager list the various operations (call them $i = 1, 2, \ldots, k$) for the process. For each operation, an operation time t_i has been estimated (as shown in Table 10-1). An ordering of the sequence of operations has been determined (illustrated by the precedence diagram of Fig. 10–2).

This information is essential for line balancing. In addition, Filmasters' executive committee must indicate the level of productivity that is expected— for example, 40 orders processed per hour.

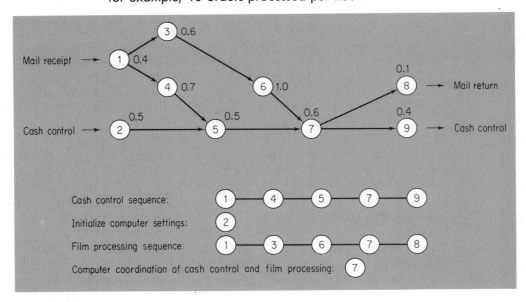

FIGURE 10-2. Filmasters' precedence diagram.

The number 40 was chosen arbitrarily, but it would be chosen by Filmasters to represent actual needs. For this example, the expected demand level is 320 orders per 8-hour day, or 1,600 orders per week. If more orders than that are received, there will be a waiting line, which will begin to disappear when less than 320 orders are received per day.

With a processing capacity of 320 orders per day, if 400 are received on a particular day, a waiting line of 80 orders will result. If on the following day 260 orders are placed, the backlog of 80 will be reduced to 20. Mail-order film customers do not like to wait too long, so the probability that more than 320 orders will be received each day should be low.

CYCLE TIME

How many work stations should Filmasters have? How should operations be assigned to stations? Will the flow shop be well-balanced? What is a well-balanced flow shop?

The answers to these questions depend on the required productivity rate, on the precedence constraints, and on the operation times.

Productivity can be directly translated into cycle time C, which is the time allowed for the job to remain at each station (see Fig. 4–2). Thus, if N orders are to be processed in a work period of T minutes, we have $N/T = 1/C$.

The productive rate of the line is measured by $1/C$ as well as by orders processed (or, in general, items produced) per unit of time. For the example, 40/60 (orders ÷ minutes per hour) equals $1/C$. Hence $40C = 60$ and $C = 1.5$ minutes.

Table 10–1 indicates that the selected productivity of 40 orders per hour may be possible. Every operation time is shorter than the cycle time of 1.5 minutes, so one or more operations can be completed at a station. We assume that the operation times cannot be shortened, that they are the smallest reasonable components into which the total job can be subdivided. Later, we allow changes in operation times resulting from technological factors and from running identical parallel operations. Let us find out what productivity rates are possible, under conditions of perfect balance.

The number of stations n must always be an integer. We cannot have 2.5 work stations. For each integer number of stations, there is an associated cycle time. In Table 10–2, we have added all the operation times ($\Sigma_i t_i$) and found the sum to be 4.8 minutes. ($\Sigma_i t_i$ is called the total work content time.) Thus, each order processed by Filmasters requires 4.8 minutes of work.

Line balancing can decrease the total work content time because of specialization, but we do not assume such savings. However, the number of stations used will determine how many orders are being worked on at the same time (although each at different stages of completion). This in turn will determine the rate at which orders are finished, or the production rate.

If we divide the total work content time by the integer number of stations, we determine the number of minutes spent by an order at each station, and thus the number of minutes elapsing between completion of orders. Equation

**TABLE 10-2 FILMASTERS' TOTAL
WORK CONTENT TIME AND LONGEST
OPERATION TIME (t_{max})**

Operation (i)	Operation Time (t_i), Minutes
1	0.4
2	0.5
3	0.6
4	0.7
5	0.5
6	1.0 (t_{max})
7	0.6
8	0.1
9	0.4
	4.8 $\Sigma_i t_i$

(10–1) gives the cycle time.

$$C = \frac{\Sigma_i t_i}{n} \qquad (10\text{-}1)$$

where n equals the integer number of work stations.

In Table 10–2, we have marked the sixth operation with t_{max}, because it is the longest operation time. Cycle time cannot be smaller than t_{max}. If it were, then the single operation must be completed at more than one station, which is not allowed. Also, cycle time must be equal to or less than $\Sigma_i t_i$ [the latter follows from Eq. (10–1), where the smallest integer value of n is one]. Thus, we have

$$t_{max} \leq C \leq \Sigma_i t_i \qquad (10\text{-}2)$$

Table 10–3 presents Filmasters' possible cycle times C and hourly productivity rates $N/T = 60(1/C)$ for all possible integer number of stations. *Warning: This is based on perfect balance, which may not be able to be achieved (see Fig. 10–4).*

Filmasters' expectation of processing 40 orders per hour seems possible with 4 stations, which with perfect balance can process 50 orders per hour. This allows a leeway of 10 orders per hour under circumstances of less than perfect balance. Another possibility is to set up more than one parallel production line. For example, with perfect balance, two production lines with 2 stations each would also be able to process 50 orders per hour.

What happens if we reduce t_{max} from 1.0 to 0.7 minutes by improving the technology of this film development step? With perfect balance, if that could be achieved, 3 stations would suffice, with a cycle time of exactly 1.5 minutes. Perfect balance is not an unreasonable goal if all operations are automated, or if sufficient allowance has already been made in estimating operation times for workers' rest and delay.

**TABLE 10-3 FILMASTERS' POSSIBLE
CYCLE TIMES, C, AND HOURLY
PRODUCTIVITY RATES
N/T = 60(1/C) FOR ALL INTEGER
NUMBER OF STATIONS, n**

n	$C = \Sigma_i t_i/n$	$N/T = 60(1/C)$
1	4.8 minutes	12.5 orders/hour
2	2.4	25.0
3	1.6	37.5
4	1.2	50.0
*5	0.96	62.5
*6	0.80	75.0
*7	0.69	87.5
*8	0.60	100.0
*9	0.53	112.5

*Not feasible, since $C < (t_{max} = 1.0)$

To obtain this answer we should note that t_{max} is now 0.7 min at operations 4 and 6. Also, $\Sigma_i t_i$ would now be 4.5 minutes. Table 10–4 presents C and N/T for all integer numbers of stations.

What happens if we reduce t_{max} from 1.0 to 0.5 minutes by installing two developing units in parallel for operation 6? Develop your own table for this answer.

Developing Station Layouts

The procedure for developing station layouts is based on the use of **precedence diagrams.** We proceed as follows. Place in station I (the first column) all operations that need not follow others. Fig. 10–2, which is Filmasters' precedence diagram, shows that operations 1 and 2 can be

**TABLE 10-4 FILMASTERS' CYCLE
TIMES AND PRODUCTIVITY FOR ALL
INTEGER NUMBERS OF STATIONS,
n; GIVEN THAT t_{max} IS REDUCED
FROM 1.0 TO 0.7 MINUTES**

n	C	N/T
1	4.5 minutes	13.3 orders/hour
2	2.25	26.7
3	1.5	40.0
4	1.13	53.3
5	0.90	66.7
6	0.75	80.0
7*	0.64	93.3
8*	0.56	106.7
9*	0.50	120.0

*Not feasible, since $C < (t_{max} = 0.7)$.

placed in station I. Then place in station II operations that must follow those in station I, 3 and 4. Note that 5 must follow 4 and therefore cannot be in the second station. Continue to the other columns in the same way. In Fig. 10–3 we have forced Filmasters' operations into the maximum number of stations required by operation sequence, not by operation times.

We observe that while sequence is fully specified, column position is not. For example, operation 2 could be done as well in station II. Note also that, for this first feasible set of 5 stations (which is the maximum number that can be required), 5 is determined by the longest chain of sequenced operations not in time, but in the number of operations.

Many orderings satisfy the precedence requirements. Intracolumn movement is totally free between operations that are mutually independent (not connected by arrows). For example, at station II, operation 3 could be done before operation 4, or vice versa. Also, elements can be moved sideways from their columns to positions to the right without disturbing the precedence restrictions. Thus, operations 3 and 6 could be done at the same work station, with 3 always preceding 6. The first kind of flexibility is called **permutability of columns,** and the second kind is called **lateral transferability.**

How well have we done? With these 5 stations, we have a cycle time of 0.96 minutes. The total operation times, idle times, and violations of cycle time at each station are shown in Table 10–5.

We have violated Equation 10–2, the condition that $C \geq (t_{max} = 1.0)$ (see $n = 5$ in Table 10–3). The cycle time of 0.96, being less than $t_{max} = 1.0$, is not permissible. Also, we have overassigned the second and third stations. This is not allowable. In fact, we require a cycle time of 1.5 to accommodate station III. We have a lot of idle time at the fourth and fifth stations.

A feasible but inefficient assignment pattern is illustrated in Table 10–6. By ''feasible'' we mean that no violations of cycle time have

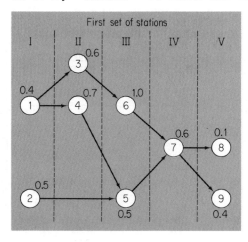

FIGURE 10-3. Filmasters' precedence diagram with 5 stations.

TABLE 10-5 FILMASTERS' FIVE-STATION LAYOUT IS NOT FEASIBLE CYCLE TIME = 0.96 MINUTES

	Station				
	I	II	III	IV	V
Operations	(1), (2)	(3), (4)	(5), (6)	(7)	(8), (9)
Total operation time	0.9	1.3	1.5	0.6	0.5
Idle time	0.06	—	—	0.36	0.46
Violations of cycle time	—	0.34	0.54	—	—

occurred. Total idle time is 2.7 minutes out of a total work time of $5 \times 1.5 = 7.5$ minutes. This is 36 percent idle time. If we decrease the number of stations, can we balance Filmasters' flow shop?

Shortly, we shall turn to heuristic methods for line balancing. These commonsense approaches are necessary for real problems that are too large for trial and error solution. First, however, let us consider perfect and imperfect balance.

Perfect Balance Equals Zero Balance Delay

If the cycle time C is fixed by design (1.5 minutes for Filmasters), then the number of stations under perfect balance would be $\Sigma_i t_i / C = n$, or $4.8/1.5 = 3.2$ stations. This is not a possible solution. The integer number of stations, $n = 3$ or $n = 4$, might qualify; the former if a lower production rate can be accepted, and the latter if higher productivity (probably reduced by idle time) is preferred.

Even if the number of stations, given perfect balance, turned out to be an integer, perfect balance may not be achievable. This is because the jigsaw puzzle of operation times cannot be fitted together so that all operations are self-contained within one station (there is no way to group operations such that the total operation times at all stations are equal).

TABLE 10-6 A FEASIBLE BUT INEFFICIENT LINE BALANCE WITH FIVE STATIONS CYCLE TIME = 1.5 MINUTES

Station	i	t_i	Station Sum	Cumulative Sum	Idle Time
I	1	0.4			
	2	0.5	0.9	0.9	0.6
II	3	0.6			
	4	0.7	1.3	2.2	0.2
III	5	0.5			
	6	1.0	1.5	3.7	0.0
IV	7	0.6	0.6	4.3	0.9
V	8	0.1			
	9	0.4	0.5	4.8	1.0

Aside from the number problem, technological factors exist that do not let operations be combined. Sometimes workers or facilities cannot be shifted between stations in such a way as to let total idle time equal zero. These physical restrictions often are referred to as **zoning constraints.**

When perfect balance is not available, we measure the system's inefficiency (or imperfect balance) by a quantity d, called the **balance delay.** The term refers to unproductive periods at the stations, also called **idle times.** Balance delay is a systems measure of idle time.

$$d = 100(nC - \Sigma_i t_i)/nC \qquad (10\text{-}3)$$

This equation for balance delay d can be better understood by observing that balance delay is zero for all cycle times listed in Tables 10–3 and 10–4. That is because:

$$nC = \Sigma_i t_i \text{ for all values of } n$$

Similarly, for the cycle time specified by Filmasters (which is 1.5 minutes), we derive $n = 3.2$ for perfect balance. Therefore:

$$d = 100[(3.2)(1.5) - (4.8)]/(3.2)(1.5) = 0$$

We must use the integer value of $n = 4$. With the cycle time of 1.5 minutes, balance delay would be:

$$d = 100[(4)(1.5) - (4.8)]/(4)(1.5) = 20\%$$

This is illustrated in Fig. 10–4 to show that balance delay is the total idle time of all stations as a percentage of total available working time of all stations.

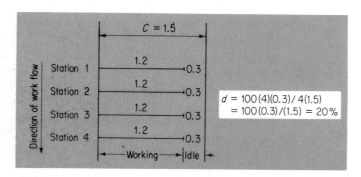

FIGURE 10-4. Filmasters' flow shop with balance delay of 20 percent.

Toyota Model of Continuous Work Flow

Figure 10–5 represents a completely balanced assembly line used by the Toyota Motor Company in Japan.[1] In the center is a box labeled "continuous work flow." It means that all materials are being worked on and passed along to the next work station. Finished cars are continuously coming off the assembly line and can be shipped because they require no reworking. Product-in-process is receiving value-added 100 percent of the time.

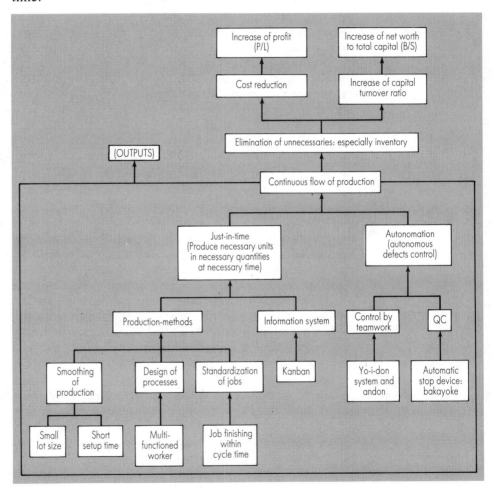

FIGURE 10-5. Toyota continuous work flow.

[1]"What Makes the Toyota Production System Really Tick?", Monden, Yasuhiro; *Industrial Engineering,* January 1981. Copyright Institute of Industrial Engineers, 25 Technology Park/Atlanta, Norcross, GA 30092.

Several parts of Figure 10–5 deserve attention. First, the top part illustrates the financial benefits of having continuous work flows. They generate a continuous stream of revenues with minimum cost and therefore large profit margins. At the left side of the figure are the material control systems used to maintain minimum, but just enough, WIP. The JIT delivery requirement for suppliers assures that the least possible space is needed for received materials used in the assembly process. Plants are near the assembly line space. Trucks deliver supplies where needed on the assembly line; the walls roll up to allow unloading. P/OM scheduling of small product runs is supported by the capability to change from one product to another in a minimum time and without creating startup defectives.

At the right side of the figure are the quality control factors that ensure producing very small numbers of defectives. There are two kinds of signals that each worker can send. One is a call for assistance (yellow light). The other is a button to stop the line (with a red light on the control panel that is seen by all workers). It is said that Toyota has never had a line stop for more than 9 seconds. Worker groups (such as Quality Control Circles) use statistical quality control charts and other means to continuously improve the quality of the product.

Innovation and Degree of Flow Shop Commitment

As the commitment to high-volume flow shop operations grows, so does the investment. Unless great pains are taken to be flexible, rigidity can set in, and the company executives find themselves fighting costly changes to the process. As a result, innovations that smaller companies might be able to introduce are shunted aside. This effect was studied by William Abernathy of Harvard University within the automobile industry and reported by him in *The Productivity Dilemma*. It was later the subject of a conference that resulted in the book, *Industrial Renaissance*.[2]

PROBLEM
SET

1. Draw a precedence diagram for changing a tire. Assume that you are going into business selling tires. Discuss the way in which this job could be done with a flow shop configuration. Why would you prefer a flow shop? Suggest a possible division of labor that could produce a reasonable line balance.

2. Draw a precedence diagram for making a deposit at the bank. How can this job be accomplished by tellers in flow shop configuration? Suggest a possible division of labor that would produce an acceptable

---

[2]William J. Abernathy, *The Productivity Dilemma*, Baltimore: The Johns Hopkins University Press, 1978, and Abernathy, William J., Kim B. Clark and Alan M. Kantrow, *Industrial Renaissance* (New York: Basic Books, 1983).

line balance. What would be the effect of allowing customers to make withdrawals also?

3. For the Filmasters' example, assume that Fig. 10–2 still applies as the precedence diagram, but the operation times in Table 10–1 are changed as follows:

Operation (i)	Operation Time (t_i), Minutes
1	1.4
2	1.5
3	1.6
4	1.7
5	1.5
6	2.0
7	1.6
8	1.1
9	1.4

   a. What productivity rates are possible with perfect balance?
   b. Develop the station layout for $n = 5$. What idle time and violations of cycle time occur (see Table 10–5)?
   c. Develop a feasible station layout. Describe its productivity and balance delay.

4. With respect to line balancing:
   a. What does permutability of columns mean?
   b. What does lateral transferability mean?
   c. To what do zoning constraints apply?

5. A flow shop system has been balanced as follows:

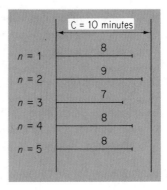

All the work is done with 5 stations.
   a. What is the productive output per hour?
   b. What is the balance delay?

6. With respect to Problem 5, if perfect balance is assumed, how many stations would be required?

7. Answer the following questions:

a. Is it realistic to use a flow shop for heart surgery?

b. If each operation takes 6 hours, how many patients can be treated in a 10-hour day?

c. What kind of charges per operation would be needed to break even?

d. Compare "normal" surgery with the flow shop system. How is quality likely to be affected? How about cost?

Section 10.2: Heuristic Line Balancing

Heuristic Models

Heuristic comes from the Greek word *heuriskein,* meaning to discover. The term has been used by Simon and Newell[3] to describe a particular approach to problem solving and decision making. Heuristic models utilize logic and common sense derived by observation and introspection. These models replace mathematical ones when formal, analytic methods have little promise of being operational. Complex formulations of linear programming (see Chapter 12) and other mathematical models have been devised to obtain solutions to the line balancing problem, but heuristic approaches are faster and offer more latitude for testing alternative hypotheses.

The essence of the heuristic approach is in the application of selective routines that reduce the size of a problem. Thus, for example, the production problem of assembly line balancing can be treated by reducing the total system to a series of simpler line balancing problems that can be studied analytically.[4] Another kind of reduction is used in which a relatively simple rule is applied repeatedly until all decisions that must be made have been made.

Looking at heuristic procedures in another way, sensible rules can be used to simulate the decision-making pattern of managers as they would normally operate in the system. The advantages of this approach are consistency, speed, and the ability to cope with more data and larger systems than is otherwise possible. Once the basic decision-making pattern is developed, it can be expanded and applied to larger system segments.

For situations that do not lend themselves to mathematical analysis for finding optimal solutions, the heuristic approach is an attractive alternative. The key is to trace out and then embody the thinking process that

---

[3]H. A. Simon and A. Newell, "Heuristic Problem Solving: The Next Advance in Operations Research," *Operations Research,* 6, 1 (January–February 1958), pp. 1–10.

[4]Fred M. Tonge, "Summary of a Heuristic Line Balancing Procedure," *Management Science,* 7, 1 (October 1960), pp. 21–39.

an intelligent decision maker would use to resolve the specific type of problem. Heuristic models do not guarantee an optimal result. Instead, they are designed to produce relatively good strategies subject to specific constraints. For the line balancing problem, we will talk about a number of heuristics and illustrate one in particular.

If the product or service output of the flow shop is expected to have a long and stable life cycle, then engineering design will override the mathematical approaches to line balancing. The technological approach using engineering knowledge of materials, mechanics, and electronics alters operation times and creates facilities that are equivalent to many fully integrated and coordinated stations.

On the other hand, when the output life cycle is not stable over a long time, shorter-term flow shops (including intermittent designs) are needed, and these are ideally suited for heuristic resolution.

Kilbridge and Wester's Heuristic

Kilbridge and Wester[5] proposed a heuristic procedure that assigns a number to each operation describing how many predecessors it has. This is easily accomplished by referring to the appropriate precedence diagram. The operations are then rank-ordered according to the number of predecessors each has.

The number 0 is ranked first in line. Next comes 1, then 2, etc. The first operations assigned to stations are those with the lowest predecessor numbers: 0, then 1, then 2. This procedure is illustrated in Tables 10–7 and 10–8.

Using the data for Filmasters, let us balance a three-station configuration where $n = 3$ and $C = 4.8/3 = 1.6$ minutes [Eq. (10-1)]. We count the number of predecessors for each operation (see Fig. 10–2) and list them in Table 10–7.

---

[5]M. D. Kilbridge and L. Wester, "A Heuristic Model of Assembly Line Balancing," *Journal of Industrial Engineering*, 12, 4 (July–August 1961), pp. 292–98.

**TABLE 10-7 OPERATIONS RANKED BY
THE NUMBER OF PREDECESSORS**

Operation	Number of Predecessors	t_i
1	0	0.4
2	0	0.5
3	1	0.6
4	1	0.7
5	3	0.5
6	2	1.0
7	6	0.6
8	7	0.1
9	7	0.4

Operations are assigned to stations in the order of the least number of predecessors. This means, for station I, we first select operations 1 and 2. They have a total operation time of 0.9 min. Since $n = 3$, then $C = 1.6$, so we can introduce either operation 3 with $t_i = 0.6$, or operation 4 with $t_i = 0.7$ into station I.

Where ties exist, another rule applies. Choose first the longest operation times that can be used. Short operations are saved for ease of manipulation at the end of the line. In this way, the earliest stations are given the least idle time possible. Operation 2 precedes Operation 1. Operation 4's time of 0.7 minutes is larger than operation 3's time of 0.6. Therefore, operation 4 is assigned to station I. This results in a total time of 1.6 minutes for station I, which is fully packed with no idle time. Turning to station II, we find that, of the remaining operations, 3 has the least number of predecessors. Next comes operation 6. Together, they have a total activity time of 1.6 minutes. Therefore, station II is also fully packed. If operation 6 has taken too long to fit in station II, then operation 5 would have been chosen. But operations 7, 8, and 9 must be saved for a later station because of precedent constraints.

When an operation with the next smallest number of predecessors has too long an operation time to be included in the station, we select that operation with the next smallest number of predecessors that fits within the station time and precedent constraints. Continuing in this way, we obtain three fully packed stations having no idle time (see Table 10–8).

The precedence diagram (Fig. 10–6) can then be subdivided accordingly. These three perfectly balanced stations can be used, if the technology permits (and this is probable because the precedence constraints have been observed), if facilities permit, and if operator movements permit.

This is an excellent solution, but production output is 37.5 orders per hour and not the 40 orders that Filmasters has set as the objective. If rest time is needed at the stations, then cycle time could be increased to, say, 1.7 or 1.8 minutes, but this would further decrease productivity to 35.3 or 33.3 orders processed per hour.

TABLE 10-8 CYCLE TIME = 1.6

Station	i	t_i	Station	Cumulative Sum	Idle Time
I	2	0.5			
	1	0.4			
	4	0.7	1.6	1.6	0
II	3	0.6			
	6	1.0	1.6	3.2	0
III	5	0.5			
	7	0.6			
	9	0.4			
	8	0.1	1.6	4.8	0

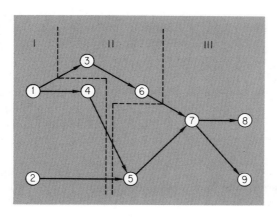

FIGURE 10-6. Filmasters' three-station assignment (Kilbridge and Wester's heuristic).

Other Heuristics

Helgeson and Birnie's Heuristic. Another heuristic suggested by Helgeson and Birnie[6] is to assign to stations first those operations whose "followers" have the largest total time, i.e., the sum t_i of all successors. They call their approach the **ranked positional weight method.**

In Table 10–9, each operation of the Filmasters' example is associated with a weight equal to the sum of all operation times that follow it. The operations are then ranked by descending order of the weight measure.

[6]W. B. Helgeson and D. P. Birnie, "Assembly Line Balancing Using the Ranked Positional Weight Technique," *Journal of Industrial Engineering,* XII, 6 (November–December 1961), pp. 394–398.

TABLE 10-9 CYCLE TIME = 1.6 MINUTES

Station	Operation in Ranked Order	Weight	t_i	Sum	Idle Time
I	1	3.9	0.4		
	3	2.1	0.6		
	2	1.6	0.5	1.5	0.1
II	4	1.6	0.7		
	5	1.1	0.5	1.2	0.4
III	6	1.1	1.0		
	7	0.5	0.6	1.6	0
IV	8	0	0.1		
	9	0	0.4	0.5	1.1
				4.8	1.6

Check Fig. 10–6 to find paths for calculating weights. For example, operations 3, 4, 5, 6, 7, 8, and 9 (not 2) follow operation 1. The sum of these operation times is 3.9. This is the weight given to operation 1 in Table 10–9. Similarly, operation 8 and 9 follow operation 7. The sum of their operation times is 0.5, which is the weight for operation 7 in Table 10–9.

Subject to the cycle time of 1.6 minutes, in the attempt to get three stations, *operations are assigned that do not violate precedence or zoning constraints.* When total time for a station is exceeded, an attempt is made to find a feasible operation further down the list that can be included. This was not possible with station I.

The heuristic requires that operations 1 and 3 be included as part of station I. Operations 2, 4, and 6 are the only ones that might then be included for completion without violating precedence. We could have operations 1, 3, and 4, but their total time is 1.7 minutes. For 1, 3, and 6, it is 2 minutes. This approach does not yield three stations but results in four stations operating under the cycle time of 1.6 minutes. The fourth station's unused capacity is particularly poor. Balance delay is:

$$d = 100(4 \times 1.6 - 4.8)/(4 \times 1.6) = 25 \text{ percent}$$

The same result can be obtained by adding up the total idle time in Table 10–9 and dividing it by total station time: $1.6/(4 \times 1.6)$. Four stations might be used with a cycle time of 1.5 minutes if a feasible station assignment can be found.

Can this be done? Yes, a better solution can be obtained in this way, again using the Helgeson and Birnie heuristic (see Table 10–10 and Fig. 10–7). However, the Kilbridge and Wester solution for $n = 3$ is much better. It has fewer stations with no idle time.

**TABLE 10-10 CYCLE TIME = 1.5 MINUTES
BALANCE DELAY = 1.2/(4 × 1.5) = 20 PERCENT**

Station	i	Weight	t_i	Station Sum	Idle Time
I	1	3.9	0.4		
	3	2.1	0.6	1.0	0.5
II	2	1.6	0.5		
	4	1.6	0.7	1.2	0.3
III	5	1.1	0.5		
	6	1.1	1.0	1.5	0
IV	7	0.5	0.6		
	8	0	0.1		
	9	0	0.4	1.1	0.4
				4.8	1.2

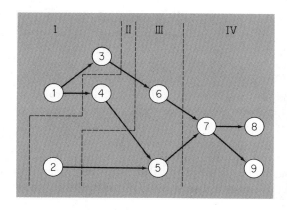

FIGURE 10-7. Filmasters' four-station assignment (Helgeson and Birnie's heuristic).

Tonge's Heuristic. Tonge[7] describes a learning (reward and penalty) precedure that selects a heuristic randomly from a catalog of heuristics. The sequence of selections provides the basis for assigning operations to stations. This is a forerunner to expert systems (ES) and artificial intelligence (AI).

When the selected heuristics produce improved solutions (i.e., less idle time), they are rewarded by increasing the likelihood that they will be selected the next time. When they produce poorer solutions, a penalty is imposed that decreases such likelihoods. Among the set of heuristics employed to choose the next operation were:

1. Longest operation time, t_i
2. Largest number of immediate followers
3. Operation i chosen at random

The choice of heuristic is determined by $p(A)$, $p(B)$, and $p(C)$. These probabilities of choice sum to 1, and initially they are all equal—i.e., 1/3. Then, according to the reduction in balance delay achieved by successive iterations, particular probabilities are increased as they appear to contribute to improved performance. Tonge concludes that this probabilistic approach results in fewer work stations than using any one individual heuristic alone, or a purely random choice of operations.

Arcus's Heuristic. Arcus randomly generated feasible sequences using probability assignments based on precedence, zoning, and feasibility relations. In addition, he used heuristic weighting to improve his results. Another forerunner to ES and AI. The computer program generates 1000 sequences, and the 1 out of a 1000 sequences that is chosen is the one that requires the minimum number of stations. On computers in the 1990s,

---

[7]Fred M. Tonge, "Assembly Line Balancing Using Probabilistic Combinations of Heuristics," *Management Science*, 11, 7 (May 1965), pp. 727–735.

large problems take, at most, a few minutes to generate 1000 sequences. Therefore, it is historically interesting to note Arcus's experience in 1966 with a relatively small problem. He reported that the generation of 1000 sequences for a system of 70 operations on an IBM 7090 required 30 minutes.[8]

Especially for large problems, the objective of minimizing the number of work stations for a given cycle time makes good sense. Usually, it is reasonable to expect that a number of alternative configurations will require the same minimum number of stations, so there is additional leeway for interpretation. All the heuristics we have described attempt to organize those operations that are free to move; some operations cannot move because they are constrained by the partial ordering determined by precedence relations.[9]

PROBLEM SET

1. Solve Filmasters' problem, but change the data by multiplying all operation times by 10. Use the Kilbridge and Wester heuristic to achieve a productivity level of 20 finished units per 8-hour day.

   Answer: To begin, convert to an hourly basis: $20/8 = 2 \ 1/2$ units per hour. Then, cycle time must be $60/2.5 = 24$ minutes, whence we derive the number of stations ($n = \Sigma_i t_i/C = 48/24 = 2$).

   The total work content is 48 and $t_{max} = 10$. The cycle time must be $10 \le C \le 48$. When $n = 2$, the value of C is given by $48/2 = 24$. This assumes zero balance delay. Using Kilbridge and Wester's heuristic, we have:

Station	i	t_i	Station Sum	Cumulative Sum
I	2	5		
	1	4		
	4	7		
	3	6	22	22
II	6	10		
	5	5		
	7	6		
	8	1	22	44
III	9	4	4	48

   This is obviously a poor arrangement. One alternative would be to include operation 9 in station II. This would necessitate changing the

---

[8]A. L. Arcus, "Comsoal: A Computer Method of Sequencing Operations for Assembly Lines," in Elwood S. Buffa, ed., *Readings in Production and Operations Management* (New York: Wiley, 1966), pp. 336–360.

[9]In spite of its antiquity, for one of the best summaries of line balancing approaches, see E. J. Ignall, "A Review of Assembly Line Balancing," *Journal of Industrial Engineering*, 16, 4 (July–August 1965), pp. 244–254.

cycle time to 26 or greater. By shifting workers or changing technology, a decrease in some t_i could be obtained. For example, try to decrease operation 6's time. Another arrangement would be to shift operation 6 to station I and put operation 4 in station II. This would produce station times of 25 and 23, respectively.

The balance delay in the case of $C = 25$ with $n = 2$ is:

$$d = \frac{100(2 \times 25 - 48)}{(2)(25)} = 4 \text{ percent}$$

If C were increased to 27 for flexibility:

$$d = \frac{100(2 \times 27 - 48)}{(2)(27)} = 11.1 \text{ percent}$$

2. Find the solution for Filmasters using the Kilbridge and Wester heuristic with $n = 4$.
   a. What is the cycle time?
   b. What is the productivity rate?
   c. How much idle time results?
   d. What do you recommend, 3 stations or 4?
   e. How about working 9 hours per day with $n = 3$?
   f. Was rest allowance made for workers so that the perfect balance (achieved with $n = 3$) is realistic?
   g. If the system is totally mechanized (there are no workers), can we speed up certain operations so that an output rate of 40 per hour is achieved?
   h. Is it possible to design a balanced flow shop that can deliver hourly output rates of 37.5, 40, and 42.5 at the flick of a switch?

Section 10.3: Stochastic Line Balancing

Another dimension of the line balancing problem occurs when operation times at the work stations are variable. Without careful planning, bottlenecks happen, and then a WIP buildup occurs. If a paced conveyor is used, it may have to be stopped or other steps taken to keep the process moving.

Beyond Deterministic Estimates

There is yet another dimension to the line balancing problem, and that is when operation times are randomly distributed. The operation times are variable within limits, or **stochastic**. To illustrate, Filmasters' operation

6 might sometimes require as little as 0.8 minutes, and sometimes as much as 1.3 minutes. The average time is 1.0 minute. Accordingly, we would consider the costs of stopping the line plus other methods of dealing with the situation when a station exceeds its time. Various line balancing algorithms minimize overall costs under stochastic conditions.[10]

Perfect Balance and the Stochastic Problem

A perfectly balanced line is the goal of engineers, especially when equipment determines timing. Mechanization and automation are the ultimate forms of perfect balance. No manager wants to approach the state of perfect balance when dealing with workers on the line. Human behavior ensures that the t_is are not deterministic, but are random variables. The more that human effort is involved on the line, the more this statement applies. Thus, some idle time is purposely maintained so that the cycle time will not be exceeded.

With a paced line, exceeding the cycle time often means that the conveyer must be stopped and all $n - 1$ stations will be idle waiting for the other station to catch up. Alternatively, the part can be removed from the line, creating a queue (or waiting line) for the station that slipped behind. Special workers can be assigned who can shift from station to station to provide extra help where needed. Each situation has its own characteristics, which determine the best thing to do.

When humans dominate the work content of the line, a rule of thumb for P/OMs is to load the stations within 90 percent of full utilization. This provides a degree of leeway for rest and changing pace. Also, it takes some of the pressure off the workers that arises with a perfectly balanced system. The resulting product quality is improved. The costs of inspection and rejects are decreased. The total cost concept should include the additional terms related to costs of exceeding cycle times when this is a possibility.

We should not overlook the fact that the **line balancing problem** refers to the way in which machines and human components of a production line are matched with respect to their characteristic production rates. The machines can be counted upon for relatively deterministic t_is, whereas the human operators of the system have significant variability. There is a substantial literature on the effects of stochastic behavior on system performance where inventories build up when a successor operation works more slowly than the preceding one.

---

[10]For a good example, see Fred N. Silverman, "The Effects of Stochastic Work Times on the Assembly Line Balancing Problem," August 19, 1974 (unpublished dissertation). Plus 2 articles by Fred N. Silverman and John Carter, "A Cost Effective Approach to Stochastic Line Balancing with Off-Line Repair" *J of Operations Management,* Feb. 1984 and "A Cost-based Methodology for Stochastic Line Balancing with Intermittent Line Stoppages," *MANAGEMENT SCIENCE,* April, 1986.

Queues can form when stochastic behavior characterizes the t_is (the operation times are statistically distributed). The word "queue" literally means a tail-like plait of hair worn behind; a pigtail. The word is commonly used to describe a waiting line for service, such as a group of people lining up while waiting for a bus).

We are dealing with a series of stations, every one of which can be considered to be an input-output process. Each station provides service through its combined operations. One or several things come to the station to claim service. Thus, we have a provider of service and a user of that service.

In the TQC environment, each next station is a customer for the supplier station that precedes it. If there are no queues, then the JIT principle has been achieved. Flow-through is continuous and WIP-less. Each station pulls work from the prior one. JIT is usually considered to contain TQC. This is because defectives stop the continuous flow of revenue-producing output. JIT is not always achieved. When it is not, queues can occur. Queueing models are ideal representations of in-line systems where one machine feeds the next one, and so on down the line. WIP can build up quickly and shut down the feeding machine when storage space is exceeded. That is why pull systems are used. They have the advantage of simulating the continuous flow of a perfectly balanced, deterministic line.

The pull system does not allow the preceding work station to supply the next work station in line with any WIP until that next work station is finished servicing all the work it currently has. The Japanese use a card called a *kanban* to signify that the next work station will be needing x number of parts to continue working. When the *kanban* calls for one part at a time, the ideal JIT flow system is achieved.

The **pull system** is contrasted with the **push system,** where each station works as hard and continuously as it can, while pushing the WIP to the next work station. A motivating factor for such diligence is the accounting system, which records the utilization factor of workers and equipment. The focus is on keeping everyone and everything busy. But the result is unnecessary production. Unnecessary storage space is filled with unsold WIP, which has unnecessary carrying costs and which tends to get damaged, stolen, or lost. The smooth-running JIT pull system has **multiplicative advantages** over the full-utilization accounting model.

A Single-Channel Service System

Consider the fundamental single-channel queueing (service) model. Figure 10–8 shows this one-service facility system, where λ is the input rate and μ is the output (or processing) rate.

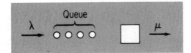

FIGURE 10-8. A single-channel service system.

A Multiple-Channel Service System

We can expand this model to a multiple-channel service system with M service facilities (see Fig. 10–9). Multiple-channel service systems can exist within work stations or between work stations of line-balanced processes. Wherever a work station has several workers and/or facilities dedicated to the same set of operations, the computations for an M channel system apply.

Knowledge of the structure of queueing models is fundamental to understanding stochastic line balancing. Queueing models are concerned with the following generalized situations:

1. *The system provides a specific service.* The service facilities might be composed of such diverse units as drill presses, milling machines, turret lathes, drop forges, plating tanks, airplane seats, hospital operating tables, supermarket checkout counters, tellers' windows, tollbooths, shipping docks, airport runways, restaurant tables, telephone trunk lines, and machine repair staff. Service is rendered within the firm to internal customers, as well as outside the firm to external customers. Suppliers provide the services.

2. *Units arrive to receive the service.* These can include materials to be machined or plated, travelers, patients, shoppers, customers, ships, airplanes, gourmets, and machines that have broken down. Extreme diversity of both materials and people needs marks these applications. This confirms our interest in goods and services, public and private sectors, especially with regard to achieving flow shop productivity whenever possible.

3. *There is an expected or average rate of servicing the units.* For example, on the average, 5 units are serviced per hour. We call this expected servicing rate μ. There is a distribution of servicing rates around a mean value. That is, sometimes more than 5 units are

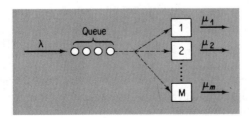

FIGURE 10-9. An M-channel service system.

serviced per hour, while at other times less than 5 units receive service.

4. *There is an expected rate of arrival of the units for servicing.* For example, on the average, 3 units arrive per hour that require service. We call this expected arrival rate λ. There is a distribution of arrival rates around a mean value. That is, sometimes more than 3 units arrive, sometimes less.

5. *Because we are dealing with distributions, a greater than average number of units can arrive for servicing.* It is equally possible that a run of units will require longer than average servicing times. Under such circumstances a queue or waiting line can develop, even though the process has ample capacity and is capable of providing more service than is normally demanded, that is, $\mu > \lambda$. At other times, less than the expected number of units can arrive or shorter than average servicing times can occur. This produces idle time for service facilities.

6. *We have as a guide to the probable behavior of a single-channel system the ratio* $\rho = \lambda/\mu$. It is called the **process utilization factor.** We must also know or make assumptions about the shapes of the distributions around the expected values of λ and μ.

7. *Service units arranged in job shop configuration show each one standing alone as an individual input/output system providing batch service.* When the flow shop configuration is used, the various service units are interrelated, and the outputs of one system become the inputs to another. This requires careful coordination and matching of the stochastic behaviors of systems that are in communication with each other.

Measures of Service Effectiveness

For the successful operation of any production process, management must decide how much service capacity is required, what type of facilities will provide optimum service, and how to group facilities in a production line. These problems are particularly demanding for the flow shop.

Whatever the specific situation, some measures of effectiveness, such as the ten shown below, are useful to evaluate the service system. Others may be found that are better suited to particular situations.

1. Average number of units in a queue. We shall call this L_q.
2. Average number of units in the system, called L. (This includes the number in the queue and the number in service.)
3. Average waiting time (delay) before service begins, called W_q.
4. Average total time spent by a unit in the system, called W. (This total delay is the sum of waiting time and service time.)

5. The probability that any delay or waiting will occur, called $P(n > M)$, where n equals the total number of units in the system, and M stands for the number of service facilities.

6. The probability that the total delay will be greater than some value of t, $P(W > t)$. (A comparable expression could be written for W_q.)

7. The probability that n units will be in the system (where M of them will be in service, given M channels) called P_n.

8. The probability that all service facilities will be idle, called P_0. (Note: $n = 0$ in 7 above.)

9. The expected percentage of idle time of the total service facility:

$$\overline{I} = \frac{M}{M} P_0 + \frac{(M - 1)}{M} P_1 + \cdots + \frac{(M - n)}{M} P_n + \frac{(M - M)}{M} P_M$$

(Again, note that P_n equals the probability that n units will be in the system, both waiting for and receiving service from M facilities.)

10. The probability of turnaways, resulting from insufficient waiting line accommodations, P_n, where $N - M$ represents the maximum number of units that can be stored or accommodated on the waiting line at any moment.

Having evaluated the characteristics of a process (or components of a process) in terms of these or other measures of effectiveness, it is possible to achieve highly productive systems. Without such measures, the P/OM will be hard pressed to achieve even a reasonably good systems design. The reason for this is that the situation is simply far too complex for intuition. Even using queueing models, one does not obtain optimum performance. Queueing models are descriptive. They cannot be optimized. Consequently, the manager designs one or more production systems and then tests them by adequate queueing criteria. Changes are made based on test results, and the system is retested. This goes on until a satisfactory configuration is obtained.

The OPT System

The **Optimum Production Technique (OPT)** focuses on bottlenecks. OPT is not a bottleneck remover, but it is a bottleneck identifier. Then production scheduling is designed to feed the bottleneck. Because OPT is intended for job shops, and not for line-balanced flow shops, it is discussed in more depth in Chapter 11.

Storage Space for WIP

A natural restriction on queue size exists if the storage facilities needed to accommodate a waiting line are limited. For example, the size of a doctor's waiting room provides a physical upper limit on queue length. The doctor's office is a kind of flow shop where the doctor is the single-channel server, and people waiting for processing queue up in the waiting room. The doctor tries to maintain continuous flow. On a production line, the in-process inventory will be limited by the amount of storage space that can be made available between operations. Figure 10–10 depicts the fact that only an inventory limited to N items can be carried between operations A and B.

We know that because of variability in both arrival and service rates a queue can form under even the most favorable process utilization ratio, ρ. When this queue has grown to size N, several different things can happen. Here are some examples:

1. *The N + 1 arrival is turned away.* This could mean that it is taken to an outside storage depot. In the case of a person arriving at the doctor's office when it is completely filled, the individual can refuse to stand outside the door and thus becomes a turnaway.
2. *The N + 1 arrival does not leave the first service facility (which we call A).* Instead, it stays there until the queue in front of the next service facility (which we call B) can accept it. In this way, A is blocked for other service and forced to be idle. This is equivalent to shutting down operation A until the bottleneck is cleared up. The problem is particularly relevant to the flow shop. Adjacent facilities must be coordinated to minimize the probability that bottlenecks will occur.

The design of the production process must take these possibilities of bottlenecks and idleness into account. It is unusual that a large in-process inventory can be tolerated. Excessive in-process inventories must be put somewhere off the line, or they must be prevented. Some production lines permit no queues. This is so where the facilities are mechanized for continuous production. The system must be stopped if there is trouble, or else the defectives are picked off the line at the output for rework. Automobile assembly lines are often like this, and can have rework rates as high as 30 percent. When all is going well, there is an uninterrupted flow of nondefective materials through the total process. (See the Toyota process, Figure 10–5).

With the process stopped, only when all operations have been com-

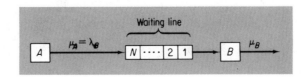

FIGURE 10-10. There is a limitation (N) on the size of the in-process inventory between operations A and B.

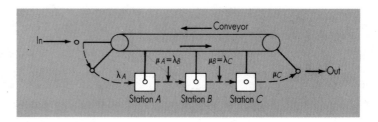

FIGURE 10-11. A production system where no waiting line is permitted.

pleted at each work station is the production line permitted to advance. This Kanban-type system is illustrated by Fig. 10–11. For such lines a breakdown of any one facility will close down the entire line until repairs are made, unless duplicate facilities are available.

Our discussion is converging on the production fundamentals of line balancing and plant layout. There are many variations of facility arrangements; Fig. 10–12 provides just a few possiblilities. Each of these three variants would perform quite differently, even though all have the same number of *A* and *B* facilities.

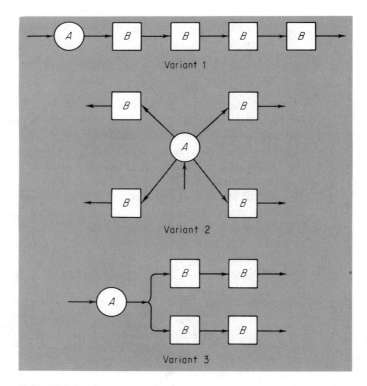

FIGURE 10-12. Alternative arrangements of facilities produce different systems' performances. Thus, three possible arrangements are shown for a system with one A facility and four B facilities.

Variable Work Rates of Adjoining Stations

Our initial line balancing analysis was based on the assumption that activity times were deterministic. Now we are considering what happens when we allow activity times to vary; that is, they are stochastic. We must examine two important questions concerning the probability distributions of activity times.

1. *Are the arrival and service rate distributions stable over time?* A rough criterion to use with respect to this requirement would be that the distribution shapes, obtained in successive periods of time, are similar. The distribution of the first sample period compared with that of the second sample period should be essentially the same. These data can then be pooled. Although such a criterion lacks rigor, it can be of practical utility if used with care. A more satisfactory criterion is supplied by statistical control theory (see pp. 267–269). Queueing models do not work with unstable distributions. If the distributions of the productioin process are changing, control methodology must be applied to stabilize the situation.

2. *What are the shapes of the distributions?* Figure 10–13 illustrates a number of possible distributions. These are **cumulative probability distributions.**

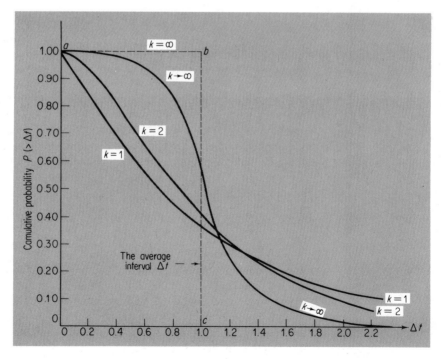

FIGURE 10-13. Some theoretical cumulative probability distributions. As the parameter k approaches infinity, the distribution takes on the shape abc.

A point on any one of the curves is the probability that the arrival or service interval will be greater than the x-axis interval Δt. Accordingly, there is 100 percent probability that the interval will be greater than zero for all distributions, and this makes sense.

For the $k = 1$ curve, there is a 50 percent probability that the interval will be greater than 0.69315 ($e^{-0.69315} = 0.5$) and a 36.78 percent probability that the interval will be greater than 1 hour ($e^{-1} = 0.3678$).

Frequently, some member of this family of theoretical curves will provide a reasonably good approximation to the observed distribution. The curve marked $k = 1$ in Fig. 10–13 is an **exponential distribution**. It is identified with the case of pure randomness. Pure randomness exists if there are no sequential patterns of long and short intervals. The exponential distribution is observed when the intervals between arrivals or the service intervals are entirely independent of the length of all previous intervals. In effect, the succession of intervals is the outcome of a random process.

A process of this type is exemplified by the succession of heads and tails of a coin. The coin has no memory of prior outcomes. The output rates of behavioral systems are often of this type. The distribution associated with $k \rightarrow \infty$ is more characteristic of machines. It is approaching a constant interval value. On the other hand, here are some examples that would not satisfy the requirement of independence. A pieceworker's rate increases with practice and decreases with fatigue, producing a cyclical pattern over the day. The speed of a machine increases as it heats up, and the temperature rises as a function of use. A maintenance crew attempts to beat the servicing times of another crew. The accident rate of an individual increases because of the psychological phenomenon of accident proneness. The lack of independence is more frequently associated with the human component in the system than with machines. But it can be found with machines.

Many situations are reasonably well described by the $k = 1$ type of distribution. We limit our attention to exponential distributions, but with the realization that process design and line balancing may involve a large variety of types of distributions which must be recognized and understood for satisfactory control.

A Line Balancing Example

Fundamental differences exist between continuous and intermittent production processes. We are familiar with such relatively continuous processes as canning, bottling, refining, automobile assembly, and production of semiconductor chips. Other goods and services, such as making clothing and toys, delivering mail, providing patient care, and printing books and newspapers, require different degrees of intermittent production. The range can be from what are basically job shops to "almost" flow shops.

For job shops, the major production problem is to find the best way to assign jobs to machines. The various methods available to help resolve this problem are discussed in Chapter 11.

With the flow shop, if the station assignments are not properly designed, serious bottlenecks can develop, resulting in extremely inefficient operations. Machine breakdowns can stop the entire line and cause a backing up of in-process inventories with only so much storage space between stations. A complete study of equipment characteristics is required. The effects of preventive maintenance on machine breakdowns must be understood.

Line balancing can be handled by simulating throughput in the system, with all the random factors that can affect the process being taken into account. These are the flows of information, materials, energy, and resources that are used by the transformation process. Such simulations can be well worth the time and effort if a large process investment is being tested (simulation is treated on pp. 369–371 and 528–534).

CASE: SORTING BULK MAIL

Another approach, which we now examine, utilizes the mathematical and statistical models derived from queueing theory. To give substance to our discussion, let us consider the flow shop problem of sorting bulk mail (see Fig. 10–14).

Our production line consists of only two stations, called I and II. The technological sequence will be fixed: I goes first, II goes second. Thus, I is sort mail by region, and II is sort mail within region. We assume that station I has an expected production output rate of 3 units per minute. This in turn describes the expected load on station II, which has an assumed process rate of 4 units per minute. Furthermore, we do not restrict the in-process (WIP) inventory accommodations between the first and second mail-sorting stages. Figure 10–15 depicts this arrangement, called Case A (where $\lambda = 3$ is the output rate of I and consequently the input rate to II; $\mu = 4$ is the process or service rate of II).

Although station II's output capacity is greater than I's, a queue can develop. This might occur if I speeds up while II remains constant at the expected value. It could also be that a queue of WIP inventory develops because II slows down while I performs according to expectation. If both

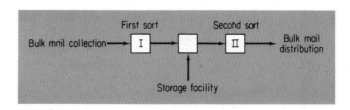

FIGURE 10-14.

FIGURE 10-15. Sorting system: Case A.

events occur simultaneously, the resultant queue can be formidable. The average number of units in the queue would be:

$$L_q = \frac{\rho^2}{(1 - \rho)}$$

where

$$\rho = \frac{\lambda}{\mu} = \frac{3}{4} = 0.75$$

Then

$$L_q = \frac{9}{4} = 2.25$$

These relationships apply when:

1. There is a very large source of mail to be sorted.
2. There are unlimited accommodations for a waiting line.
3. Service is granted on a FIFO (first-in, first-out) basis.
4. There is a single service channel.
5. The arrival and service distributions are both exponential.

We can also determine the probability distribution (P_n), where P_n equals the probability that a total of n units is in the system. Some units would be waiting for service from station II. These units comprise the WIP. The remaining unit is being served by II.

When $n = 0$, station II is idle. When $n = 1$, station II is working and the WIP inventory is zero. When $n = 2$, one unit is waiting for station II to become available, and so forth. We know:

$$P_n = (1 - \rho)\rho^n$$

The same five conditions hold as listed above.[11]

---

[11]For these and other queueing formulations, see P. M. Morse, *Queues, Inventories and Maintenance* (New York: Wiley, 1958); D. R. Cox and W. L. Smith, *Queues* (London: Methuen, 1961); T. L. Saaty, *Elements of Queueing Theory* (New York: McGraw-Hill, 1961).

Then, we can prepare Table 10–11 for station II.

TABLE 10-11

n	P_n	Probability Density	Cumulative Probability
0	$P_0 = (1 - \rho)$	$= 0.2500$	0.2500
1	$P_1 = (1 - \rho)\rho^1$	$= 0.1875$	0.4375
2	$P_2 = (1 - \rho)\rho^2$	$= 0.1406$	0.5781
3	$P_3 = (1 - \rho)\rho^3$	$= 0.1055$	0.6836
4	$P_4 = (1 - \rho)\rho^4$	$= 0.0791$	0.7627
5	$P_5 = (1 - \rho)\rho^5$	$= 0.0593$	0.8220
6	$P_6 = (1 - \rho)\rho^6$	$= 0.0445$	0.8665
7	$P_7 = (1 - \rho)\rho^7$	$= 0.0334$	0.8999
8	$P_8 = (1 - \rho)\rho^8$	$= 0.0250$	0.9249
9	$P_9 = (1 - \rho)\rho^9$	$= 0.0188$	0.9437
10	$P_{10} = (1 - \rho)\rho^{10}$	$= 0.0141$	0.9578
.	.	.	.
.	.	.	.
.	.	.	.
n	etc.	etc.	etc.

Figure 10–16 depicts the resulting probability distribution that n units are in the system. The area of the tail of this distribution (crosshatched) is the probability that the queue length will exceed some designated value of $n - 1$. (We have called this tail area α.) When there are n units in a single channel system, one unit is being serviced. Therefore, the queue length is $n - 1$, which for this example is equal to 8 with a probability $\alpha = 0.0563$ that the queue length will exceed this value.

Thus, the in-process inventory can be expected to be greater than 8 more than 5 percent of the time. If only 8 units can be stored between stations I and II, then at least 5 percent of the time the flow shop will have to be shut down. This is undesirable, and steps must be taken to decrease the probability of exceeding 8 units in queue or of providing more storage space between stations I and II.

Many other performance characteristics of this system are also apparent. Station II will be idle 25 percent of the time. We know this from the fact that $P_0 = 0.25$. Station II's output will be:

$$\text{Expected output} = (1 - P_0)\mu = (0.75)(4) = 3 \text{ units per minute}$$

which is equal to $3(60) = 180$ units per hour.

The use of line balancing to resolve the bulk mail sorting problem assumes realistic meaning when the manager begins to associate costs and value

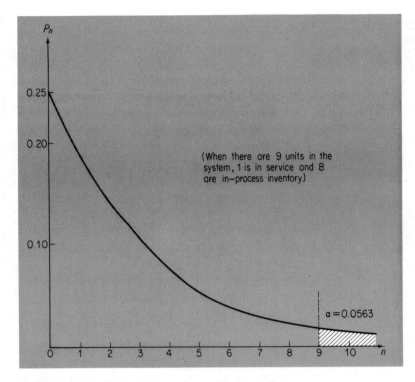

P_n

0.25

0.20

(When there are 9 units in the
system, 1 is in service and 8
are in-process inventory)

0.10

$\alpha = 0.0563$

0   1   2   3   4   5   6   7   8   9   10 n

FIGURE 10-16. Probability density distribution for $\rho = 0.75$.

with the system's performance characteristics. Thus, for example, the manager might assemble the following information:

Expected output — 180 units per hour
Output value — $0.50 (postage) per unit of dispatched bulk mail
Cost of station I* — $30 per hour
Cost of station II* — $50 per hour
Storage cost — $5 per bulk mail unit per hour

*The cost factors of the facilities would be straightforward to compute if the facilities are salaried individuals. For machines and man-machine combinations, an approximate cost figure can still be found.

Then, the net value of the configuration shown in Fig. 10–15 (called Case A) would be:

Net value ($/hr) = total output value − total input costs

$$= \left(\begin{array}{c}\text{output value} \\ \text{per unit}\end{array}\right) \left(\begin{array}{c}\text{expected output} \\ \text{per hour}\end{array}\right)$$
$$\quad - \text{ total input costs}$$
$$= (\text{output value})(1 - P_0)\mu(60) - (\text{storage cost})L_q$$
$$\quad - \text{ cost of stations}$$
$$= (\$0.50)(180) - [(\$5.00)(2.25) + \$30.00 + \$50.00]$$
$$= \$90.00 - \$91.25 = -\$1.25$$

The job shop method of sorting may well have resulted in an even greater loss than $1.25 an hour. We cannot jump to any conclusions about "how bad is bad" until we have compared this flow shop arrangement with the net value per hour of the present method. In any case, the manager does have another idea in mind. He would like to test an alternative to see which balanced configuration is superior (see Fig. 10–17, which is called Case B).

For Case B, two slower station I-type sorters, having the same combined output as the Case A facility, will be used. These are called I_1s. The combined cost of the two slower stations is $15 less per hour than that of the faster station.

Also, for Case B, two slower station II-type sorters, each having half the output of the Case A facility, will be used. These are called II_1s. The combined hourly cost of these two slower stations is the same as that of the faster station.

The manager's idea is to try two slower parallel sorting operations. Cross-overs are not allowed between channels; i.e., each I_1 is specifically paired with one II_1 and cannot supply the other one. The relevant equations are the same as those used for Case A:

For each subsystem ($I_1 \rightarrow II_1$):

$$p = \frac{1.5}{2} = 0.75$$

Therefore,

$$L_q = 2.25$$

$$P_0 = 0.25$$

$$\text{Expected output} = (1 - P_0)\mu = (0.75)2 = 1.5 \text{ units/min}$$

which is equal to 1.5(60) = 90 units/hour.

The combined expected waiting line is $2L_q$ = 4.50, The combined output is 2(90) = 180 units per hour. Then the net value for the total system is

$$\text{Net value (\$/hr)} = (\$0.50)(180) - [(\$5.00)(4.5) + \$15.00 + \$50.00]$$
$$= \$90.00 - \$87.50 = +\$2.50$$

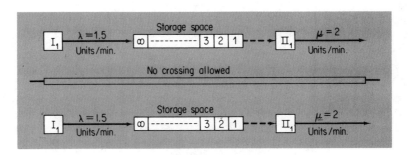

FIGURE 10-17. Sorting system; Case B.

Presumably, the Case B design would be chosen unless other alternatives existed. Other alternatives might also have been requested if none of the designs yielded a satisfactory measure of value.

We have tried to present a simple description of the kind of thinking that occurs in the stochastic line balancing problem. Far more complex situations, including many activities and stations, and a variety of alternative arrangements, can occur.

Flow Shop Simulation with Stochastic Station Times

It has been proposed that a two-station system be used to sort bulk mail in a flow shop configuration (see Fig. 10–18). The output rates of the first and second stations are expected to vary as shown in Table 10–12.

The average output rate for station I is 3.4 units per minute and for station II it is 3.6 units per minute. Since II processes at a faster rate than I, it might be supposed that the storage facility between I and II, which is of limited size, would not become a constraint on the output of station I. That is, station I must stop working when the storage queue gets larger than N.

Output rates are easily converted to "intervals between inputs from station I and to service durations at station II" by taking the reciprocals (as in column 2 of Table 10–12). Column 3 gives the probability distribution estimates, and these are converted into Monte Carlo numbers (column 4) for the following reason: We want to simulate a random process. In this case, we need to generate sequences of input intervals from station I and service intervals at station II that conform to the respective probability distributions of each station.

Monte Carlo numbers enable us to do this. However, we begin our discussion with colored chips mixed together in a bowl. Then we will show how these colored chips can be used to explain the Monte Carlo process. We count out colored chips in the quantities shown in Table 10–13.

Mix station I's chips in a bowl marked I. Mix station II's chips in a separate bowl, marked II. Withdraw a single chip from each bowl. Say they are blue and yellow. This means that the first interval between inputs

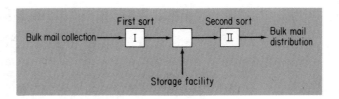

FIGURE 10-18.

TABLE 10-12

Output Rate		Interval between Inputs to Station II	Probability	Monte Carlo Number
Station I	2 units/min	0.500 minutes	0.10	00–09
	3	0.333	0.50	10–59
	4	0.250	0.30	60–89
	5	0.200	0.10	90–99
		Service Duration at Station II		
Station II	2 units/min	0.500 minutes	0.10	00–09
	3	0.333	0.30	10–39
	4	0.250	0.50	40–89
	5	0.200	0.10	90–99

to station II was 0.250 minute (blue). Then, 0.500 minute (yellow) elapses before station II completes its sorting operations on this same unit. The sequence of colors withdrawn from bowl I will represent the sequence of input intervals from station I. The sequence of colors withdrawn from bowl II will represent the sequence of service durations at station II.

Replace the chips in their respective bowls (we do not want to change the probability distributions). Make sure that the chips are well mixed in each bowl (we want to be certain that every chip has an equal likelihood of being picked). Continue picking and replacing chips in the same way until an adequate simulation sample has been achieved. A good criterion for adequate is that the frequency count of the actual colors withdrawn matches the estimated probability distribution.

Figure 10–19 graphically depicts what has occurred and makes it easy to visualize what can happen next. If the second chip withdrawn from bowl I is red, blue, or black, it will signify that a second input will arrive at station II before the first input unit has been completed. Consequently, the second arrival will have to wait. Specifically, if the second bowl I chip is red, then the unit arrives at $0.250 + 0.333 = 0.583$ and must wait:

$$0.750 - 0.583 = 0.167 \text{ min}$$

TABLE 10-13

Station I			Station II		
Input Intervals	Color	Quantity	Service Intervals	Color	Quantity
0.500 min	Green	10	0.500 min	Yellow	10
0.333	Red	50	0.333	Orange	30
0.250	Blue	30	0.250	Purple	50
0.200	Black	10	0.200	Brown	10

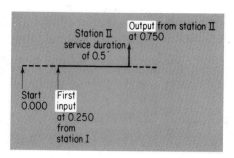

FIGURE 10-19.

On the other hand, if the second bowl I chip is green, then the unit arrives at 0.250 + 0.500 = 0.750, just as station II has completed sorting the first unit, and there is no waiting. Let us complete the analysis.

First, assume that the storage facility between stations I and II can accommodate only one unit. Two more units are completed at station I before station II has completed servicing the first unit:

One at 0.250 + 0.200 = 0.450, a bowl I—black chip

The second at 0.450 + 0.250 = 0.700, a bowl I—blue chip

Station I must shut down from 0.700 until 0.750. Then, at 0.750, station II begins servicing the waiting unit and unblocks the storage facility, which accepts the unit that has been held at station I.

Second, assume that station II completes servicing the first unit at 0.750 and that a second unit arrives at that time which is serviced in 0.200 minutes (a bowl II—brown chip). This means that station II will be idle at 0.750 + 0.200 = 0.950 if anything but a bowl I—black chip is drawn. In Fig. 10–20, the third input is a bowl I—red chip, arriving at station II at 0.750 + 0.333 = 1.083.

To understand Monte Carlo numbers, replace the colored chips with numbered chips. This is shown in Table 10–14. Instead of green chips, we now have chips numbered 00–09. There were 10 chances to pick a green chip.

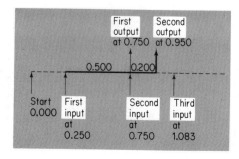

FIGURE 10-20.

TABLE 10-14

| | Station I | | | | Station II | |
Color	Monte Carlo Numbers	Quantity	Service Interval	Color	Monte Carlo Numbers	Quantity
Green	00–09	10	0.500 min	Yellow	00–09	10
Red	10–59	50	0.333	Orange	10–39	30
Blue	60–89	30	0.250	Purple	40–89	50
Black	90–99	10	0.200	Brown	90–99	10

Now there are 10 chances to pick a chip numbered 00–09, associated with an input interval from station I of 0.500 minute. Similarly, there are 50 chances of picking a chip numbered 10–59. This is the right proportion of station I input intervals of 0.333. Because we have numbers instead of colors, we can do away with the necessity for chips. Instead, we use a table of random numbers (Table 10–15). The character of the numbers in the table is that they have been randomly generated. This means that any digit 0 through 9 is as likely to appear as any other.

Therefore, following some systematic pattern of reading the numbers (vertically, diagonally, horizontally) so that we do not introduce bias in the way numbers are selected, we read off successive pairs of digits. Of every 2 pair, the first is equivalent to an input interval from station I, and the second is equivalent to a service interval at station II. We would use successive triplets of digits 000–999 if the probabilities are stated to three places, and so on.

We shall now run a hand simulation of the two-station bulk mail flow shop for sorting introduced earlier. The simulation consists of choosing successive pairs of random numbers and matching these against the input interval and service interval Monte Carlo numbers shown in Table 10–12.

The first random number pair indicates the interval until the next arrival at station II. The second random number pair tells how long service will take. When a sufficient sample is drawn, the bottleneck effect of limited storage between stations can be assessed. The idle time of station II can be estimated, and the overall quality of this flow shop configuration can be observed to determine whether an acceptable line balance has been achieved.

If we use a left to right scan of our random number table (only the starting portion of the top line is shown here), the first 2 pairs of digits are 05 and 62, representing an input interval of 0.500 and a service duration of 0.250.

05621   64483   38549   62908   71579   19203   83546

The simulation continues in Table 10–16 (especially note Arrival Time, Completion Time, Idle Time, and Queue Size).

TABLE 10-15 RANDOM NUMBERS

05621	64483	38549	62908	71579	19203	83546	05917	51905	10052
03550	59144	59468	37984	77892	89766	86489	46619	50263	91136
22188	81205	99699	84260	19693	36701	43233	62719	53117	71153
63759	61429	14043	49095	84746	22018	19014	76781	61086	90216
55006	17765	15013	77707	54317	48862	53823	52905	70754	68212
81972	45644	12600	01951	72166	52682	97598	11955	73018	23528
06344	50136	33122	31794	86423	58037	36065	32190	31367	96007
92363	99784	94169	03652	80824	33407	40837	97749	18364	72666
96083	16943	89916	55159	62184	86208	09764	20244	88388	98675
92993	10747	08985	44999	36785	65035	65933	77378	92339	96454
95083	70292	50394	61044	65591	09774	16216	63561	59751	78771
77308	60721	96057	86031	83148	34970	30892	53489	44999	18021
11913	49624	28510	27311	61586	28576	43092	69971	44220	80410
70648	47484	05095	92335	55299	27161	64486	71307	85883	69610
92771	99203	37786	81142	44271	36433	31726	74879	89348	76886
78816	20975	13043	55921	82774	62745	48338	88348	61211	88074
79934	35392	56097	87613	94627	63622	08110	16611	88599	02890
64698	83376	87524	36897	17215	74339	69856	43622	22567	11518
44212	12995	03581	37618	94851	63020	65348	55857	91742	79508
82292	00204	00579	70630	37136	50922	83387	15014	51838	81760
08692	87237	87879	01629	72184	33853	95144	67943	19345	03469
67927	76855	50702	78555	97442	78809	40575	79714	06201	34576
62167	94213	52971	85974	68067	78814	40103	70759	92129	46716
45828	45441	74220	84157	23241	49332	23646	09390	13032	51569
01164	35307	26526	80335	58090	85871	07205	31749	40571	51755
29283	31581	04359	45538	41435	61103	32428	94042	39971	63678
19868	49978	81699	84904	50163	22625	07845	71308	00859	87984
14294	93587	55960	23149	07370	65065	06580	46285	07884	83928
77410	52195	29459	23032	83242	89938	40510	27252	55565	64714
36580	06921	35675	81645	60479	71035	99380	59759	42161	93440
07780	18093	31258	78156	07871	20369	53947	08534	39433	57216
07548	08454	36674	46255	80541	42903	37366	21164	97516	66181
22023	60448	69344	44260	90570	01632	21002	24413	04671	05665
20827	37210	57797	34660	32510	71558	78228	42304	77197	79168
47802	79270	48805	59480	88092	11441	96016	76091	51823	94442
76730	86591	18978	25479	77684	88439	35112	26052	57112	91653
26439	02903	20935	76297	15290	84688	74002	09467	41111	19194
32927	83426	07848	59327	44422	53372	27823	25417	27150	21750
51484	05286	77103	47284	05578	88774	15293	50740	07932	87633
45142	96804	92834	26886	70002	96643	36008	02239	93563	66429
12760	96106	89348	76127	17058	37181	74001	43869	28377	80923
15564	38648	02147	03894	97787	35234	44302	41672	12408	90168
71051	34941	55384	70709	11646	30269	60154	28276	48153	23122
42742	08817	82579	19505	26344	94116	86230	49139	32644	36545
59474	97752	77124	79579	65448	87700	54002	81411	57988	57437

We see that all of the different performance characteristics of our system can be simulated. Complex assumptions can be made that would defy strictly mathematical analyses. For example, to this point, we have assumed that the input and service intervals are independently distributed, but if this is not so, and they are conditional upon each other or on prior states, then these conditional dependencies can be modeled in a simulation. With a computer simulation program, it would not be difficult to simulate Filmasters' line balancing problem or any much more complex situations involving hundreds of activities.

TABLE 10-16

			At Station II				
Sample Number	Random Numbers	Input Interval	Arrival Time	Service Duration	Completion Time	Idle Time	Queue Size
1	05, 62	0.500	0.500	0.250	0.750[a]	0	0
2	16, 44	0.333	0.833[a]	0.250	1.083	0.083[a]	0
3	83, 38	0.250	1.083	0.333	1.416	0	0
4	54, 96	0.333	1.416	0.200	1.616[b]	0	0
5	29, 08	0.333	1.749[b]	0.500	2.249[c,d]	0.133[b]	0
6	71, 57[e]	0.250	1.999[c,d]	—	—	0	1[c]
7	91, 92[f]	0.200	2.199[d,f]	—	—	0	2[d]
6			2.249[d,e]	0.250[e]	2.499[d]	0	1[e]
7			2.499[f]	0.200[f]	2.699	0	0[g]
8	03, 83	0.500	2.699	0.250	2.949	0	0

etc.

[a]Station II is idle from 0.750 until 0.833 (0.083 minute).
[b]Station II is idle from 1.616 until 1.749 (0.133 minute).
[c]Station II is busy, so arrival must wait from 1.999 until 2.249 (0.250 minute).
[d]A second unit joins the line at 2.199. We shall assume that there is storage space for it; otherwise, station I would have to stop at 2.199 and wait until 2.499 before it could begin again. One unit waits from 1.999 until 2.249 (0.250 minute); the other unit waits from 2.199 until 2.249 (0.050 minute).
[e]The random number 57 in the sixth sample indicates a service duration of 0.250. Thus, the sixth arrival begins to be serviced at 2.249.
[f]The seventh arrival waits from 2.199 until 2.499 to be serviced. The random number 92 indicates a service duration of 0.200.
[g]The line is cleared of waiting units. To this time, station II has been idle a total of 0.216 minute. The waiting line has been occupied by a single unit for 0.200 minute, and by two units for 0.050 minute for a total waiting time of 0.300. There has been no shutdown of station I.

PROBLEM
SET

1. The flow shop is designed to remove stochastic behaviors. Explain this statement and comment on how this objective can be accomplished. When is this objective unrealistic?

2. What is the difference between deterministic and stochastic line balancing?

3. In the bulk mail sorting problem, assume that the process rates are exponential but different $\lambda = 8$, $\mu = 10$. What kind of in-process (WIP) storage will be needed?

4. If the bulk mail sorting operations did not combine to form exponential distributions at each station but instead were constant, what then is the line balancing problem?

   Answer: Station I needs $60/(\lambda = 3) = 20$ seconds per unit, whereas station II needs $60/(\mu = 4) = 15$ seconds per unit. Consequently, a paced conveyor would have to stay the longer time of 20 seconds at both stations. This leaves station II idle $5/20 = 25$ percent of the time. The solution, if possible, is to move a 2 (or 3) second operation from station I to station II, resulting in 18 seconds at station I and 17 seconds at station II.

5. Omega Company, manufacturer of a mid-price line of hand-held telephone and memocomputers, requires a comparison of two production configurations: A: Fig. 10–15, and B: Fig. 10–17. The value of each finished unit is $40. Materials cost $10 per unit. Costs at the first A facility are $30/hr. Costs at the second are $50/hr. The process rate of the first A facility is 8 units/hr. The process rate at the second is 10 units/hr. For B, both inputs are 4/hr, and outputs are 5/hr. All four facilities cost half the amounts in A. All facilities have exponential process times. Storage costs are $2 per unit per hour. Which configuration should be used?

REFERENCES   ALFORD, L. P., ed. *Cost and Production Handbook,* 3rd ed. New York: Ronald Press, 1955.

ANSOFF, H. I., ed. *Business Strategy.* Middlesex, Eng.: Penguin Books, 1969.

ASHBY, W. R. *An Introduction to Cybernetics.* New York: Wiley, 1956.

BAUMOL, WILLIAM J. *Economic Theory and Operations Analysis,* 2nd ed. Englewood Cliffs, NJ: Prentice-Hall, 1965.

BECKETT, J. A. *Management Dynamics, The New Synthesis.* New York: McGraw-Hill, 1971.

BEER, STAFFORD. *Decision and Control.* New York: Wiley, 1967.

BELLMAN, R. *Adaptive Control Processes.* Princeton, NJ: Princeton University Press, 1961.

BLACK, GUY. *The Application of Systems Analysis to Government Operations.* New York: Praeger, 1968.

BONINI, C. P., R. J. JAEDICHE, and H. W. WAGNER. *Management Controls: New Directions in Basic Research.* New York: McGraw-Hill, 1964.

BOSTON CONSULTING GROUP. *Japan in 1980: The Economic System and Its Prospects.* London: The Financial Times Ltd., 1974.

BOWMAN, EDWARD H., and ROBERT B. FETTER. *Analysis for Production and Operations Management,* 3rd ed. Homewood, IL: Richard D. Irwin, 1967.

BROWN, R. G. *Smoothing, Forecasting and Prediction.* Englewood Cliffs, NJ: Prentice-Hall, 1962.

BUFFA, ELWOOD S. *Modern Production Management,* 3rd ed. New York: Wiley, 1969.

————, *Readings in Production and Operations Management.* New York: Wiley, 1969.

CHERRY, COLIN. *On Human Communication.* New York: Wiley, 1957.

COCHRAN, W. G., and G. M. COX. *Experimental Designs.* New York: Wiley, 1950.

COOMBS, C. A. *Theory or Data.* New York: Wiley, 1964.

CYERT, R., and J. MARCH. *A Behavioral Theory of the Firm.* Englewood Cliffs, NJ: Prentice-Hall, 1967.

EILON, SAMUEL. *Elements of Production Planning and Control.* New York: Macmillan, 1962.

FELLER, W. *Probability Theory and Its Applications,* Vol. 1, 2nd ed. New York: Wiley, 1957.

FISHER, R. A. *The Design of Experiments.* Edinburgh: Oliver & Boyd, Ltd., 1947.

FORRESTER, J. W. *Industrial Dynamics.* New York: Wiley, 1961.

GAVETT, J. WILLIAM. *Production and Operations Management.* New York: Harcourt Brace Jovanovich, 1968.

GEORGE, JR., CLAUDE S. *Management for Business and Industry,* Englewood Cliffs, NJ: Prentice-Hall, 1970.

GOETZ, B. E. *Quantitative Methods: A Survey and Guide for Managers.* New York: McGraw-Hill, 1965.

HALL, A. D. *A Methodology for Systems Engineering.* Princeton, NJ: Van Nostrand, 1962.

HEGELSON, W. B., and D. P. BIRNIE. "Assembly Line Balancing Using the Ranked Positional Weight Technique." *Journal of Industrial Engineering,* 12, 6 (November–December 1961), pp. 394–398.

HENDERSON, B. D. *The Experience Curve—Reviewed.* A series of pamphlets. Boston: The Boston Consulting Group, 1974.

HOLT, C. C., F. MODIGLIANI, J. MUTH, and H. SIMON. *Planning Production Inventories and Work Force.* Englewood Cliffs, NJ: Prentice-Hall, 1960.

IGNALL, EDWARD J. "A Review of Assembly Line Balancing," *Journal of Industrial Engineering,* 16, 4 (July–August 1965), pp. 244–254.

KILBRIDGE, M., and L. WESTER. "A Heuristic Method of Assembly Line Balancing." *Journal of Industrial Engineering,* 12, 4 (July–August 1961), pp. 292–299.

KLIR, J., and M. VALACH. *Cybernetic Modelling.* Princeton, NJ: Van Nostrand, 1967.

LEVITT, T. "Production-Line Approach to Service," *Harvard Business Review,* 50, 5 (September–October 1972), pp. 41–52.

McKEAN, R. N. *Efficiency in Government through Systems Analysis.* New York: Wiley, 1958.

McMILLAN, C., JR., and R. F. GONZALES. *Systems Analysis: A Computer Approach to Decision Models,* 2nd ed. Homewood, IL.: Richard D. Irwin, 1968.

MORSE, PHILLIP M. *Queues Inventories, and Maintenance.* New York: Wiley, 1955.

MUTH, J. F., and G. L. THOMPSON. *Industrial Scheduling.* Englewood Cliffs NJ: Prentice-Hall, 1963.

NAYLOR, T. H., et al. *Computer Simulation Techniques.* New York: Wiley, 1968.

NILAND, POWELL. *Production Planning, Scheduling, and Inventory Control.* New York: Macmillan, 1970.

OPTNER, S. L. *Systems Analysis.* Englewood Cliffs, NJ: Prentice-Hall, 1960.

PANICO, J. A. *Queueing Theory.* Englewood Cliffs, NJ: Prentice-Hall, 1969.

RIDDLE, DOROTHY I. *Service-led Growth.* New York: Praeger, 1986.

SAATY, T. L. *Elements of Queueing Theory.* New York: McGraw-Hill, 1961.

SCHONBERGER, RICHARD J. *Japanese Manufacturing Techniques.* New York: The Free Press, 1982.

STARR, MARTIN K., ed. *Management of Production.* Middlesex, Eng.: Penguin Books, 1970.

———. *Management: A Modern Approach.* New York: Harcourt Brace Jovanovich, 1971.

TIMMS, HOWARD L., and MICHAEL F. POHLEN. *The Production Function in Business: Decision Systems for Production and Operations Management,* 3rd ed. Homewood, IL.: Richard D. Irwin, 1970.

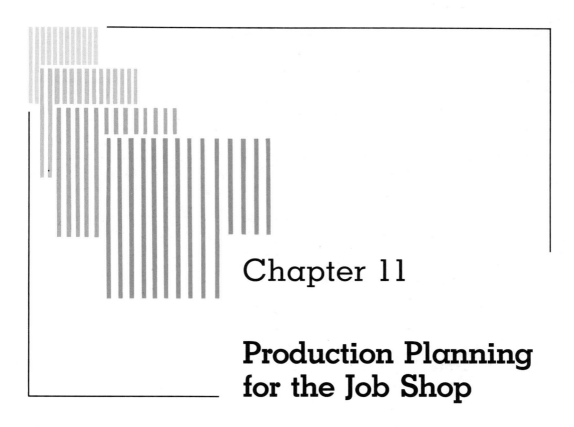

Chapter 11

Production Planning
for the Job Shop

CHAPTER
SUMMARY

Among all the kinds of work configurations, the job shop is the most complex production system to manage. If the job shop can be converted to a flow shop by aggregating volume, it should be done because of the economy of scale advantages. If it cannot be made into a flow shop, at least it can be made into a good job shop. There are many ways of running a competitively better job shop. A better job shop delivers greater margin contribution as a result of the elimination of waste and inefficiencies.

No matter what it is called, job shop management involves so many details (different jobs, machines, workers) that strong information management capabilities are essential. Information is critical for planning. Most companies maintain information in the form of blueprints, bills of materials, operations sheets, and routing sheets, as well as in computerized databases. At the aggregate scheduling level, forecasting and prediction play a critical role.

In Section 11.1 we examine the aggregate scheduling problem. The quadratic cost model created by Holt, Modigliani, Muth, and Simon (HMMS) is applied to Paintmasters' problem. Then, a transportation method approach to aggregate scheduling is explained. (These are weaker models than HMMS, but easier and faster to use.)

Shop loading is the focus of Section 11.2. The Gantt load chart is used to introduce shop loading. This graphic approach shows which jobs are assigned to which department, and the cumulative workload. The underlying character of shop loading is explained by means of the assignment model, which works by minimizing total opportunity costs.

With an understanding of opportunity costs, as developed by the assignment model, the index method for shop loading, which is a heuristic approach, is applied to Toolmasters, Inc. The index method is a strong and relatively easy way to obtain near-optimal solutions for real shop loading problems.

The third job shop problem of sequencing is described in Section 11.3. Gantt sequencing charts are introduced. Then the logic of the SPT (shortest processing time) sequencing rule is developed. It is the keystone concept of the sequencing area. An application of SPT to the scheduling problem of Information Please, Inc., provides further insights into the use of weighted processing times. Then, the sequencing problem where jobs must be sequenced for processing through more than one facility is treated.

Section 11.1 Aggregate Scheduling

Aggregate scheduling is achieved by lumping all items together to determine workforce requirements, general productivity levels, and so on. For example, a paint manufacturer has water-based and oil-based and acrylic paints. They are of many colors and come in different size containers. For aggregate planning, the paint manufacturer forecasts demand for gallons of paint, on a month by month basis, for all of next year. It might have been decided to do separate aggregate planning for each type of paint, on a week by week basis, for half a year. The idea is to aggregate demand that uses essentially the same resources for effective resource planning. To be effective, the forecast interval must provide sufficient lead time to allow the resource mix to be changed in accord with the plan. The paint company might decide to do aggregate planning every three months for the next half year (see Figure 11–6).

The Use of Standard Units of Work

We said above that "aggregate scheduling is achieved by lumping all items together." By "lumping" we mean that different parts, activities, products, and services are all described and accounted for in terms of an arbitrarily chosen but agreed-upon standard unit of work.

Thus, a gallon of Paintmasters' famous velvet white paint (known within Paintmasters as X12) requires two standard units of labor, a standardized workforce-hour of labor, or of human/machine time. Since the demand for X12 in the next quarter is expected to be 100 gallons, the X12 contribution to expected aggregate demand is 200 standard units.

This figure will be added to the expected demands of other products (or services), all of which are expressed in standard units. The aggregate total will be used for workforce planning. The aggregate schedule that is derived represents an important planning stage for management. It applies to intermittent flow shops and job shops.

Aggregating Demand for Different Products (or Services) into Standard Units of Required Production Capacity

Assume that four machines (people, departments) represent total production capacity. These machines work at different rates.

Machine 2 is fastest, so it is convenient to choose M2 as the standard machine (SM). It will be assigned an index of 1.0, and then all the other machines will have fractional indexes.

Machine 1 is half as fast (with an index of 0.5)
Machine 3 is 80 percent as fast (index of 0.8)
Machine 4 is 60 percent as fast (index of 0.6)

Each machine is ranked by an index number which when multiplied by the actual machine hours available, say, per week yields the standard machine hours (SMH) available per week. Thus:

Machine No.	Hours Available per Week	Index	SMH of Supply Available per Week
1	36	0.5	18
2*	54	1.0	54
3	80	0.8	64
4	$33\frac{1}{3}$	0.6	20
			156

*Chosen as the standard machine (SM). If machine 1 had been chosen as SM, the indices would have been 1.0, 2.0, 1.6, 1.2.

A total of 156 standard machine hours (SMH) is available per week. How many standard hours are demanded? Next week's demand prediction is shown below:

Job	A	B	C	D	E
Units demanded	300	210	240	1800	400

We use the productivity rate of the standard machine for each job.

Job	A	B	C	D	E
Production rate of the standard machine in pieces per SMH	6	7	6	30	25

Our computations are guided by the following equation (where dimensions are shown in italics):

$$\left(\begin{array}{c}\text{Demand} \\ \text{in units}\end{array}\right) \frac{pieces}{week} \div \left(\begin{array}{c}\text{production} \\ \text{rate}\end{array}\right) \frac{pieces}{SMH} = \left(\begin{array}{c}\text{demand in} \\ \text{standard hours}\end{array}\right) \frac{SMH}{week}$$

Specifically, for job A:

$$(300) \frac{pieces}{week} \div (6) \frac{pieces}{SMH} = (50) \frac{SMH}{week}$$

For all of the jobs, we obtain the table below:

Job	SMH of Demand
A	300/6 = 50
B	210/7 = 30
C	240/6 = 40
D	1800/30 = 60
E	400/25 = 16
	196 standard machine hours

Both supply and demand are now converted to the common terms of SMH, but we have only 156 standard hours available from our machines. Therefore, 196 − 156 = 40 SMH of demand will not be met.

The same reasoning applies to standard man-hours and to combinations of workforce and capital equipment. Various weighting schemes are required to bring the different kinds of estimates of supply and demand into a common framework.

The Use of Forecasts

The first requirement is a believable forecast that can then be used with various methods for achieving aggregate schedules. In fact, for every planning period (say 3 months) the need for new and revised forecasts is recurrent.

Paintmasters (a pseudonym for a large U.S. company) deserves much credit for having supported the development of aggregate scheduling methods. Its technique of using quadratic equations is explained on pp. 546–550. Aggregate scheduling gains much of its utility from the advantage of predicting aggregate phenomena as compared to the detailed components of the aggregation. The methodology of aggregate scheduling is entirely dependent on a reasonably good ability to forecast and predict.

An Aggregate Scheduling Model

Job shops require a strong methodological approach for planning ahead. Aggregate scheduling provides such an approach. Demand and production output are treated in aggregation across a variety of different work facilities and output jobs. The aggregate is treated as one job made by one facility operating under several different modes, e.g., regular and overtime production.

The organization's facilities are used to satisfy varying demand levels over time in whatever way promises to minimize total costs that vary according to the production schedule used. Demands for different outputs are aggregated by considering them all to be demand for the output capacity of the facility.

Fig. 11–1 portrays seasonal demands for several different items that have been transformed into an aggregate demand for production facilities. The demand during period t is called S_t. The amount produced during time period t is called P_t. The facilities and especially the organization's work force can vary over time. The work force level during time t is called W_t. For the prior period, called $t - 1$, the work force level is W_{t-1}. An additional variable that the P/OM wants to control over time is the inventory level, I_t.

Given a ''good'' prediction of aggregate demand over time, S_t, the problem to solve is How should we vary P_t, W_t, and I_t to optimize the system's performance? The demand forecast must be reliable. Otherwise, aggregate scheduling is meaningless.

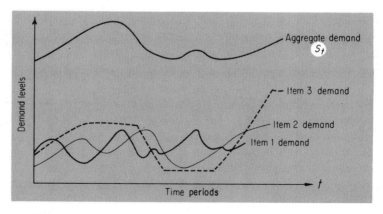

FIGURE 11-1. Determination of aggregate demand as the sum of the demand for three items during time periods t.

Two strategies suggest themselves: First, vary W_t so that P_t matches the demand S_t as closely as possible. In Fig. 11–2 this is production pattern B, which exactly satisfies demand for every period in time, i.e., $P_t = S_t$. This is the situation where workers are to be hired and fired in each time period, according to the expected demand of the period. The practice could be daily, weekly, monthly. Second, do not vary the work force, thereby keeping P_t constant over time, i.e., $P_t = P$ for all t. In Fig. 11–2 this is pattern A. The latter strategy provides a constant (or fixed) volume of production. In this case, only routine production sequences need be followed. Compared to a variable-volume shop, fixed volume creates a more stable job shop environment.

The information management problem of the variable-volume job shop is considerable. Nevertheless, there are many products and services for which variable volume of output is the best option. There are many variable-volume lines that could connect 0 and S_t in Fig. 11–2. Each line has different costs. For example, certain costs disappear when pattern A is followed instead of pattern B, but other costs increase.

We expect our solution to represent some combination of changing production rates, changing workforce size, varying degrees of overtime utilization, and fluctuating inventory levels. Fig. 11–3 captures some of the aspects of this system's interrelatedness.

What happens to the change in the work force level ($W_t - W_{t-1}$) when production pattern B (monthly variation of the workforce to match demand), is followed: $P_t = S_t$? For this case, assume that each worker can produce 10 units in every time period. Demand in the first period is 420 units: $S_1 = 420$ (see Table 11–1).

Production in the first period is 420 units: $P_1 = 420$. Production exactly matches demand, so there is no inventory: $I_1 = 0$. Cumulative inventory, $\Sigma_t I_t$, is also 0. We need 42 workers, so $W_1 = 42$. The change in workforce size is not relevant for the startup period. In the second period the work-

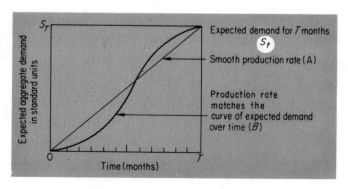

FIGURE 11-2. Expected demand S_T for period T can be satisfied with smooth production (A) or by matching demand seasonality and other fluctuations (B).

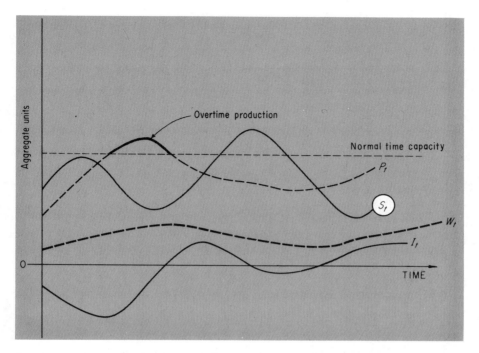

FIGURE 11-3. The aggregate scheduling problem requires period by period solutions that will optimize the total system's performance, recognizing interperiod dependencies.

TABLE 11-1   PATTERN B

t	S_t	P_t	I_t	$\sum_t I_t$	W_t	$(W_t - W_{t-1})$
1	420	420	0	0	42	
2	360	360	0	0	36	−6
3	390	390	0	0	39	+3
4	350	350	0	0	35	−4
5	420	420	0	0	42	+7
6	340	340	0	0	34	−8

force contracts to 36, a reduction of 6. The workforce expands to 39 in the third period. Inventory is never produced, so it cannot be accumulated. All orders are filled with minimum delay.

Now, let us look at the second case (A type) where the workforce is maintained at a constant level ($W_t = 38$), which means that inventory can fluctuate. At the end of the first period, production has fallen short of demand by $\sum_t I_t, = 40$ units. (see Table 11–2). This back-ordered work is shown as negative inventory.

TABLE 11-2   PATTERN A

t	S_t	P_t	W_t	$(W_t - W_{t-1})$	I_t	$\sum_t I_t$
1	420	380	38	0	−40	−40
2	360	380	38	0	+20	−20
3	390	380	38	0	−10	−30
4	350	380	38	0	+30	0
5	420	380	38	0	−40	−40
6	340	380	38	0	+40	0

We cannot tell which actual jobs will not be completed, because we are dealing with aggregates. But some jobs, or parts of jobs, are going to be **back ordered.** These customers are going to be more or less unhappy. It is even possible that some will cancel their orders. Note that in the second period, demand S_t falls 20 units behind production P_t. This adds 20 units to inventory, I_t. These units will be shipped to fill back orders. The remaining 20 back-ordered units are shown in the column of cumulative inventory $\sum_t I_t$, as −20.

Let us contrast these cases. The constant A-type workforce has produced three instances of supply being less than demand. These total to 90 units. However, back orders never exceed 40. From the cumulative inventory column $\sum_t I_t$ we see that back orders at any time vary between 0 and 40.

There is never positive cumulative inventory, but there could have been. Note that total demand for 6 periods is 2,280, which is the same as supply. Yet with the B-type rule, there is not one back-order occasion, even though demand fluctuates. Thus, in a trade off for no back orders, we are required to hire 10 workers and lay off 18. Such workforce changes have costs.

The question to be answered before deciding how to set up the job shop is this: Which approach has the lowest expected cost?

Other configurations come to mind. For example, what happens if a mixture of policies is used—if changes in the workforce level are allowed only between specific limits?

What result is obtained if a constant workforce of 39 is maintained, instead of 38 workers?

t	I_t	$\sum_t I_t$
1	−30	−30
2	+30	0
3	0	0
4	+40	+40
5	−30	+10
6	+50	+60

Back orders occur only at the end of the first period. Thereafter, inventory begins to accumulate.

There is a cost for carrying inventory. Consequently, this example illustrates another opportunity for cost tradeoffs: the wages of another worker plus the costs of carrying inventory, versus a reduction in the number of back orders.

What result would have occurred if the demand series $t = 1$ through 6 had occurred in reverse order: 340, 420, 350, 390, 360, 420, and the workforce was held constant at 38? This result is worth discussing. When P_t varies with S_t, workforce adjustment costs occur. This could represent the costs of a constant-size workforce engaged in overtime, or a fluctuating workforce size, with or without overtime. Consider the opposing costs that have been encountered in these cases. When the production rate over time P_t is smooth, then hiring, training, and other workforce adjustment costs, such as overtime, go to 0. Further, when P_t is constant, demand fluctuations produce inventory costs for overstocks and back-order costs for understocks. The extent of these costs depends on the demand fluctuation.

The optimal size for the workforce should be determined by the cost tradeoffs between adjustment costs, including wages and the over and understock costs. If production rates match demand rates, then inventory-type costs disappear, but quality problems may arise because of workforce adjustments.

Fig. 11–4 illustrates these opposing costs. For such systems analysis there is a total cost, composed of inventory costs and workforce adjustment costs, which reaches a minimum value for some particular production schedule. Also, a large constant-size workforce will decrease back-order costs and increase inventory carrying costs.

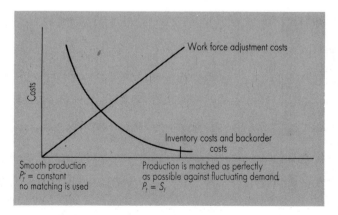

FIGURE 11-4. The x axis represents the degree to which production rates P_t match demand rates S_t.

The Quadratic Cost Model (HMMS)

Production requirements for many items can be expressed in aggregate figures using standard processing hours. Then a reasonable time series of forecast demand (in standard processing hours) can be developed. Next, costs of carrying inventory, back orders, workforce level changes, and so forth, are estimated. All of these can be united in an aggregate scheduling model that will produce minimum total cost work schedules.

Work done by Holt, Modigliani, Muth, and Simon (in a paint factory) has provided an important aggregate scheduling model, which we will call the HMMS model.[1] They examined all relevant costs (hiring, layoff regular and overtime payroll, setup, back ordering, and inventory carrying costs), using both linear ($y = cx$) and quadratic ($y = cx^2$) cost functions as required to provide adequate approximations of the cost systems. Their predictions of sales were based on a method of moving averages we have previously covered (pp. 157–159).

The paint factory experienced significant fluctuations in demand, and although large inventories were maintained, outages occurred frequently. As a result, sales were lost or significant overtime and hiring costs were incurred. Worker morale was low and efficiency poor as workers stretched out their jobs during demand downturns.

HMMS built a mathematical model that involved minimizing a quadratic total cost equation:

$$\text{Minimize } \sum_{t=1}^{T} C_t \text{ where}$$

$$C_t = C_1 W_t + C(W_t - W_{t-1})^2 + C_3(P_t - C_4 W_t)^2 + C_5 P_t - C_6 W_t + C_7(\sum_t I_t - C_8 - C_9 S_t)^2$$

subject to the necessary inventory constraint:

$$\sum_t I_{t-1} + P_t - S_t = \sum_t I_t$$

This equation is equivalent to the cumulative inventory measure, $\sum_t I_t$ as used in the tables on pp. 543, 544. The variables are identified as follows:

C_1 = costs related to payroll, i.e., absolute size of the work force.

C_2 = hiring and layoff costs, in terms of work force *changes*.

C_3, C_4, C_5, C_6 = different kinds of overtime costs.

C_7, C_8, C_9 = different kinds of inventory costs.

[1]C. C. Holt, F. Modigliani, J. F. Muth, and H. A. Simon, *Planning Production Inventories and Work Force* (Englewood Cliffs, NJ: Prentice-Hall, 1960).

S_t = demand forecast for period t.

$\sum_t I_t$ = on hand inventory minus back orders at the end of period t.

P_t = the *aggregate* production rate in period t.

W_t = the size of the work force for period t.

To understand how the costs were derived, see Fig. 11–5. Note that the payroll costs $C_1 W_t$ are treated as being linear, whereas the other costs are approximated by quadratic (squared) terms.

Often the quadratic approximations are more realistic than linear ones, which are assumed by other aggregate scheduling models.

The HMMS Model Applied to Paintmasters

The best way to understand the HMMS aggregate scheduling model is to use it in an example. Because there are many calculations, the example is kept small, limiting the analysis to only two time periods.

Let us contrast the two cases we previously studied.

1. The workforce level is kept at constant size.
2. Production output rate matches demand.

Assume that Paintmasters has determined that its costs are as follows:

$$
\begin{array}{lll}
C_1 = 100 & C_4 = 10 & C_7 = 0.1 \\
C_2 = 3 & C_5 = 2 & C_8 = 60 \\
C_3 = 0.2 & C_6 = 20 & C_9 = 0.2
\end{array}
$$

1. Constant size work force policy (it is assumed that each worker can produce 10 units in each time period)

t	W_t	P_t	S_t	I_t	$\sum_t I_t$
0	38	380	380	0	0
1	38	380	400	−20	−20
2	38	380	350	+30	+10

$$
\begin{aligned}
C_{t=1} &= 100(38) + 3(0)^2 + 0.2[380 - 10(38)]^2 + 2(380) - 20(38) \\
&\quad + 0.1[-20 - 60 - 0.2(400)]^2 \\
&= 6360
\end{aligned}
$$

$$
\begin{aligned}
C_{t=2} &= 100(38) + 3(0)^2 + 0.2[380 - 10(38)]^2 + 2(380) - 20(38) \\
&\quad + 0.1[10 - 60 - 0.2(350)]^2 \\
&= 5240
\end{aligned}
$$

$$
C_{t=1} + C_{t=2} = 11{,}600
$$

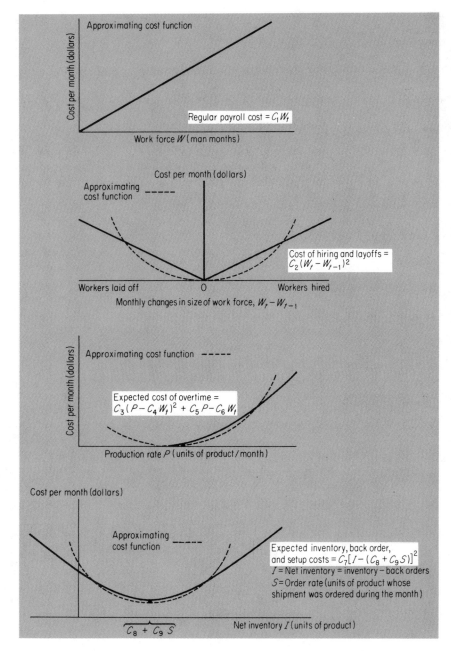

FIGURE 11-5. Hypothetical cost behavior as a function of planning variables [From Charles C. Holt, Franco Modigliani, and Herbert A. Simon, "A Linear Decision Rule for Production and Employment Scheduling," *Management Science,* Vol. 2, No. 1 (October 1955). Reprinted by permission of the Institute of Management Sciences.]

2. The policy that matches production output with demand

t	W_t	P_t	S_t	I_t	$\sum_t I_t$
0	38	380	380	0	0
1	40	400	400	0	0
2	35	350	350	0	0

$$
\begin{aligned}
C_{t=1} &= 100(40) + 3(2)^2 + 0.2[400 - 10(40)]^2 + 2(400) - 20(40) \\
&\quad + 0.1[0 - 60 - (0.2)(400)]^2 \\
&= 5972
\end{aligned}
$$

$$
\begin{aligned}
C_{t=2} &= 100(35) + 3(-5)^2 + 0.2[350 - 10(35)]^2 + 2(350) - 20(35) \\
&\quad + 0.1[0 - 60 - (0.2)(350)]^2 \\
&= 5265
\end{aligned}
$$

$$
C_{t=1} + C_{t=2} = 11{,}237
$$

Thus, policy 1 produces a total cost that is $363 less than policy 2. But this does not mean that Paintmasters should match demand and production output. There may be a mixed-policy solution that is even better. For example, consider the use of overtime in periods 0 and 1. This is shown in problem 3.

3. A mixture of policies with overtime allowed

t	W_t	P_t	S_t	I_t	$\sum_t I_t$
0	35	390	380	+10	+10
1	36	400	400	0	+10
2	35	350	350	0	+10

$$
\begin{aligned}
C_{t=1} &= 100(36) + 3(1)^2 + 0.2[400 - 10(36)]^2 + 2(400) - 20(36) \\
&\quad + 0.1[10 - 60 - 0.2(400)]^2 \\
&= 5693
\end{aligned}
$$

$$
\begin{aligned}
C_{t=2} &= 100(35) + 3(-1)^2 + 0.2[350 - 10(35)]^2 + 2(350) - 20(35) \\
&\quad + 0.1[10 - 60 - 0.2(350)]^2 \\
&= 4943
\end{aligned}
$$

$$
C_{t=1} + C_{t=2} = 10{,}636
$$

This pattern of aggregate scheduling gives the best result so far. Total cost at $10,636 is $964 less than the policy 2 result and $601 less than the policy 1 result.

Note that the $t = 0$ period costs have been ignored. This startup effect would not apply to ongoing systems, but could be taken into account if need be. We could keep trying different combinations, and choose the best mixed policy we discover. However, we will never know what the optimal result is, and how close we have come to it. A method is required to obtain the optimal solution, and such a method does exist.

The HMMS model can be solved for optimum values of W_t, P_t, and I_t, for each time period $t = 1, 2, 3, \ldots, n$. These solutions (for minimum total cost) will differ according to the planning period n that is used. A better systems solution is obtained as n increases, but the reliability of demand forecasts usually decreases as n moves further into the future. As a rule of thumb, the best planning interval would be about a quarter (or 3 months), but specific circumstances could dictate that shorter or longer intervals be used.

The planning interval T in Fig. 11–6 does not have to coincide with the updating interval D. The intervals D and T could coincide, but when forecasts for the period T should be altered to account for actual occurrences and new information, then D would be smaller than T. For example, say that monthly updating of the quarterly schedule would be used.

The method for obtaining the optimal solution is fully detailed in the book referenced in footnote [1] in this chapter. It is not a difficult method (although it does surpass the level of mathematics required by this text). To employ the model does not require mathematical capability. The P/OM would have the equations of the model programmed for computer solution, since a great deal of computation is involved.

Paintmasters should derive the same kind of benefits from using the HMMS model as did the company that supported the original research: Employee morale improved; and there were lower process and freight costs, smaller inventories, higher sales, and numerous intangible benefits.

The complexities of managing a large job shop are awesome. The HMMS model provides a means for organizing the great amount of information that characterizes the job shop: the composition of aggregate demand forecasts, the costs associated with overstock, understock, overtime, hiring, training, laying off, setups, changeovers, and so on. Although other models have been designed that treat aggregate scheduling (such as the transportation method, described below) none of them is as detailed, thorough, and realistic as the HMMS model.

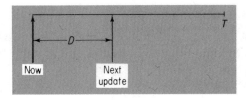

FIGURE 11-6. Every D months the aggregate schedule for the planning period of T months ahead is updated.

Transportation Method for Aggregate Scheduling

The transportation matrix provides a convenient representation of the aggregate scheduling problem. It can provide an optimal aggregate schedule based on relatively simple assumptions. As was previously shown (on pp. 441–453), it is quite easy to solve transportation problems using network algorithms.

It is also possible, but more difficult, to resolve the transportation matrix using linear programming (see pp. 609–621).[2]

Two transportation matrices are presented. The first one (Table 11–3)

TABLE 11-3

Sales Periods

	1	2	3	Final Inv.	Slack	Supply
Initial Inv.	0	c	2c	3c	0	I_0
Regular 1	r	r + c	r + 2c	r + 3c	0	R_1
Overtime 1	v	v + c	v + 2c	v + 3c	0	O_1
Regular 2	x	r	r + c	r + 2c	0	R_2
Overtime 2	x	v	v + c	v + 2c	0	O_2
Regular 3	x	x	r	r + c	0	R_3
Overtime 3	x	x	r	v + c	0	O_3
Demand	D_1	D_2	D_3	I_f	S	Grand total

where c = carrying cost per unit for the interval of time.
r = regular production cost per unit.
v = overtime production cost per unit.
I_0 = initial inventory
I_f = final inventory.

<hr />

[2]J. F. Magee and D. M. Boodman, *Production Planning and Inventory Control* (New York: McGraw-Hill, 1967), pp. 369–73.

allows no back orders. The second one (Table 11–4) has back order costs. Other costs are explained under the first matrix. These include regular time production costs, overtime production costs, and inventory carrying costs. The column totals are demand levels in the first, second, and third periods. Final inventory is specified at the bottom of the fourth column. Slack is listed at the bottom of the fifth column. That slack balances supply and demand. Supply is shown as the row totals. The first row is initial inventory. Thereafter, rows alternate in presenting production supply for regular time and for overtime.

The objective is to minimize total cost. Constraints reflect the availability of regular and overtime production capacity. Alternatives can be examined where capacity can be added or removed. Standard units are required to aggregate different kinds of product, such as small cans, large cans, white paint, green paint. The flexibility of the transportation model is a boon. It does not require a square matrix. A slack column or row can be added to balance supply and demand. The solutions are relatively easy to obtain on a personal computer. On the other hand, the model is linear, since unit costs or profits are not able to be changed as a function

TABLE 11-4

Sales Period

	1	2	3	I_f	Slack	Supply
I_0	0	c	$2c$	$3c$	0	I_0
R_1	r	$r + c$	$r + 2c$	$r + 3c$	0	R_1
O_1	v	$v + c$	$v + 2c$	$v + 3c$	0	O_1
R_2	$r + b$	r	$r + c$	$r + 2c$	0	R_2
O_2	$v + b$	v	$v + c$	$v + 2c$	0	O_2
R_3	$r + 2b$	$r + b$	r	$r + c$	0	R_3
O_3	$v + 2b$	$v + b$	v	$v + c$	0	O_3
Demand	D_1	D_2	D_3	I_f	S	Grand total

of volume. Each matrix applies to a specific period. No allowance is made for interdependencies over time.[3]

Table 11–3 presents the aggregate scheduling—transportation matrix that does not allow back orders. The regular transportation method (pp. 451–453) is used for solution, but in this matrix back orders are prohibited (by *x*). (See Problem 9. and Table 11–5 below for a numerical example of this problem.)

Table 11–4 present the aggregate scheduling transportation matrix where back orders are allowed. This matrix has the additional new cost, *b*, which is the back order cost per unit. Both matrices can be solved by conventional transportation techniques. (See Problem 10 and Table 11–6 below for a numerical example of this problem.)

1. We expect that seven jobs will be in the shop next week. The demand in units for each job (called *D*), and the production rate of the standard operator in pieces per standard operator hour (called *PR*) are given below.:

Job	A	B	C	D	E	F	G
D	600	1000	500	50	2000	20	800
PR	60	20	25	10	40	2	40

What production capacity in standard operator hours is required to complete all these jobs?

2. Why do forecasts for aggregate scheduling have an advantage over forecasts for disaggregated scheduling of specific jobs?

3. Can the effects of seasonal demand be taken into account for aggregate scheduling? Explain.

4. In some job shop industries, a smooth production rate is preferred. In others, the workforce size is altered to match the expected demands. Give some examples of each kind of situation.

---

[3]The original citation is E. H. Bowman, "Production Scheduling by the Transportation Method of Linear Programming," *Operations Research*, 4, 1 (February 1956), 100–03. Further discussion will be found in E. H. Bowman and R. B. Fetter, *Analysis for Production and Operations Management,* 3rd ed. (Homewood, IL: Richard D. Irwin, 1967), pp. 134–36.

5. At one time, the canning industry was totally dependent on harvest dates. As a result, major workforce alterations occurred sporadically. After careful study, steps were taken to smooth the demand patterns. What measures do you think might have been effective?

6. Actual monthly demands for the past year are available for item Z54, a microswitch.

Month	Demand	Month	Demand
1	621	7	708
2	415	8	615
3	380	9	422
4	763	10	669
5	845	11	810
6	550	12	396

Can you find any useful patterns that will enable you to proceed with an aggregate scheduling problem?

7. With reference to the analyses on pp. 543–544, find the total cost for the following aggregate scheduling policy:

t	W_t	P_t	S_t	I_t	$\sum_t I_t$
0	35	380	380	to be filled in	
1	36	390	400		
2	37	370	350		

How does this policy (called 4) compare with policies 1, 2, and 3? What type of policy is 4?

8. Use the HMMS model with the data in problem 6 grouped into quarterly demands. Assume simple values for all the costs based on reasonable patterns for the curves in Fig. 11–5. Determine the optimum values for each of the four quarters of the coming year. *Note:* The solution to this problem requires the use of calculus.

9. The aggregate scheduling transportation matrix with no back orders allowed (Table 11–3) has been given numerical values, as follows:

TABLE 11-5

Sales Periods

	1	2	3	Final Inv.	Slack	Supply
Initial Inv.	0	c	2c	3c	0	I_0
Regular 1	r	r + c	r + 2c	r + 3c	0	$R_1 = 100$
Overtime 1	v	v + c	v + 2c	v + 3c	0	$O_1 = 200$
Regular 2	x	r	r + c	r + 2c	0	$R_2 = 300$
Overtime 2	x	v	v + c	v + 2c	0	$O_2 = 200$
Regular 3	x	x	r	r + c	0	$R_3 = 100$
Overtime 3	x	x		v + c	0	$O_3 = 50$
Demand	$D_1 = 200$	$D_2 = 300$	$D_3 = 200$	I_f	S	Grand total

where
- c = carrying cost per unit for the interval of time = \$1
- r = regular production cost per unit = \$2
- v = overtime production cost per unit = \$3
- I_0 = initial inventory = 50
- I_f = final inventory = 200

Complete the matrix and interpret the numbers to explain the situation.

10. The aggregate scheduling transportation matrix with back orders allowed (Table 11–4) has been given the same numerical values in Table 11–6 as in Table 11–5. Also, b = \$4.

Complete the matrix and interpret the numbers to explain the situation.

Overview

In Fig. 4–11, we showed the three problem stages involved in managing the job shop. We have just addressed the first problem. Now it is time to move to the second problem, shop loading, which is the subject of Section 11.2.

Table 11-6

Sales Period

	1	2	3	I_f	Slack	Supply
I_0	0	c	$2c$	$3c$	0	$I_0 = 50$
R	r	$r+c$	$r+2c$	$r+3c$	0	$R_1 = 100$
O_1	v	$v+c$	$v+2c$	$v+3c$	0	$O_1 = 200$
R_2	$r+b$	r	$r+c$	$r+2c$	0	$R_2 = 300$
O_2	$v+b$	v	$v+c$	$v+2c$	0	$O_2 = 200$
R_3	$r+2b$	$r+b$	r	$r+c$	0	$R_3 = 100$
O_3	$v+2b$	$v+b$	v	$v+c$	0	$O_3 = 50$
Demand	$D_1 = 200$	$D_2 = 300$	$D_3 = 200$	$I_f = 200$	S	Grand total

Section 11.2: Shop Loading

Shop loading is required to assign specific jobs to equally specific facilities. But shop loading does not specify the order in which jobs should be done at each facility. Sequencing methods (Section 11.3) provide this detail. For example, ten patients are assigned to the third floor medical clinic for treatment. In what order should they be processed? The answer can make a big difference. Both shop loading and sequencing epitomize job shop management techniques.

Shop Loading Responsibility

Shop loading for the job shop is a regular, repetitive managerial responsibility. The requirement is to determine which facility (machines, equipment, individuals, areas) will be assigned specific jobs. We say that each facility carries a certain "load," which is why the term **shop loading** is used. Individual jobs and facilities are identified. In aggregate scheduling, jobs are grouped together as demand and facilities are grouped together as supply. Further, demand has to be forecast for aggregate scheduling whereas for shop loading, the jobs are real tasks, on hand, that must be done.

Gantt Shop Loading Charts

The first structured shop-loading methods were based on Gantt charts. Henry L. Gantt recognized that only by means of some formal device could the problem of assigning jobs to facilities be suitably organized. Gantt charts provided a better tool than anything that had existed before.

Fig. 11-7 typifies a Gantt load chart. It has a time scale running along

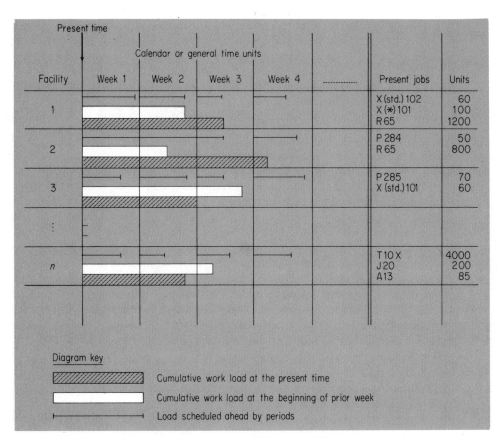

FIGURE 11-7. The Gantt load chart.
Cumulative work load is the sum of unfinished jobs at each facility. These jobs are identified by their code names such as R65 and T10X.

the top. The rows are intended to represent machines, departments, or whatever facilities will be required to do the job. The time scale can be labeled in calendar time or using intervals (such as weeks). The left-hand side of the chart is now, whether that be May 21 or merely time 0. Bars and lines, running from left to right, convey various kinds of information. These are interpreted by the diagram key. We can read off the cumulative load that exists with respect to each facility. (Note that the load chart does not indicate the sequence for doing the jobs.[4]

The backlog of jobs is shown as it exists at the beginning of the present week.[5] It is also shown as it existed at the beginning of the prior week.

We are interested in this information to find out whether load and backlog are increasing, decreasing, or staying about the same. The backlog has increased for facilities 1 and 2. The backlog has decreased for facilities 3 and n.

The way in which the manager has scheduled work in the weeks ahead is also shown on the chart. The criterion for a good loading or a change for the better might be will depend upon the configuration of a job shop facilities and the load situation. Thus, the Gantt load chart will reveal whether we have sufficient resources and capacity available to handle the work that has been accumulating. It also helps to determine whether the load is equally distributed among facilities. Perhaps most important of all, it can point out the fact that the load level is changing.

The Assignment Method: To Minimize Costs

When alternative facilities exist for processing jobs, a decision must be made concerning which jobs are to be done at each facility. For example, when there are 3 jobs that can be done at any one of three available facilities, but with different costs, an assignment problem exists. To understand the basic nature of this problem, we are going to develop the assignment model in which there are costs for not making the best possible assignments of jobs to facilities. These are called opportunity costs. The reason that we cannot always make the best possible assignments is that jobs often compete for available time on those facilities for which they are best fitted with respect to productivity or cost or both. Consider Table 11–7 (called Matrix 1) of cost per part for jobs 1, 2, and 3 at facilities A, B, and C.

Jobs 1 and 2 achieve their lowest cost per part when made at facility B. They are therefore in direct competition with each other for the use of this facility. What should be done?

First, note that job 3 is best assigned to facility A, and it is not competing with any other job for that facility. Yet this assignment cannot be made

---

[4]See the Gantt sequencing (or layout) chart on p. 575.

[5]It is also listed (see column Present Jobs) in Fig. 11–7.

TABLE 11-7 MATRIX 1 OF COST PER PART

		Facilities A	B	C
	1	0.10	0.09	0.12
Jobs	2	0.08	0.07	0.09
	3	0.15	0.18	0.20

until we have resolved the conflict between jobs 1 and 2. All the numbers in the matrix are interrelated. Therefore, we must regard this as a systems problem. It might turn out that to resolve the conflict, job 3 should not be assigned to facility A.

The assignment model develops comparisons of penalties that must be paid for making an assignment other than the best possible one. To get these comparisons, subtract the smallest number in each row from all other numbers in that row. This yields Table 11–8 (called Matrix 2).

TABLE 11-8 MATRIX 2

	A	B	C
1	0.01	0	0.03
2	0.01	0	0.02
3	0	0.03	0.05

The numbers in Matrix 2 are the opportunity costs per part for not assigning each job to the best possible facility for that job.

Wherever there is a zero, we would like to make an assignment, but we cannot do that in this case, because jobs 1 and 2 have their only zero opportunity cost assignment at facility B. Also, we are making the assumption that the orders are of the same size. Otherwise, we should be thinking in terms of total costs (see Problems 2, 3 and 8 in the Problem Set for further discussion of this point). We could have used column subtraction, which yields the opportunity costs at a given facility for assigning jobs that are not the best jobs.

Return to Matrix 1. Subtract the smallest number in each column from all other numbers in that column. The opportunity costs of each facility with respect to jobs obtained by column subtraction are shown in Table 11–9 (called Matrix 3).

TABLE 11-9 MATRIX 3

	A	B	C
1	0.02	0.02	0.03
2	0	0	0
3	0.07	0.11	0.11

Job 2, having all zero opportunity costs in its row, is the preferred job at each facility. Based on our analysis so far, there is no feasible assignment. Therefore, using Matrix 3, subtract the smallest number in each row from all other numbers in that row. This will give us the combined opportunity costs for each job's being assigned to less than the best facility, and each facility's being assigned to less than the best job. See Table 11–10 (Matrix 4).

TABLE 11-10   MATRIX 4

	A	B	C
1	0	[0]	0.01
2	0	0	[0]
3	[0]	0.04	0.04

Note that all jobs could be assigned to facility A with zero opportunity cost. If we would permit this (assuming there was other work for facilities B and C), then we have a sequencing problem at facility A (that is, which job goes first, which goes second, which goes third?). Sequencing, you will recall, is the third kind of problem in the job shop (see Fig. 4-11). Given that we must assign a job to each facility, there is now one feasible set of 0 opportunity cost assignments for this case. They are shown by the squares in Matrix 4. There is only one 0 in column C. Job 2 must be assigned there. There is only one 0 in row 3. Job 3 must be assigned to facility A. That forces the assignment of job 1 to facility B.

For completeness, let us return to Matrix 2, which was derived by using row subtraction first. This yielded the opportunity costs of each job being assigned to less than the best facility. Now use column subtraction first and derive Table 11–11 (Matrix 5).

TABLE 11-11   MATRIX 5

	A	B	C
1	0.01	[0]	0.01
2	0.01	0	[0]
3	[0]	0.03	0.03

We have obtained the same assignment solution as in Matrix 4. Although the final matrices are not identical, it is always equally correct to use either row or column subtraction first. Sometimes it turns out to be easier to use one way rather than the other to reduce the matrix to an assignable set of zeroes. There is no way of prejudging this beforehand.

**TABLE 11-12 MATRIX 6 OF NEW
COSTS PER PART**

		Facilities	
	A	B	C
1	0.11	0.09	0.13
Jobs 2	0.08	0.07	0.09
3	0.18	0.15	0.20

There is one additional complication we shall demonstrate with a new set of costs. Assume that the initial cost per part matrix is changed, as shown in Table 11–12 (Matrix 6). After row and column reduction, we obtain Table 11–13 (Matrix 7). Either row or column subtraction can go first. We still cannot make an assignment. Jobs 1 and 3 are both assigned to facility B without any other options. Facility A and facility C have been assigned job 2 without any alternatives. There is no further basis for row and/or column subtraction, since a zero exists in each row and in each column. To resolve this situation, remember that each zero signifies an acceptable assignment. Therefore, we want to move any one of the zeroes to another position in the matrix in order to remove the deadlock.[6]

TABLE 11-13 MATRIX 7

	A	B	C
1	0.01	0	0.02
2	0	0	0
3	0.02	0	0.03

The best place to move a zero is to the position of the lowest opportunity cost in the matrix. This is 0.01 for job 1 at facility A. Thus, to assign job 1 to facility A imposes an extra cost of 0.01 to any assignment at facility B. Accordingly, we add 0.01 to all entries in column B. Similar reasoning applies to job 2. An assignment of job 1 to facility A imposes an extra cost of 0.01 to any assignment of job 2, so we add 0.01 to all entries in row 2. We had to break the deadlock, and we did it with the smallest opportunity cost (0.01).

Note that at the intersection of row 2 and column B, 0.01 is added twice. This results in Table 11–14 (Matrix 8).

---

[6]The generalized methodology for resolving assignment problems that are deadlocked after row and column subtraction is described on pp. 562–563.

TABLE 11-14 MATRIX 8

	A	B	C
1	0	0.01	0.02
2	0.01	0.02	0.01
3	0.02	0.01	0.03

Whether we use row or column subtraction, we achieve the same final assignments in Table 11–15 (Matrix 9). *Note:* The maximization assignment problem is described in the Burgermasters Case below.

TABLE 11-15 MATRICES 9

	Row Subtraction				Column Subtraction		
	A	B	C		A	B	C
1	[0]	0.01	0.02	1	[0]	0	0.01
2	0	0.01	[0]	2	0.01	0.01	[0]
3	0.01	[0]	0.02	3	0.02	[0]	0.02

The Generalized Methodology for the Assignment Model

Step 1. Set up the matrix for the assignment model with minimization as the objective.

Step 2. Use row subtraction (arbitrarily chosen before column subtraction).

Step 3. Use column subtraction.

Step 4. Use the minimum number of lines through rows and columns to cover all zeroes. For example:

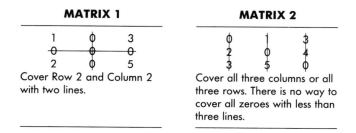

MATRIX 1

1	0	3
0	0	0
2	0	5

Cover Row 2 and Column 2 with two lines.

MATRIX 2

0	1	3
2	0	4
3	5	0

Cover all three columns or all three rows. There is no way to cover all zeroes with less than three lines.

Step 5. If the minimum number of marked rows and columns to cover all zeroes is equal to n for our $n \times n$ matrix, then the assignment problem is solved. See Matrix 2 in Step 4. If this is not the case, go to Step 6.

Step 6. Take the smallest uncovered value and subtract this number from every uncovered number in the matrix including itself. Then add this value to every intersection of the covering lines. Using Matrix 1 in Step 4 as an example, we obtain Matrix 3.

MATRIX 3

0	0	2
0	1	0
1	0	4

Step 7. Use row (or column) subtraction. If the final assignment solution is not obtained (Steps 4 and 5), then repeat Step 6. In this case, we need go no further. Matrix 4 shows the final solution as A1, B3, and C2. *Note:* Alternative solutions are available when additional zeroes provide assignment flexibility.

MATRIX 4

	A	B	C
1	0	0	2
2	0	1	0
3	1	0	4

The assignment model captures the essence of the opportunity cost basis for shoploading assignments. Before we go on to a broader modeling use of these concepts, let us try our hand at another assignment problem, which introduces some additional aspects of the methodological strengths of opportunity cost analysis.

CASE: BURGER-MASTERS, INC.

This fast foods franchiser is planning to open three new company-owned outlets (A, B, and C). Managers are sought. Out of numerous applicants, four candidates (1, 2, 3, and 4) remain. They have been interviewed and rated with respect to their qualifications for managing each store, on a scale of 0 (worst) to 10 (best). The matrix of qualifications is shown below.

MATRIX OF QUALIFICATIONS

		Stores		
		A	B	C
Candidates for Manager	1	9	5	6
	2	x	10	4
	3	5	8	9
	4	7	7	7

Note: Candidate 2 is unable to be considered for store A because of travel distance from home and unwillingness to move.

Three new problems confront us in this assignment problem.

1. We are asked to maximize the total value of the assignments. For jobs and facilities, this could have been to maximize productivity or profit.
2. One of the possible assignments is prohibited.
3. We are forced to choose 3 assignments from among 4 candidates. This could have been 4 jobs to be assigned to 3 facilities.

Let us consider each of these in turn.

To maximize the total benefits of a set of assignments, subtract all numbers from the largest number in the matrix, and then proceed with row and column substraction, as was done for minimization. The subtraction of all numbers from the largest has created a set of costs for not doing as well as the best that can be done. Thus, candidate 2 at store B has a zero cost, because that assignment is the best that can be obtained.

To handle the blocked assignment, enter a large enough cost to prohibit assignment. These steps have been taken in the matrix below.

		Stores		
		A	B	C
Candidates	1	1	5	4
for	2	100	0	6
Manager	3	5	2	1
	4	3	3	3

To deal with the extra candidate for manager, create a dummy store, called D. All costs at the dummy store will be zero, meaning that we are indifferent as to which candidate is assigned to that store. Whichever candidate is so assigned will not be hired. Thus:

		Stores			
		A	B	C	D
Candidates	1	1	5	4	0
for	2	100	0	6	0
Manager	3	5	2	1	0
	4	3	3	3	0

Using column subtraction, we obtain a final solution.

	A	B	C	D
1	⓪	5	3	0
2	99	⓪	5	0
3	4	2	⓪	0
4	2	3	2	⓪

	Value in the Original Matrix
Candidate 1 goes to store A	9
Candidate 2 goes to store B	10
Candidate 3 goes to store C	9
	28

There is no set of assignments that can have a higher value than 28. Often, alternative, equally good assignments do occur in assignment problem solutions, but not in this case.

The Index Method for Shop Loading: A Heuristic Method

A major weakness of the assignment model is that each job can be assigned to only one facility. That is, jobs cannot be divided. Another weakness is that only one job can be assigned to each facility, even though some jobs may be long and others short. Thus, the sizes of jobs are not properly related to the available working capacity of the facilities. The transportation method has been used to overcome these difficulties, but it requires certain restrictive assumptions that are often not met in reality. With the transportation method, split assignments can be made, but the application of standard hours assumes that strict proportionality exists between the facilities. For example, on page 539, the standard machine (2) is twice as fast as machine 1. Machine 3 is 0.8 as fast, and so on.

If reasonable proportionality exists, the transportation method provides a satisfactory solution. When it does not, the index method should be used. The index method also allows some assumptions to be made about setup times, which the other assignment methods ignore. All in all, the index method offers a shop loading technique with assumptions that conform nicely to reality. Being a heuristic method, it does not produce an optimum solution. But it has been used in practice with satisfying results.[7]

The basic idea behind this method is opportunity cost analysis. In this case, the opportunity costs are viewed in ratio to the value of the best assignment, and these are called index numbers.

CASE: TOOL- MASTERS, INC.

Toolmasters, Inc., is an established and well-known manufacturer of metal cutting tools used for lathes, milling machines, drill presses, etc. The company has employed Gantt charts for shop loading as long as the division manager can recall.

The manager has reviewed some new techniques and has decided in favor of the heuristic approach (the index method). This is not surprising. The activity of shop loading is repeated so often that a relatively fast heuristic

---

[7]See R. O. Ferguson and L. F. Sargent, *Linear Programming* (New York: McGraw-Hill, 1958), pp. 149–159.

**TABLE 11-16 TOOLMASTERS'
SCHEDULE CARD FOR CUTTING
TOOL 4x.**

Part Name—

Machine	A	B	C
Time per part (hr)	$2/5$	1	$4/5$
Cost per hour	$4	$2	$3

which allows multiple job assignments and job assignment splitting with simple computation is highly desirable.

To begin with, a row of index numbers is computed for each job i with respect to its performance at the places it can be done, such as machine centers j.

When the performance criterion is of the cost per part type, the ith row of index numbers will be $(c_{ji} - c_{ji}^*)/c_{ji}^*$. When the performance criterion is for profit per part, we have $(p_{ji}^* - p_{ji})/p_{ji}^*$. (In both cases, the asterisk represents the ideal machine assignment—lowest cost or highest profit per part.)

These index numbers show the relative penalties of assigning each of the given jobs to the different machine centers. In many job shops, for every part that is reordered by certain customers, a schedule card is maintained that presents relevant information concerning processing times and costs on different machines. For example, Toolmasters has the data for Part 4x as shown in Table 11–16.

An order has been received for 100 cutting tools of type 4x. The schedule card is modified to an index card reflecting the order quantity of 100 units. Indices are developed for total time and total cost (see Table 11–17). Examination of the data in Table 11–17 shows that machine A is the most productive facility that can be used, turning out 100 units in 40 hours at a total cost of $160. Machine B is the least productive facility. It requires 100 hours to do the same job, yet it is less costly than machine C. Thus, although machine C can do the entire job in 80 hours, it does so at an expense of $240 versus $200 for machine B.

**TABLE 11-17 TOOLMASTERS' INDEX CARD
FOR CUTTING TOOL 4x; ORDER
QUANTITY = 100.**

Part Name: 4x Machine	A	Order Quantity: 100 B	C
Time per part (hr)	$2/5$	1	$4/5$
Total time (hr)	40	100	80
Cost per hour	$4	$2	$3
Total cost	$160	$200	$240
Total time Index	0	$3/2$	1
Total cost Index	0	$1/4$	$1/2$

Let us review the calculation of the index numbers. At machine A, each cutting tool requires 2/5 hour. Consequently, to make 100 units of 4x takes 40 hours. Similarly, the order will spend 100 hours with machine B and 80 hours with machine C.

We want to minimize total time, so the best time is 40 hours at machine A. Thus, using $(c_{ji} - c_{ji}^*)/c_{ji}^*$ because as with cost, best is smallest, we obtain:

Machine	A	B	C
Total time index	$\dfrac{40 - 40}{40} = 0$	$\dfrac{100 - 40}{40} = \dfrac{3}{2}$	$\dfrac{80 - 40}{40} = 1$

To compute total cost at each facility, we multiply the cost per hour by the total time. The lowest total cost is at machine A. Then we obtain the total cost index numbers.

Machine	A	B	C
Total cost index	$\dfrac{160 - 160}{160} = 0$	$\dfrac{200 - 160}{160} = \dfrac{1}{4}$	$\dfrac{240 - 160}{160} = \dfrac{1}{2}$

What are the total time index numbers for Part 1x?
Given:

Machine	A	B	C
Time per part (hr)	$\frac{1}{4}$	$\frac{1}{5}$	$\frac{3}{8}$
Order quantity—200 cutting tools			

In fact, Toolmasters has on hand orders for 5 types of cutting tools, all of which can be made at machines A, B, and C. The sizes of the orders are reflected by the total times to complete the jobs, listed in Table 11–18.

TABLE 11-18 TOTAL TIMES (IN HOURS) TO COMPLETE JOBS

		Machines	
Job	A	B	C
1x	50	40	75
2x	25	40	50
3x	27	30	54
4x	40	100	80
5x	20	100	50

Additional information is required concerning the availability of machines A, B, and C during the next week: There are 2 machines of each kind:

Machine	A	B	C
Total time (hr)	50	40	75
Total time index	$\dfrac{50-40}{40} = \dfrac{1}{4}$	$\dfrac{40-40}{40} = 0$	$\dfrac{75-40}{40} = \dfrac{7}{8}$

Every machine is able to work 40 hours per week, less preventive maintenance time, which is 2 1/2 hours per week. Accordingly, 75 hours each of A, B, and C facilities are available in the next week, for a total of 225 hours. From this information, a matrix of: total times, total time index numbers, and available times at the facilities is prepared (see Table 11–19).

TABLE 11-19

Machines

Job	A	B	C
1x	[1/4] 50	[0] 40	[7/8] 75
2x	[0] 25	[3/5] 40	[1] 50
3x	[0] 27	[1/9] 30	[1] 54
4x	[0] 40	[1.5] 100	[1] 80
5x	[0] 20	[4] 100	[1.5] 50
Available Time	75	75	75

The index numbers have been entered into the little boxes in the upper right-hand corner of each cell of the matrix. Available time is the capacity constraint at each center. An investment in another type A machine would be required to increase the total available time at facility A to 112.5 hours.

The Heuristic Rule

First assignments are always made to 0 index measures. Then, to satisfy capacity constraints if some machines are overloaded, jobs are shifted to other machines that have the lowest possible alternative index numbers. The reassignments are done in the order of increasing index values. In our example, the assignments based on 0 index would be as shown in Table 11–20.

TABLE 11-20

		Machines	
Jobs	A	B	C
1x		40	
2x	25		
3x	27		
4x	40		
5x	20		
Available Time	75	75	75
Assigned Time	112	40	0
Excess	+37	−35	−75

Machine A is overloaded with an excess of 37 hours (shown as +37 in Table 11–20). Machines B and C are underutilized (shown as −35 and −75 in Table 11–20). If we do not use the index method at all, and simply choose an assignment that is feasible (i.e., assigned time at each facility is equal to or less than available time), we could obtain the result shown in Table 11–21. We can use this casually produced result of 205 hours as an upper bound solution. That is, we do not have to accept any solution that has a total time that is greater than 205. When we obtain a new solution that requires less total time, it will replace 205 as the new upper bound.

Let us now apply the heuristic rule to Table 11–20. We will shift job 3x, because in its row the smallest alternative index appears—namely, 1/9 at 3x, column B. When we shift 3x from A to B, it takes 30 hours to do the job instead of 27 (see Tables 11–19 and 11–22). The heuristic rule can be applied in several ways at this point. For example, since 1/4 is now the next best index, at 1x, A, this would mean that 1x, B should be shifted to 1x, A. Generally, however, we refuse to further overload a machine center, and instead try to move jobs from it to the best possible alternative positions. Here, for machine A, either 2x, 4x, or 5x could be shifted from A to C. Since 5x's index for C is larger than the others, we eliminate it as a choice. Job 4x, when moved, will cause an overload at

TABLE 11-21

		Machines	
Jobs	A	B	C
1x			75
2x		40	
3x		30	
4x	40		
5x	20		
Available Time	75	75	75
Assigned Time	60	70	75
Excess	−15	−5	0
Total time = 60 + 70 + 75 = 205 hours			

TABLE 11-22

Jobs	A	Machines B	C
1x		40	
2x	25		
3x		30	
4x	40		
5x	20		
Available Time	75	75	75
Assigned Time	85	70	0
Excess	+10	−5	−75

center C, so move 2x. The index for job 2x at machine R is smaller than at machine C. Therefore, we move as much as we can of job 2x to machine B and the remainder of job 2x to machine C. This requires job splitting.

We should note the difference between assigning several jobs to one facility and the splitting of one job between several facilities. Assigning several jobs to one facility is shown in Tables 11–20, 11–21, and 11–22. It could not be done with the square matrix of the assignment model. Splitting one job between several facilities is shown in Table 11–23.

We can assign no more than 5 hours at machine B. The entire job 2x requires 40 hours at machine B. We are using only 5/40 or 1/8 of this time. Consequently, 7/8 of the job 2x remains to be completed at machine C. Job 2x requires 50 hours at machine C. Thus, we assign 7/8 of 50 hours (or 43.75 hours) to machine C for completion of job 2x. The result, producing a total job time of 178.75 hours, becomes our new upper bound. It represents an improvement of 12.8 percent over our previous upper bound of 205 in Table 11–21.

Still further improvement is available (if we allow additional splitting), because machine A, which is fast for every job except 1x, is underutilized. (For the next solution, see Table 11–24.) We have returned 15 hours of job 2x to machine A. This completes the available time at machine A.

Job 2x, if done entirely at machine A, consumes 25 hours. We are doing 15/25 (or 3/5) of job 2x at machine A. Previously, we noted that

TABLE 11-23

Jobs	A	Machines B	C
1x		40	
2x		5	43.75
3x		30	
4x	40		
5x	20		
Available Time	75	75	75
Assigned Time	60	75	43.75
Excess	−15	0	−31.25
Total time = 60 + 75 + 43.75 = 178.75 hours			

TABLE 11-24

Jobs	A	Machines B	C
1x		40	
2x	15	5	13.75
3x		30	
4x	40		
5x	20		
Available time	75	75	75
Assigned time	75	75	13.75
Excess	0	0	−61.25
Total time = 75 + 75 + 13.75 = 163.75 hours			

5/40 (or 1/8) of job 2x is completed at machine B. This leaves $1 - 3/5 - 1/8$ (or 11/40) of 50 hours required by job 2x at machine C, $(11/40) \times 50 = 13.75$ hours. The result reduces the total job time to 163.75 hours, an improvement of 8.3 percent over the previous upper bound of 178.75 hours, or a total improvement of 20.1 percent over the first upper bound of 205 hours.

Perhaps we could still improve on the 163.75 hour solution, but it is a good one, and likely to be good enough. The index method promises only "approximately optimal" solutions, with a degree of directness that captures the real elements of the shop loading problem and with simplicity that permits large problems to be resolved by hand, or with inexpensive calculator or computer operations. The best solution we could get, assuming that we had additional capacity at machine A, will be found in Table 11–20 as $112 + 40 = 152$. This represents a 7.1 percent improvement over the 163.75 hour solution. Given the existing capacity constraints, we are willing to say that total time of 163.75 hours is "likely to be good enough".

If no splitting is allowed, can we find a better total time solution than 205 hours? We rearrange Table 11–22, which is not a feasible solution. Shifting all of job 2x to machine C is a good option.

Jobs	A	Machines B	C
1x		40	
2x			50
3x		30	
4x	40		
5x	20		
Available time	75	75	75
Assigned time	60	70	50
Excess	−15	−5	−25
Total Time = 60 + 70 + 50 = 180 hours			

We reduce total time from 205 to 180 hours. This is an improvement of 12.2 percent.

1. The Gantt load chart (see p. 557) can be used to determine whether the "load" is equally distributed among facilities. The same kind of issue applied to resource leveling for projects. Discuss the relationship of these two situations.

2. Here is a total cost matrix for jobs 1, 2, and 3 at facilities A, B, and C:

	A	B	C
1	1000	900	1200
2	800	700	900
3	1500	1800	2000

Was the opportunity cost analysis of the cost per part matrix appropriate? See pp. 558–562. Explain how you can tell.

Answer: Yes, it was appropriate. In fact, the two matrices are equivalent given that each job had 10,000 parts. By finding the minimum cost per part assignment, we also found the minimum total cost solution.

3. In the terms of Problem 2 (above), assume that the order sizes of the jobs are:

Job	Size
1	10,000
2	10,000
3	5,000

What assignment do you recommend?

4. The executive offices for 5 vice presidents of a large bank are on the tenth floor of the bank's new building. The president wants to assign the offices in such a way as to maximize total satisfaction. She therefore asks each vice president to rank his preference for the available offices. The president receives the information in the following form:

Office	VP_1	VP_2	VP_3	VP_4	VP_5
O_1	1	1	2	3	2
O_2	5	3	1	2	3
O_3	4	2	5	1	1
O_4	3	5	4	3	4
O_5	2	4	3	5	5

Rank 1 is the preferred location.
a. What is the best assignment plan?
b. How does this relate to production schedules?

5. Use the assignment method to achieve a satisfactory shop loading arrangement for an intermittent flow shop where the per unit profits are given in the matrix below and relatively continuous production (in the quarter) can be expected for each assignment.

			Machines		
Jobs	A	B	C	D	E
1	19	17	15	15	13
2	12	30	18	18	15
3	13	21	29	19	21
4	49	56	53	55	43
5	33	41	39	39	40

6. For the data in Problem 5, a new machine F has become available that can only work on jobs 1, 2, or 3, with unit profits of 14, 11, and 12. Would it be worthwhile to replace one of the present machines with F? After analysis, what information is still lacking?

7. Use the data below to develop an index shop loading analysis where splitting of assignments is permitted and assumed to have negligible costs. Assume that the objective is to minimize total job times.

	Parts per Hour at Facility				
Job	A	B	C	D	Demand/Week
1	7.5	15	10	20	400
2	4.5	9	6	12	300
3	3	6	4	8	200
Available Hours per week	40	40	40	40	

8. With respect to Problem 2, relating to the opportunity cost analysis in the text (pp. 558–562), assume that the order sizes of the jobs are:

Job	Size
1	10,000
2	20,000
3	5,000

What assignment do you recommend?

Section 11.3 Sequencing Operations

Shop loading assigns work to facilities without regard to the order in which the jobs will be done. Sequencing establishes the order for doing the jobs at each facility. In effect, sequencing reflects job priorities by the arrangement of queues. As we will see, there are different costs associated with the various orderings.

Sequencing in a typical job shop is done over and over again. Each time there is a saving, albeit a small one. The nature of that saving must be fully explored to appreciate how total savings can accumulate to a substantial sum. When there are many jobs and facilities, sequencing rules take on considerable economic importance.

Gantt Sequencing Charts

Gantt was a master chartmaker. In addition to all the previous charts described, he developed a chart to formalize the sequencing problem. Let us consider this chart, called a **layout chart.** It reserves specific times on the various facilities for the particular jobs on hand.

First-in, First-out (FIFO) Sequence Rule

The most natural ordering is that the first jobs into the shop get worked on first. We call this **FIFO (first-in, first-out).** It is appealing because it seems to be the fairest rule to follow. However, by at least one measure, FIFO is unfair, because it penalizes the average customer more than other sequencing rules. The penalty is extra waiting time for the average processing time order. Consistent customers, who submit orders to the same job shop regularly, will benefit if that job shop does not employ the FIFO rule, but uses instead a rational rule. Sequencing is one of the most highly repetitive decisions made in the job shop. Even if only a small savings can be realized each time by using a rational rule, these savings accumulate to substantial sums over time. Using the Gantt layout chart, shown in Fig. 11–8, we can sequence specific jobs at particular facilities, over some given period of time. Concurrently, past sequences of work can be monitored to discover the state of completion of those jobs that were scheduled to be run in prior time periods. Thus, Gantt charting provides work schedule control, but offers little help in determining what the best sequences might be. For each facility, we observe the job schedule and its state of completion. The present date is indicated by the arrow and its associated vertical line.

The chart is divided into time past, present, and future. Looking ahead, we can observe what the load is, but not in the cumulative form of the load chart, which does not specify sequence. Thus, the difference between loading and sequencing is that the latter specifies the time of assignments. With sequencing, future assignments are specific time reservations on the facility. They block other assignments from being made. Because sequencing charts are revised regularly, assigned time can be unblocked if it appears to permit a better schedule. A little time is usually allowed between jobs to account for machine maintenance, to absorb divergences from estimates and minor variabilities, and to allow for setups and take-

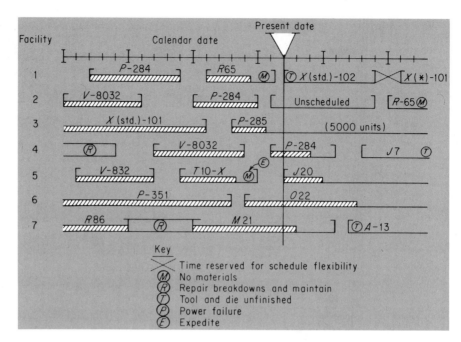

FIGURE 11-8. The Gantt layout chart (a reserved time planning system)
Status: (1) job P-284 is ahead 2 days; (2) jobs J20 is ahead 3.0 days; (3) job O-22 is ahead 5.5 days; (4) job M21 is ahead 1.0 day; (5) job R65 is 2 days short of completion—and 2.5 days late waiting for materials (M); (6) job P-285 is 1.5 days short and 1.5 days late (breakdown delay); (7) job T10-X is 1.5 days short and about 3.5 days late (M) and (E).

downs. Frequently, additional symbols are attached to these charts to indicate why a job has not been completed and to convey other kinds of useful information by means of a succinct shorthand notation. The Gantt layout or sequencing chart must be continually updated. Jobs must be rescheduled, so that the chart can serve its intended function of providing reasonably good work schedules.

Classification of Sequencing Rules

There are at least four factors that are essential for classifying sequencing problems.[8] First, describe the job arrivals. This means knowing when each job arrives and how long it will take to complete once it is begun. The symbol n refers to the number of jobs that are waiting to be sequenced through the facility. Typically, in the job shop, n is a number that varies a good deal. Second, it is necessary to specify the number of facilities, m, through which the jobs must pass. Also, we want to know how much time each job spends at each facility. Third, the flow pattern

---

[8]R. W. Conway, W. L. Maxwell, and L. W. Miller, *Theory of Scheduling* (Reading, MA: Addison-Wesley, 1967), p. 1.

in the shop must be identified. When a set of jobs follows a fixed ordering, the conditions exist for an intermittent flow shop. On the other hand, when many technological orderings are required, job shop sequencing prevails. The sizes of orders, the number of alternative facilities for doing each job, the length of production runs, the importance of setups and takedowns, and so on, are the ultimate determinants of what type of shop exists. Fourth, a variety of criteria exist for evaluating the performance of the schedule.

Evaluatory Criteria

To determine how good a sequence is, we use sequence evaluation measures called **flow time** and **mean flow time.** These are defined in the following way. Three jobs (11, 12, and 13) in Fig. 11–9 are sequenced

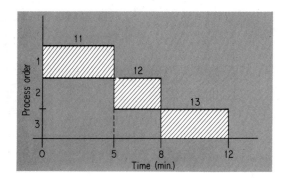

FIGURE 11-9.

through a facility in that order. Job 11, which goes first, is completed after 5 minutes. Meanwhile, jobs 12 and 13 have waited 5 minutes. Job 13 then must wait an additional 3 minutes (while job 2 is being worked on) before it can begin its own processing.

We define for job i a waiting time, W_i, and a processing time, t_i. If we assume that job 11 begins at time zero,[9] then the completion time is:

$$C_i = W_i + t_i.$$

For our three jobs this yields the following table:

Job i	W_i	t_i	C_i
11	0	5	5
12	5	3	8
13	8	4	12
Sums	13 +	12 =	25

---

[9]That is, the **release time,** often called r_i, equals zero (say at the start of the day).

The $\Sigma_i C_i$ is the *flow time*, in this case 25, and *mean flow time* would be $\Sigma_i C_i/n = 25/3$.

Part of flow time and mean flow time is job waiting time, W_i. We would like the total waiting time to be as small as possible on the assumption that all customers want to have their orders filled as quickly as possible. Therefore, if we minimize the mean flow, this is equivalent to minimizing the mean waiting time (since the processing times t_i are fixed). If the average completion time $\sum_i C_i/n$ is as small as possible, the average customer's order is delayed the minimum necessary time. This is a primary objective in determining rational sequence priorities.

Other measures are used in evaluating operation sequences. For example, there are promised delivery times. Thus, define d_i as the due date of a job. Then, $L_i = C_i - d_i$ is a measure of the lateness of job i. To minimize average lateness, we should minimize mean flow time, assuming that the promised dates are reasonably determined.

The degree of facility idleness may also play a critical role in sequence determination. The fact is, however, that sequencing models become increasingly difficult to handle with optimizing models, as the number of facilities through which the jobs must pass becomes large. Since the jobs take different times at each facility, what is the best sequence at one location may not be the best at another. The information problem is enormous. Consequently, heuristics have been developed to try to cope with the level of detail involved in making the highly repetitive sequencing decisions required by many job shops.

The SPT Rule for n Jobs: $m = 1$ Facility

As we have stated, a common objective of facility sequencing is to minimize mean flow time. For reasons apparent from our previous discussion, in many problems this is equivalent to minimizing average job waiting times, i.e.:

$$\min \frac{\sum\limits_i^n C_i}{n} = \min \frac{\sum\limits_i^n (W_i + t_i)}{n} = \min \frac{\sum\limits_i^n W_i}{n}$$

A simple rule applies. Namely, if a set of n jobs in one facility's queue are ordered so that the operations having the **shortest processing times (SPT)** are done first, the mean flow time, mean completion time, and mean waiting time will all be minimized. It also turns out that facility idleness is often minimized. Ordering jobs according to shortest processing times is called the **SPT rule**.

Using this rule, we can rank-order jobs by least t_i, as in Fig. 11–10. Note that the area under the curve is minimized. Fig. 11–10 provides an example of SPT, the shortest processing time rule, where $t_4 < t_5 < t_2 <$

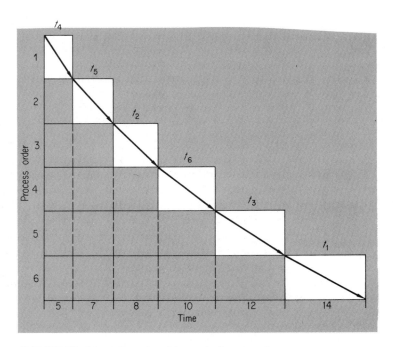

FIGURE 11-10. Jobs ordered by ranked process times.

$t_6 < t_3 < t_1$. There are $n = 6$ jobs and $m = 1$ facility. The computation of flow time follows in Table 11–25.

On the other hand, in Fig. 11–11, the jobs are randomly ordered without regard to SPT, and the area under the curve is not minimized, nor is mean flow time. The random ordering is quite like the expected sequence of jobs if FIFO is employed, since any job is as likely to enter the shop first as any other.

Fig. 11–11 provides an $n \times 1$ problem where SPT is not used. There are $n = 6$ jobs and $m = 1$ facility. Table 11–26 provides the results. The areas under the curves in Figs. 11–10 and 11–11 can be approximated by multiplying each job's processing time t_i by the number of jobs waiting (plus the job being worked on).

TABLE 11-25

Job i	W_i	t_i	C_i
4	0	5	5
5	5	7	12
2	12	8	20
6	20	10	30
3	30	12	42
1	42	14	56
	109 +	56 =	165

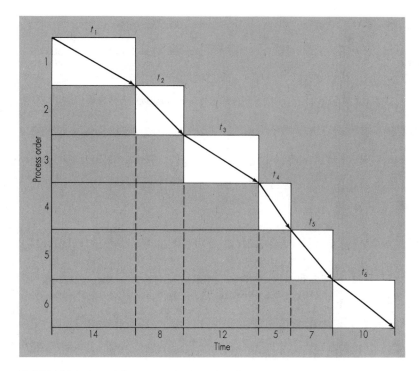

FIGURE 11-11. Jobs are randomly ordered.

In each figure, there are columns of blocks which represent the number of jobs waiting plus those being processed. The columns are the jobs, and each job carries its stack of waiting jobs, except the last one. When we multiply the stack size by the processing times, we obtain the product, called **job time spent in the system.** Thus, for Fig. 11-10, we have Table 11-27.

This is the same value we obtained in Fig. 11-10 for flow time $\sum_i C_i$. Note how the larger values of t_i are multiplied by the smaller value of the number of jobs waiting and working, i.e., of the sequence 6, 5, 4, 3, 2, 1.

TABLE 11-26

Job i	W_i	t_i	C_i
1	0	14	14
2	14	8	22
3	22	12	34
4	34	5	39
5	39	7	46
6	46	10	56
	155 +	56 =	211

TABLE 11-27

t_i	$\times$	number of jobs waiting and working	$=$	job time spent in the system
5	$\times$	6	$=$	30
7	$\times$	5	$=$	35
8	$\times$	4	$=$	32
10	$\times$	3	$=$	30
12	$\times$	. 2	$=$	24
14	$\times$	1	$=$	14
		Total job time spent in the system	$=$	165

When we go through the same multiplication operation for the random ordering of jobs (Fig. 11–11), we obtain Table 11–28. This is the same value we obtained in Fig. 11–11 for flow time $\sum_T C_i$. Now, the largest value of t_i happens to be multiplied by the largest value of the number of jobs waiting and working. This is not a logical ordering of the sequence aimed at achieving the minimum possible total job time spent in the system. With this evidence before us, we can see why ordering jobs by the SPT rule also succeeds in minimizing average delivery lateness L_i (the purpose is to maximize fulfillment of delivery promises).

Modified SPT Rule: Sequence Influenced by Job Importance

As an additional strength, the SPT rule can be modified to take into account the fact that some jobs are more important than others. This is done by dividing each job time t_i by the relative importance of that job, w_i.

Thus, t_i/w_i are rank ordered. The job having the smallest value of t_i/w_i is placed first. An important job will have a large value of w_i, resulting in

TABLE 11-28

t_i	$\times$	number of jobs waiting and working	$=$	job time spent in the system
14	$\times$	6	$=$	84
8	$\times$	5	$=$	40
12	$\times$	4	$=$	48
5	$\times$	3	$=$	15
7	$\times$	2	$=$	14
10	$\times$	1	$=$	10
		Total job time spent in the system	$=$	211

a small number t_i/w_i. This will place the job earlier in the sequence than would otherwise have been the case.

In Fig. 11–12, the importance weight, w_i, alters the height of the blocks, and thereby the slope of the arrows. Previously (in Fig. 11–10 and 11–11) the w_is were all equal to one. Now, the most vertical arrow (the largest slope) will belong to the job with the smallest ratio t_i/w_i.

As shown in Fig. 11–12, the ratio of t_3/w_3 is smallest. Therefore, job 3, with processing time t_3, is placed first in the sequence. It is clear that this ratio rule assures a smooth (convex) function that will minimize the area under the curve.

CASE: INFORMATION PLEASE, INC.

This small but growing company receives requests by telephone from clients who seek all sorts of information, such as the number of automobiles registered in Costa Rica in 1988, the value of the soybean crop in The Peoples Republic of China in 1950, and so on. At first, the company processed orders in FIFO fashion. Then, after it discovered the SPT rule, its efficiency jumped by more than 30 percent. New clients were signed up, and existing clients increased their contract levels. One problem marred the picture. Estimates of t_i were made by a small group of people whose track records in estimation were excellent, and who, with feedback of how well they had done, continued to improve. So the SPT ordering was very good, but jobs with very high estimates of t_i were continually bounced to the end of job sequences and would get done only when the client complained.

The president of Information Please, Inc., decided to resolve this problem by using SPT with weighted processing times. Her decision rule was to set $w_i = 1$ for all new requests for information. Any order that had not begun

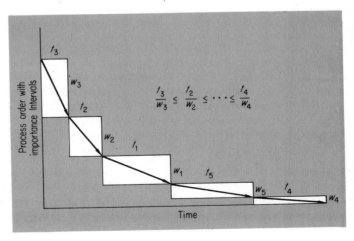

FIGURE 11-12. Jobs ordered by smallest ratios of weighted processing time.

processing on the first day was given a weighting factor $w_i = 2$ for the second day's sequence decisions, and $w_i = 3$ for the third day's decisions, etc.

For example, at the beginning of one particular day, there were 100 requests on hand. One of 15 researchers was carrying the following load:

Job	Estimated ti (minutes)	wi	Job	Estimated ti (minutes)	wi
1	20	1	6	64	2
2	12	1	7	30	1
3	120	2	8	13	1
4	5	1	9	366	2
5	180	1	10	93	3

How should these be sequenced? First, in line with the straight SPT rule? Second, in accord with the president's decision to use weighted processing times?

If straight SPT is used, the sequence would be 4, 2, 8, 1, 7, 6, 10, 3, 5, 9. If weighted processing times are used, the sequence would be: 4, 2, 8, 1, 7, 10, 6, 3, 5, 9. Will the president's modified rule benefit the company? (See problem 4).

Sequencing with More Than One Facility

The SPT character of the sequencing problem is epitomized by n jobs and 1 facility. But the complexity of sequencing becomes increasingly evident as we consider larger numbers of facilities. We now treat situations with more than 1 facility.

Consider n Jobs with $m = 2$ Facilities

The SPT concept still applies when jobs must pass through 2 facilities in a given technological ordering. For example, facility 1 (F1) drills the part. This is followed by facility 2 (F2) which deburrs from the drilling.

For this example we use a medical case, where diagnosis is followed by treatment, not vice versa. In this case, jobs are people and facilities are doctors; see Table 11–29.

S. M. Johnson's algorithm[8] solves this problem for all "no passing" cases in terms of minimum completion time. "No passing" means that the order of processing jobs by the first facility must be preserved for all subsequent facilities. To use the algorithm for the table above, where F1

---

[8]S. M. Johnson, "Optimal Two- and Three-Stage Production Schedules with Set-up Times Included," *Naval Research Logistics Quarterly*, (March 1954), pp. 61–68.

Table 11-29

Job (Person)	F1 (Diagnosis)	F2 (Treatment)
a	6	3
b	8	2
c	7	5
d	3	9
e	5	4

must be first, select the job (or person) with the shortest processing time on either F1 or F2. If this minimum value is in the F2 column, place the person last in sequence (here in fifth place). If it is in the F1 column, award that person first place. For our example, person b with 2 in the F2 column will be treated last. Remove person b from further consideration, then continue in the same way.

Select the smallest number remaining in the matrix. If it is in the F2 column, assign that person to the last place, if available, or the next to last place if not. If the smallest number is in the first column, that person is given first place or next to first place. (Ties are resolved by randomly selecting either position for assignment.) For the example above, person b goes last. Person d goes first in sequence. Person a goes next to last. Person e is treated next to next to last. Person c fills the remaining slot. The minimum total completion time is 31. See the Gantt chart in Fig. 11–13.

Consider n Jobs with m = 3 Facilities

Johnson proposed a variant of his two-facility algorithm that will obtain the optimal sequence for three facilities. But this can only be done if

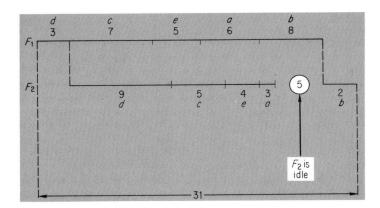

FIGURE 11-13. Gantt chart.

certain conditions are met. Suppose that we have three facilities with the technological ordering F1, F2, F3. As before, no passing is allowed, and we define t_{ij} = processing time of the ith person at facility j.[9]

If at least one of the following restrictions holds, we can apply Johnson's method:

$$\min t_{i1} \geq \max t_{i2}$$

or

$$\min t_{i3} \geq \max t_{i2}$$

In words, the middle facility may not have any operation times that are greater than the minimum operation times of both the other facilities.

For example, the method can be applied to Table 11–30's matrix of processing times. If there had been a 4 in the F2 row, the method we are about to describe could not be used.

We reformulate the problem as a two-facility system. That is, let:

$$p_i = t_{i1} + t_{i2}$$

and

$$q_i = t_{i2} + t_{i3}$$

For the numbers in the matrix:

	a	b	Person c	d	e
(F1 + F2)p	6	8	7	3	5
(F2 + F3)q	3	2	5	9	4

TABLE 11-30

Facility	a	b	Person c	d	e	
F1	4	7	5	3	3	Min t_{i1} = 3
F2	2	1	2	0	2	Max t_{i2} = 2
F3	1	1	3	9	2	Min t_{i3} = 1

---

[9]There is no solution that allows passing which can produce a shorter completion time than the no-passing solution for up to $n = 3$. See Conway et al., pp. 80–83.

Then, we proceed as we did before: Person i should precede Person k in the optimal sequence if:

$$\min(p_i, q_k) < \min(p_k, q_i)$$

So the optimal sequence is unchanged from the one previously developed for the $n \times 2$ case. Giglio and Wagner applied this method to a series of problems where the restrictive condition did not hold and found that fairly good results were achieved.

Of the 20 problems solved, the optimal sequence was achieved in 9 cases, and in 8 others it would have been reached if two adjacent jobs in the sequence exchanged positions. More important, the average error—measured from the true optimum that was found by enumeration—was under 3 percent for the twenty problems tested. Therefore, by relaxing the restrictive conditions and applying Johnson's algorithm, we have what amounts to a heuristic method for finding a pseudo-optimum sequence.

Consider n Jobs with m Facilities

There is no general solution for any problem where $m > 2$. But there are heuristic approximations of the optimal solution. Campbell, Dudek, and Smith report on the successful performance of a heuristic algorithm that generates a series of sums for each job similar to the two new sets of sums generated in the prior discussion of $n \times 3$ systems.[10]

With m facilities, we can develop $m - 1$ two-column sets of job times that can then be treated by the S. M. Johnson $n \times 2$ algorithm, assuming the technological ordering:

$$1 \longrightarrow 2 \ldots \longrightarrow m \text{ and no passing}$$

For example, consider the following 6-person, 4-facility problem (Table 11–31).

TABLE 11-31

Person	1	2	3	4
a	50	43	15	4
b	89	99	95	77
c	7	47	20	98
d	8	64	12	94
e	61	19	65	14
f	1	80	66	78

[10]H. G. Campbell, R. A. Dudek, and M. L. Smith, "A Heuristic Algorithm for the n Job, m Machine Sequencing Problem," *Management Science*, 16, 10 (June 1970), pp. B630–B637.

For our first two-facility subproblem, we need to reformulate the Table 11–31 so that we are considering the times for facilities 1 and 4 only. Our new Table 11–32 is:

TABLE 11-32

Person	Facility 1	Facility 4
a	50	4
b	89	77
c	7	98
d	8	94
e	61	14
f	1	78

Applying the 2-facility algorithm, we get (*fcdbea*) as the solution to our first subproblem.

The second subproblem is based on adding the processing times for facilities (1 + 2), creating the first column of Table 11–33, and then adding the processing times for facilities (3 + 4) found in the second column of Table 11–33.

Solving this subproblem, we find the solution to be the sequence (*cdfbea*).

The last subproblem to be solved, in this case, consists of combining facilities (1 + 2 + 3) and facilities (2 + 3 + 4). In Table 11–34, first, we obtain the sums of the times on facilities 1, 2, and 3. Then we combine the times spent on facilities (2 + 3 + 4). That is, we obtain the sums of the times on facilities 2, 3, and 4.

The solution sequence for this subproblem is the same as for subproblem 2, (*cdfbea*). Each of the subproblem sequences is evaluated in terms of total flow time. The results are shown below:

Sequence	Total Processing Time
(fcdbea)	512
(cdfbea)	487

TABLE 11-33

Person	Facility (1 + 2)	Facility (3 + 4)
a	50 + 43 = 93	15 + 4 = 19
b	89 + 99 = 188	95 + 77 = 172
c	7 + 47 = 54	20 + 98 = 118
d	8 + 64 = 72	12 + 94 = 106
e	61 + 19 = 80	65 + 14 = 79
f	1 + 80 = 81	66 + 78 = 144

TABLE 11-34

Person	Facilities (1 + 2 + 3)	Facilities (2 + 3 + 4)
a	50 + 43 + 15 = 108	43 + 15 + 4 = 62
b	89 + 99 + 95 = 283	99 + 95 + 77 = 271
c	7 + 47 + 20 = 74	47 + 20 + 98 = 165
d	8 + 64 + 12 = 84	64 + 12 + 94 = 170
e	61 + 19 + 65 = 145	19 + 65 + 14 = 98
f	1 + 80 + 66 = 147	80 + 66 + 78 = 224

On the basis of these figures, we would choose the sequence (cdfbea) as our quasi-optimal solution for this problem. Actually, our chosen sequence did not fare badly at all with the true optimum for the problem. By enumeration we would find that the sequences (cdbfae) and (cdbfea) are optimal, with a total processing time of 485. Thus, we could calculate the degree of error as:

$$\frac{487 - 485}{485} \times 100 = 0.41 \text{ percent error}$$

PROBLEM SET

1. Our company has 4 orders on hand, and each must be processed in the sequential order:

Department A—press shop
Department B—plating and finishing

The table below lists the number of days required by each job in each department. For example, Job IV requires 1 day in the press shop and 1 day in the finishing department.

	Job I	Job II	Job III	Job IV
Department A	8	6	5	1
Department B	8	3	4	1

a. Assume that no other work is being done by the departments. Use a Gantt layout chart to try to find the best work schedule. By best work schedule, we mean minimum time to finish all four jobs.

b. Find the best sequence, treating each department separately. How does that compare with your Gantt chart solution?

2. Examine several alternative sequences for the following n × 1 system, with 6 jobs and processing times ti.

i	t_i	i	t_i
a	5	d	9
b	4	e	12
c	6	f	8

Especially study SPT and also the effect of LPT (longest processing time).

3. For Problem 2 above, what effect does the information that jobs a, b, and c are half as important as jobs d, e, and f have on the sequence solution?

4. For the problem faced by Information Please, Inc. determine the mean flow times with and without the president's weighting system. See pp. 581–582. Will the president's policy be helpful?

5. Do Gantt sequencing (or layout) charts reflect a preference for first come-first serve ordering or for the SPT rule? Discuss your answer.

REFERENCES   AGEE, M. H., R. F. TAYLOR, and P. E. TORGERSEN. *Quantitative Analysis for Management Decisions.* Englewood Cliffs, NJ: Prentice-Hall, 1976.

BOWMAN, E. H., and R. B. FETTER. *Analysis for Production and Operations Management,* 3rd ed. Homewood, IL: Richard D. Irwin, 1967.

BROWN, ROBERT G. *Smoothing, Forecasting, and Prediction of Discrete Time Series.* Englewood Cliffs, NJ: Prentice-Hall, 1963.

BUFFA, ELWOOD S., and WILLIAM H. TAUBERT. *Production Inventory Systems: Planning and Control.* Homewood, IL: Richard D. Irwin, 1972.

————. *Modern Production Management,* 3rd ed. New York: Wiley, 1969.

————, ed. *Readings in Production and Operations Management.* New York: Wiley, 1966.

CONWAY, RICHARD W., WILLIAM L. MAXWELL, and LOUIS W. MILLER. *Theory of Scheduling.* Reading, MA: Addison-Wesley, 1967.

EILON, S. *Elements of Production Planning and Control.* New York: Macmillan, 1962.

ELMAGHRABY, S. E. *The Design of Production Systems.* New York: Reinhold, 1966.

GARRETT, L. J., and M. SILVER. *Production Management Analysis.* New York: Harcourt Brace Jovanovich, 1968.

GAVETT, J. W. *Production and Operations Management.* New York: Harcourt Brace Jovanovich, 1968.

GEORGE, C. S. *Management in Industry,* 2nd ed. Englewood Cliffs, NJ: Prentice-Hall, 1964.

GOLD, BELA. *Foundations of Productivity Analysis.* Pittsburgh: University of Pittsburgh Press, 1955.

HALL, ROBERT W. *Attaining Manufacturing Excellence*, Irwin, Homewood, IL, 1987.

HOPEMAN, R. J. *Systems Analysis and Operations Management.* Columbus, OH: Charles. E. Merrill, 1969.

HOTTENSTEIN, M. P. *Models and Analysis for Production Management.* Scranton: International Textbook Co., 1968.

HOLT, C. C., F. MODIGLIANI, J. F. MUTH, and H. A. SIMON. *Planning Production Inventories and Work Force.* Englewood Cliffs, NJ: Prentice-Hall, 1960.

JOHNSON, R. A., W. T. NEWELL, and R. C. VERGIN. *Operations Management.* Boston: Houghton Mifflin, 1972.

KRAJEWSKI, L. and L. RITZMAN. *Operations Management-Strategy and Analysis,* Addison-Wesley, Reading MA, 1987.

MAGEE, J. F., and D. M. BOODMAN. *Production Planning and Inventory Control,* 2nd ed. New York: McGraw-Hill, 1967.

MUTH, JOHN F., and GERALD L. THOMPSON, eds. *Industrial Scheduling.* Englewood Cliffs, NJ: Prentice-Hall, 1963.

NILAND, POWELL. *Production Planning, Scheduling, and Inventory Control.* New York: Macmillan, 1970.

Progress in Operations Research, Vol. I, Russell L. Ackoff ed., 1961; Vol. II, David B. Hertz and Robert T. Eddison, eds., 1964; Vol. III, Julius Aronofsky, ed., 1969. New York: Wiley.

STARR, M. K., ed. *Management of Production.* Middlesex, Eng.: Penguin Books, 1970.

———. *Systems Management of Operations.* Englewood Cliffs, NJ: Prentice-Hall, 1971.

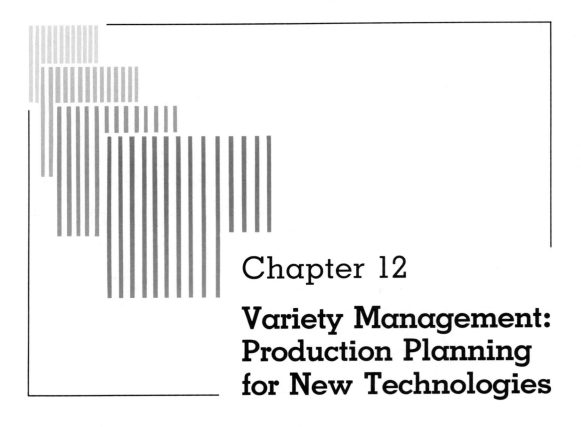

Chapter 12

Variety Management: Production Planning for New Technologies

CHAPTER SUMMARY   Production planning for processes that employ computer drivers to achieve output variety is different from production planning for familiar, traditional job shops or flow shops. There are many names for these flexible process systems and there will be many more. During the next decade there will be an explosion of inventions related to flexible, programmable, and even intelligent processes. Section 12.1 examines the characteristics of these flexible systems.

Linear Programming (LP) is a production scheduling method with particular applicability for flexible systems. Section 12.2 first studies the nature of LP, and then looks at the applicability of LP for scheduling flexible production systems.

Section 12.1 Flexible Systems

Among the names given to flexible systems that are familiar at this time are FMS and CIM. We have also generalized the terminology applicable to programmable equipment and work transfer paths by speaking about FPS (flexible and programmable systems). See Section 4.3 for the discussion of FPS.

Let us review some of these ideas. FMS means flexible manufacturing systems. FPS applies to both manufacturing and service processes. As such, it includes FMS as a subset. We will use FPS to represent both kinds of systems except when just manufacturing applies. The important characteristic of such systems is that they can produce variety at low unit cost.

Information Systems

All kinds of computerized information systems that have flexibility built into database management and telecommunications are examples of FPS that are not directly FMS. Yet increasingly, manufacturing processes are becoming information-driven systems. Figure 12–1 shows how the information support systems of both manufacturing and services are converging on similar menu-driven choice systems.

FMS is a subset of FPS. It is also a subset of CIM. The reason is that CIM represents the entire manufacturing system as an integrated entity,

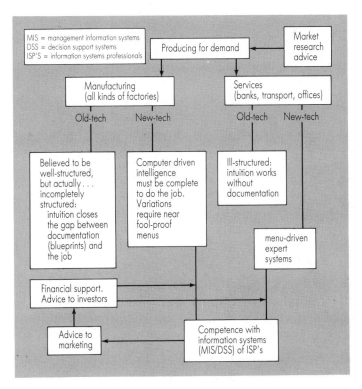

FIGURE 12-1. Convergence of information systems for manufacturing and services.

whereas the FMS can consist of a few machines connected by a work-transfer arm. Later, we will address the whole question of how to categorize the computer-driven technologies that are emerging. For the moment, we will acknowledge that what they all have in common is the ability to produce a great variety of high-quality work, at low unit cost. They all enjoy low setup, takedown, and changeover costs.

In particular, **CIM (computer-integrated manufacturing)** experts readily acknowledge the fact that **information architecture** is the key to successful CIM applications. Figure 12–2 illustrates the complex of factors that interact to form a CIM system. If any of the parts of the two outer rings are not included, the system will not work. In fact, all the elements must be tied to the core at the center; this is integrated systems architecture.

The CIM analogy with architecture goes further than words. The parts that are represented in Figure 12–2 are like the elements of a building that must work together in a coherent way for the structure to function. Imagine how difficult it would be to get a permit for an office building for which there was no coordinated planning of elevators, staircases, space allocation, placement of windows, plumbing, electrical fixtures, and entrances.

For CIM, the coordination starts with people and their training, as the workers go in the front door. They are coordinated with machines, materials, computers, engineering design, and so on, in the process of manufacture. Quality and scheduling are involved as the product is sold going out the shipping doors.

Why was integrated systems architecture not needed before the computer began to manage large portions of the input-output process? First, because human abilities to size up the situation, and to take appropriate action, made up for lack of understanding of system dynamics. This is an information collection and decision problem. Second, the systems were smaller and less complex. Less information was required to manage them. Third, process control systems, decision support systems, artificial intelligence, and expert systems require a constant supply of relevant information to operate effectively. CIM architecture is responsible for the timely collection and dissemination of relevant information.

Economies of Scope

The best of both worlds is available when FPS and/or CIM can be justified. Flexible and programmable systems can produce the great variety of the job shop with higher quality and lower unit costs. The economies of scale that the flow shop offers are available because setup times (also called changeover times) are negligible. The production system adjusts instantly to produce each new product. From the process point of view, any piece in its repertoire can be played with equal ease. It is not as if the same product were being made over and over, but the differences

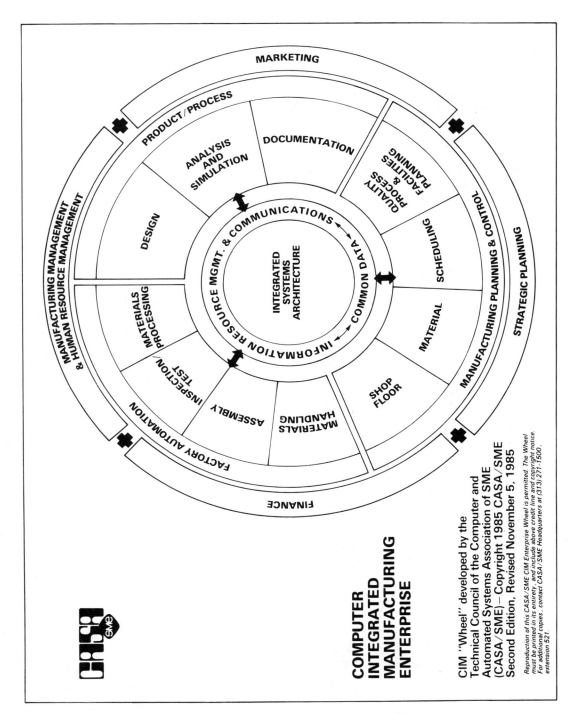

COMPUTER INTEGRATED MANUFACTURING ENTERPRISE

CIM "Wheel" developed by the
Technical Council of the Computer and
Automated Systems Association of SME
(CASA/SME) — Copyright 1985 CASA/SME
Second Edition, Revised November 5, 1985

FIGURE 12-2.

are programmed and the changeover times are negligible. Each product calls up its own software programming. The shift from one to the other is costless. This is referred to as **economies of scope.**

Because of FPS's ability to generate variety with no setup costs, this computer technology has been described as providing economies of scope. Figure 12–3, compares the character of economies of scale with those of economies of scope. However, in preparing for each new product to be made by the FPS, there can be large one-time software costs and problems because the technology is not yet entirely understood. Such costs and delays need to be considered when making the choice of FPS-type work configurations.

Effect on Organizational Size

Say that the company, using traditional technology, is producing and shipping V units per day. Assume that this is 100 percent of its capacity. Since CIM, FPS, and FMS are 24-hour, 7-day systems, with a little time out for maintenance, a smaller flexible system can produce the same output as the traditional one. However, it is seldom possible to design a flexible system that has scaled-down volume proportional to the original demand levels. Consequently, the flexible system has larger output capacity than the traditional system it replaces. This means that for a well-run flexible system, there has to be enough work to keep the FPS busy about 160 hours each week.

The production process will therefore begin to **push marketing** with new product designs. This is far different from the usual relationship, which is for marketing to **push production.** So this and other ways, the organization is affected by the existence of FPS and FMS capabilities.[1]

---

[1]M. K. Starr and A. J. Biloski, "The Decision to Adopt New Technology—Effects on Organizational Size," *OMEGA*, Vol. 12, No. 4, pp. 353–361, 1984.

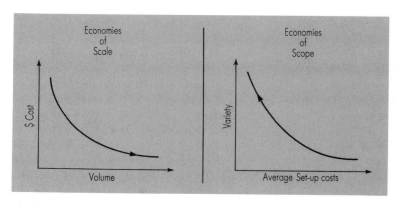

FIGURE 12-3. Comparing economies of scale and scope.

595
*Variety
Management:
Production
Planning for
New
Technologies*

Timing of Adoption of New Technologies

Numerical controlled machines (NC) and computer numerical controlled equipment (CNC) have been available since the 1960s. The NCs use a punched tape to instruct the machine. The CNCs provide direct computer instruction. Most companies have absorbed these technologies, but there are many departments within companies that still consider them experimental. In the present technological environment, the timing for learning such technology has really passed.

The higher levels of technological achievement include these:

Computer Aided Design (CAD), which assists the designer with computer graphics and computer structural analyses. Where design responsiveness is important, CAD should be employed regularly.

Computer Aided Manufacture (CAM), which converts the CAD design into instructions for the manufacturing equipment. CAM should be at least experimental, following experience with CAD. Again, efforts should be made to embody CAM in order to be competitive on a global scale.

Computer Aided Engineering (CAE) is another aid. Usually, work stations with sophisticated computer equipment assist engineers. Still experimental in many locations, the adoption of CAE should be rapid in companies that rely upon the fastest and the best engineering responses.

Global competitors are moving into these high technologies, so it is important to study them and to experiment with them. On the other hand, large commitments to production facilities must be carefully considered. Timing of full-scale commitment is crucial, since knowledge of how to use these technologies is still not complete, and the technology itself is constantly evolving.

Classification of Flexible Systems

Many different classification systems are in use; changes are occurring so fast that there is no agreement. However, we should call attention to an early distinction by Mikell Groover[2] between two basic types of flexible systems. These are: (a) dedicated FMS, and (b) random FMS. Dedicated FMS have low variety levels because of commitments to particular parts and sequences. Random FMS have high part variety levels because they are less constrained by sequence.

At the present time, a four-level structure is often used for classifying flexible systems:

1. **Stand-alones** reflect machine flexibility. For example, NCs and CNCs are viewed as improved versions of the basic machines and they

---

[2]Mikell P. Groover, *Automation, Production Systems, and Computer-Aided Manufacturing* (Englewood Cliffs, NJ: Prentice-Hall, 1980).

are used in the same way as if a machine operator was working the facility.

2. **Machine cells** are groups of flexible machines with operators transferring work between them. The routines are predesigned, since the volume of work is sufficiently large to enable the engineering of the process. In other words, there is integration of the facilities so that work is different from that of a worker moving between standalones. There is process flexibility, but automatic transfers are not available.

3. **Islands of automation** are parts-oriented arrangements of equipment. There is routing flexibility, which permits group technology (pp. 140–144) to be used. Automatic transfer of parts between machines is built into the system. Often tool sharing is designed into the arrangement. Small run sizes are sought. Therefore, both quality control of output and production scheduling are not well understood.

4. **Flexible factories** are complete ensembles that produce products. Toyota's flexible factory makes a variety of autos in Japan, and in West Germany, Messerschmidt has a flexible factory for making military fighter planes. The U.S. Air Force has been expanding its capabilities to produce military planes in flexible factories. IBM has semiconductor facilities that qualify as flexible factories.

The difference between an island of automation and a flexible factory may be difficult to distinguish. For example, John Deere Company has a crankshaft line that would qualify as a flexible factory for a parts manufacturer, but not for a manufacturer of farm equipment.

Another useful classification for flexible systems is based on the character of the system components:

The machine tools
The materials handling system
The storage for WIP
The computer controls

Also, the difference between manufacture and assembly has to be sorted out. In many of the new plants, these activities are mixed together. Adaptive automation of metal cutting is different from that of assembly. These and other taxonomy questions are being further clarified each day.

Another Classification System

Nothing is settled yet; lest the assumption be made that we now know the structure of flexibility, consider the many aspects of flexibility that are presently being considered. In a joint paper entitled "Classification of Flexible Manufacturing Systems'',[3] the authors list eight types of flexibilities. Notice the international backgrounds of the authors to understand the global significance of flexible systems.

We are paraphrasing the article, but note the number of different names that have been suggested for category 2. A similar situation exists for other categories. Also, consider our use of FPS and CIM. The diversity of names should help us to recognize the present state of flexible nomenclature and the concepts that must underlie useful taxonomies. It also indicates the fact that efforts are being made to find agreement.

1. *Machine Flexibility:* the ease of making the changes required to produce a given set of part types. Flexibility might be measured as the time to make such changes as replacing worn-out or broken cutting tools; changing tools in a tool magazine to produce a different subset of parts, and so on.

2. *Process Flexibility:* the ability to produce a given set of part types, each possibly using different materials, in several ways. Buzacott (1982) calls this ''job flexibility''; Gerwin (1982) calls this ''mix flexilibity.''[4]

3. *Product Flexibility:* the ability to change over to produce a new set of products.

4. *Routing Flexibility:* the ability to handle breakdowns and to continue producing the given set of part types.

5. *Volume Flexibility:* the ability to operate an FMS profitably at different production volumes. A higher level of automation increases this flexibility, partly as a result of both lower machine setup costs and lower variable costs such as direct labor.

6. *Expansion Flexibility:* the capability of building a system, and expanding it as needed, easily and modularly.

7. *Operation Flexibility:* the ability to interchange the ordering of several operations for each part type. There is usually some required partial precedence structure for a particular part type.

8. *Production Flexibility:* the universe of part types the FMS can produce. This flexibility is measured by the level of existing technology.

In the same article, the authors list four kinds of flexible systems which are somewhat like the four classes given previously in the classification

[3]Jim Browne, University College, Galway; Didier Dubois, Centre d'Etudes et de Recherches de Toulouse; Keith Rathmill, Cranfield Institute of Technology, U.K.; Suresh P. Sethi, University of Toronto; and Kathryn E. Stecke, The University of Michigan: *The FMS Magazine*, pp. 114–117, April 1984.

[4]J. A. Buzacott, "The Fundamental Principles of Flexibility in Manufacturing Systems," *Proceedings of the First International Conference on Flexible Manufacturing Systems*, Brighton, UK, October 20–22, 1982. Donald Gerwin, "Do's and Dont's of Computerized Manufacturing," *Harvard Business Review*, 60, 2 (March–April 1982, pp. 107–116.

of flexible systems. For contrast, we list these, but do not go into their characteristics in depth. They are:

Type I FMS: Flexible Machining Cell: one general-purpose CNC machine tool interfaced with automated materials handling for input and output.

Type II FMS: Flexible Machining System: real-time, on-line control of part production. It is highly machine, process, product, and routing flexible.

Type III FMS: Flexible Transfer Line: for all part types, each operation is performed on only one machine; this results in a fixed route for each part through the system.

Type IV FMS: Flexible Transfer Multiline: multiple Type III FMSs that are interconnected. The duplication does not increase process flexibility. The main advantage is redundancy in a breakdown situation.

According to the authors (p. 117): "In general, The FMS's of the United States and the Federal Republic of Germany tend to be more like the Type II FMS, while those of Japan are more similar to Type III. The second floor of Fanuc's Fuji complex, consisting of four flexible transfer lines, is an example of an operating Type IV FMS." It is useful to note that the Type II FMS tends to be more flexible than Type III.

International Comparisons of Variety Levels

Figure 12–4 illustrates the different degrees of variety that are produced in three countries.[5] The reasons for this difference in performance needs to be explained. The United States produced the least variety for its investments in flexibility. The reason seems to be that the U.S. engineers seek to design total flexible automation. In contrast, the West Germans and Japanese interface their flexible systems with engineers who reach human decisions at various steps in the sequence. See Figures 12–5 and 12–6 help to illustrate the differences between **total system automation** and **interruptive automation**.

---

[5]R. Jaikumar, *Technology Review,* July, 1985.

Country	Number of FMS	Average variety produced
Japan	50	30
USA	30	8
West Germany	20	85
	100	

FIGURE 12-4. Three-country comparisons of FMS variety. Source: R. Jaikumar, *Technology Review,* July 1985.

599
*Variety
Management:
Production
Planning for
New
Technologies*

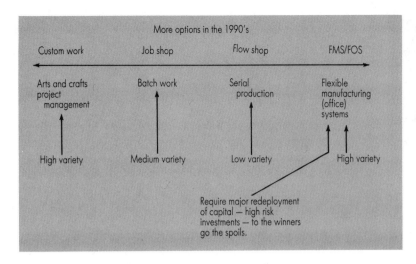

FIGURE 12-5. Span of variety by work configuration.

Justification of CIM

Because there are large initial outlays of capital for a real CIM system, justifying expenditures in the normal fashion has been questioned. Robert Kaplan has marshaled a number of the answers.[6] The problem is that large initial expenses are incurred. A substantial period of time is required before payback is achieved. The normal use of discounted cash flow (DCF) described on pp. 467–470 would discriminate against acceptance of CIM investments. Kaplan notes that the intangible CIM benefits are treated as though they have zero value, whereas it is reasonable to assume that intangibles have some value.

What are these intangible values? First, there is 24-hour on-line capacity. When the capacity is teamed with flexible product line, there is

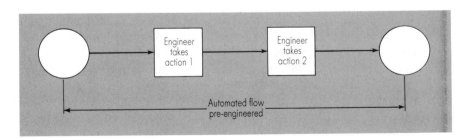

FIGURE 12-6. Interruptive automation.

[6]Robert S. Kaplan, "*Must CIM Be Justified by Faith Alone?*" *Harvard Business Review*, 64 (March–April 1986), pp. 87–95.

greater marketing opportunity. The equipment can be operated on a 24-hour basis with remote telecommunication controls, which means that facilities all over the world can be instructed from a central location to provide for regional markets. In spite of the high variety produced, the quality can be as good or better than from any other process. WIP can be maintained at the lowest possible levels. Consequently, the FMS requires minimum space, so space charges are lower. Lead times can be maintained at minimums. Cycle times can be driven down and kept low, which means that throughput time is at a minimum, and output rates are maximized.

Meanwhile, it should be noted that a comparison of FMS with the present system, whatever it might be, should recognize the declining value of the present system. First, it is aging. Second, it is being used up. Third, it is not of the same class as FMS technology. Also, for survival, each company must learn the strengths and weaknesses of FMS for its own situation. Otherwise, it will cease to be globally competitive with companies that learn over time to use the new technologies successfully.

Operating against approval of large CIM investments is the common practice of letting P/OMs have the signoff responsibility for small to medium expenditures for capital investments, but not for large investments. Human nature leads the P/OMs to invest gradually. It is easier to use incremental changes which they can approve, rather than proposing a massive restructuring of the system that must be approved by the CEO and/or the board of directors.

The Effects of Flexible Systems

The Boston Consulting Group has listed five effects of flexible automation:[7]

1. Scale effects will be reduced. Smaller-scale operations can compete successfully. Multiple-shift utilization of equipment will become more critical than overall scale.

2. Labor rate differences will lose importance. Location choices will depend on proximity to customer, not on the price of labor. Advantages of concentration in a central facility will be diminished.

3. Suppliers will have closer contact with customers. Special knowledge and capabilities such as customized software for varieties needed by each customer will lead to one-on-one relationships. Also, flexible systems allow delivery times to be reduced.

4. There will be more price differentiation. Premium prices will be achieved for both consumer and industrial goods as products are

---

[7]Heinrich N. Rutt, "Flexible Automation", *Perspectives,* Boston Consulting Group pamphlet, 1985.

601
*Variety
Management:
Production
Planning for
New
Technologies*

tailored to specific customer needs and delivered faster than by a general supplier.

5. Organizations will have to be more flexible. There will be job reductions and changes that have to be accepted. The process of becoming flexible will require realignments over a period of a decade or more. Short delivery times require better coordination between manufacturing and distribution. Unused FMS capacity requires better coordination between marketing managers and P/OMs.

Effects of CIM on Production Scheduling

Flexible systems pull things together, and they change organizations in many ways. Figure 12–7 shows how manufacturing flexibility relates product and process flexibility with infrastructure flexibility. Figure 12–8 illustrates some terminology differences that relate production scheduling volumes of output to cost and variety levels. In all cases, quality is assumed to be at the highest possible level.

The production flow from input to output is shown in Figure 12–9. An integration of shop floor controls with the production schedule is coordinated by the CIM, or the flexible system that is driving the output. The same flow diagram that was used in Figure 12–9 is revised to reflect the use of such control systems as MRP, MRPII, JIT, and TQC in Figure 12–10.

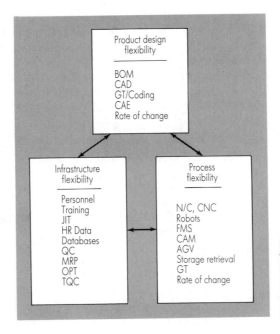

FIGURE 12-7. Manufacturing flexibility. Adapted from Paul M. Swamidass, *Manufacturing Flexibility*, Monograph No. 2, Figure 6, OMA, January 1988. Naman and Schneider Associates Group.

Flexibility in automation	Low cost	High volume	Low variety
Flexibility in manufacturing	Mid cost	Mid volume	Mid variety
Flexible custom manufacturing	High cost	Low volume	High variety

FIGURE 12-8. Production costs and variety of volume. Adapted from Paul M. Swamidass, *Manufacturing Flexibility*, Monograph No. 2, Figure 6, OMA, January 1988. Naman and Schneider Associates Group.

The Variety Problem as a Function of Level

At the global level, the variety problem is one of diversification. With respect to diversification, a major issue is the extent to which an organization's assets are convertible. Where there is high resource convertibility, the company's planning can be extremely flexible. We know that management ability is supposed to be highly transferable. In reality, when focus is lost in diversification, the company's performance seems to suffer. Variety at the global level has to be carefully managed for long-term benefits, although mergers and acquisitions are based, for the most part, on short-term benefits.

Technological knowledge may be the least convertible managerial resource, but the manager is generally somewhat flexible with respect to the kind of technological system that can be managed. The manager may have difficulty dealing with both flow shops and job shops. There will be even more difficulty integrating projects with batch production or flow systems. Crossing between old and new technologies increasingly is being done with success.

At the next level, operating within the accustomed framework of limited

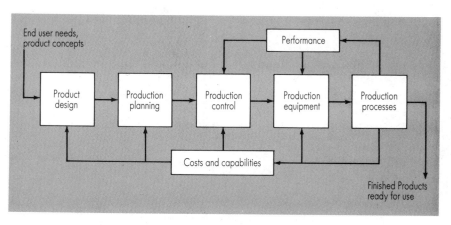

FIGURE 12-9. Integration of functions in a computer integrated manufacturing system.

603

*Variety
Management:
Production
Planning for
New
Technologies*

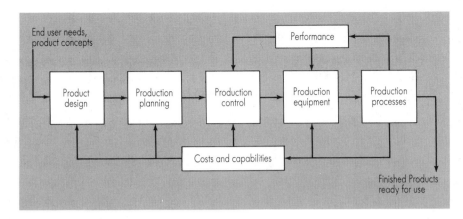

FIGURE 12-10. Production scheduling with TQC and JIT.

resources, a company must determine its optimal product or service mix. The optimal mix is defined as that mix of products and services, using the existing resources and facilities of the company, that will maximize benefits, such as profit. For determination of optimal mix, the financial, marketing, and production managers must pool their knowledge. This need for interfunctional cooperation is facilitated through unifying models such as the breakeven model and the LP model.

The next step could be called the level of product style; it has less to do with alternative uses of resources and facilities. At this level, the questions asked concern the number of flavors, colors, or package design alternatives that should be considered for a particular item. Thus, for sales promotion reasons, the question is: How many tastes, images, styles, or variations on a theme should be developed? The question at this level that needs to be addressed is: What effects do these product variations have on process costs? To the extent that the effect is minimal (there are negligible changeover times), then the process is flexible with respect to styles.

Choice potential (variety) interacts with the customer's selection process, producing a greater sales volume than could otherwise be obtained. This is due to the fact that a varied offering can offset boredom for the individual customer, while appealing to a larger number of specialized segments of consumers. If you get tired of vanilla you can try chocolate, but there are some people who like only chocolate. The company would lose both types of chocolate sales if it offered only vanilla.

But variety costs money. There are more items to stock, more records to keep, more materials to buy (at lesser quantities, so that discounts will be lower), and so on. And there are line changeover costs, or big investments in flexible systems to avoid them.

There is an optimal number of varieties. The product and service-mix models of linear programming can help to determine what this level should be. However, the LP method is not genuinely suited for the style problem or for the diversification problem. Also, LP must be fitted into the usual intermittent flow shop or A-type (of the ABC Curve) job shop environment. As we have said, this is because of setup costs and times. With flexible systems, this setup problem goes away, and LP is admirably suited for resolving problems.

In the first and third cases, the concept of using up limited resources must be stretched to fit the situation. Even so, as a first approximation, the LP model can be applied. And it is ideally suited for second-level problems, having zero setup costs, where the various activity outputs use up different amounts of the same resources. For example, there are problems where:

The scarce resource is machine time, and the production mix can be different numbers of nuts and bolts (Manufacturing)

The scarce resources are land and fertilizer, and the potential activities are the production of different amounts of peas and beans (Agriculture)

The scarce resources are teachers and rooms, and the decision must be the mix of graduate students and undergraduates (Service system)

It is easy to draw similar comparisons for drill presses and milling machines, for secretaries and office jobs, for doctors and patients, for different petroleum crude stocks to be blended at the refinery, or for perfume blends (or whiskey blends), and for cattle or poultry feed mixtures, which must deliver sufficient nutrition at minimum cost.

The Economic Advantages of Variety

Variety is of two kinds. One is the difference perceived by the customers between one item and another, or between one service and another. This is often based on perceptions of appearance and/or the functional utilities rendered. Another is the difference in process that exists between making or serving one item and another. The customer may not even be able to spot this second kind of variety. For example, the leads for one company's modular telephone jack may be gold-plated, with a thickness that is ten times that of another company's jack. Both are so thin that the customer cannot see the difference.

Marketing Aspects

Marketing managers enjoy variety. They can react quickly to specific customer needs. They can also charge more for the product. Their customers are more loyal because the fundamental software is in their (suppliers') hands, as are the varieties that have been fashioned from it.

605
*Variety
Management:
Production
Planning for
New
Technologies*

Confident and knowledgeable management is required to deal with the risks of FPS. The large investments deliver variety with high quality and low unit costs. But the management of a process designed for variety is a challenge to the P/OM's ability to learn and adapt. Also, there is the FPS challenge to marketing. This challenge arises because of the FMS ability to deliver a larger volume of output, which embodies variety that may be less market-driven and more production-driven. Consider the scenario where the P/OM decides to make a Model XT sportscar without any order on hand because the flexible process system has adequate inventory on hand that is not being used. The inevitable fear of finished goods inventories cannot be readily dismissed until the P/OM costs out the XT and shows that if it sold at a 20 percent discount, it would still make the expected profit margin.

Production and Design Aspects

One of the fundamental design questions that management must resolve is this: What variety of products or services should it supply? Given that the strategic answers have been reached in this regard, various design possibilities exist, and there is a real opportunity to introduce variety that can lead customer choice into the line of goods and services offered.

Variety has marketing advantages; it has several economic production benefits as well. The first production benefit is related to the manner in which production capacity is used and the consequent economic utilization of resources. This is the subject of Section 12.2, where the product/service mix problem is treated by means of linear programming (LP). The second production benefit stems from high-volume production of certain components or ingredients that are used in as many end products as possible. Such modular production allows the benefits of flow shop operations to be realized.

LP and Variety

The variety issue is intricately bound up with life cycle planning. One approach to solving the variety problem is by means of the linear programming model. Therefore, life cycle planning and LP are interrelated.

The LP model provides an economically sound solution (indicating how much of each kind of product to make or to offer as a service). This solution must then be considered in life cycle terms of market demand changing (increasing) over time, plus changes in production capacity that attempt to match demand. The LP solution must be altered accordingly, possibly by using an iterative procedure.

LP is particularly well suited for job shop variety problems. Interdependencies of production, marketing, and finance become apparent. A difference in the interpretation of the LP solution will be found depending upon whether the facilities have already been purchased or are in the planning stages and could be altered. If the facilities exist, there are constraints. If the facilities do not exist, their type and optimum size can be determined.

Life Cycles and Production Configurations

Depending on marketing needs and production capabilities, variety will be generated in the output. When we speak of variety, we refer to the use of the production system to produce different end products or services over some given period. The design function can come up with new varieties that have never been seen before, as they are needed. This ability is entirely new to both production and marketing. How much and what kind of variety is a major issue in life cycle planning, because often the output varieties are brought to the customer through the same distribution channels.

The variety may provide alternative choices to the customer that are relatively the same and therefore substitutable. When this is the case, variety speeds up the rate of acceptance of a new product line or service mix. It increases the life of the established set of goods and services, and it postpones the decay of sales volume.

Whether or not the varieties of output are distributed through the same channels and are relatively substitutable, there may be a basic economic production advantage to be gained by producing variety. This functional aspect of variety is captured by the LP model.

Work Configurations

Flow shops can be designed to produce a high degree of variety. Usually, the only penalty to be paid is the downtime required to switch the line from one output to another. For example, several different blends of coffee could be made and packaged using the same flow system, with time out between successive blends to change coffee beans, labels, and so on. Petroleum refineries can change the blending formulas of crudes to produce a broad range of fuel outputs on a relatively automatic basis. The point to be noted is that such output variety can have both marketing advantages and the economic motivation of using production resources in the best possible fashion.

On the other hand, job shop variety is often a function of orders received that must be processed with as little delay as possible. However, when the job shop configuration is being used to add to inventory rather than to fill an order, the advantages of variety that we have already mentioned remain entirely applicable.

Life cycle management involves juggling production and marketing issues. Financial goals and constraints are always in the picture. This can be seen by considering the Petromasters' problems, in Section 12.2.

Section 12.2 Linear Programming and Flexible Systems

The fundamental model in determining optimum variety is linear programming. Optimal is defined from a process point of view, not in terms of customer satisfaction. **Linear programming (LP)** is a quantitative method for the optimal allocation of resources. By optimal, we mean that *only* a single objective such as profit or sales volume can be maximized. On the other hand, minimization is used if the problem is stated in terms of costs. LP is a powerful and much used management science model for optimal resource allocation.

CASE: PETRO-MASTERS

Petromasters has on hand specific petroleum crudes that can be blended in a number of ways. Each way produces a different set of fuels (say A, B, and C) which sell at different prices and yield alternative profits. Petromasters has been using LP for over 30 years to determine the optimal product mix which maximizes total profit.

The objective needs to be clearly formulated. For example, Petromasters managers wish to determine how much output of each different fuel should be made to maximize profit, subject to the resource constraints of the crudes. A possible solution might be to make 200 gallons of A, 150 gallons of B, 30 gallons of C. Will this maximize Petromasters' profits? Now, assume that the profit per unit is largest with A-type fuels. Why not make more gallons of A and less of B and C? The answer is that the crude resource contraints may limit what can be made. The LP model determines the best (optimal) product mix for whatever constraints exist on resources.

In general, each output type requires different amounts of available resources (such as pounds of materials, hours of machine time, numbers of widgits). Below, we discuss the fundamentals of the LP technique and explain why this form of mathematical programming is called linear.

LP and FMS, FPS and CIM

What product mix should be made on an FMS, FPS or CIM? This question can, in large part, be answered by using linear programming. In fact, LP is well suited for scheduling the output of the flexible systems described previously. It is difficult to use LP when substantial changeover costs exist. Fortunately for Petromasters, changeover costs for blending are very small relative to the value of the product. But in many instances, such as metal cutting and assembly, the existence of real and substantial setup times and costs has made it difficult to use LP to plan production quantities. Since FPS do not have significant setup costs, LP provides a powerful means for production planning. LP can help in planning what to make, but it does not provide instructions about how to sequence the various products through the production process. For that consideration, see pp. 573–587.

LP assigns a percentage of existing capacity needed to make each unit of product in such a way as to maximize total profit. How much to make of each kind of unit is represented by x_i. That is, x_i = how much to make of the ith kind of item. Such x_is, representing the product mix, are the direct variables of the LP.

Every linear programming problem can be rearranged so that the direct variables are transformed into a different set of variables. These new variables reflect the value of the resources that have previously set the resource constraints. They are called **shadow prices** or **dual variables.** When capacity is not fully utilized, the shadow price is equal to zero. Shadow prices greater than zero establish the values of the scarce productive resources. They define the FPS tools that are bottlenecking the system.

CASE: PAINTMASTERS, INC.

The manufacturing facilities of Paintmasters, Inc., are arranged in a flow shop configuration. Each time a different color of paint (1, 2, 3, ... n) is to be produced, the process is stopped and converted to the next color. There are constraints on ingredients and storage space. The sales department would like to have as many colors as possible in stock. Colors can be made in quantities of $x_1, x_2, x_3, ... x_n$

Various sets of values for these x_is create feasible mixtures or blends. The production department calls on its P/OM staff to study the problem. Shortly thereafter, a report is submitted which states that:

$$x_1 = 5000 \text{ gallons of } 1$$

$$x_2 = \text{making zero gallons of } 2$$

$$x_3 = \text{making zero gallons of } 3$$

$$x_4 = \text{making 1000 gallons of } 4$$

will minimize production costs for the company. LP was used to derive this answer.

The sales department is understandably unhappy. It has market research personnel who also understand LP. The sales manager calls on the market research group to use the same data, but instead of minimizing production costs, the objective is to maximize company sales volume.

This LP maximization often yields a different solution than an LP minimization solution. A compromise is required by asking all parties involved to accept the LP solution that maximizes company profits.

609
*Variety
Management:
Production
Planning for
New
Technologies*

Note the different objectives:

1. Minimize production costs
2. Maximize sales volume
3. Maximize profits

Some of the difficulties cannot be straightened out through the use of LP. For example, consider one aspect of the life cycle characteristics of this product line. One class of paint colors is mature and stable. There is always demand for that class. Another class of colors is faddish. Yet another class is stable and seasonal.

The sales department would like to have as many colors as possible in stock. To this we can now add the fact that faddish colors are considered particularly important. But production would like to minimize inventories of raw materials and of finished goods. Also, only large quantities of dyes can be purchased at good discounts.

Unlike FPS systems, intermittent flow shops (such as the one Paintmasters uses) incur costs for changeovers. Small runs are costly in many ways, but especially because each time the color is changed, the process has to be stopped, the vats must be cleaned out, and production time is lost.

The dilemma is apparent, but it will be resolved because Paintmasters must do something. A compromise between the LP solutions and the other factors that prevail will be found.

Linear Programming Modeling

Applying it to flexible and programmable systems is a new way of using the ubiquitous LP model. There are strengths and weaknesses in the application. And there are really many objectives expressed in the LP model. Only one objective can be maximized (say market share) or minimized (say errors). The set of constraints includes all other objectives (such as not exceeding the service capacity of each department, or using no more raw materials than are held in inventory). Optimizing the single objective is achieved by employing different activities in various amounts. This requires using up specific amounts of limited resources.

Each possible product or service design that can be made with existing facilities (or possible with a new facility) is an activity that can be considered as a separate variable by the model. The set of activities optimizes one objective, subject to the constraint objectives not being violated.

According to the number of units of each design that will be made, the limited resources of departmental capacities will be used up. In the simplest case (which applies to a very large number of real situations), we use linear forms to express the way in which resources are used up; that is, the same amount of resource is required for each unit of a particular design that is made. The same reasoning applies to profit, which is to be maximized. Each unit sold of a particular design contributes an equal amount of profit. The assumption that all units are sold is basic to the structure of the LP model.

How LP Works: A Graphic Explanation of the Maximization Problem

The explanation of the linear programming technique is easier with an example. The situation can be kept manageable by considering the possibility of a two-product line. This permits a two-dimensional graphic representation. Assume that Partmasters makes only P_1 at the present time. Two departments are required to make the product. First, the press shop blanks, draws, and forms the part. Blanking is cutting out the flat piece in the size that is needed. Drawing and forming refer to operations used to shape the part (such as a doorknob formed from a flat metal blank). Then the item is sent to the second department, where it is chrome-plated. Although it applies here, the specific processing order is not a requirement of the LP method.

From Table 12–1, we see that the full capacity of the first department is utilized when 10 units of P_1 are made per day. On the other hand, only 83 1/3 percent of the plating department's capacity is used. Assume this results from the fact that the minimum plating tank capacity that could be purchased was capable of handling less than 10 units per day. The next largest size, accommodating 12 units per day, was purchased. The departmental capacities are the resource constraints in this particular problem. The item called P_1 returns a profit of $3 per unit.

The manager, wishing to get fuller utilization of equipment, and knowing that marketing has been pushing for greater line variety, suggests that the company consider adding another product to the present line, using only the existing facilities. The new product, which marketing has designated P_2, is developed. A prototype is made and test marketed. The relevant cost and capacity utilization estimates are made. The marketing department feels that the new product should be sold at a lower price than P_1. Table 12–1 shows that P_2 costs less to make. Twenty units could be made in the press shop with full equipment and workforce utilization. Only 12.5 of such units could be processed per day by the plating department if it made only P_2. Thus, for P_2, the capacity of the plating tank is the dominant constraint. Working together, the managers agree that the per-unit profit of P_2 will be $2. All this information is summarized in Table 12–1.

These questions have to be answered:

1. Should P_2 be added to the line?
2. If so, how many units per day of P_2 (called x_2) should be made?

611

*Variety
Management:
Production
Planning for
New
Technologies*

TABLE 12-1

		x_1 Units/Day of P_1	x_2 Units/Day of P_2	Restriction of Full Utilization
	Department 1 (press shop)	10%/unit	5%/unit	100%
	Department 2 (plating)	8⅓/unit	8%/unit	100%
Objective:	(Maximize) profit	$3.00/unit	$2.00/unit	

The table is read as follows:

x_1 = number of units of product type P_1 that will be made per day

x_2 = number of units of product type P_2 that will be made per day

Each unit of the P_1 type that is made uses up 10 percent of the daily capacity of department 1, and 8 1/3 percent of the daily capacity of department 2. Each unit of P_2 consumes 5 percent of the daily capacity of department 1, and 8 percent of the daily capacity of department 2.

If we make only P_1—as is presently done—we can produce a maximum of 10 units (department 1 is the limiting resource). If we make only P_2, we can produce a maximum of 25 units every two days (department 2 is the limiting resource). We should note at this point that if we could make only one or the other, we would prefer to make P_1 because it promises a daily profit of $30, compared to $25 for P_2. Although we can make more of P_2 than of P_1, we cannot make sufficiently more to counterbalance the fact that P_2 has a lower profit per unit. Neither making only P_1 nor making only P_2 will provide full utilization of all plant facilities and resources. Therefore, we can consider a mixture that might provide better utilization of capacity.

It is important to note that better utilization might, but also might not, provide a greater profit. The product mix is subject to the departmental constraints, and our objective remains to maximize profit. Because of the size of this problem, it is relatively easy for a P/OM to determine what should be done without recourse to linear programming. Various methods can be used to solve the problem. For example, an algebraic approach could be used. Normally, complex problems would be solved by means of a matrix method, such as the simplex algorithm of linear programming. The simplex algorithm is presented in brief form on pp. 620–621. Many computer programs are available for solving LP problems. These approaches and appropriate software known as LINDO and GINO are discussed on p. 631.

However, to understand what is involved in obtaining a solution, the method that best serves to explain, and that can be used in this case, is a geometrical resolution of the problem. First, let us refer to Table 12–1 so that we can construct the following inequations:

$$10x_1 + 5x_2 \le 100 \left.\right\}$$
$$8\tfrac{1}{3}x_1 + 8x_2 \le 100 \left.\right\}$$

The symbol $\le$ is read equal to or less than, expressing the fact that any combination of x_1 and x_2 which does not use up more than 100 percent of each department's capacity can be considered. These inequations fit the constraint format of the linear programming model. They state the way in which each department's capacities will be utilized for different production schedules of P_1 and P_2.

Inequations allow more solutions than do equations. That is because inequations can be satisfied with values equal to or less than the amount to which the x_is sum (in this case, 100). The inequations express the fact that it is impossible to utilize more than 100 percent of any department's capacity. Thus, for example, if $x_1 = 10$, department 1 is fully utilized. On the other hand, if $x_1 = 5$ and $x_2 = 5$, then only 75 percent of the first department's capacity has been used up. We say that the remaining 25 percent is **departmental slack.** By substituting different values for x_1 and x_2 we can determine whether either departmental constraint has been violated and also what profit would result from such a plan.

The objective is to maximize profit; that is:

$$\text{maximize } [3x_1 + 2x_2].$$

Furthermore, we can never produce negative quantities of a product, thus:

$$x_1 \ge 0, x_2 \ge 0$$

These inequations express the fact that negative amounts of production cannot be allowed to occur, since they have no basis in reality.

The Trial and Error Method

Table 12–2 shows a number of different combinations of x_1 and x_2 values that might be tried. Several of the plans violate the departmental restric-

TABLE 12-2 EVALUATION BY TRIAL AND ERROR

Plan	x_1	x_2	Department 1 Slack	Department 2 Slack	Profit
Plan$_1$	5	5	25%	18.3%	$25
Plan$_2$	10	5	violation	violation	violation
Plan$_3$	5	10	0%	violation	violation
Plan$_4$	6	5	15%	10%	28
Plan$_5$	7.83	4.35	0%	0%	32.20

613
*Variety
Management:
Production
Planning for
New
Technologies*

tions. For this particular set of trial and error plans, maximum profit of 32.20 is obtained with the fifth plan, which is a feasible product-mix strategy—i.e., it does not violate any of the inequations.

Trial and Error: An Inefficient Approach

Trial and error is an inefficient approach for solving even small problems, but it is useful for learning. Care to try some other combinations? We suggest a few possibilities, and you can supply some of your own.

Plan	x_1	x_2	Department 1 Slack	Department 2 Slack	Profit
Plan$_6$	0	0	100%	100%	$0
Plan$_7$	7	5	5%	1⅔%	31
Plan$_8$					
Plan$_9$					
Plan$_{10}$					

Refer now to Fig. 12–11. All the plans in Table 12–2 can be found on it. The two solid lines that cross each other within the first quadrant represent the two departmental constraints. The first quadrant has only positive values of x_1 and x_2. (The first quadrant is, by convention, the

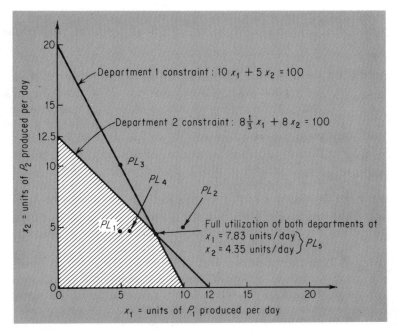

FIGURE 12-11. Feasible solution space for the product-mix problem Points PL_1 through PL_5 refer to the five plans shown in Table 12-2.

upper right-hand portion of any graph.) Each line is labeled with its appropriate equation. The area under each of the two constraint lines is the equivalent of the mathematical statement of an inequation that has the directional sense of less than ($<$). Thus, all points that fall in the first quadrant and meet the requirements of both constraints must lie within the crosshatched area or on its perimeter. We call this the **feasible solution space.**

The first quadrant is defined by the feasibility constraints $x_1 \geq 0$, $x_2 \geq 0$. Any combination of x_1 and x_2 that forms an allowable product mix must be part of the crosshatched space or on the boundary lines that enclose the space. It is simple enough to check and see that any combination of values for x_1 and x_2 that falls on a solid line produces 100 percent utilization of whichever department that line describes. Thus, each solid line stands for the full utilization of the respective department.

We should also note that for this case, there is only one combination of x_1 and x_2 values that yields full utilization of both departments' capacities. It is the crosspoint of the two solid lines.

Now, let us ask a question but defer the answer until later. Why does it not automatically follow that any combination of x_1 and x_2 that fully utilizes all production capacity (the crosspoint, in this case) would be the optimal product-mix solution?

Our purpose is to maximize profit. At least one point in the feasible solution space will achieve this result. It is unnecessary to use trial and error methods to determine which point will maximize profit. We will superimpose a family of dashed profit lines over Fig. 12–11. The result is shown in Fig. 12–12. Each of the dashed parallel lines represents many different combinations of x_1 and x_2. All combinations of x_1 and x_2 that fall on any particular profit line produce one and only one specific level of profit. Thus, consider the line $3x_1 + 2x_2 = 18$. Here, profit always equals 18. If we substitute any one pair of x_1 and x_2 values that falls along this line, that combination (or product mix) will produce a profit of $18. Note that all the points that lie on this profit line of $18 fall within the feasible solution space. This is not true when profit equals $30.20.

We can obtain a profit of $18 in many ways. Is it possible to obtain even greater profit? Let us consider the profit line labeled $30. If we test the profit of each x_1, x_2 pair that falls on this line, we find that they all yield a profit of $30. In this case, however, as previously noted, part of this line does not fall within the feasible solution space. Those x_1, x_2 combinations that are outside the feasible space cannot be used for the product mix. Nevertheless, because some points do meet the departmental capacity constraints, a profit of $30 could be obtained. However, as we will see, this is still not the maximum possible profit.

As we consider other profit lines further upward and toward the right, the profit level increases. We should therefore choose that member of the family of (parallel) profit lines which is the last one to touch the feasible solution space as the isoprofit lines move upward. Each isoprofit line is

615
*Variety
Management:
Production
Planning for
New
Technologies*

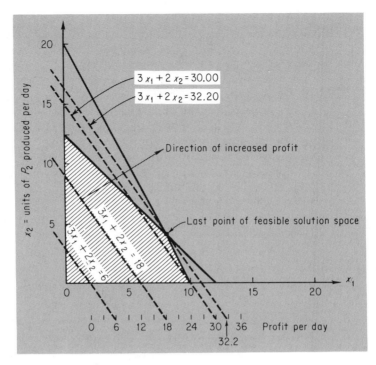

FIGURE 12-12. Family of dashed profit lines superimposed on the feasible solution space.

a line of equal profit. There is one such line for every possible profit level; we have shown just a few. This last profit line to touch the feasible space is the line of maximum profit. For this example, it occurs at the intersection of the two department constraint lines. The production values for this solution are as follows:

$$x_1 = 7.83$$

and

$$x_2 = 4.35$$

With this solution, there is no departmental slack for either department: The profitability is $32.20 per day.

The values of x_1 and x_2 in this solution are fractional. If this violates the sense of the solution, then we must utilize the technique of integer programming. Frequently, it is quite satisfactory to round off fractional numbers so that a reasonable solution is obtained that is very close to optimal and that meets the system's constraints.

Now, let us answer the question previously posed but left unanswered. We do this by raising a different question. What would the optimal product mix be if the relative profitabilities of the different units in the product mix were changed? Let us consider an example where the profitability of the first product has been made equal to $2 per unit and the profitability of the second item has been raised to $3 per unit. This produces a change in the solution, as shown in Fig. 12–13. This solution leaves 37.5 percent [$100 - (5 \times 12.5)$] unused capacity in department 1. Even so, because of the orientation of the profit line, profit can be maximized only by ignoring the attraction of full utilization of facilities. The real issue is one of appraising the value of the resources as they contribute to the profit objective. LP methods help a great deal in such an evaluation.

We can show that:

1. A solution must always occur at a vertex.
2. As a special case, the solution can occur simultaneously at two adjacent vertices. When this happens, all points on the line that connects the vertices will be optimal product mix solutions.

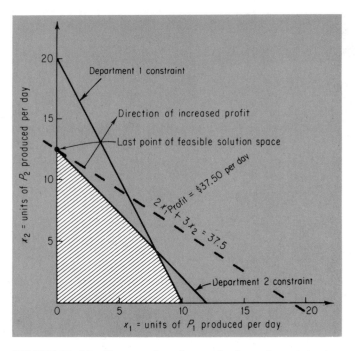

FIGURE 12-13. The optimal product mix for the profit maximization problem changes when P_1 produces $2 of profit per unit and P_2 produces $3 of profit per unit. Thus: maximize $2x_1 + 3x_2$. The solution is: produce 12.5 units of P_2 and no P_1. Total profit = $37.50 per day.

617
Variety
Management:
Production
Planning for
New
Technologies

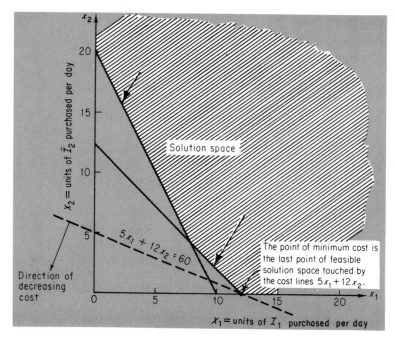

FIGURE 12-14. For cost minimization, the feasible solution space is $\geq$ the constraints, and the optimum solution is associated with the last possible cost line to leave that space, moving down and left. Assume that I_1 costs $5 per unit and I_2 costs $12 per unit; then, minimize $5x_1 + 12x_2$. The solution is: purchase 12 units of I_1 and no I_2. Total cost = $60 per day. Nothing less costly will satisfy the minimum vitamin constraints. We have obtained 120 units of vitamin B_1 and the required 100 units of B_{12}.

The Cost Minimization Solution

Let us illustrate this point by considering a cost minimization problem. In this case, the solution is obtained by determining the last possible cost line to leave the solution space as we move down and toward the left with our cost lines (see Fig. 12–14).

The objective is to minimize the cost function. For cost minimization, the feasible solution space lies on or above the equal to or greater than constraints. The optimum solution is associated with the last possible cost line to leave that space, moving down and left. To give meaning to the two constraints being used in our cost minimization example, we will reformulate the problem. Replace department 1's capacity resources with vitamin B1 requirements for cattle feed. In the same sense, replace department 2's capacity resources with vitamin B12. The resources are now the vitamin content of different cattle feed ingredients. The two ingredients we are considering purchasing contain the two B vitamins in different amounts. We will buy x_1 of the first ingredient I_1 and x_2 of the second ingredient I_2. Table 12–3 summarizes this situation, and adds some additional information.

The inequations are now written:

$$10x_1 + 5x_2 \geq 100 \qquad (x_1, x_2 \geq 0)$$

$$8\tfrac{1}{3}x_1 + 8x_2 \geq 100$$

And cost is to be minimized:

$$\text{Objective: MINIMIZE } [5x_1 + 12x_2].$$

It should be evident that linear programming is not a substitute for ingenious product planning or creative new product development. The character of the product or service mix is strictly a function of whatever designs or components the operations manager has been able to conceive.

If the various products that are competing for available capacity are individually excellent, then the product or service mix will produce a large profit. Otherwise, the best that can be done may not be good enough. The same applies to ingredients as well as other formulations of the LP model.

Functional Interdependencies

Marketing, finance, and production must cooperate whenever LP is used. Estimates of the profit coefficients require sales price strategy as well as confirmation that linearity will be a good enough description of the market's response to $x_1, x_2, \ldots$, etc., quantities of goods or services. When new products or services are to be offered, such estimates can only come from marketing.

Underlying every LP is a process with specific capabilities and re-

TABLE 12-3

	I_1 x_1 Pounds/Day of Ingredient 1	I_2 x_2 Gallons/Day of Ingredient 2	Minimum Vitamin Requirements per Day
Vitamin B_1	10 units of vitamin B_1/pound	5 units of vitamin B_1/gallon	100 units
Vitamin B_{12}	$8\tfrac{1}{3}$ units of vitamin B_{12}/pound	8 units of vitamin B_{12}/gallon	100 units
Objective: (Minimize) cost	$5/pound	$12/gallon	

619
*Variety
Management:
Production
Planning for
New
Technologies*

quirements. The resource utilization coefficients of the process (often called technological coefficients) can be quite different, depending on the fixed investments required for the particular production configuration that is used. Constraints can describe limits to production capacity, including labor and machines, as well as raw materials, energy, and capital. Decisions concerning all these require good coordination between finance and production. With LP, the effects of using different processes on all these factors can be explored.

The assumption of linear constraints as well as the specification of the resource utilization coefficients is a production and operations management responsibility. Using methods engineering and value analysis (see pp. 222, 315–316) it may be possible to improve the resource utilization coefficients by decreasing them so that greater output can be obtained. Such changes in the constraint coefficients could lead to other solutions. This result, which might change the product or service mix, would be of more than casual interest to marketing.

Functional interdependencies begin with the selection of the objective function and the set of constraints. Different solutions will be obtained in most cases for each of the following: profit maximization, cost minimization, sales volume or brand share maximization, inventory minimization, and productivity maximization. Together, all members of the management team can assess the degree to which a linear model fits the actual circumstances. Even if minor deviations from linearity exist, LP generally provides a good enough solution. For certain kinds of major distortions, the LP model is easily modified to take into account nonlinearities, such as when profit increases at a decreasing rate with increasing sales volume. In other circumstances, nonlinear programming must be used.

LP Software

A variety of linear programming software is available. The way these programs can be used for planning production and operations with FMS and FPS is valuable information that changes quite rapidly. We will list and explain only the software that has persisted over a long period of time, albeit with changes and improvements.

Lindo

Although Lindo uses the mathematics of the Simplex Method (see pp. 620–621), it has the advantage of bypassing the need to understand the mathematics. Instead, the routines that are required to input data, to run the programs, and to read and interpret the results, are stressed. The computer application of Lindo is referenced in Appendix A, on pp. 628, 631.

Gino

Gino is nonlinear optimization programming. The computer application of Gino is referenced in Appendix A, on pp. 628, 631.

The Simplex Algorithm for Linear Programming

At one time it was considered essential to understand how to use the simplex algorithm to solve LP problems. Recently, because of powerful software such as Lindo, it is less rewarding to spend time in this way. In fact, the simplex cannot handle the level of complexity that Gino represents with its nonlinear programming. Nevertheless, we deem it useful for all P/OM students to know what the simplex looks like and how it works.

There are straightforward mathematical methods that are computer programmable for solving linear programming problems. One of the first and most understandable algorithms is the **simplex method**. We can understand this mathematical approach by observing the iterative procedures which are shown in Fig. 12–15 and described below:

    I. Begin by selecting any vertex of the area or volume that is formed when two or more axes are involved. (The Cartesian coordinates of the two-dimensional geometric approach—shown on pp. 615–617—must be extended when more than two types of products or ingredients are to be mixed.) This is equivalent to a first feasible solution.

    II. Test to determine whether an improvement in profit can be made by moving to another vertex.

    III. If improvement is possible, attempt to find the best possible change to make.

    IV. Make the indicated change—choose the new, improved vertex solution. Operations II through IV are repeated until condition V occurs.

    V. Stop, because the test (in II) reveals that no further improvement is possible.

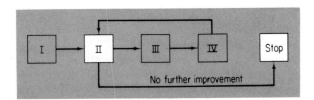

FIGURE 12-15.

The specifics of the simplex method are described in many texts. A number of these are listed in the references. The point to keep in mind is that the graphic explanation on pp. 610–616 of the text is the concept base that drives Lindo and the simplex method.

1. We begin with a set of m inequations and n unknowns. (For this example, $m = 3$ and $n = 4$.)

$$6x_1 + 4x_2 + 8x_3 + 2x_4 \leq 24$$

$$2x_1 + 6x_2 + 4x_3 + 8x_4 \leq 36$$

$$8x_1 + 2x_2 + 6x_3 + 4x_4 \leq 40$$

Although the numbers are hypothetical, their use simplifies our explanation of the method.

2. Then we appoint slack variables x_5, x_6, x_7. The slack variables are used to convert our inequations into equations; see (4) below. Since $m = 3$, there are three slack variables.

3. Next, we write the appropriate objective function. (For this illustration the objective is maximization of profit Z_n, where n is the iteration number. All the numerical values are hypothetical.)

MAXIMIZE:

$$Z = 5x_1 + 4x_2 + 6x_3 + 3x_4 + (0)x_5 + (0)x_6 + (0)x_7$$

4. The inequations are converted to equations.

$$6x_1 + 4x_2 + 8x_3 + 2x_4 + x_5 \qquad\qquad = 24$$

$$2x_1 + 6x_2 + 4x_3 + 8x_4 \qquad + x_6 \qquad = 36$$

$$8x_1 + 2x_2 + 6x_3 + 4x_4 \qquad\qquad + x_7 = 40$$

5. The feasibility conditions include the slack variables:

$$x_j \geq (j = 1, 2, 3, 4, 5, 6, 7)$$

6. The simplex method operates on rules for making a new variable active and, in turn, inactivating a variable. Only those changes are allowed which maintain or increase the value of Z_n. That is, at each successive calculation of Z_n, the value of profit must either increase or remain unchanged. It cannot decrease unless a mistake has been made.

1. To what extent can the essential elements of the problem of diversification be modeled by LP?

2. What is the solution to the following LP problem (based on the two-department example, pp. 610–612)?

	x_2 Units/Day of P_1	x_2 Units/Day of P_2	Restriction of Full Utilization
Department 1 (press shop)	10%/unit	5%/unit	100%
Department 2 (plating)	11%/unit	6%/unit	100%
Objective: (Maximize) profit	$3/unit	$2/unit	

Explain the result.

3. What is the solution to the following LP problem (based on the two-department example, pp. 610–612)?

	x_1 Units/Day of P_1	x_2 Units/Day of P_2	Restriction of Full Utilization
Department 1 (press shop)	10%/unit	5%/unit	
Department 2 (plating)	$8\frac{1}{3}$%/unit	8%/unit	100%
Objective: (Maximize) profit	$3/unit	$1.50/unit	

Explain the result.

4. Apply the 54 questions listed on pp. 61-64 to Paintmasters. Assume that management is considering relocating to a better sales distribution area, and altering the process so that it automatically outputs specified quantities of any color. A recent technological change accounts for this new process capability. Make further assumptions as required.

5. Explain the economic consequences of variety.

6. The fundamental theorem of LP states that there cannot be more activities used in the final solution than the number of constraints. Why is this notion important?

Answer: Assume that an organization has 10 items in its product line, but can identify only three viable constraints on capacity and input materials. An investigation is warranted, which should reexamine constraints and check on the linearity assumptions. If the number of constraints is correct and linearity holds, and if several of the varieties are not relatively identical in resource requirements and price, there is strong reason to advise this organization to decrease the product line. Market considerations can override this advice.

7. A greeting card manufacturer, wishes to diversify its line. Its designers have been experimenting with a new plastic material. It is available in thin sheets and lends itself to some unusual effects. The designers have come up with two alternative card designs. Both appear to be totally acceptable. Because special equipment is required to print and cut this

623

Variety
Management:
Production
Planning for
New
Technologies

new material, the P/OM wants to consider carefully the advantages of either card or the possibility of making both. The following data have been made availible to the manager:

	Card A	Card B
Time to print card on one special machine	2.4 min	2.4 min
Time to cut and fold card on one special machine	4.8 min	1.6 min
Material required	80 in.^{2}	240 in.^{2}
Estimated profit per card	$0.70	$0.80

The company works a 40-hour week; it has 833 square feet of the material on hand and cannot obtain more in the near future. Assume no cutting waste and the requirement that the job be completed within one week. What product mix should the production manager plan to use? Discuss your answer.

Answer: This is a straightforward linear programming problem. The card printing machine creates the following restraint:

$$2.4x_A + 2.4x_B \leq 2400$$

where x_A = the number of A-type cards that will be made and x_B = the number of B-type cards that will be made. There are 2400 = (60)(40) minutes in a week. The cut and fold requirements may be expressed as:

$$4.8x_A + 1.6x_B \leq 2400$$

The material restraints are:

$$80x_A + 240x_B \leq 120,000$$

where $120,000 \approx (833)(144)$ square inches of material.

Plotting these three lines, we can develop the area that includes all the feasible solutions (those which do not violate any of the constraints). Then by drawing the profit lines,

$$0.70x_A + 0.80x_B = K$$

We may locate the line with largest K which has at least one point in common with the feasible solution space. In our example, this point occurs at the intersection of the cut and fold constraint and the material constraint. The coordinates of this point are:

$$x_A = 375, \ x_B = 375 \text{ cards}$$

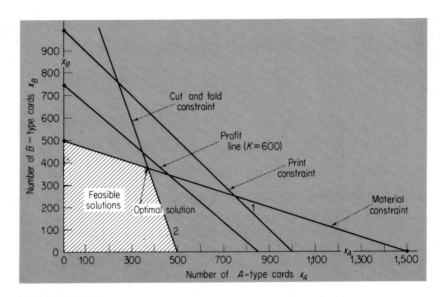

FIGURE 12-16.

The maximum profit that can be obtained with this product mix will be $562.50; see Fig. 12–16.

REFERENCES

ALDERSON, WROE. *Marketing Behavior and Executive Action.* Homewood, IL.: Richard D. Irwin, 1957.

ASIMOW, MORRIS. *Introduction to Design.* Englewood Cliffs, NJ: Prentice-Hall, 1962.

BIERMAN, HAROLD, and SEYMOUR SMIDT. *The Capital Budgeting Decision,* 2nd ed. New York: Macmillan, 1966.

CHASE, R. B., and N. J. AQUILANO. *Production and Operations Management (A Life Cycle Approach),* 4th ed. Homewood, IL: Richard D. Irwin, 1984.

DREYFUSS, HENRY. *Designing for People.* New York: Simon & Schuster, 1955.

FORRESTER, JAY. *Industrial Dynamics.* Cambridge, MA: MIT Press, 1961.

FRIEDLAND, SEYMOUR. *The Economics of Corporate Finance.* Englewood Cliffs, NJ: Prentice-Hall, 1966.

GERLACH, J. T., and C. A. WAINWRIGHT. *Successful Management of New Products.* New York: Hastings House, 1968.

GHISELIN, BREWSTER. *The Creative Process.* New York: New American Library, 1960.

GLEOG, G. L. *The Design of Design.* Cambridge, Eng.: Cambridge University Press, 1969.

GORDON, W. J. J. *Synectics.* New York: Harper & Row, 1961.

GREEN, P. E., and D. S. TULL. *Research for Marketing Decisions,* 3rd ed. Englewood Cliffs, NJ: Prentice-Hall, 1974.

625
*Variety
Management:
Production
Planning for
New
Technologies*

HARRIS, R. D., and M. J. MAGGARD. *Computer Models in Operations Management*, 2nd ed. New York: Harper & Row, 1977.

HERTZ, DAVID B. "Risk Analysis in Capital Investment," *Harvard Business Review* (January–February 1964), pp. 95–106.

IMAI, MASAAKI, *KAIZEN: The Key To Japan's Competitive Success*. New York: Random House Business Division, 1986.

KAUFMANN, A., M. FUSTIER, and A. DREVET. *L'Inventique, Nouvelles Methodes de Creativité*. Paris: Entreprise Moderne D'Edition, 1970.

KILMANN, RALPH H. *Beyond the Quick Fix*. Jossey-Bass Publishers, 1985. San Francisco, CA, Washington, DC.

LUCE, R. DUNCAN. *Individual Choice Behavior*. New York: Wiley, 1959.

MACHLUP, FRITZ. *The Production and Distribution of Knowledge in the United States*. Princeton, NJ: Princeton University Press, 1962.

MAYER, MARTIN. *Madison Avenue U.S.A.* New York: Harper & Row, 1958.

MILLER, DAVID W., and MARTIN K. STARR. *Executive Decisions and Operations Research*, 2nd ed. Englewood Cliffs, NJ: Prentice-Hall, 1969.

MORITA, AKIO, *Made In Japan*, E. P. Dutton, NY, 1986.

MORTON, J. A. *Organizing for Innovation*. New York: McGraw-Hill, 1971.

NEWTON, NORMAN T. *An Approach to Design*. Cambridge, MA: Addison-Wesley, 1951.

PETERS, TOM, *Thriving on Chaos*, Alfred A. Knopf, NY, 1987.

REHDER, R., R. HENDRY and M. SMITH. "NUMMI: The Best of Both Worlds?", *Management Review* (December 1985), American Management Association.

SCHON, DONALD A. *Technology and Change*. New York: Delacorte Press, 1967.

SHUBIK, MARTIN. *Strategy and Market Structure: Competition, Oligopoly, and the Theory of Games*. New York: Wiley, 1959.

STARR, MARTIN K. "Product Planning from the Top Variety and Diversity," *University of Illinois Bulletin*, 65, 144, *Proceedings, Systems: Research and Applications for Marketing*, July 26, 1968, pp. 71–77.

———. *Product Design and Decision Theory*. Englewood Cliffs, NJ: Prentice Hall, 1963.

STARR, MARTIN K., and NANCY E. BLOOM. "The Performance of Japanese-Owned Firms in America: Survey Report," Columbia University, Graduate School of Business, Center for Operations, New York, February 1985.

STARR, MARTIN K., and PATRICE A. HALL. "The Performance of Japanese-Owned Firms in America: 1982–1985," Survey Report—No. 2, Columbia University, Graduate School of Business, Center for Operations, New York, February 1987.

STOCKTON, R. STANSBURY. *Introduction to Linear Programming*, 2nd ed. Boston: Allyn and Bacon, 1963.

VAN HORNE, JAMES C. *Financial Management and Policy*. Englewood Cliffs, NJ: Prentice-Hall, 1971.

VASZONYI, A. *Scientific Programming in Business and Industry*. New York: Wiley, 1958.

WATERMAN, ROBERT H., Jr., *The Renewal Factor*, Bantam Books, NY, 1987.

WILLIAMS, J. D. *The Compleat Strategyst*. New York: McGraw-Hill, 1954.

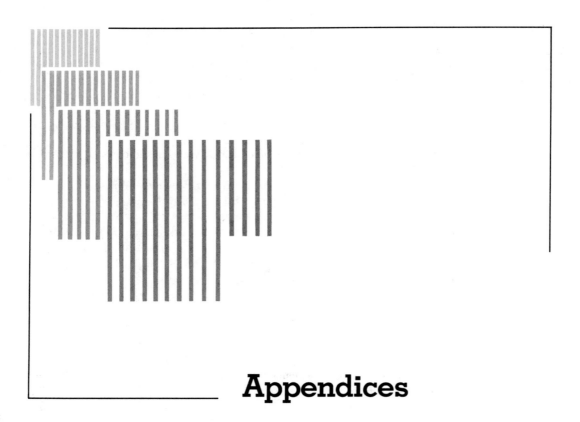

Appendices

Appendix A. Personal Computer Software that Compliments the Text: Managing Production and Operations (MPO)

Many thousands of personal computer (p.c.) programs exist that are related to the planning and control methods explained and used in this P/OM text (called MPO). These programs are on diskettes which (when inserted in the computer) aid and prompt the student in their use. The programs are designed to solve the quantitative problems typical of P/OM decisions. Each program has different equipment specifications which must be satisfied. For example, the amount of RAM memory, mono or color monitor, color graphics or other type of board, and type of printer.

Rather than choose 15 or 20 programs, on a one by one basis, from among thousands of possibilities, we have chosen two main systems (called QSB and STORM). In addition, we have selected several supplementary systems. This spares the student (and the computer lab) having to go in search of many different sources of diskettes and their manuals. The two main systems, when taken together, cover most of the programs we need. The supplementary software programs are included because neither of the two main systems covers all of the materials explained in the MPO text.

In particular, one of the supplements called THE BUSINESS COURSEWARE LIBRARY (BCL) Educational Software Services, Richard D. Irwin, Inc., 1988 has developed uniquely different programs which fill some gaps that are not likely to be satisfied by other software systems in the near future. A loose-leaf format is intended for BCL which allows the selection of those programs which fit the instructor's course plan.

The first of the two main systems is QUANTITATIVE SYSTEMS FOR BUSINESS by Yih-Long Chang and Robert S. Sullivan (Prentice-Hall, Inc., Englewood Cliffs, NJ, 1986). To refer to this system, we use the abbreviation, QSB. Also, QSB is what we enter for the computer to call up the menu of programs. QSB treats about 75% of the models that are explained in our text, Managing Production and Operations (MPO). The QSB computer programs are described by their authors as being "User Friendly". With two diskettes, access is available to all 14 algorithms which are listed below. The price of the diskettes and manual is reasonable for students.

Because MPO and QSB have the same publisher, (viz., Prentice Hall of Simon & Schuster) updates of the computer programs will be brought to the students' attention without delay. Also, there are special site licensing and pricing arrangements that are applicable.

The second of the two main systems is STORM: QUANTITATIVE MODELING FOR DECISION SUPPORT by Hamilton Emmons, A. Dale Flowers and Kamlesh Mathur (Holden-Day, Inc., Oakland, CA, 1986). To refer to this system, which is classed as "User Friendly", we employ the abbreviation, STORM. Also, STORM is what we enter for the computer to call up the menu of programs. With two diskettes, access is available to all 13 STORM algorithms which are listed below. The diskettes and manual are reasonably priced for students. Both STORM and QSB have been classroom tested.

The supplementary programs (SP) that we have chosen have varying degrees of user-friendliness. A number of them require LOTUS. We should note that even the most "User Friendly" programs (including QSB and STORM) have eccentricities that often cause confusion and manuals which can puzzle sophisticated users. In this regard, we interpret "User Friendly" as meaning that the confusion can be cleared up and the puzzles solved without too much pain.

STORM treats about 75% of the models that are described in Managing Production and Operations. However, it is not the same 75% of the models that QSB treats. About half of the models treated by QSB and STORM overlap. Such overlap provides many choice opportunities since the same program name (e.g., linear programming, inventory management or transportation) reflects different capabilities of maximum problem size, data entry requirements, user-friendliness, etc. For one situation, the student may prefer QSB, for another STORM.

Table A1 (below) indicates where QSB, STORM and the SP's overlap. It also shows where they do not. The way that QSB, STORM and the SP's apply to the 12 chapters of this text, Managing Production and Operations (MPO) is documented in matrix form by Table A1. Software of the Business Courseware Library are indicated by BCL, and the component BCL programs are described at a later point. All of these programs, including the SP's, are designed for P.C.'s. They are menu-driven with simple data entry and have manuals that are relatively easy to use.

The 14 programs in the QSB software package are shown with their abbreviations and chapter designations in Table A2.

Not all of these 14 programs are used for our MPO text. We designate with (*) the algorithms that do not apply. However, it is useful to note that they could be utilized by anyone familiar with the Operations Research and Management Science literature.

The 13 programs in the STORM software package are shown with their chapter designations in Table A3. All of the STORM programs can be applied to the MPO text.

Another alternative exists which is COMPUTER MODELS FOR MANAGEMENT SCIENCE, 2nd Edition, by Warren J. Erikson and

TABLE A1

MPO Chapter	QSB Chapter	STORM Chapter	SP Programs
1: No available software is pertinent to this chapter.			
2: Models dealing with cash flow, return on investment (ROI), payback period and present value (PV).		13	MIRAGE (BCL)
3: Critical path methods (CPM) and PERT models for project management.	9,10	9	PAC-MICRO (AGS)
4: Forecasting with time series methods, moving averages, exponential smoothing and regression analysis.	17	14,17	
5: Decision models with expected values (EV's). Also breakeven analysis and capacity planning.	15		CAPACITY (BCL)
6: Quality control models.			STATPAD
7: Inventory models including EOQ and discounts. Also, ELS models and ABC models. Reorder points, safety stock and MRP.	12	10,16	INGRAF (BCL)
8: Interactive human resource management (HRM) exercise programs.			HRM (BCL)
9: Facility layout models.		11	
10: Line balancing models with cycle time.	13,14	8,12	ALB (BCL) QPAK (BCL)
11: Transportation and assignment models. Also, production scheduling models with simulations.	6,7	6,7,15	XCELL + SOAPMKR (BCL)
12: Linear programming including sensitivity analysis.	4,5	5	LINDO/GINO

TABLE A2

1. Linear programming (LP)   Chapter 4
*2. Integer linear programming (ILP)   Chapter 5
3. Transportation problems (TRP)   Chapter 6
4. Assignment problems (ASMP)   Chapter 7
*5. Network modeling (NET)   Chapter 8
6. Critical path method (CPM)   Chapter 9
7. Program Evaluation and Review Technique (PERT)   Chapter 10
*8. Dynamic programming (DP)   Chapter 11
9. Inventory theory (INVT)   Chapter 12
10. Queuing theory (QUEUE)   Chapter 13
11. Queuing system simulation (QSIM)   Chapter 14
12. Decision and probability theory (DSPB)   Chapter 15
*13. Markov process (MKV)   Chapter 16
14. Time series forecasting (TSFC)   Chapter 17

Owen P. Hall (Addison-Wesley Publishing Co., Reading, MA, 1986). We designate it by E/H. The 11 programs in the E/H software package are more like QSB than STORM. E/H does not have the benefits of coordinated up-dating and pricing which are available to users of the QSB text because QSB and MPO have the same publisher, i.e., Prentice-Hall of Simon and Schuster. The programs of E/H are listed in Table A4 with their chapter designations.

Not all of these 11 programs are used for our MPO text. We designate with (*) the algorithms that do not apply. However, it is useful to note that they could be utilized by anyone familiar with the Operations Research and Management Science literature.

The normal time available for the P/OM course does not allow full utilization of either QSB, E/H or STORM in a term. As a result, it is recommended that only one of these software packages be purchased by

TABLE A3

1. Linear Programming   Chapter 5
2. The Assignment Problem   Chapter 6
3. The Transportation Problem   Chapter 7
4. Queueing Analysis   Chapter 8
5. Project Management (CPM/PERT)   Chapter 9
6. Inventory Management   Chapter 10
7. Facility Layout   Chapter 11
8. Assembly Line Balancing   Chapter 12
9. Investment Analysis   Chapter 13
10. Forecasting   Chapter 14
11. Production Scheduling   Chapter 15
12. Material Requirements Planning   Chapter 16
13. Regression Analysis   Chapter 17

TABLE A4

1.	Linear programming	Chapter 3
*2.	Integer programming	Chapter 4
3.	Transportation model	Chapter 5
4.	Assignment model	Chapter 6
*5.	Network models	Chapter 8
6.	Project scheduling	Chapter 7
7.	Decision Analysis Models	Chapter 9
*8.	Decision Tree Model	Chapter 10
9.	Inventory Models	Chapter 12
10.	Queuing Models	Chapter 13
*11.	Markov Models	Chapter 11

the students. The exception is where the student desires to have relatively complete computer coverage. It is also possible to make arrangements with the computer lab to carry QSB, E/H, STORM and selected software of the SP's. In that way, mixtures of the various system's capabilities can be tapped.

QSB, E/H and STORM together do not cover all of the models described in the MPO text. That is why we have added the SP's. Among them, The Business Courseware Library (BCL) treats human resource management (HRM), capacity planning (CP), financial evaluation (MIRAGE) and additional issues that are not available in the other existing software. Another important missing program that applies to quality control is covered by the SP called Statpad. In addition, we supply supplemental programs for project management (Pac-Micro), linear programming (Lindo), integer linear programming (Gino) and production scheduling simulation for the job shop (Xcell+). These latter programs (which are discussed below) permit large (realistic) problems to be solved on a personal computer.

The Business Courseware Library (BCL) programs that are directly applicable to this text (MPO) include:

1. MIRAGE (MPO, Chapter 2) examines cash flow and breakeven analysis. MIRAGE requires the use of LOTUS. The STORM program in Chapter 2 provides an easier way to begin cash flow analysis.

2. CAPACITY (Explained in detail in Chapter 5 of MPO) analyzes linear and non-linear breakeven situations and combines them with forecast data to obtain expected values used for decision-making. CAPACITY also presents a size-planning model in which price elasticity interacts with economics of scale to yield different values of margin contribution. The production system is selected which maximizes margin contribution.

3. INGRAF (MPO, Chapter 7) is a graphical tutorial for using inventory control models that apply to both deterministic and stochastic situations.

4. HRM (MPO, Chapter 8) presents scenarios that raise personnel problems and (ethical) dilemmas for Human Resources Managers. The simulations offer role playing opportunities to the students. Another name for the program is DILIM—DILemmas In Management

5. ALB (MPO, Chapter 10) allows students to balance an assembly line using heuristic procedures that lead to a relatively good solution in a realistic context of many tasks.

6. QPAK (MPO, Chapter 10) employs the tools of queueing theory without the burden of computing statistics to describe the performance of service systems. The program provides both analysis and simulation.

7. SOAPMAKER (MPO, Chapter 11) is an interactive production management game. It is so-named because it stimulates decisions about production scheduling that a detergent plant manager has to make in response to various market conditions.

The BCL has many other programs which are not explained in this Appendix because they are less applicable to the MPO text.

Concerning the remaining SP's, we briefly list their sources and characteristics.

1. Pac-Micro Project Management System (from AGS Management Systems, Inc., King of Prussia, PA) is an integrated set of programs for project planning. It is designed to organize many activities with supporting graphics and systems reporting capabilities.

2. Statpad is useful for many different forms of Quality Control including frequency polygons, x-bar and standard deviation charts, p-charts and sampling plans. (Available from John A. Clements, Professional Applications Development, 12 Sandy Way, Weymouth, MA, 02191, Tel.: 617-331-4062.) Statpad requires the use of Lotus.

3. XCELL and XCELL + (Factory Modeling Systems, available from The Scientific Press, Redwood City, CA). Both programs permit realistic simulations of job shop production schedules. There are shop floor graphics and reporting systems for performance measures. XCELL + is a more powerful version requiring a color graphics board.

4. LINDO/PC and GINO/PC (for Linear and Non-linear Programming, from The Scientific Press, Redwood City, CA). With the ''SuperSystem'' version, Lindo can solve an LP problem matrix having up to 120 rows and 300 variables. Lindo also handles integer programming and performs a wide range of sensitivity analyses. Gino solves non-linear, constrained optimization problems. For comparison, we note that QSB can solve up to 40×40 LP's and 20×20 integer LP's while STORM can handle up to 25×40 LP's.

Appendix B

TABLE OF THE NORMAL DISTRIBUTION

AREAS UNDER THE NORMAL CURVE FROM K_α to ∞

$$\alpha = \int_{K_\alpha}^{\infty} \frac{1}{\sqrt{2\pi}} e^{-x^2/2}\,dx$$

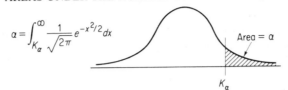

Area $= \alpha$

K_α

K_α	0.00	0.01	0.02	0.03	0.04	0.05	0.06	0.07	0.08	0.09
0.0	0.5000	0.4960	0.4920	0.4880	0.4840	0.4801	0.4761	0.4721	0.4681	0.4641
0.1	0.4602	0.4562	0.4522	0.4483	0.4443	0.4404	0.4364	0.4325	0.4286	0.4247
0.2	0.4207	0.4168	0.4129	0.4090	0.4052	0.4013	0.3974	0.3936	0.3897	0.3859
0.3	0.3821	0.3783	0.3745	0.3707	0.3669	0.3632	0.3594	0.3557	0.3520	0.3483
0.4	0.3446	0.3409	0.3372	0.3336	0.3300	0.3264	0.3228	0.3192	0.3156	0.3121
0.5	0.3085	0.3050	0.3015	0.2981	0.2946	0.2912	0.2877	0.2843	0.2810	0.2776
0.6	0.2743	0.2709	0.2676	0.2643	0.2611	0.2578	0.2546	0.2514	0.2483	0.2451
0.7	0.2420	0.2389	0.2358	0.2327	0.2296	0.2266	0.2236	0.2206	0.2177	0.2148
0.8	0.2119	0.2090	0.2061	0.2033	0.2005	0.1977	0.1949	0.1922	0.1894	0.1867
0.9	0.1841	0.1814	0.1788	0.1762	0.1736	0.1711	0.1685	0.1660	0.1635	0.1611
1.0	0.1587	0.1562	0.1539	0.1515	0.1492	0.1469	0.1446	0.1423	0.1401	0.1379
1.1	0.1357	0.1335	0.1314	0.1292	0.1271	0.1251	0.1230	0.1210	0.1190	0.1170
1.2	0.1151	0.1131	0.1112	0.1093	0.1075	0.1056	0.1038	0.1020	0.1003	0.0985
1.3	0.0968	0.0951	0.0934	0.0918	0.0901	0.0885	0.0869	0.0853	0.0838	0.0823
1.4	0.0808	0.0793	0.0778	0.0764	0.0749	0.0735	0.0721	0.0708	0.0694	0.0681
1.5	0.0668	0.0655	0.0643	0.0630	0.0618	0.0606	0.0594	0.0582	0.0571	0.0559
1.6	0.0548	0.0537	0.0526	0.0516	0.0505	0.0495	0.0485	0.0475	0.0465	0.0455
1.7	0.0446	0.0436	0.0427	0.0418	0.0409	0.0401	0.0392	0.0384	0.0375	0.0367
1.8	0.0359	0.0351	0.0344	0.0336	0.0329	0.0322	0.0314	0.0307	0.0301	0.0294
1.9	0.0287	0.0281	0.0274	0.0268	0.0262	0.0256	0.0250	0.0244	0.0239	0.0233
2.0	0.0228	0.0222	0.0217	0.0212	0.0207	0.0202	0.0197	0.0192	0.0188	0.0183
2.1	0.0179	0.0174	0.0170	0.0166	0.0162	0.0158	0.0154	0.0150	0.0146	0.0143
2.2	0.0139	0.0136	0.0132	0.0129	0.0125	0.0122	0.0119	0.0116	0.0113	0.0110
2.3	0.0107	0.0104	0.0102	0.00990	0.00964	0.00939	0.00914	0.00889	0.00866	0.00842
2.4	0.00820	0.00798	0.00776	0.00755	0.00734	0.00714	0.00695	0.00676	0.00657	0.00639
2.5	0.00621	0.00604	0.00587	0.00570	0.00554	0.00539	0.00523	0.00508	0.00494	0.00480
2.6	0.00466	0.00453	0.00440	0.00427	0.00415	0.00402	0.00391	0.00379	0.00368	0.00357
2.7	0.00347	0.00336	0.00326	0.00317	0.00307	0.00298	0.00289	0.00280	0.00272	0.00264
2.8	0.00256	0.00248	0.00240	0.00233	0.00226	0.00219	0.00212	0.00205	0.00199	0.00193
2.9	0.00187	0.00181	0.00175	0.00169	0.00164	0.00159	0.00154	0.00149	0.00144	0.00139

K_α	0.0	0.1	0.2	0.3	0.4	0.5	0.6	0.7	0.8	0.9
3	0.00135	0.0^3968	0.0^3687	0.0^3483	0.0^3337	0.0^3233	0.0^3159	0.0^3108	0.0^4723	0.0^4481
4	0.0^4317	0.0^4207	0.0^4133	0.0^5854	0.0^5541	0.0^5340	0.0^5211	0.0^5130	0.0^6793	0.0^6479
5	0.0^6287	0.0^6170	0.0^7996	0.0^7579	0.0^7333	0.0^7190	0.0^7107	0.0^8599	0.0^8332	0.0^8182
6	0.0^9987	0.0^9530	0.0^9282	0.0_9149	$0.0^{10}777$	$0.0^{10}402$	$0.0^{10}206$	$0.0^{10}104$	$0.0^{11}523$	$0.0^{11}260$

Appendix C

TABLE OF LOGARITHMS

N	0	1	2	3	4	5	6	7	8	9
10	0000	0043	0086	0128	0170	0212	0253	0294	0334	0374
11	0414	0453	0492	0531	0569	0607	0645	0682	0719	0755
12	0792	0828	0864	0899	0934	0969	1004	1038	1072	1106
13	1139	1173	1206	1239	1271	1303	1335	1367	1399	1430
14	1461	1492	1523	1553	1584	1614	1644	1673	1703	1732
15	1761	1790	1818	1847	1875	1903	1931	1959	1987	2014
16	2041	2068	2095	2122	2148	2175	2201	2227	2253	2279
17	2304	2330	2355	2380	2405	2430	2455	2480	2504	2529
18	2553	2577	2601	2625	2648	2672	2695	2718	2742	2765
19	2788	2810	2833	2856	2878	2900	2923	2945	2967	2989
20	3010	3032	3054	3075	3096	3118	3139	3160	3181	3201
21	3222	3243	3263	3284	3304	3324	3345	3365	3385	3404
22	3424	3444	3464	3483	3502	3522	3541	3560	3579	3598
23	3617	3636	3655	3674	3692	3711	3729	3747	3766	3784
24	3802	3820	3838	3856	3874	3892	3909	3927	3945	3962
25	3979	3997	4014	4031	4048	4065	4082	4099	4116	4133
26	4150	4166	4183	4200	4216	4232	4249	4265	4281	4298
27	4314	4330	4346	4362	4378	4393	4409	4425	4440	4456
28	4472	4487	4502	4518	4533	4548	4564	4579	4594	4609
29	4624	4639	4654	4669	4683	4698	4713	4728	4742	4757
30	4771	4786	4800	4814	4829	4843	4857	4871	4886	4900
31	4914	4928	4942	4955	4969	4983	4997	5011	5024	5038
32	5051	5065	5079	5092	5105	5119	5132	5145	5159	5172
33	5185	5198	5211	5224	5237	5250	5263	5276	5289	5302
34	5315	5328	5340	5353	5366	5378	5391	5403	5416	5428
35	5441	5453	5465	5478	5490	5502	5514	5527	5539	5551
36	5563	5575	5587	5599	5611	5623	5635	5647	5658	5670
37	5682	5694	5705	5717	5729	5740	5752	5763	5775	5786
38	5798	5809	5821	5832	5843	5855	5866	5877	5888	5899
39	5911	5922	5933	5944	5955	5966	5977	5988	5999	6010
40	6021	6031	6042	6053	6064	6075	6085	6096	6107	6117
41	6128	6138	6149	6160	6170	6180	6191	6201	6212	6222
42	6232	6243	6253	6263	6274	6284	6294	6304	6314	6325
43	6335	6345	6355	6365	6375	6385	6395	6405	6415	6425
44	6435	6444	6454	6464	6474	6484	6493	6503	6513	6522
45	6532	6542	6551	6561	6571	6580	6590	6599	6609	6618
46	6628	6637	6646	6656	6665	6675	6684	6693	6702	6712
47	6721	6730	6739	6749	6758	6767	6776	6785	6794	6803
48	6812	6821	6830	6839	6848	6857	6866	6875	6884	6893
49	6902	6911	6920	6928	6937	6946	6955	6964	6972	6981
50	6990	6998	7007	7016	7024	7033	7042	7050	7059	7067
51	7076	7084	7093	7101	7110	7118	7126	7135	7143	7152
52	7160	7168	7177	7185	7193	7202	7210	7218	7226	7235
53	7243	7251	7259	7267	7275	7284	7292	7300	7308	7316
54	7324	7332	7340	7348	7356	7364	7372	7380	7388	7396

N	0	1	2	3	4	5	6	7	8	9
55	7404	7412	7419	7427	7435	7443	7451	7459	7466	7474
56	7482	7490	7497	7505	7513	7520	7528	7536	7543	7551
57	7559	7566	7574	7582	7589	7597	7604	7612	7619	7627
58	7634	7642	7649	7657	7664	7672	7679	7686	7694	7701
59	7709	7716	7723	7731	7738	7745	7752	7760	7767	7774
60	7782	7789	7796	7803	7810	7818	7825	7832	7839	7846
61	7853	7860	7868	7875	7882	7889	7896	7903	7910	7917
62	7924	7931	7938	7945	7952	7959	7966	7973	7980	7987
63	7993	8000	8007	8014	8021	8028	8035	8041	8048	8055
64	8062	8069	8075	8082	8089	8096	8102	8109	8116	8122
65	8129	8136	8142	8149	8156	8162	8169	8176	8182	8189
66	8195	8202	8209	8215	8222	8228	8235	8241	8248	8254
67	8261	8267	8274	8280	8287	8293	8299	8306	8312	8319
68	8325	8331	8338	8344	8351	8357	8363	8370	8376	8382
69	8388	8395	8401	8407	8414	8420	8426	8432	8439	8445
70	8451	8457	8463	8470	8476	8482	8488	8494	8500	8506
71	8513	8519	8525	8531	8537	8543	8549	8555	8561	8567
72	8573	8579	8585	8591	8597	8603	8609	8615	8621	8627
73	8633	8639	8645	8651	8657	8663	8669	8675	8681	8686
74	8692	8698	8704	8710	8716	8722	8727	8733	8739	8745
75	8751	8756	8762	8768	8774	8779	8785	8791	8797	8802
76	8808	8814	8820	8825	8831	8837	8842	8848	8854	8859
77	8865	8871	8876	8882	8887	8893	8899	8904	8910	8915
78	8921	8927	8932	8938	8943	8949	8954	8960	8965	8971
79	8976	8982	8987	8993	8998	9004	9009	9015	9020	9025
80	9031	9036	9042	9047	9053	9058	9063	9069	9074	9079
81	9085	9090	9096	9101	9106	9112	9117	9122	9128	9133
82	9138	9143	9149	9154	9159	9165	9170	9175	9180	9186
83	9191	9196	9201	9206	9212	9217	9222	9227	9232	9238
84	9243	9248	9253	9258	9263	9269	9274	9279	9284	9289
85	9294	9299	9304	9309	9315	9320	9325	9330	9335	9340
86	9345	9350	9355	9360	9365	9370	9375	9380	9385	9390
87	9395	9400	9405	9410	9415	9420	9425	9430	9435	9440
88	9445	9450	9455	9460	9465	9469	9474	9479	9484	9489
89	9494	9499	9504	9509	9513	9518	9523	9528	9533	9538
90	9542	9547	9552	9557	9562	9566	9571	9576	9581	9586
91	9590	9595	9600	9605	9609	9614	9619	9624	9628	9633
92	9638	9643	9647	9652	9657	9661	9666	9671	9675	9680
93	9685	9689	9694	9699	9703	9708	9713	9717	9722	9727
94	9731	9736	9741	9745	9750	9754	9759	9763	9768	9773
95	9777	9782	9786	9791	9795	9800	9805	9809	9814	9818
96	9823	9827	9832	9836	9841	9845	9850	9854	9859	9863
97	9868	9872	9877	9881	9886	9890	9894	9899	9903	9908
98	9912	9917	9921	9926	9930	9934	9939	9943	9948	9952
99	9956	9961	9965	9969	9974	9978	9983	9987	9991	9996

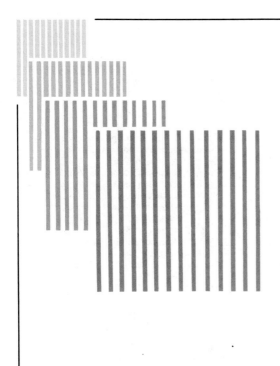

Index

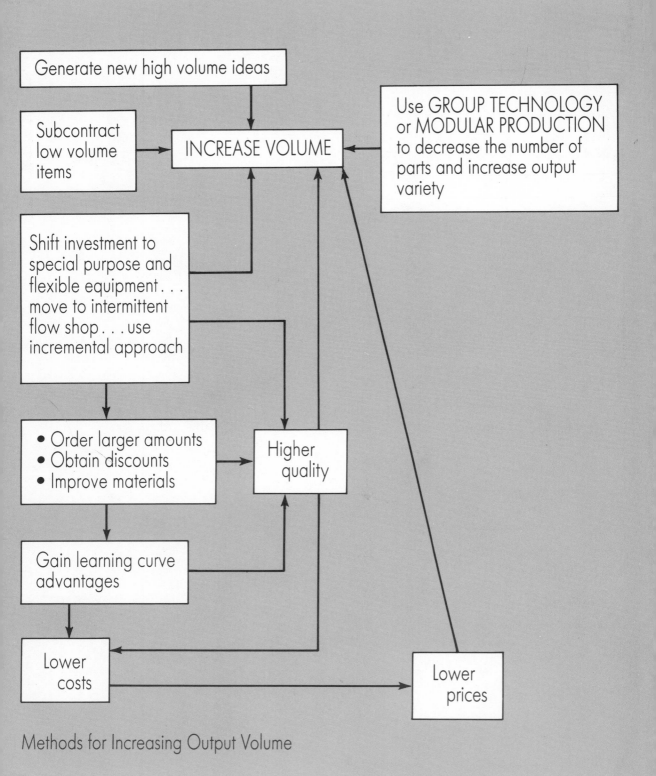

Methods for Increasing Output Volume